The Concise DICTIONARY of the CHRISTIAN TRADITION

Doctrine • Liturgy • History

J.D. Douglas
Walter A. Elwell
Peter Toon

The Concise Dictionary of the Christian Tradition

Regency Reference Library is an imprint of Zondervan Publishing House,
1415 Lake Drive, S.E., Grand Rapids, Michigan 49506

Library of Congress Cataloging in Publication Data

Douglas, J. D. (James Dixon)
The concise dictionary of the Christian tradition : doctrine, liturgy, history / J. D. Douglas, Walter A. Elwell, Peter Toon.
p. cm.
ISBN 0-310-44320-2
1. Christianity–Dictionaries. I. Elwell, Walter A. II. Toon, Peter, 1939– . III. Title.
BR95.D67 1989
203–dc20 89-10349
CIP

Printed in the United States of America

90 91 92 93 94 / DH / 10 9 8 7 6 5 4 3 2

A

A CRUCE SALUS (Lat. "*salvation comes from the *cross"). The salvation *God provides is centered in *Jesus' death on the cross.

A.D. See ANNO DOMINI.

A PRIORI, A POSTERIORI Latin phrases meaning "from before" and "from after" and used with reference to human experience in the world of observable facts. Thus, *a priori* statements are made without reference to observation or examination of the world (e.g., "morality cannot exist without *God"). Other statements are *a posteriori*—observation shows them to be true (e.g., "Plants breathe carbon dioxide").

ABBA (Aram. "father"). Used in the *NT (Mark 14:36; Rom 8:15; Gal 4:6) as the expression of an intimate relationship with *God the Father. It was probably a featured part of a primitive *confession of *faith and *assurance at *baptism in the early church. See also ADOPTION (THEOLOGICAL).

ABBESS Female *superior of a nunnery, most commonly of the *Benedictine *rule. The title was in use by the early 6th century. In the Middle Ages an abbess sometimes ruled a double *monastery of monks and *nuns. She had to be at least forty years old and had to have professed for at least ten years. She had complete spiritual authority over her nuns but no sacramental jurisdiction.

ABBOT *Superior of a monastic community of the *Benedictine *rule. An abbot (Aram. *abba,* "father") must be at least thirty years old, of legitimate birth, and an ordained *priest. His election (by secret ballot) must be ratified by the *pope or other designated authority. Though traditionally a life appointment, the post is sometimes limited to six to ten years.

ABBOT, GEORGE (1562–1633). *Archbishop of Canterbury from 1611. Strong Royalist and former *bishop of London, his moderate *Calvinism was less acceptable after the death of James I, when High Church views were pressed by William *Laud. Abbot's accidental shooting of a gamekeeper while hunting sparked off a famous controversy.

ABBOTT, LYMAN (1835–1922). Congregationalist minister and writer. Briefly a lawyer, he studied *theology and ministered in Indiana and the South before becoming editor of the *Illustrated Christian Weekly* (1870). In 1876 he transferred to the *Christian Union*, becoming its chief editor in 1881 and vigorously using it to apply *Christianity to social problems. *The Theology of an Evolutionist* (1897) reflects his Darwinist outlook. He followed H. W. *Beecher at Plymouth Congregational Church, Brooklyn (1888–1899).

ABECEDARIANS Followers of Nicholas *Storch (d. 1525), a German *Anabaptist who saw human knowledge as a barrier to religious understanding and held that even knowing the alphabet was unnecessary.

ABELARD, PETER (1079–1142). French philosopher and theologian. Born in Brittany, he was a popular and original lecturer in Paris until his secret marriage to Heloise (1118), who bore his child. Incensed by his apparently insensitive attitude, Heloise's uncle had him castrated. Abelard retired to a *monastery; Heloise became a *nun. His theological writings challenged the *orthodoxy of his day and led to condemnation by the Councils of *Soissons (1121) and *Sens (1141). His views on the *Atonement and on the *Trinity were regarded as defective, notably by *Bernard of Clairvaux (whose influence prejudiced Pope Innocent II against Abelard). Nevertheless, his independent mind and profound scholarship had a significant effect on many later Roman Catholic scholars.

ABJURATION A solemn act of renouncing (in set forms of words to be read) what is recognized as a false *doctrine or opinion, including (throughout church history) *apostasy, *heresy, *schism, public *sins, *Judaism, Islam, and unacceptable persons. It still exists legally in both the Roman Catholic and the *Orthodox churches but is not used as much today as in earlier times.

ABLUTIONS (Lat. *ablutio,* "cleaning"). In the *Eucharist, the ritual cleansing of the *paten, the *chalice, and the *priest's fingers and mouth before the consecration of the bread and wine. Also the washing of the fingers and the chalice after Holy *Communion has been given and received.

ABOLITIONISM Nineteenth-century reform movement in the U.S. that sought for the abolition of slave trade and the emancipation of slaves. Leaders of the movement such as James Birney; Theodora Weld; and Harriet Beecher *Stowe, author of *Uncle Tom's Cabin,* stung the conscience of a nation into action, even if stridently at times. The Thirteenth Amendment to the Constitution of the United States in 1865 following the Civil War achieved the abolitionists' ultimate goals.

ABOMINATION OF DESOLATION A biblical phrase (Dan 9:27; 11:31; 12:11; Matt 24:15; Mark 13:14) indicating idolatrous, desolating *sacrilege. Antiochus Epiphanes' placing of an idol in the temple of Jerusalem in 168 B.C. was known as a desolating sacrilege (1 Macc 1:54; 6:7; 2 Macc 6:2). In Matthew and Mark it may refer to the profanation of the temple in the Jewish War in A.D. 68.

ABORTION The removal of a living fetus from the womb so that it cannot survive. A miscarriage is a natural abortion and raises no special moral problems. An abortion induced by taking drugs or by direct surgical interference raises moral problems for the *Christian because the fetus is recognized as being the beginning of a human life. However, many would condone induced abortion if the life of the mother is in danger or if it is known that the baby will have serious physical and/or mental deficiencies.

ABSALON (1128–1201). *Archbishop of Lund. Born into a prominent Danish family, he studied in Paris and was ordained there. He led military campaigns against the Slavs, was responsible for the construction of a stronghold that developed into Copenhagen, and was a lifelong battler for his country's independence from the *Holy Roman Empire. He became *bishop of Roskilde in 1158, archbishop of Lund in 1178. A builder of many churches and an encourager of *monasticism, he introduced Western church customs into Denmark.

ABSOLUTE, THE A general description of *God as being totally free from limitations of any kind. A more common use is in idealist philosophy since *Kant (1724–1804) and in writers such as *Hegel (1770–1831). For Hegel the absolute was the totality of what really exists, which is spiritual reality.

ABSOLUTION The act of setting a person free from *sin and its penalties. *Jesus claimed to do this in granting *forgiveness (e.g., Mark 2:5–11). He also gave the apostles authority to pronounce others forgiven (John 20:23). In some *worship services, after the congregation has confessed its sins and expressed *repentance, presiding ministers normally pronounce a declaration of forgiveness. Absolution also follows private *confession to a *priest, as in the Roman Catholic *sacrament of *penance.

ABSTINENCE The refusal, for religious purposes, to satisfy one's natural appetites—i.e., sexual intercourse, all or a part of normal food, alcoholic drinks, and worldly pleasures generally. Traditionally there have been special days or periods each year when the church has required its members' abstinence—normally from food. The best example is *Lent, particularly the week before *Easter *Sunday. Some religious *orders maintain high levels of abstinence (e.g., the *Trappists). The purpose of abstinence is to develop control over the *body in order to give oneself more completely to *God.

ABSURD Used in *existentialism to express the nonrationality and meaninglessness of life and of human activity. Realizing this can lead to *angst (a feeling of *anxiety and dread), which, if rightly directed, can lead (e.g., *Christian existentialists) to *authentic existence.

ABUNA Meaning "our father," this is the title given to the *patriarch of the *Ethiopian church.

ACACIAN SCHISM (484–519). A rift between Eastern and Western churches caused after Emperor Zeno and *Patriarch Acacius of Constantinople issued an edict that Pope Felix III held to be against the *canons of the Council of *Chalcedon. The latter had condemned the Monophysite *heresy (which denied that *Christ was wholly human and wholly divine). When Acacius refused to justify or withdraw the edict, Felix pronounced him excommunicate. The *schism came to an end when the accession of a pro-Chalcedonian emperor, Justin I, favored the conditions laid down by Pope *Hormisdas.

ACADEMIES, DISSENTING See DISSENTING ACADEMIES.

ACATHISTUS (Gk. "not sitting"). A *hymn sung in honor of the Virgin *Mary at the end of the fifth week of *Lent in the Greek Orthodox church. It has twenty-four stanzas of varying length, and each begins with one of the twenty-four letters of the Greek alphabet.

ACCIDENT(S) A term much used in medieval and traditional Roman Catholic *theology. Taken from Aristotle, it cannot be understood except in relation to *substance. "Accidents" *accede* to a "substance"—e.g., the substance of a door is wood, but its accidents are its size, shape, etc. Accidents are more than the paint and label on a door, for they actually determine the way in which the wood of the door is experienced by us. See also TRANSUBSTANTIATION.

ACCIDIE (Gk. "negligence"). A word used primarily by writers on the spiritual life of monks and *nuns, this refers to a state of mind in which it is difficult, perhaps impossible, to pray or to work. Thus it is the neglecting of duties to *God or man.

ACCOMMODATION When used of *God's self-disclosure to humankind this refers to the way in which he uses familiar terms, images, and pictures to convey knowledge—e.g., God calling himself "King" in the image of the absolute monarchy of Egypt and Assyria. Some theologians also say accommodation occurs if a meaning given to an *OT passage was not the original meaning of the author or speaker (e.g., if it was addressed to *Israel and is now applied to the church) or if, in *preaching, careful attention is paid to the intellectual world and *culture of the hearers.

ACOLYTE Sometimes also called an altar boy. A boy or man who assists the *deacon and *priest in the *Eucharist. He is not ordained, and his usual tasks are to carry the *cross, light the candles, ring the bells, and carry the *Bible. He may also assist in the distribution of Holy *Communion.

ACOSMISM An exaggerated form of *pantheism. It claims that the world we know (the physical world) does not really exist, for the only true reality is the *absolute spirit of which the world is the expression or the phantom. It is often associated with the name of Bernard de Spinoza (1632–1677).

ACROSTIC An arrangement (of words, lines, or verses) on which letters or syllables (occurring in the key position of first or last) together make up a word, phrase, or alphabetic sequence. Examples of this in the *Bible occur where there are alphabetic sequences in Hebrew (e.g., Pss 9, 10, 25, 34, 37, 119). A famous *Christian example is the Greek word for *fish (*ichthus*).

ACT Act, action, and agent are all derived from Latin *agere,* "to do." Thus in human behavior the "agent" is the person, the "act" is the deed done, and the "action" is the doing of the deed. To separate "act" and "action" is always difficult. A distinction is made between *actus hominis*, someone's act that is not specifically human (e.g., eating an apple when hungry), and *actus humanus*, a human act that involves the exercise of the conscience and *will (e.g., spending money on a new car). See also ACTUS PURUS.

ACTON, JOHN EMERICH EDWARD DALBERG (LORD ACTON) (1834–1902). Roman Catholic English historian. He was educated in Germany, where he became closely associated with J. J. I. von *Döllinger. Acton, at *Vatican Council I, organized resistance against the proposed definition of papal *infallibility but stopped short of rebellion such as led to Döllinger's *excommunication. A close friend of W. E. *Gladstone, Acton was made a peer after a brief parliamentary career as a liberal; in 1895 he became regius professor of history at Cambridge, where he organized the *Cambridge Modern History* project. He held that a country's freedom would be judged by the amount of security enjoyed by minorities. To him also is attributed the aphorism "Power tends to corrupt; absolute power corrupts absolutely."

ACTS OF UNIFORMITY See UNIFORMITY, ACTS OF.

ACTUAL SIN A *sin that results from the act of the person's *will (e.g., telling a half-truth). It is contrasted with *original sin, which, as the result of being a descendant of Adam, is not related to personal choice.

ACTUS PURUS (Lat. "pure act"). A medieval, philosophical definition of *God. Since *God does not have unrealized potential within himself, he is pure act, or pure actuality. God is unchangeable, for he is always perfect, *holy *love. If he could improve his being, he would not be perfect.

AD MAJOREM DEI GLORIAM (Lat. "for the greater glory of *God"). The motto of the *Jesuits (Society of Jesus) but used by many other Christians also.

ADALBERT (956–997). *Bishop of Prague. A man of high principle who urged moral reformation on an uncaring country, he evangelized also in other lands. Twice he left Prague (of which, at the age of twenty-six, he had become the first Czech bishop) because of dissatisfaction with contemporary attitudes to *Christianity. Finally, in 995, with papal permission, he went as a *missionary to Prussia, where he was martyred.

ADAM OF MARSH (d. 1258). English *Franciscan monk and scholar. A pupil of *Grosseteste (whom he accompanied to the 1245 Council of *Lyons), he was consulted by king, pope, and the *archbishop of Canterbury because of his learning and *wisdom. Known as

"Doctor Illustris," he was the first Franciscan master in *theology at Oxford.

ADAMNAN (c. 625–704). Ninth *abbot of *Iona. One of *Columba's greatest successors, he nonetheless moved against the island community's autonomy in trying unsuccessfully to impose Roman customs, particularly concerning the dating of *Easter, wherein the Celtic church differed. He traveled in England and Ireland, achieving notable humanitarian reforms, but he is best known for his biography of Columba (a valuable historical document, despite legend and embellishment).

ADAMSON, PATRICK (1537–1592). *Archbishop of St. Andrews, the last to bear that title until the modern reestablishment of the Roman Catholic *hierarchy. Ordained in the post-*Reformation church, he spent some years in Geneva, was minister of Paisley, and then in 1576 was named archbishop by Regent Morton (though evidently never consecrated). He fought a bitter battle with the Presbyterians, who made his position untenable.

ADESTE FIDELES The opening words of a famous but anonymous *Christmas *hymn. Known either in its Latin form or as "O Come, All Ye Faithful" (trans. Frederick Oakeley [1802–1880]).

ADIAPHORA (Gk. "things indifferent"). Church *rites/ceremonies that are neither commanded nor forbidden in the *Bible. Examples are special dress for *clergy and *choir, set *liturgies, use of candles, etc. Some—especially Anglicans and Lutherans—maintain this principle; other *denominations claim that only what is actually commanded in *Scripture should be a part of *worship. The term came into prominence when moderate Lutherans of the 16th century (led by *Melanchthon, criticized by *Calvin), partly under political pressure, took a softer line on some things that *Luther had condemned.

ADIAPHORISTS Those who claimed that certain *Christian practices were *adiaphora.

ADJURATION A solemn command or request that uses the name of *God or of a *holy person/thing. The famous example is the high priest's command to *Jesus (Matt 26:63). It is used in *exorcism when a *demon is commanded to leave.

ADONAI (Heb. "my lord"). The word is used 134 times in the *OT for the *God of the Hebrews (e.g., Exod 23:17; 34:23; Isa 1:24; 3:15; 10:16; Amos 8:1). Later when the Jews did not pronounce God's true name of *Yahweh (Jehovah), Adonai was used as a substitute. There is an old tradition in *liturgy of addressing the *eternal *Son of God as "O Adonai"—e.g., in the *antiphon and in the *Magnificat on December 18 in the Roman Catholic Church. See also JEHOVAH.

ADOPTION, LEGAL The legal process whereby a child becomes a member of a family that is not that of his/her natural, blood parents. In most Western countries an adopted child now has the same rights and obligations as a natural child in the family he has joined. The placing of children for adoption is seen as an important sphere of *Christian ministry by the church, and so many adoption agencies are Christian.

ADOPTION, THEOLOGICAL The act of *God the Father including believers in *Christ in his family and giving them the Holy *Spirit, "the Spirit of adoption" (Gal 4:5; Eph 1:5). *Jesus, the Incarnate Son, is the true, only-begotten Son; believers become adopted sons and daughters, adopted by *grace. Adoption is closely connected with *justification.

ADOPTIONISM A *heresy (also spelled "adoptianism") taught in Spain by Elipandus of Toledo and Felix of Urgal in the 8th century and condemned by Pope *Leo III at a *synod in Rome in 799. It was claimed that *Jesus, at some point in his life (e.g., at his *baptism), was adopted by the

Father, thereby creating the Son and incorporating him into the Godhead. Thus it denies the *eternal existence of the Son and his *incarnation as Jesus of Nazareth. See also MONARCHIANISM.

ADORATION Worship that belongs to *God alone. In Latin this act is *latia*—in Greek, *latreia*. When in some quarters a lesser reverence is given to the Virgin *Mary, or perfected *saints, different words are used—*dulia* (Lat.) and *proskunesis* or *douleia* (Gk.). See also VENERATION.

ADRIAN I (d. 795). Pope from 772. His *pontificate was entirely within the reign of *Charlemagne, with whom he had a comparatively harmonious relationship from the outset, when Charlemagne routed the Lombards who were attacking papal possessions and threatening Rome itself. Adrian nonetheless was alert in fighting off imperial interference in spiritual affairs. He was a strong defender of *orthodoxy, and he worked to alleviate the lot of the *poor, undertook extensive construction work in Rome, and laid the foundation of Western *canon law.

ADRIAN II (792–872). Pope from 867. Weak and indecisive, the elderly Adrian could not maintain the standards set and progress made by his predecessor *Nicholas I. His interventions in French affairs were rebuffed, and though by a prudent stroke he won the loyalty of the Moravians, it was through his vacillation in East-West relations that Bulgaria was lost to Roman Catholicism. He did, however, initiate the significant outreach of *Cyril and *Methodius to the Slovaks.

ADRIAN IV (c. 1110–1159). Pope from 1154. Born Nicholas Breakspear, he was the only Englishman to have held the papal office. He had served earlier in France, Italy, and Scandinavia. In 1155 he crowned *Frederick I (Barbarossa) as Holy Roman emperor after Frederick had handed over to him would-be church reformer *Arnold of Brescia. Relations soon deteriorated as papal pretensions clashed with imperial ambitions. In other areas, too, Adrian was confronted by unsettling troubles and demands, but his able if brief rule enhanced the *papacy. In a *bull later refuted, Adrian ostensibly gave hereditary possession of Ireland to *Henry II of England.

ADRIAN VI (1459–1523). Pope from 1522. Born Adrian Florensz Boeyens, he was the only Dutch pope and the last non-Italian to hold the office until *John Paul II in 1978. A notable theologian from the University of Louvain and tutor to the future emperor *Charles V, he sought to crush Martin *Luther. He planned far-reaching church reforms, but he died before they could be implemented, after only twenty months in office.

ADULTERY Sexual intercourse between a married person and another who is not the married partner. It is forbidden by the Mosaic Law (Exod 20:14) and by *Jesus (Matt 5:27–30). See also DIVORCE, FORNICATION.

ADVENT (Lat. "coming"). The season in which the church thinks of *Christ's first and *second comings to earth—first as a babe and second as the Judge of all. It covers the four *Sundays before *Christmas Day.

ADVENTISTS, ADVENTIST CHURCHES Protestant groups that originated in the mid-19th century in the U.S. as a result of, or connected with, the *preaching of William *Miller (1782–1849). His calculations and predictions of the advent of *Christ to inaugurate the Millennium proved wrong. However, those who held to the essence but not the details of his teaching formed such *denominations as the Advent Christian church (which has c. 32,000 members in North America) and the *Seventh-Day Adventist church.

ADVOCATE (Gk. *parakletos,* "advocate, intercessor, comforter, counselor, *paraclete"). A title of *Christ (1 John 2:1) and of the Holy *Spirit (John 14:16, 26; 15:26; 16:7).

ADVOCATUS DIABOLI See DEVIL'S ADVOCATE.

AELFRIC (c. 953–c. 1015). *Anglo-Saxon writer and *abbot. Belonging to the second generation of monastic reformers, he wrote works in English that improved the education and morals of *clergy and people. In 1005 he became the first *abbot of Eynsham in Oxfordshire. Aelfric denied the *Immaculate Conception and evidently opposed also the *doctrine of *transubstantiation, which views led to a revival of interest in his work at the *Reformation.

AEON (Gk. *aion,* "age, epoch, long period of time"). The *NT often speaks of two aeons: the present (*evil) age (Gal 1:4)—beginning with Adam and ending with the Last *Judgment—and the future age of the *kingdom of *God (Heb 6:5). See also ETERNITY.

AETIOLOGY (lit. "the science or philosophy of causation" or "the enquiry into origins"). When studying certain biblical stories, some scholars assume that stories were told in prescientific *cultures in order to explain the origins of familiar customs or natural phenomena. Thus, e.g., they say that the account of Lot's wife turning to salt (Gen 19:26) and the account of the Tower of Babel (Gen 11:1–9) may be stories to explain strange rock formations.

AFFUSION (INFUSION) The pouring of water over the head of one being baptized. *Baptism is also performed by *immersion in water and by *aspersion (sprinkling) water over the head.

AFRICAN METHODIST EPISCOPAL CHURCH Organized in 1816, it developed out of a group of blacks who formed a congregation some three decades earlier because of discrimination in a Philadelphia church. The AME church's first *bishop, Richard *Allen, was consecrated by Francis *Asbury in 1816. The church spread into the South after 1865 and now has some 1.25 million members in approximately 5,800 churches.

AFRICAN METHODIST EPISCOPAL ZION CHURCH Like the *African Methodist Episcopal church, it arose out of white discrimination. A group of black members of a church in New York City met together in 1796, built their own church in 1800, and organized a national body in 1821. Their first *bishop, James Varick, was elected in 1822. Currently it has about 1.35 million members in 5000 churches.

AGAPE A Greek word for *love. John described *God's *agape* and its effects (1 John 4:7–12), and Paul described its place in the *Christian life (1 Cor 13). The word is also used to describe a Christian *fellowship meal (a love feast), held either with or distinct from the *Lord's Supper. Such a practice occurred in the primitive Corinthian church and has been part of revival movements (e.g., early *Methodism) and liturgical movements (e.g., in the form of parish breakfasts or lunches after the Lord's Supper).

AGAPEMONISM English religious *sect. Henry James Price (1811–1899), an Anglican clergyman inhibited because of bizarre views, founded at Spaxton in Somerset, with his former rector Samuel Starky, a community called Agapemone (Abode of Love). Pronouncing judgment on Christendom, Price induced followers to sign over their possessions to him. A notorious court case exposed this practice and moral irregularities, but the sect survived into the early 20th century.

AGAPETUS (d. 536). Pope from 535. A champion of *orthodoxy, he traveled to Constantinople and there deposed its *patriarch Anthimus and consecrated a successor free of Monophysite tendencies. Not only did he carry this through despite the opposition of the empress Theodora; he took the opportunity to pronounce against *heresy generally. Agapetus died in Constantinople, but his remains were brought back for *burial in Rome.

AGATHO (d. 681). Pope from 678. Sicilian by birth, he formally declared to the *Eastern Church the *inerrancy of the Roman Catholic Church, condemned the *Monothelites, and intervened on behalf of *Bishop *Wilfrid of York against the high-handed action of *Archbishop Theodore of Canterbury. Agatho is said to have been more than a hundred years old when he was elected.

AGE OF REASON The age of a child (usually between seven and twelve years old) at which church and state recognize that the child is responsible in the sense of knowing right from wrong.

AGGIORNAMENTO An Italian word that became common outside Italy during the *papacy of *John XXIII (1958–63). It means "bringing matters up to date" and is used of bringing traditional *Roman Catholicism into the modern age without losing its essential character.

AGGREY, JAMES EMMAN KWEGYIR (1875–1927). African educator. Educated at a Methodist *mission school in Ghana and at a North Carolina college where he taught for twenty years, he was the only black member of the Stokes-Phelps Commission that studied educational affairs in Africa. He helped to establish Achimota College in what was then the Gold Coast and was greatly beloved as a *mediator between races and *cultures.

AGLIPAY CRUZ Y LABAYAN, GREGORIO (1860–1940). First *bishop of the Philippine Independent church. When revolutionaries with whom he sympathized proclaimed the republic in 1898, they named Aglipay, a Roman Catholic *priest, head of the Philippine church, which for centuries had been dominated by Spanish *friars. The word "Independent" was added when the *pope refused to appoint Filipino bishops. Excommunicated by Rome, Aglipay was consecrated bishop by twelve priests, an early church practice, and remained supreme bishop until his death.

AGNELLUS OF PISA (1194–1236). Founder of the *Franciscan *order in England. Recruited by Francis himself, he served in Paris until 1224, when he came to England with eight colleagues of piety and scholarship. He established a school at Oxford and brought to it as a lecturer R. *Grosseteste, one of the most erudite men of the 13th century, who helped to make it a renowned center of learning.

AGNOSTICISM (lit. "not knowing"). A term coined by T. H. Huxley (1825–1895). Used in a strong sense, the term "agnostic" indicates someone who believes it is impossible in practice—some would say even in principle—on the basis of the available evidence or the limits of the human intellect to affirm or deny the existence of *God. A weaker meaning relates to the hesitancy of *theists to claim to know aspects of the *mystery of God (e.g., agnosticism about the working of God's mind in a matter like *predestination).

AGNUS DEI (Lat. "Lamb of *God"). Based on John 1:29 and used of the words recited by the Roman Catholic *priest or sometimes sung by the *choir in the *Eucharist/*Mass just before the receiving of *Communion. The formula (normally "O Lamb of God . . . have mercy upon us") is said three times, addressed to *Christ, now believed to be present in and through the sacramental bread and wine.

AGRICOLA, JOHANN (1494–1566). German Reformer. Recording secretary to *Luther at the Disputation of Leipzig, he became in 1525 head of the Latin school at Eisleben. There he rejected the law ("To the gallows with Moses!") as unnecessary in bringing the sinner to *repentance. This view (*antinomianism) brought Agricola into dispute first with *Melanchthon, then with *Luther himself. In 1540 Agricola retracted his views, but he again alienated orthodox Protestants by contributing to the Interim of *Augsburg.

AGRICOLA, MIKAEL (c. 1510–1557). Finnish Reformer, often called the "father of Finnish literature." Influenced toward the *Reformation by fellow countryman Peter *Sarkilax, he studied in Wittenberg (1536–1539) and returned commended by *Luther. He was principal of the theological school at Abo (southwestern Finland), then *bishop of the *diocese. Pious and scholarly, his translations of *Scripture and other religious *works made a vital contribution in the growth of the Finnish church.

AIDAN (d. 651). "Apostle of Northumbria" and first *bishop of Lindisfarne. Irish by birth, he left *Iona in order to work among the barbarous people of northeastern England. He evangelized extensively, founded churches and *monasteries and a school for boys who would continue his work. The Venerable *Bede, who disapproved of Aidan's *Celtic church loyalties, nevertheless testified to his learning, concern for the *poor and oppressed, and simple lifestyle. J. B. *Lightfoot, 19th-century bishop of Durham said, "Not Augustine, but Aidan, is the true apostle of England."

AILRED (AELRED) (1109–1167). English *Cistercian *abbot. Reared at the court of David I of Scotland, whose biographer he became later, he entered the Cistercian *order and in 1147 was appointed *abbot of Rievaulx in Yorkshire. He exercised great influence on the political scene, traveled widely on his order's business, but remained essentially a pious ascetic. He produced some of the best medieval writings and was known as "the English St. Bernard."

ALAIN (ALAN) OF LILLE (c. 1120–1202). French theologian and philosopher. So versatile as to earn the title "Doctor Universalis," his robust but highly personal defense of *Christianity had eclectic tendencies. To Alain, whose opponents ranged from Waldensians to Saracens, the truths of the *faith were self-evident. He made notable contributions in many areas, including medieval Latin poetry and *preaching theory, and his writing was said to have given inspiration to Dante and Chaucer. He died at Citeaux, apparently as an ordinary *Cistercian lay brother.

ALACOQUE, MARGUERITE MARIE (1647–1690). *Visitandine nun. She entered a French convent in 1671 and reportedly was commissioned by Christ in a vision to establish devotion to his *Sacred Heart. This involved *Communion on the first Friday of the month, the Holy Hour on Thursday, and observance of the Feast of the Sacred Heart annually. Not until the latter part of the following century was the devotion recognized; she was subsequently canonized (1920).

ALB The (normally) white linen *vestment worn by the minister in the *Eucharist, covering the whole *body from neck to ankles and fastened at the waist with a *cincture, a type of belt. The whiteness symbolically points to the need for purity of heart and life.

ALBAN (d. c. 304). First British *martyr. According to *Bede, he served in the Roman army and was martyred in place of a fleeing *priest with whom he changed clothes. Some scholars suggest that the execution occurred, not under the *Diocletian persecution, but under an earlier one.

ALBERT OF BRANDENBURG (1490–1545). *Cardinal *archbishop of Mainz. A cultured man, he is remembered chiefly because it was he whom *Luther attacked over the sale of *indulgences. He nonetheless had some sympathy for the *Reformation in its initial stages, and even when he reverted to support of the papacy he disliked strong action taken against the Reformers.

ALBERT OF PRUSSIA (1490–1568). Grand master of the Order of *Teutonic Knights. In 1523 the *order was dissolved by Albert on the advice of *Luther, and East Prussia subsequently became a hereditary duchy under *Sigismund I of Poland, despite the resistance of emperor *Charles V. In 1544 Albert founded the University of Konigsberg, and after a time of turmoil he made his territory a stronghold of orthodox *Lutheranism.

ALBERTUS MAGNUS (ALBERT THE GREAT) (c. 1200–1280). *Dominican scholar. After teaching in his native Germany and in France, he returned home to serve the newly founded Dominican *order. Briefly *bishop and papal legate, the latter part of his life was devoted to writing. One of the greatest scholars of medieval times (Thomas *Aquinas was among his pupils), Albert's encouragement of the study of natural science owed a great deal to Aristotle, but he was careful to stress the primacy of revelation over human reason. A contemporary called him "a man so superior in every science, that he can fittingly be called the wonder and the miracle of our time."

ALBIGENSIANS Medieval French heretical *sect. Originating from Albi in southern France in the mid-12th century, the name was applied particularly to groups such as *Bogomils, who sought to revive the teaching of the 3d-century Manichees. They denied *Christ's true humanity, crucifixion, and *resurrection. The Albigensians created their own *clergy, freed from the *evil and corruption they saw in the church. *Salvation was attainable through liberation from matter. They recognized two categories: the "perfect" (who were baptized by the Holy *Spirit by the laying on of hands and who adhered to a strict lifestyle) and the "believers" (who led normal lives but vowed to receive the *baptism when in danger of death). Forcibly suppressed by the mid-13th century, they had disappeared by the end of the 14th century. The Albigensians challenged the church, particularly *Dominicans and *Franciscans, to concern themselves with deepening the spiritual life of the common people.

ALBRIGHT, JACOB (1759–1808). Founder of the Evangelical Church in the U.S. Son of German immigrants in Pennsylvania, converted in 1790, licensed as a Methodist lay preacher, and ordained by his own congregation, in 1807 he became first *bishop of a new movement he organized along Methodist lines, later called the Evangelical Association (1816) and the Evangelical Church (1922).

ALBRIGHT, WILLIAM FOXWELL (1891–1971). Eminent American biblical archaeologist. Born in Chile, son of a Methodist *missionary, he obtained his doctorate at Johns Hopkins University and was professor of Semitic languages there for some thirty years until 1958. He was a tireless opponent of liberal theories on the *OT, an active fieldworker whose excavations at Tell Beit Mirsim set the pattern for future archaeological work in the region, longtime editor of the prestigious *Bulletin of the American Schools of Oriental Research*, and a prolific author whose writings included *From the Stone Age to Christianity* (1957) and *The Archaeology of Palestine* (1960).

ALCUIN (c. 732–804). English scholar and prime mover in the Carolingian Renaissance. Master of the famous cathedral school in York, he accepted an invitation by *Charlemagne in 781 to Aachen, which became a center of *culture and discussion. Alcuin made significant contributions in educational and liturgical matters and continued to exercise a notable influence in church and state after he left the court in 796 to become *abbot of Tours.

ALEANDRO, GIROLAMO (1480–1542). Roman Catholic scholar and *cardinal. Italian by birth, he was rector of Paris University when in 1520 Pope *Leo X commissioned him to lead the opposition to *Luther at the Diet of *Worms. Aleandro instituted strong action against *Reformation supporters in Brussels and was a leading advocate of the need for the Council of *Trent.

ALESIUS (ALANE), ALEXANDER (1500–1565). Scottish Lutheran theologian. As canon of St. Andrews, he was chosen to reclaim Patrick *Hamilton from Lutheran opinions, but was himself converted, imprisoned, and forced to flee to Germany in 1532. Alesius unsuccessfully tried to persuade *Luther to adopt less extreme views, arranged debates among Protestant parties, wrote many theological works, and was a signatory of the *Augsburg Confession.

ALEXANDER (d. 328). *Patriarch of Alexandria from 312. He realized and tirelessly sought to counter the fundamental *heresy taught by *Arius, one of his *priests who denied the true divinity of *Jesus Christ. Alexander excommunicated Arius, and with his young *deacon (and future successor) *Athanasius, a perceptive counselor, upheld orthodox *doctrine at the Council of *Nicea in 325.

ALEXANDER, ARCHIBALD (1772–1851). Father of the so-called *Princeton Theology. He was professor of *theology at Princeton Theological Seminary, where he developed his particular blend of 17th-century Protestant *scholasticism, Scottish common sense realism, and *Reformed theology, all with a heavy emphasis on human reason and a skeptical attitude toward *mysticism. He was followed in this by Charles *Hodge, A. A. *Hodge, and B. B. *Warfield, who succeeded him at Princeton.

ALEXANDER, SAMUEL (1859–1938). Jewish pantheistic philosopher. He combined Spinoza's basic ideas with a form of emergent evolution that saw a hierarchical set of levels arise from a space-time matrix, ultimately fashioning a "deity." He held that the religious life of man lies in actively participating in the emergence of good, thus in the ultimate victory of deity over *evil. He wrote *Space, Time, and Deity* (1916–1918 Gifford Lectures).

ALEXANDER I (d. before 120). Pope for about a ten-year period between 105 and 119. Claimed to have been the fifth pope after Peter, he is said (probably erroneously) to have introduced *holy water, and the practice of mixing *Communion wine with water. The suggestion that he died a *martyr has never been substantiated.

ALEXANDER II (d. 1073). Pope from 1061. Known also as Anselm of Lucca (of which *diocese he was *bishop from 1057, and which gives the same name to his nephew with whom he is often confused), Alexander was a reforming pope who dealt vigorously with *simony and upheld clerical *celibacy. He was, moreover, a champion of Jews who were undergoing severe persecution in southern France and Spain. Despite initial opposition from an *antipope named by *Henry IV, the future emperor, he consolidated the *papacy's influence against secular powers.

ALEXANDER III (c. 1105–1181). Pope from 1159. As a *cardinal he strongly resisted the aim of *Frederick I (Barbarossa) to make the *pope subordinate to the emperor. When he himself became pope, Alexander found himself confronted by an *antipope who was Frederick's man. Twice exiled through imperial action that brought a seventeen-year *schism to the church, Alexander successfully led the Lombard League against Frederick, who was forced to acknowledge defeat and to seek reconciliation in 1177. Alexander's patience (some say ambivalence) saw him through the crisis that preceded and followed the murder of Thomas *Becket in 1170. Alexander is esteemed in *Roman Catholicism as the first great lawyer-pope.

ALEXANDER V (c. 1339–1410). Pope from 1409–1410, a status disputed by some scholars who classify him as an *antipope. Born in Crete, he was elected by the Council of *Pisa, which thought thereby to end the *Great Schism but merely added a third claimant to the *papacy. Foul play was said to have been involved in his mysterious death.

ALEXANDER VI (c. 1431–1503). Pope from 1492. Spanish by birth and one of the Borgia family, he became in his mid-twenties a *cardinal appointed by his uncle *Callistus III. Elected pope through the bribery and corruption that were to mark his whole career, he pronounced the New World divided between Spain and Portugal, had *Savonarola executed, fathered illegitimate sons, and so disgraced the *papacy as to contribute substantially toward the *Reformation.

ALEXANDER VII (1599–1667). Pope from 1655. Born into a prominent Sienese family, he was a tireless upholder of his church's rights, particularly against *Jansenism, and less successfully against *Louis XIV of France who refused to help in the *pope's plans to mount an offensive against the encroaching Turks. Alexander was an encourager of foreign *missions and the arts.

ALEXANDER VIII (1610–1691). Pope from 1689. He brought an end to the disputes between the *papacy and *Louis XIV, condemned *Jansenism and the *Gallican Articles, and implemented humanitarian reforms in the *papal states. He was interested also in the possibility of restoring the Stuart monarchy in England.

ALEXANDER OF HALES (c. 1170–1245). English theologian and philosopher. From 1220 he taught in Paris, where, having become a *Franciscan about 1236, he established a famous school where Aristotelian thought and its theological implications were studied in depth. Alexander was enlisted to act as peacemaker in the 1235–1236 negotiations between England and France. Basically *Augustinian, he exercised a profound influence on his students, among whom was *Bonaventura.

ALEXANDRIAN THEOLOGY The method and context of the *theology taught in the church of ancient Alexandria and by those associated with it. Usually it is contrasted with the *Antiochene theology associated with the church in ancient Antioch. It was particularly important in two periods.

1. From c. 190–c. 255 under the leadership of *Clement and *Origen. The *Christian *faith was expounded with reference to the leading ideas of current Greek philosophy. Also, it is a way of interpreting the *Bible as if it were *allegory, *truth expressed in rich symbolism.

2. From c. 325–c. 451, when there was much controversy in the church concerning precisely how *Jesus Christ, as the *God-Man or Incarnate Son, should be described in theological terms. The mood of Alexandria tended to underplay the full humanity of the *Lord Jesus while emphasizing his deity. *Athanasius and *Cyril were well-known Alexandrian theologians.

ALFORD, HENRY (1810–1871). Dean of Canterbury. Author of well-known *hymns and first editor of the *Contemporary Review,* he is remembered best for a durable edition of the Greek *NT (1849–1861).

ALFRED THE GREAT (849–899). King of England from 871. He routed the Danish invader, sowed the seed for monastic reform, and fostered a great revival of learning throughout the kingdom. Himself a cultured and ascetic man, he was in a cosmopolitan group of scholars that provided English translations of *Christian classics by writers such as *Augustine and *Gregory I.

ALIENATION A theological term arising from three sources—Karl Marx, modern sociologists, and certain existentialist philosophers, e.g., M. Heidegger (d. 1976). In *theology it is usually a way of describing the effects of *sin. So it is claimed that a man is alienated from his true self, from the society in which he lives, and from his Creator and Redeemer. In other words there is the lack of true harmony and wholeness in his life and relationships.

ALL SAINTS' DAY The feast to celebrate all *saints, known and unknown, and kept on November 1. The evening before is known as *Halloween—All Hallows Eve.

ALL SOULS' DAY The feast to celebrate the faithful departed and kept on November 2 (or November 3 when November 2 is a *Sunday).

ALLEGORY, ALLEGORICAL INTERPRETATION A particular way of interpreting *Scripture. Behind the plain history or the literal meaning, a deeper symbolic, or spiritual, truth is seen. E.g., Paul saw Abraham's two sons (Isaac and Ishmael) as the symbolism of two *covenants (see Gal 4:21–15:1; Gen 21:8–14). Misuse of this method brings into question the credibility of the biblical narratives as history. *Jesus sometimes used allegory in his parables (e.g., Matt 13:18–23), but more often they had one obvious point. See also EXEGESIS, HERMENEUTICS.

ALLEINE, JOSEPH (1634–1668). English *Presbyterian minister. One of the famous Oxford Puritans, he was ejected after the *Restoration and in 1663 was imprisoned for *preaching to his own family. He is remembered for his *Alarm to the Unconverted,* to which classic a debt was acknowledged by many, including George *Whitefield and C. H. *Spurgeon.

ALLEN, RICHARD (1760–1831). Founder of the *African Methodist Episcopal church. Born into a slave family, he bought his freedom in 1786 and became a leader in a Methodist Episcopal church in Philadelphia. Restricted in his ministry to fellow blacks, he organized in 1787 an independent body from which emerged the first black congregation in the country. In 1816 he founded the AME church and was elected its first *bishop.

ALLEN, WILLIAM (1532–1594). English *cardinal. An Oxford graduate, he became principal of St. Mary's Hall there (1556) but had to leave England on refusing to take the *oath acknowledging *Elizabeth I as head of the Church of *England. He was ordained a Roman Catholic *priest in Belgium and founded and headed an English *seminary in France (1568–1585), where he directed production of the *Douay-Reims version of the *Bible and organized *Jesuit *missions to England. He encouraged *Philip II to conquer England, a project that ended with the defeat of the Armada in 1588.

ALLOIOSIS A Greek figure of speech used by U. *Zwingli (1484–1531) to deny that *Jesus' *suffering and death could be said to be the suffering and death of the *eternal *Son of God. The experience of the humanity the Son of God assumed in the *Incarnation cannot be that of the divine *nature.

ALMONER An officer responsible for the distribution of *alms to the *poor—thus, a social worker in a hospital, a chaplain in an orphanage, and also (in France) a chaplain in the army. Normally associated in church history with a religious institution, the term often applies to one holding an honorary secular post or to a trained social worker.

ALMS An archaic word referring to gifts collected in divine *worship.

ALPHA AND OMEGA A title of *Christ (Rev 1:8) and of *God (21:6). It is based on the first and last letter of the Greek alphabet and suggests that God is not only the source but also the goal of everything.

ALSTED, JOHANN HEINRICH (1588 – 1638). German *Calvinist. Trained in German and Swiss universities, he returned to teach at the Reformed Academy at Herborn and was one of the representatives at the Synod of *Dort (1618–1619). His premillenarian work *Beloved City* contributed to the contemporary debate on *eschatology.

ALTAR (holy table). In many churches the central piece of furnishing. Used as a synonym for table, being the place on which the bread and wine of the Holy *Communion are consecrated. The use of the word "altar" need not imply that a *sacrifice is being offered to *God, i.e., that *Christ's sacrifice is being symbolically offered again. As church architecture evolved, and as the importance of the *Eucharist/*Mass developed in the medieval period, so the beauty and centrality of both stone and wood altars became more prominent. In modern times, with new emphases, this trend has often been reversed with interest in simple movable tables.

ALTHAUS, PAUL (1888–1966). German Lutheran *NT scholar, preacher, and theologian. He is best remembered as the cofounder of the *Zeitschrift für Systematische Theologie*, the president of the *Luthergesellschaft*, author of *Die Letzten Dinge* (1922) and *Die sogenannte Kerygma und der historische Jesus* (1958), and his involvement in the NT commentary *Das Neue Testament Deutsch*. His apparent compromise with National Socialist politics during the 1930s casts a dark cloud over an otherwise distinguished career.

ALTRUISM (Lat. *alter*, "the other"). A way of life or theory of life that is the opposite of egoism or self-centeredness. It is a selfless devotion to the needs and well-being of others because they actually need help. If this is done in and for the *love of *God, then it may be described as *Christian; but if it is done for humane reasons only, then it is a high point of *humanism or another philosophy of life.

ALUMBRADOS ("enlightened"). Spanish mystical *sect. Its adherents, often known as *Illuminati, many of them *Franciscans or *Jesuits, held such things as *sacraments and good *works to be unnecessary for those who had achieved direct communion with *God. Beginning about 1512 (just before the *Reformation), the movement was held to have links with the latter and was condemned by the *Inquisition, not least for gross carnality. It survived into the 17th century, but the excesses of some of its leaders prevented it from being a greater threat to traditional *Roman Catholicism.

AMANA CHURCH SOCIETY *Pietistic *sect, otherwise known as the Community of True Inspiration. Originating in Germany in 1714, the group held that direct inspiration from *God was still available and that true *Christianity is to be characterized by simplicity of life. In 1842 more than eight hundred members went to the New World in search of religious freedom, settling finally in Iowa in 1855. In 1932 communistic practices were replaced by private enterprise, and the church subsequently separated from very profitable business concerns. The society now numbers only a few hundred people.

AMANUENSIS A secretary. It is probable that Paul dictated some of his epistles to a secretary who wrote them down (see, e.g., Rom 16:22 and 2 Thess 3:17, where Paul appears only to have added the greeting in his own hand). In Roman society educated slaves often had the role of secretaries.

AMBROSE (c. 339–397). *Bishop of Milan. Orphaned early, he was brought up in a *Christian family and received an excellent training in arts and law. He was a provincial governor in imperial service and a Christian by conviction when he unwillingly, but by public acclamation, was pressed into succeeding an Arian as bishop of Milan (374). Still only a *catechumen, he was baptized, ordained, and consecrated within a few days. He gave his inheritance to the *poor, lived austerely, was a fearless champion of *orthodoxy against paganism and *Arianism, and of the church's independence of secular rulers. A notable preacher and writer whose knowledge extended to Greek *theology (a rare feature in the Western church at that time), Ambrose brought *Augustine of Hippo into Christian *faith and service.

AMBROSIANS Sixteenth-century *Anabaptist *sect, named for its leader, Ambrosius. Its adherents, claiming to base their position on John 1:9, stressed divine *revelation from *God that rendered priestly mediation or interpretation unnecessary and called in question the unique character of the *Bible. The name had been borne also by a number of Roman Catholic *religious congregations between the 9th and 16th centuries who regarded *Ambrose as their *patron.

AMEN (Heb. "firm, established"). Jesus is called the "Amen" (Rev 3:14—the trustworthy and reliable one). Some of Jesus' sayings begin with "Amen" ("Truly, truly"; "Verily, verily")—e.g., John 1:51; 5:19, 24, 25; 6:26, 32, 47, 53. The word is also used to conclude *prayers. This is not a convenient way to end but an affirmation of the acceptability of a prayer to *God offered in the name of *Jesus Christ.

AMERICAN BAPTIST CHURCHES A *denomination made up of some six thousand congregations. It originated in 1907 when a number of local and state associations formed a national grouping known as the Northern Baptist Convention, which developed into the American Baptist Convention in 1950 and assumed its present title in 1972. Its ministries reflect a greater diversity of theological stance than most American denominations.

AMERICAN BOARD OF COMMISSIONERS FOR FOREIGN MISSIONS An organization formed in 1810 during the *Second Great Awakening to support those pledged to *missionary service. The impetus came from New England *Congregationalists, but they were soon joined by Presbyterians and *Reformed. The first missionaries left in 1812 for India and Ceylon; work among American Indians began in 1817.

AMERICANISM Conflict within the Roman Catholic Church during the late 19th century concerning the degree to which traditional Catholic policy could be accommodated to a New World setting. Father Walter Elliot, *Archbishop John Ireland, and *Bishops John Keane and James Gibbons spearheaded the movement in America but were rebuked by the papal letter of *Leo XIII (January 22, 1899) *Testem benevolentiae*. These issues were to crop up again in *Vatican II.

AMES, WILLIAM (1576–1633). English *Puritan theologian. Graduate of Cambridge, he expressed himself so forcefully against trends in the Church of *England that he had to leave for Rotterdam in 1610. In the *Dutch Reformed Church he found a congenial base for attacking *Arminianism. As professor of *theology at Franeker (1622–1633) he produced weighty treatises, especially one on *Christian *ethics later translated into English as *Conscience* (1639).

AMICE (from Lat. *amictus,* "that which is wrapped around"). Originally a rectangular piece of linen used as a neckerchief to catch sweat. Now it is usually a neckerchief and a hood worn along with the *alb as a *vestment by ministers taking part in the *Eucharist.

AMILLENNIALISM Modern term for the belief that the Millennium is presently in existence and the denial that Revelation 20:4ff. refers to a literal period of a thousand years. The viewpoint may be traced back to the early church.

AMISH A *Christian group in North America known also as Amish *Mennonites. Their roots go back to 17th-century Europe, when Swiss Mennonite *elder Jacob Amman took a hard line on *doctrine and practice, more particularly on *excommunication, views his church would not accept. To his breakaway group he introduced such things as uniformity of dress, *footwashing during church services, and avoidance of state church services. Their immigration to the New World began in 1720. They settled first in Pennsylvania, then moved west and into Canada. Though depleted by unions and defections, the so-called Old Order Amish Mennonite church is still known for simple lifestyle, rejection of modern amenities, and suspicion of education above elementary level.

AMSDORF, NIKOLAUS VON (1483–1565). German Reformer. One of *Luther's strongest supporters, he accompanied him to the Leipzig Disputation (1519) and the Diet of *Worms (1521). Formerly a theological professor, he became *bishop of Naumburg (1542–1547) until deprived because of political developments. Amsdorf retired to Magdeburg but continued to fight for Lutheran *orthodoxy against what he regarded as the liberalizing tendencies of *Melanchthon and others. He took the initiative in the founding of the staunchly Lutheran University of Jena.

AMSTERDAM ASSEMBLY (1948). The meeting at which the *World Council of Churches was constituted. One hundred thirty-five *denominations from 44 countries were represented. Because a conference of *Orthodox churches in Moscow the previous month had condemned the WCC's aims as political, only the Greek church and the *ecumenical patriarchate of Constantinople reflected that tradition. The assembly declared: "The World Council of Churches is composed of churches which acknowledge *Jesus Christ as *God and Saviour. They find their unity in him. They do not have to create their unity; it is the gift of God. But they know that it is their *duty to make common cause in the search for the expression of that unity in work and life."

AMSTERDAM CONFERENCE (1983). What was claimed to be the first such conference in church history occurred when four thousand participants from 133 nations came to Amsterdam for the International Conference for Itinerant Evangelists. Its main purpose was to stimulate thoughtful and creative discussion and planning about the evangelistic task of the church today. In addition to major addresses by Billy *Graham and others, numerous workshops provided instruction on a wide variety of subjects. All the material was incorporated in the official conference report, *The Work of An Evangelist* (1984).

AMYRALD (AMYRAUT), MOSES (1596–1664). French Protestant *pastor. Trained in law and *theology and respected in high government circles, he became professor at Saumur in 1631. Temperamentally a peacemaker, he sought to build a bridge between Lutheran and *Reformed theology. He evolved a system (*Amyraldism) that was Calvinist in upholding the sovereignty of *God, but *Arminian in its declaration that God wills all men to be saved. God's purpose is, however, thwarted because of the universalism of man's sinfulness, and the actual *salvation of all men does not result.

AMYRALDISM A system of *theology named after M. *Amyrald (1596–1664), a French Protestant professor at the Academy of Saumur. Also called "New Methodism" because it advocated a new understanding of the *eternal decrees of *God, one that contrasted with that of the orthodox *Calvinism at that time. The double decree (*election to eternal life and to *eternal *damnation) was replaced by a decree of universal *redemption (achieved by *Jesus' death and *resurrection) and a decree of *election to life with no decree of *reprobation/damnation.

ANABAPTISTS Sometimes called the left-wing of the *Reformation, they were known by this description used from the 4th century of those who advocated rebaptism in certain cases. The 16th-century Anabaptists went further, rejecting their *baptism as infants as useless because it lacked that public *confession of *sin and *faith that they regarded now as inseparable from true baptism. They upheld the primacy of *Scripture and the separation of church and state, refused to take civil *oaths, and (in most cases) were pacifists. The movement began in Zurich where the first baptisms took place in 1525. Many were executed for their beliefs. Among the leaders of the different groups into which Anabaptists divided were C. *Grebel, T. *Münzer, and S. *Franck.

ANACLETUS (latter 1st century). Pope c. 79–92. Listed as the third *bishop of Rome (after Peter and Linus), he is said to have known Peter and to have died a *martyr during the reign of the emperor Domitian.

ANAKEPHALAIOSIS (Gk. "summary, recapitulation"). Its use in *theology is derived from the phrase in Eph 1:10, "to unite all things in him [*Christ]." *Irenaeus (c. 130–c. 200) used the idea with reference to the *Incarnation. He taught that in and by Christ fallen humanity is restored to *fellowship with *God and that the history of God's redeeming activity is completed and "summed up" in the life and work of Christ. Later theologians took up and developed the idea.

ANALOGIA FIDEI (Lat. "analogy of *faith"). The phrase, in its Greek equivalent, occurs in Romans 12:6. When used in *theology it means that every statement of *doctrine has to be made in the light of the total understanding of the faith. When used in biblical interpretation it means that the obscure parts are to be interpreted in the light of what is clear in the rest of *Scripture, and that the *OT is to be interpreted in the light of the *NT. See also Exegesis, Hermeneutics.

ANALOGUE Refers to the human or earthly reality that has a real analogy to something or someone other than itself, to which it points. For example, kingdom/kingship is an analogue of the sovereign rule of *God, and fatherhood is an analogue of an important aspect of the character of God. So it is appropriate to speak of God's *kingdom/kingship and God's fatherhood.

ANALOGY (Gk. *analogia,* "proportion"). The recognition of valid or true relationships. The way of analogy (*via analogia*) in *theology is to speak of *God in terms used of human beings and their world. This is possible because there is a definite relationship (*analogia entis*, "analogy of being") between God and man: God created man in his own image and likeness (Gen 1:26). So the way of analogy allows us to speak meaningfully of God as father, judge, rock, bridegroom, and *Savior and to claim that he loves, chastises, blesses, and curses. This way of explaining how religious language functions was given a sound, theoretical basis by Thomas *Aquinas (c. 1225–c. 1274), the great medieval philosopher; and it has been developed by others since his time. The main point is that what is being attributed to God is done so in a way that is appropriate to him as *eternal, *infinite, and Creator. Therefore he is Father in a manner appropriate to his own being and not some bearded old gentleman living beyond the sky.

ANALYSIS FIDEI (Lat. "analysis of *faith"). An expression used by Roman Catholic theologians in their investigation of living faith. They enquire into such questions as, "Does the believer believe *directly* in *God or indirectly by believing words spoken by God?" and "What is the relation of faith to a life of obedience?"

ANALYTIC AND SYNTHETIC STATEMENTS It is possible to distinguish between statements by the nature of the evidence required to establish their *truth. The statement "All clergymen are male" is an analytic proposition and truth because the concept of the predicate (male) is included in the concept of the subject (clergymen). However, the statement, "A red light indicates *stop*" is different, for the idea of stopping is not included by definition in the idea of a red light. So it is a synthetic proposition, for it is only true by virtue of the laws of a country and by people obeying the law. So a statement is an analytic truth if it is true in the light of the words it contains; a statement is a synthetic truth if it is true in virtue of the world as it happens to be.

ANALYTICAL PHILOSOPHY One of several names (others being linguistic analysis, linguistic philosophy, and logical empiricism) given to a modern and predominantly British philosophy. It is concerned not with ultimate questions and speculative theories, as was older philosophy. Rather its purpose is to analyze the language that we use daily to describe our everyday life, in order to clarify the function of language. Its most influential exponents have been Ludwig Wittgenstein (1889–1951), J. L. Austin (1911–1960), Gilbert Ryle (1900–1976), and A. J. Ayer. This approach to language raises particular problems for religious believers; and some *Christian philosophers, notably *Bishop I. T. Ramsey, have sought to justify religious language on the principles of this philosophy.

ANAMNESIS (Gk. "remembrance, recollection, memorial, commemoration"). Used particularly with reference to the *Lord's Supper or *Eucharist. According to Luke 22:19 and 1 Corinthians 11:24, *Jesus said, "Do this for my *anamnesis*." Thus the "recalling," or "calling back," of the *passion and death of the *Lord Jesus is done in the Lord's Supper in the belief that what was achieved once for all and forever by *Christ on the *cross will be received by the worshipers as they partake of the bread and wine.

ANAPHORA (Gk. "offering"). Used primarily to describe the *prayer of *consecration in the *Eucharist or *Lord's Supper. Along with this prayer, the bread and wine are offered to *God so that, having his blessing, they can become symbols of the *body and *blood of *Jesus Christ for the believer. Although this is the most widely used name, others used are *eucharistia* (thanksgiving), *oratio oblationis* (the prayer of offering), *canon (rule) and *prex eucharistica* (eucharistic prayer). The normal parts of the *anaphora* are: thanksgiving, reference to the institution of the Lord's Supper, the remembrance (*anamnesis) of God's saving work, request for the coming of the *Spirit, and praise.

ANATHEMA (Gk. "suspended"). In the *Septuagint it translates the Hebrew *cherem*, which means "placed under the ban" or "accursed" (see Lev 27:28–29; Num 21:3; Deut 7:26). Paul made use of the idea (see, e.g., Rom 9:3; Gal 1:8–9; cf. also Acts 23:14). Within the churches sentences of *anathema* (*excommunication) were pronounced against heretical *doctrines (e.g., *Arianism) from early times.

ANASTASIS (Gk. "*resurrection"). Used to refer to *Jesus' resurrection.

ANASTASIUS I (d. 401). Pope from 399. His short rule was praised by *Jerome and *Augustine not least for his condemnation of the writings of the influential *Origen. He also encouraged the African *bishops in their fight against *Donatism.

ANCHORITE; ANCHORESS Formerly synonymous with "hermit," the term was used of one who renounced the world in favor of a silent and solitary life of *prayer, *contemplation, and *mortification. It was an individual matter (as with Simeon the *Stylite) until anchorites in the early 4th century were organized under the rules of the church and confined to their cells. Both types of solitaries have long ceased to exist in their original forms, but a modified type of anchoritic life is still found among groups such as *Carthusians.

ANCIENT OF DAYS A title of *God in Daniel 7:9, 13, 22. A literal translation of the original is "advanced in days." Thus God is presented in the image of an old, wise judge who rules the world.

ANDERSON, SIR ROBERT (1841–1918). Lay theologian and policeman. Born in Dublin and converted at age nineteen, he trained as a lawyer, served as a government adviser, and in 1888 became head of Scotland Yard's criminal investigation department. All this time this *Presbyterian layman's *preaching and writing on biblical themes had immense popular appeal. His books included *The Coming Prince* (1882) and *The Bible and Modern Criticism* (1902).

ANDOVER CONTROVERSY Late 19th-century controversy at Andover Theological Seminary during which "Progressive Orthodoxy" (liberalism) was being substituted for a more traditional conservative *Calvinism. Specifically, it dealt with the idea of "future probation," whereby one was given a chance after death to respond to the *gospel. Bitter infighting among faculty, administration, and board was ultimately brought to the Massachusetts Supreme Court, which overturned the conservatives, thus allowing the liberals eventual victory.

ANDREW OF CRETE (c. 660–740). One of the greatest *hymn writers of the Greek Orthodox church. Born in Syria, he became archbishop of Gortyna in Crete about 692, backed the *Monothelites in 712, but recanted the following year. His *hymns and *canons are still used in the Greek *liturgy.

ANDREWES, LANCELOT (1555–1626). *Bishop of Winchester. A devout High Churchman whose linguistic expertise helped to prepare the *King James Version of the *Bible (1611), he opposed *Puritanism and Romanism equally and appealed in church affairs for "apostolic handsomeness and order." He declined two episcopal posts under *Elizabeth I because she appropriated church revenues, but under *James I he became successively *bishop of Chichester (1605), Ely (1609), and Winchester (1613), and a popular court preacher.

ANDREWS, CHARLES FREER (1871–1940). *Missionary to India. Son of a Catholic *Apostolic church minister, he became an Anglican and in 1904 joined the Cambridge Mission in Delhi. He wrote the biography of Sadhu Sundar *Singh, became a friend of Gandhi and the poet Tagore, and identified himself thoroughly with his adopted country and the plight of those called by Tagore "the poorest, the lowliest, and the lost."

ANGEL OF THE LORD Theophanic figure in the *OT. He is identified with the *Lord in some passages (Gen 16:13; Judg 6:14) yet distinguished from him in others (Exod 23:23; 32:34). Many Christians, including some of the church *fathers, identify this figure with the preincarnate *Christ, hence making his appearances Christophanies, but it is unclear if the *NT supports this idea.

ANGELICO, FRA (c. 1400–1455). Florentine painter. He became a *Dominican at twenty and worked first on illuminated manuscripts. One report says he was offered the archbishopric of Florence but was not willing to leave his art, which included paintings such as *The Last Judgment* and *Deposition from the Cross*. *Eugenius IV and *Nicholas V commissioned him to undertake work in the *Vatican.

ANGELS On the basis of scriptural evidence the church has accepted the existence of both good and bad angels. Angels were originally created good, but those who defected from *God became the bad angels. Discussion of angels, or angelology, as a part of *systematic theology, began in the medieval church with Thomas *Aquinas. This study investigates the relation of angels to God, *Christ, and man, their place in God's providence and administration of *salvation. Many *Christian *liturgies presuppose the existence of angels by inviting worshipers to join angels in worshiping the *Lord. See also Demon, Devil, Satan.

ANGELUS The commemoration of the announcement to *Mary by the angel Gabriel (Luke 1:26ff.) that she would bear a son who would be the *Savior of the world. It is a Roman Catholic devotional practice performed at 6:00 A.M., noon, and 6:00 P.M. In Latin it begins *Angelus Domini nuntiavit Mariae* ("The angel of the *Lord declared unto Mary . . .").

ANGLICAN COMMUNION, ANGLICANISM Those churches whose origin may be traced directly or indirectly to the Church of *England are known as the *Anglican Communion of churches. They are called "Episcopal," "Anglican," "the Church of ——," or "the Church of England in ——." They look to the *archbishop of Canterbury as the senior archbishop, they maintain a succession of *bishops that may be traced to the English *bishops of the 16th century; they use *liturgies that have a strong "family" resemblance, and their doctrinal basis is the *Bible with the catholic creeds (*Apostles' and *Nicene). The bishops of the *dioceses meet regularly at the Lambeth Conference, but their decisions are only advisory as each part of the communion is independent.

ANGLO-CATHOLICISM A movement (*Oxford Movement) or ethos within the *Anglican Communion of churches, it began in 1833 in the Church of *England and was known originally as *Tractarianism. Early leaders were J. H. *Newman, E. B.

*Pusey, and John *Keble. Later in the 19th century the influential leader was *Bishop Charles *Gore. The Tractarians emphasized the Roman Catholic (non-Protestant) aspects of the heritage of the Church of England (e.g., episcopal succession, the centrality of the *Eucharist, and auricular *confession to a *priest). Thus "Anglo-Catholic" was coined to describe the Tractarians. Under Charles Gore and others the movement sought to preserve its "Catholic" emphasis while receiving what it took to be the sound findings of science and of scholarly study of the *Scriptures (*biblical criticism). In recent times Anglo-Catholics have made changes in their approach to *worship because Roman Catholics, to whom they look for guidance, have made significant changes. Anglo-Catholicism is a small but significant movement in *Anglicanism.

ANGLO-SAXON CHURCH A title for the period from the landing in England of *Augustine of Canterbury (597) down to the Norman Conquest (1066). During those centuries *Christianity slowly spread throughout the land, with the earliest *dioceses established in Canterbury, London, Rochester, and York. Among the pioneers of the *gospel in England were *Aidan, *Theodore of Tarsus, Dunstan, and *Wulfstan, who often had to labor despite difficulties caused by famine, lingering paganism, and Scandinavian invasion. *Monasticism flourished in many places such as Canterbury, Glastonbury, Melrose, and Lindisfarne; and by the 11th century a *parish system had developed with sixteen *dioceses.

ANGST (Ger. "anxiety, dread, terror"). Its common usage in theological literature is to be traced to the influence of S. *Kierkegaard (1813–1855). When a person truly examines himself and recognizes the mystery of his existence in the context of the threat that death gives and the immensity of the universe, he has *angst*. See also ABSURD, EXISTENTIALISM.

ANHYPOSTASIS (Gk. "without a hypostasis," "autonomous mode of existence"). A technical term used in discussion of *Jesus Christ as the "Word made flesh" or "the *eternal Son made man." It is a way of saying that the human *nature of the Incarnate Son is not an individual human being but true humanity without an individual existence. It exists only as belonging to the *Son of God. So it is without its own mode of existence, for its mode of existence is in the *person of the *Lord Jesus, the Incarnate Son. Following the early church *fathers, Karl *Barth (1886–1968) expounds this *doctrine in his *Church Dogmatics*.

ANIMA CHRISTI (Lat. "soul of *Christ"). The first words of a traditional *prayer, "Soul of Christ, sanctify me; Body of Christ, save me." It originated as a prayer in the 14th century and was made famous by *Ignatius of Loyola (1491–1556).

ANIMA NATURILATER CHRISTIANA A Latin expression used by *Tertullian of Carthage (d. c. 225) meaning "the *soul is naturally *Christian." He meant that *God has so made man that as a spiritual being man has the capacity to know God. Only in finding God is the soul satisfied. It does not mean that he is born a Christian, but that he will find his true *nature only in being a Christian.

ANIMISM The belief that natural objects such as trees, rivers, stones, waterfalls, and springs are inhabited by spirits or *demons who in some way determine the nature of the objects. Animism is found among many but not all primitive peoples.

ANNATES A tax on the first year's income from an ecclesiastical benefice given by a newly installed incumbent to the *pope or to his *bishop. The practice is first recorded in 1306, when *Clement V put a levy on minor British benefices.

ANNE (1665–1714). Queen of Great Britain from 1702. Daughter of the Roman Catholic *James II, she was raised as a Protestant and sided with her brother-in-law *William III against James in 1688. A High Church Anglican (a position reflected in her episcopal appointments), she disliked Roman Catholics and *Nonconformists. She married a Danish prince but died heirless. Nonetheless she took steps to ensure the Protestant succession subsequently embodied in the Hanoverian dynasty.

ANNIHILATIONISM The *doctrine that the *souls of wicked people will not endure *eternal *punishment in hell but will be destroyed, or annihilated, after the Last *Judgment. On this view the soul is not necessarily immortal but can be so by the *grace of *God. Thus *immortality is given to the souls of the righteous by God. Annihilationism has been taught and condemned at various periods of history. It is held today by *Adventist churches. See also CONDITIONAL IMMORTALITY.

ANNO DOMINI (Lat. "in the year of our *Lord"). Usually written and spoken as A.D., the supposed year of the birth of *Jesus. The fixing of our present calendar, and therefore of the A.D., was carried out by Dionysius Exiguus (d. c. 550).

ANNULMENT An official ecclesiastical declaration that a contract (especially of marriage) was invalid and is thus null and void.

ANNUNCIATION (OF THE VIRGIN MARY) The announcement by the angel Gabriel to *Mary that she had been chosen by *God to be the mother of God's *Messiah (Luke 1:26–38). In the Roman Catholic, Anglican, and *Orthodox churches this is celebrated on March 25.

ANOINTING (OF THE SICK) The biblical basis for this act is James 5:14–16. Anointing the sick, together with *prayer for their recovery, occurs in many *Christian churches. However, a development of this basically simple act led to what is known as the *sacrament of unction in the medieval church. This is the anointing with oil of a person who is dying in the confident *hope that his *sins will be forgiven before he dies. See also CHRISM, UNCTION.

ANOMOEANS (from Gk. *anomoios,* "unlike, dissimilar"). In the Arian controversy of the 4th century the most extreme group was known as *anomoeans* because they insisted that in terms of their true and essential *natures the Father and the Son were dissimilar. They were related only in that *Jesus, the Son, did the *will of the Father. Leading exponents were Aetius (d. 370) and Eunomius (d. 394). See also HOMOEANS, HOMOIOUSIOS.

ANONYMOUS CHRISTIANS An expression used in modern *theology to designate those who, though they do not realize it, are in fact *Christians. They show by their commitment to what they know and what they experience that they truly love *God and desire to please him. See also BAPTISM OF DESIRE.

ANSELM OF CANTERBURY (1033–1109). *Archbishop of Canterbury from 1091. Born in Italy, he was *prior (1063) and *abbot (1078) of the famous *Benedictine *monastery at Bec, Normandy. The Canterbury post was urged on him by William II (Rufus), who imagined he was dying. Anselm accepted only when concessions were made to the church by this most rapacious of English kings who in the event survived and who with his successor Henry I made Anselm's a turbulent primacy. In *theology Anselm followed *Augustine. He wrote what became the classic statement of the *Atonement as satisfaction in **Cur Deus Homo* (1094–1098). This theory asserted that *Jesus satisfied the honor and justice of *God by atoning for human sin. Anselm insisted that *faith must precede *reason: "I do not seek to understand in order that I may believe, but I believe in order to understand." His theology influenced many theologians, including Karl *Barth.

ANSGAR (ANSKAR) (801–865). *Archbishop and *missionary to Scandinavia, hence the title "Apostle of the

North." Born a Frank and educated at the famous *Benedictine *monastery at Corbie, he lived as an ascetic and had a special concern for the *poor. Ansgar worked for the evangelization of Denmark and Sweden, held the sees of Hamburg and Bremen, and despite political conditions and resurgent paganism, laid the foundation for the espousal of *Christianity in Scandinavia during the following century.

ANTE CHRISTUM (Lat. "before *Christ"). Often written as B.C., denoting the time before the birth of *Jesus Christ. See ANNO DOMINI.

ANTELAPSARIANISM (lit. "before the *Fall"). The view that God's decree to give *eternal life to some was not dependent on the Fall, or *sin, of humanity; it was made of his pure good pleasure. See also PREDESTINATION, SUPRALAPSARIANISM.

ANTHEM Probably an anglicized form of *antiphon, though the origin is not wholly clear. Originally an anthem was a sacred *hymn sung alternately by two *choirs, but now it refers to the singing of sacred music by a choir.

ANTHROPOCENTRISM The view that man is "the measure of all things," that man does not need *God, and that man is autonomous. It covers a wide range of views and philosophies that deny the existence of God and place man at the center of all things.

ANTHROPOLOGY (from Gk. *anthropos*, "man"). Used to mean four things: (1) the science that studies the physical development of man; (2) the study of human beings as they live in communities with specific *traditions, customs, and ceremonies; (3) the description of a theologian or biblical writer's view of human beings—e.g., Paul's anthropology; (4) the part of *theology that deals with the creation of man, his *sin, and his relation to *God. See also MAN, CHRISTIAN VIEW OF.

ANTHROPOMORPHISM (from two Gk. words meaning "man" and form"). The describing of *God as if he were in the form of man. The *Bible has a noble type of anthropomorphism in which God is described as "walking," "talking," "hearing," "seeing," "smelling," and even "whistling" (Isa 5:26). He is said to have a heart, a face, eyes, ears, and nostrils (Exod 15:8; Ps 18:15). Human words and images are all that we possess to describe God, and if they are used correctly, they are perfectly proper. See also ANALOGY, MODEL.

ANTHROPOSOPHY (lit. "*wisdom about man"). Often used today to describe the teaching of Rudolf Steiner (1861–1925), the educator who believed that the development and cultivation of the spiritual perceptions of human beings were the most important tasks facing man. The key to *wisdom and happiness lies within the human person.

ANTIBURGHERS See BURGHERS.

ANTICHRIST The word occurs in the *Bible only in the letters of John (1 John 2:18, 22; 4:3; 2 John 7). The spirit of antichrist opposes *God's *Messiah. He is referred to as the "man of sin" (2 Thess 2:3–12) and as the "beast" (Rev 13:1–8). In church history various opponents of the *Christian *faith have been called "antichrist" (e.g., various Roman emperors, Islamic kings, and dictators). Many Protestants have regarded the *pope as the antichrist, believing that *Roman Catholicism is a false *religion that opposes true *Christianity.

ANTICLERICALISM General hostility to the authority and privilege of the *clergy, either from within or outside the church. While such a view goes back to the Middle Ages, it found its clearest manifestation in France, particularly during the French Revolution. The movement spread throughout Europe and into Latin America, not always clearly articulated. It is linked with the misuse of clerical privilege and the rise of liberal thinking in politics and *culture. Modern totalitarian systems have encouraged it on grounds of ideology or expediency.

ANTIDORON (Gk. "instead of the gift"). The bread from which the bread for Holy *Communion has been cut that is distributed to the congregation at the end of the *liturgy of the *Eucharist in *Orthodox churches. For noncommunicants it functions "instead of the gift" (consecrated bread of Holy Communion), and for all who have been *fasting it provides sustenance. In French and Canadian Roman Catholic churches a similar practice recently existed and the bread was known as *pain bénit* (i.e., "blessed bread").

ANTILEGOMENA (Gk. "disputed writings"). Used by Eusebius of Caesarea (d. c. 340) to describe those books that nearly did not become, or in fact never became, a part of the collection known as the *NT. The ones eventually included are James, Jude, 2 Peter, 2 John, and 3 John. Those left out include the Shepherd of *Hermas and the Epistle of Barnabas.

ANTINOMIANISM The view that Christians are free from moral obligations since they are saved by *grace and not through any effort of their own. Paul strongly denies that this was any part of his teaching (Rom 3:8). Some trace this *heresy to *Gnosticism, and similar views reappeared at the *Reformation when *Luther himself is said to have been the first to use the word "Antinomian" in countering the argument of J. *Agricola.

ANTINOMY (from Lat. *antinomia,* "conflict of laws"). The general meaning is paradox or contradiction. Used in philosophy, it refers to one of a pair of opposites: one of a pair of mutually conflicting principles or sequences of thought. These can be called "thesis" and "antithesis." An example would be: (a) *God is the cause of everything; (b) I have freedom. As used by Immanuel Kant (1724–1804) antinomy became an argument against *metaphysics and in favor of the human reason dealing only with experience received through the senses.

ANTIOCH, COUNCILS OF Among the church gatherings in this ancient city (modern Antakya in Turkey) were the following: in 268, when *Paul of Samosata was condemned and deposed for *heresy; in 325, when *Arianism was condemned; in 341, when 97 Eastern *bishops rejected the charge of Arianism, declared that the Son was begotten before all ages and coexisted with the Father, and attacked the *doctrine of *Marcellus of Ancyra; and in 375, when 153 Eastern bishops gave assent to reconciliation with the Western church.

ANTIOCHENE THEOLOGY The *theology of the *bishops or leading thinkers of the church of Antioch in Syria or of churches closely associated with that church. The expression is normally used of the theology of such writers as *Marcellus of Ancyra (d. c. 374), *Chrysostom (d. 407), *Theodore of Mopsuestia (c. 356–428), and Nestorius (d. c. 451). In the 5th century, Antiochene and *Alexandrian theology were distinctly opposed to each other. Antiochene theologians worked from Aristotelian, not Platonic philosophy; they emphasized the humanity of the *Lord Jesus and appeared to be satisfied with a loose or imprecise union of the human and divine in *Jesus.

ANTIPHON (from Gk. "something sung alternately by two *choirs"). Used of the chanting or saying of *Psalms and *canticles when the two sides of the choir (or congregation), or a soloist and choir, read alternate verses. It is also used of specific verses from *Scripture sung before or after the Psalms and Canticles and of the four *anthems addressed to *Mary sung at *compline.

ANTIPOPE One set up in opposition to, and claiming to supersede, the Roman pontiff. Such disputes around the *papacy, whether for doctrinal, political, procedural, or other reasons, beginning in the early 3d century, have seen the emergence of up to forty antipapal contenders, though the description "antipope" does not seem to have been used until the late 14th century. Sometimes the incumbent pope has been challenged by two rivals at the same time, most notably during the *Great Schism (1378–1417). The last antipope relinquished his claim to be Felix V in 1449, whereupon Pope *Nicholas V bestowed on him a *cardinal's hat.

ANTI-SEMITISM Feelings and acts of prejudice and hostility toward Jews. An irrational hatred of Jews as Jews. The church has not been free of this tendency, and in medieval and early modern times persecuted Jews ruthlessly. It was held that they were guilty of the crime of killing *Jesus and so deserving of *punishment. In recent times both the Roman Catholic Church and the *World Council of Churches have stated that anti-Semitism is wrong and is a *sin against *God.

ANTITYPE (Gk. *antitupos,* "copy, antitype, representation"). Found in 1 Peter 3:21 and Hebrews 9:24. Certain *OT practices and people are called *types in that they point to a fuller reality to come. That fuller reality is the antitype. Thus, in Hebrews 9:24 the presence of *God in *heaven is the antitype of the temple, the type.

ANTONELLI, GIACOMO (1806–1876). *Vatican secretary of state to *Pius IX. Made *cardinal in 1847, his was the controlling hand in the papal states for most of the time until they were absorbed officially into the Italian state in 1870. While criticism was often directed against his moral laxity, nepotism, and acquisition of *wealth, he was a shrewd if authoritarian diplomat, whose policies greatly benefited the *papacy.

ANTONY OF EGYPT (c. 250–c. 355). Generally regarded as the founder of Christian *monasticism. Born of *Christian parents in middle Egypt, he gave away his property and possessions in order to devote himself to an ascetic life and the quest for perfection. He attracted a number of would-be hermit followers and spent about five years trying to instruct them before withdrawing again into a life of solitude. When nearly ninety, he visited Alexandria to add his voice to the defense of *orthodoxy against *Arianism. His biography, written by *Athanasius in 356 and later translated into Latin, had a powerful influence on Christendom.

ANTONY OF PADUA (1195–1231). Known as the *patron *saint of the *poor. Born in Lisbon, he became an *Augustinian (1210) and later transferred to the *Franciscans (1220), hoping to find *martyrdom in Africa, but illness soon compelled his return to Europe, and he chose a life of seclusion. His superiors had other plans for him, and in 1223 he became the first teacher of his *order, carrying out his duties in various French and Italian centers of learning. In 1230 he was permitted to devote himself to *preaching, in which he was so compelling that 30,000 were said to have assembled on one occasion to hear him, to their great spiritual benefit and with far-reaching results. Antony was known to be especially effective in recalling heretics to orthodox *faith.

ANXIETY See ANGST.

APARTHEID An Afrikaans word used in South Africa to describe the rigid and rigorous form of racial *segregation and development enforced by law. Its existence has caused severe moral problems for the *Christian churches in South Africa. On the one side biblical and theological arguments have been used to support it, while on the other different arguments from the same sources have been used to oppose it. The *World Council of Churches has strongly condemned it, and so have numerous other Christian organizations.

APOCALYPTIC (Gk. *apocalupsis,* "*revelation, unveiling"). From 200 B.C. to 100 A.D. there appeared in *Judaism a way of describing *God, his relationship to the world, and especially his *kingdom to come that made use of strange and mysterious symbolism. This religious approach is known as apocalyptic, and the literature that contains it is apocalyptic literature. Examples are *The Assumption of Moses*, *The Apocalypse of Baruch*, and *The Testaments of the Twelve Patriarchs*. Such books have the following characteristics: They are attributed to a great name of the past (pseudonymous), they employ rich symbolism, and they predict the future in terms of God's entering human affairs.

APOCATASTASIS (Gk. "restoration"). Found in Acts 3:21. In *theology it was used by *Clement (d. c. 215) and *Origen (c. 185–c. 254) of Alexandria to mean universal restoration at the end of the age in which all human beings would be given *eternal *salvation. This *doctrine covers not only sinful human beings but also fallen *angels and devils. The Council of Constantinople of 543 condemned it as *heresy after *Augustine of Hippo (354–430) had attacked it. In modern times it has been known as *universalism.

APOCRYPHA (Gk. "the hidden things"). Books that the early church received as part of the Greek version of the *OT but that are not included in the Hebrew *Bible: 1 Esdras; 2 Esdras; Tobit; Judith; Additions to Esther; Wisdom of Solomon; Ecclesiasticus; Baruch; The Letter of Jeremiah; The Prayer of Azariah and The Song of the Three; Daniel and Susanna; Daniel, Bel and the Snake; The Prayer of Manasseh; 1 Maccabees; 2 Maccabees. They were included in the Latin translation of the OT known as the *Vulgate. Thus they have been included in Roman Catholic Bibles. In general Protestants make no doctrinal use of the Apocrypha.

APOLLINARIANISM A view of the *Lord *Jesus associated with the name of Apollinarius (d. c. 390), an extreme representative of *Alexandrian theology. He said that "the Word became flesh" meant that the humanity that the *eternal *Son of God assumed consisted of *body and *soul but not of *spirit (or mind). He believed that a man has a body, soul, and spirit, but that in Jesus the divinity functioned in place of the human spirit or mind. This was possible, he taught, since the eternal *Logos (Word, Son) is the prototype of the human spirit or mind. His teaching was rejected on the basis that it taught that Jesus was only two-thirds human.

APOLOGETICS (from Gk. *apologia*, "a defense"). Used in Acts 26:2 and 1 Peter 3:15. *Apologists* are *Christian intellectuals who defend the Christian *faith in terms suitable to the times and *culture in which they live. The word is used particularly of a group of writers in the early church including Justin *Martyr, *Athenagoras, and *Tertullian who lived from A.D. 120–220. *Apologetics* is providing an apology, the defense of the faith on intellectual principles. While it is recognized that no one can be argued into acceptance of *Christianity, it is claimed that reasoning can remove barriers to faith and show that to believe is not to be irrational. As thought-forms change from age to age and culture to culture, the form that apologetics takes will differ accordingly even though its task is always the same.

APOLYSIS (Gk. "dismissal"). Used of the concluding blessing in the *liturgy of the *Eastern Orthodox Church and said by *priest or *bishop.

APOPHATIC THEOLOGY (Gk. *apophatikos*, "negative"). A way to the knowledge of *God that proceeds by negations, by saying what God is not. It is a form of *mystical *theology, is only possible in the context of *prayer and *meditation, and is held to be the highest form of theology in the *Eastern churches. It is the opposite of *cataphatic theology, which proceeds by positive, rational propositions about God.

APOSTASY (Gk. *apostasia*, "rebellion, abandonment, apostasy"). Its normal use is of the deliberate rejection of the *Christian *faith which has once been held. It is also used of less dramatic rebellions—e.g., of leaving a *religious *order and abandoning *vows made for life.

APOSTLE (Gk. *apostolos*, "one who is sent with authority to act on behalf of another"). Used in the *NT of the men chosen by *Jesus to be eyewitnesses of the events of his life, to see him after his *resurrection, and then to tell the world what they knew (Matt 10:2–42; Acts 1:21–22; 1 Cor 9:1). After the *suicide of Judas Iscariot, Matthias was appointed (Acts 1:15ff.), and he was joined later by Paul (1 Cor 9:1). Also used in a less technical sense of spiritually gifted leaders who labored for *Christ—e.g., Barnabas (Acts 13:2; 14:4, 14). In the history of the church it has been used of important *Christian leaders, *evangelists, and pioneers–e.g., of Martin *Luther.

APOSTLES' CREED A statement of *faith used very widely in churches in the Western world and in churches started by Western *missionaries. Its origin is not the *apostles but the church in Rome where it began use as a baptismal *confession of faith—"I believe. . . ." It was elaborated to be used in daily acts of *worship. Most of the churches of the *Reformation accepted it, and so it is now shared by both Roman Catholics and Protestants. It has three parts concerned with *God, *Jesus Christ, and the Holy *Spirit. The *Orthodox churches do not normally use it.

APOSTOLATE What the *apostles (and thus the church that they founded) do. The bearing of the *gospel by the whole people of *God to the whole world in the name of *Christ and in the *love of God by every means.

APOSTOLIC AGE The first period of the history of the church covering the lifetime of the *apostles—e.g., from c. A.D. 30 to c. 90. The period immediately after 90 is usually called the subapostolic age. The apostolic and subapostolic ages are often also called the period of the primitive church.

APOSTOLIC BLESSING The blessing given by the *pope at the end of the *Mass on very special occasions—e.g., *Easter and immediately after his election.

APOSTOLIC CONSTITUTIONS (more correctly, "Ordinances of the Holy Apostles Through Clement"). A collection of eight books of church law purportedly compiled by the *apostles and passed on to the church by *Clement of Rome. It is generally held, however, that they were of late 4th-century Syrian origin, from a source sympathetic to *Arianism. The work, which covers a wide range of liturgical and pastoral subjects, was condemned by the Trullan Synod in 692.

APOSTOLIC FATHERS The name given to a number of early *Christian writers who were said to have known the *apostles. The name seems to have been known from the 6th century but to have been in common use only since the 17th. Included in the designation are *Clement of Rome, *Ignatius, *Polycarp, *Hermas, *Papias, and several writers whose works, but not names, are known.

APOSTOLIC SEE A church or *diocese believed to have been founded by an *apostle. Used particularly of the church of Rome because of the claim that Peter and Paul were involved in its foundation and early history.

APOSTOLIC SUCCESSION Originally the passing on of sound and faithful *doctrine from *apostles to their successors as leaders of the young churches. Then also used of the succession of *ordination—the apostles set apart men to be their successors, these men (*bishops) consecrated others, and so on. From this claim of historical continuity of ordination and *consecration of bishops the *doctrine that only those ordained by bishops in this line are truly ordained has been set forth—e.g., by *Orthodox and Roman Catholic churches. This claim has been challenged on doctrinal and historical grounds, and the concept is further questioned because some Episcopal churches reject as invalid the ministry of other Episcopal churches.

APOSTOLICITY The church is described in the *Nicene Creed as "one, *holy, catholic, and *apostolic*." It is built upon the foundation of the *apostles (Eph 2:19–22) and so follows their *doctrine and practice. Apostolic may be understood also in terms of tracing the history of the church back to the apostles through a succession of *bishops (the *apostolic succession). As a further use, it refers to *missions—going out into the world as did the apostles. See also NOTES OF THE CHURCH.

APOSTOLICUM A title used in Europe for the *Apostles' Creed.

APOTHEOSIS (Gk. *apo,* "expressing completion"; and *theos,* "*God"). Glorification of someone as God. It was a pagan custom in the Roman empire to call emperors "gods" from the time they sat on their thrones. Domitian (A.D. 81–96) was worshiped as a god. It has been argued, though not very successfully, that the origin of the *veneration of *saints in the medieval church is to be traced to this pagan custom.

APPARITIONS Used especially in the Roman Catholic Church to describe a psychical experience, aided by the Holy *Spirit, in which a vision is received. The effect of such a supernatural experience is said to be that of creating a new love for *God or new devotion to him. Some of the most famous apparitions have been those of the Virgin *Mary, e.g., those to *Bernadette in the grotto near Lourdes in 1858.

APPROPRIATION(S) Used in reference to the *doctrine of the *Trinity when an attribute that properly belongs to the Godhead or common essence is particularly applied to one *person. This is done because the attribute seems to apply particularly to this person. E.g., creation may be applied to the Father, *redemption to the Son, and *sanctification to the Holy *Spirit, even though all three may be said to be involved in creation, redemption, and sanctification.

APSE A vaulted semicircular or polygonal recess in a church, especially at the end of the *chancel. It is an adaptation of the design of Roman basilicas (law courts). In it was the *altar.

AQUINAS, THOMAS (1225–1274). Greatest theologian and philosopher of *Roman Catholicism. He became a *Dominican in 1244, studied further under *Albertus Magnus at both Paris and Cologne, and taught at Paris for much of his working life. He wrote commentaries on the work of Peter *Lombard, on *Boethius, on *Scripture, and on Aristotle, but he is remembered most for his two great *Summae* (summaries of human knowledge). One defended "the *truth of the Catholic *faith against the pagans" by clearly distinguishing between *reason and faith; the other summarized all that was known about *God and man. Much of his work reflects the influence of *Augustine of Hippo. He wrote highly regarded *hymns that have played a prominent part in Roman Catholic *liturgy.

Aquinas composed the order of service for the *Mass of *Corpus Christi and wrote poetry that later became familiar *Communion hymns: "Now, My Tongue, The Mystery Telling" (*Pange lingua*), "O Saving Victim," and "Humbly I Adore Thee, Verity Unseen."

Aquinas left unfinished his **Summa theologiae* in 1273, for after a spiritual experience he said, "All I have written seems to me like so much straw compared with what I have seen and what has been revealed to me."

Aquinas was declared a Doctor of the Roman Catholic Church in 1567 by Pius V.

ARAMAIC A language of Mesopotamia, the Palestinian form of which was the language spoken at the time of *Jesus. Some Aramaic phrases are found in the Gospels, e.g., "*Talitha cumi*," and "*Ephphatha*," reflecting the use of Aramaic by Jesus. Parts of the *OT are in Aramaic (Dan 2:4–7:28; Ezra 4:8–6:18; 7:12–26).

ARCHANGEL A chief angel (Jude 9; 1 Thess 4:6). Two are named in the *NT—Michael in 1 Thess 4:16 and Gabriel in Luke 1:26. Raphael is often associated with the moving of water at the pool of Bethesda (John 5:1ff.). Other names, taken from the apocryphal Book of Enoch, include Uriel, Raguel, and Sarial.

ARCHBISHOP The *bishop of a prominent or distinguished see—e.g., Canterbury and York.

ARCHDEACON A senior clergyman who has particular legal and administrative duties given to him by the *bishop within the *diocese. He is given a title such as "archdeacon of Winchester."

ARCHDIOCESE A *diocese whose *bishop is always an *archbishop—e.g., Canterbury.

ARCHIMANDRITE (from Gk. *archimandrites*, "the ruler of a fold"). Originally used in the *Eastern Orthodox churches to describe the head of a *monastery or group of monasteries and so, similar in meaning to *abbot. In modern times it is often used as a title of honor for one who is a member of a monastic *order and not necessarily its head.

ARGUMENT FROM SILENCE Expression used when an argument is either put forward or destroyed, not on any specific evidence, but rather on the lack of it. An example is the silence of the *NT on the *baptism of infants and arguments made on this basis.

ARGUMENTS FOR THE EXISTENCE OF GOD In answer to the question "Does *God exist?" Christians have attempted to provide a rational answer. There are four traditional arguments or proofs for God's existence. The first represents *a priori reasoning and the last three *a posteriori reasoning.

1. *The Ontological Argument*. This has been principally presented by *Anselm (1033–1109) and *Descartes (1596–1650). In Anselm's definition *God is "a being than which nothing greater can be conceived." Yet it is one thing for an object to be in my understanding and another thing for it to exist in reality. Conscious of this, Anselm replied that if God exists only in my understanding, then he is not the "being than which nothing greater can be conceived." In the case of God, and of God alone, to move surely from existence in thought to existence in reality is possible.

2. *The Cosmological Argument*. This was presented by *Aristotle (384–322 B.C.) and by Thomas *Aquinas as the *Five Ways. It points out that everything in the world need not exist and does not necessarily exist. The reason for the existence of a table, a chair, or a human being is not in them but outside of them. To explain contingent and dependent existence there must be a reality that necessarily exists, whose reason for existence is within itself. Such a reality is *God.

3. *The Teleological Argument*. Also known as the argument from/to design. It is particularly associated with W. *Paley (1743–1805) and simply asserts that the universe has design and purpose. It is ordered for the sake of an end. Thus it must have a designer, and that designer is God.

4. *The Moral Argument*. Particularly associated with Immanuel *Kant (1724–1804). He held that in the inner life of man there is freedom to choose among values. In making a choice a man feels an obligation; he feels he ought to do something. This ought comes as a demand, as an imperative. There is no other possible explanation for this universal phenomenon than the existence of *God, the source of the moral law and the highest good. The moral order and the natural order are brought together meaningfully only by supposing God's existence.

ARIANISM Fourth-century *heresy concerning Jesus and his relationship to *God. It bears the name of Arius, a *presbyter of the church of Alexandria, who began teaching it c. 319. The teaching was condemned at the Council of *Nicea (325) but was widely held in a weak form for most of the 4th century. The core of the *heresy is that

*Jesus Christ is not the *eternal *Son of God become man. Rather he is a spiritual being made by God before the creation of the world, who is given the title "Son of God." Thus the Son does not share the essence or substance of the Father. Some Arians held that the Son was dissimilar in essence from the Father, others that he was of a similar essence. But only the orthodox held that he was of the *same* essence. See also ANOMOEANS, HOMOEANS, SEMI-ARIANISM.

ARIMINUM, SYNOD OF (359). A church council in modern Rimini attended by Western *bishops while the Eastern *bishops met at Seleucia. *Arianism still had the support of an influential minority, and though the majority at Ariminum decided to adhere to the orthodox position established at *Nicea in 325, the emperor Constantius II, himself pro-Arian, put pressure on the bishops to change their minds and later to accept an Arian *creed. The latter was rejected by Pope Liberius, who pronounced the council to be without authority.

ARISTIDES (2d century A.D.). *Christian writer. His *Apology for the Christian Faith,* addressed to the emperor *Hadrian (117—138) and referred to in the work of *Eusebius of Caesarea, is the oldest known work of its kind. It divides humankind into three categories: barbarians, Greeks, and Jews, but goes on to say that only the Christians, the "new nation," had a true *vision of *God by which they could revive the world. In the late 19th century, Armenian and Syriac fragments of the apology came to light, and subsequently a medieval Christian legend was found to have incorporated it, enabling a reconstruction of the complete Greek text to be made.

ARISTOTELIANISM The philosophy formulated in the Middle Ages that took much of its terminology and concepts from Aristotle (e.g., *substance, *accident, matter, and form). The major formulators were *Albertus Magnus (c. 1200–1280) and his pupil Thomas *Aquinas (1224–1274). This philosophy was married to *theology so that *systematic theology took its method and concepts from Aristotelianism. Before being adopted by *Christian thinkers Aristotle's teaching had been developed by Arabs, especially in the form of *Averroism. See also NEOPLATONISM, SCHOLASTICISM.

ARIUS See ARIANISM.

ARMAGEDDON The site where the last battle of the world will be fought, thus ending this age and ushering in the new age of *God. It is mentioned only once in the *Bible (Rev 16:16) as the place where the bowls of God's wrath will be poured out upon the rebellious kings of the earth and their armies, epitomized in "Babylon the Great."

ARMENIAN CHURCH Because *Christianity in Armenia was held to have been brought by Bartholomew and Thaddaeus, its official name is the Armenian Apostolic (*Orthodox) Church. Armenia adopted Christianity about the beginning of the 4th century through the evangelistic labors of *Gregory the Illuminator. Two centuries later, however, it embraced *Monophysitism and repudiated the *doctrines of the Council of *Chalcedon. The country lost its autonomy in the later Middle Ages, and from 1893 its people have suffered cruelly from the genocidal activities of Turkish and Soviet governments. The church has been torn by dissension, reflected in the existence of two *primates (catholicoi) in Echmiadzin (USSR) and Antilyas (Lebanon), and patriarchates in Jerusalem and Constantinople. Apart from Monophysite tendencies, the Orthodox Armenian Church (numbering some 3.5 million worldwide) generally shares the doctrinal position of Eastern *Orthodoxy.

ARMINIANISM The approach to the *doctrines of *God and his *salvation that had its origin with Jacobus *Arminius (1560–1609), the Dutch theologian. The doctrines of Arminius were articulated in the conviction that the teaching of the successors of John *Calvin (1509–1564) in the Calvinist churches was developing in an unsatisfying and unbiblical way. The doctrines were set forth in the *Remonstrance (1610). This document taught that God eternally elected in *Christ all who will believe in Christ, that Christ died for every person, that each believer must be regenerated by the Holy *Spirit, that it is possible to resist the *grace of God, and therefore that the possibility of falling completely from *grace must be seriously entertained. The orthodox Calvinists responded to these articles by their own five articles produced at the Synod of *Dort (1618–1619). Arminianism is used also of two English theological movements. First, that associated with *Archbishop *Laud in the 1620s and 1630s; and second, that taught by John *Wesley, the founder of the Methodist church. Methodist teaching is often called Arminianism.

ARMINIUS, JACOBUS (1560–1609). Dutch theologian. Born in the Netherlands during the Spanish occupation, he was one of the first students enrolled in the new University of Leiden (1576). There he adopted the controversial *theology of Peter Ramus before going on to study in 1582 at the Geneva academy headed by *Beza. In 1588 he became one of the ministers of Amsterdam and soon came under attack by strict Calvinists who disliked his views on *grace and *predestination. In 1592 he was accused of *Pelagianism and other deviations, but it was later, as professor of theology at Leiden (1603–1609), that he was involved in more serious disputes in his attempt to give the human *will a more active role in *salvation than orthodox *Calvinism conceded. His views, always defended from *Scripture, were reflected by the *Remonstrance in 1610.

ARNAUD, HENRI (1641–1721). Waldensian *pastor. Born in France of Italian parents, he studied *theology in Switzerland and in 1685 went to his ancestral homeland in Piedmont as pastor among the Waldensians, or Vaudois, at a time when Protestants were being persecuted by the duke of Savoy. Forced to flee, he returned to Switzerland, where he organized Waldensian exiles who, supported by English and Dutch money, fought their way home across the mountains to Piedmont. During Arnaud's lifetime the Waldensians were tolerated sporadically, usually when foreign invaders threatened. Arnaud founded a settlement at Schönenberg for the many exiles and supervised there the cultivation of alfalfa and mulberries.

ARNAULD, ANTOINE (1612–1694). French theologian and Jansenist. Born in Paris, he studied law and *theology at the Sorbonne and was ordained as a *priest in 1641. An anti-*Jesuit work called "On Frequent Communion" (1643) caused an uproar and identified him as the new leader of *Jansenism in France. Expelled from the Sorbonne for his views, he led the Jansenists through a period of severe persecution (1661–1669). Arnauld also distinguished himself as a scientist and philosopher. His last twelve years were spent in Brussels.

ARNDT, JOHANN (1555–1621). German theologian and writer. Although a Lutheran *pastor, he argued against the *real presence view of the *Eucharist, which he regarded as symbolic observance. His tendency toward *mysticism is seen in his most famous book, which was translated into English as *Four Books on True Christianity* (1606). This volume was to contribute much to the *Pietistic movement later in the century.

ARNOLD, EBERHARD (1883–1935). Founder of the modern Bruderhof movement in Germany. Early influenced by the 16th-century *Anabaptists, he spoke out against the rise of national socialism and warned that "the most sinister powers of our civilization are . . . the State, the military, and the capitalist structure." Harassed by the Gestapo, he arranged for all Bruderhof children to be removed to Switzerland and laid the groundwork for the extension of the Bruderhof in England and the U.S.

ARNOLD OF BRESCIA (c. 1100–c. 1155). Italian radical religious reformer. As *prior of a *monastery in Brescia in 1137, he joined a movement against unworthy *clergy and the church's temporal *wealth. He was banished first from Italy, then from France, and finally was excommunicated in 1148. He helped establish at Rome a commune independent of the *papacy. Betrayed finally by a leadership not yet ready for republicanism, Arnold was captured by imperial forces, condemned for *heresy by an ecclesiastical tribunal, and hanged. His *body was burned, his ashes thrown in the Tiber.

ARNOT, FREDERICK STANLEY (1858–1914). Scottish *missionary and explorer. Member of the *Christian Brethren, he went to South Africa in 1881 and soon began the first of many journeys into the hinterland. A man of independent mind like David *Livingstone, whose family he knew, he too was criticized by those dubious about missionaries who doubled as explorers. He preached the *gospel in remote areas of Central Africa, endured incredible hardship, established mission stations, and was elected Fellow of the Royal Geographical Society. Among those he brought to Africa was Dan *Crawford.

ARS MORIENDI (Lat. "the art of dying"). A type of book widely used in the late Middle Ages, it dealt with spiritual preparation for death.

ARS PRAEDICANDI (Lat. "the art of *preaching"). A type of book produced by the *friars in the 13th and 14th centuries giving instruction concerning preaching.

ART, CHRISTIANITY AND By art is meant not only painting and sculpture but also literary and musical art. In the history of the church in the West it is possible to discern at least four different attitudes to art.

1. In the medieval period art was seen as a product of men made in the *image of *God* and as a definite means of assisting the *worship of God. The architecture and decoration of places of worship set the scene and context for praise of God, while the musical and rhetorical arts provided the means of expressing that praise. The Gothic *cathedral and the Gregorian *chant are good examples. This is a positive approach to art.

2. In the *Renaissance, art and *Christianity began to be separated. Art was seen as autonomous and was patronized by the rich. It was still seen as related to *God the Creator, but the tendency toward *secularization had begun and was to continue. Aspects of the *Reformation, especially the *iconoclasm, helped to drive a wedge between art and Christianity.

3. Therefore it is not surprising that in parts of *Protestantism there was a retreat from art. In a definite desire not to be "worldly," the view gained ground that art was a sensuous temptation and so was to be avoided. To go to the theater, to dance, and even to paint were seen as sinful, and only certain types of music and poetry were allowed or encouraged. Meanwhile, in Western *culture, art became the vehicle of expression for a variety of views and philosophies of life, and so it continued to raise acute problems for *Christian believers.

4. A positive approach to art by Christians is a possibility today. Art must be seen as a creative gift of God that may be used for his glory or abused by human sinfulness. Art has to be encouraged on Christian principles by the Christian community so that it reflects the thought and ideals of Christianity. Yet it has to be encouraged not only for providing the setting for *liturgy but also as providing a reflection of God's glory within society.

ARTICLES OF RELIGION The twenty-five articles dating from 1784 that form the doctrinal standard of the United Methodist Church of America. All but one were edited or rewritten by John *Wesley from the *Thirty-Nine Articles of the Church of *England. The twenty-fifth article pledged loyalty to the American government after the War for Independence.

ARTICLES OF RELIGION, THE THIRTY-NINE See THIRTY-NINE ARTICLES, THE.

ARTICLES OF WAR A *Salvation Army document that every new soldier is required to sign. A world-renouncing statement that proscribes alcohol, drugs, bad language, and unbecoming behavior, it demands strict discipline, *sacrifice, and total commitment to the "*salvation *war."

ARTICULI FIDEI FUNDAMENTALIS The fundamental *doctrines of *Christianity that one must hold to gain *salvation. The *deity of *Christ is usually seen as one such doctrine.

ARTICULI FIDEI MIXTI The *doctrines gained from natural and supernatural (or revealed) knowledge of *God, e.g., God as Creator.

ARTICULI FIDEI PURI The *doctrines of pure *faith as doctrines supernaturally revealed, e.g., *God as three in one and one in three.

ARUNDEL, THOMAS (1353–1414). *Archbishop of Canterbury. Aristocratic by birth, he became *bishop of Ely when only twenty-one. He sided with the nobles against Richard II and served twice as *chancellor of England before going to Canterbury in 1396. Soon deprived of his see by a king who remembered old grievances, he resumed the primacy on *Henry IV's accession in 1399 and coupled this with two further terms as chancellor. Arundel initiated a cruel campaign of persecution against the Lollards.

ASBURY, FRANCIS (1745–1816). American Methodist *bishop. An itinerant preacher in England, he went to North America in 1771 and became assistant to John *Wesley. In 1778 he declined appointment by Wesley as general superintendent but was elected to that office by his colleagues, *consecrated by them, and took the title of bishop. This greatest leader of American *Methodism traveled many thousands of miles on horseback to foster the young church, which at his death had 412 societies and a membership of 214,235.

ASCENSION OF CHRIST *Christ's departure into *heaven after his *resurrection. From Acts 1:3–11 it seems to have occurred forty days after the Resurrection, although in Luke 24:50–51 it appears to be on the day of the Resurrection. In Paul's letters Christ's ascension and resurrection are closely linked (Rom 8:34; Eph 1:20; Col 3:1; 1 Tim 3:16). By his ascension *Jesus became the *vicegerent of the Father, "sitting at his right hand," sharing his rule, and representing as intercessor all who believe the *gospel. Ascension Day is a major festival for most churches, held on the sixth Thursday after *Easter Day (forty days). The theological significance of the Ascension is that our human *nature, which the *eternal *Son of God made his own, has been exalted into *God's presence. This has implications for our *salvation both here and in the *kingdom to come.

ASCETICAL THEOLOGY The systematic consideration of the truths and problems of the *Christian life in order to give practical guidance to *pastors and spiritual directors who guide the faithful. As a recognized discipline, it has existed in the Roman Catholic Church since the 17th century, though its origins are much earlier. It is to be distinguished from *mystical and *moral *theology. It is often divided into three parts: purging of selfishness, illumination by the mind and example of *Christ, and awareness of union with *God.

ASCETICISM (from Gk. *askesis*, "training, discipline, renunciation"). Thus it is the combination of all forms of discipline that is necessary for the individual *Christian to experience conformity to *God's *will. Negatively, it means giving up those things that, though good in themselves, do not assist in loving God and doing his perfect will (e.g., perhaps not getting married). Positively, it means imitating *Christ. This demanding approach is to be traced to the idealism of the monks of the 14th century and the later monastic *tradition. The Reformers of the 16th century. rejected it, relating the *Christian life to *justification by *faith. It has persisted in the *Orthodox and Roman Catholic churches, though today there is much questioning concerning what asceticism really means in the complexity of modern society. Asceticism aims at overcoming all obstacles to loving *God that are found in the human person so as to conform the disciplined believer to the God of *love.

ASEITY (from Lat. "being from itself"). A quality that no created being can possess, for such a being is derived from another. Only *God, the *eternal *Lord, has the quality of aseity, for his being is derived from no other. A mother gives life to a child, but no one gives life to God, who is eternal.

ASH WEDNESDAY The first day of *Lent and so named because on it ashes are blessed and placed on the heads of the faithful as a sign of *penitence and sorrow for *sin.

ASKEW (ASCUE), ANNE (c. 1521–1546). English Protestant *martyr. Tried in *Henry VIII's reign for allegedly heretical views on the *Eucharist, she was tortured, refused to recant, and was burned at the stake at Smithfield, London.

ASPERGES The first word in Latin of the *antiphon "Thou shalt purge." Before the principal Roman Catholic *Mass on *Sundays the president/-*priest often sprinkles holy water over the *altar and congregation. As he does this the *choir sings, "Thou shalt purge me with hyssop, and I shall be clean."

ASPERSION A way of baptizing in which the water is sprinkled on only the head of the candidate. It is a variant of *affusion, in which water is poured over the head. See also BAPTISM.

ASSEMBLIES OF GOD (GENERAL COUNCIL OF) A large Pentecostal *denomination formed in 1914 in Arkansas. It has more than 1.3 million members in the U.S. in approximately 9,300 churches. With a mixture of Congregational and *Presbyterian polity, it holds to evangelical doctrines in its treatment of the *Bible, to *premillennialism in its *eschatology, and to *believers' *baptism. It claims that the *gifts of the Spirit are available today for the people of *God and sees *glossolalia as evidence of being baptized in the *Spirit. See also PENTECOSTALISM.

ASSUMPTION (OF THE BLESSED VIRGIN MARY) The teaching of the Roman Catholic church that *Mary, mother of *Jesus, did not enter *purgatory but was taken directly into *heaven by a supernatural act of *God. It was held by many Christians from the 6th century but did not become a *doctrine of the Roman Catholic church until 1950, when it was defined by Pope *Pius XII in a document entitled *Munificentissimus Deus*. In the *Eastern Orthodox Church the *doctrine is widely believed but in a less precise way. Protestants generally reject it as it is not taught by the *NT. Among Roman Catholic theologians there is discussion as to whether Mary died and then entered the heavenly glory or whether she did not experience physical death. In either case she is now presented as the true model of the believer and the church.

ASSUMPTIONISTS (AUGUSTINIANS OF THE ASSUMPTION) Founded in France in 1843, the Assumptionists' stated purpose was "to restore higher education according to the mind of St. Augustine and St. Thomas, to fight the Church's enemies in secret societies under the revolutionary flag; to fight for the unity of the Church. . . ." Banished by an *anticlerical French government in 1900, in many lands it consolidated a ministry in welfare, education, literature, and *missions.

ASSURANCE Believers' experience of certainty that they are truly *God's children, a result of the Holy *Spirit's witness in the human *spirit (Rom 8:15–17). There is a question as to whether a believer is given assurance from the first moment of true belief in *Christ when the Spirit enters the heart or whether assurance is given later as the loving obedience of Christ develops. A further question concerns what realities help to give or develop assurance (e.g., the regular receiving of *Communion, the *fellowship of believers, etc.).

ASSYRIAN CHURCH In the West, the name now given to those who trace their origins back to Nestorius, rejecting his condemnation by the 5th-century Councils of *Ephesus and *Chalcedon. Known often as *Nestorians, the Assyrian church through the centuries has been greatly diminished by defection, *schism, and partial union with other churches, and has suffered particularly during World War I from massacre and disease. Its *patriarch now resides in the U.S.

ASTROLOGY The study of the influence of the stars and planets on human destiny. The position of the stars at the birth of a baby is considered by astrologists to supply information to forecast the general pattern of future life. Common in popular Hinduism and found in a lesser or greater degree in Christendom, not a few theologians of the past thought it to be compatible with *Christianity, though most now consider it under the general heading of the *occult.

ATHANASIAN CREED A *Christian statement of *faith, formerly attributed to *Athanasius (d. 373), that is now thought to have originated in southern France about the beginning of the 5th century. This Latin document (also called the *Quicunque Vult* [''Whosoever will''] from its opening words) was unknown to the *Eastern church until the 12th century; but from the 16th or 17th century it has been highly regarded in Russian and Greek *Orthodox churches. The *Eastern Orthodox churches never formally adopted it. It provides a useful summary of *Augustine's interpretation of the *doctrine of the *Trinity and of the teaching of the Council of *Chalcedon (451) on the *person of *Christ. In addition to its status in the Roman Catholic Church, Anglicans and Lutherans regard it as authoritative. The creed chiefly expounds orthodox teaching on the Trinity and the *Incarnation and opens and ends with warnings that these beliefs are indispensable to *salvation. See also APOSTLES' CREED, NICENE CREED.

ATHANASIUS (c. 293–373). *Bishop of Alexandria. Although only a *deacon at the Council of *Nicea, he became there and subsequently the chief defender of orthodox *Christianity against *Arianism. Bishop of his native Alexandria from 328, his determination to uphold the true *doctrine of *God involved him in exhausting controversies with highly placed Arians in church and state. He was banished several times, returning finally only about six years before his death. By his faithful ministry, steadfast character, significant writings, and zeal for God's *truth, he contributed much toward the triumph of *orthodoxy at the Council of *Constantinople eight years after his death.

ATHEISM The rejection of belief in *God. Two approaches are taken. First, some say it is meaningful but false to say that God exists—i.e., such belief contradicts reason. Second, according to logical positivists, since it is meaningless to speak of God (who cannot be seen or touched), to believe in him is a futile exercise. However, in popular usage atheism often means *agnosticism or the rejection of a concept of God that Christians articulate. Atheism exists only in relation to a stated belief in, and description of, God.

ATHENAGORAS (2d century). Greek *Christian apologist. Writing from Alexandria about 177, he addressed a work to Roman emperor Marcus Aurelius in which he refuted charges that Christians were atheists (i.e., that they disbelieved in pagan gods), cannibals, and incestuous. On the contrary, he pointed out that they lived by a strict moral code that forbade such things as *abortion and second marriage. Athenagoras produced the first systematic argument for the *Christian *doctrine of the triune *God.

ATHOS, MOUNT A self-governing Orthodox community in northern Greece comprised of twenty monasteries and their dependencies. It sits on a 130-square-mile promontory of which the highest point is Athos (6,670 feet). Monastic life began there in the 10th century; the youngest *monastery dates from 1542. In this community of about 1,700 men (women are barred, as are female animals), many *Byzantine art and literary treasures are to be found.

ATONEMENT The making *at one* of *God and human beings who were previously estranged (Rom 5:11). This is essentially *reconciliation, for sinful humanity is brought into a state of friendship with God through the *Lord *Jesus Christ. The death and *resurrection of *Christ are seen as the focal points of the act of God in achieving "at-one-ment." Various theories of how atonement/reconciliation was achieved have been put forward on the basis of what God did in *Christ. Major ones are: (1) Ransom to *Satan. Jesus paid a debt to release humans from Satan's lordship. Popular in the early centuries. (2) Satisfaction to God's honor. Sin, being an *infinite offense to God, had to be satisfied. Jesus provided that infinite satisfaction to divine *justice, for he was God made man. Popular in the Middle Ages. (3) Penal substitution. Jesus took the place of sinners and suffered the *punishment due to them. Popular in *Protestantism. (4) Christ's victory over *sin, death, *hell, and Satan, as the second Adam, the representative man. This was taught in the early church, by some Reformers of the 16th century, and today. See also CROSS AND CRUCIFIX; DEVIL RANSOM; RECONCILIATION; REDEMPTION; SATISFACTION; SUBSTITUTE, CHRIST AS.

ATONEMENT, EXTENT OF THE Theological discussion on the intention (and purpose) of *God with respect to *Jesus' atoning death. The theory of *limited atonement or particular *redemption directly connects *Christ's atoning work with the decree of election and limits its saving effect to a particular group, the elect. The theory of general redemption or unlimited atonement argues that Jesus' death was intended to provide *salvation for everyone generally; those who reject the offer are lost. There are many variations on these two basic positions.

ATTRIBUTES OF GOD Traits belonging uniquely to *God, often divided into two groups. (1) The metaphysical, or incommunicable: (a) *aseity—God's existence depends on no one else; (b) simplicity—God has one perfect essence; (c) *infinity and eternity—God is unlimited by time and space; (d) immutability and *impassibility—God is not subject to change in himself. (2) The religious, moral, or communicable, including the perfections of *will, life, and intelligence. Therefore *holy *love, *omnipotence, *omniscience, perfect freedom, and *righteousness are intended. See also ANALOGY; THEISM, CHRISTIAN.

ATTRITION (Lat. *attritio*, "*repentance"). In Roman Catholic teaching, a sorrow for *sin that comes from the motive of fear—fear of *punishment from *God or man. By contrast, *contrition is said to be *repentance proceeding from *love for God. Attritionism is the teaching that attrition is sufficient for a valid reception of Holy *Communion. At the *Reformation *Luther denied this teaching, but it was upheld by the Roman Catholic Council of *Trent (1545–1563).

AUBURN AFFIRMATION (1924). Proclamation drafted in Auburn, New York, by 150 *Presbyterian (USA) clergymen in defense of a liberalized position on such matters as the *Virgin Birth, the inerrancy of *Scripture, *miracles, the *satisfaction theory of the *Atonement, and *Jesus' bodily *resurrection. By May of 1924 at the General Assembly of the Presbyterian Church, USA, more than 1,270 had signed the affirmation.

AUBURN DECLARATION (1837). Document issued from Auburn, New York, by New School Presbyterians after a somewhat protracted conflict in which four New School *synods were expelled from the General Assembly. The declaration affirmed the New School's faithfulness to traditional *Presbyterian standards in an attempt to breach the gap with the Old School. The reconciliation was not effected until 1868 when Old School conservatives accepted the intent of the document.

AUFKLÄRUNG (Ger. "enlightenment"). Used by historians to describe a particular type and movement of thought found in Germany in the 18th century. The idea of the supernatural was denied, and the all-sufficiency of human reason was affirmed. It preserved belief in *God and the dignity of man; it denied *doctrines such as the *Incarnation, *miracles, and *original *sin. Leaders in the movement were G. E. Lessing, H. S. *Reimarus, and J. G. Herder. German pastors and teachers were deeply affected by its ideas and ethos. Some reacted strongly against it, while others accepted its major presuppositions. See also Enlightenment, The.

AUGSBURG, CONFESSION OF (1530). Written by Philip *Melanchthon and presented to Emperor *Charles V, it was meant to explain Lutheran *doctrine in the context of traditional and contemporary *Christianity; and it became an important statement of *faith for *Lutheranism. It is divided into two parts. The first sets forth the distinctive Lutheran doctrines in twenty-one articles, explaining particularly the idea of *justification by *grace through faith. In the second the abuses needing remedy are listed—e.g., compulsory *celibacy. In later years minor modifications were made so that the Lutheran churches of today receive the text of 1580, the "Invariata," as authoritative.

AUGSBURG, INTERIM OF (1548). A temporary agreement between Roman Catholics and Protestants in Germany, drawn up on the instigation of Emperor *Charles V. While it allowed clerical marriage and *Communion in both groups, the document, twenty-six articles long, largely expressed the Roman Catholic viewpoint, causing some Protestants to redress the balance by their own declaration at Leipzig later that year. Not until the Peace of *Augsburg in 1555 was a religious settlement effected in Germany.

AUGSBURG, PEACE OF (1555). A religious settlement made by civil authorities whereby Germany came to terms with the need for both *Roman Catholicism and *Lutheranism to exist within its borders. Prudently, however, only one *denomination was permitted in each territory, which choice was to be determined by the ruler. Migration for individuals to a more congenial territory was provided for, but Roman Catholics and Protestants were allowed to coexist in the imperial cities. It was an uneasy compromise that brought up many problems, but it largely saw Germany through a period when civil *war might have torn it apart.

AUGUSTINE OF CANTERBURY (d. 604–605). First *archbishop of Canterbury. A *Benedictine *prior in Rome, he was appointed by *Gregory I to lead a forty-strong *mission that began work in largely pagan southern England in 597. Welcomed by King Ethelbert of Kent who gave them a base in Canterbury (and was himself an early convert), the *missionaries evangelized so effectively that, before the end of the 7th century, *Christianity had been accepted by all of the Saxon kingdoms of England. *Augustine, who had been *consecrated in France, was subsequently given *metropolitan status by Gregory and authorized to consecrate twelve *suffragan *bishops.

AUGUSTINE OF HIPPO (354–430). *Bishop of Hippo (modern Annaba, Algeria). Born and educated in North Africa, he became a teacher of rhetoric, a profession continued when he went to Milan in 384. Influenced by that city's bishop, *Ambrose, he forsook *Manichaeism for *Christianity. While visiting Hippo in 391 he was reluctantly ordained, and in 395 he was consecrated as successor to Bishop Valerius. He defended Christianity against attacks by Manichees, *Donatists, pagans, and *Pelagians, and showed himself a faithful *pastor, preacher, administrator, and encourager of *monasticism. Augustine is often called the greatest thinker in *Christian antiquity. His writings include *The Confessions* (c. 399) and *The City of God* (c. 413–427). His *Confessions* is considered to be the first instance of Christian spiritual autobiography.

His basic understanding of theology was that "I believe in order that I may understand"—"*credo ut intelligam.*"

AUGUSTINIAN CANONS The first Roman Catholic *religious *order of men in which *priests followed a full common life. Claiming to have been founded in the 4th century and revived in the 11th, it was greatly diminished because of the hostility shown during the *Reformation and the French Revolution. Otherwise known as Black or Austin or Regular Canons, the order now lists over a thousand members and engages in pastoral, educational, *missions, and hospital work.

AUGUSTINIAN HERMITS (AUSTIN FRIARS) Established as a *mendicant *order in the mid-13th century by Pope Alexander IV, it brought together a number of independent Italian *monasteries and belied its name by active work in cities, universities, the New World, and the Far East. Once including Martin *Luther and the great Austrian scientist Gregor Mendel, membership now exceeds four thousand.

AUGUSTINIANISM Refers to particular aspects and developments of the teaching of *Augustine of Hippo (d. 430) who exercised such a tremendous influence over *Christian thought. The word can refer to his influence on both *theology and philosophy in *Roman Catholicism and *Protestantism.

1. Theology. Here it is primarily but not exclusively Augustine's teaching on divine *grace that is in view. He taught that such is the sinful state of man that only the efficacious and irresistible *grace of *God can cause a sinner to begin to love and obey God. In the Roman Catholic church the major exponents of Augustinianism have been H. Noris (1631–1704), F. Belleli (1675–1742), and J. L. Berti (1696–1766). In Protestantism the influence of Augustinianism on *Calvin and *Luther was great.

2. Philosophy. Here the dominant ideas are that all human knowledge is derived from direct divine *illumination and that the human *will enjoys a priority over the intellect. The major exponents belong to the Middle Ages and are *Alexander of Hales (c. 1170–1245), *Bonaventura (1221–1274) and William of Auvergne (c. 1180–1249).

AULÉN, GUSTAF EMANUEL HILDEBRAND (1879–1978). Swedish theologian. Successively theological professor and *bishop with a great influence in his homeland, he was also known abroad for his strong *ecumenism, his opposition to Nazism, and his books, which included *Christus Victor* (1931) and *Reformation and Catholicity* (1959).

AUTHENTIC EXISTENCE A term made famous by Martin Heidegger (1889–1976) the German philosopher. It refers to the approach to life and understanding that is possible for a human being who recognizes fully the certainty of his own death. Avoiding the full and serious recognition of death leads to inauthentic existence and the missing of true selfhood. Theologians have adopted this approach as a means of conveying to modern people what Christian commitment entails or what "living in the Spirit" means in contrast to "living in the flesh." See also ABSURD, EXISTENTIALISM.

AUTO-DA-FÉ A Portuguese term which, translated "act of *faith," denoted the public ceremony for the reading of sentences passed on those brought before the *Inquisition. The occasion included an elaborate *ritual that featured a solemn *mass and a *sermon. The victims, usually *heretics of various kinds, might be sentenced to anything up to life imprisonment (only the civil authority could impose the death penalty). The first auto-da-fé took place in Spain in 1481, the last in Mexico in 1850.

AUTONOMY The power to determine action in freedom from external forces. Since it is the rejection of any law or principle except that which emerges from one's own being, Christians cannot subscribe to it, because they look to *God's *will for their principles. See also HETERONOMY, THEONOMY.

AUTOPISTIC (Gk. "self-evident *faith"). Used of the impact *God's self-disclosure or *revelation makes on the heart. God reveals himself and creates by the Holy *Spirit the faith by which the receiver actually believes.

AVE MARIA (Lat. "Hail Mary"). A *prayer addressed to *Mary in two parts. The first is taken from Luke 1:28, 42; and the second is "Holy Mary, Mother of God, pray for us sinners now and at the hour of our death."

AVE MARIS STELLA (Lat. "Hail Star of the Sea"). A metrical *hymn of seven strophes, each with four lines. Dating from the 9th century, it is a *prayer to *Mary, who is addressed as "Star of the Sea" and as the Virgin through whose cooperation with *God *evil was overcome and *salvation came.

AVERROISM The system of philosophy developed by Averroes (1126–1198), a Spanish Muslim. He wrote commentaries on the works of Aristotle, the ancient Greek philosopher, and in them produced elaborate *doctrines of *God and the world. After being generally received in the *Christian centers of learning, Averroism was condemned as erroneous, and it died a gradual death.

AWAKENING The *revival or renewal of a *Christian community/church so that its *worship, *fellowship, and *evangelism are enhanced and deepened. It is a term used by historians to describe what happened as a result of the *preaching of famous *evangelists like John *Wesley and Charles *Finney. However, an awakening can occur without the intervention of visiting preachers.

AXIOLOGY The rational or philosophical study of values, especially in *religion and *ethics. Questions such as the following are asked and answered: What makes anything/anyone valuable? What various types of value are acknowledged? What criteria can be set forth by which to judge value?

AXIOM A statement for which no proof is required and therefore which occurs as the premise (basis) of many arguments but the conclusion of none. E.g., the statement "*God exists" is regarded as axiomatic by the community of believers.

AYER, WILLIAM WARD (1891–1985). Widely known Baptist *pastor, author, and conference speaker. During his fifty-year ministry he pastored churches in Gary, Indiana (1927–1932), Hamilton, Ontario (1932–1936), Canada, and New York City (1936–1949); and he was heard on radio throughout the United States.

AYLWARD, GLADYS (1902–1970). *Missionary to China. Daughter of a London postman, she was converted at eighteen while in domestic service. She overcame educational and financial difficulties and went on her own initiative to China, where she subsequently destroyed her British passport and adopted a Chinese lifestyle in order to reach the people more effectively. After the 1940 Japanese invasion, her incredible feat in leading a hundred children on a long, arduous journey to safety was made the basis of a Hollywood film. Later she founded an orphanage in Taiwan.

AZARIAH, VEDANAYAKAM SAMUEL (1874–1945). First Indian *bishop of the Anglican church. Son of an Anglican *priest in Madras state, he worked for the YMCA among students, was ordained in 1909, and became bishop of Dornakal in 1912. Host at the great 1938 *Tambaram Conference, he was a pioneer of Indian *ecumenical talks that led after his death to two major church unions in India.

AZUSA STREET REVIVAL The revival that took place 1906–1913 at the Apostolic Faith Mission on Azusa Street in Los Angeles, California. Restorationism, frontier *revivalism, the *Holiness movement, and premillennialism came together here in what is generally considered the beginning of the *Pentecostal movement. The leading figure in the revival was William J. *Seymour.

B

B.C See ANTE-CHRISTUM.

BABYLONIAN CAPTIVITY Used of the period 1309–1377 when the *popes (*Clement V through *Gregory XI) resided for political reasons in Avignon, France. The allusion is to the captivity of the Jews in ancient Babylon after 586 B.C. The expression was used by Martin *Luther in his famous treatise, *The Babylonian Captivity of the Church* (1520), to describe the situation in the church being captive to the *pope and needing the liberation of the *gospel.

BACH, JOHANN SEBASTIAN (1685–1750). German composer and organist. Born in Eisenach and orphaned at ten, he was a church and court organist before becoming musical director to Prince Leopold of Kothen (1717–1723) and thereafter cantor at Leipzig's renowned Thomasschule. In 1748 his sight began to fail, and by the time he died he was totally blind. Bach's large output of choral music (surprisingly little of which was published in his lifetime) included more than two hundred cantatas, the *Mass in B Minor*, and three settings of the *Passion (one lost). A strong Lutheran who was regarded as contentious by many colleagues, he strove for what he called "a well-regulated church music to the glory of *God." He is regarded as the greatest of all composers for the organ. The total output of his music, especially the church cantatas, has been called "the Fifth Gospel."

BACKSLIDING The retreat from *Christian commitment or the implication of Christian *faith. It was used in the *OT to describe *Israel's rejection of the *will of *God (Jer 3:6, 8, 11, 14; 5:6; 8:5). Thus it came to be used in the church of baptized Christians who reject the obvious implications of their baptismal commitment after having given good promise of such commitment.

BACKUS, ISAAC (1724–1806). American Baptist minister. Originally a *Congregationalist ordained in 1748, he was influenced by George *Whitefield and Jonathan *Edwards. Subsequently he became a Baptist and rose to prominence. He is chiefly remembered for his robust efforts in the cause of religious freedom.

BACON, ROGER (c. 1220–1292). English philosopher and scientist. After studying at Oxford and teaching at Paris, he joined the *Franciscans about 1257, chiefly in order to further his scientific experiments. He produced Greek and Hebrew grammars and three works that formed a kind of encyclopedia. Like many original minds, he chafed under traditional authority that criticized his "suspected novelties." He is popularly credited (he himself made no such claims) with having invented gunpowder and an early form of telescope.

BAILLIE, JOHN (1886–1960). Scottish theologian. After holding chairs of *theology in North America, he returned to Edinburgh as professor of divinity (1934–1956). A president of the *World Council of Churches and prominent participant in *ecumenical enterprises, he was also a prolific and appealing writer. Among his works were *A Diary of Private Prayer* (1936) and *Invitation to Pilgrimage* (1942).

BAILLIE, ROBERT (1599–1662). Scottish minister and writer. One of the early *Covenanters who resisted the attempt to impose *episcopacy on Scotland, he participated in the *Westminster Assembly. After the *Restoration he became principal of Glasgow University, but his policy of moderation was shattered when *Charles II, from whom he had expected so much, reimposed episcopacy. His *Letters and Journals* offer a valuable commentary on events of the time.

BALFOUR DECLARATION (1917). Official declaration (November 2, 1917) made by the British Foreign Secretary Arthur James Balfour regarding the establishment of a homeland in Palestine for the Jews. The declaration reads, "His Majesty's Government views with favour the establishment in Palestine of a national home for the Jewish people, and will use their best endeavours to facilitate the achievement of this object, it being clearly understood that nothing shall be done which may prejudice the civil and religious rights of existing non-Jewish communities in Palestine, or the rights and political status enjoyed by Jews in any other country."

BANCROFT, RICHARD (1544–1610). *Archbishop of Canterbury from 1604. A staunch opponent of *Puritanism, *Presbyterianism, and state meddling in church affairs, he became *bishop of London in 1597. At the *Hampton Court Conference he defended Anglican practices against Puritan objections. He also supervised the preparation of the *King James Version of the *Bible but died before its publication.

BANNS OF MARRIAGE The reading of the names of those who are to be married in church. It is done in public *worship, and opportunity is given for legal objections to be made to the planned marriage. The custom goes back to the rules promulgated by the Emperor *Charlemagne in the 9th century. It has most relevance in countries where there is a *state church.

BAPTISM The sign or *rite of entering the *Christian community. A few Christian groups, e.g., *Salvation Army and *Society of Friends, do not use it. It began in the apostolic period (Acts 2:41) and has been universal since then. For Paul it was the symbol of union with *Christ (Rom 6:1ff.).

Over the centuries many forms of water baptism have emerged (e.g., *affusion, *aspersion, and *immersion). Also there has been a difference of opinion concerning whether it is lawful to baptize infants or children who have not reached the age of personal responsibility for their *faith. So both *infant baptism and *believers' baptism exist in the church.

In *theology baptism is often call a *sacrament. By this is meant that it was instituted by *Christ (Matt 28:19) and that the outward sign (water) accompanies an inward reality (*God's work in the heart). The normal formula in baptism is "in the name of the Father, Son, and Holy *Spirit," but some use "in the name of Jesus."

BAPTISM, BELIEVERS' See BELIEVERS' BAPTISM.

BAPTISM, INFANT The *baptism of the children of members of the church. Most of the major churches practice this; they claim that it is perfectly agreeable with the teaching of *Scripture and in accord with the primitive practice of the early church. In the *OT all sons of the *covenant people were given the sign of membership (circumcision), and so it is argued that the children of believers should likewise receive the sign of membership in the new covenant. Boys and girls receive the sign of the new covenant, whereas only boys received the sign of the old covenant (Acts 2:39). Though there are no explicit statements that babies were baptized in the apostolic period, proponents of infant baptism see it as highly probable that they were included in the households which were baptized (Acts 16:15, 31).

BAPTISM FOR THE DEAD A practice mentioned by Paul in 1 Cor 15:29. It has been understood in at least three ways: (1) vicarious *baptism: being baptized for one who has died (practiced by Mormons); (2) baptism of someone actually dying and "as good as dead"; (3) baptism performed over the grave of someone who has been recently buried.

BAPTISM OF DESIRE A *baptism without water and without the express knowledge of the one baptized. Some modern Roman Catholic theologians claim that sincere religious people who follow the highest elements in their *religion (e.g., Buddhism) are in fact seeking *God. Their search is reckoned by God as the equivalent of a water baptism; it is a baptism of desire. So such a person is reckoned by God to be in the same state of *grace as one baptized into the triune name of God.

BAPTISM IN THE SPIRIT. Expression used in *Pentecostal and *Charismatic circles describing a special act of the Holy *Spirit accompanying or subsequent to *salvation, endowing the receiver with extraordinary spiritual abilities, such as *speaking in tongues, miraculous powers, prophesying, or *healing. The nature of these gifts, the experience itself, the timing of the event, its relation to water *baptism, and its relation to salvation are much debated both in and out of Charismatic circles, with opinions ranging from a complete denial that such exist at all to the requirement that they be experienced for salvation.

BAPTISMAL REGENERATION The *doctrine that the Holy *Spirit places divine life or *grace within the human *soul/heart at or closely connected with the act of *baptism by water. This occurs in both infants and adults at baptism. Such a belief is found in the Roman Catholic and *Orthodox churches as well as in some Protestant churches (e.g., Anglican and Lutheran). It has to be understood in the context of a *sacrament of grace in which water is the external sign and *God's renewing grace is the invisible reality. Some Protestants have strongly opposed this teaching because they have suspected that the idea is that the act of baptism conveys grace automatically. In fact, the *faith of the one being baptized or the faith of the sponsors of an infant is integral to the context of this doctrine.

BAPTIST WORLD ALLIANCE Founded in 1905 to promote *fellowship and cooperation among all *Baptists, there are international and regional meetings for study and *evangelism, and the Alliance works also in the cause of religious liberty. World congresses are held every five years.

BAPTISTS Those churches and *denominations that practice *believers' baptism and reject *infant baptism. Their origins may be traced to the *Anabaptists of the 16th century. However, it is more accurate to see their beginnings as a distinct part of English *Puritanism (and then of *Separatism) in the 17th century. Most are Calvinistic in *theology. While they have enjoyed a moderate growth in Europe, they have become, since the 17th century, a major force in American *Christianity (about 30 million in 1980). They are found in a variety of denominations of which the largest is the Southern Baptist Convention; a minority exist in wholly independent congregations. They emphasize their commitment to the authority of the *Bible but also hold to the major *doctrines of the early church (*Trinity and *person of Christ) and of the *Reformation (*salvation by *grace through *faith). Virtually all churches, whether inside or outside Baptist denominations, are congregationally governed. Since the late 18th century they have done vigorous *missionary work throughout the world so that Baptist churches are found today in most countries.

BARCLAY, JOHN (1734–1798). Founder of the *Bereans. A licentiate in the Church of *Scotland, he was censured for alleged deviations from *Presbyterian *doctrine. Invited to minister to a *secessionist group in Edinburgh, he was ordained by an English *presbytery in 1773. He founded churches in London and Bristol as well as in other parts of Scotland.

BARCLAY, ROBERT (1648–1690). Scottish *Quaker. Descended from the 12th-century David I of Scotland, he was educated in Paris, became a Quaker in 1665, and later became one of their leading apologists. A prolific writer, his most significant work, *Apology for the True Christian Divinity* (1678), became a strong statement of Quaker *doctrine. He held that both church and *Scripture were secondary to the work of the Holy *Spirit (the "inner light") in believers. Harassed and imprisoned initially, he was later received favorably by *Charles II and became friendly also with the Roman Catholic duke of York (later *James II). The result was a patent enabling Barclay's brother and William *Penn to establish a Quaker settlement in East Jersey, of which Robert Barclay (who never crossed the ocean) was appointed nominal governor.

BARCLAY, WILLIAM (1907–1978). Scottish biblical scholar. After graduation from Glasgow University and *ordination, he was for thirteen years in a *parish on industrial Clydeside before teaching (divinity and biblical criticism) *NT at Glasgow (1946–1974). He spoke and wrote lucidly for ordinary people. His *Study Bible*, a commentary consisting of daily readings, sold more than five million copies in English and were translated into many different languages.

BARMEN DECLARATION (1934). The statement of *faith composed by the first *synod of the German Confessing church (*Bekennende Kirche*) meeting at Barmen, May 29–30, 1934. It represents a witness to *God and a battle cry against all teaching (e.g., that of the Nazi party) that stands in the place or the way of *Jesus Christ; the church must listen to Jesus Christ alone. Behind this emergency declaration is the influence of Karl *Barth and *Barthianism.

BARNARDO, THOMAS JOHN (1845–1905). Philanthropist and pioneer in social work. Dublin-born, he joined the *Plymouth Brethren after conversion in 1862, and in 1866 he began medical studies in London in preparation for medical missions. While a student he was touched by the plight of poor boys, and in 1870, helped by the Earl of *Shaftesbury, this "father of nobody's children" founded in Stepney the first of more than ninety homes for destitute children. His lifetime saw an outreach to 250,000 children and a further 60,000 admitted to his homes, of whom one-third found new lives in Canada.

BARNES, ALBERT (1798–1870). Controversial *Presbyterian minister who figured prominently in the New School–Old School debate. His widely read *Notes: Explanatory and Practical* continued the promulgation of his denial of *original *sin and insistence that men were free moral agents. Twice charged with *heresy by the Philadelphia Synod in the 1830s, he was acquitted by the General Assembly. His early connection with Union Theological Seminary (New York) allowed him to promote social reform, *social action, and *abolition.

BARNES, ERNEST WILLIAM (1874–1953). *Bishop of Birmingham. A former Cambridge mathematics lecturer who was Prime Minister Ramsay MacDonald's first episcopal appointment (1924), he was a thorn in the flesh of the episcopal establishment during four *primacies and three decades at Birmingham. He was a fearless opponent of Anglo-Catholic deviations, a radical theologian whose *Rise of Christianity* (1947) caused a furor, a pacifist, and an advocate of alliance between *Christianity and the F. D. Maurice-Charles *Kingsley type of socialism. Barnes upheld sexual purity, was rigorous in personal devotions, and wanted the

Anglican *Communion service open to all Christians.

BARNHOUSE, DONALD GREY (1895–1960). American *Presbyterian minister and radio preacher. After work with the Belgian Gospel Mission (1919–1927) he became minister of Tenth Presbyterian Church, Philadelphia. He immediately began a remarkable radio outreach that included an eleven-year series of weekly broadcasts. He preached worldwide and wrote thirty books.

BARROW, HENRY (c. 1550–1593). Early *Congregationalist *martyr. Born in Norfolk and educated at Cambridge, he was converted about 1581 and embraced Puritan views. He became a lawyer in London and accepted the *separatist ideas of Robert *Browne and John Greenwood, who advocated the formation of churches independent of the Church of *England. Barrow held that the true church was "a company of faithful people, separated from the unbelievers and heathen of the land, gathered in the name of *Christ." He upheld the autonomy of each congregation and the *priesthood of all believers. With religious *nonconformity considered a threat to national security, Barrow and Greenwood were found guilty of separatist activities and died together on the scaffold.

BARTH, KARL (1886–1968). Swiss theologian. Born in Basel and educated in Switzerland and Germany, he served as *pastor in his homeland (1909–1921) before becoming successively professor at Göttingen (1921), Münster (1925), and Bonn (1930). He courageously supported the *Confessing church against Hitler, was deprived of his chair for refusing to swear loyalty to the German leader, and returned to Switzerland in 1935 as professor of *theology at Basel. While he did not hesitate to change his views if so convinced, he consistently strove to restore biblical and *Reformed theology to its rightful place in *Christian life and thought. In his view too much had been made of natural *theology and not enough of a transcendent *God who had revealed himself through *Christ. He said that all Christian *preaching must be tested against *Scripture and that the chief end of man is to glorify God. Barth's writings, from his commentary on Romans (1919) onward, particularly his monumental *Church Dogmatics* (which began to appear in 1932), confirm that he was the greatest Protestant theologian of his age.

BARTHIANISM The *theology of Karl *Barth (1886–1968) or of his immediate *disciples. Since he had a positive attitude to classical, *patristic theology (e.g., in the *Nicene Creed) and to *Reformation theology, his teaching has been called *neoorthodoxy, the new *orthodoxy. Since he held that all human institutions, including religious *denominations, were judged by *God's self-disclosure in *Christ, his views were referred to as a *crisis theology (where crisis implies judgment). Further, since he emphasized that human reason cannot apprehend God in any meaningful way, his teaching has been called *dialectical theology; we can only say yes or no to God, who reveals himself to us. Finally, since Barth stressed that God is known in Christ, the *eternal *Word, and nowhere else, his theology has been called a theology of the Word; the *Scriptures are the written *revelation of God in *Jesus Christ.

BARTHOLOMEW'S DAY, MASSACRE OF (1572). The mass murder of *Huguenots in Paris on the eve of St. Bartholomew's Day (August 23–24). The act was prompted by Catherine de' Medici, who feared the influence of Gaspard de *Coligny, the Huguenot leader. The killings were repeated throughout France, and some 30,000 Huguenots were slain, including Coligny.

BASEL, CONFESSION OF (1534). A document containing twelve articles, it is generally regarded as a moderate statement of *Reformed *doctrine. The work successively of John *Oecolampadius and Oswald *Myconius, and reflecting a position between that of *Luther and that of *Zwingli, it was adopted by the citizens of Basel and later by the city of Muhlhausen. Until 1872 all ministers of Basel had to affirm it.

BASEL, COUNCIL OF (1431–1449). A general council of the Roman Catholic Church. Its major problems were the question of papal supremacy, high tax demands, how the church should deal with the followers of Jan *Hus, and the threat to Christendom posed by Turkish encroachments. Having sturdily rejected the attempt by *Eugenius IV to adjourn the council ostensibly because of sparse attendance, the council declared that its authority came not from the *pope but directly from *God. It subsequently agreed to the reception back into communion of most of the Hussites (1436); but thereafter Eugenius, who had belatedly backed the council, sensed danger from proposed reforms and announced the council's transfer to Ferrara (1437). When a minority resisted the move, Eugenius excommunicated them. They in turn declared him deposed and later elected an *antipope, Felix V (1439). The much depleted Council of *Basel survived and served various vested political interests until 1449, when it recognized Eugenius's successor, *Nicholas V.

BASIL THE GREAT (c. 329–379). *Cappadocian Father. Born into an aristocratic *Christian family, the brother of *Gregory of Nyssa, he was educated in Cappadocia, Constantinople, and Athens. On his return home he was ordained about 365 and followed an ascetic existence until made *bishop of Caesarea (370) at a time when the *Arians were troubling the *Orthodox Church. Basil developed into a notable theologian and teacher. His great gifts and irenic temperament made him an excellent *mediator between Eastern and Western churches. Among those whose writings he influenced were *Augustine of Hippo and *Leo I.

BAUR, FERDINAND CHRISTIAN (1792–1860). German radical theologian. Born near Stuttart, he was professor of *theology at Tübingen (1826–1860). He rejected the apostolic origin of most of the *NT, held that only four of the letters attributed to Paul were genuinely his, that this Paul was different from the one referred to in Acts, and that the *gospel writings were largely based on an earlier gospel. Later in his life Baur turned to church history. His five-volume history of the *Christian church subjected *Christianity to critical historical examination. Much influenced by German philosophers (notably *Schleiermacher and *Hegel), Baur declared, "Without philosophy, history seems to me dumb and dead." He was founder of the so-called Tübingen school of theology.

BAVINCK, HERMAN (1854–1921). Prominent Dutch theologian and professor of *systematic theology (Kampen [1882–1902], Free University of Amsterdam [1902–1920]). Only the second volume, *The Doctrine of God*, of the four-volume *magnum opus, Gereformeerde Dogmatiek* is available in English. Bavinck devoted his manifold talents to engaging the thought of his time and attempting a renewal of scholastic Reformed *theology. He stressed theology as the study of *God revealed in *Christ and the *Scriptures, summarized in the church's *creeds and confessions.

BAXTER, RICHARD (1615–1691). English *Puritan minister. Though physically frail, he read extensively and was ordained in the Church of *England in 1638. Becoming minister of Kidderminster in 1641, his spiritual influence transformed the community. Though he served as chaplain with the Parliamentary troops in the British Civil War, he supported the *Restoration, at which time he was made a royal chaplain. He was ejected from the church by the 1662 Act of *Uniformity and later served an eighteen-month prison term for alleged sedition. More *Presbyterian than Anglican, Baxter was tolerant in an intolerant age. His writings include the classic, *The Saints' Everlasting Rest* (1650).

BAY PSALM BOOK (1640). The first book in English to have been printed in the American colonies. The work of John Eliot and two colleagues, it aimed at a literal translation of the Psalms, one that could be used in congregational singing in the Massachussetts Bay Colony. Their goal was "Conscience rather than elegance, fidelity rather than poetry." Officially called *The Whole Book of Psalms Faithfully Translated into English Metre,* it was approved by the colony. Its use spread to other colonies and even to Britain.

BEADLE Originally a mace-bearer at Oxford and Cambridge universities, the beadle in Scottish *Presbyterianism is the minister's man or attendant.

BEATIFIC VISION The fulfillment of the promise, "Blessed are the pure in heart for they shall see *God" (Matt 5:8) within the future *kingdom of God. In their spiritual bodies the redeemed will experience God's nearness and glory through *Jesus Christ. The word "vision" is used because it is recognized that even in the glorious kingdom of God the redeemed will "see" God only in and through their *Mediator, the *Lord Jesus. In the Middle Ages there was a protracted controversy as to the precise nature and content of the vision. In modern times theologians recognize that we can only speak of it in symbolical and metaphorical terms (see Rev 21, 22). The final perfection of the whole person in *heaven is known as a state of beatitude.

BEATIFICATION The act by which the *pope permits the *veneration of a faithful *Christian who has died. Such a person is given the title of "Blessed." Normally the permission relates only to a given geographical area, a monastic *order, *diocese, or other limited group. Beatification by the pope does not require Roman Catholics to venerate those called "Blessed," but *canonization does. A clear distinction is drawn between veneration offered to a faithful Christian and *worship offered to *God himself.

BEATITUDES Promises made by *Jesus Christ of present and future blessings and happiness. In Matt 5:3–11 there are nine, and in Luke 6:20–22 there are four. They describe the perfect *Christian character in terms of inner *spirituality and outward *love for others.

BECKET, THOMAS (c. 1118–1170). *Archbishop of Canterbury from 1162. Born in London of Norman parents and trained in law, he was ordained and became *archdeacon of Canterbury. A close friend of *Henry II, he was *chancellor of England from 1155 and was even seen in full armor in France during a siege. After his elevation to the primacy it soon became apparent that the king had overestimated Becket's pliability. Becket's lifestyle changed, and he put loyalty to church and *papacy above that to the king. Henry took action against Becket, who fled into exile in France; and when he returned in 1170 and disciplined those *bishops who had furthered the king's policies in his absence, Henry's utterance of unguarded words encouraged four knights to murder the archbishop in his cathedral. The deed provoked widespread horror and forced Henry to do public penance in the same place in 1174.

BECON, THOMAS (c. 1512–1567). English Reformer. A Cambridge graduate of Protestant sympathies who became chaplain to Protector Somerset and Thomas *Cranmer, he was arrested on the accession of Mary *Tudor, released evidently by mistake, fled to the continent, and survived to become under *Elizabeth I a *canon of Canterbury, holding a series of benefices. His writings on the Protestant cause became increasingly robust and were widely read.

BEDE, THE VENERABLE (c. 673–735). "Father of English church history." Born in County Durham, he entered the *monastery at seven and evidently never traveled outside Northumbria. His disciplined habits and *love of scholarship, nonetheless, made him one of the greatest scholars of his time. His *Bible commentaries were highly esteemed during the Middle Ages, and his church history of the English people, completed in 731, was the first work on the subject.

BEECHER, HENRY WARD (1813–1887). American Congregational minister. Son of Lyman *Beecher, he became a *Presbyterian minister in Indiana and soon won fame as a preacher and as a writer with his *Seven Lectures to Young Men* (1844). In 1847 he went to Brooklyn as minister of Plymouth Congregational Church, where his oratory and undemanding type of *Christianity drew crowds of 2,500 or more. He became a persuasive opponent of *slavery, on which he lectured also in England; pressed for women's suffrage; and supported the evolutionary theory. The charges of immorality that clouded his latter years were dismissed by Congregational and other denominational bodies.

BEECHER, LYMAN (1775–1863). American *Presbyterian minister. A graduate of Yale, he served churches in New York and New England (1799–1832) before going west to Ohio as president of the new Lane Theological Seminary (1832–1850) and minister of Second Presbyterian Church, Cincinnati (1832–1842). A founder of the American Bible Society and active in the antislavery movement, he assailed the *evils of intemperance and *Roman Catholicism and preached for conversions, but his less rigid view of *Calvinism led more conservative colleagues to unsuccessful action against him in the church courts in 1835. The careers of his thirteen children, among them Henry Ward *Beecher and Harriet Beecher *Stowe, earned him the title of "the father of more brains than any other man in America."

BÉGUINES, BÉGHARDS Communities of females and males, respectively, originating in the 12th-century Netherlands and taking their name apparently from a revivalist preacher called Lambert le Bègue ("the Stammerer"), who died in 1177. Taking no irrevocable *vows, their austerity self-imposed, they engaged in philanthropic and welfare work. Suffering persecution and severe criticism by ecclesiastical authority in 1311, both communities maintained their existence in modified form. The Béghards survived until the end of the 19th century; the Béguines are still to be found, especially in Belgium.

BEHAVIORISM A theory and method of psychological investigation based on the observation and analysis of human and animal behavior. In its strong form the theory denies the reality of what is traditionally called "mind" and explains everything by physiological processes. Often it is found in a weak form as a method of studying humans. Even so, it is difficult to see its relationship to *Christianity, which insists that humans do have minds (or *souls) and are responsible to *God for their behavior.

BEING, BECOMING In ancient Greek philosophy these were contrasted. Being is perfection and cannot change: to become is to change. In medieval *theology *God was considered as pure Being, and his essential activity is to be himself. A biblical foundation was found for this in Exodus 3:14, "I am who I am." Creatures were seen as dependent beings, dependent on pure Being.

The word Being is also found in some modern theologies, but here it has a different meaning. E.g., Paul *Tillich (d. 1965) spoke of *God as "Being itself" and of encountering "New Being" in *Jesus Christ. Being as divine activity rather than as a perfection already enjoyed is found in both modern theological *existentialist and *process theology.

BEISSEL, JOHANN CONRAD (1690–1768). Founder of the *Ephrata Society. German-born, his *Pietist view brought persecution, to escape which he went to America in 1720, settling in Pennsylvania. After the Ephrata Society had been founded he changed his name to Gottrecht Friedsam ("godly and peaceable").

BELGIC CONFESSION (1561). A Calvinistic statement of *faith drawn up by Dutch Protestants trying to secure *toleration from *Philip IV. Its thirty-seven articles, systematically expressed and based on the 1559 French Confession, were translated into Dutch, German, and Latin. The Belgic Confession was accepted after revision by the Synod of *Dort (1619) and became a symbol of the *Reformed Churches in the Low Countries, and of the (Dutch) *Reformed Church in America.

BELIEVERS' BAPTISM *Baptism of those who have previously made a *confession of *faith in *Jesus as *Lord. This is the normal procedure in Baptist churches. It is based on the conviction that such baptism was the norm in the apostolic period. Those who advocate only this form of baptism (which may be *affusion or *immersion) give no weight to the church *tradition that allows for baptizing the children of Christians.

BELL, GEORGE KENNEDY ALLEN (1883–1958). Anglican *bishop and ecumenist. Formerly dean of Canterbury, he became bishop of Chichester in 1929 and was active on behalf of refugees from Nazi Germany and in developing relations with the *Confessing church there. A warm advocate of church reunion, he courageously spoke out against the World War II bombing that led to heavy civilian casualties. His persistence in this, as his later condemnation of nuclear weapons, irritated many in high places and may have blocked his elevation to the primacy.

BELLARMINE, ROBERT (1542–1621). Roman Catholic *cardinal and apologist. Born in Tuscany, he became a *Jesuit (1560) and in the face of resurgent *Protestantism was drafted in 1569 to teach *theology in Belgium. There he became the first Jesuit professor at the University of Louvain. *Gregory XIII brought him back to teach in the Roman College in 1576. Made cardinal in 1599 and *archbishop of Capua in 1602, he reluctantly carried out the task of admonishing *Galileo, but generally he showed himself an enlightened scholar. Such was his active concern for the *poor that he died penniless.

BEMA A Greek word meaning a platform and used by the *Eastern Orthodox to describe that part of the church that is raised above the level of the main part (nave). It is separated from the nave by the *iconostasis (screen) and contains the *altar.

BENEDICITE (Lat. "Bless ye the *Lord"). A song of praise sung by Shadrach, Meshach, and Abednego as they faced Nebuchadnezzar from the hot furnace. It occurs only in the Greek and Latin texts of the Book of Daniel and so does not appear in Protestant *Bibles, which are based on the Hebrew text. The song is found in the extra section beginning at Dan 3:23. As a *hymn it has been used in *worship since the 5th century.

BENEDICT (c. 480–c. 550). Commonly called the "Father of Western *monasticism." A saintly seeker after solitude much admired by kindred spirits, he founded twelve monasteries of twelve monks each but later established the famous *monastery at Monte Cassino. His *Benedictine *rule became the standard for Western *monasticism and demanded personal *poverty, manual labor, spiritual reading, regular recitation of the divine *office, and a *vow to remain in the *monastery until death. *Abbots were, however, specifically instructed to show also gentleness and tolerance for human weakness.

BENEDICT XII (d. 1342). Pope from 1334. French-born and a *Cistercian, he was the third of the *popes to rule from Avignon during the Babylonian Captivity. His *pontificate saw the start of the *Hundred Years' War, despite papal mediation. In 1336 he issued the *bull *Benedictus Deus,* which held that the *souls of the just are granted a *vision of *God immediately after death. He was a church reformer despite opposition, and he contributed to the restoration of Rome's dilapidated churches. Far from returning the *papacy to Rome, he built a magnificent papal palace at Avignon.

BENEDICT XIII (c. 1328–1423). *Antipope. Born in Spain, he became professor of *canon law at Montepellier, then was made *cardinal in 1375. When the *Great Schism began in 1378, he supported *Clement VII who had been set up in opposition to *Urban VI, and he succeeded Clement in 1394. Benedict held on to his claim for nearly thirty stormy years, outliving several rivals, rejecting decisions of the Councils of *Pisa and *Constance, and even naming four new *cardinals in the year before his death.

BENEDICT XIII (1649–1730). Pope from 1724. When elected, this aged *Dominican had been a *cardinal for fifty-two years and had helped elect five other popes. A man who lived modestly, and ineffectually criticized the extravagance and worldliness of his *cardinals, he allowed papal foreign policy to deteriorate against the pretensions of 18th-century national monarchs. He would make no concessions to *Jansenism but favored somewhat similar tendencies in his own Dominicans.

BENEDICT XIV (1675–1758). Pope from 1740. An enlightened man who advocated moderation and promoted scientific studies, he also encouraged agriculture, reduced taxes, and showed wise diplomacy in political and ecclesiastical disputes. He nonetheless condemned *Jesuit concessions to converts in Asia, though he was more conciliatory toward French *priests who held *Jansenist views.

BENEDICT XV (1854–1922). Pope from 1914. Elected just after the outbreak of World War I, his problems were largely involved with *war and its aftermath. Seeking to follow a strictly neutral course, he worked for the alleviation of human misery. He persuaded Switzerland to take in soldiers with tuberculosis, and he set up an office to reestablish contact between prisoners of war and their families. His attempt at mediation in 1917 was hampered by the pro-Axis views of most of his *cardinals (a factor that weakened the papal influence in postwar planning). His *papacy saw diplomatic relations with France resumed and the accreditation of a British representative to the *Vatican for the first time since the 17th century. Benedict made himself accessible to all, and so generous was his almsgiving that the Vatican had to borrow money to bury him.

BENEDICTINES The Order of Saint Benedict is composed strictly of confederated congregations of monks and *nuns, each exercising autonomy. The *rule, named after the 6th-century native of Nursia, offers a comprehensive manual for the physical and spiritual welfare of its monastic followers. The *monasteries multiplied and prospered and were the centers of *culture and teaching in Western Europe until the mid-12th century, by which time other forms of *monasticism, such as *Carthusians and *Cistercians, had begun to emerge. Benedictinism declined but revived after reform measures in the 15th century. Thereafter the cycle of revival and decline was continued after the *Reformation. In 1893 *Leo XIII departed from *tradition by creating the office of *abbot *primate as head of the federation of autonomous congregations. In the early 1970s membership of the *order was about 11,000.

BENEDICTION This word has two meanings in the context of *worship: (1) the blessing pronounced at the end of a worship service—"The blessing of *God Almighty, Father, Son, and Holy *Spirit be with you . . ."; (2) a worship service found in the Church of Rome and in parts of the Anglican communion. The consecrated bread of Holy *Communion is exposed to the view of the congregation with suitable ceremony, and prayers or *hymns to the *Lord *Jesus are offered; it is held that his presence is in and with the consecrated bread. Protestants have usually seen this service as verging on *idolatry.

BENGEL, JOHANN ALBRECHT (1687–1752). German Lutheran theological writer. His edition of the *NT, published in 1734, marked the start of modern textual criticism. His word-by-word *exegesis of the Greek NT text (1742) was highly regarded by John *Wesley, who published much of the material in *Notes Upon the New Testament* (1755). Bengel's eschatological writings also made a notable contribution to the study of NT *theology.

BENSON, EDWARD WHITE (1829–1896). *Archbishop of Canterbury from 1883. Cambridge graduate and patristics scholar, he was appointed in 1877 to the new *diocese of Truro. While dogmatic in many situations, Benson eventually was a conciliatory force over the vexing matter of *ritualism. He was a supporter of *missions and of sponsoring or reestablishing links with churches in other countries.

BERDYAEV, NIKOLAI ALEKSANDROVICH (1874–1948). Russian philosopher and religious writer. A Marxist sympathizer during student days at Kiev, he was exiled for three years. Even when, influenced by *Dostoevsky, his views changed and he joined the Russian Orthodox Church (1907), he remained nonconformist by criticizing church authority. He escaped *punishment because of the Russian Revolution (1917), after which he became professor of philosophy at Moscow University (1920). Finding orthodox Marxism distasteful, he was exiled in 1922 and with other exiles founded the Academy of Philosophy and Religion, which in 1924 was transferred from Berlin to Paris. He held that *God's *will was that man should be free and that *truth was the result of "a light that breaks through from the transcendent world of the Spirit" into a confusing environment.

BEREANS This name, taken from Acts 17:10–11, was applied by John *Barclay in 1773 to those who followed him out of the Church of *Scotland into secession. Barclay, a moderate Calvinist who regarded *Scripture as the sole repository of *truth, held that our knowledge of *God derives from *revelation, not nature. He founded congregations in London, Bristol, and several Scots towns. Most of them found their way into Congregationalism during the 19th century.

BERGGRAV, EIVIND (1884–1959). Norwegian Lutheran *bishop. After studies in Norway, England, Germany, and Switzerland, he was ordained, was a teacher (1909–1918), a country *pastor, a prison chaplain, and the first bishop of Tromso (1928) then of Oslo (1928–1950). A versatile scholar and educator, he published works on many subjects and always sought to maintain links between church and *culture. He was *interned for his criticism of the Nazi occupation (1942–1945). Even after retirement for health reasons he was active in the *ecumenical movement, serving as a president of the *World Council of Churches (1950–1954).

BERKHOF, LOUIS (1873–1957). *Christian Reformed church theologian and president of Calvin Theological Seminary (1931–1944). Widely versed, Berkhof taught both *OT and *NT subjects, but he is best remembered for his well-formulated, if unoriginal, *Systematic Theology* (1938). Heavily dependent upon Herman *Bavinck and Abraham *Kuyper, this work or versions of it have been extensively used in conservative circles worldwide.

BERNADETTE (MARIE BERNARDE SOUBIROUS) (1844–1879). French visionary born in Lourdes. In 1858 she was chronically ill and claimed to have had a series of visions of the Virgin *Mary. She did not waver when those experiences were challenged by parents, *clergy, and civil authorities. She subsequently joined the Sisters of Notre-Dame, where, despite constant pain and sickness, she displayed a piety and serenity that impressed everyone. She was *canonized in 1933.

The shrine at Lourdes is named after her.

BERNARD, JOHN HENRY (1860–1927). Irish scholar and *archbishop. Born in Bengal, he graduated at Trinity College, Dublin (1880), where between 1884 and 1911 he was a faculty member and professor, combining this from 1902 with the Anglican deanery of St. Patrick's. He became *bishop of Ossory in 1911 and archbishop of Dublin in 1915, but he returned to Trinity as provost in 1919 and held that post until his death. A Protestant leader in Roman Catholic society pressing for independence from Britain, he strove to maintain harmony in church and state. He published works on philosophy, church history, and Irish *hymns, but he is chiefly remembered for commentaries on the Pastoral Epistles (1899), 2 Corinthians (1903), and John's Gospel (1928).

BERNARDINO OF SIENA (1380–1444). *Franciscan preacher. Born into a noble family but orphaned at six, he joined the Franciscans in 1402. In 1417 he began his famous preaching tours throughout north and central Italy in which he sought to counter the lawlessness and immorality of the age. He took part in the Council of *Florence in 1439, supported the short-lived union between Greek and Roman churches, and was a notable scholar. In 1444 he set out to evangelize the kingdom of Naples but died on the way.

BERNARD OF CLAIRVAUX (1090–1153). *Cistercian *abbot. Born in Burgundy, he entered the *monastery at Citeaux in 1112, and in 1115 he was commissioned to found a monastery at Clairvaux. A solitary man of austere habits, he sought to combine the *worship of *God with the service of humankind. One of the more influential churchmen of his day, his counsel was sought by successive popes. Bernard opposed the heretical teaching of *Abelard and the theories of *Arnold of Brescia.

BÉRULLE, PIERRE DE (1575–1629). French *cardinal and mystic. Educated by the *Jesuits and at the Sorbonne, he played a prominent part in the 17th-century revival of *Roman Catholicism in France. He founded the French Oratory (1611) for *priests who would establish new *seminaries, improve *preaching, and promote theological studies. He cooperated with *Richelieu in the suppression of Protestants, and he would have taken stronger measures against them had Richelieu's political instinct not prohibited it.

BESSARION, JOHN (1403–1472). Greek *cardinal and theologian. Born in Trebizond (modern Trabzon, Turkey), he became a monk in 1423 and *archbishop of Nicea in 1437. At the Council of *Florence he supported the union of Eastern and Western churches at a time when the Turks were threatening invasion, a view unacceptable to his fellow *Byzantines. Made *cardinal by *Eugenius IV in 1440, he remained in Italy and carried out many papal embassies. He was an eminent scholar who contributed greatly to the revival of philosophical and literary studies and to the spread of Greek language and learning.

BEZA, THEODORE (1519–1605). French Protestant theologian. Formerly a Paris lawyer, he became professor of Greek at Lausanne (1549) and Geneva (1558) before succeeding *Calvin as professor of *theology and leader of *Reformed *Protestantism. He strove to help the persecuted French Protestants, and despite English protests, complained about unreformed tendencies in the English *Prayer Book. More diplomatic and flexible than Calvin, whose biographer he became, Beza consistently sponsored higher education and was a renowned biblical scholar.

BIBLE The collection of books of the *OT and *NT. The thirty-nine OT books were written in Hebrew (parts in Aramaic), and the twenty-seven NT books were written in Greek. Some Bibles (in the Roman Catholic and *Orthodox churches) also include the *Apocrypha (fifteen books written in Gk.) as part of the OT.

BIBLE (ENGLISH VERSIONS) The major ones are: (1) the Authorized Version, or *King James Version (1611): AV, KJV; (2) the Revised Version (1881–1885): RV; (3) the American Revised Version (1901): ARV; (4) the Revised Standard Version (1952): RSV (a later edition was known as the Common Bible [1966]); (5) the New English Bible (1970): NEB; (6) Today's English Version: The Good News Bible (1976): TEV; (7) the New International Version (1979): NIV. The Jerusalem Bible (1966) and the Living Bible (1971) are other popular versions.

BIBLE CHRISTIANS Sometimes called Quaker Methodists, the group was founded in Devon in 1815 by William *O'Bryan (1778–1868), a dissident Methodist preacher. Women played a prominent part in the group's outreach, which stressed the inner light of the *Spirit. From the west of England the Bible Christians spread to some other parts of the country—as far north as Northumberland. O'Bryan was proved unpopular with his colleagues and finally withdrew from the movement. The group's most prominent personality in its ninety-two-year history was Billy Bray. By the mid-19th century the work had spread to North America and Australia. Bible Christians in 1907 became part of the *United Methodist church.

BIBLE SOCIETIES While the movement arose in early 18th-century German *Pietism, the first English-speaking body was the British and Foreign Bible Society (1804), founded "to encourage the wider circulation of the Holy *Scriptures, without note or comment." Similar bodies were founded in Europe, and in America in 1816. In 1825 there was division over the inclusion of the *Apocrypha, which persisted into recent times. The need for closer cooperation led in 1946 to the organization of the United Bible Societies, with regional centers in four countries. Papal *encyclicals during the 19th century had banned Bible societies, but *Vatican Council II gave them an approving nod, and Pope *Paul VI ordered an enquiry into the possibility of joint distribution of the *Scriptures. Scriptures are now available in some 1,600 languages. Bible society work is conducted on a noncommercial basis.

BIBLICAL CRITICISM The application to the study of the *Bible of "scientific" methods developed for use in other literary and historical studies. "Criticism" does not imply criticism in the popular sense but rather critical analysis in a technical sense. However, sometimes the critical analysis has proceeded from presuppositions that deny, for example, the supernatural and the possibility of miracles. A distinction is often made between lower and higher criticism. Lower relates to the work on the text of the Bible in order to restore the original words. Higher criticism is the application of the critical methods referred to above. For further details see also FORM CRITICISM; REDACTION CRITICISM; SOURCE CRITICISM; and TEXTUAL CRITICISM.

BIBLICAL THEOLOGY The doctrinal teaching of the *Bible. This can be understood in two ways. (1) The arrangement of the *doctrines of the Bible in a systematic way but preserving the biblical images and world-view. This is what is usually attempted by biblical scholars in studies of *OT and *NT *theology. It is to be distinguished from *systematic, or *dogmatic theology, which is the presentation of biblical doctrines in contemporary thought-forms. However, even where the attempt is made to present biblical teaching in its own terms and images, modern presuppositions inevitably enter (e.g., in how the material is arranged). (2) A modern theology that rejects anything but the authority of *Scripture in its attempt to present *Christian *truth. Strictly, this means that no use is made of the church's teaching over the centuries, especially when that teaching is expressed in nonbiblical concepts or images (e.g., the doctrine of the *Trinity in the *Nicene and *Athanasian Creeds).

BIBLIOLATRY The *worship of a book. A pejorative or derogative way of referring to an extreme veneration of the *Bible because it is believed to be verbally inspired by *God.

BIEDERWOLF, WILLIAM EDWARD (1867–1939). American *Presbyterian *evangelist. Graduate of Princeton, much of his career was devoted to evangelistic work, including the direction of the well-known Winona Lake Bible School of Theology. He organized also the Family Altar League in 1909.

BILOCATION The capability of being in two places at one and the same time. It has been used in *theology in two ways: (1) the risen, exalted *Christ present in many places at one time when the *Lord's Supper is celebrated; (2) the presence of certain Roman Catholic *saints in two places at one time. Bilocation has been claimed of Philip Neri (d. 1595) and Alphonsus Liguori (d. 1787).

BINDING AND LOOSING A power or authority given by *Jesus Christ to Peter (Matt 16:19) and to all the *apostles (18:18). The authority certainly referred to the discipline exercised by the apostles in the early church, and it could also possibly refer to their authority in *Christ's name to forgive *sins (John 20:23). The same power and authority is claimed for ordained ministers in modern *denominations, although how the phrase is understood is not uniform.

BINGHAM, HIRAM, JR (1831–1908). *Missionary to Micronesia. Born of missionary parents in Hawaii, he was educated and then taught on the American mainland before going under the *American Board of Commissioners for Foreign Missions in 1856 as the first missionary to the Gilbert Islands. He evangelized in the widely scattered islands, and by 1890 he had translated the whole *Bible into Gilbertese.

BINGHAM, HIRAM, SR (1789–1869). *Missionary to Hawaii (the Sandwich Islands). Born in Vermont, he was sent by the *American Board of Commissioners for Foreign Missions to Hawaii in 1820, built the first church in Honolulu in 1821, established schools, helped create a written language for the islanders, and participated in the translation of the *Bible published in 1839. His counsel was sought by the native people, not least when profit- and pleasure-seeking Americans came to the islands.

BINITARIANISM The teaching that there are two persons, Father and Son, in the Godhead rather than three. As a consciously held *theology this has not been very common in the church. Often, however, it represents an undeveloped (see 1 Cor. 8:6) or imprecise way of speaking of *God in which the Holy *Spirit is not mentioned. See also Trinity, Doctrine of the.

BIRETTA The rigid square cap sometimes worn by some Roman Catholic *clergy. For *priests it is black, for *bishops purple, for *cardinals red, and for *abbots white. In origin it was a part of academic dress.

BIRTH CONTROL The adoption of methods to prevent conception through sexual intercourse. This is achieved by a variety of means—e.g., by making a man or woman infertile or sterile and by using artificial means to prevent the sperm from fertilizing the egg. Such procedures raise a cluster of moral questions. E.g., is sexual intercourse without the possibility of procreation justifiable? Does the prevention of the possibility of conception interfere with what *God has ordained? Will constant use of birth control lead to selfishness and seeking only physical gratification by the couple? The Roman Catholic Church has officially condemned all means except that known as the rhythm, or safe-period, method. Protestants tend to leave the whole matter to the individual *conscience.

BIRTH, THE NEW See Regeneration.

BIRTHRIGHT MEMBERSHIP A rule adopted by the London Yearly Meeting of *Quakers in 1737 that extended membership to wives and children of members without any requirement of profession of *faith. This practice, which inevitably diluted spiritual fervor, continued until the beginning of the 20th century.

BISHOP (from Lat. *biscopus* and Gk. *episcopus,* meaning "an overseer"). Though used in the *NT as a title for a *presbyter (Phil. 1:1), it soon came to be the title of the chief *pastor—the one who presided at the celebration of the *Eucharist and who ordained presbyters and *deacons. There developed in the early church a *hierarchy of ordained ministers, deacon, presbyter-priest, and *bishop. As the church expanded, some bishops became more important than others, and so such titles as *archbishop and *patriarch arose. At the *Reformation some Protestants rejected the office of bishop as the chief pastor and insisted on the equality of the ordained presbyters. The traditional office of bishop was preserved in the Church of *England and in Scandinavian Lutheran churches.

BISHOPS' WARS (1639–1640). The clashes between king and *Covenanters because of *Charles I's determination to force a thoroughgoing *episcopacy on *Presbyterian Scotland. With Charles beginning to be caught up in those parliamentary troubles in England that were to lead to his execution, the Scots emerged victors. Episcopacy was duly abolished in the country until the *Restoration.

BLACK THEOLOGY A method of presenting *Christian *doctrine that begins within the cultural framework and consciousness of black people. The expression is particularly used in the U.S. and South Africa but is sometimes used as a synonym for *theology from the Third World. The idea is that much Western theology, Protestant and Roman Catholic, begins from within the white *culture with its overtones of cultural and racial superiority and does not therefore easily speak to black people. It may be seen as a form of *liberation theology and as an expression of black consciousness. Its most well-known exponent in the 1970s was James Cone of Union Seminary (New York).

BLAKE, WILLIAM (1757–1827). English poet and artist. Son of a London hosier, he began to write poetry early but made his living as an engraver. He later gained fame for his painting and water-color drawings. A visionary genius whose religious views were unorthodox and elusive (he was said to have been greatly influenced by *Swedenborg), he saw as his task to "open the mortal Eyes of Man inwards into the worlds of Thought." Blake produced much highly original poetry of lasting value and has been called the earliest of the romantics.

BLASPHEMY Speech or activity that dishonors, manifests contempt for, or defames *God's name. In the *OT it was punished by stoning (Lev 24:16). Many countries in the past legislated against it though most Western nations hardly make use of this legislation now. Some Arab nations strictly enforce such laws.

*Jesus referred to blasphemy against the Holy *Spirit as the *unpardonable *sin (Matt 12:31–32; Mark 3:28–29; Luke 12:10). This is often understood as having arrived at a spiritual and moral position in which one cannot discern good from *evil, God from the *devil.

BLESSING See BENEDICTION.

BLOOD OF CHRIST The blood of *Jesus that flowed from his *body in crucifixion and represented, therefore, his sacrificial and atoning death. The essential background is the *OT sacrificial system. His shed blood sealed a new *covenant between *God and the human race (Matt 26:28; Mark 14:24; Luke 22:20). Biblical scholars disagree as to whether "blood" refers to "life poured out in death" and then (mysteriously) made available to others, or (more probably) to the fact of a violent, sacrificial, and atoning death (Rom 5:9–10; Col 1:20).

BODELSCHWING, FRIEDRICH (1831–1910). German Lutheran *pastor. Soon after four of his own children had died within a few weeks in 1869, he became superintendent of an epileptic institution later called Bethel, near Bielefeld. This work, part of the outreach of the *Innere Mission, grew to include also the mentally sick, refugees, destitute, and young people in need of help. It also trained *deacons and *deaconesses and provided schools and educational facilities for the study of *theology.

BODELSCHWING, FRIEDRICH (1877–1946). German Evangelical church leader. He succeeded his father (see previous entry) in overseeing and expanding the work at Bethel and in addition was elected *reichsbishop of the German Evangelical church (1933). When the appalling command came from Hitler that the Bethel sick should be consigned to euthanasia, Bodelschwing stoutly resisted. The Nazis subsequently dropped the project.

BODY The concrete totality of an individual person as existing in this world and as subject to natural forces and conditions. A human being exists in a body, but if the body is destroyed, he as an individual personality is not obliterated (Matt 10:28; Luke 12:4). In the age to come the redeemed also will have resurrected, spiritual bodies (1 Cor 15:35ff.). See also SOUL.

BODY OF CHRIST Used in four different ways: (1) an image of the church (Rom 12:5); (2) the bread used in Holy *Communion, which is symbolically the body of *Christ; (3) the human body that the *eternal *Son of God received from *Mary and that was raised from death and received into *heaven as a glorified body; (4) in Latin, *Corpus Christi, as the title of a feast in the Roman Catholic Church kept in honor of the *sacrament of Holy Communion.

BOEHLER, PETER (1712–1775). *Moravian *missionary. Born and educated in Germany, he was influenced by *Zinzendorf to become a *missionary to slaves in North Carolina. Later he led the migration of Moravians to Pennsylvania. He spent six years in England as superintendent of the Moravian church and was consecrated *bishop in 1748. He later returned to Pennsylvania for eleven years. Boehler greatly influenced John and Charles *Wesley.

BOEHME, JACOB (1575–1624). Mystical theologian and writer. Influenced by earlier esoteric Jewish and *Christian writings, Boehme developed a complicated numerological system that bordered on *pantheism and the dissolution of ethical boundaries. He was highly influential, and his ideas later reappeared in German idealism and in British writers such as William *Blake.

BOETHIUS (c. 480–524). Roman philosopher and statesman. A *Christian consul's son who himself attained the same rank under Theodoric (510), he was educated in Athens and Alexandria. Due to the breadth of his scholarship, many regard him as a leading exponent of what became the Middle Ages. When his espousal of unpopular causes landed him in prison, he wrote the *Consolation of Philosophy*—a standard text for more than a thousand years, which traces the true source of human happiness to the pursuit of *wisdom and the *love of *God. He produced other works on philosophy and wrote also on *theology, music, and science. Falling from imperial favor, he was executed for alleged treason and magic.

BOGOMILS A religious *sect originating in 10th-century Bulgaria but holding views similar to *Manichaeism. They attributed the creation of the world and the human *body to the *devil, regarded matter as *evil, and rejected such *Christian *doctrines as the *Incarnation and the *Cross, *baptism and the *Eucharist. They also rejected marriage, meat, alcohol, worldly possessions, and everything that called for physical contact. These views prevailed among those of them numbered among "the Perfect," *obedience to whom was mandatory for the ordinary member, who could receive "spiritual baptism" on his deathbed.

The movement spread into Italy and France, where adherents were known as Patarines or *Cathari, and to other parts of Europe. Despite action taken against it by civil and church authorities, the *sect survived until the 15th century. After the Ottoman conquest of southeastern Europe, many Bogomils became Muslims.

BOHEMIAN BRETHREN Otherwise known as Unitas Fratrum, a mid-15th-century religious group in Bohemia and Moravia, whose principles originated in Jan *Hus. Their lifestyle was simple. They taught nonviolence and regarded the *Bible as the sole *rule of *faith and *Christ as the only *Mediator. They celebrated the *Eucharist but denied *transubstantiation. They spread into Poland in the 16th century. In 1627 an imperial edict suppressed all Protestants, and the Brethren lost all their buildings and were faced with conformity to Rome or exile. J. A. *Comenius was one who chose the latter course. Among those who trace their origin to the Bohemian Brethren are the *Moravian Church and the Czech Evangelical Brethren Church.

BONAR, ANDREW ALEXANDER (1810–1892). Scottish minister. Leaving the Church of *Scotland at the 1843 *Disruption, he joined the *Free Church of Scotland and had a long ministry in Glasgow. His many writings include a biography of R. M. *McCheyne, the best-known edition of Samuel *Rutherford's *Letters,* and his own remarkable *Diary*. After a visit to Palestine in 1839 he wrote on the condition of the Jews there. He also visited America at the instigation of D. L. *Moody.

BONAR, HORATIUS (1808–1889). Scottish minister and *hymn writer. Like his brother Andrew *Bonar, he joined the *Free Church of Scotland at the *Disruption and ministered in Kelso and Edinburgh. He edited several religious periodicals. His *Hymns of Faith and Hope* (3 vols., 1857–1866) were sung throughout the English-speaking world. They included "I Heard the Voice of Jesus Say" and "Here, O My Lord, I See Thee Face to Face."

BONAVENTURA (1221–1274). *Franciscan theologian. Born in Italy, he joined the Franciscans about 1244, became head of the *order's school in Paris, and in 1257 was elected minister general. He declined the archbishopric of York in 1265, but became *cardinal *bishop of Albano (Italy) in 1273 after his influence had secured the *papacy for Gregory X. One of the most prominent medieval theologians, Bonaventura was known for personal piety and was notable for his rejection of the *doctrine of the *Immaculate Conception.

BONHOEFFER, DIETRICH (1906–1945). German *pastor and theologian. Son of a doctor, he had a wide-ranging education in various countries before becoming a theological lecturer. As the Nazis began to control the country more rigidly he became a leading protester on behalf of the *Confessing church. During World War II he allied himself with those who opposed Hitler, and this led to his execution after a two-year imprisonment and only a month before the end of the *war. Many of his writings were translated into English, notably *Letters and Papers from Prison* (1948).

BONIFACE (c. 675–754). "Apostle of Germany." Born in England and originally called Wynfrith, he was educated by *Benedictines, was ordained, and in 719 was assigned by Pope *Gregory II to a broad *missionary jurisdiction among the pagans in Germany. He worked in Thuringia, Frisia, and Hesse, and in 722 is reputed to have baptized thousands of Hessians. That year also he was consecrated as missionary *bishop by Gregory in Rome. As papal legate to Germany in 738 he organized the church in Bavaria and established new bishoprics and abbeys to consolidate the gains made in evangelization. He worked on the reform of the Frankish church (742–47), became *archbishop of Mainz in 752, but was murdered by Frisians two years later.

BONIFACE I (d. 422). Pope from 418. His reign was marked by internal strife in the church, notably the opposition of Eulalius, who had been acclaimed pope by a faction that held the Lateran. The rivalry ended when Eulalius tried to disrupt an attempt at arbitration, whereupon Boniface was declared the legal *pontiff. He was a shrewd diplomat and upheld the cause of *orthodoxy by his support of *Augustine of Hippo against *Pelagianism.

BONIFACE II (d. 532). Pope from 530 and the first of Germanic origin. His *pontificate was at first disturbed by the claims of an *antipope, Dioscorus of Alexandria, sponsored by a majority of the Roman Catholic *clergy, but he died after only three weeks. Boniface upheld the decisions of the second Council of *Orange (529), which condemned *Semi-Pelagianism.

BONIFACE VIII (c. 1235–1303). Pope from 1294. An autocratic man who favored his own family in the disbursement of offices and lands, he is best remembered for the long and bitter struggle against the actions and pretensions of *Philip IV of France, who thwarted papal control of the French *clergy. In the famous *bull *Unam Sanctam* the *pope reaffirmed the supremacy of spiritual over temporal power. The forces of Philip, who had brought the most serious charges of misconduct against Boniface, held the pope captive in Italy for two days and probably ill treated him. Boniface died a broken man soon afterwards.

BONIFACE IX (c. 1355–1404). Pope from 1389. His *pontificate was dominated by the need to raise money, not least in order to maintain his position against the claims of two successive *antipopes at Avignon. He alienated many by selling preferments, exemptions, and *indulgences; and while he did not personally profit from this, his pontificate was not unjustly characterized later as "the crooked days of Boniface IX."

BONN CONFERENCES (1874–1875). Two church conferences held in the German city to promote reunion between churches professing historic *Christianity. Directed by the *Old Catholics, the gathering also included representatives of Eastern *Orthodoxy, the *Reformed churches of Germany and the Netherlands, and the Church of *England. Some disagreement emerged between East and West on the *doctrine of the Holy *Spirit and on the validity of Anglican *orders.

BONNER, EDMUND (c. 1500–1569). *Bishop of London. Having shown himself a loyal supporter of *Henry VIII, especially over the king's attempt to have his marriage to Catherine of Aragon annulled, Bonner was consecrated bishop of London in 1540. On Henry's death in 1547, he transferred his allegiance in religious matters from *Edward VI to the *pope, was deprived of his bishopric, and imprisoned (1549–1553). Restored under Mary *Tudor, he was criticized for not stepping up the prosecution of Protestants. On the accession of *Elizabeth he was again dismissed for refusing to acknowledge her headship of the Church of *England. He spent his remaining ten years in prison.

BOOTH, CATHERINE (1829–1890). "Mother of the *Salvation Army." Having married William *Booth in 1855, she was associated with him in the evangelistic work that led to the founding of the Salvation Army. She herself carried on a remarkable ministry among women and put them to work in an organization that has always encouraged them to play an equal part with men.

BOOTH, EVANGELINE CORY (1865–1950). *Salvation Army general. Daughter of William *Booth, she took charge of the Army's work in Canada (1896) and the U.S. (1904), where she greatly expanded its social service program. She was elected general in 1934, held that supreme post for four years, then returned to the U.S. for the last twelve years of her life.

BOOTH, WILLIAM (1829–1912). Founder of the *Salvation Army. Born in Nottingham and converted in 1844, he was a Methodist preacher; but chafing under *denominational restrictions, he left in 1861 to pursue independent evangelistic work that led him to London's East End. Out of his "Christian Mission" there developed the Salvation Army (1878). Booth was a tireless fighter against such things as squalid slums, uncaring authority, abused children, drink, forced labor conditions, internal dissension, and unfounded charges, but chiefly against the *devil and all his *works. His book *In Darkest England—and the Way Out* (1890) became a best seller. He traveled 5 million miles and preached nearly 60,000 *sermons. Forty thousand people attended his funeral in London.

BORIS I (d. 907). Ruler of Bulgaria. Having succeeded his father in 852, he led the *conversion of his subjects to *Christianity and founded a national church. Though of the Orthodox *faith, he rejected Constantinople's claim to overlordship of the Bulgarian church and ensured at the Fourth Council of Constantinople (869–870) the establishment of an autonomous archbishopric for Bulgaria. Boris was a great promoter of Slavonic literature. He abdicated and became a monk in 889 but reentered political life briefly in 893 to replace one of his sons with another who was less vulnerable to pagan tendencies.

BORN AGAIN See REGENERATION.

BORROMEO, CHARLES (1538–1584). *Archbishop of Milan and a leader of the *Counter-Reformation. Appointed by his uncle, *Pius IV, as *cardinal and archbishop at the age of twenty-one, he played a prominent part in the closing stages of the Council of *Trent and in implementing its decisions. A humane, able courteous *prelate, he demanded high ideals of his *clergy, established *seminaries and colleges, was active in welfare work, and bravely carried on his ministry during the plague of 1576. He worked hard for the reconversion of Swiss Protestants.

BOSCO, JOHN (1815–1888). Founder of the *Salesians. As a *priest in Turin he built up an extensive social, educational, and religious work among boys who came to seek employment in the city. In 1859 he founded the Salesians, and in 1872 the Salesian Sisters for kindred work among girls. By the time of Bosco's death the work had spread to other European countries and to Latin America.

BOSSUET, JACQUES BENIGNE (1627–1704). Roman Catholic *bishop of Meaux and leading exponent of *Gallicanism. Bossuet was an outstanding preacher, writer, and churchman who defended the rights of the French Catholic church against excessive demands of the *papacy. He was the principal author of the Four Gallican Articles (1682), the proposals that outlined the essential autonomy of the French church. See also GALLICANISM.

BOSTON, THOMAS (1676–1732). Scottish minister and writer. Graduate of Edinburgh and a Hebrew scholar, he ministered faithfully in the Scottish border country. In 1718 he was responsible for the reprinting of a 17th-century work, *The Marrow of Modern Divinity,* which contained extracts from the Reformers and an exposition of the *Ten Commandments in terms unacceptable to the legalism of the ruling *moderate party in the Church of *Scotland. The general assembly condemned the book as heretical, but its defenders ("Marrowmen") saw this action as an attack on *evangelical *doctrine. Boston is regarded as one of Scotland's greatest theologians. His works include *Human Nature in Its Fourfold Estate* (1720) and *A View of the Covenant of Grace* (1734).

BOUNDARY SITUATION (Ger. *Grenzsituation*). Used by existentialists to describe those points in life in which a person becomes conscious that there is a dimension to life that may be called the transcendent—the recognition that reality is more than mere existence. Boundary situations are normally times or moments of crisis caused by illness, dramatic events, or feelings of inadequacy. By them a person is challenged to live authentically. See also ANGST, ANXIETY, EXISTENTIALISM.

BOURDALOUE, LOUIS (1632–1704). French *Jesuit, described as the "king of orators and the orator of kings." A preacher in Paris from 1669 until his death, *Louis XIV reportedly said he would rather hear Bourdaloue on an old theme than anyone else on a new one. Consistently orthodox in *doctrine and an effective foe of *Jansenism and other deviations, he was also highly regarded as a wise spiritual director and teacher.

BOURGEOIS, LOUIS (c. 1510–1561). French *Huguenot musician. Born in Paris, he was a friend of *Calvin and lived with him in Geneva (1545–1557). His alterations in the conventional Psalm tunes led to his imprisonment there, but he was released on Calvin's intervention. Later composers used his melodies, the best known of which is the "Old Hundredth." In the *Genevan Psalter* he was responsible for some eighty-five melodies. He found the spiritual climate of Geneva repressive and spent his last four years in Paris.

BOURIGNON, ANTOINETTE (1616–1680). French religious enthusiast. A Roman Catholic who identified herself with the "woman clothed with the sun" (Rev. 12:1; cf. Elspet Buchan, founder of the *Buchanites), she felt commissioned to restore the true spirit of the *gospel to the churches and to assail all religious organization, Catholic or Protestant. She attracted followers of all kinds and several nationalities—notably in *Presbyterian Scotland, where her views so persisted that the general assembly condemned them three times (1701–1711).

BOURNE, HUGH (1772–1852). Founder of the *Primitive Methodist Church. A Wesleyan Methodist local preacher, he was expelled for importing the *camp-meeting type of gathering from the U.S. He founded the Primitive Methodist body to aim at restoring *Methodism to its early simplicity. When he died thirty-two years later, it had 110,000 members. By the union in 1932 the membership had grown to almost a quarter of a million. Bourne was a carpenter and builder and for most of his ministry worked manually to avoid being a charge on his church.

BOYS' BRIGADE The first uniformed voluntary organization for youth. It was begun in Scotland by William A. *Smith in 1883. Its aim: "The advancement of *Christ's Kingdom among boys and the promotion of habits of obedience, reverence, discipline, self-respect, and all that tends towards a true *Christian manliness." In 1971 the Brigade reaffirmed its Christian basis. The movement spread throughout the world, and in 1984 it had a reported membership of 582,000.

BRADFORD, JOHN (c. 1510–1555). English Protestant *martyr. Chaplain first to Nicholas *Ridley and then to *Edward VI, he was charged with seditious *preaching when Mary *Tudor became queen in 1553. He refused to renounce *Protestantism and was burned at Smithfield, London.

BRADFORD, WILLIAM (1590–1657). Governor of Plymouth Colony. Born in Yorkshire and orphaned at eight, he left England for Holland in 1607 with a group of fellow Protestants in search of religious freedom. In 1620 he was a leader on the *Mayflower*'s voyage to the New World, and a framer of the famous *Mayflower Compact. In 1621 he was unanimously elected as governor of the Plymouth Colony and served thirty further single-year terms between 1621 and 1656. He insisted on democratic government, discouraged *sectarian labels, and ensured tolerance toward all *separatist groups who joined the colony. His *History of Plymouth Plantation* is a fascinating historical record.

BRADWARDINE, THOMAS (c. 1290–1349). *Archbishop of Canterbury. An

Oxford scholar of great distinction who became chaplain to Edward III about 1335, he was a tireless servant of church, crown, and country. In 1346 he strove to reconcile England, Scotland, and France. He became *archdeacon of Lincoln in 1347, and two years later, archbishop of Canterbury. Six weeks after his appointment he was a victim of the Black Death. An able theologian, he championed *orthodoxy against *Pelagianism.

BRAINERD, DAVID (1718–1747). *Missionary to American Indians. Born in Connecticut, he was converted in 1739, went to Yale, and was expelled in 1742, reportedly for overmuch religious zeal. Appointed missionary to the Indians of eastern Pennsylvania, he labored despite rigorous hardships and saw more than 130 of them converted by 1746. Ill health forced his retirement, and he died at the home of Jonathan *Edwards. Brainerd's *Journal* has had a tremendous influence in turning many to the *mission field.

BRAY, THOMAS (1656–1730). Anglican clergyman. Formerly a rector in Warwick, he was sent to organize Anglican churches in Maryland (1699–1700). Back in London he continued to promote the colony's interests. He founded free libraries and helped establish the Society for the Promoting of Christian Knowledge (1698) and the Society for the Propagation of the Gospel (1701).

BRÉBEUF, JEAN DE (1593–1649). *Jesuit *missionary to Canada. Born in France, he was sent in 1625 to what was then called "New France," and from 1626 he labored amid primitive conditions among the Huron in Ontario, produced a Huron grammar and a translation of the *catechism, and greatly impressed the Huron on one occasion by predicting a lunar eclipse (then *preaching about hellfire when it was happening). In a savage *war launched against the Huron by the Iroquois, he and his colleague Gabriel Lalemant were captured and tortured to death. Their serenity amid all astounded their murderers.

BRENT, CHARLES HENRY (1862–1929). Anglican *bishop and ecumenist. Born in Ontario, ordained in 1887, he ministered in Boston and later became *missionary bishop in the Protestant Episcopal Church in the Philippines (1901–1917); there he led in the fight against the opium traffic. In 1918 he became bishop of western New York and later took charge of the Episcopal churches in Europe. He was president of the 1927 *Lausanne Conference and wrote several religious works.

BRENZ, JOHANN (1499–1570). German Reformer. Influenced by *Luther and *Oecolampadius toward the *Reformed position, he stopped celebrating the *Mass. In Württemberg he initiated educational and welfare projects. Forced to flee before the imperial forces in 1548, he became a minister in Stuttgart. He contributed to Lutheran teaching, particularly the *doctrine of the *Eucharist.

BRETHREN (DUNKERS) In origin they were *separatists from the state church in Germany. They arrived in the U.S. in the early 18th century. They called themselves Baptist Brethren or Fraternity of German Baptists. Others called them Dunkers or Dunkards. Their particular emphases included *pacifism, *believers' baptism (by threefold *immersion), *footwashing, and the *love feast (*agape). After various divisions, there are now in the U.S. the Church of the Brethren (Conservative Dunkers), the Brethren Church (Progressive Dunkers), and the Old German Baptist Brethren (Old Order Dunkers).

BRETHREN, PLYMOUTH See PLYMOUTH BRETHREN.

BRETHREN IN CHRIST (RIVER BRETHREN) A North American Protestant church. It originated toward the end of the 18th century among European settlers (mostly *Anabaptists and *Pietists) who had come to Pennsylvania about thirty years earlier. Emphasizing *conversion and *NT simplicity, the church accepts the *Bible as the inspired *Word of *God, is pacifist, practices *believers' baptism, and looks for the *second coming of Christ. It currently has about 14,000 members in 187 churches in the U.S. and Canada.

BRETHREN OF THE COMMON LIFE A religious community organized in the Netherlands by Gerhard *Groote in the late 14th century. Adopting a simple lifestyle, they were self-supporting and had a common fund. They stressed *Bible reading, *meditation, and the pursuit of holiness. The movement spread to Germany and Switzerland, and houses for women also were opened. They earned money by copying manuscripts and later by printing books. Many religious leaders such as Thomas à *Kempis, *Erasmus, and *Luther owed much to the movement. The Brethren survived until the early 17th century.

BREVIARY The book containing the *Scripture lessons, Psalms, *hymns, and portions for meditation to be recited or read daily by Roman Catholic *clergy and such *laity as are required or desire to do so. The present breviary was issued in 1971 by Pope *Paul VI. It contains an office of readings that can be said at any time of day, lauds (Morning Prayer), a midday office, *vespers (evening *prayer), and *compline.

BREWSTER, WILLIAM (c. 1567–c. 1644). Plymouth Colony leader. Born in Nottinghamshire, he became one of the founders of a *separatist congregation in 1606. In 1608 he went to Holland with other nonconformists seeking escape from harassment. He made his living as a printer of Protestant books until that source of income and disaffection was stopped by the English government. He sailed on the *Mayflower* in 1620, and on settlement in New England became the effective leader of the church, regulating its *doctrine and *worship until a minister was ordained in 1629. He then continued as one of William *Bradford's counselors.

BRIDGET OF SWEDEN (c. 1303–1373). Founder of the *Brigittines. Daughter of a provincial governor, she became the mother of eight children, but on her husband's death in 1344 she retired to a life of *penance and *prayer. A lifelong visionary, she felt called to found a new *religious *order. She made *pilgrimages to the Holy Land, and to Rome where she ministered and preached to all who would listen, denounced clerical abuses, and urged an end to the *Babylonian Captivity.

BRIGITTINES (BRIDGETTINES) An *order of cloistered *nuns founded by *Bridget of Sweden in 1344. Officially named the Order of the Most Holy Savior, it was first approved by Urban V in 1370. The order, which stressed simplicity and promoted *culture, spread to other parts of Scandinavia, to Germany, and to England. To each house was attached a *monastery whose monks shared the same liturgical life under the jurisdiction of the abbess. The order suffered great losses during the *Reformation period, but four autonomous houses of nuns remain (two in Holland, one in England, and one in Germany). A modern offshoot was begun in 1911 and now has houses in Europe, India, and the U.S. A contemplative order, it is concerned with the reunion of Christendom and the return of Scandinavia to the Roman Catholic Church.

BRITISH–ISRAEL THEORY The view that the British (Anglo-Saxon) people and the Indians of North America descended from the ten tribes of *Israel who were taken capture by the Assyrians in 711 B.C. The fate of these tribes is not wholly known, and so various theories have been put forward to explain where their descendants are now. The British–Israelite theory is held by the Worldwide Church of God founded by Herbert W. Armstrong.

BROAD CHURCH Used particularly in the Church of *England to describe the position of those who interpret the historic *faith in a broad, or liberal, way. It originated in the mid-19th century at a time when new views of science and history were emerging. A. P. *Stanley (d. 1881), Thomas Arnold (d. 1842), and Benjamin Jowett (d. 1893) were among the early leaders. A broad churchmanship had been anticipated in the 17th century by *latitudinarianism.

BROOKE, ALAN ENGLAND (1863–1939). English biblical scholar. Cambridge graduate, he spent his working life there, eventually as provost of King's College. For the ten years he held a university chair of divinity he was also a *canon of Ely, and he liked to preach in the villages of the *diocese. He was coeditor of the larger Cambridge edition of the *Septuagint (an important work of scholarship), and his other published work included a commentary on the Johannine Epistles (1912). He was elected a Fellow of the British Academy in 1935, an honor not given to many clergymen in modern times.

BROOKS, PHILLIPS (1835–1893). American preacher. Author of the *hymn "O Little Town of Bethlehem," he ministered in the *Protestant Episcopal Church, notably for twenty-two years at Trinity Church, Boston. He won initial fame as a preacher of liberal *Christianity, published many volumes of *sermons, declined a Harvard professorship, but became *bishop of Massachusetts in 1891. His *Lectures on Preaching* (1877) were delivered originally at Yale.

BROTHER LAWRENCE (LAWRENCE OF THE RESURRECTION) (c. 1605–1691). Christian mystic. Born Nicholas Herman, he was a soldier and domestic servant until the middle of his life when he became a *Carmelite lay brother in Paris. Assigned to kitchen work, which he loathed, he developed the habit of doing all things, including menial tasks, to the glory of *God. This philosophy is reflected in the spiritual classic *The Practice of the Presence of God,* compiled and published after Lawrence's death.

BROTHERS HOSPITALLERS As "*Hospitallers of St. *John of God" the *order was founded in 1537 in Spain. A largely lay order that came under *Augustinian *rule, it demands *vows of *chastity, hospitality (that binds them to work for the sick), *obedience, and *poverty. It established hospitals in Europe and overseas, and though it suffered a severe setback from the French Revolution (1789), it has revived and now has a membership of well over two thousand.

BROWN, WILLIAM ADAMS (1865–1943). Liberal *Presbyterian theologian and leading exponent of the *social gospel. Believing in the essential goodness of man and the social nature of the kingdom of *God, Brown sought to minimize denominational boundaries and promote *ecumenical endeavors. Primarily a teacher (over forty years at Union Theological Seminary in New York City), Brown spread his influence through students and writings, notably his *Christian Theology in Outline* (1906), one of the most influential *liberal *theology texts of its day.

BROWNE, ROBERT (1550–1633). Leader of early English *separatists, often called Brownists. An unlicensed minister in Norwich about 1580, he held that the true church was limited to a chosen few. He suffered three terms of imprisonment. Considered by many to be the founder of Congregationalism, he later modified his views, was episcopally ordained in 1591, and was a rector in Northamptonshire, where he died in prison after assaulting a policeman.

BRUCE, ALEXANDER BALMAIN (1831–1899). Scottish theologian. A farmer's son who graduated at Edinburgh, he ministered in the *Free Church of Scotland in whose Glasgow college he became professor in 1875. Some of his writings on biblical criticism raised the suspicions of more conservative minds, notably *The Kingdom of God* (1889), but no action was taken against him.

BRUCE, ROBERT (1554–1631). Scottish minister. Descendant of a family famous in Scottish history, he became a minister in Edinburgh and was moderator of the general assembly at thirty-three. He opposed *James VI's aim to impose episcopacy on Scotland, was banished from the capital, and spent his last thirty years in no fixed home, highly venerated by the people. His remarkable *sermons on the *sacraments were republished in 1843.

BRUNNER, HEINRICH EMIL (1889–1966). Swiss theologian. As a longtime professor at Zurich, he stressed the preeminence of divine *revelation and held that *faith was primarily *obedience. Only in *Christ the *Mediator is there enablement. He denied the *infallibility of *Scripture and the concept of *hell and detested Nazism and communism. After retirement from Zurich he was professor of *Christian philosophy in the International Christian University of Tokyo (1953–1955) and then became a worldwide itinerant lecturer.

BRUNO THE CARTHUSIAN (c. 1030–1101). Founder of the *Carthusian *order. Ordained in his native city of Cologne in 1057, he served the church as educational director in Reims for twenty years but refused to become *archbishop there. He and six companions built a *monastery at Chartreuse and, without intending to do so, founded the order (1084), adapting the *Benedictine *rule as their basis. Bruno declined another archbishopric and established also a community in Calabria.

BRYAN, WILLIAM JENNINGS (1860–1925). Populist, editor, Chautauqua lecturer, secretary of state, and opponent of evolution. He practiced law, was a congressman, and—gaining national prominence through his "Cross of Gold" speech—was three times candidate for the presidency. A *Presbyterian *elder, he defended the *Bible and the *doctrine of creation at the Scopes trial in Dayton, Tennessee, in 1925. Bryan College there was built in his memory.

BUCER (BUTZER), MARTIN (1491–1551). German Protestant Reformer. Originally a *Dominican, he withdrew after studying the humanists, *Luther, and the *Bible. Despite persistent attempts, he failed to reconcile Luther and *Zwingli. Invited to England by Thomas *Cranmer, he became a professor at Cambridge (1549) and helped to produce the Book of *Common Prayer.

BUCHANAN, GEORGE (1506–1582). Scottish humanist. Educated at Paris and St. Andrews, he was twice imprisoned for Protestant views and later, though he had been the friend and tutor of *Mary Queen of Scots, he supported the *Reformation in his homeland. One of the most famous scholars of his time, he became in 1570 tutor to the four-year-old *James VI, but in 1579 he published *De Jure Regni apud Scotos,* a treatise that claimed that the people could call wicked rulers to account, a view later espoused by the *Covenanters.

BUCHANITES A Scottish *sect founded in 1783 by Elspet Buchan, a Glasgow potter's wife who claimed to be the woman mentioned in Rev. 12:1 (cf. Antoinette *Bourignon). Her group numbered no more than fifty but included a *Presbyterian minister, a marine lieutenant, and the town prosecutor of Irvine. They settled in southern Scotland, renounced worldly connections, and looked for *Christ's return. When Mrs. Buchan died in 1791, her followers expected her to rise again, and a court order had to be obtained to have her buried. "The sheriff with his warrant," it was said, "closed the grave over all her pretensions." By 1839 only two Buchanites survived.

BUCHMAN, FRANK NATHAN DANIEL (1878–1961). Founder of the *Oxford Group. Born in Pennsylvania and ordained a Lutheran, he was converted in 1908 at Keswick. He engaged in work among students. In 1929 the

Oxford Group was founded; it developed into Moral Re-Armament in 1938. He called the latter a "*God-guided campaign to prevent *war by a moral and spiritual *awakening."

BUGENHAGEN, JOHANN (1485–1558). German Reformer. An ordained *priest, *Luther's writings convinced him of his church's errors (1520), and he became an enthusiastic Reformer. From 1522 until the end of his life he was minister of the collegiate church in Wittenberg, except for a five-year absence when he organized the Danish church at the invitation of Christian III. Bugenhagen was a close friend of Luther and published a commentary on the Psalms.

BULGAKOV, SERGEI NIKOLAEVICH (1871–1944). Russian theologian and philosopher. Influenced by Marxism to abandon *theology for economics, he studied at home and abroad before teaching at the universities of Kiev (1901–1906) and Moscow (1906–1918). Disillusioned with Marxism, he was converted, became a *priest in 1918, and was expelled from his homeland in 1923. From 1925 until his death he was theological professor and dean of the Russian Orthodox Theological Institute in Paris. His numerous writings, which reflected the influence of medieval *mysticism and modern philosophy, contained elements regarded as heretical by Orthodox theologians.

BULL (Lat. *bulla*, "a seal"). A written mandate or instruction from the *pope. Originally sealed in wax with the pope's signet ring, it is now sealed in a less ornate manner. Today the most important bulls are signed by the pope and *cardinals, while the others only have the pope's signature.

BULLINGER, JOHANN HEINRICH (1504–1575). Swiss Protestant Reformer and successor to *Zwingli in Zurich in 1531. Author of the *Second Helvetic Confession (1566) and numerous theological works, he is best remembered for his *Decades* (1549–1551), a compendium of *theology in fifty lengthy sections that were originally *sermons. He was a moderate who sought to heal rifts and bring Protestants together.

BULTMANN, RUDOLPH (1884–1976). German *NT scholar. After teaching at other German universities he became professor of NT at Marburg (1921–1951). He is associated with the attempt to "demythologize" the NT, a position exhaustively developed in his many published works. He was strongly anti-Nazi and a supporter of the *Confessing church.

BUNYAN, JOHN (1628–1688). Author of *Pilgrim's Progress*. Born near Bedford, son of a tinker, he was converted through writings recommended by his godly wife. He joined an independent congregation, became a preacher, and by 1660 was well known as an *evangelist. After the *Restoration, as an unlicensed preacher, he was imprisoned for much of the period 1660-1672, when his main reading was the *Bible and Foxe's *Book of Martyrs*. On his release he resumed *preaching, holding strongly that the world was the scene of a deadly struggle against the forces of darkness, with the *soul's *eternal destiny at stake. His other writings include *Grace Abounding to the Chief of Sinners* (1666) and *The Holy War* (1682).

BURGHERS Scottish *secessionist group. When certain cities required of their burgesses an *oath that acknowledged the national *religion, the issue split Scottish seceders in 1747. The Burghers agreed to take the oath, the Anti-Burghers would not. Both groups had a further split, but nearly all in the four groups ended up either in the *United Secession Church (1820) or in the *Free Church of Scotland (1852).

BURGON, JOHN WILLIAM (1813–1888). Anglican scholar and controversialist. He wrote the well-known *Lives of Twelve Good Men* (lively sketches of *High Churchmen of the time) and defended the **Textus Receptus* against *higher criticism and the Revised Version.

BURIAL The traditional *Christian method of disposing of those who have died. It can be in the earth, in a cave, or in a large receptacle. An area of several graves is known as a cemetery. *Burial in contrast to *cremation has seemed more in line with the Christian *hope of the *resurrection of the *body and of the belief that the earthly body is the temple of the Holy *Spirit.

BURNEY, CHARLES FOX (1868–1925). English biblical scholar. Son of the Royal Navy's paymaster-in-chief, he graduated from Oxford (1893) and remained there as a fellow of St. John's, university librarian, and divinity professor. A versatile and original writer, his many works included *Outlines of Old Testament Theology* (1899), a commentary on Judges (1918), and *The Aramaic Origin of the Fourth Gospel* (1922). In a comprehensive obituary notice *The Times* [London] hailed him as "beyond dispute the foremost Old Testament Semitic scholar in this country."

BUTLER, JOSEPH (1692–1752). Anglican *bishop and theologian. Son of a *Presbyterian, he was ordained in the Church of *England and won fame as a preacher. He became bishop of Bristol in 1738 and of Durham in 1750. He is said to have declined the primacy. His *Analogy of Religion* (1736) influenced many scholars and demolished the arguments of *deism.

BYZANTINE That which was produced in Byzantium (= Constantinople = Istanbul) or its empire when it had *Christian emperors (4th–14th centuries), especially art, architecture, and literature. The Byzantine text of the *NT is the standard text in the *Orthodox churches; the Byzantine church is the family of churches that developed from the Church of the Empire. The Byzantine *liturgy is the name given the services of *worship used in the patriarchate of Constantinople and the Greek Orthodox churches, and Byzantine *theology is the Greek theology that forms the theological *tradition of Orthodox churches today.

C

CABRINI, FRANCES XAVIER (1850–1917). Founder of the Missionary Sisters of the *Sacred Heart. Born in Lombardy, she wanted to become a *missionary in China. *Leo XIII instead sent her to the United States (1889), nine years after she had founded her *order, to work among Italian immigrants. Despite indifferent health, she traveled widely (she was to die of malaria). The sixty-seven houses she established included some located in different parts of Europe and Latin America. She was naturalized in 1909, making her the first American citizen to be canonized (1946).

CADBURY, HENRY JOEL (1883–1974). American *NT scholar. A prominent *Quaker whose various teaching posts included a twenty-two-year stint at Harvard, he was a translator of the Revised Standard Version and a meticulous scholar who published works especially on the Gospel of Luke and the Book of Acts.

CAEDMON (d. c. 680). First known English poet. According to *Bede's *Ecclesiastical History,* he was an illiterate cowherd to whom a stranger appeared in a dream, commanding him to sing of "the beginning of things." "He began at once," says Bede, "to sing lines in praise of God the Creator, verses he had never heard before." Such was his gift of utterance that the *abbess *Hilda persuaded him to enter her double *monastery in Yorkshire. The monks there would expound *Scripture to him, and he would render it into vernacular poetry. He was the first Anglo-Saxon writer of religious verse. Of his many works, only the nine lines of his creation *hymn are extant.

CAESARIUS OF ARLES (c. 470–542). *Archbishop of Arles. He became a monk at twenty, was soon advanced to *abbot, and then, as archbishop of Arles (502), was promoted to the *primacy of Gaul and Spain. Loved because of his saintliness and benevolence, he was the initiator of the Second Council of *Orange (529), which upheld a moderate *Augustinianism against the threat posed by *Semi-Pelagianism, causing the latter to be declared heretical by *Boniface II.

CAESAROPAPISM The government of both state and church by the civil ruler (e.g., the rule of *Charlemagne [742–814] and of the czars of Russia). The term is often erroneously applied to the *Byzantine emperors, but with a few exceptions they did not interfere in doctrinal and liturgical matters.

CAJETAN (TOMMASO DE VIO) (1469–1534). *Dominican theologian. Having joined the Dominicans at sixteen, he studied at Naples and Bologna and taught at Padua, Pavia, Milan, and Rome. Appointed master general of the Dominicans (1508–1518), he defended the *order against *Savonarola, upheld papal authority against the Council of *Pisa (1511), and sent the first Dominican *missionaries to the New World. As papal legate in Germany, he helped secure the election of *Charles V, entered into discussions with *Luther, and later helped to prepare the *bull that condemned the reformer (1520). Cajetan became *bishop of Gaeta in 1519 and worked closely with *Adrian VI, who shared his reforming ideas. His greatest work, still highly regarded by Thomist scholars, was his commentary on the *Summa Theologiae* of Thomas *Aquinas.

CALAMY, EDMUND (1600–1666). Puritan minister. Graduate of Cambridge and episcopally ordained, he opposed the *High Church policies of William *Laud, advocated *presbyterian views as a compromise, participated in the *Westminster Assembly, disapproved of the execution of *Charles I, and hoped much from the *Restoration. He declined a bishopric, refused to obey the 1662 Act of *Uniformity, was ejected, briefly imprisoned, and spent his last years in retirement.

CALASANCTIUS, JOSEPH See Joseph Calasanctius.

CALCED Members of a *religious *order who wear shoes, in contrast to the *discalced, who wear sandals or go barefoot.

CALENDAR Until 1582 the Julian calendar, in general use since 47 B.C., set the year at 365¼ days, with February 24 occurring twice every fourth year. Since, however, the year was fractionally less than 365¼ days, the discrepancy had by 1582 totaled ten whole days. *Gregory XIII rectified matters by a *bull announcing that October 4 would be followed by October 15. Future discrepancies would be avoided by regarding as leap years only those century years divisible by 400 (e.g., 1600, 2000). The Gregorian calendar was not implemented by the British until 1752; the Russians ignored it until after the 1917 revolution. A large section of Eastern Orthodoxy still does not accept it and is now thirteen days behind those who do.

CALENDAR, LITURGICAL The system of commemorations and feasts used by the church to regulate its year. This begins with *Advent (late November or early December). Prominent parts of the calendar are the commemorations of the birth (*Christmas), death and *resurrection (*Easter), and *ascension (Ascension Day) of *Christ, and the coming of the Holy *Spirit (*Pentecost/*Whitsuntide). Of secondary importance are the days on which the *apostles, the Virgin *Mary, and the *saints are remembered.

CALIXTINES The moderate group among the followers of Jan *Hus, who demanded that communicants should receive the wine as well as the bread. Their name comes from *calix,* the Latin word for *chalice or cup.

CALIXTUS, GEORG (1586–1656). German theologian. Professor at Helmstedt from 1614 and an admirer of *Melanchthon, he strove tirelessly to effect reconciliation among the parties divided by the *Reformation. His attempts at moderation and peacemaking were misunderstood by both fellow Lutherans and by Roman Catholics, and his efforts to bring them and the Calvinists together on the basis of common ground brought the term "*syncretism" into prominence. Calixtus also reawakened interest in the study of early church history.

CALL, CALLING See Vocation.

CALLISTUS I (d. 222–223). Pope from 217. Elected after the death of *Zephyrinus in 1217, he was, according to *Hippolytus who opposed the election, originally a slave consigned to the Sardinian mines for fraud (c. 186–189). Callistus excommunicated *Sabellius, but his attitude on that matter and his leniency in disciplinary cases caused Hippolytus to set himself up as the first *antipope. Callistus was martyred under unknown circumstances.

CALLISTUS II (d. 1124). Pope from 1119. *Archbishop of Vienne from 1088 and a strong opponent of *Henry V's rights in the matter of ecclesiastical appointments, he gained prominence as a reformer within the church. His predecessor having died at Cluny, the *cardinals there elected him, and he promptly had Henry and an *antipope excommunicated at the Council of *Reims. Matters were resolved and the *Investiture Controversy was finally settled when the Concordat of *Worms took place in 1122; and its provisions were ratified the following year by the first *Lateran Council to be held in the West.

CALLISTUS III (1378–1458). Pope from 1455. Spanish by birth, he proved an able diplomat in the papal cause, became *bishop of Valencia in 1429, and was elected pope as a compromise candidate between two powerful Italian factions. He launched a crusade with mixed success against the Turks, reversed the trial of *Joan of Arc by proclaiming her innocence, and advanced unworthy members of his own family to high positions in the church.

CALOVIUS, ABRAHAM (1612–1686). German Lutheran scholastic. Calovius argued that all revealed *truth was necessary for *salvation as opposed to Georg *Calixtus, who held that the *Apostles' Creed was sufficient. On this ground Calovius condemned all who disagreed with his rigid Lutheran *orthodoxy, including other Lutherans, Calvinists, Anabaptists, and Roman Catholics, among others. His major theological work, *Systema Locorum Theologicorum (1655–77),* epitomized the Lutheran scholastic approach.

CALVIN, JOHN (1509–1564). French Protestant reformer. Born in Picardy, he studied *theology in Paris and law at Orleans and Bourges, during which time he came under Protestant influence. He broke with *Roman Catholicism in 1533 after a *conversion experience in which he felt called to restore the church to its original purity. Forced to leave Paris because of rising feelings against *Protestantism, he settled in Basel and in 1536 published the *Institutes of the Christian Religion* in Latin. His studious inclinations were disrupted when, on a visit to Geneva in 1536, he unwillingly agreed to become William *Farel's colleague in organizing the *Reformation there. Appointed preacher and professor of *theology, he excluded the unworthy from *Communion and proposed other reforms. The result was the expulsion of Calvin and Farel from the city in 1538. In Strasbourg for the next three years he got to know Martin *Bucer and Philip *Melanchthon, and he published a commentary on Romans. Welcomed back to Geneva in 1541, he established a regime with a strong *OT emphasis that gave the supreme council under Calvin wide powers over the private lives of citizens. *Adultery, *blasphemy, and *heresy were punishable by death. Calvin and *Calvinism controlled church and state. Calvin preached regularly, introduced congregational singing into the *Reformed church services, and gave lectures that brought students from near and far. His Bible commentaries are still hailed as classics. He was also a champion of the *Huguenots, welcomed Protestant refugees from Mary *Tudor's England, trained John *Knox for his leadership of the Scottish Reformation, and counseled Protestants in other lands. Calvin believed that *virtue should be practiced for its own sake, regardless of future *rewards and *punishments.

CALVINISM The teaching of John *Calvin (1509–1564) or of one of his successors or followers. Calvin's own *theology is summarized in his *Institutes of the Christian Religion*. It represents an attempt to expound the meaning of *Scripture in the light of the experience of the church before and during the *Reformation. Thus aspects of traditional theology are retained (e.g., the *doctrine of the *Trinity and the *person of *Christ) and other aspects are renewed and restated (i.e., the new emphasis on *justification by *faith). Calvinism was developed by his successors as they were in debate with Roman Catholics, Lutherans, and among themselves. Classic expositions of developed Calvinism are found in the Canons of the Synod of *Dort (1618) and the *Westminster Confession of Faith (1647). This may be described as *Reformed orthodoxy,

High Calvinism, or simply Calvinism. See also Five Points of Calvinism.

CALVINISTIC METHODISM Otherwise known as the *Presbyterian Church of Wales, it originated in the 18th-century Methodist *revivals in the principality. Among its early leaders were Howel *Harris and Daniel *Rowland. Methodism in Wales, unlike that in England that followed John *Wesley, was Calvinist inasmuch as it accepted the *doctrine of *predestination held by George *Whitefield. Methodism in Wales remained within the Church of *England until 1811. In 1823 it adopted its own *confession of faith, which, based on the *Westminster Confession, is *Presbyterian, as is its church government. Membership in 1983 was 75,092.

CAMBRIDGE PLATFORM (1648). A polity statement of New England Congregationalism. In church government it upheld the autonomy of the local congregation, but it provided a fellowship of churches. In *doctrine it accepted the *Westminster Confession. The platform remained the basis of American Congregationalism until the mid-19th century.

CAMBRIDGE PLATONISTS A 17th-century group of Anglican theologians who, reacting against strict *Calvinism on one hand, the High Churchmanship of William *Laud on the other, denied that precise *dogmas or *ritualism were essentials of *Christianity. Claiming to find links between the *OT and *Platonism, they aimed to reconcile *faith and *reason, *Christian *ethics, and the humanist spirit of the *Renaissance. Among their leaders were Benjamin *Whichcote, Henry *More, and Ralph *Cudworth. They have been criticized because, living in Cambridge at a time of fierce political and religious unrest (1633–1688), they did not become involved.

CAMERONIANS Seventeenth-century Scottish *Covenanter group. Named after the field preacher Richard Cameron, killed by royalist dragoons in 1680, they fought for religious freedom under *Charles II and *James VII. Even after the accession of *William III, many of them regarded the religious settlement as defective and would not rejoin the Church of *Scotland. Their descendants were from 1743 known as the *Reformed Presbyterian Church.

CAMILLUS OF LELLIS (1550–1614). Founder of the Ministers of the Sick (Camillians). Born in the kingdom of Naples, he lived dissolutely as soldier and gambler until converted in 1575. Despite physical incapacity, he began his order in Rome about 1582 and received papal approval for his twelve-strong group of priests to engage in hospital work in 1586. Camillus was general of the order until 1607, when he resigned to give more time personally to sick people. The Camillians did much to improve hospital conditions and to give spiritual help to the dying. At the time of the founder's death, they had 330 members in fifteen Italian cities. They are still found in Europe, the Americas, and Asia, operating hospitals, clinics, and nursing homes.

CAMISARDS Protestant militants in southern France who organized resistance when as a result of *Louis XIV's revocation of the Edict of *Nantes (1685) the king sought to impose *Roman Catholicism on all French people. Beginning with the murder of a persecuting archpriest in the Cevennes (1702), the Camisards aimed to destroy churches and even to kill *priests. The government took savage reprisals, burning villages and massacring many citizens in the Camisard regions. The revolt was put down but continued fitfully until 1710. The Camisard excesses prevented toleration toward more responsible Protestants for much of the 18th century.

CAMP MEETINGS Open-air gatherings held on the American frontier during the 19th century. Due to the lack of churches, thousands of people would pitch their tents around a forest clearing and spend three or four days in religious *worship and social contact. *Baptisms and weddings were a common feature also. By 1811 Francis

*Asbury found more than four hundred such gatherings were held annually from Georgia to Michigan. Revivalistic in character, they brought an element of moral discipline to the unruly life of the frontier.

CAMPBELL, ALEXANDER (1788–1866). Cofounder of the *Disciples of Christ. Born in Ireland, he emigrated to the U.S. in 1809, following his father, Thomas *Campbell, who had settled in Pennsylvania. Both Campbells embarked on a program of religious reform and *Christian unity. Alexander and his followers were baptized by *immersion in 1812, but after differences their links with the *Baptists ended in 1830. As the Disciples of Christ (Campbellites) from 1832, augmented by another group led by Barton *Stone, they opposed *revivalism and controversial divinity, debated with secularists, stressed the *second coming of *Christ, and founded Bethany College in West Virginia in 1840, of which Campbell was president until his death. He began a denominational magazine and published many books.

CAMPBELL, JOHN MCLEOD (1800–1872). Scottish theologian. Five years after his 1825 induction to the *parish of Rhu in Dunbartonshire, he was found guilty by the *presbytery of preaching "the *doctrine of universal *atonement and *pardon through the death of *Christ, and also the doctrine that *assurance is of the essence of *faith and necessary to *salvation." The 1831 *general assembly deposed him from the ministry, and Campbell became minister of an independent congregation in Glasgow (1833–1859). His book *The Nature of the Atonement* was a landmark in the development of modern Scottish *theology.

CAMPBELL, THOMAS (1763–1854). Cofounder of the *Disciples of Christ. Formerly a *Presbyterian minister in Ireland, he emigrated to the U.S. and founded a *Christian association in Pennsylvania in 1807. He became known as an itinerant preacher and usually made his living by teaching school. Associated with his son Alexander *Campbell in founding the Disciples of Christ, he lost his sight late in life and spent his last years with Alexander in West Virginia.

CAMPION, EDMUND (c. 1540–1581). English *Jesuit. University teacher at Oxford and Anglican *deacon, he was converted to Roman Catholicism and in 1573 became a Jesuit in Rome. He taught in a Jesuit school in Prague, where he was ordained in 1578, and two years later he was part of a Jesuit *mission sent to minister to Roman Catholics who under *Elizabeth were forbidden to practice their *religion. He preached secretly and under different names in various parts of England, distributed a pamphlet in Oxford denouncing Anglicanism, and was arrested in 1581. Despite torture, he refused to recant; he was convicted on fabricated charges of treason and was hanged, drawn, and quartered in London.

CANADA, UNITED CHURCH OF See UNITED CHURCH OF CANADA.

CANDLEMAS The feast that commemorates the *purification of *Mary according to Jewish law and the presentation of *Jesus in the temple after his birth (Luke 2:22ff.; Lev 12:1–4). As there is a special blessing of candles during the *Eucharist on this feast day, it is traditionally called Candlemas. In modern *liturgies it is usual to call this feast The *Presentation of the Lord or The Presentation of Christ in the Temple.

CANDLISH, ROBERT SMITH (1806–1873). Scottish minister. As minister of historic St. George's, Edinburgh, he was one of the leading figures among those who for conscience' sake left the Church of *Scotland at the *Disruption and formed the *Free Church of Scotland in 1843. He was described as "a wonderfully electric preacher," and some said he prayed like an inspired Hebrew prophet. He made notable, but not unchallenged, attempts to widen the discussion of *systematic theology in the very conservative new body, of whose college in Edinburgh he became principal in 1862. He had also been one of the founders of the *Evangelical Alliance (1845).

CANISIUS, PETER (1521–1597). *Jesuit reformer, often called the "Second Apostle of Germany." Born in the Netherlands, he joined the Jesuits in 1543 and became their spokesman and apologist in Cologne. A strong foe of *Protestantism, he was a theological consultant at the Council of *Trent and produced the Triple Catechism (1555–1558), with 400 editions in 150 years—the clearest exposition of Roman Catholic *dogma produced by the *Counter-Reformation. Canisius taught and preached with marked success in Germany, Bohemia, Switzerland, and Austria. His personality and his writings won or kept the allegiance of many able men for *Roman Catholicism.

CANON (Gk. *kanon*, "a straight bar or a rod"). It has at least four meanings in the church: (1) the list of books that constitute the *Bible (the canon of *Scripture), (2) the rules that govern church *worship, especially the *Eucharist (liturgical canons), (3) the rules by which the church is organized and ruled (canon law), and (4) a title originally given to *priests in the *bishop's household, later extended to nonmonastic priests attached to a *cathedral or collegiate church. In the modern Church of *England, residentiary canons form the cathedral *chapter, with the dean at its head, and are responsible for the maintenance and services of the cathedral. The title can be conferred also on nonresidentiary canons who hold regular livings in the *diocese.

CANON LAW The rules imposed by a church upon its membership for the regulation of its life. Beginning with the *ecumenical councils in the 4th century there grew up a body of regulations governing aspects of church life—from who may be baptized to how the dead are to be buried. Collections of such rules were made from time to time, the most famous being the *Decretum* of Gratian of 1140. At the *Reformation the Protestant churches made major changes in canon law, but the Roman Catholic church did not. However, between 1904 and 1917 a major revision took place in the latter church resulting in the *Codex Iuris Canonici*. Some Protestant churches have also recently revised their canon law (e.g., the Church of *England).

CANON OF SCRIPTURE The books received by the church as the *rule of faith. The canon of the *NT was recognized by synods at Hippo and Carthage (North Africa) in the late 4th century, but no general council in the early church ever authorized the canon. It was received without major questioning by the whole church. There is, however, not one uniform rule for the *OT, since some churches (Roman Catholic and Orthodox) receive the *Apocrypha as *Scripture while other churches (Protestant) reject it as such. The difference in the OT is between the Greek and Hebrew versions of it. The former contains the Apocrypha.

CANONESS The term seems to derive from the mid-8th century, denoting a member of a female community under vows of *celibacy and *obedience. Where formerly *nuns lived under a more austere regime than canonesses, there came to be little difference between them.

CANONICAL HOURS The specific times of day when the services are to be read by monks and *clergy of the Roman Catholic, Orthodox, *Eastern, and parts of other churches. Traditionally there are seven in the Western church: *matins with lauds, prime, terce, sext, none, *vespers, and *compline. For the Orthodox there are eight beginning with vespers, since they count the day as beginning at sundown. Recently the Roman Catholic Church has revised the hours. See also BREVIARY.

CANONIZATION The process by which the *pope decrees that a member of the Roman Catholic Church be listed among its recognized *saints, considered worthy of profound respect and *veneration, and called upon anywhere in the world to pray for sinners on earth. Superseding the previous local recognition of *martyrs, the first official saint canonized by a pope was Ulrich, *bishop of Augsburg (973). In the 18th century, *Benedict XIV wrote extensively on the subject, and the procedures promulgated in the Code of Canon Law, which became effective in 1918, were based on his work. In Eastern Orthodoxy, canonization does not result from a long process but is made by solemn proclamation after spontaneous *worship has been directed toward the person concerned.

CANONS, BOOK OF A collection of rules (canons) accepted by the Church of *England Convocations of Canterbury (in 1604) and York (1606). Numbering 141, they were necessary to clear up the changes and confusion caused by the English *Reformation. The canons deal with such things as the position of the Church of England (including the monarch's supremacy over it); the conduct of divine service; and regulations regarding the *clergy and church courts and buildings.

CANONS OF THE SYNOD OF DORT The Synod of *Dort (1618–1619) condemned *Arminianism in a series of ninety-three canonical rules. These asserted unconditional *election, limited *atonement, *total depravity, the irresistibility of divine *grace, and the final *perseverance of the *saints. This victory for strict *Calvinism led to the deprivation of some two hundred dissentient ministers, one of whom was beheaded and another sentenced to life imprisonment.

CANTATA A composite musical form that may include an organ/orchestral prelude, an overture, arias, duets, and choruses. In *Lutheranism it became an integral part of 17th- and 18th-century *worship and was performed between the Epistle and *Gospel, being directly related to one or both of them. In other traditions it has not had such a basic relation to the *liturgy.

CANTATE DOMINO The opening words of Psalm 98 in Latin meaning "O sing to the Lord." This psalm is much used in *liturgy because of its powerful call to praise the Lord.

CANTICLE (Lat. *canticulum*, "a little song"). A song from *Scripture. The four most used in liturgical *worship are: *Benedicite (Dan 3:35–66), Benedictus (Luke 1:68–79), *Magnificat (vv. 46–55), and Nunc Dimittis (2:29–32). Other songs from the *Bible commonly used include the Song of Habakkuk (Hab 3:2–19), the Song of Hannah (1 Sam 2:1–10), the Song of Isaiah (Isa 26:1–21), the Song of Jonah (Jonah 2:2–9), and the Songs of Moses (Exod 15:1–19; Deut 32:1–43).

CANTOR The person who sets the pitch and leads the singing in *worship. If there is no musical instrument, this is an important function. See also PRECENTOR, SUCCENTOR.

CAPITAL PUNISHMENT The use of the death penalty for specific crimes. Over the centuries the majority of Christians have believed that the taking of life by the *state in certain cases was right, a number of texts being cited (e.g., Gen 4:14; 9:16; Acts 25:11; Rom 13:4). Today the whole basis of the traditional *theology of *punishment is being reexamined by Christians, and so there is no consensus. Whether or not the carrying out of the death penalty is morally acceptable and justifiable depends on a theory of punishment. Factors such as whether the death penalty is a deterrent, whether punishment should reform rather than destroy, and whether anyone should be asked to perform the actual penalty on behalf of the state have to be carefully weighed.

CAPITAL SINS, CAPITAL VIRTUES (Lat. *capitalis*, "principal"). The principal sins and virtues that are the source of other sins and virtues. In contrast these are: (1) *pride/humility, (2) avarice/liberality, (3) lust/*chastity, (4) anger/meekness, (5) gluttony/:N: *temperance, (6) envy/brotherly *love, and (7) sloth/diligence.

CAPITO, WOLFGANG FABRICIUS (1478–1541). Swiss reformer. Roman Catholic *priest and professor of *theology at Basel, his views progressively changed through contact with *Oecolampadius, *Luther, and *Zwingli. He became *cathedral preacher and *chancellor at Mainz (1519–1523) but finally resigned to join the Protestant ranks in Strasbourg. With *Bucer he tried unsuccessfully to mediate between Luther and Zwingli, but unlike Bucer he remained for a time on friendly terms with *Anabaptists and other *dissenters from mainline *Protestantism. A distinguished scholar who held degrees also in law and medicine, Capito edited the *psalter in Hebrew and wrote on church discipline and pastoral theology. He died of the plague while returning from the Colloquy of *Ratisbon.

CAPPADOCIAN FATHERS Three theologians from Cappadocia who defended the *doctrine of the *deity of *Christ and developed that of the Holy *Spirit. They were Basil of Caesarea (*Basil the Great [c. 329–379]), his brother *Gregory of Nyssa (335–c. 395) and Basil's friend, *Gregory of Nazianzus (330–389). Basil also made an important contribution to the development of *monasticism.

CAPSULA A short, round metal vessel used in Roman Catholic churches to reserve the consecrated bread (*host) for use in the service of *Benediction.

CAPUCHINS Officially the Order of Friars Minor Capuchin, it was founded in 1528 as an autonomous branch of the *Franciscans by Matteo da Bascio (d. 1552), who advocated a return to stricter observance of the rule of *Frances of Assisi. This extended to dress: the order took its name from a pointed hood (*capuccino* in Italian) devised by da Bascio. Despite a strict regime, papal restrictions on their ministry, the opposition of regular Franciscans, and the *conversion to *Protestantism of their *vicar general, Bernardino *Ochino (1524), their numbers had risen to 17,000 by 1574 and reached a peak of 34,000 some eighty years later. They made a significant contribution to the *Counter-Reformation and worked valiantly through sundry epidemics. The order, which concentrates on *missionary and parochial work, still has a membership of some 14,000.

CARDINAL A holder of the highest rank in the Roman Catholic Church after the *pope; one who with others forms the Sacred College whose responsibility includes electing the pope and acting as his chief adviser. In 1586 *Sixtus V fixed their number at 70, but *John XXIII (1958–1963) abrogated this, and by August 1978 there were 128 cardinals. The college has three *orders (*bishops, *priests, and *deacons). Cardinals are appointed only by the pope and receive the red hat and *biretta as *symbols of their office.

CARDINAL VIRTUES (Lat. *cardo*, "a hinge"). Those virtues that are the "hinge" or "fulcrum" of the moral life of human beings. They are: prudence, *justice, *temperance, and *fortitude. See also THEOLOGICAL VIRTUES.

CAREY, WILLIAM (1761–1834). *Missionary and educator in India. Born in Northamptonshire and a shoemaker by trade, after his *conversion (1779) he combined shoemaking with schoolteaching, preaching, and learning languages. He became a Baptist in 1783. Concerned for the spread of the *gospel throughout the world, he founded with others the Baptist Missionary Society, of which the first two representatives were Carey and a medical colleague who went to Calcutta in 1793. He became superintendent of an indigo plant in Bengal in 1794, translated the *NT into Bengali, and preached as an itinerant in the villages. In 1800 he moved to Serampore, which was to be his base until he died. He became professor of Bengali, Sanskrit, and Marathi at Fort William College (1801), and translated *Scripture into thirty-five languages and dialects. His educational work earned him the title of "father of Bengali prose." He established a printing press, planted churches, evangelized, provided medical relief, encouraged agriculture, and urged the government to ban Hindu practices such as infanticide and suttee. Often regarded as the father of modern *missions, Carey's life exemplified the advice he had given at a missionary meeting in 1792: "Expect great things from God; attempt great things for God."

CARLSTADT, ANDREAS RUDOLF BODENSTEIN VON See KARLSTADT.

CARMELITES Known as the Brothers of the Blessed Virgin *Mary of Mount Carmel, the *order emerged from *hermits on the mountain in 12th-century Palestine after the establishment of the Latin Kingdom there. These devout men, said to have been formerly pilgrims and crusaders, had settled themselves about 1155 near the traditional fountain of Elijah, whom the monks were to claim as the founder of *monasticism. *Honorius III approved the rule in 1226. With the setbacks sustained by the crusaders having made Mount Carmel unsafe, the Carmelites migrated to Europe; their first general *chapter meeting was held in England in 1247. The hermits became *mendicant *friars and spread throughout western Europe. An order of Carmelite *nuns was founded in the Netherlands in 1452, but both sections suffered decline until reforms initiated in the latter 16th century by *Teresa of Avila and *John of the Cross. During the 19th and 20th centuries a number of different congregations of Carmelite sisters were founded in Europe, America, and India; and apart from contemplatives, they engage in various kinds of ministry.

CARMICHAEL, AMY WILSON (1867–1951). *Missionary to India. Born in Northern Ireland, she was briefly a missionary in Japan, but in 1895 she began her fifty-five-year unbroken association with India. She had a remarkable ministry in rescuing girls from a shameful existence in Hindu temples, and this led to the opening of a children's home in Tinnevelly, South India, and the establishment of the Dohnavur Fellowship. Disabled through arthritis from 1931, she remained very much the focal point of the fellowship and of the work among women and girls. She also had a wider ministry in her devotional books, which became popular because of their rare blend of *mysticism and her very practical approach to *Things as They Are* (the title of one of her books).

CARNELL, EDWARD JOHN (1919–1987). American Protestant theologian. Professor of ethics and philosophy of religion (and president from 1954–1959) at Fuller Theological Seminary, Carnell sought to present historic *orthodoxy in a rationally defensible manner, sometimes in a pronounced anti-Fundamentalistic manner. His many books helped to establish him as one of the most original minds of American Evangelicalism.

CARNIVAL (Lat. *carnem levare*, "to put away flesh meat"). The season of feasting and merrymaking immediately before *Lent. The "last fling" before the rigors of *fasting.

CAROLINE DIVINES, THE The Church of *England theologians who lived in the reigns of Charles I (1625–1649) and Charles II (1660–1685) and expounded high views of the place of *bishops, *sacraments, and *liturgy (high in contrast to Puritan views). The first of these is Lancelot *Andrewes (d. 1626), and included is William *Laud (d. 1645).

CARROLL, JOHN (1735–1815). First Roman Catholic *bishop in America. Born in Maryland and educated in France, he became a *Jesuit in 1753, taught philosophy and *theology, and returned to America in 1773. Active in the movement for independence, friend of Benjamin Franklin, and promoter of education and *culture, he helped make the Roman Catholic Church in the U.S. independent of English oversight. In 1790 he was consecrated in England as bishop of Baltimore, becoming *archbishop in 1808 when four new *sees were carved out of his *diocese.

CARTESIANISM The basic philosophical principles and method taught by

Rene *Descartes (1596–1650), the founder of modern philosophy. He posed the problems that have kept thinkers busy from his time to ours. Desiring to bring together the developing natural and mechanistic sciences and traditional theological knowledge, he emphasized the duality and distinction of matter and mind. The scientists had matter and the theologians had mind. Also he systematically doubted everything but was left with his own doubt—*dubito ero sum* ("I doubt, therefore I am"). He is best known for his claim, *cogito ergo sum* ("I think, therefore I am").

CARTHUSIANS A contemplative *order of monks founded at Chartreuse, France, in 1084 by *Bruno the Carthusian and six colleagues. Part of the reform movement in monastic life, it reflected a rigorous regime, with strict regulations about food and drink, *fasting, the wearing of hair shirts, the observance of silence, and lengthy *prayer periods. Attached to each *monastery was a community of lay brothers who looked after the material needs of the house. By 1521 the order included 195 houses, but it suffered severe losses during the *Reformation, during the 18th-century nationalist movement in various countries, and during the Revolutionary and Napoleonic periods in France. Regulations governing the order have changed remarkably little through the centuries; it is said that it has never required and never experienced reform.

CARTWRIGHT, PETER (1785–1872). American *circuit rider. Converted in a Kentucky *camp meeting in 1801, he became a Methodist preacher and served in Southern circuits before moving to Illinois in 1824 in protest against *slavery in the South. He served in the Illinois legislature and lost an election for congressman to Abraham Lincoln in 1846. He is said to have baptized more than twelve thousand people during his seventy years in the ministry.

CARTWRIGHT, THOMAS (1535–1603). Puritan scholar. His strongly *Reformed views interrupted his studies at Cambridge on the accession of Mary *Tudor in 1553, but even under *Elizabeth he was in trouble. For criticizing the *Elizabethan church settlement he was deprived of his divinity chair after holding it for only one year (1570). He fled abroad (1573–1585) and spent some time with *Beza in Geneva and in ministering to the English congregation in Antwerp. He was imprisoned briefly by the *Court of High Commission in 1590. Perhaps the most learned and able of the 16th-century Puritans, he helped to draft the *Millenary Petition to *James I.

CASSIAN, JOHN (360–435). Monk, ascetical writer, and defender of *semi-Pelagianism. Born in Romania, he became successively a monk in Bethlehem, a learner from the ascetics of the Egyptian desert, and a disciple in Constantinople of John *Chrysostom, who ordained him deacon. When Chrysostom was deposed and exiled, Cassian was sent to Rome in 404 to enlist *Innocent I's help. Cassian evidently stayed in the West, founded two monasteries in France (415), and wrote works on the ascetic life that were reverenced for centuries.

CASSOCK The long garment worn principally by *clergy. *Deacons and *priests usually wear black or white, *bishops wear purple or violet, and *cardinals wear red. It is ankle-length with long narrow sleeves.

CASSOCK-ALB A modern liturgical garment, worn especially by *clergy taking part in the *Eucharist. Instead of wearing an *alb or a *surplice over a *cassock, this white or light-colored garment combines the two.

CASTELLIO, SEBASTIAN (1515–1563). Protestant theologian. A native of Savoy, he became a Protestant in 1540 after meeting *Calvin in Strasbourg. In 1541 he became rector of the college at Geneva. He disagreed with Calvin doctrinally and probably temperamentally and was one of the few who spoke out against the execution of *Servetus. Castellio was professor of

Greek at Basel from 1553. Among his writings were Latin and French translations of the *Bible and theological works that challenged strict *Calvinism and favored religious *liberty.

CASUISTRY The application of general moral principles to particular cases of *conscience. As a theological science it developed from the advice given to those who made private *confession to a *priest (*sacrament of *penance) in the medieval period. Since then different approaches have developed in the Roman Catholic church (e.g., *equiprobabilism, *probabilism, *probabiliorism). In *Protestantism casuistry is less developed and more flexible, since private confession is not widespread.

CATACOMBS Underground rooms and tunnels used for *burial of the dead. Since the early Christians, like the Jews, did not practice *cremation, they buried their dead. As there was not always space at ground level, they dug underground burial rooms. In and around the city of Rome are forty known *Christian catacombs. Excavations in them and others have brought to light interesting inscriptions, paintings, and sarcophagi.

CATAPHATIC THEOLOGY (Gk. *cataphasis*, "affirmation"). Used especially in Greek *theology as a contrast to and a complement to **apophatic* theology (the way of negation). It is the way of affirmation in that *God is described on the basis of his self-revelation (contained in the *Bible) in positive terms. In the Latin West it was known as *Via Affirmationis* or *Via Affirmative* ("the way of affirmation").

CATECHETICAL SCHOOLS Educational institutions in early *Christian times for teaching the *faith. Less accurately, the name is used also of Christian academies, such as the one at Alexandria begun in the late 2d century of which *Clement and *Origen successively became head. This was the best known, greatly influencing the development of Christian *theology, especially among those with a background of classical *culture.

CATECHETICS, CATECHESIS, CATECHIST, CATECHUMEN (Gk. *katecheo*, "to instruct"). Catechetics is the study of the principles and methods involved in teaching the *faith. Catechesis refers to the actual instruction given to those being prepared for *baptism or *confirmation. The catechumen is the one undergoing the instruction. In the primitive church the catechist was the teacher of catechumens but in the modern church, especially in developing countries, the catechist is the local, native preacher and teacher who is not ordained.

CATECHISM A book(let) presenting *Christian *doctrine usually in a question-and-answer form. They were much used by the Protestant churches in and after the *Reformation. Famous examples include *Luther's *Smaller Catechism* (1529), the **Heidelberg Catechism* (1563), and the **Westminster Larger Catechism* (1647).

CATECHIST The title given in the early church to one who gave *Christian instruction to those being prepared for *baptism. It is still used in some churches for those who teach children, and on the *mission field denotes a native teacher.

CATEGORICAL IMPERATIVE A term introduced by the philosopher Immanuel *Kant (1724–1804) to describe the obligation to do one's *duty. He expressed it in the words: "Act only on such a maxim as you can will that it should become a *universal law." It refers to absolute moral law that human *reason recognizes as binding. It is contrasted with the hypothetical imperative that would work as follows: "Water your plants if you wish them to grow." For a *Christian the categorical imperative is the known *will of *God revealed in the *Bible.

CATENA (Lat. "a chain"). A collection of passages or quotations usually from the early Fathers used to expound a biblical passage or expound a theme. The most famous of these in

Latin is the *Catena Aurea* of Thomas *Aquinas, a running commentary on the four Gospels. The modern use of the word *catena* is based on this title in the 1484 edition.

CATHARI Heretical *Christian *sect. While the name had been held by some earlier groups, it is generally associated in western Europe with a movement known in France by 1017 that seems to have links with the *Bogomils of 10th-century Bulgaria. They repudiated matter as *evil, rejected sex and procreation, repudiated the *Incarnation and the *Resurrection, and approved of *suicide and *usury. The sect did not survive the 14th-century *Inquisition.

CATHEDRA, CATHEDRAL (Gk. "a chair or throne"). Used of the chair of the *bishop in his principal church—hence "cathedral." It is placed in the center of the *apse or in the *chancel. A cathedral is the mother church of a *diocese.

CATHERINE OF SIENA (1347–1380). Mystic and *patron *saint of Italy. At sixteen she became a tertiary of the *Dominican order in Siena and was soon known for holiness and *asceticism. She traveled widely and worked unsuccessfully to settle the strife that embroiled church and *papacy. Less irenically she tried to raise support for an onslaught against the Muslims. Her letters and spiritual writings are still highly prized. She and *Francis of Assisi were named chief patron saints of Italy in 1939.

CATHOLIC APOSTOLIC CHURCH An English religious body begun about 1832. It developed out of a desire on the part of a group of ministers and laymen, including Henry *Drummond, to see restored to the church the gifts of the *apostolic age. Owing much to the teaching of Edward *Irving (who was not, however, one of its founders), it appointed twelve *apostles, developed an elaborate *ritual, and was associated with such things as *speaking in tongues, *prophecy, and the imminence of *Christ's return. The last apostle died in 1901, and the movement has gradually declined, though it still has a few hundred members in Great Britain and Germany.

CATHOLIC, CATHOLICITY (Gk. *katholikos*, "universal"). It is used: (1) of the *universal church in contrast to the local, (2) of holding orthodox *truths (e.g., those of the *Nicene Creed), (3) of the Roman Catholic Church, and (4) by those who wish to affirm that they belong to the one, historical church of *God (e.g., *Old Catholics and "Catholic" Anglicans).

CATHOLIC EPISTLES Those *NT Letters that are not addressed to specific churches—James; 1 and 2 Peter; 1, 2, and 3 John; and Jude. Technically 2 and 3 John should not be included, for they are addressed to specific recipients, but in *Christian *tradition they have been grouped with 1 John.

CATHOLICOS The title of the heads of the *Armenian, Georgian, and *Nestorian churches. In former times the designation of a superior *abbot, it came to denote first a senior *bishop and thereafter became synonymous with *patriarch. In the case of the head of the *Chaldean Christians the title patriarch-catholicos is used.

CAUSA SUI (Lat. "cause of itself" or "of himself"). Applied to *God as the One who cannot be produced by, or be dependent on, anything or anyone else.

CAUSE, FIRST Applied to *God as the final and ultimate explanation of all created reality. See also Five Ways, The.

CELEBRANT The proclamation and the receiving of the *gospel or of an aspect of *God's *salvation is called "celebration." It is that in which the congregation engages when attending the *Eucharist. So the president of the Eucharist is sometimes called the "celebrant."

CELESTINE I (d. 432). Pope from 422. He upheld *orthodoxy against *Nestorianism and *Pelagianism, sent a *mission to deal with the latter *heresy in Britain, and commissioned *Palladius as the first *bishop in Ireland, in which work he was to be succeeded by *Patrick.

CELESTINE III (c. 1106–1198). Pope from 1191. Friend of Peter *Abelard and Thomas *Becket, he was about eighty-five when he was elected. A patient and moderate man, he was continually thwarted by the pretensions and successes of the emperor Henry VI, whom a stronger pope would have excommunicated for blatant misdeeds. Celestine offered to resign in 1197, but the *cardinals would not permit him to do so.

CELESTINE V (1215–1296). Pope for five months of 1294, and the first pope to abdicate. Previously a *hermit under the *Benedictine rule, in about 1260 he became he became head of a group later called Celestines. A life of *asceticism, however, had ill-equipped him to deal with administration, diplomacy, and *cardinals. He relinquished the *papacy, but his successor, *Boniface VIII, would not allow him to return to his hermitage and kept him *interned until his death. *Petrarch expressed high admiration for Celestine, but Dante gave him a lower place.

CELESTIUS (5th century). *Pelagian heretic. Formerly a lawyer in Rome, he was condemned by a church council in Carthage (412) for denying *original *sin and the *remission of sins by *baptism. Celestius and his friend Pelagius were opposed by *Jerome and *Augustine of Hippo, and they were excommunicated by *Innocent I in 416, a stance later confirmed after some hesitation by Pope *Zosimus. The Council of *Ephesus (431) repeated the condemnation of Celestius.

CELIBACY (Lat. *coelebs*, "a bachelor"). The acceptance of the single state as a *duty to *God. This may be expressed in a *vow, but this is not necessary unless required by the church or community. The idea of celibacy for God's sake can be traced to Matt 19:10ff. and 1 Cor 7:20ff. The Roman Catholic Church requires celibacy of *clergy as well as of monks and *nuns. In the *Orthodox church parochial clergy are allowed to marry if they do so before *ordination. Protestants believe that God must individually *call a person to celibacy and that the normal state is the married state. See also VIRGINITY.

CELTIC CHURCH The term usually denotes the church in the British Isles before the arrival of *Augustine of Canterbury in 597. Little is known of its beginnings, but it sent representatives to church *synods at Arles in 314 and *Ariminum in 359. From mainland Europe early in the 5th century came two influences: the *heresy of *Pelagianism and the practice of *monasticism, of which *Ninian and *Patrick were leaders. Much more far-reaching in mid-century were the Saxon invasions that resulted in the abandonment of *Christianity except in the more isolated areas. For sixty-six years after Augustine's mission reestablished links with Rome, the Roman and Celtic *traditions clashed on various issues, such as the date of *Easter and the form of the tonsure, until differences were resolved at the Synod of *Whitby (664).

CENOBITES A name once used to describe monks who lived in communities, to distinguish them from the more solitary existence chosen by *hermits and *anchorites. *Benedictines and *Cistercians are contemporary examples of cenobitism.

CENSURES Reprimands or *punishments imposed by a church upon those who have transgressed ecclesiastical law.

CERULARIUS, MICHAEL (d. 1059). Patriarch of Constantinople. Delegated in 1043 after having been a monk for only three years, he showed himself a fierce opponent of Western church practices and claims. He closed the Latin churches in Constantinople after an impracticable ultimatum. The outcome was that pope and patriarch excommunicated each other, and the severance of relations between Eastern and Western churches known as the *Great Schism began.

CHAFER, LEWIS SPERRY (1871–1952). *Presbyterian theologian, educator, and writer. Founder and president of Dallas Theological Seminary (1924–1952) and professor of *systematic theology. Chafer championed dispensationalist *premillennialism, giving it academic respectability through his own personal skill as a teacher and his best-remembered work, *Systematic Theology* (8 vols., 1947–1948). He was strongly influenced by C. I. *Scofield.

CHAIN OF BEING A metaphor for the *order, unity, and completeness of the *universe. The idea is of a chain that extends to include all types and forms of existence from *God at one end to the smallest electron at the other. It was a popular metaphor in the *Renaissance and has been made widely known in modern times by the book *The Great Chain of Being* (1936) by A. O. Lovejoy (d. 1962).

CHALCEDON, COUNCIL OF (451). The fourth *ecumenical council of the *Christian church. The largest of the early councils, it repudiated the so-called Robber Synod of *Ephesus (449) that had favored *Monophysitism, reaffirmed the condemnation of *Eutyches and Nestorius, upheld the *Nicene Creed and the Tome of Leo, and adopted *canons to rectify the disorder within the *Eastern Church. The council was also an important step in the development of the Roman *primacy.

CHALCEDON, THE DEFINITION OF (451). A statement composed at and authorized by the fifth *ecumenical council of Chalcedon (451). It contains a definitive pronouncement concerning the relation of the human and divine *natures in *Jesus, the *Christ. He is described as being truly *God and truly man (two natures) in one *person. The two natures are said to coexist "without confusion, without change, without division and without separation." See also HYPOSTASIS, PHUSIS, PROSOPON.

CHALDEAN CHRISTIANS A section of the descendants of the ancient Nestorian branch of *Christianity, which after an internal disagreement with other Nestorians in the 17th century recognized the papal authority. It nevertheless retained some distinctive features: its *patriarch is elected without confirmation from Rome; *bishops are elected by the Chaldean *hierarchy, though papal confirmation is necessary for *consecration; and *secular *clergy are not canonically bound to *celibacy. Most married *priests are converts from *Nestorianism.

CHALICE (Lat. *calix*, "a cup"). The cup, usually of silver, in which the wine used as a *symbol of the *blood of *Christ is held during Holy *Communion. The bread, symbolizing the *body of Christ, is kept on the *paten.

CHALMERS, JAMES (1841–1901). Scottish *missionary and explorer in the South Seas. A former Glasgow city missioner, he went under *Congregationalist auspices to the New Hebrides in 1867, in the footsteps of the famous John *Williams. In 1877 he went on to pioneer in New Guinea, planting a line of mission posts, encouraging an indigenous church, making significant geographical findings, helping to establish British rule in northern New Guinea, but always pushing on to places where no missionary had been. It was this determination that led to his death at the hands of tribesmen in an island off the south coast of Papua.

CHALMERS, THOMAS (1780–1847). Scottish minister and social reformer. He was the leader of those ministers who for *conscience' sake left the national church at the 1843 *Disruption and formed the *Free Church of Scotland. Earlier as a minister in Glasgow he had worked actively to apply *Christian *ethics to social problems and had occupied the chair of moral philosophy at St. Andrews. He was the Free Church *general assembly's first *moderator and was principal of its New College in Edinburgh, but he did not long survive that appointment.

CHANCEL (Lat. *cancellus*, "a screen"). The part of a church in which the *altar/*holy table and the stalls for *choir and *clergy are located. In medieval times a screen often separated the chancel from the nave—hence the name chancel.

CHANCELLOR Secretary to a *cathedral *chapter in medieval times, he is now in the Church of *England the *bishops' representative in administering the temporal affairs of the *diocese. He issues marriage licenses and hears complaints of *immorality against the *clergy. In modern *Roman Catholicism he is a *priest with special responsibility for diocesan archives; but very often the bishop, particularly in the U.S., delegates some of his episcopal powers to him.

CHANNING, WILLIAM ELLERY (1780–1842). American *Unitarian minister. Harvard graduate and *Congregationalist minister in Boston, he denied basic *Christian *doctrines such as the *Trinity, the *Incarnation, *original *sin, and substitutionary *atonement. He was one of the leading influences in the establishment of the American Unitarian Association in 1825.

CHANT The vocal melody belonging to specific parts of *liturgy. It may be a recitation of a scriptural text on a single pitch or more elaborate melodies sung by clergyman or *choir. The *Christian use of chant developed from that of the *synagogue of the Jews. There are different kinds of chant—e.g., Gregorian, *Byzantine, and Syrian.

CHAPMAN, JOHN WILBUR (1859–1918). American *pastor and *evangelist. Born in Indiana, he held various *Presbyterian pastorates but is known most for his association as evangelist first with D. L. *Moody, then with Charles M. Alexander from 1910. He crossed the Pacific and the Atlantic on evangelistic tours and was the first director of the Winona Lake Bible Conference.

CHAPTER The term derived originally from the monastic practice of gathering to hear the reading of a chapter of the *rule of the body/society to which the *clergy belonged. The meeting place came to be known as the chapter-house, and the assembly as the chapter. It is used especially of the clergy of a *cathedral. In a modern Anglican cathedral or collegiate church the chapter comprises the dean and *canons (thus "the Dean and Chapter"). It is also used more generally of any group of clergy attached to specific foundations or houses.

CHARACTER, SACRAMENTAL (Gk. *charakter*, "distinctive mark"). Used of the spiritual and indelible imprint of divine *grace upon the *heart and *soul as a result of the action of *God in the *sacraments of the church when faithfully received. This is a *theology developed from Rev 7:2–8, the seal with which the elect are marked, and it began in the medieval period. It is particularly used by Roman Catholics of *baptism, *confirmation, and entry into holy *orders.

CHARISMA, CHARISMATA, CHARISMATIC (Gk. *charisma*, "a gift"). Paul used *charismata* (pl.) in listing the *gifts of the Spirit (e.g., 1 Cor 12:8–11, 28). To be charismatic is to possess one or more of these gifts. However, the word is used generally as meaning "dynamic" — hence the term "charismatic leadership." To speak of the Charismatic movement is to refer to the search for, and the use of, the gifts of the Spirit in many *denominations. This phenomenon reached a peak in the 1960s and 1970s and affected many parts of the world in that whole congregations or small groups within congregations were involved. It is sometimes called *Neo-Pentecostalism.

CHARISMATIC MOVEMENT Contemporary religious phenomenon that embodies a renewed emphasis on the *person and work of the Holy *Spirit. Beginning in the late 1950s and early 1960s non-Pentecostal Christians, many from the mainline *denominations, began experiencing Pentecostal visitations that included *speaking in tongues, divine *healings, *prophecies, and various physical phenomena such as prostrations and fainting, in a way reminiscent of the great *awakenings of the past. It created a vast unrest and rethinking on the part of traditional non-Pentecostal Christians, including the Roman Catholics, of what place such gifts and experiences ought to play in the *Christian life. Voluminous literature and over one hundred official denominational documents have discussed its value pro and con with the general feeling (although not universally held) that one ought not to bridle the Holy Spirit, who "blows where he will," but still one must "test the spirits" to see if they are of *God.

CHARITY (Lat. *caritas*; Gk. *agape*; "*love"). The Old English word for *God's love and the love God places in human *hearts. This is expounded by Paul (1 Cor 13) and by John (1 John 4) (see the KJV for its use in these chapters). Charity, or love, is the greatest of the *theological virtues.

CHARLEMAGNE (CHARLES THE GREAT) (742–814). King of the Franks and emperor of the West. Son of *Pepin III and grandson of Charles Martel, he became sole ruler of the Franks in 771, subdued the Lombards in 774, and moved thereafter to conquer the Saxons, northern Spain, Bavaria, and eastward to the land of the Slavs. On *Christmas Day in 800, Pope *Leo III, who was in need of a powerful ally against local enemies, crowned Charles in Rome as emperor of the West. Charles regarded himself as the guardian of the *papacy, orthodox *Christianity, and the morals of the *clergy (whatever his own private practices); and he was the prime mover in the Carolingian *Renaissance.

CHARLES I (1600–1649). King of Great Britain and Ireland. Born in Scotland where his father was *James VI, he inherited and expanded James's belief in the *divine right of kings. When that conflicted after his accession (1625) with the Puritan-dominated Parliament in London, he dissolved that body and ruled without it (1629–1640) until he had to seek funds for the subjection of *Presbyterian Scotland. Civil *war broke out in 1642, with parliamentarians joined by the Scots against the king from 1644. Charles finally surrendered to the Scots, who handed him over to the English on the condition that his life be spared—a promise that was not kept. Charles's autocratic tendencies were out of step with an age that demanded more civil and religious *liberty than he was prepared to give.

CHARLES II (1630–1685). King of Great Britain and Ireland. Son of *Charles I, he was crowned by the Scots in 1649 but was defeated by the forces of Oliver *Cromwell when he tried to advance his cause in England. He was exiled on the Continent until the *Restoration in 1660. Devoid of the high, albeit misguided, principles of his father, Charles was dissolute and operated on the basis of expediency. Strong legislation against dissent was taken in England, while in Scotland even more savage measures were directed against the *Covenanters. For monetary gain he made common cause with *Louis XIV against the Protestant Dutch, and in England favored *Roman Catholicism, which he is said to have professed on his deathbed.

CHARLES V (1500–1558). King of Spain (1516–1556) and Holy Roman emperor (1519–1556). Born in Ghent, son of Philip of Burgundy, he has been regarded as the last emperor to think in terms of a unified empire covering the whole *Christian world. The *doctrines of *Luther and the growing strength of *Protestantism, coupled with Turkish encroachments, the opposition of the French, and the hostility of the *pope, all made Charles's an uphill task. Disillusioned at the failure of attempts at moderation, he abdicated and spent his last two years in a Spanish *monastery.

CHASTITY The preservation of sexual purity in all states of life—e.g., *virginity for girls, loyalty to the married partner in marriage. Chastity is violated by *fornication and *adultery. Positively, chastity is directing *love in legitimate channels according to *God's will. Monks and *nuns take a *vow of chastity.

CHASUBLE The outermost vestment worn by a *priest or *bishop when celebrating the *Eucharist. It is used in *Orthodox churches (where it is called the phelonion), Roman Catholic churches, and some Lutheran and Anglican churches. Its color varies according to the church year, and it is normally made of a rich and pliant material.

CHAUNCY, CHARLES (1705–1787). American *Congregationalist minister. He held the pastorate of First Church, Boston, for sixty years, from 1727, during which time he clashed with Jonathan *Edwards and certain features of the *Great Awakening in New England, resisted Anglican claims to a favored position in Massachusetts, and preached and wrote against an undue enthusiasm that misunderstood authentic *Puritanism.

CHELCICKY, PETER (c. 1390–c. 1460). Czech writer. Greatly influenced by John *Wycliffe and Jan *Hus, he formulated views later developed by the *Bohemian Brethren. Unlike the militant section of the Hussite movement, he condemned violence and secular authority, rejected *monasticism, and wanted a return to primitive *Christianity.

CHEMNITZ, MARTIN (1522–1586). Lutheran theologian. Supporter of Philip *Melanchthon, he became superintendent of the churches of Braunschweig in 1567 and strove to reunite the Lutheran church, which had divided over theological differences. This task, in which he worked with fellow scholar Jakob Andreae, ended successfully with the Formula of *Concord in 1577. Chemnitz was the author of many theological works upholding *Lutheranism.

CHESTERTON, GILBERT KEITH (1874–1936). English writer. Author of many works of social and literary criticism, he had written on *religion in *Orthodoxy* (1909) but gave increasing emphasis to that area after converting to *Roman Catholicism in 1922. His works included *St. Francis of Assisi* (1923), *The Everlasting Man* (1925), and *St. Thomas Aquinas* (1933). He became famous for his ability to use *paradox effectively in the discussion of *Christian *theology, saying it reflected "*truth standing on its head."

CHEYNE, THOMAS KELLY (1841–1915). *OT scholar. Most of his life was spent at Oxford, where from 1885 he was Oriel professor of the interpretation of *Scripture, which he approached from the standpoint of one deeply influenced by German radical criticism. Author of many works on the OT, he was coeditor of the *Encyclopaedia Biblica* (1899–1903).

CHICAGO CALL, THE (1977). An appeal to Evangelicals to reconsider their historic roots and continuity, fidelity to the *Bible, creedal identity, idea of holistic *salvation, sacramental integrity, *spirituality, idea of church authority, and unity. It was signed in Chicago on May 3, 1977 by forty-two leading evangelicals and then published. It was explained in the book *The Orthodox Evangelicals* (ed. R. Webber, 1978).

CHICAGO SCHOOL OF THEOLOGY Liberal Protestant point of view emanating from the University of Chicago Divinity School from the 1920s through the 1960s stressing in various ways *higher criticism, a sociological approach to *religion, *pragmatism, and an empirical *theology. Shailer *Mathews, Henry Nelson Weiman, and Edward Scribner Ames were loosely the spokesmen for the movement and were vigorous in their attack upon theological conservatives during the so-called Fundamentalist-Modernist controversy.

CHICAGO STATEMENT ON BIBLICAL INERRANCY, THE (1978). A document produced at an international conference of Evangelicals held in Chicago in October 1978. Its purpose was to state and explain the traditional conservative evangelical approach to, and *doctrine of, the *Bible as being inerrant.

CHICAGO-LAMBETH ARTICLES Otherwise known as the Chicago Quadrilateral, they embodied four principles adopted by the *bishops of the American Protestant Episcopal Church in 1886 and proposed as steps toward *Christian unity. They were: (1) *Scripture as the ultimate standard of *faith; (2) the *Apostles' Creed and the *Nicene Creed; (3) the *sacraments of *baptism and the *Lord's Supper; (4) and a belief in the historic episcopate. A revised form of the articles (the *Lambeth Quadrilateral) was accepted by the Lambeth Conference in 1888.

CHILD OF GOD A *Christian as seen as a member of the family of *God. One who has been adopted by the *grace of God into the family in which *Christ is the Elder Brother (Rom 8:16; 1 John 3:1). See also ADOPTION.

CHILIASM (Gk. *chilioi*, "a thousand"). The *doctrine that there will be a reign of *Christ, or of Christ and his *saints, on earth for a thousand years before the final *judgment of the nations and the beginning of *eternity future. A biblical base is claimed in Rev 20:1–5. See also MILLENARIANISM.

CHILLINGWORTH, WILLIAM (1602–1644). Anglican clergyman. An Oxford graduate who loved disputation, he was converted to *Roman Catholicism and in 1630 went to France. Four years later he was back in England and back in Anglicanism, convinced that it contained the few fundamentals necessary to *salvation. He served with the king's forces during the Civil War and died after having been captured by parliamentary forces. He wrote *Religion of Protestants, a Safe Way to Salvation* (1638).

CHOIR Used in two ways. (1) Architectural. Another word for the *chancel or *sanctuary. The place in a church where the *clergy sit. (2) Musical. The group (usually robed) that sings alone or leads the congregation in singing in worship. Ancient *cathedrals have choir schools to ensure a choir each day for the singing in divine service.

CHOREPISCOPUS (Gk. "a country bishop"). A *bishop of a country area who is subject to a bishop in the nearby town or city. Such bishops were numerous in Asia Minor in the 4th century, but their functions were taken over by *priests and *archdeacons.

CHRISM (Gk. *chrio*, "to anoint"). The holy oil (a mixture of olive oil and balsam) used especially in the *sacraments of *baptism, *confirmation, and *ordination in Roman Catholic and *Orthodox churches. It *symbolizes the gift and action of the Holy *Spirit. It is also used in other ceremonies of dedication—of churches, *chalices, church bells, etc.

CHRISMATION A practice in the *Eastern churches that follows *baptism. The anointing of the newly baptized with oil and the *sign of the cross on forehead, eyes, nostrils, lips, ears, breast, hands, and feet. As this is done the *priest says, "the seal of the gift of the Holy *Spirit." Sometimes called "chrism."

CHRIST (Gk. *Christos*; Heb. *Messiah*; Lat. *Christus*; "anointed one"). The name given by Jews to the One whom they believed *God would send as their King and *Savior. He would be *God's agent in bringing into being the new age of *righteousness and peace. Thus this title summed up the expectations expressed in a variety of ways (e.g., Son of David; *Son of Man; *Servant of the Lord) in the Hebrew *Scriptures.

The disciples of *Jesus came to recognize with the help of divine illumination that he was the Christ (Matt 16:16–20). After his *resurrection they were confident that he truly was the Christ, and they proclaimed this message to the Jews (Acts 2:22–36). So it became common for the early Christians to speak of Jesus, the Christ, which was shortened to *Jesus Christ or Christ Jesus (Rom 1:1–4). The church in its worship and the theologians in their teaching tended to use "Christ" as the one word that contained the other names and titles of the One they served and worshiped. They knew that he could only be the Christ because he was preexistent as the *Son of God; thus Christ came to include the idea of preexistence and also of true humanity as Jesus of Nazareth. One title that was encouraged and preserved as either a synonym or as a complementary description alongside Christ was "*Lord" (Gk. *Kyrios*), which was particularly meaningful to people living in a Greek *culture.

Thus it has become common for theologians to look at the Lord Jesus Christ in terms of (1) the *person of Christ and (2) the *work of Christ. The former is a study of his preexistence as Son of God, his *incarnation, and his present heavenly identity. The latter is a study of what he did and what he now does for the *salvation of the world. The two themes are separated in conceptual analysis, but of course in the one Christ there was no distinction between who he was (is) and what he did (does), for the two are inextricably intertwined. See also CHRISTOLOGY; EXALTATION OF CHRIST; HUMILIATION OF CHRIST; KINGSHIP OF CHRIST; LORD; MESSIAH; PRIEST, CHRIST AS; PROPHET, CHRIST AS; SON OF GOD.

CHRISTADELPHIANS A *sect founded in 1848 by John Thomas (1805–1871), a physician who had left England for America in 1832 and had settled in New York. Formerly a member of the *Disciples of Christ, he left because of differences concerning *doctrine and organization. The Christadelphians ("Brothers of Christ") view the *Bible as their sole authority; reject the *orthodox view of the *Trinity and *Christ's expiatory death; stress good works; and look for the return of Christ, who will reign in Jerusalem, at which time the saved will dwell with him and the wicked will be annihilated. British membership may be about 25,000; the figure for the U.S. is slightly less.

CHRISTENING (from the Anglo-Saxon *cristnian*, meaning "naming with a *Christian name"). Another word for *infant baptism.

CHRISTIAN, CHRISTIANITY According to Acts 11:26, "Christian" was a name given to *disciples of *Jesus to distinguish them from Jews and other religious people. Today it has the same function, distinguishing the follower of *Christ from adherents and members of other religious and antireligious groups. Christianity is that to which Christians are committed, the Christian *religion and Christian *faith.

CHRISTIAN BRETHREN See PLYMOUTH BRETHREN.

CHRISTIAN CHURCH (Disciples of Christ). Group founded by Thomas and Alexander Campbell, Barton Stone, and Walter Scott on the American frontier in the early nineteenth century. The "Christian" group of Stone merged with the "Disciples" group of Alexander Campbell in 1832 to become the Christian Church (Disciples of Christ) as it is called today, although both names are still used. The *Churches of Christ split from this group over the questions of missionary society organization and instrumental music in the church. In 1968 the formerly congregational church was totally reorganized as a representative church body. Currently it has 1.26 million members in the U.S. and Canada.

CHRISTIAN ENDEAVOR SOCIETY A nondenominational youth organization begun in Portland, Maine, in 1881 by Congregational minister F. E. *Clark. Within ten years of its beginning it had a half million members. Each society is part of a local church. Its weekly meetings are conducted by and for young people. The movement's aim is "to lead young people to commit themselves to *Jesus Christ as *Lord; to bring them into the life of the church; to sustain and train them for the service of *Christ; and to release them through all channels of human activity in the service of God and man." The movement has spread to seventy-five countries and was reported as having a membership of about three million.

CHRISTIAN REFORMED CHURCH American Protestant *denomination. Originating in a disagreement among Dutch immigrants in 1857, it picked up two other groups of *dissenters (1882, 1890). An orthodox Calvinist body, the church adheres to documents such as the *Heidelberg Catechism (1563), the *Canons of the Synod of Dort (1618–1619), and the *Belgic Confession (1561). Dutch has been superseded by English as the language used in services. Its current membership is about 287,000 in 750 churches.

CHRISTIAN SCIENCE A religious body that developed out of a society formed by Mary Baker *Eddy in Massachusetts in 1875. Its newspaper is *The Christian Science Monitor*, and it has more than two thousand churches in the U.S. alone. Christian Science, as expounded by Mrs. Eddy, holds that "nothing is real and *eternal; nothing is *spirit—but *God and His ideal; *evil has no reality." Matter and *evil, *sin and sickness, sorrow and death, have no reality—except what man gives them. God is viewed as Spirit and as All in all. "*Healing" consists in having spiritual understanding that disease is not actually real, that it has no reality.

CHRISTIAN SOCIALISM A term used from the mid-19th century to describe various movements that sought to apply *Christian principles to modern society. Among its advocates in England were J. M. F. Ludlow, J. F. D. *Maurice, and Charles *Kingsley. They wrote against social injustices, established a working men's college in London, sponsored cooperative workshops, and organized practical relief work.

CHRISTIAN AND MISSIONARY ALLIANCE A body of independent *evangelical churches in North America. It began in the work of A. B. *Simpson, who left the *Presbyterian Church for an independent ministry in New York City. His Christian Alliance was founded in 1887, his International Missionary Alliance in 1889, and the two combined in 1897. The C&MA, which has about 193,000 members in North America, considers itself interdenominational, a movement among all Christians, stressing *Christ the "*Savior, Sanctifier, Healer, and Coming King." It has an extensive *missions work, concentrating on areas neglected by other *missionary agencies. Currently, there are about 4,500 churches with more than 332,000 members in forty-six nations and territories.

CHRISTMAS The festival commemorating the birth of *Jesus. In all churches, except the Armenian (who observe it on January 6) it is held on December 25. At the center of the celebration is the service of *worship (*Eucharist, or *Mass) proclaiming the birth; thus we get the name "Christmass."

CHRISTOCENTRIC Any system of thought of which *Christ is the center. Thus a *systematic *theology or system of *Christian *ethics that is built around the person of, or the fact of, Christ in a self-conscious way is Christocentric. Sometimes Matthew 11:27 is given as a *justification of this method.

CHRISTOLOGY The *doctrine of *Christ or the study of Christ. In particular the study of precisely who *Jesus, called the Christ, is. This study usually proceeds by one of two methods. "Christology from above" begins with the idea of the *eternal *Son of God who took on human *nature and became incarnate. This is the traditional method, and it is given a biblical basis in John 1:1ff. "Christology from below" starts with the fact of Jesus of Nazareth and what he said and did. From this basis it makes deductions as to his true and full identity. This method is very common in modern *theology, but it rarely appears to lead to a *doctrine of Christ that affirms that he is wholly *God and wholly man in one person. Classical christology is stated in the Definition of the Council of *Chalcedon (451).

CHRISTOTOKOS (Gk. "the Christ-bearer"). Title used by Nestorius (d. 451) to describe *Mary as the mother of Jesus. He preferred this title to *Theotokos (God-bearer). The Council of *Ephesus (431) condemned him as a heretic.

CHRISTUS VICTOR "*Christ the Victor." The theme of Christ as victorious over *sin, death, *hell, and *Satan runs through the whole of *Christian devotion and literature. He was especially victorious in what he did in his atoning death and glorious *resurrection and *ascension. He overcame all the enemies of humanity so that friendship and *fellowship between *God and humankind could be wholly restored and maintained.

CHRYSOSTOM, JOHN (c. 347–407). *Patriarch of Constantinople. Born in Antioch, he became a *hermit about 373 and damaged his health by self-imposed discipline. He returned to Antioch in 381, was ordained, and gained a reputation for *preaching that led to the description "golden-mouthed" (*chrysostomos*), which was was attached to his *Christian name in the 6th century. Appointed patriarch in 398, his reforming zeal led to his being exiled twice on specious charges to which a rigged Synod of the *Oak (403) gave credence. John died in exile, but his cause was vindicated three decades later.

CHURCH ARMY An organization of lay *evangelists in the Church of *England. It began in 1882 after a Kensington curate, Wilson Carlile (1847–1942) began to train lay preachers. Church Army officers (men and women) serve *parish churches or work in specialized ministries (armed services, prisoners, children, elderly). Some serve as *missionaries overseas. The Church Army has autonomous branches in the U.S., Canada, New Zealand, and Australia.

CHURCH EXPECTANT, MILITANT, TRIUMPHANT The whole church of *God consists of those who are alive in *Christ, those who have died in Christ, and those who are yet to be born to believe in Christ. This totality may be called the catholic church. The church militant is the church on earth fighting against *sin and *Satan and for *righteousness. The church triumphant is the church in God's presence in *heaven, the company of those who have died in the *faith of Christ. And the church expectant is the company of the faithful (as Roman Catholics explain) passing through *purgatory on their way to heaven.

CHURCH GOVERNMENT The method used to govern a local church, *denomination, national church, or international church. Examples are the episcopal (in which *bishops have the final authority), *presbyterian (with a series of church courts beginning with that of the local congregation), and congregational (where the democratic vote of the members is final). In reality most systems include features found in others. Most scholars agree that there is no clear model or teaching in the *NT commending a particular type of government that is applicable to all times and places.

CHURCH GROWTH MOVEMENT Contemporary Protestant movement stressing numerical growth in a church as an index to its vitality and the fulfillment of its divine *mission. It is closely associated with C. Peter Wagner, Donald McGavran, Win Arn, and the Fuller Theological Seminary Graduate School of World Mission. Principles of growth have been delineated, such as emphasizing the need for homogeneity in a congregation; use of the *laity in *evangelism; contextualizing the *gospel message; and beginning evangelism among families and friends of believers. The movement has been criticized as being more interested in the quantity, rather than the quality, of growth.

CHURCH OF THE BRETHREN Found in the U.S. with some 175,000 members, they trace their origins to German Pietist protest in 1708 against the *state church at Schwarzenau. They came to America in 1719 to escape persecution. They are pacifists; they oppose *oaths, worldliness in every form, and secret societies; and they hold to *believers' *baptism, *anointing the sick, and congregational *church government.

CHURCH OF GOD (Anderson, Ind.). A movement rather than a denomination, consisting of a loose coalition of churches with a common theological position that combines the Wesleyan Holiness tradition with the Anabaptist believers' church view. The group has a national office and operates several schools, including Anderson University and Anderson Seminary. Since it does not consider itself a denomination, there is no formal membership; the number of people affiliated in the U.S. is estimated at approximately 190,000, the number worldwide at twice that.

CHURCH OF GOD (Cleveland, Tenn.). One of the largest Pentecostal denominations, with a membership of 1,650,000. Founded in 1886 as the Christian Union, a number of its members experienced glossolalia and healings in 1896. The parallel experiences that were reported from California, especially from the *Azusa Street Revival, encouraged the small church to preach aggressively the baptism in the Holy Spirit. The first overseer of the church was A. J. Tomlinson, who later formed the Church of God of Prophecy.

CHURCH OF GOD IN CHRIST The largest black North American Pentecostal body, led for over a half-century by Charles *Mason. The COGIC saw phenomenal growth in the sixties and seventies, from fewer than 400,000 members to more than 3,700,000. Its leaders have been accepting of the charismatic movement, a stance unique among black denominations.

CHURCHES OF THE BRETHREN See BRETHREN (DUNKERS).

CHURCHES OF CHRIST (U.K.) Originating partly from *Glasites and Scottish *Baptists in the early 19th century, they are *congregationalist in *church government, *evangelical in *theology, and emphasize a special *grace conferred at *baptism by immersion on *confession of *faith. *The Lord's Supper is the central act of the *Sunday morning service, *Christian reunion is one of their chief interests, and the name "Campbellites" sometimes given to them reflects the link with the *Disciples of Christ. The British churches, numbering about 3,500 members in 1981, united at that time with the *United Reformed Church.

CHURCHES OF CHRIST (U.S.) Made up of autonomous churches with their roots in the *Disciples of Christ, they have been separately identified since 1906, partly on the basis of opposing organized *missions and the use of instrumental music. *Sunday *worship still debars the latter, but individual congregations now sponsor extensive *missionary work. The churches have no documented creed, regard the *Bible as the sole *rule of *faith and practice, and do not take part in *ecumenical activities. Currently there are about 2.5 million members in more than 17,000 independent congregations.

CHURCHES OF GOD In the U.S., the name is used in one form or another by more than two hundred independent religious bodies. A large number of these is *Pentecostal, among them such substantial bodies as the *Church of God (Cleveland, Tenn.), which has some 1,650,000 members, and the *Church of God in Christ, with a reported membership of 3,709,661. Other Churches of God stand in the Wesleyan Holiness tradition, among them the *Church of God (Anderson, Ind.). In Britain the name came from a split in the *Plymouth Brethren in 1892, with a further division in the breakaway group in 1904. A group that is generally rejected as unorthodox is the Worldwide Church of God, founded by Herbert W. Armstrong.

CHURCH OFFICERS Those who hold pastoral or administrative office in the local or larger church unit. Their titles (and the precise meaning of them) vary from group to group. Among the more common are *archbishop, *bishop, *archdeacon, *priest, *deacon, *deaconess, *elder and *pastor.

CIBORIUM (Gk. *kiborion*, the hollow seedcase of the Egyptian water lily and by deduction a drinking cup). In the church it has two meanings. (1) The canopy over an *altar and supported by four columns (also *called *baldacchino*). (2) A vessel with a lid used to hold a large number of wafer breads for the celebration of the *Eucharist.

CINCTURE (Lat. *cinctura,* "a girdle"). A long cord used to hold the *alb at the waist.

CIRCUIT RIDER An itinerant Methodist preacher on the American frontier. John *Wesley had developed the practice of itinerancy in England, and Francis *Asbury adapted it to American conditions about 1771. Circuit riding involved traveling long distances for weeks at a time, thus calling for a degree of fitness and dedication. Circuit riders made a significant contribution to the religious and moral life of the frontier. By the mid-19th century more churches had been established, and the need for itinerant preachers had declined.

CIRCUMCISION The cutting off of the foreskin of the male penis. It was a sign of the *covenant between *God and Abraham (Gen 17:9–14). The church did not maintain it, deciding that it was not obligatory for Gentiles (Acts 15:6ff.). Paul opposed the imposition of it on Gentiles (Gal 5:6; 6:15) and saw it as fulfilled in the cleansing of the *heart (Rom 2:29; Phil 3:3). Thus it is practiced by Christians now for medical reasons and has no religious significance.

CIRCUMINCESSION A Latin equivalent of the Greek **perichoresis*, meaning *coinherence. A technical term to indicate that the three persons of the Holy *Trinity interpenetrate each other. What the Father is and does must in some sense (difficult to define) be what the Son and the Holy *Spirit are and do, for they all share one Godhead. The biblical basis for this is sought in John 10:28–38.

CISTERCIANS A monastic *order founded by *Robert of Molesme (c. 1027–1111) and others at Citeaux (hence the name), France, in 1098. The impetus came from a group of *Benedictine monks dissatisfied with the easy life at their *abbey of Molesme and seeking a return to a strict interpretation of the Rule of Benedict. Included in the new regulations, which were developed conspicuously under the third *abbot (1109–1133), Stephen *Harding, were a simplified *liturgy; a rigorous *asceticism of life, the rejection of feudal revenues, and the reintroduction of manual labor. The *order was greatly boosted by *Bernard of Clairvaux, who joined it about 1112 and at whose death in 1153 the number of abbeys had sprung to 338 all over Europe. A decline set in toward the end of that century, but the 16th and 17th centuries saw reform movements, particularly through the breakaway by the *Trappists in 1664. Both orders still prosper and have experienced a *revival of literary work.

CITY OF GOD The title of a famous book by Augustine of Hippo (354–430). In it the city of *God (human society controlled by the *love of God) is contrasted with the city of man/earth/*devil (human society controlled by self-love).

CIVIL DISOBEDIENCE An act contrary to laws deemed not in the best interest of the *state or its citizens. Usually such acts are nonviolent, done on the basis of principle and with the person so acting willing to suffer whatever consequences might arise, even to the point of death. Such acts have occurred as a regular part of church life from the very beginning, especially in repressive societies. However, Dr. Martin Luther *King, Jr., showed that it might be necessary in democracies as well in order to awaken the *conscience of a nation.

CIVIL RELIGION. That set of generalized beliefs, values, *rites, and *symbols that binds persons of diverse ecclesiastical *faiths together into a political unit, providing a basis for the exercise of power, as well as a criticism of it. Sometimes this secular or public *religion makes reference to a transcendent dimension, in which case it overlaps with traditional religion, sometimes not, running the danger of absolutizing the *state. Widespread discussion surrounding this concept arose in America in the 1950s and 60s, but its roots may be traced back to antiquity.

CLAPHAM SECT A group of Evangelicals, living mainly in Clapham, England, who during the period 1790 to 1830 worked to abolish *slavery and to promote missions at home and abroad. Among them were William *Wilberforce and Henry *Venn. Some were members of Parliament and promoted legislation for prison reform and against such things as cruel sports and gambling. They espoused many philanthropic and educational causes. Evidently they were not given the name Clapham Sect until the early part of the 19th century.

CLARENDON CODE A name commonly but inaccurately given to legislation passed during a four-year period from 1661. Directed against English *dissenters, it comprised four acts: the *Corporation Act (1661), the *Act of Uniformity (1662), the *Conventicle Act (1664), and the *Five Mile Act (1665).

CLARK, FRANCIS EDWARD (1851–1927). Founder of the *Christian Endeavor movement. He was *pastor of Williston (Congregational) Church in Portland, Maine (where he founded the movement in 1881), then spent four years at Phillips Church, South Boston, before giving his whole time to Christian Endeavor, whose magazine he edited and on whose business he traveled the world.

CLARKE, ADAM (c. 1762–1832). Methodist theologian. Born in northern Ireland and educated in Bristol. At John *Wesley's instigation, he became a Methodist preacher in 1782. From 1805 he lived in London and three times presided over the Methodist conference. Clarke was a remarkably versatile scholar. Though generally orthodox, he questioned *Christ's *eternal sonship while accepting his divinity. He produced an eight-volume *Bible commentary (1810–1826) and was much in demand as a preacher throughout the British Isles.

CLARKE, SAMUEL (1675–1729). English theologian and philosopher. Born in Norwich and educated at Cambridge, before he was thirty he had written *A Demonstration of the Being and Attributes of God* and *A Discourse Concerning the Unchangeable Obligations of Natural Religion,* the former of which drew fire from David Hume. Chaplain to Queen *Anne from 1706, Clarke was also a friend of Isaac Newton's, whose mathematical views he espoused. A later work of Clarke's, *Scripture Doctrine of the Trinity* (1712), caused a furor and brought an accusation of *Arianism against him.

CLARKE, WILLIAM NEWTON (1840–1912). American theologian. Baptist *pastor and teacher, in 1890 he became professor of *Christian *theology at Colgate Theological Seminary. Eight years later he published his *Outline of Christian Theology,* which was regarded as a major work in liberal circles. It has been described as a combination of Christian theology and evolutionary thinking.

CLARKSON, THOMAS (1760–1846). Abolitionist. A Cambridge graduate and *deacon of the Church of *England, he determined to give his life to the abolition of the slave trade. His published writings brought him into alliance with William *Wilberforce and others and earned him the support of leading statesmen of the time. He traveled around the ports gathering evidence, and though powerful vested interests moved against his cause, he and his colleagues were rewarded in 1807 when Parliament passed a bill for the abolition of slave trade and in 1833 when *slavery itself was abolished. His two-volume history of the trade (1808) contributed greatly toward its condemnation in other major countries.

CLASS MEETING A weekly gathering within *Methodism begun by John *Wesley in 1742 for the understanding of the *faith and the deepening of the spiritual life and for the collecting of church funds. Members divide into groups under a lay leader for "*fellowship in *Christian experience.

CLAVER, PETER (1581–1654). Spanish *Jesuit *missionary. Catalan by birth, he became a Jesuit in 1601 and went to Cartagena, Colombia, in 1610 to alleviate the plight of African slaves. It is estimated that this "*Apostle of the Negroes" converted and baptized more than 300,000 people by 1651.

CLEMENT I (CLEMENT OF ROME) (latter 1st century). Various church *fathers hold him to have been the third pope after Peter, to have been consecrated by Peter himself, and to have been a contemporary of the apostles and identified in Phil 4:3. *Eusebius of Caesarea gives Clement's *pontificate as A.D. 92–101. He is thought by some scholars to have been the author of certain writings and to have been martyred, but nothing is known about him with certainty.

CLEMENT V (c. 1260–1314). Pope from 1305. French by birth and formerly *archbishop of Bordeaux, he was elected through the influence of *Philip IV and was the first pope to make his residence in France, thus beginning the *Babylonian Captivity. Philip found Clement more pliable than his predecessor in the *papacy, *Boniface VIII. During his *pontificate, the church lost ground to secular authority, the *Knights Templars were suppressed, a branch of the *Franciscans was charged with *heresy, and anti-imperial policy was pursued. Clement was guilty of nepotism and *simony.

CLEMENT VII (1342–1394). The first *antipope of the *Great Schism in the Western church. Known also as Robert of Geneva, and formerly *archbishop of Cambrai, he led the *cardinals who opposed *Urban VI's election and was himself elected by them in 1378. Europe divided over the rival claimants, and Clement had the support of France and the *Eastern Church, among others. Clement died, still having powerful support and still convinced that he was the true pope.

CLEMENT VII (1478–1534). Pope from 1523. He was a cousin of *Leo X, who made him *archbishop of Florence and a *cardinal (1513). After his election, Clement was at first uncertain whether to support Francis I of France or the emperor *Charles V, and his final choice of the former led to the sack of Rome by imperial soldiers in 1527 and to the *pope's imprisonment for a time. Clement forbade *Henry VIII's remarriage, dealt weakly with growing *Protestantism, and advanced the interests of his own family.

CLEMENT VIII (1536–1605). Pope from 1592. A Florentine by birth and known for integrity and diligence, he was concerned with the political troubles between France and Spain and with the promotion of the *Counter-Reformation. He helped rejuvenate the church in France and tried to help Roman Catholics in England and Scotland. He shrewdly appointed *Francis de Sales as *bishop of Geneva to win back the erring Swiss, furthered the cause of *missions, and ordered a new edition of the *Vulgate.

CLEMENT XI (1649–1721). Pope from 1700. A versatile scholar and former papally appointed governor in Italy, he was caught up in the political strife leading to the War of the Spanish Succession (1701–1714), was faced with both religious revolt and *heresy in France, and because of inept handling threatened to ruin the *missionary outreach in China. His missionary plans in other areas were more successful.

CLEMENT XII (1652–1740). Pope from 1730. Born into an influential Florentine family, he suffered ill health and total blindness for much of his *pontificate. He jailed a scandalous *cardinal, carried out extensive relief work, and had fair success in confronting clerical and doctrinal problems in France. He encouraged *missionary enterprises (except for continuing Clement XI's disastrous policy on China), and forbade Roman Catholics to join the growing *Freemasonry movement on pain of *excommunication.

CLEMENT XIII (1693–1769). Pope from 1758. Venetian by birth and a former civil governor appointed by the *pope, he was elected at a time when strong antipapal tides were running among European rulers, especially in France and Germany. The attack came largely against the *Jesuits, who during a nine-year period from 1759 were expelled from Portugal, France, and Spain, and their respective dominions—Naples, Sicily, and Parma. Clement, despite strong threats, refused demands for the worldwide suppression of the *order.

CLEMENT XIV (1705–1774). Pope from 1769. His *pontificate was dominated by incessant pressure put upon him by France, Spain, and Portugal, who wanted the *Jesuits suppressed. Finally Clement yielded in 1773, ostensibly in order to restore peace to the church and because the Jesuits could not achieve their original ends. Clement was severely disturbed because of this decision, which was not reversed until 1814. He received seven *Nestorian *bishops into union with Rome in 1771 and abandoned official papal support for the exiled English Stuarts.

CLEMENT OF ALEXANDRIA (c. 150–c. 215). Early *Christian scholar. Born probably in Athens, he became head of the catechetical school of Alexandria in 190. Twelve years later, the imperial persecution forced him to flee to Jerusalem where he was welcomed by the *bishop, *Alexander, his former student, with whom he remained until his death. He wrote works to commend the Christian *faith, particularly to those with a classical background, to defend *orthodoxy against *Gnosticism and to deal with practical problems of the Christian life.

CLEMENT OF ROME See CLEMENT I.

CLERGY, CLERICAL (Gk. *kleros*, "portion," "inheritance," "lot"). The modern meaning is developed from 1 Peter 5:3 where the plural, *kleroi*, appears. A clergyman has a *pastoral sphere, a flock to tend. Since *clergy were often the only literate people in medieval society the word clerical came to mean that which is done by the clerk—writing. A clergyman is thus a clerk in *holy orders, a man with a particular portion and task from *God.

CLERMONT, COUNCIL OF (1095). An assembly that made various decisions on church reform and other matters but chiefly remembered because it was there that *Urban II launched the first of the *Crusades against the Muslims.

CLINICAL THEOLOGY The study of the relationship of psychic, mental, spiritual, and emotional factors as they affect the well-being of people. Such study requires the cooperation of a trained *pastor and medical experts.

CLOUD OF UNKNOWING Classic book on the mystical experience. Written by an anonymous author of the 14th century, this work describes the work of contemplation that recognizes that all language and images about God limit both his Being and our awareness of him. It is a way of quieting the thoughts and centering in the spirit which alone can come to discern and know the Invisible and Unknowable One. It is meditating on nothing but the Cloud of God's Presence, which is intellectually unknowable; it is being and becoming supremely open to the working of God's grace upon the person, to be attentive to God without effortful "work" or human strain. In the 20th century this contemplative practice has been popularized by Basil Pennington in *Centering Prayer*.

CLOVIS (465–511). Founder of the Frankish kingdom. He had conquered northern Gaul by 494, was converted to *Christianity about 496, and later further consolidated his dominions by defeating the Arian king of the Visigoths in 507. The first national church *synod, held at Orleans in 511, accepted Clovis's supremacy. He made his capital at Paris and laid the foundations of the modern French nation.

CLOWES, WILLIAM (1780–1851). Cofounder with Hugh *Bourne of the *Primitive Methodist Church. Converted in 1805, he combined *preaching with his trade as a potter in Staffordshire, but in 1810 he was expelled from mainline *Methodism for supporting innovations. He gained the support of some local Methodists who hired him as full-time preacher. He combined with Hugh Bourne and his group to form the Primitive Methodist Church in 1811.

COCCEIUS, JOHANNES (1603–1669). Professor of *theology at Leiden and *covenant theologian. Cocceius balked at the prevailing views of his day that sought to impose foreign presuppositions on the *Scriptures, whether Cartesian, *Reformed, or Lutheran, and postulated that Scripture should be interpreted by Scripture.

CODEX A Latin word describing sheets of vellum or papyrus laid on top of each other to form a book. This replaced the older scroll. Important manuscripts of the *NT are in codex form, e.g., Codex Alexandrinus.

COFFIN, HENRY SLOANE (1877–1954). American *Presbyterian minister and educator. After serving two charges in New York City (1900–1926) he was appointed president of Union Theological Seminary in the same city (1926–1945). One of the most eloquent preachers of his time, he traveled widely and was a keen ecumenist and a liberal theologian of marked social concern. He authored twenty books.

COINHERENCE The mutual indwelling of the three persons of the Trinity. See also CIRCUMINCESSION, PERICHORESIS.

COKE, THOMAS (1747–1814). Methodist *bishop. A Welsh-born Oxford graduate, he was dismissed from his Anglican curacy for Methodist sympathies. He became a Methodist preacher in 1778, presided over the first Irish Methodist conference in 1782, urged sponsorship of foreign *missions, joined John *Wesley in ordaining Methodist ministers for America, and himself went to Baltimore in 1784 as superintendent (a title the 1787 American conference changed to bishop—an enactment of which Wesley disapproved). His outspoken opposition to *slavery aroused hostility. He vainly proposed an Anglican-Methodist union in America (1792) and England (1799) and the establishment of bishops in English *Methodism. After much transatlantic travel he remained mostly in England from 1803 but died on board ship in the Indian Ocean while going to establish a mission in India.

COLENSO, JOHN WILLIAM (1814–1883). *Bishop of Natal. A rector in Norfolk before his *consecration in 1853, he had a remarkable ministry among Zulus, but in dealing with their simple questions he began to doubt the historical accuracy of the *Pentateuch. For his modernistic *theology, his critical attitude toward the *OT, his rejection of the *doctrine of *eternal *punishment, and his toleration of *polygamy among the converts, he was found guilty of *heresy (1864) but was acquitted on appeal to the privy council in London (1865). The *archbishop of Capetown nonetheless excommunicated him in 1866 and later appointed a new bishop, but Colenso remained in legal possession of diocesan property and income until his death.

COLET, JOHN (c. 1466–1519). Dean of St. Paul's. Son of a former lord mayor of London, he studied extensively at home and abroad before returning to lecture at Oxford in 1497. A friend of *Erasmus and Thomas *More, he was appointed dean of St.

Paul's in 1505 and soon afterwards founded St. Paul's School where boys could receive a good *Christian and classical education. A strong critic of worldliness in the church and of *clerical misbehavior, Colet was a leading humanist who promoted *Renaissance *culture in England.

COLIGNY, GASPARD DE (1519–1572). French *Huguenot leader. A distinguished soldier who was made admiral of France in 1552, he gave public support to the *Reformation from 1560 and demanded religious *toleration for fellow Protestants in France, though it was said that his chief motivation was the maintenance of public order. At the instigation of Catherine de' Medici, the death of the Huguenot leaders was ordered, the Massacre of *Bartholomew's Day began, and de Coligny was among the victims.

COLLECT A short set *prayer for use on particular days and at particular moments in divine *worship. There are collects for every *Sunday of the year and for each special feast or commemoration.

COLLEGIALISM The view expressed in the 17th and 18th centuries that church and state are voluntary organizations (*collegia*) and that in each is vested appropriate final power and authority. Thus the church cannot be told what to believe and how to administer internal discipline by the civil authority. An opposing view is *territorialism.

COLLEGIALITY (Lat. *collegium*, "a body"). An assembly of bishops of the Roman Catholic Churrch is sometimes called a college. Collegiality affirms that they are not merely a collection of individuals but that they corporately represent the whole church and make decisions for all.

COLLIER, JEREMY (1650–1726). Anglican clergyman. Imprisoned twice for supporting the deposed *James II and outlawed for absolving two would-be assassins of *William III, he nevertheless returned to London in 1697. By attacking immorality in stage plays, Collier produced a notable controversy with William Congreve and others, which led to much-needed reform. He became "*bishop of the *Nonjurors" in 1713 and wrote a church history of Great Britain.

COLORS, LITURGICAL The use of different colors for the seasons of the ecclesiastical year. There is no common rule applying to all churches. That of the Roman Catholic Church is as follows: white for *Easter and *Christmas, red for *Palm Sunday, *Good Friday, and *Whitsunday, violet for *Advent and *Lent, rose for Gaudete Sunday (Advent III) and Laetare Sunday (Lent IV), and green for general use.

COLUMBA (c. 521–597). Irish *abbot. Of a noble family in County Donegal, he was ordained about 551, founded churches and *monasteries, then settled in 563 with twelve followers on the Scottish island of Iona, aiming to use it as a base for the *conversion of the mainland. He trained *priests, evangelized among all classes, established more *monastic houses, and is regarded as the most illustrious Irish churchman of the 6th century.

COLUMBANUS (COLUMBAN) (c. 543–615). *Celtic church leader and scholar. Born in Leinster, he left Ireland with twelve monks about 590 and established three *monasteries in Burgundy which became centers of learning. He was expelled from France for denouncing the vices in church and state, and he finally founded a monastery at Bobbio in northern Italy. A strong supporter of Celtic church practices and a vigorous defender of *orthodoxy, Columbanus was also a notable expositor and poet.

COMENIUS, JAN AMOS (1592–1670). Czech educational reformer and religious leader. An ordained *priest of the *Bohemian Brethren, he left the country and settled in Poland when the law proscribed all non-Roman Catholic *clergy. He became rector of the gymnasium at Leszno, and soon his work and writings became widely known. On a visit to London (1641–1642) he unsuccessfully suggested the establishment of a pansophic college, and he was one of the first modern advocates of education for women. He later reformed the Swedish and Hungarian educational systems. When Leszno was burned in 1656, Comenius lost many valuable manuscripts. He settled in Amsterdam for the rest of his life and there produced many of his books. He exercised a profound religious influence and strove unceasingly for the unification of Christendom.

COMMANDMENTS, THE TEN The commandments given by *God to Moses on Mount Sinai for the people of *Israel to obey (Exod 20:1–7). *Jesus accepted them as reflecting the moral demands of God (Matt 5:17). And they have been used in the church as a summary of the *duty of human beings to *God, their Creator. The precise function of these laws in the life of the committed *Christian has been debated, especially between Lutherans and Calvinists. This debate centers on what is known as the third use of the law.

COMMANDMENTS OF THE CHURCH The five duties that are traditionally said to be required of Roman Catholics of seven years and above: (1) to keep *Sunday and holy days, (2) to attend the *Eucharist on these days, (3) to *fast on prescribed days, (4) to confess *sins to a *priest at least once a year, and (5) to receive Holy *Communion in the period of *Easter.

COMMON GRACE The goodness and kindness of *God to all people everywhere in terms of natural blessings (Matt 5:45). See also GRACE.

COMMON PRAYER, THE BOOK OF The one official service book of the Church of *England from 1662 to 1980 and of the Protestant Episcopal Church in America from 1789 (when a new book, the Alternative Service Book, was made optional). It contains the daily services (*matins and *evening prayer), the Holy *Communion, the services for *baptism, the psalms, the *collects, *Sunday readings, and other material.

COMMON SENSE PHILOSOPHY Known also as Scottish realism. It was an attempt to refute the philosophy of both David Hume (1711–1776) and Immanuel *Kant (1724–1804), for their teaching was a threat to the philosophical foundations of the Calvinistic *faith of the Scottish church. Expounded by Thomas Reid (1710–1796), it became the dominant philosophy at Princeton College and Seminary in New Jersey. Thus it was used by the great Calvinistic divines (e.g., A. A. *Alexander and Charles *Hodge) as the basis of their exposition of *Christian *doctrine and their interpretation of the *Bible.

COMMUNICATIO ESSENTIAE A technical phrase. The communication of the *essence (*substance) of the Godhead eternally from the Father to the Son and from the Father (and the Son) to the Holy *Spirit. See also TRINITY, DOCTRINE OF THE.

COMMUNICATIO IDIOMATUM (Lat. for the sharing or communication of attributes). *Jesus Christ is described in classic *theology as having two *natures, human and divine. So as the one *person possesses as his very own both deity and humanity, it can be said for example that the *Son of God died on the *cross. As man he really and truly died, but as *God he did not die. However, in the *communicatio idiomatum* it is possible to say that the *Son of God died. Thus the communication of idioms is a way of expressing the mystery of the *Incarnation.

COMMUNICATIO OPERATIONUM (Lat., the sharing or communication of operations). Expounded by Lutheran theologians (e.g., Martin *Chemnitz [d. 1586]) to express their understanding of the presence of *Christ in the bread and wine of Holy *Communion. They spoke of a transference of ubiquity from the divine to the human *nature of Christ with the result that the *symbols of the humanity of Christ contained the divine, spiritual presence of Christ.

COMMUNION, HOLY Either, in general, the whole service of the *Lord's Supper (*Eucharist) or in particular, the reception of the consecrated bread and wine. The latter is the primary meaning, and the former is a development from it. In Protestant churches, Communion is received by both *clergy and *laity in two kinds, bread and wine. In the Roman Catholic Church, while the clergy receive in two kinds, the laity often receive in one kind only, bread. In the *Orthodox churches the clergy receive in both kinds, and the laity receive bread on which wine has been sprinkled. All churches believe that the receiving of the bread (or bread and wine) symbolizes a spiritual communion with the *Lord *Jesus and with other Christians. See also CONSUBSTANTIATION, EUCHARIST, RECEPTIONISM, TRANSUBSTANTIATION, VIRTUALISM, ZWINGLIANISM.

COMMUNION OF SAINTS. A phrase from the *Apostles' Creed translating the Latin *communio sanctorum*. Since *sanctorum* can refer to things or persons, the phrase has two possible meanings: (1) a communion in "*holy things"—*fellowship in the *Lord's Supper and other means of *grace; (2) a fellowship between all Christians of all times and places because they are all in spiritual union with *Christ through the *Spirit.

COMMUNION TOKENS Evidence of fitness to receive *Communion. Sometimes inscribed metal tokens, less often written tickets, they were used in England during *Henry VIII's reign and in France during the second half of the 16th century. In the Church of *Scotland they were widely used from the *Reformation, a custom that survived into modern times in remoter parts of the country.

COMPARATIVE STUDY OF RELIGION The study and comparison of the various religions of the world. This is an immense task that not only requires vast knowledge but also some experience of the religions as living realities. Thus comparison often only amounts to a comparison of one aspect or another (e.g., ideas of *God, types of *prayer, and views on survival after death). There is a variety of *Christian approaches to this study. See also RELIGIONSGESCHICHTLICHE SCHULE.

COMPASSION The sense of pity and concern felt for those in need. *Jesus often displayed it (Matt 9:36; 14:14; 15:32; Mark 6:34; 8:2; Luke 7:13; 10:33; 15:20). *God is the source of *compassion (James 5:11), and Christians are called to be compassionate (Col 3:12).

COMPLINE (LITURGY OF THE HOURS) The last of the *traditional services of the day in the Western church. It is made up of a *hymn, *canticle(s), and psalms and is said before going to rest. The corresponding service in the Greek Orthodox Church is the *Apodeipnon* (lit. "after supper").

CONCELEBRATION The recitation in unison of the central part of the *Eucharist by several *priests or a *bishop and priests. Only one breaks the bread, but the others mime the part. Since 1963 the practice has become widespread in *Roman Catholicism but is rarely used in Protestant churches.

CONCILIARISM The teaching that an *ecumenical council has supreme authority over the whole church. In particular the word has been used to describe the position that such a council is superior to the *pope (a *doctrine condemned by the First *Vatican Council of 1869–1870).

CONCLAVE The term is used to describe both the locked area of the *Vatican Palace in which the *cardinals elect a new pope and the actual meeting of those cardinals. The practice originated in 1274. All cardinals must vote at each ballot, no contact with the outside world is permitted, and no notes of the proceedings may be taken away.

CONCOMITANCE The Roman Catholic *doctrine that fullness of spiritual communion with the *Lord *Jesus is possible through receiving either the consecrated bread or the consecrated wine. Therefore *Communion in one kind is made theologically justifiable, and so for centuries *laity have received only the consecrated bread of the *Eucharist. The theological idea is that the whole *Christ is sacramentally present in both the bread and wine.

CONCORD, BOOK OF (1580). The collected doctrinal standards of the Lutheran Church. It comprises various writings from Lutheran sources, three creeds (*Apostles', *Nicene, and *Athanasian), and a collection of citations from the early church *fathers. Its aim was to heal the divisions that had broken out after *Luther's death and to maintain certain distinctive Lutheran emphases. See also CONCORD, FORMULA OF.

CONCORD, FORMULA OF (1577). Lutheran *confession, drawn up by Jacob Andrea, Martin *Chemnitz, and others. Basically upholding the teaching of the *Augsburg Confession, the twelve-article document deals with such questions as *original *sin, *free *will, *justification, *good works, *law and *gospel, the *Eucharist, *predestination, and *adiaphora.

CONCORDANCE An alphabetical list of *Bible words with references where each occurs. Famous concordances are by Alexander *Cruden (1737) and R. Young (1879). With new translations of the *Bible in circulation, new concordances are beginning to appear—e.g., *An Analytical Concordance to the RSV* (ed. C. Morrison, 1979), and *The Complete NIV Concordance* (ed. Edward W. Goodrick and John R. Kohlenberger, III, 1981).

CONCORDAT OF 1801 An agreement between *Pius VII and Napoleon Bonaparte that ended the breach caused by the French Revolution. It defined the position of *Roman Catholicism in France and served as a model for numerous 19th-century concordats with other countries; it was abolished in 1905.

CONCUPISCENCE (Lat. *concupiscentia*, found in the Latin *Bible in Rom 7:7–24; Gal 5:24). It refers to the great power of *sin in the human *heart and is usually held to be the consequence of *original sin. It is also used to describe the powerful emotion of desire in the heart that because of sin is often directed to *evil purposes.

CONCURRENCE, DIVINE (Lat. *concursus divinus*). The way in which the activity of *God and that of human beings concurs or coincides. Used mostly by Roman Catholic theologians, it attempts to describe how in the (secret) *providence of God in the world he acts along with the activity of men without causing the activity of men to be that of robots.

CONDITIONAL IMMORTALITY The view that the human *soul is not by *nature immortal and only receives *immortality by the gift and *grace of *God. Thus a wicked person will have no existence after death or after *judgment by God. In popular usage conditional immortality is often incorrectly equated with the *doctrine of *annihilationism. The latter presupposes the inherent immortality of the soul and its extinction by God for its wickedness.

CONFESSING CHURCH The Protestant movement in Germany in reaction to Hitler's policy of using the churches for his political ends. His so-called *German Christians had gained the ascendancy in the Evangelical church and had introduced the specious *doctrine of Aryan racial superiority. Resistance was organized by Martin *Niemöller, Hans Lilje, and others, who issued a statement at Barmen in 1934 that became the mark of the Confessing church. Its adherents protested against *euthanasia and the persecution of Jews and were increasingly driven underground. In 1937 Niemöller and other *pastors were arrested. The movement nonetheless continued during World Ward II, and the Confessing church existed until 1948 when the

Evangelical church in Germany was reorganized.

CONFESSION OF 1967 The statement of *faith produced as part of the merger of the United Presbyterian Church of North America and the Presbyterian Church of the U.S. to form the United Presbyterian Church in the U.S.A. It was presented as an exposition of the *Reformed *faith for the 20th century, based on the theme of *reconciliation. It became part of a book of confessions that includes the *traditional *Reformed and Calvinist confessions and the *Barmen Declaration.

CONFESSION OF FAITH Although this expression can be used of the *Apostles', *Nicene, and *Athanasian Creeds, it is usually reserved for the Protestant statements of *doctrine. Of these the first was the Lutheran *Augsburg Confession (1530). The idea is of declaring to *God and to the whole church what is believed on the basis of God's *revelation recorded in *Scripture (Rom 10:9). The major *Reformed (Calvinistic) ones are: (1) *Tetrapolitan Confession (1530), (2) First Confession of Basel (1534), (3) First *Helvetic Confession (1536)—also known as the Second Confession of Basel, (4) Lausanne Articles (1536), (5) Geneva Confession (1536), (6) *Gallican Confession (1559), (7) *Scottish Confession (1560), (8) *Belgic Confession (1561), (9) *Second *Helvetic Confession (1566), (10) *Canons of the Synod of *Dort (1618), and (11) *Westminster Confession (1647). See also Catechism; Concord, Book of; Thirty-Nine Articles, The.

CONFESSION A *prayer to *God acknowledging *sin and expressing sorrow. When an individual confesses to God via a *priest, the practice is called auricular confession. Confession (*confessio*) also refers to a tomb of a *martyr/confessor—e.g., the confession of Peter in the *Vatican at Rome.

CONFESSIONALISM The view that the commitment to a *confession of *faith is necessary for the existence of a church or *denomination. If the commitment is an exclusive one, then the implication is that the body making such a confession has a better or clearer understanding of *doctrine than others.

CONFIRMATION The complement to *baptism, or the completion of the process of initiation into full church membership, including the first reception of the Eucharist. The Roman Catholic Church sees it as a *sacrament, but Lutherans and Anglicans regard it only as the completion of the sacrament of baptism. It involves the laying of the *bishop's or *priest's hands on the candidate after he or she has made a public commitment to *Christ. Roman Catholic and *Orthodox churches include anointing with oil in the *ritual.

CONGREGATIONALISTS Protestants who hold to a form of church order based on the autonomy of each congregation, and the belief that a church is composed of Christians joined together for *worship, *fellowship, and service. All members have equal rights and regard themselves as part of the church *universal, of which *Christ is the sole Head. Congregationalism began with the *Reformation and took its early principles from Lutheran and Anabaptist teaching. As *separatists they opposed *Elizabeth's claim to be head of the church; as *independents they formed the backbone of Oliver Cromwell's support. In New England they established colleges, notably Harvard and Yale. In 1795 they were the prime movers in the founding of the London Missionary Society. *Ecumenical in tendency, Congregationalists have made the greatest impact in the U.S. In England they merged with Presbyterians in 1972 to form the *United Reformed Church.

CONGRUISM A theory attempting to reconcile the effectiveness of the *grace of *God and the freedom of the human *will. It was expounded especially by *Jesuit theologians of the 17th century and opposed by Protestants who held that too much credit was being given to the human participation in receiving God's grace and *salvation.

CONNECTIONAL, CONNEXIONAL The form of church organization adopted by Methodists. There are local societies (churches) organized into circuits, and circuits make up districts. From each circuit representatives attend the annual conference. The system goes back to the organization instituted by John *Wesley.

CONSCIENCE (Lat. *conscientia*, Gk. *suneidesis*, "consciousness" or "self-awareness"). It is used today in a variety of ways, all of which point to some kind of moral self-awareness. Four uses are a moral conviction, a consciousness of basic value, a consciousness of a feeling that can give "pangs," and (in psychological terms) the suppression of the libido in the name of the superego. Theologically it may be described as the internal means by which a sinful human being can progressively learn and know the *will of *God as he lives in *fellowship with God and his people.

CONSCIENTIOUS OBJECTION The refusal, on moral grounds, by an individual to serve in the armed forces or to support military action. Those who support *pacificism take this position. Christians who adopt it are usually of two kinds: (1) those who take Exodus 20:13 and Matthew 5:3–11 literally and believe that all violence is wrong, and (2) those who argue that in the particular case they are facing the conflict cannot be called a just *war and so cannot be supported on moral grounds. Only the first is pure pacificism.

CONSECRATION The act (*ritual and words) by which a person or thing is set apart for *holy use—e.g., a church, a *bishop, and the bread and wine of the *Eucharist. It is also sometimes used to describe a richer *Christian life that is wholly committed to *God.

CONSENT OF THE FATHERS Agreement among the *fathers (leading theological teachers) of the church (especially in the first five or six centuries) on matters of *faith. This includes such *doctrines as the *Trinity and of the *person of *Christ.

CONSERVATIVE BAPTIST ASSOCIATION OF AMERICA An association of independent Baptist churches founded in the U.S. in 1947. Its formation was prompted by what were regarded as defective attitudes on the part of the American Baptist Convention to *Scripture, *doctrine, and *missions. The association has headquarters in Wheaton, Illinois, and lists about 300,000 members.

CONSERVATIVE EVANGELICALISM The position of those Protestant Christians who hold to the full inspiration and authority of *Scripture, the *deity of *Christ and his substitutionary *atonement, the *doctrine of the *Trinity, the need for personal *conversion to *God, and a personal, ongoing *fellowship of the believer with his or her *Lord. As such this phenomenon is found in most *denominations, while some denominations claim to be explicitly conservative *evangelical. It is most obviously reflected in *parachurch organizations such as Inter-Varsity Christian Fellowship and in colleges such as London Bible College and Wheaton College, Illinois.

CONSISTORY As used by *Reformed churches this refers to a church court and is the equivalent of the *session or (in France) the *Presbytery. It is the meeting of the ordained minister and the lay *elders.

CONSTANCE, COUNCIL OF (1414–1418). Sixteenth *ecumenical council of the Roman Catholic Church. Under pressure from Emperor *Sigismund the council was converted to reunite the church, of which there were three claimants to the *papacy; to examine the teachings of John *Wycliffe and Jan *Hus; and to institute reforms. The antipope *John XXIII, who had summoned the council, fled in the hope that his absence would render it inoperative, but the assembly affirmed the superiority of a general council over a pope. All three rivals were deposed or resigned, the council elected *Martin V, and the *Great Schism of the Western church officially ended. The council condemned Wycliffian teaching, delivered Hus to the secular power to be burned, and made reforms that were to prove inadequate.

CONSTANTINE THE GREAT (c. 274/280–337). First *Christian emperor of Rome. Brought up at the court of *Diocletian, he became Western emperor after a military victory near Rome in 312, which he attributed to the *God of the Christians. The Edict of *Milan in 313 decreed full *toleration and other advantages for Christians, including the restitution of confiscated property. In 325, by now sole emperor of East and West, Constantine summoned the Council of *Nicea to settle the Arian controversy. He presided at the opening sessions. The result was a victory for *orthodoxy, but Constantine had no theological discernment and was soon thereafter swayed by *bishops of Arian tendencies. In 330 he established a new capital in the East, which he called Constantinople.

CONSTANTINOPLE, FIRST COUNCIL OF (381). Attended by only about 150 bishops, all from the East, it deposed the Arian *bishop of Constantinople, upheld the findings on *Arianism made at the Council of *Nicea, and condemned all heretical views, notably those of Sabellius and Apollinarius. Among other findings, it gave Constantinople the *primacy of honor next to Rome.

CONSTANTINOPLE, SECOND COUNCIL OF (553). The fifth *ecumenical council of the *Christian church. Attended by 168 *bishops, nearly all from the East, it condemned *Theodore of Mopsuestia and *Theodoret of Cyrrhus, who were prominent Nestorians (a condemnation which the *pope and the Western bishops refused to ratify). This council also condemned *Origenism and declared the *perpetual virginity of the Virgin *Mary. Pope *Vigilius, after some hesitation, accepted the council and its decisions.

CONSTANTINOPLE, THIRD COUNCIL OF (680–681). The sixth *ecumenical council of the *Christian church. Called to restore *orthodoxy at a time of Islamic advance, this thinly attended assembly condemned the *Monothelites and their supporter Pope *Honorius I (which was to provoke a controversy over papal infallibility at *Vatican Council I). This council led to the separation from Eastern Orthodoxy of Nestorians and Monophysites.

CONSUBSTANTIALITY The three *persons of the Holy *Trinity share the one divine *Being or *substance. Thus they are consubstantial. The term is not used in the *NT but is developed from John 1:1ff., Heb 1:1–4, and similar passages. See also Homoousios.

CONSUBSTANTIATION A theory as to how *Christ is present in the *Eucharist. The *body of Christ is said to be conjoined to the bread, and the *blood of Christ to the wine, so that there is a true receiving of both Christ and of bread and wine. The bread is always bread and the wine always wine, but to these Christ is sacramentally united. The Lutheran *doctrine of the presence of Christ is often called consubstantiation. See also Impanation, Transubstantiation.

CONTEMPLATION A way of approaching *God in *prayer that is not the result of the use of the rational/logical powers of the mind. Rather it is intuitive, a viewing of God in the light of *truth already known. As such it may develop naturally from *meditation or, as mystics have found, may be caused by the direct action of the Holy *Spirit. It is a spiritual activity in which only a small number of Christians appear to engage, and it is encouraged especially by *religious *orders, some of which are known as contem- plative orders. The "contemplative life" is often contrasted with the "active life."

CONTINGENCY A condition that exists in dependence on *God the Creator and could have been different from what it is. E.g., the *universe is contingent because it is dependent on God, who could have made it different than he did. Usually "contingent being" is contrasted with "necessary being," and it is claimed that the latter belongs only to God. Anything that need not have existed, need not have happened, or need not be as it is, is contingent.

CONTRACEPTION Methods of preventing conception by means that do not include abstinence from sexual intercourse. Most Christians believe that if used wisely contraceptive devices are acceptable. Pope *Paul VI, however, in his famous letter, *Humanae Vitae* (1963), condemned artificial methods of contraception but called upon scientists to search for more reliable means of ascertaining the so-called safe period in the feminine ovulatory process. See also BIRTH CONTROL.

CONTRA-REMONSTRANTS Strict Calvinists in the early 17th-century Netherlands. The name originated in a *remonstrance issued in 1610 by the supporters of *Arminius, who had tried to soften the rigors of *Calvinism. The Contra-Remonstrants replied in the following year, and their views prevailed at the Synod of *Dort seven years later.

CONTRITION A deep, inward sorrow for a *sin or sins committed. This sorrow flows not only from fear of *God's wrath (for such sorrow is only *attrition) but also from *love of God and a desire to please him. Ps 51 is a classical, biblical example of contrition.

CONTROVERSIAL THEOLOGY A Roman Catholic term to describe their study of the *theology of other churches and *denominations. There are three basic types: (1) the polemical method, which attempts to show that *doctrines are erroneous or heretical; (2) the irenical method, which attempts to understand why particular doctrines are believed; (3) the *symbolics method, which compares and contrasts the different doctrines. Often these types are all found in the writings of one theologian.

CONVENTICLE ACT (1664). Parliamentary legislation for the suppression of *Nonconformity in England after the *Restoration. All gatherings of five persons, apart from family members, were declared illegal on pain of a fine for the first offense, transportation (banishment to a penal colony) for the third. Later modified, the act remained in force till 1689.

CONVERSION A term with several uses. The most general is to describe a turning from a life of *sin or self-service to a life of serving *God. Theologians differ as to whether conversion is wholly the work of God's *grace or whether there is a freely motivated cooperation by the person concerned in his or her response to the grace of God. Further, conversion may refer to the move from paganism to *Christianity, from *atheism or *agnosticism to Christianity, or from nominal Christianity to committed Christianity. The term may mean changing churches (e.g., "a convert to Rome") or changing theologies (e.g., "a convert to Calvinism"). Conversion in the sense of a new life of serving *Jesus Christ is a basic biblical idea (see Acts 15:3; Rom 16:5; 1 Cor 16:15; 2 Thess 2:13). Closely associated with it, as such, are such themes as *faith and *repentance.

CONVICT, CONVICTION In John 16:8 the Holy *Spirit is said to convict to the world of *sin. People are aware of sin when they recognize that they have no communion with *God because they do not believe in the *Lord *Jesus. To convict is to make aware of sin, and the result is conviction of sin. Theologians differ as to whether or not all whom the Holy Spirit convicts are eventually led to repentance and true *faith in *Christ.

COPERNICUS, NICOLAUS (1473–1543). Founder of modern astronomy. Born in Poland, he studied at Cracow and in Italy and returned home about 1503 fully trained in mathematics, medicine, astronomy, and *theology. From

1512 he took up ecclesiastical duties at Frauenburg Cathedral, of which he had been made a *canon some years before, and used his medical skill chiefly in the service of the poor. He had earlier criticized the Ptolemaic theory of the *universe, which held that the earth was a stationary body about which the sun, planets, and stars revolved daily, suggesting rather that the earth moved round the sun. Though he wrote extensively on the subject, his conclusions were not generally accepted for some time. The Protestant reformers opposed them because they thought them at variance with the *Bible. Copernicus is significant not merely for his scientific achievements but because of the stimulation he gave to the spirit of enquiry.

COPTIC CHURCH The main *Christian church body in Egypt. Claiming to originate from Mark the evangelist, the Christian church in Egypt is distinctive because of its official adherence to *Monophysitism since the Council of *Chalcedon (451). The land in which *monasticism had developed was thereafter disrupted by religious and political strife, followed by centuries of Muslim domination that has persisted into modern times, despite an official policy of religious *toleration. The Coptic church gives communion in one kind only, combines *baptism with *confirmation, emphasizes *fasting, and has an elaborate *ritual.

COREDEMPTRIX A title given to *Mary, mother of *Jesus, in *Roman Catholicism to indicate the part she played, in being his mother, in the redemption of the world. Since the expression has often been an embarrassment to Protestants, the Second *Vatican Council did not use the word, hoping that this would help to lead to an *ecumenical understanding of the role of Mary in *God's redemptive purpose.

CORPORATION ACT (1661). Passed by the cavalier Parliament of *Charles II, the first of a series of repressive measures, it confined membership of municipal bodies to Church of *England communicants. Such officials were required to renounce the *Solemn League and Covenant, take the *oath of nonresistance to lawful authority, and receive the *Lord's Supper according to the Anglican form (thus degrading the *sacrament into a political test). The act remained theoretically in force until 1828.

CORPUS CHRISTI (Lat. "*body of *Christ"). A feast in the Roman Catholic Church in honor of the presence of Christ in the *Eucharist. The annual celebration began in the 14th century, and a central feature is a procession after the *Mass. In this the carrying of the consecrated bread is central. The feast is held on the Thursday after Trinity *Sunday.

COSMOGONY A theory of the origins of the physical *universe. It is used of both primitive myths or stories about how the world began as well as of the speculative theories of modern scientists. A *Christian approach to this subject has to take seriously the teaching of such biblical passages as Genesis 1–3 and John 1:1–15.

COSMOLOGICAL ARGUMENT, THE See FIVE WAYS, THE.

COSMOLOGY The study of the *universe. Normally the word describes the world-view of a particular age. In recent times cosmology has been dominated by the theories of Albert Einstein while in earlier times it was under the influence of such theorists as Aristotle, Ptolemy, and *Copernicus. There seems to be agreement among biblical scholars that in the *Bible there is no particular theory of the *universe apart from the strong theme that *God is Creator and Sustainer.

COSMOSCOPE A world-view. Used particularly by modern Calvinists to indicate that they have a philosophy of the *universe based on biblical premises. Important among the latter are that man is *God's appointed viceroy on earth, that through *sin he lost this privilege, and that in *Christ he is reinstated as viceroy. A leading exponent of a Calvinist world-view was the late Herman *Dooyeweerd, professor at the Free University, Amsterdam.

COTTON, JOHN (1585–1652). New England Puritan leader. Formerly a Cambridge don and an Anglican *vicar, he fell foul of the *Court of High Commission because of Puritan views, sailed for America (1632), and became *pastor of the First Church of Boston (1633–1652). Even in *Congregationalist New England he never lost his Erastian tendencies, and this brought him into contention with Roger *Williams. A man of piety, learning, and strong *convictions, Cotton exercised a profound influence in the affairs of New England. One of the more lucid of Protestant writers, he helped draw up the *Cambridge Platform (1648).

COUNSELS, EVANGELICAL Advisory direction based on the words and example of *Christ. They are contrasted with *precepts (commandments of obligation), for they are to be embraced freely in order to live a joyful *Christian life. Traditionally the counsels are said to be *poverty, *chastity, *obedience, and loving one's enemies. They are *evangelical in that they are said to be based on the *Gospels (Matt 19:11–12; Mark 10:17; 9:35; Luke 6:27, 35).

COUNTER-REFORMATION Often regarded as Roman Catholic reaction to the Protestant *Reformation, it describes with equal accuracy the reform movement within *Roman Catholicism. This had manifested itself even before the Reformation, but the *papacy was slow to act, and even the decisions of the Council of *Trent (1545–1563) were criticized as offering too little too late. The *Inquisition and the exercise of force by *Charles V and *Philip II were dubious allies of true *Christianity, while Roman Catholic theologians of the age were on the whole no match for *Luther and *Calvin. It was in the work and outreach of the *religious *orders, especially in *missions, that the old church was seen to better advantage.

COUNTESS OF HUNTINGDON'S CONNEXION An *evangelical Protestant group sponsored by the countess (Selina Hastings, 1707–1791) and formed into an association in 1790. A Methodist who supported *Whitefield rather than *Wesley and who appointed evangelical Anglicans as her chaplains, she opened several chapels and aimed to reach the upper classes. She also established an *evangelical theological college to train her *clergy. Anglican hostility forced her to register her chapels as *Nonconformist places of *worship and caused the withdrawal of her Church of *England chaplains. Her association survived into the second half of the 20th century, by which time most of the *pastors had become *Congregationalists.

COURT, ANTOINE (1695–1760). French *Reformed *pastor. Even before *ordination in 1718 he was working toward the *revival of the Protestant church in France after *Louis XIV's 1685 revocation of the Edict of *Nantes had flung that church into disarray. Despite his restraint, his activities in the Protestant cause brought renewed persecution, and he spent some periods in Switzerland where he founded and directed a theological *seminary to train ministers for what he called the "Church of the Desert." His writings, published and unpublished, are of considerable value in tracing the history of the period.

COURT OF HIGH COMMISSION Originally one of the devices by which *James VI of Scotland enforced his ecclesiastical policy, it was revived in 1664 by *Archbishop James *Sharpe against the *Covenanters. Its wide-ranging powers permitted arrest without explanation, scourging, branding, selling into *slavery, and the public whipping of women. Under its savage regime many left Scotland and found religious *liberty in Ulster. The bloodthirsty *prelate was overruled by the civil power, and the court was suppressed in 1666.

COVENANT Binding agreement between two parties. In the *Bible the term is used to describe the action of *God on behalf of humankind whereby he agrees to be their God and to bless them on the condition that they fulfill the terms of the agreement, which are *faith and *obedience. The covenant was renewed at various times throughout *Israel's history, culminating in the new covenant of *Jesus Christ (promised in Jer 31:31ff.) in whom all the blessings of God's *salvation are to be found.

COVENANT THEOLOGY An exposition of the relationship between *God and man in terms of *covenants. In the Calvinist *tradition it is often called *federal *theology. Basic to it, in its developed 17th-century form, are two covenants: (1) that of *works, which God made with Adam as the head of all humanity; and (2) that of *grace, made with *Christ as the Head of the new humanity (the elect). Sometimes there is reference to another covenant, that of *redemption, made between the three persons of the *Trinity in *eternity. In this the Father chooses the elect, the Son agrees to redeem the elect, and the Holy *Spirit to sanctify the elect. Such theology was commonplace in the Calvinist tradition from the 17th to the 19th centuries but has lost ground recently party because of the recognition that *Calvin himself had no developed covenant theology.

COVENANTED COMMUNITIES An expression of the understanding within the *charismatic movement that the gifts of the Spirit are given for the renewal of the body of Christ. Covenanted communities are groups of people committed to a corporate lifestyle in "households." These households may live under one roof or may be "nonresidential." In either case, the purpose of these communities is to express in practice the power of the Holy Spirit in everyday life, as a witness to others. Two well-known communities (primarily RC) are the Word of God Community in Ann Arbor, Michigan (with its own publishing house, Servant Publications), and the Mother of God Community in Gaithersburg, Maryland.

COVENANTERS The Scots who signed the *National Covenant of 1638 and the *Solemn League and Covenant of 1643 and their like-minded successors during the reigns of the last two Stuart kings. Dissatisfied with the moderate *episcopacy imposed on Scotland by *James VI, his son *Charles I overreached himself when, with the connivance of William *Laud, he tried in 1637 to impose a new *liturgy on the northern kingdom, leading to the first covenant. After the *Restoration of 1660, *Charles II permitted a relentless persecution of those who denied his supremacy over the church, and who fought for "Christ's Crown and Covenant." Covenanting ministers were ejected from their *parishes and freedom of *worship was stifled. Many were brutally murdered or executed with a pretence of legality; others were imprisoned or banished. The Killing Times persisted until *James VII/II fled the country in 1688 and the cause of the Convenanters was vindicated in the reestablishment of *Presbyterianism by *William III.

COVERDALE, MILES (1488–1568). *Bible translator and Protestant reformer. Graduate of Cambridge, he was ordained in 1514 and later joined the *Augustinian Hermits. He became interested in church reform, preached against *confession and *images, and was forced into exile. On the Continent he produced in 1535 the earliest complete Bible in English. In 1539 he collaborated with Richard Grafton in the "Great Bible," presented to *Henry VIII by Thomas *Cromwell, who ordered it to be placed in every English church. In 1551 Coverdale became *bishop of Exeter, but Mary *Tudor's reign exiled him. Debarred later as bishop, presumably by his marriage, he ministered in London and helped prepare the Geneva Bible (1560). He was a popular preacher and a leading Puritan.

COX, RICHARD (c. 1500–1581). *Bishop of Ely and Protestant reformer. Graduate of Cambridge, he was dean successively of Christ Church, Oxford (1547), and of Westminster (1549), and he helped compile the *Prayer Books of 1549 and 1552. On Mary *Tudor's accession he was imprisoned and then exiled. In the English congregation at Frankfurt he collaborated uneasily with John *Knox. On *Elizabeth's accession he became bishop of Ely (1559–1580), but some of the remnants of popery tolerated by Elizabeth led to his resignation the year before his death.

CRAIG, JOHN (1512–1600). Scottish reformer. Formerly a *Dominican *friar, he was converted to *Protestantism and condemned to death by the *Inquisition, but he escaped to become the favorite preacher at the imperial court and returned to Scotland during the *Reformation in that country (1560). He joined John *Knox in ministering at St. Giles', Edinburgh; became a royal chaplain; and was largely responsible for the *King's Confession of 1581.

CRANACH, LUCAS (1472–1553). German painter and engraver. Portrait painter of the emperor Maximilian and *Charles V, he is best known for his portraits of his reformer friends—*Luther, *Melanchthon, and others. One of his pictures (1518) now at Leipzig features a dying man's *soul rising to meet the *Trinity, illustrating the *doctrine of *justification by *faith alone.

CRANMER, THOMAS (1489–1556). First Protestant *archbishop of Canterbury and a *martyr. Formerly adviser and chaplain to *Henry VIII, he became *primate in 1532 and annulled Henry's marriages with Catherine of Aragon (1533) and Anne Boleyn (1536). After Henry's death in 1547 Cranmer became one of *Edward VI's most trusted counselors. His ideas developing increasingly in a Protestant direction, he arranged for continental theologians such as Peter *Martyr and Martin *Bucer to come to England. He took a leading part in abolishing Roman Catholic ceremonies, in destroying *images and other *relics, and in compiling the 1549 *Book of Common Prayer* (probably his greatest achievement). On the accession of Mary *Tudor, Cranmer was charged with treason; was finally tried for *heresy; and after revoking various recantations, was burned at the stake in Oxford.

CRASHAW, RICHARD (c. 1613–1649). English mystical poet. Son of a Puritan divine, he refused to sign the *Solemn League and Covenant, became a Roman Catholic, and finally was appointed *canon at the *cathedral of Santa Casa in Loreto, Italy. He died of fever within a month. His poetry, which exercised great influence on *Milton, Pope, and Coleridge, was capable of soaring to heights of devotion never surpassed. His published works include a volume of sacred poems, *Steps to the Temple* (1648).

CRAWFORD, DANIEL (1870–1926). *Missionary to Africa. A Scot by birth and a member of the *Plymouth Brethren, he accompanied F. S. *Arnot to central Africa in 1889. Apart from a four-year absence (1911–1915), he remained there until his death. His famous book *Thinking Black* expressed his principle and practice: that the missionary must identify himself with the people. A marked individualist dependent on no society for support, he was a tireless itinerant who preached for *conversions.

CREATION, DOCTRINE OF The *Christian position is that *God created the *universe out of nothing (*ex nihilo*), and therefore the final explanation and purpose of the *universe is with and in God. Where Christians differ is on the extent of scientific data included in the biblical account of creation (Gen 1–3) and how that data harmonizes with modern scientific theories.

CREATIONISM The view that the human *soul of each person is directly created by *God at conception in the womb. An alternative view is *traducianism, which asserts that the soul is transmitted from parents to child. Another aspect of creationism involves the late 20th-century Fundamentalist difficulty with scientific and historical textbooks that espouse Darwin's theory of evolution, to the neglect or dismissal of the biblical account of creation. In America this battle became focused in the trial of John T. *Scopes in 1925.

CREED(S) (Lat. *credo*, "I believe"). A summary statement of the chief items of *Christian belief. There are brief creeds in the *NT (e.g., "*Jesus is *Lord"). From such there developed creeds used at *baptisms, and from baptismal creeds the famous *Apostles' and *Nicene Creeds evolved. Creeds may be in the singular, "I believe," or in the plural, "We believe."

CREED, JOHN MARTIN (1889–1940). English theologian. He spent most of his working life as a Cambridge don and was a strong believer in the place of the Church of *England in the life of the nation. During the last years of his life he was Ely professor of divinity (1926–1940). He published a commentary on Luke's Gospel and a history of *Christian *doctrine and was one of the editors of the prestigious *Journal of Theological Studies*.

CREMATION The reducing of human corpses by fire. This has become increasingly common in the Western world in recent decades. Traditionally *Christianity has had a strong commitment to *burial, since this appeared to harmonize with the *hope of the *resurrection of the *body and the belief that the body is the temple of the Holy *Spirit. However, arguments based on public hygiene, convenience, and conservation of land have been accepted within the churches, and so cremation is becoming increasingly common.

CRISIS THEOLOGY The teaching of Karl *Barth, Emil *Brunner, and those associated with them in the period after World War I. "Crisis" has various meanings, which together point to the character of this *theology. There was a crisis in theological confidence—*liberalism had shown itself to have no answer to the moral and spiritual needs of humankind. There was a crisis in terms of civilization—World War I and its aftermath. Finally there was the *krisis* (Gk. "judgment") of *God—God has judged *sin, and the only way to please him is to receive his free *grace through *Jesus Christ. See also BARTHIANISM, DIALECTICAL THEOLOGY.

CRITICISM, BIBLICAL See BIBLICAL CRITICISM.

CROMWELL, OLIVER (1599–1658). Lord Protector of England. Member of Parliament for Cambridge in 1640, he fought for annual Parliaments and the abolition of *episcopacy. When the Civil War divided the country he became a general in the parliamentary army and reluctantly supported the execution of *Charles I. He was made Lord Protector in 1653, refused the title of king, supported religious *toleration, and reorganized the Church of *England, for which he stressed the need of faithful *pastors. Strongly *Christian, he was unselfish to a high degree, and while his work seemed to be undone at the *Restoration of 1660, he notably contributed to the perpetuation of parliamentary democracy in England.

CROMWELL, THOMAS (c. 1485–1540). English statesman. A merchant's son who rose to high office in the state, he encouraged *Henry VIII to assert the royal supremacy over the church, which led subsequently to the confiscation of monastic property in 1540. He supported the publishing of the Great *Bible in 1539, was sympathetic to *Lutheranism, and took the initiative in furthering an alliance with the German Protestant princes by arranging Henry's marriage to Anne of Cleves. This was a disaster, and Cromwell, though he had just been made earl of Essex, was tried for *heresy and treason, found guilty, and beheaded.

CROSS AND CRUCIFIX From the 2d century the *sign of the cross was traced by the fingers as part of *Christian devotion. The biblical ideas that informed it are found in a few passages

(Matt 16:24; 1 Cor 1:23; Gal 5:24; 6:14). The use of painted pictures of the cross along with wooden and metal crosses/crucifixes (*images of *Christ on the cross) developed later. After the *Iconoclastic controversy in the 8th century, *veneration of the cross/-crucifix was clarified by the Second Council of *Nicea (787). *Latria was being offered to *Christ himself when a cross was truly venerated. The earliest representations of Christ on the cross date from the 5th century and are of Christ reigning as king. The presentation of the suffering Christ on the cross came into general usage in the 13th century.

CROWTHER, SAMUEL ADJAI (c. 1809–1891). Anglican *bishop. Born in Nigeria, he was rescued from a slave ship and educated in a Sierra Leone mission school. Under the auspices of the Church Missionary Society he was trained in London and ordained in 1843. He initiated the Niger Mission in 1857, and in 1864 he was consecrated as bishop of western Africa—an appointment somewhat inhibited by European *missionaries who rejected his jurisdiction despite his abilities and personal integrity.

CRUDEN, ALEXANDER (1701–1770). Compiler of the best-known English *Bible *concordance. A graduate of Aberdeen, he was confined in an asylum three times for brief periods. After an initial lukewarm response, second and third editions of his concordance brought him fame. He was generally scoffed at, however, when he regarded himself as divinely charged to be guardian of public morality, especially when he was denouncing swearing and Sabbath-breaking.

CRUSADES A series of military expeditions launched by the *Christian West between 1095 and 1291, with the aim of recovering the Holy Land from the Muslims and establishing Christian rule there. Popes preached support of the Crusades, financed them, sent legates to lead them, and indulgenced even those who pillaged towns and massacred women and children in the name of *Christ, notably in the sacking of Constantinople in 1203. Though often hailed as a model of cooperation between European nations, many of them found it hard to maintain a united front over a long period and were dictated by political rather than religious considerations. Not surprisingly, their main objective failed, but they did help to establish new trade routes to the East.

CRYPTO-CALVINISM A way of describing the teaching of Philip *Melanchthon (d. 1560) and especially his views on the presence of *Christ in the *Lord's Supper. As a Lutheran, Melanchthon was accused by rigid Lutherans of adopting Calvinist ideas.

CUDWORTH, RALPH (1617–1688). Probably the most distinguished of the Cambridge Platonists. Professor of Hebrew at Cambridge from 1645, he was a strong advocate of revealed *religion, pointed to the logical impossibility of *atheism, and stressed the reality of moral freedom and responsibility. He supported Cromwellian rule, hoping that it would foster a lasting religious *toleration. He died just before this was to a large extent realized under *William III.

CUIUS REGIO, EIUS RELIGIO (Lat. "a territory's *religion is that of its prince"). This was the formula adopted by the Religious Peace of Augsburg (1555) in order to decide how princes of the *Holy Roman Empire were to settle the question of the major *religion (*Lutheranism or *Roman Catholicism) in their territories.

CULT A religious group that is sometimes called a "*sect" and is reckoned not to hold orthodox *Christian *doctrine. Some sociologists identify a cult by its small size, its reference to one particular area, its dependence on a leader with a strong personality, and beliefs and *rites that are different from mainstream *religion. Others use broader categories of identification. Thus *Satan worshipers, *Jehovah's Witnesses, and *Mormons are all sometimes called cults.

CULTURAL RELATIVISM Used by some scholars to suggest that the basic teaching of the *Bible expresses the thought world of ancient *culture to the extent that it may be impossible to make that teaching, in part or in whole, meaningful for today. Such a position is unnecessarily negative.

CULTURE The totality of ideas, images, and emphases that give a specific pattern to the life of an identifiable group of people. It is a neutral word describing the social behavior of a particular human group. Thus a *theology of culture is an attempt to face the fact that the *gospel must be preached, taught, and lived in a way that makes sense in a given culture.

Culture, however, is sometimes used of a particular attainment in what are seen as the "higher" aspects of general culture—e.g., in literature, music, art, and philosophy. Often the church has been closely linked with such "higher" aspects of culture.

CUMBERLAND PRESBYTERIAN CHURCH American Protestant church founded in 1810. It arose from a dispute within the Presbyterian Church in the U.S.A. after the latter's Cumberland *presbytery had been dissolved (1806). The new body was *evangelical in outlook and rejected the view of *predestination held by the mother church. When the latter point was put right in 1906, a majority of the Cumberland Presbyterians rejoined the larger body, but many would not do so and continued a church that, largely found in the South, has some 90,000 members.

CUMMINS, GEORGE DAVID (1822–1876). Founder and first *bishop of the *Reformed Episcopal Church. Ordained in the *Protestant Episcopal Church in 1845, he became assistant bishop of Kentucky in 1866, but his *evangelical views made it difficult for him to cope with the growing *ritualism. Under pressure from other dissidents he organized the Reformed Episcopal Church in 1873.

CUNNINGHAM, WILLIAM (1805–1861). Scottish theologian. One of those who left the Church of *Scotland at the *Disruption, he became principal of the *Free Church of Scotland college in Edinburgh when Thomas *Chalmers died in 1847. Considered to have been one of Scotland's greatest theologians, he produced his two-volume *Historical Theology* (1862), which is still held to be a classic.

CUR DEUS HOMO The title of a famous book by *Anselm of Canterbury completed in 1098. It means, "Why (did) God (become) man?" It was a major contribution to the *doctrine of the *Atonement and taught that *Christ satisfied the honor and *justice of *God for humankind.

CURATE One who is charged with or entrusted with the care of something. A *priest in charge of a *parish was known as a curate—a usage preserved in the French *curé*. However, in modern usage a curate is normally the assistant priest in a parish, working with a rector or *vicar.

CURIA ROMANA (Lat. "Roman curia"). The total organization that surrounds and assists the *bishop of Rome in the performance of his duties. In it there are now ten congregations (e.g., Education, *Evangelism, *Worship, and *Sacraments) and several secretariats (e.g., *Christian Unity). Although the organization evolved over the centuries, it was reformed in 1967 in order to streamline it, making it relevant to modern conditions.

CURSILLO MOVEMENT A charismatic renewal movement within the Roman Catholic Church. The name derives from the Spanish for "Little course." The movement seeks, primarily through retreats, to produce vital Christians who as a committed community will lead in the development of parish (lay?) spirituality. It has been adapted by other denominations, including the United Methodists (Emmaus Walk) and the Episcopal Church (Episcopal Cursillo).

CYPRIAN (c. 200/210–258). *Bishop of Carthage. Born into a pagan family in Carthage, he became a notable teacher of rhetoric, was converted about 246, and was ordained and then promoted to bishop three years later. During the persecution under *Decius, Cyprian left the *diocese, and in his absence those Christians who had lapsed under trial were treated leniently, a decision Cyprian regarded as irregular. A serious controversy developed over this and also later with Pope Stephen I over different interpretations on *baptism (Cyprian disapproving of traditional Roman acceptance of heretical baptism)—an issue that might have led to excommunication for Cyprian had not the *pope died in 257. He also had grave misgivings about the Roman claim to outrank other bishoprics. The imperial persecution was resumed, and Cyprian was first banished, then beheaded. Some of his ecclesiastical problems arose from his *OT emphases, which were not always relevant to *Christian situations.

CYRIL AND METHODIUS (c. 827–869; c. 825–885). "*Apostles of the Slavs." Brothers and scholars from Thessalonica, they were sent to evangelize the Slavs in 862 as a result of a request from Moravia. There they devised an alphabet, introduced Slavonic into the *liturgy, and circulated Slavonic *Gospels (thus incurring the hostility of Bavarian *priests in Moravia). The brothers also trained *disciples to carry on the work. Cyril died in 869. His brother was consecrated *bishop by Pope Adrian II and returned to his work in Moravia. He was imprisoned for a time and released at the instigation of Pope *John VIII, who made him *archbishop of Pannonia. Details about the two brothers are often uncertain, but in southeastern Europe their names are still held in high esteem.

CYRIL OF ALEXANDRIA (c. 375–444). *Patriarch of Alexandria. Succeeding his uncle in that post in 412, he took strong issue with pagans, Jews (whom he had expelled from Alexandria), and heretics, especially *Nestorius, whose deposition he secured at the Council of *Ephesus in 431. Cyril's major contribution was his defense of the unity of *Christ in the face of Nestorian and other deviations.

CYRIL OF JERUSALEM (c. 310–387). *Bishop of Jerusalem. Born into a *Christian family in Jerusalem, he was ordained and about 350 became bishop. He was exiled three times through Arian influence. He finally returned in 378 and was acclaimed as the champion of *orthodoxy. He played a significant part in the First Council of *Constantinople (381).

D

D A supposed source of the *Pentateuch, written by the Deuteronomist. See also DOCUMENTARY HYPOTHESIS.

D.V. (Lat. *Deo volente,* "*God willing"). Used as an expression of belief in the *providence of God.

D'AILLE, JEAN (1594–1670). French Protestant theologian. Ordained in 1623, his forty-four-year pastorate at Charenton saw him win renown as an orator and suffer attack from Roman Catholics and others for his relegation of *tradition and his emphasis on the *Bible as the sole *rule of *faith and practice.

D'AUBIGNE, JEAN HENRI MERLE (1794–1872). Swiss Protestant church historian. Professor at Geneva and greatly influenced by *Neander, he wrote a much acclaimed history of the *Reformation (13 vols., 1835–1878). A tolerant man, he held that the church should not be financed by the *state, and he advocated *presbyterian polity as the most biblical form.

DABNEY, ROBERT (1820–1898). American *Presbyterian theologian. One of the prime movers in the founding of the Southern Presbyterian Church in 1881, he taught at Union Seminary in Richmond, Virginia, from 1859 to 1883, apart from a five-year period (1861–1866) when he served with Stonewall Jackson during the Civil War. From 1884 he taught philosophy at the University of Texas and helped to found Austin Theological Seminary. He is regarded as one of the great theologians of his *denomination.

DALE, ROBERT WILLIAM (1829–1895). Congregational minister. An activist with strong political and social concerns, and a theological liberal, he produced a highly acclaimed work on the *Atonement (1875). His forty-two-year ministry at Carr's Lane Chapel, Birmingham, from 1853 was an outreach to all classes. He was a warm supporter of D. L. *Moody when the American came to Birmingham in 1875, and he gave the Lyman *Beecher Lectures at Yale in 1877.

DALMAN, GUSTAF HERMANN (1855–1941). Biblical scholar. Having spent more than thirty years in Palestine working in the field of archaeology and antiquities, he produced authoritative works, including an Aramaic grammar, *The Words of Jesus* (Eng. transl. 1902), and *Sacred Sites and Ways* (Eng. transl. 1935).

DALMATIC The outer vestment worn by the *deacon and occasionally by the *bishop at Roman Catholic *High *Mass. It is open at the sides, covering from the shoulders to below the knees, and with wide, short sleeves. The name comes from its place of origin, Dalmatia. The equivalent garment in the Orthodox church is called the *sakkos*.

DAMASUS I (c. 305–384). Pope from 366. Earlier involved in internal squabbles around the *papacy, he was active against *Arianism and other heresies during his *pontificate, which saw the Roman assertion of *primacy over Constantinople. He was the first pope to call Rome the Apostolic See. Damasus commissioned his secretary *Jerome to revise the Latin translations of the *Bible (later called the *Vulgate), introduced Latin as the language of the *Mass, and sponsored the restoration of *catacombs and churches.

DAMIAN, PETER (1007–1072). Roman Catholic reformer. Born in Ravenna, Italy, he became a *Benedictine in 1035. From 1057 he served as a *cardinal under three popes. A lifelong reformer with a robust turn of phrase that lashed the decadence of the *clergy and simoniacal practices, he was theologically conservative, which is reflected in his many extant writings.

DAMIEN, FATHER (JOSEPH DE VEUSTER) (1840–1889). Roman Catholic *missionary to Hawaii. Belgian by birth, he went as a missionary to Hawaii (Sandwich Islands) in 1863. From 1873 he took charge of an isolated colony of lepers that an uncaring authority had practically written off. Damien was everything from *priest to manual worker. He brought order and *hope to those outcasts and saw their numbers grow to more than a thousand. Though he contracted the disease himself in 1884, he stayed at his post until the month before his death.

DAMNATION The condemnation to *eternal *punishment in *hell that *Christ will pronounce at the Last *Judgment upon those who have rejected *God's *salvation (Matt 25:41–46). As this appears to be a harsh *doctrine, many *Christians have rejected it or explained it in such ways (e.g., the deprivation of the good only, or *annihilationism) as to soften its impact.

DANTE ALIGHIERI (1265–1321). Italian poet. Born in Florence, he eagerly absorbed learning of all kinds, became one of his city's chief magistrates, and opposed papal interference in civic matters. The result was a false charge brought against him in 1302, leading to banishment, loss of possessions, and threat of death if he returned to Florence. Dante spent the rest of his life in exile. His crowning achievement was the work that came to be called the *Divine Comedy*. It portrayed the author's journey through hell, purgatory, and heaven. Its people and situations were realistic, even identifiable, and its aim was to warn humankind that reward or penalty would meet them hereafter. The work has been translated into many languages. Dante is regarded as the national poet of Italy.

DARBY, JOHN NELSON (1800–1882). *Plymouth Brethren leader. Born in Ireland and educated at Trinity College, Dublin, he was called to the Irish Bar in 1822 and ordained in the Church of Ireland in 1825. Two years later he left his *curacy and soon became leader of a group that met in Dublin for *prayer and the breaking of bread. During 1838–1845 he was in France and Switzerland. With the growing Brethren movement came controversies that divided the ranks into exclusive (Darbyites) and open. He traveled the world on *preaching *missions, edited the *Christian Witness,* and was also a *hymn writer, *Bible translator, and humanitarian.

DARWINISM The theory of Charles Darwin (1809–1882) that all living things developed from simple forms through a process of evolution and natural selection. His views were expressed in *The Origin of the Species* (1859) and *The Descent of Man* (1871) and caused great controversy. Many Christians see his theory of evolution as contrary to the *Christian view of origins. See also EVOLUTION, THEISTIC.

DAVENANT, JOHN (1576–1641). *Bishop of Salisbury. Divinity professor at Cambridge, he and three others were sent by *James I in 1618 to represent the Church of *England at the Synod of *Dort, where Davenant read an address advocating the *doctrine of universal *redemption. James evidently approved, for Davenant went to Salisbury in 1621. Even his very moderate *Calvinism, however, was unacceptable to *Charles I, and Davenant was publicly rebuked after *preaching a court *sermon on *predestination. Thereafter he dutifully carried out William *Laud's policies in church matters. Among his works is a much praised commentary on Colossians.

DAVID, CHRISTIAN (1691–1751). *Moravian Brethren leader. A former carpenter and lay *evangelist, after *conversion in 1717, he helped *Zinzendorf found his *Herrnhut community. Sent to Greenland in 1733, he clashed with Hans *Egede, whose Lutheran *orthodoxy did not take to the more devotional Moravian approach. David visited the U.S. and twice returned to Greenland before dying at Herrnhut.

DAVIDSON, ANDREW BRUCE (1831–1902). Scottish theologian. Graduate of Aberdeen, schoolmaster, then divinity student at Edinburgh, he became in 1863 professor of Hebrew and *OT at the *Free Church College, Edinburgh. A pioneer in introducing historical methods of OT study in Scotland, it was said he made the *prophets come alive for his students. His writings include an *Introductory Hebrew Grammar,* which was still used in Scottish divinity colleges in the mid-20th century. He helped produce the 1884 Revised Version of the *Bible.

DAVIDSON, RANDALL THOMAS (1848–1930). *Archbishop of Canterbury, 1903–1928. Born into a *Presbyterian family in Edinburgh, he was educated in England, episcopally ordained, and became chaplain to archbishop *Tait. His promotion was swift: dean of Windsor (1883), *bishop of Rochester (1891), bishop of Winchester (1895). He was highly regarded by Queen Victoria, was a strong ecumenist, and protested against religious persecution in Russia. In the Church of *England he strove to reconcile extremists, particularly over the use of *ritual in church services. He was made a peer on his retirement.

DAVIES, SAMUEL (1723–1761). Regarded as the founder of the *Presbyterian Church in the U.S. (Southern Presbyterian Church). Born in Delaware, he was ordained as a Presbyterian *evangelist in 1747 and became an active promoter of the *Great Awakening in Virginia and North Carolina. He visited Britain with Gilbert *Tennent in 1753, made a great impression there through his *preaching, and raised support for two notable causes: the College of New Jersey (now Princeton), of which he succeeded Jonathan *Edwards as president in 1759, and the fight for legal status for Presbyterians in Virginia—a battle won after Davies's early death at age thirty-eight.

DAY, DOROTHY (1897–1980). Roman Catholic social activist and writer. In her early years she wrote for the socialist and communist press. She converted to Catholicism in 1927 and helped found the Catholic Worker Movement. With another colleague she began the publication *Catholic Worker,* which interpreted social issues in terms of the Gospel. She also founded many homes and shelters for the homeless. Many Catholics see her as a contemporary saint of the church.

DAY OF CHRIST Term used by the *apostle Paul to denote the *second coming of *Christ (1 Cor 1:8; Phil 1:10; 2:16; et al.), based upon the *OT idea of the Day of the *Lord. It will be a day of judgment, surprise, *reward, consummation, and blessing, when *God in Christ will become all in all. It is variously expressed in the *NT, being referred to as the "Day of the Lord *Jesus" (2 Cor 1:14), "Day of Christ" (see references above), "Day of the Lord" (1 Thess 5:1), "his Day" (Luke 17:24), and "Day of God" (2 Peter 3:12).

DE BRUYS, PETER (d. c. 1130). French heretic. Reportedly a deposed *priest, he rejected infant *baptism and church buildings, the *Real Presence in the *sacrament, and *prayers for the dead. The valid points in his teaching were offset by the violence of his followers and by his own provocative behavior that led him to burn *crosses. A hostile mob, in the end, burned him.

DE FIDE (Lat. "concerning the *faith"). This term means that the statements of faith that the church teaches are revealed by *God and must not be denied. Such are the *Apostles' and *Nicene Creeds.

DE NOBILI, ROBERT (1577–1656). Born in Tuscany, he was sent to India in 1605 and served as a *Jesuit *missionary for thirty-six years in Madura. He dressed and lived as an Indian and declined to make his converts Europeans as well as Christians, which led to his suspension for some time. An eminent linguist and an author of numerous books, he traveled widely and reportedly made some 100,000 converts.

DE RANCÉ, ARMAND-JEAN LE BOUTHILLIER (1626–1700). Founder of the *Trappists. Family benefices were his from an early age, including a number of French abbacies. Even after his *ordination in 1651 it took the the death of two close friends to effect a *conversion that led to his becoming a *Cistercian in 1663. He made the *monastery at La Trappe (one of his former posts of which he was truly *abbot from 1664) a center of French spiritual life. In his emphases on *prayer, austerities, and manual labor he excluded study, for which he was often criticized.

DEACON (Gk. *diakonos,* "a servant or minister"). As servants of *Christ and his church deacons are named in Phil 1:1 and 1 Tim 3:18. The seven of Acts 6:1–6 are often called deacons, but in the passage the word is not used. In the early centuries a deacon had liturgical and social *duties. He assisted in the *Eucharist and at *baptisms, and he helped to administer the *charity of the church. However, in the West the diaconate became merely a short preparation for the entry into the priesthood (presbyterate), and so it is today in both the Roman Catholic and Anglican churches. In the *Eastern churches the traditional idea of a deacon has been preserved. Protestant churches have made various attempts to revive the *order of deacons, while in some churches (e.g., Baptist) a deacon is much the same as an *elder.

DEACONESS A female *deacon (Rom 16:1; 1 Tim 3:11). In the early church her *duty was to care for the sick and *poor, to instruct women in preparation for *baptism, and to help at the baptism of women. From the 6th century until recent times the office became virtually obsolete. It has been revived in *Lutheranism, *Anglicanism, and *Methodism.

DEAD, PRAYER FOR THE The practice of making petitions to *God for his blessing upon those who have died as Christians. It is presumed that they are in *purgatory and that the *prayers of the faithful on earth help the process of purification of *souls on their way to *heaven through purgatory. The biblical basis for such prayers is from the *Apocrypha (2 Macc 12:39–46). It has no explicit support in the *NT but is practiced by the Orthodox and Roman Catholics.

DEAD SEA SCROLLS Documents (from c. 150 B.C.–A.D. 70) found in Judean wilderness caves beginning in 1947 that were apparently the library of the *Qumran community, a strict religious *sect living on the edge of the desert. More than four hundred different documents have been identified, of which over a hundred are biblical texts. They cover basically the theological, ethical, and moral life of the community, dealing with such subjects as the end of the world; their views of priesthood, *sacrifice, and *obedience; the *law; leadership by "the Teacher of *Righteousness"; the *evil of the world; and the need for constant vigilance against defection. There are some similarities between ideas found here and in the *NT, but the differences are equally striking.

DEADLY SINS, SEVEN Sometimes called cardinal *sins. See also CAPITAL SINS, CAPITAL VIRTUES.

DEATH OF GOD THEOLOGY, THE A description of certain forms of radical *theology of the 1960s. Its basic idea appears to have been that *God has lost relevance for modern westerners; life can be explained without him. Advocates were T. J. J. Altizer, William Hamilton, and Gabriel Vahanian. They claimed to follow *Jesus and attempted to (radically) reinterpret *Christianity for a secular, scientific society.

DECALOGUE See COMMANDMENTS, THE TEN.

DECISION FOR CHRIST An expression used by some *evangelical Christians to denote an acceptance of the *gospel. This acceptance often occurs in a public meeting and is signified by putting up one's hand or by walking to the front. Theologically a decision of this kind cannot be described simply. It may represent a genuine interest in *Christianity, a desire to be known as a committed *Christian, an acceptance of the *faith learned at home or at church, or one of several things.

DECIUS (c. 201–251). Roman emperor. The first to launch organized persecution against the Christians. He began this persecution when many of them refused to perform religious *sacrifice in the name of the emperor. *Pope *Fabian and two other bishops were slain. Public opinion condemned the violence, and it ceased after a year. Decius and his son were killed soon afterwards in battle against the invading Goths.

DECLARATIONS OF INDULGENCE See INDULGENCE, DECLARATIONS OF.

DECREES, GOD'S ETERNAL The act of *God's *eternal *will putting into effect and operation his plan of *salvation. Speculation on this matter was common in medieval *theology and continued in Protestant *theology. Theologians differ as to whether there is only a decree of *predestination unto eternal life or whether with this there is a decree of *reprobation. All agree that there was a decree to create the *universe and uphold it when created.

DECRETALS Letters containing papal rulings on matters of law, notably those of canonical discipline. Binding only in the case under consideration, such decretals (rescripts) are sometimes decreed by the *pope to be general church law. The first known decretal (385) is often credited to Pope *Siricius.

DEDICATION OF INFANTS A service of thanksgiving for the birth of an infant and a time of *prayer for the child's future. This occurs instead of a service of infant *baptism and is common in Baptist churches. The child is entrusted to *God's care, and the parents pledge to raise the child according to *Scripture.

DEESIS (Gk. "entreaty"). An *icon found in the Greek *Orthodox Church. It has three parts. In the center is *Christ, on his right is *Mary, his mother, and on his left is John the Baptist. Mary and John face Christ, extending their hands in a gesture of *prayer.

DEFENDER OF THE FAITH A title conferred on *Henry VIII by Pope *Leo X in 1521 as a *reward for the king's pamphlet *Defence of the Seven Sacraments* against *Luther. The title was withdrawn by *Paul III after Henry had broken with Rome but was restored by Parliament in 1544 and is still used by English monarchs. The letters "F.D." (*Fidei Defensor*) have appeared on the coinage from the reign of George I (1714–1727).

DEFINITION, DOGMATIC A precise declaration by the church in an area of *doctrine. While such a declaration can never be the equivalent of *Scripture and must be subject to possible improvement at a later date, it represents the clearest expression of *truth at which the church has arrived. See also DOGMA, INFALLIBILITY.

DEHAAN, MARTIN R (1891–1965). Skilled *Bible expositor. This 20th-century physician-turned-preacher was a *pastor, a well-known conference speaker, the author of twenty-five books, and for over a quarter of a century the teacher on the "Radio Bible Class," which he founded in 1938. This worldwide ministry has been carried on by his son Richard and expanded with the addition of the television program "Day of Discovery."

DEIFICATION Being made like *God. The idea is developed from 2 Peter 1:4: "becoming partakers of the divine nature."

DEISM The view that our only knowledge of *God comes through *reason rather than through *revelation. On that broad base developed several strands of deism, but in England its "natural *religion" was expressed most lucidly in John *Toland's *Christianity Not Mysterious* (1696) and Matthew Tindal's *Christianity as Old as the Creation* (1730). Deism dispensed with the need for *faith or personal religion. Joseph *Butler's *Analogy of Religion* was welcomed as a weighty and decisive reply to deism.

DEISSMANN, ADOLF (1866–1937). German *NT scholar. Professor at Heidelberg (1897) and Berlin (1908), he was a pioneer in work on newly discovered Greek papyri. He wrote works that included *Light from the Ancient East* (Eng. transl. 1910). He was also an early encourager of the *ecumenical movement.

DEITY OF CHRIST See CHRIST, CHRISTOLOGY.

DELITZSCH, FRANZ JULIUS (1813–1890). German Lutheran theologian. Of Jewish descent, he was professor at Erlangen (1850), then at Leipzig (1867). He was an acknowledged master of Jewish studies, founded a Jewish *missionary college, and translated the *NT into Hebrew (1877). More conservative than *Wellhausen, he published several commentaries on *OT books and gained respect as a thoughtful scholar of independent mind.

DEMETRIUS (d. c. 231). *Bishop of Alexandria. Consecrated in 189, he appointed *Origen as head of the famous *catechetical school about 203. Differences arose between the two when Origen (a layman) preached in Caesarea (216) and later allowed himself to be ordained there (228). Demetrius objected to both actions.

DEMIURGE (Gk. *demiourgos,* "a craftsman"). Plato and certain early *Christian writers used this word to describe *God as the Creator. However, it was also used by heretics, especially Gnostics, to describe the inferior being (not God himself) who made the world. See also GNOSTICISM.

DEMON, DEMONOLATRY, DEMONOLOGY A demon is an *evil *spirit. *Jesus accepted the reality of their existence and delivered people from their power (Mark 1:34, 39). Paul saw their power behind paganism and false teaching (1 Cor 10:20–21; 1 Tim 4:1). Demonolatry is the *worship of demons. Once common in ancient times it is enjoying a revival in western civilization. Demonology is the study of "fallen *angels," *Satan, and *evil spirits; this may be pursued out of *Christian concern to identify them and their powers or for other motives. See also ANGELS, PRINCIPALITIES AND POWERS, SATAN.

DEMYTHOLOGIZATION A method of interpreting the *Bible pioneered by Rudolph *Bultmann of Marburg (1884–1976). It presupposes that *God's word in *Scripture is wrapped within a thick, cultural (mythological) clothing. Therefore it has little immediate meaning to modern people. So it is held that by demythologizing, the *truth is set free from its ancient cultural moorings in order to be good news for today. Bultmann chose to use modern existentialist philosophy to express God's word for today.

DENCK, HANS (c. 1495–1527). *Anabaptist leader. Born in Bavaria and trained as a humanist, he studied further under *Oecolampadius in Basel (1521). As a school rector in Nuremberg he was influenced by *Münzer and *Karlstadt and was expelled from the city for *heresy (1525). He was baptized by *Hubmaier and soon became prominent among the Anabaptists. A knowledgeable *OT scholar, Denck discarded many of the *doctrines held by the reformers, including the authority of *Scripture and the sufficiency of *Christ's *atonement.

DENNEY, JAMES (1856–1917). Scottish theologian. Minister of the *Free Church of Scotland, he was called to teach *systematic *theology (1897), then *NT (1900) in that church's Glasgow college, the latter post combined with the principalship from 1915. In both disciplines he wrote notable volumes, the best known of which are his commentary on *Romans* (1900) and his theological masterpiece *The Death of Christ* (1903). He held that the only theology he was interested in was that which could be preached. Denney helped establish his church's union with the *United Presbyterians in 1900 and thereafter took a prominent part in the courts of the *United Free Church.

DENOMINATION An association of churches with a particular name and a particular *confession of *faith. The word came into common usage only in the 19th century to describe the emergence of new, powerful groupings of churches that were not the old state and established churches. There are now hundreds of Protestant denominations—Baptist, Congregationalist, *Presbyterian, Methodist, etc. When a body of churches or people denies basic *Christian *doctrine (e.g., the *Trinity), they are usually called a *sect, for denomination is normally reserved for churches that hold to basic *orthodoxy.

DEONTOLOGY (Gk. *deon*, "*duty"; *logos*; "science, study"). The ethical theory that takes duty as the basis of morality. Some acts are obligatory without regard to their consequences. Such a view is particularly associated with the name of Immanuel *Kant (1724–1804).

DEPOSIT OF FAITH The *truths entrusted to the church by *God (see 1 Tim 6:20; 2 Tim 1:12, 14). The expression is used particularly by Roman Catholics of that which the church must faithfully preserve and infallibly expound.

DEPRAVITY See TOTAL DEPRAVITY.

DESCARTES, RENÉ (1596–1650). French philosopher and scientist. Educated by *Jesuits, he studied law but from 1619 gave himself to philosophy. From 1629 he lived in Holland. While he remained Roman Catholic, he challenged many of his church's traditional ideas by insisting on the use of human thought to establish certainties such as the existence of *God. See also CARTESIANS.

DESCENT INTO HELL (HADES), THE The creedal term to describe what is referred to in some *Scripture passages (Matt 27:52ff; Luke 23:43; Eph 4:9ff.; 1 Peter 3:18–20; 4:6). This clause from the Apostles' Creed has been variously interpreted in various ways: (1) *Christ's victory in death and *resurrection over *Satan, death, and *evil powers; (2) Christ's agony expressed on the *cross ("My God, My God, why hast thou forsaken me?"); and (3) Christ's visit to *Hades to preach to the believing dead or to the unbelieving dead.

DESIGN, ARGUMENT FROM See TELEOLOGY.

DETERMINISM A system of thought advocating that all events and human activity are subject to an inexorable, rigid law of cause and effect. There is no place for human *free *will. Where determinism operates in such disciplines as sociology and psychology, human freedom is denied, for environment and heredity are seen as the means of determinism. In *theology, determinism is found in extreme *doctrines of *predestination; here the freedom of the individual to choose or reject *God's offer of *salvation is denied.

DEUS A SE (Lat. "*God as he is in himself"). The inner being of God that we cannot know. This contrasts with **Deus pro nobis* (Lat. "God for us, God as he is towards us").

DEUS ABSCONDITUS (Lat. "the hidden *God"). Based on Isaiah 45:15, this phrase was used by Martin *Luther to emphasize that only by God's self-revelation can we know him; by *reason alone we cannot know him, for his *being is hidden from us.

DEUS EX MACHINA (Lat. "*God from a machine"). The introduction of the idea of God into a discussion or debate in order to solve a difficulty or bring the matter to an end.

DEUS PRO NOBIS (Lat. "*God for us, God on our behalf"). Either a description of God who reveals himself to his people and as he is toward them or, more particularly, the work of God for us in *Jesus Christ in the saving, substitutionary work on the *cross.

DEUS REVELATUS (Lat. "the revealed *God"). The belief that in *Christ we meet the revealed God, in contrast to the hidden God, **Deus absconditus*.

DEUTEROCANONICAL Of the second *canon. A term used by Roman Catholics to describe the books included in their *OT that are not in the OT used by Protestants. They were not written originally in Hebrew but in Greek. They are Tobit, Judith, 1 and 2 Maccabees, Wisdom, Ecclesiasticus, Baruch, and certain additions to the books of Daniel and Esther. Protestants usually refer to these books as the *Apocrypha.

DEVELOPMENT OF DOGMA See DOCTRINE, DEVELOPMENT OF.

DEVIL (Gk. *diabolos,* "accuser"). The chief of the fallen *angels and known also as *Satan (Heb. "the accuser"). He is seen as the origin of *sin in the world (Gen 3), for before the creation of Adam and Eve he had rebelled against *God. *Christ did battle with him and his associates (devils or demons) in his ministry and in his death and *resurrection (John 14:30). Though the devil is defeated, God allows him to keep his power until the end of the age, when at the Last *Judgment, he and all fallen angels will be condemned (Matt 25:41).

DEVIL RANSOM Popular name given to an early theory of the *Atonement. The view postulated that *Satan had become the rightful owner of sinful humanity, but *God took pity on them and offered his Son *Jesus as a ransom for them. *Satan accepted, and when Jesus entered into the realms of death he gathered up his own, taking them with him at his *resurrection. Thus, Satan lost both humankind and the ransom. This view or variations of it was quite popular until *Anselm's day when his *satisfaction theory replaced it. It has been revived recently in a demythologized form by Gustaf *Aulén in his book *Christus Victor* (1931).

DEVIL RANSOM THEORY A *doctrine of the *Atonement suggested by Mark 10:45 ("a ransom for many"; cf. Rom 3:24; Col 1:14; Eph 1:7; 1 Peter 1:18). Though not taught in the *Bible, some have said that *Christ paid *Satan the ransom of his life as the price to liberate people from Satan's grasp.

DEVIL'S ADVOCATE A popular name used of an official of the Roman Catholic Sacred Congregation for the Causes of Saints. His task is to present anything unfavorable about the candidate and to ask pertinent and difficult questions of those who wish to have a *Christian (having died) declared "blessed" (*beatification) or a "*saint" (*canonization). His opponent, who supports the proposal, is called God's Advocate.

DEVOTIO MODERNA (Lat. "modern devotion"). A form of spiritual life exemplified in *The Imitation of Christ* by Thomas à *Kempis (1380–1471). It cultivated devotion to the *Eucharist, *meditation on the *humanity of *Christ, and imitation of the *virtues of Christ. As a school of thought it was anti-intellectual and came to an end in the 16th century. Its positive aspects were picked up by other schools of *spirituality.

DIACONICUM (Gk. *diakonikon*, "appertaining to the *deacon"). In the Greek and *Eastern churches a small room to the south of the *sanctuary looked after by the *deacons. The *vestments, service books and holy *vessels are kept here. Thus it is similar to the *sacristy in the West.

DIALECTIC(S) As taught by *Hegel (d. 1831), this describes the logical pattern that thought must follow. It proceeds by contradiction and the reconciliation of contradiction. This is the way of thesis, antithesis, and synthesis. Out of two polarities arises the synthesis. Marxism has made use of this pattern of analysis and so, in general terms, has *dialectical *theology.

DIALECTICAL THEOLOGY Another term for *crisis *theology. Liberal theology is rejected. *God, the living *Lord, cannot be confined in cut-and-dried expressions. Divine *truth cannot be equated with a set of *dogmatic statements. Divine truth appears as a *paradox. Thus the method of stating truth is in terms of statement and counterstatement. God is at once the God of *grace and the God of *wrath and *judgment. He is the God of *eternity and of time.

DIASPORA The dispersion of the Jews from Palestine (538 B.C.). At the time of *Christ, thousands of Jews living outside Palestine in the Roman Empire looked to Jerusalem as their spiritual home, and many attended festivals there. The dispersion may be seen as the fulfillment of *Scripture (Deut 4:27; 27:64). It provided a base and launching pad for *Christian *missionaries in the Roman Empire, for they went first to the *synagogue of the Jews.

DIBELIUS, MARTIN (1883–1947). German theologian. Professor of *NT at Heidelberg from 1915, he founded a school of thought known as *form criticism. It advocated a new approach to the study of *Gospel narratives. A prolific writer, he was also deeply interested in the *ecumenical movement and concerned that it should have a proper theological basis.

DIBELIUS, OTTO (1880–1967). *Bishop of the Berlin-Brandenburg Church. A *pastor of the German *Reformed Church, he resisted Hitler's attempt to control the church and was dismissed as Lutheran superintendent in Berlin. He was arrested three times for continued resistance and was forbidden to speak or publish. After World War II he became bishop of divided Berlin and was as courageous against communism as against Nazism. He was a president of the *World Council of Churches (1954–1961).

DICHOTOMISM The view that a human being is composed of *body and *soul. In essence this is a philosophical *doctrine, but it can be expressed in *Christian terms. The unity of the human person is known under two basic aspects—body and *soul. In contrast *trichotomism is the view that there are three basic aspects to a human being, body, *soul, and *spirit.

DICKINSON, JONATHAN (1688–1747). American *Presbyterian minister. Ordained as a *Congregationalist after graduation from Yale, he soon joined the newly organized *Presbyterian movement, and it was under that polity that he ministered for thirty years to the church at Elizabethtown, New Jersey. Calvinist in *theology, he was irenic in dealing with those who differed over the contemporary *revival movement (which he supported). Friend of *Whitefield and *Brainerd, he secured the charter for the College of New Jersey (Princeton) and was elected its first president shortly before his death.

DIDACHE (Gk. "teaching"). Used either of the basic teaching given to new converts (and thus contrasted with *kerygma*, which is proclaimed before *conversion) or of the early *Christian manual on morals and church practice written c. A.D. 100. The full title of the latter is *The Teaching of the Twelve Apostles*.

DIDYMUS THE BLIND (c. 313–c. 398). *Eastern Church theologian. Though blind since childhood, he was appointed by *Athanasius as head of the catechetical school at Alexandria, where *Jerome was one of his students. Like Athanasius, Didymus was a strong opponent of *Arianism, but he himself was charged with *Origenism by Jerome, and probably for this reason his works were not copied during the Middle Ages. Only fragments of his writings survive, but he is known to have been one of the most learned commentators and ascetics of his age.

DIGAMY A second marriage after the termination of the first by the death of one of the parties. Where marriage is regarded as a *sacrament there is opposition to the idea of second marriages. In the Orthodox churches there is a different *prayer of blessing for a second marriage, and this reflects the general hesitation about such marriages. Digamy is different from bigamy in that the latter normally refers to having two wives both alive at the same time.

DIOCESE (Gk. *dioikesis,* "administrative unit"). A geographical, territorial unit of the church under the care of a *bishop. In the East it is called an *eparchy. Often diocesan boundaries in Europe follow civil territorial divisions and are named after the city in which the bishop resides.

DIOCLETIAN (245–316). Roman emperor. Born in Dalmatia and a general by 284, he was acclaimed as emperor by his soldiers, and in 285 was in control of both Eastern and Western areas. In 293 he split the empire into four administrative divisions and introduced order and reform. His zeal in consolidating the unity of his territories led to the major persecution of Christians that marred the last two years of his reign. He abdicated in 305.

DIODATI, GIOVANNI (1576–1649). Calvinist theologian. Born in Geneva of Italian parents, he became professor of Hebrew there in 1597, *pastor in 1608. He succeeded *Beza as professor of *theology in 1609 and was Genevese representative at the Synod of *Dort (1618–1619). His Italian translation of the *Bible (1607), revised and enlarged with notes in 1641, is still highly regarded for accuracy and clarity.

DIONYSIUS (d. c. 268). Pope from 259. Greek by birth, his was the task of reorganizing the church after the persecution during which his predecessor *Sixtus II had been martyred. He sent help to beleaguered Christians in Cappadocia, and he helped to further the concept of the *primacy of Rome by resolving a charge of *heresy against Bishop Dionysius of Alexandria.

DIONYSIOS THE AREOPAGITE (c. 500). Traditionally considered Paul's convert mentioned in Acts 17:34. Now called Pseudo-Dionysius, his many mystical writings were enormously influential on the theology of the Middle Ages. They greatly influenced scholasticism and were avidly read by *Erigena, *Grosseteste, and Thomas *Aquinas. They possibly introduced *neoplatonism and the *theology of *angels into the West. His best known works are *The Divine Names* and *The Mystical Theology,* classics of the **apophatic* approach to *God.

DIONYSIUS THE GREAT (c. 200–c. 265). *Bishop of Alexandria. A student of *Origen's at the *catechetical school in Alexandria, he became *bishop of that city in 247. He was exiled twice (during the persecutions under *Decius and *Valerian), and on his final return about 260 he was caught up in various theological conflicts, notably against the *Sabellians, who accused him of *heresy, a case referred to Pope *Dionysius.

DIOSCORUS (d. c. 454). *Patriarch of Alexandria. Having opposed the condemnation of *Eutyches by a *synod at Constantinople in 448, he presided over the Robber Synod of *Ephesus in 449 and was responsible for reinstating Eutyches, excommunicating Pope *Leo I, and deposing *Flavian of Constantinople for opposing the *Monophysitism that Dioscorus professed.

He himself was deposed by the Council of *Chalcedon (451), but the Monophysite churches still venerate him as a *saint.

DISCALCED From a Latin word meaning "unshod," the description is applied to *religious *orders whose members wear sandals or, like earlier monks, go barefoot (cf. Matt 10:10). The word "calced" is applied to those who wear shoes.

DISCIPLE, DISCIPLESHIP (Lat. *discipulus*, "learner, pupil"; Gk. *mathetes*, "follower, pupil"). Occurs over 250 times in the *NT. A *Christian disciple is one who follows *Christ and learns from him (Acts 6:1; 11:26; 21:16). In the Gospels it covers both ordinary disciples and the inner circle of apostles (Matt 10:1; 11:1; Luke 10:1–17). Discipleship is the activity and result of being a disciple and has a particular reference to *obedience to the whole of Christ's teaching in all of life.

DISCIPLES OF CHRIST A name given to the body originally founded by Thomas and Alexander *Campbell in the early 19th century. It subsequently developed into three different groups: the *Churches of Christ, the *Christian Church (Disciples of Christ), and the Undenominational Fellowship of Christian Churches and Churches of Christ.

DISCIPLINA ARCANI (Lat. "discipline of the secret"). The practice in the early church of concealing certain *doctrines and practices from both pagans and those being prepared for *baptism. The purpose was to safeguard the *faith against misunderstanding, misrepresentation, and profanation. In times of persecution this seemed very reasonable and sensible.

DISCIPLINE, BOOKS OF Two documents (1560, 1581) issued by the post-*Reformation Church of *Scotland. The first book, the work of John *Knox and five colleagues (all appointed by Parliament), made declarations on uniformity in *doctrine, *sacraments, *election, and sustenance of the ministry, ecclesiastical *discipline, caring for the *poor, and the advancement of education. It was never ratified by the Scottish Parliament, many of whose members were less single-minded. The second book formulated in a more systematic way the specific principles of Scottish *Presbyterianism, reducing the authorized offices in the kirk to those of *pastors, doctors, elders and *deacons, and proposing to add to assemblies and *synods a more local court called the *presbytery, and defining the relationship between church and state. Largely the work of Andrew *Melville, it has been called the charter of Presbyterianism.

DISCRIMINATION The distinction made in favor of, or against, a person solely in terms of his/her class, race, nationality, *religion, or sex. The humanity, the personhood, the fact of being made in God's image and likeness, is not the primary norm of evaluation and judgment; another norm supersedes. It is often a difficult area of modern life to expose with clarity, for it is such an emotive issue.

DISPENSATION A word with several meanings. (1) A synonym for covenant—the old and new dispensations, the Mosaic dispensation, etc. *God is the Dispenser through the covenant. (2) To dispense the *sacraments is to administer them. (3) The license granted by ecclesiastical authority to do what is normally forbidden by church (not God's) law.

DISPENSATIONALISM A view of the development and distinctiveness of *God's activity in history seen in terms of *dispensations. Each dispensation is a period of time in which human beings are tested in respect of their response to some specific *revelation of God's *will. There are seven such dispensations covering the period from the Creation to the Last *Judgment. This view is expounded in the *Scofield Reference *Bible* and may be traced to the teaching of J. N. *Darby (1800–1882). It is very influential in American *Fundamentalism.

DISPERSION See DIASPORA.

DISRUPTION, THE (1843). A division in the Church of *Scotland, when 451 of its 1,203 ministers left to form the *Free Church of Scotland. During the *Ten Years' Conflict that led up to the break, many had felt that an established church was a church in subjection to the *state and therefore betraying the principles gained at great cost by their ancestors. Even Thomas *Chalmers, however, held that a church could be established and yet remain *holy and independent. In a number of notorious cases the patron's nominee was forced upon a congregation by decision of the civil courts. After an adverse decision in the House of Commons in 1843, the *kirk's general assembly that year had barely begun when, in a dramatic move, Thomas *Chalmers, George *Candlish, and other ministers and elders left the hall and formed their own assembly in a nearby hall. Patronage was abolished in the Church of Scotland in 1874.

DISSENTERS Those who separate themselves from the established or national church on grounds of *conscience. In England this term covered *Presbyterians, *Congregationalists, *Baptists, and Roman Catholics from 1662 to c. 1850, then being replaced by the term "*nonconformists."

DISSENTING ACADEMIES Educational institutions begun in post-*Restoration England for the training of nonconformists. With non-Anglicans barred from the universities, the first academy was held in a Coventry house in 1663. The 1689 *Toleration Act allowed academies to expand, though political and social sanctions on non-Anglicans remained. Some of the academies, such as that run by Philip *Doddridge, offered a high standard of teaching; out of them sprang the famous Congregational colleges in London and Oxford. The academies disappeared in the 19th century when English universities accepted nonconformists.

DISSOLUTION OF THE MONASTERIES Action taken by *Henry VIII to raise funds and to underline his claim to royal supremacy over the church. By applying to all *monasteries the corruption reflected in some, the king through Parliament had the smaller houses suppressed in 1536 and the greater *monasteries suppressed in 1539–1540. Some compensation was made to religious males, but the dissolution caused much suffering among *nuns.

DIVINATION (Lat. *devinare,* "to foresee, predict"). The art of predicting the future through *occult forces. The forms include augury (interpretation of omens—e.g., the flight of birds), chiromancy (interpreting the lines on a palm of a hand), and *necromancy (consulting the *souls of the dead; *spiritualism). Divination is condemned by the *Bible (Lev 29:31; 20:27) and is incompatible with true *faith and trust in *God.

DIVINE ("FATHER"), MAJOR J. (d. 1965). Born George Baker in Georgia, he was originally a Baptist. After he moved to New York, he founded his own Peace Mission Movement, with an emphasis also on *temperance and frugality. He founded a chain of "Peace Restaurants" and other establishments for the benefit of poor blacks. Father Divine was a millionaire. He claimed to be God and to have 22 million followers at one time.

DIVINE RIGHT OF KINGS A theory found among the later Stuart monarchs in Britain that held that the power of making laws resides solely in the king. Originally a *Byzantine conception, it did not make the same impression in the West, chiefly because of papal opposition. The Stuarts nonetheless expressed the view that Parliaments were expedient, but that members sat there only through a special privilege accorded by the ruler. It was this theory that led *Mary, Queen of Scots, and her grandson *Charles I to execution and that eventually spelled the end of the Stuart dynasty.

DIVORCE The legal dissolution of a marriage. In modern times there is a growing gulf between secular and *Christian views of the grounds for divorce, which is becoming easy to obtain in civil courts. Christian services of marriage declare that marriage is a lifelong union to the exclusion of others, and so divorce is incompatible with this idea. However, on the basis of Matt 5:32 divorce has been allowed (by some Protestants but not by Roman Catholics) for *adultery. Today with the growth of divorcees in society, the churches are having to find ways of ministering to them. To uphold traditional and biblical ideas of marriage and to be compassionate are at the center of this ministry. It also includes the difficult question of the remarriage of divorcees in church or in services conducted by *clergy.

DIX, GREGORY (1901–1952). Anglican *Benedictine monk. Graduate of Oxford, where he briefly lectured in history. He was ordained in 1925, became a monk at Nashdom Abbey in 1926, and became *prior in 1948. A well-known broadcaster and liturgical scholar, his work on *Christian *worship, *The Shape of the Liturgy* (1945), had a great influence on the Church of *England.

DIXON, AMZI CLARENCE (1854–1925). Baptist minister and writer. Born in North Carolina and ordained in 1876, he ministered in the U.S., notably at Moody Memorial Church, Chicago (1906–1911), before going to the Metropolitan Tabernacle, London (1911–1919). Called by his biographer a "strong and militant fundamentalist," he was a well-known speaker at conferences and crusades, published many books, and collaborated with R. A. *Torrey in *The *Fundamentals*.

DOCETISM (Gk. *dokein*, "to appear to be"). Early *Christian *heresy that said that *Jesus was *God in the appearance of a man but not genuinely a man: he did not actually die on the *cross; this led to a denial of his *resurrection and *ascension. Docetism arose out of the conception of matter as essentially *evil—a significant element in *Gnosticism. The *Bible teaches that Jesus was God made man (e.g., Col 2:8ff.; 1 John 4:2; 5:6).

DOCTORS OF THE CHURCH A term originally applied to four theologians of outstanding merit and holiness of life (*Ambrose, *Augustine of Hippo, *Gregory the Great, *Jerome), then also used of *Athanasius, John *Chrysostom, *Basil the Great, and *Gregory of Nazianzus. From the 16th century, *Roman Catholicism has added others so that the list has over thirty names, including *Thomas Aquinas and several women—e.g., *Catherine of Siena (1347–1380) and *Teresa of Avila (1515–1582).

DOCTRINE Teaching such as is found in books on *theology, *creeds, and *confessions of *faith. It is the attempt to put into modern language and thought forms the teaching of the *Bible in response to questions asked at any time—e.g., on the nature of man, the identity of *Jesus Christ, and the ending of the world. When a doctrine is stated by a competent church body to be true, it may be called a *dogma (cf. the dogma of the *ecumenical councils).

DOCTRINE, DEVELOPMENT OF The way in which different *doctrines are stated with clarity and approval at different points in the history of the church—e.g., the *Trinity in the 4th century and *justification in the 16th. Further, it is the relationship of these doctrines, when stated, to earlier statements and especially to basic biblical teaching. This topic is of fundamental importance to Roman Catholics, for they hold both to the authority of the *Bible and to the *truth of these doctrines defined by *ecumenical councils and by the *pope. It is also not without importance to Protestants for whom a specific *confession of *faith or doctrinal *tradition affects the way in which the Bible is read and understood.

DOCUMENTARY HYPOTHESIS A theory about the origins of the five books of Moses—Genesis through Deuteronomy. Many scholars believe that there are four principal strata of written material, coming from different periods of Israelite history. These are designated by the letters *J (Jahwist), *E (Elohist), *D (Deuteronomist), and *P (Priestly Code). The hypothesis is that editors put together these documents to form the *Pentateuch, the Five Books of Moses. Certain scholars also believe that the documents can be traced in Joshua as well. In general, conversative *evangelical scholars either receive this hypothesis cautiously or reject it. It is a part of what is called the *higher *criticism of the *Bible.

DODD, CHARLES HAROLD (1884–1973). British *NT scholar. An ordained Congregational minister, he taught at Manchester and then became the first non-Anglican since 1660 to hold a divinity chair at Cambridge. A liberal in *theology, he produced many scholarly works, including a commentary on Romans (1932), *The Parables of the Kingdom* (1934), and *The Apostolic Preaching and Its Development* (1935). He was general director of the New English Bible translation. On his death a memorial service was held in Westminster Abbey—a rare honor for a Free churchman.

DODDRIDGE, PHILIP (1702–1751). *Nonconformist minister. The most prominent of those who organized *dissenting academies, he trained many students. From 1729 he was also *pastor of a large independent congregation in Northampton. He evidently taught a modified *Calvinism and, like most moderates, was accused of a variety of *heresies. He distributed *Bibles and wrote books and *hymns (e.g., "O God of Bethel" and "Hark the Glad Sound!").

DODS, MARCUS (1834–1909). Minister of a Glasgow *Free church, he became professor of *NT at New College, Edinburgh, in 1889. Conservative churchmen often challenged his *orthodoxy, chiefly that he denied the *inerrancy of *Scripture, but the *general assembly ruled in his favor.

DOGMA *Doctrine that has become the official teaching of the church or of a *denomination. Thus the doctrine of the *Trinity is the dogma of the whole church, while the *infallibility of the *pope is a dogma only of the Roman Catholic Church. The problem of how a given dogma relates to earlier teaching is known as the development of dogma (development of *doctrine).

DOGMATICS, DOGMATIC THEOLOGY The scientific study of *doctrine and *dogma. It is the systematic presentation of the teaching of the church, showing how each part relates to other parts and how it is derived from *Scripture. Obviously in different *Christian traditions—Lutheran, Orthodox, *Reformed, Roman Catholic—it is different. The most famous of modern dogmatics is that of Karl *Barth's *Church Dogmatics*.

DÖLLINGER, JOHANNES JOSEPH IGNAZ VON (1799–1890). Roman Catholic scholar. As professor of church history in Munich, he showed a belief in national and religious freedom that brought down on him papal displeasure. He particularly disliked the *dogma of the *Immaculate Conception of *Mary. The *Syllabus of Errors in 1864 condemned some of his ideas. In 1869 he wrote a series of articles under a pseudonym that were later published as *The Pope and the Council,* in which he attacked the Council of *Trent and suggested that the decrees of a general council are dependent on the consent of the church. In 1871 Döllinger was excommunicated for refusal to accept the dogma of papal *infallibility and was soon deposed from his chair. He conferred with those who founded the *Old Catholic Church but did not join them formally. Later he differed from them when they moved against *clerical *celibacy and *confession. He nonetheless received the last *rites from an Old Catholic *priest.

DOMINIC (1170–1221). Founder of the *Dominicans. Born in Spain, he lived under the *Augustinian rule. On a visit to France with his *bishop, he encountered *Albigensians and then worked zealously to bring them back to the church. He got papal permission in 1215 to found a *religious *order devoted to *preaching and the *conversion of heretics. Dominic, who three times refused the offer of bishoprics, was conspicuous for *prayer, *mortification, and *love of neighbor. His aim was "to speak only of *God or with God."

DOMINICANS (ORDER OF FRIARS, PREACHERS; OFTEN CALLED BLACK FRIARS) Founded by *Dominic at Toulouse in 1215. He had preached *Christian *doctrine there with the intention of converting the *Albigensians. Both contemplative and active, with a democratic form of government, the *priests belonged, not to one of a number of autonomous houses, but to the *order itself, and could be sent anywhere at any time. There was emphasis on theological study, and, by the mid-13th century, influential Dominican scholars were to be found teaching in the universities of Europe, among them *Albertus Magnus and Thomas *Aquinas. Meanwhile the *evangelistic outreach continued; Dominicans were to be found accompanying the Spanish and Portuguese explorers. Though generally conservative in *theology, many of them have been active in the reform sparked by *Vatican Council II. Dominicans form one of the four great *mendicant orders of the Roman Catholic Church.

DOMITILLA, FLAVIA (d. c. 100). Early *Christian *martyr. Her husband, though a consul and a cousin of the emperor Domitian, was reportedly put to death for professing *Christianity. His wife was first banished, then killed. Her property was used as a Christian *burial place, and traces of it remain. Some scholars hold there were two women of similar name: the one mentioned here and her niece by marriage.

DONATION OF CONSTANTINE A document in which *Constantine the Great supposedly granted Pope Sylvester I (314–335) and his successors not only *spiritual supremacy over the other great patriarchates but also spiritual and temporal power over Rome and the whole Western Empire. It boosted the position of the *papacy until the 15th century, when it was proved to be an 8th-century forgery. The document was said to have been the result of Constantine's gratitude for being healed of leprosy and converted to *Christianity.

DONATISM A movement in the North African church (3d–7th century). Donatus (d. 355) was one of its early *bishops, and it is named for him. It began, in a period of persecution, over the question: Should a clergyman who had handed over the *Scriptures to the authorities be allowed to continue as a clergyman and to preside at the *Eucharist? The Donatists said no, insisting on the holiness and purity of the church. The dispute broke out after Caecilian had been consecrated as bishop of Carthage before some of the bishops had arrived, but there were mixed doctrinal and social motives involved in the opposition. Two successive Western church councils confirmed Caecilian as bishop, but in 312, Donatus, bishop of Casae Nigrae, led the dissidents into a *schism that broke with orthodox *Christianity and opposed Roman rule and influence in North Africa as well as state interference in church affairs. They sought refuge in *apocalyptic, the more extreme among them courting martyrdom. Despite persecution and exile, they grew and were for thirty years the majority party in North African Christianity. Their schismatic church did not live up to its high claims and was destroyed in the Muslim invasion of North Africa.

DONNE, JOHN (1572–1631). English poet and dean of St. Paul's. After a varied and checkered career in public service, he was ordained in 1615 and was appointed dean of St. Paul's six years later, attracting large congregations by his *preaching. A highly original poet who developed *paradox and imagery in a sometimes startling way and displayed a deep sense of *sin, he wrote prose rather than poetry after his *ordination.

DOOYEWEERD, HERMAN (1894–1977). Dutch *Reformed theologian and philosopher. Basing his system upon revelation rather than *reason, Dooyeweerd criticized all of Western philosophy as neglecting the religious dimension of decision making and thought. He then built up a positive system that consisted of a complex set of interrelated created "spheres," each of which must be kept autonomous to be understood. Dooyeweerd promulgated his views from his chair of legal philosophy at the Free University of Amsterdam, which he held from 1926–1965, and in the philosophical journal *Philosophia Reformata,* which he founded along with D. H. Th. Vollenhoven. His major work was *A New Critique of Theoretical Thought* (4 vols., 1953–1958). See also COSMOSCOPE.

DORMITION OF THE VIRGIN The feast of the falling asleep (*dormitio*) of *Mary, the Blessed Virgin. Observed by the Orthodox churches on August 15, it is the equivalent of the Roman Catholic feast of the *Assumption.

DORNER, ISAAC AUGUST (1809–1884). Lutheran historian and theologian. Dorner is best remembered for his monumental *History of the Development of the Person of Christ* (5 vols., 1846–50) and *A System of Christian Doctrine* (4 vols., 1879–1881). His influence was also exercised through his long tenures as teacher (Tübingen, Kiel, Königsberg, Bonn, Göttingen, and Berlin) and in the academic journal *Jahrbücher fúr deutschen Theologie,* which he cofounded. He was a moderate theologian in days when the radical *Tübingen School held sway. He developed an original view of the *Incarnation that was akin to that *Irenaeus, but it was never widely accepted.

DORT, SYNOD OF (1618–1619). An assembly of *Reformed churches that met at Dort (Dordrecht) in the Netherlands. Only the *Westminster Assembly is more important in *Reformed history. Confronted by the challenge of *Arminianism that sought to soften the rigors of *Calvinism, the *synod would not permit supporters of the former view to state their case in public session. Rather, they condemned them in the canons of the Synod of *Dort and had them deposed. The synod reaffirmed acceptance of the *Belgic and *Helvetic Confessions and so consolidated in Holland a strict Calvinism that lasted for two centuries.

DOSITHEUS, CONFESSION OF A statement of *doctrine from the Greek Orthodox Church (1672). It was drafted to meet the challenge of *Protestantism, and its principal author was Dositheus, *patriarch of Jerusalem (1669–1707).

DOSTOEVSKY, FYODOR (1821–1881). Russian writer. Born in Moscow, he trained as an engineer, but in 1846 he gave up a military career to devote himself to literature. Soon he won fame, but his involvement in a group that pressed for social reform brought him a death sentence that was commuted to imprisonment in Siberia, about which he wrote *The House of the Dead* (1861). Released in 1854 after a deep *spiritual transformation, his keen psychological and religious insights are apparent particularly in *Crime and Punishment* (1866) and *The Brothers Karamazov* (1880).

DOUAY BIBLE The first Roman Catholic English version of the *Bible (*NT in 1582, *OT in 1609–1610), it was done at the Roman Catholic College of Douai (then in the Spanish Netherlands but now in France). See also BIBLE, ENGLISH VERSIONS.

DOUBLE PREDESTINATION The view that *God, solely of his good pleasure and without regard to the time, place, and manner of one's birth, eternally elected some people to *eternal life and others to eternal damnation. It is found, though not exclusively, in high forms of *Calvinism. See also PREDESTINATION.

DOUBLE PROCESSION OF THE HOLY SPIRIT The *doctrine that within the *eternal life of the Godhead the Holy *Spirit proceeds from the Father and the Son. This is the teaching of the Western version of the *Nicene Creed; however, the original Eastern version states that the Spirit proceeds from the Father alone. These two views reflect different approaches to the doctrine of the *Trinity in the East and West.

DOUKHOBORS (DUKHOBORS) Eighteenth-century Russian *sect; the word means "spirit-wrestlers." A reaction to the Westernizing tendencies of the Czar Peter and the liturgical reforms of the *patriarch *Nikon, they rejected *spiritual and temporal authority and were guided by personal *revelation and an oral body of *tradition called the "Book of Life." They had no *priests or *sacraments, resisted conscription, and suffered persecution. *Tolstoy persuaded the Czar to let them emigrate, and 7,500 had reached Canada by the end of the 19th century. Some were absorbed into Canadian society, others still withhold taxes and avoid education for their children, bringing them into conflict with the law. There are some 20,000 Doukhobors in Canada today.

DOWIE, JOHN ALEXANDER (1847–1907). *Evangelist and *faith healer. Born in Scotland, he became a Congregational *pastor in Australia in 1870 but later took to independent *evangelism and faith *healing. He extended his activities to the U.S., founded the "Christian Catholic Church" there in 1896, and in 1901, with some five thousand followers, established Zion City on the shores of Lake Michigan. The community prospered under his strict regime, but financial and other problems caused his deposition in 1906.

DOWNGRADE CONTROVERSY The term seems to have emerged in London after C. H. *Spurgeon published an article (1887) lamenting *evil days and downward tendencies and criticizing ministers who questioned *cardinal *doctrines of the *faith. He left the Baptist Union and the London Baptist Association as a result. While most Baptist ministers remained within the union, Spurgeon's action made an impact among *evangelical ministers of all *denominations, and many wrote to thank him. It was nonetheless a bitter struggle and is said to have hastened his death in 1892.

DOXOLOGY A formula or *hymn of praise addressed to *God. The most common is "Glory be to the Father, and to the Son, and to the Holy Ghost" (or "Holy *Spirit"). A popular one is that by Thomas Ken: "Praise God from whom all blessings flow. . . ." In the *Bible there are many (e.g., 1 Tim 1:17; Jude 24; Rev 7:12).

DRIVER, SAMUEL ROLLES (1846–1914). *OT scholar. Professor of Hebrew at Oxford from 1883, he was a prominent figure in OT textual and critical studies. His works include commentaries, *Introduction to the Literature of the Old Testament* (1897 and many later editions), and a share in the monumental Brown-Driver-Briggs *Hebrew and English Lexicon of the Old Testament* (1906).

DRUMMOND, HENRY (1851–1897). Scottish writer and *evangelist. As a *Free Church of Scotland theological student, he left his studies to assist D. L. *Moody for the latter's two- year campaign in Britain (1873–1875). From 1877 he taught natural science at the Free Church College in Glasgow, where he became professor after *ordination in 1884. Though a gifted scientist, he gave his life to evangelistic work and became known and loved, particularly among students the world over. Among his writings were *Natural Law in the Spiritual World* (1883) and an address he gave that was published with the title *The Greatest Thing in the World*.

DUALISM The view that there are two basic, fundamental realities that are opposed to each other and that cannot be reconciled (e.g., a power of good and a power of *evil in the *universe). *Christianity rejects dualism, teaching that *God as Creator is the only source of everything and that at the end of the age all powers now contrary to his *will are to become subservient, so that all apparent dualism ceases.

DUFF, ALEXANDER (1806–1878). *Missionary to India. The first to be sent to India by the Church of *Scotland, Duff had been greatly influenced by Thomas *Chalmers's emphasis on education. In Calcutta, Duff's policy of an educational *mission reached Hindu and Muslim communities hitherto untouched. Transferring, like most Evangelicals, to the *Free Church of Scotland at the *Disruption in 1843, he had to relinquish the Indian property and to embark on a rebuilding program. Though dogged by ill health that finally forced his early retirement from the field in 1864, he helped establish Calcutta University and founded the *Calcutta Review*. From 1867 he was professor of *evangelical *theology at New College, Edinburgh.

DULIA (Gk. *douleia,* "servitude"). The reverence of a *disciple for his master. Thus the honor paid to *angels and *saints in *heaven by the faithful on earth.

DUNKERS See BRETHREN (DUNKERS).

DUNS SCOTUS, JOHN (c. 1264–1308). *Franciscan philosopher. Born in Scotland, he became a *Franciscan, studied at Oxford, was ordained in 1291, and taught at Oxford, Paris, and Cologne. Against Thomas *Aquinas he argued that *faith could not be established through *reason or speculation but was a matter of *will and practice. His theological system stressed 2 Cor 5:18: "All this is from *God, who through *Christ reconciled us to himself."

DU PLESSIS, DAVID J. (1905–1987). South African *ecumenical and *Pentecostal spokesman (later became a naturalized U.S. citizen). Du Plessis experienced the *baptism in the Holy *Spirit in 1918. By 1935 he was a leader in the *Apostolic Faith Mission, the strongest Pentecostal church in South Africa, where he served until 1947, when his worldwide ministry began. He was more successful than anyone else in linking the Pentecostal, ecumenical, and *charismatic movements.

DÜRER, ALBRECHT (1471–1528). German painter and engraver. Born and settled in Nuremberg, he introduced new concepts of *art to his country after spending some time in Italy. In 1498 he completed his magnificent engraving of the *Apocalypse. In 1512 he completed an engraving of Jerome. His many religious paintings include *The Madonna and Child* and *The Adoration of the Magi*. His woodcuts and engravings exist in collections throughout the world. He is often considered the inventor of etching. A man of serene character, he remained a Roman Catholic, but he respected and was respected by Luther and other Protestants.

DUTCH REFORMED CHURCH At the *Reformation the initial influence of Ulrich *Zwingli in the Netherlands soon gave way to a thoroughgoing *Calvinism. Despite a challenge at the Synod of *Dort in 1618–1619, this was the national *creed until the 19th century. The liberal policies of William I's reign (1814–1840) led to a series of *schisms that left Holland with three *Reformed churches, each claiming to be the true custodian of Reformed *Christianity. In 1848 the original church was disestablished. In its church courts the Dutch Reformed Church resembles those of Scottish and American *Presbyterianism. Immigrant Dutchmen established their church in America and South Africa (where it became the chief representative of Christianity). Dutch Calvinists of various branches have contributed much also to political and social life.

DUTCH REFORMED CHURCH (SOUTH AFRICA) The church appeared on the Cape with the first Dutch settlement in 1652. When the British took over the area in the late 18th century, the South Africans of Dutch origin moved northward and organized their churches in the independent territories of Transvaal and the Orange Free State. These too came under British control in the early 20th century. The Dutch Reformed Church continued side by side with the English-speaking churches but reestablished ascendancy when the Republic of South Africa was formed soon after World War II. The Dutch Reformed Church adheres to a strict *Calvinism and has countenanced the *apartheid policies of the *state (with notable individual exceptions) to an extent that has caused dismay and brought criticism from churches in other countries.

DUTY The moral obligation either to do or not to do something; also that which must be done or omitted. Christians define duty primarily in terms of *God's *will and purpose and thus see their duty as pleasing God. Duty to parents, society, etc., is seen under this general duty to God.

DWIGHT, TIMOTHY (1752–1817). Congregational theologian and educator. Graduate of Yale, he was a *Congregationalist *pastor before becoming president of Yale College (1795–1817). A grandson of Jonathan *Edwards, he was a moderate Calvinist, an effective spiritual counselor of students, and a supporter of the *Second Great Awakening.

DYOPHYSITISM (Gk. *duo*, "two"; *phusis*, "nature"). A description of the position of those who defended the teaching of the Council of *Chalcedon. They taught that *Christ is one *person with two *natures.

DYOTHELETISM (Gk. *duo*, "two"; *thelema*, "*will"). The teaching that since *Christ has both a human and a divine *nature, he must also possess a human and a divine will, which are free but never in conflict. This is the teaching of the Third Council of *Constantinople (680–681).

DYSTELEOLOGY The opposite of *teleology. Used by philosophers to denote the idea that nature is without an obvious purpose. This view gained popularity after the publication of Darwin's views on natural selection in *evolution, which appeared to prove that there was not any great purpose observable in or deducible from the world of nature. Christians hold that there is purpose and that this is revealed by *God in the *truth written in *Scripture.

E

E The supposed source of the *Pentateuch that used *Elohim for *God. See also DOCUMENTARY HYPOTHESIS.

EADMER (c. 1060–c. 1130). English historian and *Benedictine monk. He was greatly indebted to *Anselm, whose chaplain he became at Canterbury in 1093. He was elected *bishop of St. Andrews in 1120 but relinquished the see when the Scots refused to recognize the authority of Canterbury. Among Eadmer's works are a history of England between 1066 and 1122 and a life of Anselm, both of which are of great value to historians.

EASTER The festival of the *resurrection of *Jesus Christ. Its date is fixed with reference to the full moon, and it always occurs between March 21 and April 25. It is the center of the liturgical year; before it comes *Lent and *Holy Week, and after it comes Ascension Day and *Whitsuntide (*Pentecost). The origin of the word "Easter" is uncertain. It may be from "Eastre," the Teutonic goddess of spring.

EASTER, DATING OF Among Western Christians, Easter is celebrated on the first *Sunday after the full moon that occurs on or next after the vernal equinox (i.e., between March 22 and April 25). During the early centuries there had been controversy between East and West about the manner and date of Easter, until the matter was decided by the Council of *Nicea in 325. Differences nonetheless persisted in certain parts of Christendom until the 8th century. Even today, because a slightly different calculation is followed, the *Eastern Orthodox celebration of Easter, while sometimes coinciding with that of the West, can fall one, four, or five weeks later.

EASTERN CHURCHES Churches that evolved or developed from the patriarchates of Constantinople, Alexandria, and Antioch in the eastern half of the Roman Empire. Of great importance for their history were the divisions caused by the Nestorian and Monophysite controversies as well as those between Rome and Constantinople. Thus the Eastern churches of today include the Nestorian Church, the Monophysite (Non-Chalcedonian) Church, the *Orthodox Church, and churches in communion with Rome (known as the *Uniats). The largest of these groupings (the Orthodox Church) recognizes the primacy of the *patriarch of Constantinople.

EASTERN ORTHODOX CHURCH A federation of autonomous churches that claims unbroken descent from the church established by *Christ and his *apostles. It follows the *faith and practice laid down by the first seven *ecumenical councils (325–787); its official designation is "the Orthodox Catholic Church." For the *Eastern churches, the highest authority in doctrinal disputes was the ecumenical council, hence it differed radically from the Western church where ultimate authority was claimed by the *pope. These different concepts led to the *Great Schism between East and West in 1054. In Eastern Orthodoxy, the ecumenical *patriarch of Constantinople holds honorary primacy, followed by the three other ancient patriarchates of Alexandria, Antioch, and Jerusalem.

EASTERN RITES The different *liturgies and forms of *worship found in the *Orthodox, Nestorian, Monophysite, and *Uniat churches of eastern Europe, the Middle East, and India. These are usually said to be the Alexandrian, Antiochene, Chaldean, Armenian, and *Byzantine *rites. The latter is the most widely used, being that of the largest church, the Orthodox. All the rites are characterized by their antiquity and by the pomp and splendor of their ceremony.

EASTON, BURTON SCOTT (1877–1950). American *NT scholar. An ordained Anglican clergyman, he taught at Western Theological Seminary, Chicago (1911–1919), and at General Theological Seminary, New York (1919–1948). He earned an international reputation as an exegete, notably for his commentaries *Luke* (1926) and *Pastoral Epistles* (1947).

EBIONITISM From the Hebrew meaning "poor men," it specifically refers to the teaching of a *sect of Jewish Christians who lived in Palestine in the early *Christian centuries. They taught that Jesus was the true son of Joseph and *Mary and that the Holy *Spirit descended upon him so that he became the *Son of *God. They also placed great emphasis on keeping the law of Moses. However, it is also used to describe any very low view of the *person of *Jesus Christ.

ECCLESIA (EKKLESIA) A Greek and Latin word meaning "an assembly of people" and used in the *NT to describe the community of *disciples of *Jesus Christ. It is often translated as "church."

ECCLESIA REFORMATA SED SEMPER REFORMANDA (Lat. "the church reformed but always in need of reform"). One of the fundamental principles of the Protestant *Reformation of the 16th century. It has been taken over by the Roman Catholic Church and is echoed in the teaching of the Second *Vatican Council (1962–1965).

ECCLESIOLOGY The branch of *systematic theology that studies the *doctrine of the church (*ecclesia*). It involves a study of the biblical teaching on the church and ways in which that teaching has been understood and put into practice in the history of the church. The term is also used of the science of designing, building, and decorating places of *worship.

ECK, JOHANN (1486–1543). Roman Catholic theologian. Professor of *theology at Ingolstadt from 1510, he is best known for his opposition to *Luther, to whose *Ninety-Five Theses he produced a reply, and with whom he conducted a public disputation in 1618. Eck, who helped secure Luther's *excommunication in 1520, became the acknowledged champion of *Roman Catholicism in Germany against *Protestantism. He also countered the work of *Melanchthon and *Zwingli.

ECKHART, MEISTER (ECKHART VON HOCHHEIM) (c. 1260–1327). German mystic. Entering the *Dominican *order at an early age, he was *vicar general of Bohemia by 1307 and later became in Cologne one of the most renowned preachers of his day and the "father of German *mysticism." He taught that every man had a divine spark in him, but his attempt to explain the relation between *God and man in realistic terms led to ambiguities and charges of *heresy.

ECONOMIC TRINITY A view of *God that asserts the full deity of the Father (God) but claims that the Son and the *Spirit came to exist as functions (economies) of God only for the purposes of creation and *redemption. God is only threefold as he relates to the created order: he is not threefold in himself eternally, as the orthodox *doctrine of the *Trinity asserts.

ECONOMY, DIVINE (Gk. *oikonomia*, "plan" or "arrangement"). The plan of *God—Father, Son, and Holy *Spirit—for the creation and *redemption of the world as seen in its execution in space and time. Particularly God's plan is seen in the *incarnation of the Son as *Jesus Christ, *Savior of the world (Eph 3:9).

ECSTASY The state of being overcome by an overpowering experience. *Christian mystics have claimed ecstatic experiences produced by the Holy *Spirit. At such times the normal functions of the *body appear to be in suspension while a tremendous sense of the presence and power of *God is felt. St. *Teresa of Avila describes this in her *Interior Castle*. For examples of ecstasy in the *Bible see 1 Sam 10:5; 2 Kings 3:15; Acts 10:10; 11:5; 22:17.

ECUMENICAL, ECUMENICAL MOVEMENT, ECUMENISM (Gk. *oikumene,* "the whole inhabited world"). With the modern concern for *Christian unity, ecumenical has the meaning of "working for unity and reunification." Ecumenism is everything involved in this process—ethos, methods, and activities. The origin of the ecumenical movement is usually taken as the 1910 *Edinburgh Missionary Conference. The *World Council of Churches was formed in 1948 and is now the focal point of this work for unity. Since much of the *evangelical Christianity in the world remains outside the movement, it is not as yet truly ecumenical (covering all the world).

ECUMENICAL COUNCILS Meetings of *bishops of the whole church. Before the *Great Schism of 1054, seven councils were recognized as *ecumenical by Rome and Constantinople—*Nicea I (325), *Constantinople I (381), *Ephesus (431), *Chalcedon (451), *Constantinople II (553), *Constantinople III (680–681), and *Nicea II (787). Rome alone recognized an eighth: the Council of Constantinople IV (869–870), which excommunicated the *patriarch of Constantinople. Since then the Roman Catholic Church has recognized a further thirteen councils as ecumenical, including *Vatican Council II (1962–1965). To be considered ecumenical, a council has to be called by the *pope and to have had its decisions promulgated by him.

ECUMENICAL COUNCILS (ROMAN CATHOLIC) Those councils of the Western Roman Church counted as ecumenical by the Roman but not by the Orthodox churches. They begin after the Second Council of *Nicea and are: Constantinople IV (869–870), Lateran I (1123), Lateran II (1139), Lateran III (1179), Lateran IV (1215), *Lyons I (1245), *Lyons II (1274), *Vienne (1311–1312), *Constance (1414–1408), *Florence (1438–1445), Lateran V (1512–1517), *Trent (1545–1563), *Vatican I (1869–1870), and *Vatican II (1962–1965).

ECUMENICAL CREEDS Statements of *faith used by the whole church. Only one *creed, the *Nicene Creed (produced at the Councils of *Nicea [325] and *Constantinople [381]) can be called universal. In the West the *Apostles' Creed is widely used by Roman Catholics and Protestants, but it is rarely used in the *Eastern churches.

ECUMENICAL PATRIARCH A title given to the *patriarch of Constantinople, the see that since the 5th century has had the primacy of honor in the *Eastern Orthodox Church. Even after Constantinople had fallen to the Turks in 1453, the patriarch was given civil authority over all Christians within the Turkish Empire. The 20th-century Turks have threatened to be less tolerant, for the Greek presence in Turkey and Greek discrimination against the Turkish minority in Cyprus (until the invasion in 1974) have had political implications. The ecumenical patriarch in modern Istanbul is now restricted to ecclesiastical affairs in a steadily shrinking constituency.

EDDY, MARY BAKER (1821–1910). Founder of *Christian Science. Born into an old New England family, and with little formal education, she suffered early from a chronic spinal ailment. In 1862 she claimed to have been healed by Phineas Quimby, a blacksmith from Maine who practiced hypnotism and *healing through the use of the mind. Later she was to combine this with her reading of the *NT in the writing of what became known as *Science and Health with Key to the Scriptures*. The First Church of Christ, Scientist, was formed in Boston in 1879 and is still known as the mother church. Branches were established in other cities. The year 1883 saw the start of the publication known since 1908 as *The Christian Science Monitor,* a newspaper highly regarded in the secular world.

EDICT OF NANTES See NANTES, EDICT OF.

EDINBURGH CONFERENCE (1910). An interdenominational gathering to discuss the *missionary task of the church. Under the chairmanship of John R. *Mott, aided by the secretary, J. H. *Oldham, the 1,300 delegates discussed reports from eight preparatory commissions. The subjects included taking the *gospel to non-Christians and to those of other *religions, the relation of missions to governments, the place of education, and the promotion of unity. This conference is generally regarded as the beginning of the modern *ecumenical movement.

EDINBURGH CONFERENCE (1937). Second Conference on *Faith and Order, the first of which had been held at *Lausanne in 1927. The 500 delegates from 123 churches debated four main subjects: *grace, the *ministry and *sacraments, the *Word of *God, and the church's unity. On the latter point the conference approved the formation of a *World Council of Churches, but this had not been implemented when World War II broke out in 1939.

EDWARD VI (1537–1553). King of England. He was only nine when he succeeded his father, *Henry VIII, so inevitably power was first in the hands of the duke of Somerset, who in 1549 was displaced by the future duke of Northumberland. Edward's reign was significant, for it saw the Church of *England move in a more Protestant direction, notably in the second Book of *Common Prayer (1552) and in the exercise of religious *toleration.

EDWARDS, JOHN (1637–1716). Anglican clergyman. A faithful *pastor in Cambridge even amid the dreaded plague, he became unpopular in the university because of his Calvinist views. In 1683 he moved to Colchester, but after three years of declining health and popularity (under the later Stuarts the Calvinists had a lean time), he retired to rural Cambridgeshire to study and write. He published more than forty works and was said to have been "the Paul, the *Augustine, the *Bradwardine, the *Calvin of his age."

EDWARDS, JONATHAN (1703–1758). American theologian. Graduate of Yale, he was ordained as a *Congregationalist minister and as *pastor of the church in Northampton, Massachusetts, where his powerful *preaching stimulated the *Great Awakening. From 1751 he ministered in Stockbridge, combining this with outreach to the Indians. In 1758 he reluctantly accepted the presidency of Princeton; one month later he died from a smallpox injection. Edwards, a strong Calvinist throughout his life, is regarded as the greatest theologian and philosopher of American *Puritanism. He held that the kingdom of *Christ would have its first foothold in America, and then true spiritual enlightenment would radiate throughout the world. This is one of the aspects of his teaching especially discussed in the modern revival of interest in Edwards.

EFFICACIOUS GRACE The *grace of *God that achieves what God intends in the human *heart, *mind, and *will. It is the secret work of the Holy *Spirit that causes the human being to do what God wants but to do it in such a way as to exercise his own free will. This is an important concept in the Calvinist view of grace. See also GRACE.

EGEDE, HANS (1686–1758). "*Apostle of Greenland." A *pastor in the Norwegian church, he went to pagan

Greenland in 1721, learned the Eskimo language, countered their superstitions, translated for them *Luther's *catechism, and spread the *gospel. The first converts were baptized about 1725. Egede faced several setbacks: when the government sent immigrants whose lives did not commend *Christianity, when a *missionary trading venture failed, when the king ordered the colony to be abandoned (Egede was permitted to remain temporarily), and when smallpox all but wiped out the first *mission colony. Broken in health himself, Egede returned to Copenhagen in 1736, leaving his son Paul to carry on. The father became head of a missionary training school in Copenhagen.

EKKLESIA See Ecclesia.

ELDER (Gk. *presbyteros*). In the *NT a man of mature years who is *pastor in a church (Acts 20:17). The word, used in a variety of *denominations and *sects (e.g., *Mormonism) to indicate a form of leadership, most often indicates a church officer in the Calvinist/*Presbyterian churches. An elder today may be either a teaching elder (*pastor) or a ruling elder. See also Priest.

ELECTION *God's special choice of some people. In the *OT, *Israel is the chosen or elect people, while in the *NT the *saints, or *believers, are the elect of God. Election is an act of God's *will. Theologians have debated in what way that act is related to *faith and holiness of life in those who become and are called the elect. See also Predestination.

ELIOT, JOHN (1604–1690). "*Apostle to the Indians" of North America. A graduate of Cambridge and clergyman of the Church of *England, he sailed for America in 1631. He became teacher to the church in Roxbury, Connecticut, and from 1646 combined this post with work among the Indians, whose dialect he had mastered. The first Indian church was founded in 1660. Money was contributed, some from England, for the consolidation of self-governing Indian communities. Eliot was a pioneer also in championing the rights of blacks, helped prepare the *Bay Psalm Book, produced *Scripture translations and a grammar for the Indians, and published a *Harmony of the Gospels* (1678).

ELIOT, THOMAS STEARNS (1888–1965). Poet, dramatist, and critic. Born in Missouri and educated at Harvard, Paris, and Oxford, he was schoolmaster, banker, and editor after settling in London. He became a major literary force with his poem *The Waste Land* (1922), in which he expressed disenchantment with the modern world, the pretensions of which he scoffed at also in *The Hollow Men* (1925). A British citizen from 1927, he produced a number of religious works, notably *Murder in the Cathedral* (1935), and won the Noble prize for literature in 1948.

ELIZABETH I (1533–1603). Queen of England. Daughter of *Henry VIII and Anne Boleyn, she succeeded her sister Mary *Tudor in 1558, and by her handling of religious affairs in the *Elizabethan Settlement she reversed the Roman Catholic predominance in the country. She made a significant contribution to the *Reformation in Scotland (1560), and brought much-needed order to the Church of *England by appointing Matthew *Parker as *archbishop of Canterbury.

ELIZABETHAN SETTLEMENT (1559). The year after she became queen of England, *Elizabeth oversaw a change of direction in English religious life. The settlement that she approved, among other things, once more abolished papal power in the land, repealed her sister's legislation that restored Roman Catholic practices, imposed penalties for violations, required all subjects to acknowledge Elizabeth as "Supreme Governor" of the church and to attend services conducted according to the 1552 *Prayer Book, made orders about the use of *vestments and ornaments, and dissolved the *monasteries.

ELOHIM The Hebrew word the *OT uses most often for *God. Its plural form points to the inexhaustible fullness of the Godhead. See also YAHWEH.

EMANATIONISM A form of *pantheism. Everything came into existence through the outpouring or overflowing of the being of *God. Thus God did not create the world out of nothing; it is an extension of himself. Its clearest and most influential exponent was Plotinus (d. 270). Such teaching has influenced *Christian and Jewish teaching at different times and was condemned by the First *Vatican Council (1869–1870).

EMBER DAYS Four groups of three days (Wednesday, Friday, and Saturday) in the church's year. Traditionally they have been times for special *prayers and *fasting. The needs of those to be ordained have often been in view. Ember days remain in the new *liturgies of *Anglicanism and *Roman Catholicism; their purpose is now seen as more flexible, and their number is subject to local variation.

EMBURY, PHILIP (1728–1773). The first Methodist minister in America. Born in Ireland and converted in 1752, he became a Methodist preacher in 1758 and in 1760 settled in New York City. For six years he followed his trade as a carpenter, then in 1766 he founded the first known Methodist congregation in America. In 1770 he moved to upstate Washington County, organized another society there, worked as a carpenter during the week, and doubled also as the civil magistrate.

EMERSON, RALPH WALDO (1803–1882). American essayist and poet. Born in Boston and educated at Harvard, he became in 1829 minister of the Second Church of Boston. Traditional Congregationalism and his radical views did not go together, and in 1832 he resigned and devoted himself to lecturing and writing. His unitarian views, his boundless optimism about human nature, and his stress on the power of thought and *will soon gathered around him a group called Transcendentalists. His many writings include *Nature* (1836), *Essays* (1841, 1844), and *The Conduct of Life* (1860).

EMMONS, NATHANAEL (1745–1840). American Congregational minister. Graduate of Yale, he was *pastor at Franklin, Massachusetts (1772–1827), where he was responsible also for training theological students. A *Calvinist in the succession of Jonathan *Edwards, his standpoint was less rigid than others of that school, for he could not accept that in *regeneration a person was a wholly passive agent. He was an abolitionist and a keen patriot during the War of Independence. His works (6 vols.) were published posthumously (1861–1863).

EMPIRICISM The teaching that all human knowledge is rooted in experience. It has its intellectual background in the philosophy of John Locke (1632–1704), George Berkeley (1685–1753), and David Hume (1711–1776). Its origins are closely connected with the beginnings and early success of experimental science. The growth of knowledge is seen as a slow, self-correcting process based on experiment and observation. An empirical *theology is built on the observation of religious experience, not on theoretical principles. Such an approach to theology had a center at Chicago Divinity School before World War II.

ENCHIRIDION (Gk. "something to have in hand"). A handbook, manual, or concise textbook. The term is used especially of Roman Catholic manuals, of which the most famous is the collection of doctrinal statements known as the *Enchiridion Symbolorum* (ed. H. Denzinger, 1854; 32d ed. 1963).

ENCOUNTER The revelation of *God, as personal being, to man. It is an emphasis particularly associated with the *theology of Emil *Brunner (1889–1966). God is said to disclose himself, not through a series of correct statements, but in a personal act of encounter; and *Scripture is the major means, when read and preached, through which the personal encounter occurs.

ENCYCLICAL A word related to correspondence that in a *Christian context came to mean communications of a *bishop to his *diocese. It is now used almost exclusively of a pastoral letter written by the *pope for his worldwide constituency.

ENERGIES, DIVINE An *Eastern Orthodox way of describing the presence and action of *God in the universe. It is God-as-he-is-toward-the-world rather than as he is in himself. Thus an important distinction is made between the divine essence (*substance,* *being) and divine energies.

ENGLAND, CHURCH OF The national and legally established church that has its origins in Roman Britain at least from the 3d century. Despite the efforts of such as *Augustine of Canterbury, *Aidan, and *Archbishop Theodore of Canterbury (*Theodore of Tarsus), relations with the see of Rome were fitful and often stormy until the primacy of Lanfranc (1070–1089). Even afterwards there was frequent church-state conflict, notably in the murder of *Becket, though sometimes king and church were united in opposition to Roman claims. *Henry VIII led the Church of *England into reformation and established himself as its head. The modern Church of England reflects a great amount of religious diversity, including William *Laud and John *Wesley, William *Temple and Ernest *Barnes. Regarded as the mother church of the *Anglican Communion, it is divided into forty-three *dioceses plus one in Europe, twenty-six of whose *bishops are members of the House of Lords. The electoral rolls total about 1.8 million members.

ENHYPOSTASIA (Gk. *en*, "in"; *hypostasis*, "person"). The teaching based on the Definition of *Chalcedon (451) that the full humanity of *Christ was preserved but included within the *person of the *eternal *Son of *God. Thus while the eternal Son of God did and could exist only with his divine *nature, the humanity that he took in his *incarnation could not exist alone as the man, *Jesus of Nazareth. Thus the Son of God in incarnation made the human nature his so that its *hypostasis is the same as that of the divine nature. See also ANHYPOSTASIS.

ENLIGHTENMENT, THE (Ger. *Aufklarung*). The new movement of ideas that gained ascendancy in 18th-century Europe. Basic to them was the *conviction that *truth could only be reached through *reason, observation, and experiment. Thus traditional *Christianity as well as *culture and politics were often challenged by a new, often hostile, secularism. However, some theologians attempted to accommodate Christian teaching to the new ideas, and the result was a *theology of *reason, discounting a theology of *revelation.

ENTHUSIASM Extravagant religious claims and/or devotion. Used by contemporaries to describe the fervor of the early *Quakers, Methodists, and other groups. It may be understood as a reaction to formalism in religious *worship and practice.

EPARCHY See DIOCESE.

EPHESUS, COUNCIL OF (431). A general council of the church called to resolve the Nestorian controversy, it duly deposed and excommunicated Nestorius, reaffirmed the *doctrine laid down at the Council of *Nicea, anathematized *Pelagianism, and decided the autonomy of the church of Cyprus. The Syrian *bishops, arriving late and resenting the fact that proceedings had begun without them, set up a rival *synod, but the original one under *Cyril of Alexandria was ratified.

EPHESUS, ROBBER SYNOD OF (449). Called by emperor Theodosius II and influenced by the Monophysite *patriarch of Alexandria, it reinstated *Eutyches (deposed at a *synod of Constantinople in 448) and deposed his opponents. Two years later the Council of *Chalcedon reversed those decisions.

EPHRATA SOCIETY American Protestant community in Lancaster County, Pennsylvania. It was founded in 1732 by Johann Conrad *Beissel, a German Seventh Day Baptist who, with his followers, embraced ascetic principles, including *celibacy. They were pacifists, and they observed the *Sabbath on the seventh day. The thrifty, diligent community had its numbers greatly reduced through an outbreak of smallpox in the 1770s. Some were integrated into other groups of German origin, and the community dissolved in 1934. Ephrata now has a council and a manager and a population of about nine thousand.

EPICLESIS (Gk. *epiklesis,* "*prayer"). In the context of the *Eucharist it has the particular meaning of the prayer that requests *God the Father to send the Holy *Spirit upon the bread and wine so that they truly become the *body and *blood of *Christ for the faithful. Some *liturgies include a definite prayer for this "descent," while others either omit or presuppose such a prayer. It is regarded as essential to the Eucharist in the *Orthodox churches.

EPIPHANY (Gk. *epiphaneia,* "manifestation"). The church festival that celebrates the manifestation of *Christ to the Gentiles at the visit of the *Magi (Matt 2). In the *Eastern churches it is a celebration of the manifestation of Christ to the world at his *baptism. In modern Western *liturgies these two aspects are sometimes combined. In some traditions it celebrates Jesus being baptized in the Jordan and his first miracle at Cana. The evening before Epiphany was known as Twelfth Night.

EPISCOPACY (Gk. *episkopus,* "an overseer"; Lat. *episcopus,* "a *bishop"). The system of church government whose central feature is the rule of a *diocese by a bishop—e.g., Roman Catholic, *Orthodox, and Anglican churches. It is seen as the continuation of the system that quickly became the norm in the early church after the time of the *apostles. See also CHURCH GOVERNMENT.

EPISCOPI VAGANTES (Lat. "wandering *bishops"). Either *missionary/itinerant bishops of the early church or in modern times those who have been consecrated as bishops in an irregular or fraudulent way.

EPISCOPIUS, SIMON (1583–1643). Dutch Protestant theologian. A former student of *Arminius who shared with him a modified view of *predestination, he was one of the leading Remonstrants ousted at the Synod of *Dort (1618–1619). In exile until 1625, he subsequently taught *theology at the Remonstrant college in Amsterdam. Much less orthodox than Arminius, he disliked *dogma, emphasized practice, and questioned the full divinity of *Christ.

EPISTEMOLOGY The study of, or inquiry about, human knowledge. This involves questions concerning how the mind acquires and uses knowledge as well as what is *truth and certainty. The position adopted in epistemology determines the way in which *theology is understood and practiced.

EQUALITY Various meanings of this word are: (1) Absolute social equality. This is impossible to attain or implement in society. (2) General social equality. The right of citizens to receive what belongs to them as citizens—e.g., equality of opportunity in education, work, housing, and sports. (3) Political equality. A guarantee of civil rights that excludes discrimination. (4) Equality of dignity (embracing 2 and 3)—based on the *doctrine that all are made in the image of *God. (5) Equality of dignity and service in the church.

EQUIPROBABILISM Roman Catholic moral theory for resolving doubts about practical behavior. It stands between *probabiliorism and *probabilism—but nearer the latter. It teaches that when two opposing opinions are roughly equal in probability, it is morally permissible to take the opinion in favor of liberty when the doubt is on the existence of (appropriate) law but in favor of *obedience when the only doubt is whether the law is still in operation.

ERASMUS, DESIDERIUS (c. 1466–1536). Dutch humanist and first editor of the Greek *NT. Educated largely at Deventer by the *Brethren of the Common Life, he early acquired an enthusiasm for *Bible study, became an Augustinian (1486), and was ordained (1493). In Paris where he went to study *theology (1495) he was dismayed at the *dogmatic theologians whom he found intolerant, violent, and hostile to new ideas. Soon he began to write about the ignorance and corruption of the age, particularly in *The Praise of Folly*. He pointed to the primitive church and to the *Fathers for his ideal of reform rather than to the accretions of later scholastics; for Erasmus, the test of *theology was its reflection in *Christian living. Meanwhile, by his classical writings he had established himself as the foremost scholar in northern Europe. He was appointed professor at Cambridge during one of his visits to England. In 1516 he published his edition of the *NT that gave priority to the Greek text. When the *Reformation came, both sides appealed to Erasmus, who remained a Roman Catholic while urging reform. He published editions of *Irenaeus, *Augustine, *Ambrose, Epiphanius, *Chrysostom, and *Origen, and became the first best-selling author in history. At his death one of this friends said, "Most holy was his living, most holy his dying." His writings were banned by Pope Paul IV in 1559 and by *Sixtus V in 1590.

ERASTIANISM The subordination of ecclesiastical jurisdiction to the *state, so called from Thomas Erastus (1524–1583), a Swiss physician and *Reformed theologian. This view denies to the church even the right to inflict *excommunication and other disciplinary penalties. Frequently misunderstood, Erastus applied his argument only to "the case of a State where but one *religion is permitted." Erastus wrote against Calvinist views on discipline in a book later rendered into English as *The Nullity of Church Censures*. Erastianism became one of the burning issues at the *Westminster Assembly.

ERIGENA, JOHN SCOTUS (c. 810–c. 877). Medieval scholastic philosopher and theologian. Erigena postulated that *reason and *revelation were coequal in our understanding of reality, hence philosophy and *theology were ultimately the same. This brought the great Greek thinking of antiquity into the mainstream of *Christian speculation, especially Aristotle. Erigena's own thought was a blend of neoplatonic, Aristotelian, and *Patristic thought, synthesized in his *De Divisione Naturae,* which was ultimately condemned by the Roman Catholic Church in the 13th century.

ERSKINE, EBENEZER (1680–1754). Founder of the *Secession Church in Scotland. Son of a Covenanting minister ousted after the *Restoration, he was ordained (1703) in more peaceful times and ministered for twenty-eight years in central Scotland, often *preaching in the open air so that more could hear him. In 1731 he spoke out against patronage in the Church of *Scotland. He was first rebuked, then with dubious legality suspended, and with three colleagues constituted the "Associate *Presbytery." Attempts at reconciliation having failed, Erskine and seven others were deposed by the national church in 1740. The breach was not healed until 1956 when the original Secession Church rejoined the Church of Scotland.

ESCHATOLOGY (Gk. *eschata*, "the last things"). The branch of *systematic *theology that examines what the *Bible says concerning the end of the age, Christ's *second coming, the Last *Judgment, *heaven, and *hell.

ESSENCE (Lat. *esse,* "to be"). What a thing is. When used of *God it is what God is in himself; it is the one Godhead shared by Father, Son, and Holy

*Spirit. Thus it is the equivalent in meaning of **ousia* and *substance.

ESSENTIAL TRINITY The classical *doctrine of *God as *Trinity and sometimes called Immanent Trinity. God is eternally a Trinity in unity and a unity in Trinity. Because God is truly three in one, he is experienced and known by his creatures as Father, Son, and Holy *Spirit.

ETERNAL, ETERNITY Without beginning, succession, or ending. Only *God is truly eternal, possessing the fullness of eternity, since he has no beginning, does not change, and will never end. Believers have *eternal life in that God, the Eternal One, gives his life to them. They are not *eternal in their own right.

ETERNAL GENERATION The relation of the *eternal Son to the eternal Father within the one eternal Godhead (the *Trinity). The Son is "eternally begotten" or "eternally generated" by and from the Father.

ETERNAL LIFE An expression used in John's *Gospel to describe membership of *God's *kingdom and enjoyment of his *salvation. Such life is achieved on earth in spiritual union with *Jesus Christ through the indwelling Holy *Spirit. After death this sharing in God's life reaches its fulfillment and consummation in the life of *heaven.

ETERNAL PUNISHMENT The teaching that after the Last *Judgment those who have been declared guilty of rejecting *God's *righteousness and *grace will endure *eternal (everlasting) suffering in *hell.

ETERNAL SECURITY See FINAL PERSEVERANCE.

ETHICS The science of human conduct. The determination of right and wrong in human behavior. Another term is moral philosophy. When the *Christian view of *God and humanity is basic to the study, it is called Christian ethics or *moral *theology.

ETHIOPIAN CHURCH Originating in the 4th century through evangelistic efforts of *Frumentius and a colleague, the church adopted *Monophysitism, as did the *Coptic church in Egypt. Contact with other *Christian churches was lost with the spread of Islam, and even when it was restored, evangelization was hindered by squabbles and coercion in the national church and by defective *missionary strategy. Ethiopia opened up to the West after the Italian invasion of 1935, but missionary work was restricted to Italians. In 1959 the Ethiopian church became autonomous. Its *canon includes some of the apocryphal books; the ark is found in every church; it holds to circumcision and to differentiation between clean and unclean meats; and much of the educational system has been controlled by the church. More secular education became available when the military deposed Emperor Haile Selassie in 1974.

ETILOGY See AETIOLOGY.

***EUCHARIST** (Gk. *eucharistein*, "to give thanks"). See COMMUNION, HOLY.

EUDAIMONISM (EUDEMONISM) (Gk. *eudaimonia*, "well-being"). The theory that happiness is the highest good. If happiness is seen in terms of the *Beatitudes (Matt 5), then this theory can become a *Christian approach to *ethics. Its weakness is that it encourages *love of *God and man because of the happiness loving brings to those who love, not because God deserves love.

EUGENICS (Gk. *eugenes*, "well born"). Used as an applied science of the breeding of the genetically fit; genetic engineering. This is common practice in agriculture where beneficial results have been achieved for humankind. Its application to human procreation raises serious moral problems—e.g., would it mean the separation of procreation from the personal relation within marriage?

EUGENIUS III (c. 1153). Pope from 1145. A *disciple of *Bernard of Clairvaux, he was the first *Cistercian pope. He was in trouble at home when the reforming activities of *Arnold of Brescia forced him into exile (1146–1148), and his reputation in other countries was not enhanced with the failure of the Second Crusade, which he had authorized. Eugenius was nonetheless a diligent pope and a man of austere simplicity of life.

EUGENIUS IV (c. 1383–1447). Pope from 1431. Venetian by birth and Augustinian by profession, he found the first six years of his *pontificate absorbed by the struggle with the Council of *Basel over church reform and its affirmation (1433) of conciliar superiority over the *pope. Notable features also of his reign were the reunion negotiations between Roman Catholic and Greek churches leading in 1439 to a short-lived merger, and the attempts to limit papal power in France through the *Pragmatic Sanction of Bourges.

EUSEBIUS OF CAESAREA (c. 265–c. 339). "Father of Church History." A sufferer under the Roman persecutions, he became *bishop of Caesarea about 313 and was accused of *Arianism when he tried to steer a middle course at the Council of *Nicea in 325. Eusebius, who subsequently accepted the orthodox stance decreed by that council, is famous for his historical works, which give valuable insights into events during the first four centuries of the *Christian church.

EUSEBIUS OF NICOMEDIA (d. c. 342). *Bishop of Nicomedia and later *patriarch of Constantinople. Probably Syrian by birth and Arian in tendency, he gave shelter to *Arius in 323 and espoused his cause at the Council of *Nicea in 325. He continued to battle on behalf of *Arianism, played a key part in the deposition of *Athanasius in 335, and battled against the Nicene *orthodoxy at a *synod in Antioch in 341. Eusebius baptized *Constantine in 337.

EUSEBIUS OF SAMOSATA (d. 380). *Bishop of Samosata. A strong supporter of Nicene *orthodoxy against *Arianism, he became *bishop of his Syrian *diocese in 361. Though subject to physical threats, banishment for a time, and persecution, he carried on a traveling *ministry of encouragement to fellow believers. He was restored to his see in 378 but was killed by a brick thrown by an Arian woman in Dolikha.

EUSEBIUS OF VERCELLI (d. c. 371). *Bishop of Vercelli (Italy). A saintly man who warmly supported the doctrinal position of *Athanasius, he combated *Arianism all his life. Consecrated in 345, he was also the first Westerner to unite *monasticism and *ministry. For refusing at the Council of Milan (355) to join in the condemnation of *Athanasius for his anti-Arian stance, Eusebius was exiled to the East for some years and, ironically, pardoned by *Julian the Apostate. He was soon battling again for the restoration of *orthodoxy, working in cooperation with Hilary of *Poitiers.

EUSTATHIUS OF ANTIOCH (d. c. 337). *Bishop of Antioch, sometimes called Eustathius the Great. After the Council of *Nicea (325), he returned to Antioch to take strong action against Arians in his *diocese. His opponents later effected his deposition and banishment to Thrace in 330, where he remained until his death. The Second Council of *Nicea (787) acknowledged his faithfulness to orthodox *doctrine.

EUTHANASIA (Gk. "an easy death"). The termination of human life in order to end misery and suffering. It is a form of mercy-killing as, e.g., when a person has an incurable disease. Traditionally Christians have rejected it because it takes away *God's lordship over life. Modern medicines that keep people alive when previously they would have died, and modern life-support systems that keep a *body alive when mental life has virtually ceased have added to the complexity of the problem.

EUTYCHES (c. 375–c. 454). Often considered to be the father of *Monophysitism. *Archimandrite of a *monastery in Constantinople, he fiercely opposed *Nestorianism but went to the other extreme by not acknowledging the two *natures of *Christ, bringing upon himself the condemnation of *Flavian, *patriarch of Constantinople. The Robber Synod of *Ephesus (449) brought in favor of *orthodoxy, and Eutyches was again condemned.

EUTYCHIANISM The teaching of Eutyches (d. 455) that *Christ had only one *nature—the divine. The human nature was said to be absorbed into the divine. It is a form of *Monophysitism.

EVANGELICAL A word with several meanings. (1) When used in Germany, it usually refers to the Lutheran *state church. (2) In the Church of *England it refers to a party, or school (often called "*Low Church"), who trace their origins to the "Evangelical Revival" of the 18th century. (3) In a general context it refers to a particular conservative Protestant form of *Christianity that especially emphasizes the *inspiration and authority of the *Bible and the need for personal *conversion to *God.

EVANGELICAL ALLIANCE An association founded in 1846 in London, with the object of enabling Christians worldwide "to realize in themselves and to exhibit to others that a living and overlasting union binds all true believers together in the fellowship of the church." It was thus in the best sense a forerunner of the modern *ecumenical movement. Popery and *Puseyism alike were to be resisted, and "the interests of a scriptural *Christianity" promoted. Fifty *denominations were represented among the nine hundred delegates gathered for the inaugural sessions, among them Christian leaders from the United States, Switzerland, France, and Germany. From the start, the Alliance determined to disregard denominational origin, which fact is reflected in its motto: "We are one body in Christ." In 1958 the Evangelical Missionary Alliance was formed, and this grew to embrace more than seventy member societies.

EVANGELICAL AND REFORMED CHURCH American Protestant church, a 1934 union of the *Reformed Church in the United States and the Evangelical Synod of North America. Comprising both Reformed and Lutheran elements, it accepted in addition to the *Bible (the final arbiter) *Luther's *Catechism (1529), the *Augsburg Confession (1530), and the *Heidelberg Catechism (1563). In 1957 the Evangelical and Reformed Church united with Congregational Christian churches to form the *United Church of Christ.

EVANGELICAL CHURCH (ALBRIGHT BRETHREN) Founded by Jacob *Albright to meet the needs of German-speaking people in Pennsylvania, the group sometimes called "Albright People," held their first annual conference of preachers in 1807. Called the Evangelical Association from 1816 and the Evangelical Church from 1922, it merged with the *United Brethren in Christ to form the Evangelical United Methodist Church in 1968.

EVANGELICAL COVENANT CHURCH OF AMERICA Until 1957 the Swedish Evangelical Mission Covenant of America, an 1885 union of two groups of Swedish immigrants. Its only standard of *faith and *doctrine is the *Bible, and it stresses personal religious experience. With headquarters in Chicago, the church currently has a membership of 88,000, with 620 churches.

EVANGELICAL FOREIGN MISSIONS ASSOCIATION Beginning with sixty member groups, it was formed in Chicago in 1945 "to provide a medium for voluntary united action among the *evangelical foreign *missionary agencies." Currently almost 65,000 *missionaries (including short-term) and 700 agencies are associated.

EVANGELICAL FREE CHURCH OF AMERICA Organized in 1950 as a merger of the Swedish Evangelical Free Church and the Evangelical Free Church Association, this is a body of independent churches whose members trace descent from Scandinavian immigrant groups of the latter 19th century.

*Conversion is necessary for church membership, and practical *Christian living is emphasized. It currently has about 700 churches, with 100,000 members.

EVANGELICAL LUTHERAN CHURCH IN AMERICA Denomination founded in 1987 in the U.S. by the merger of three Lutheran bodies—The American Lutheran Church, The Lutheran Church in America, and the American Evangelical Lutheran Church. It has a more inclusive view of theology than does the Lutheran Church—Missouri Synod, the other major Lutheran body in the U.S., and is open to dialogue with others, including the Roman Catholics. Currently it has about 5.3 million members in 11,175 churches.

EVANGELICAL UNITED BRETHREN CHURCH An American *denomination formed by the 1946 union of the *United Brethren in Christ and the *Evangelical Church, which itself in 1968 joined with the Methodist Church to form the *United Methodist Church.

EVANGELISM (Gk. *euangelion,* "good news"). The proclamation of the good news of *Jesus Christ, crucified and risen, so that people are brought through the power of the Holy *Spirit to put their trust in *God for *salvation. The aim is to persuade people to accept Jesus Christ as *Savior from the *guilt and power of *sin, to follow and serve him as their *Lord in the *fellowship of the church and in whatever vocation he gives to them. Recently there has been much debate as to whether ministering to the social and material needs of people is an essential part or related activity of evangelism. The *evangelist is the proclaimer of the Good News.

EVANGELIST One who proclaims the *gospel (*euangelion*). The role of being an evangelist is a gift of *Christ (Eph 4:11). Philip was an evangelist (Acts 21:8), and Timothy was called to do the work of an evangelist (2 Tim 4:5). In church tradition the authors of the four *Gospels have been called evangelists. In modern times traveling preachers who seek to gain converts for Christ are called evangelists.

EVANS, CHRISTMAS (1766–1838). Welsh Baptist preacher. Born on Christmas Day, his early links were with Presbyterians; but lacking academic attainments, he became a Baptist minister in 1789 and soon afterwards experienced *conversion. Crowds flocked to hear the man who could make them laugh and cry in quick succession; he became known as "the Bunyan of Wales." He was held in high honor despite a certain autocratic temperament. His *sermons were published in Welsh, and he wrote some *hymns and tracts in Welsh.

EVANS, WILLIAM (1870–1950). American *Bible expositor. Born in England, he took theological training in the U.S. and served several *Presbyterian pastorates. He joined the staff of Moody Bible Institute in 1901 and subsequently won a reputation as "one of the foremost Bible teachers in the nation." He wrote more than forty books on the Bible.

EVANSTON ASSEMBLY (1954) Second assembly of the *World Council of Churches. With its main theme "Christ, the Hope of the World," the assembly drew 132 member-church representatives to Northwestern University in suburban Chicago. Among the subjects discussed were *eschatology, the church in the world, evangelization, and racial and ethnic tensions.

EVENING PRAYER The evening service of Anglican churches and the equivalent of vespers in the Roman Catholic Church. It includes psalms, *canticles, *Bible readings, the *Apostles' Creed, and *prayers.

EVENSONG The old English name for *vespers or *evening prayer.

EVERLASTING LIFE See ETERNAL LIFE.

EVIL That which is the opposite of good and which occurs when *God's *will is broken. Often a distinction is made between moral evil—the result of disobedience to God's will (e.g., a murder)—and nonmoral evil—the resulting suffering and misery caused solely by earthquake, flood, tornado, etc.

EVIL SPIRIT See DEMON; DEMONOLATRY, DEMONOLOGY.

EVOLUTION, THEISTIC The acceptance of a theory of the origins of species based on the theories of J. B. Lamarck (1744–1829) and/or Charles Darwin (1744–1829) or developments from them with the added emphasis that the whole process of evolution has been and is being guided by *God.

EX CATHEDRA (Lat. "from the chair"). Used to refer to the *pope when speaking from his *bishop's chair in an official capacity as *vicar of Christ on earth. Thus what he says on such an occasion is seen by Roman Catholics as infallible.

EX OPERE OPERANTIS (Lat. "in virtue of the act of the doer"). A technical term relating to the value of a *sacrament being determined by the moral or spiritual fitness of the officiant.

EX OPERE OPERATO (Lat. "in virtue of the act performed"). A technical term relating to the value of a *sacrament in and of itself; thus the benefit for those who receive it is not affected by the moral fitness of the officiant.

EXALTATION OF CHRIST The *resurrection of *Jesus Christ from death and his *ascension into *heaven considered as one mighty act of *God. As the exalted *Lord he "sits at the right hand of the Father," and from there he will return to earth to judge the living and the dead. He is the exalted *Prophet, *Priest, and King of the people of God and the *Mediator between God and man. See also HUMILIATION OF CHRIST.

EXCLUSIVE BRETHREN See DARBY, JOHN NELSON; PLYMOUTH BRETHREN.

EXCOMMUNICATION The exclusion of a person from *worship and *fellowship of a church. This is done by the proper church authority and is usually because of some serious offense against *God or his people. In some churches if a person dies in the state of excommunication that person does not have the right of *Christian *burial. In modern Western society where there is a variety of churches it is very difficult to impose discipline and sustain it, and thus excommunication is rare. It has real meaning when the church is found only in one form and where the environment is hostile to *Christianity. Thus it was a powerful reality in the early church.

EXEGESIS The act of explaining a text, e.g., a book of the *Bible. The general rules that govern the explanation are provided by *hermeneutics, and so exegesis involves the application of these rules to particular passages or portions of books. It is reading the meaning from the text, not reading a meaning into the text (eisegesis). As such it is of fundamental importance to all Christians involved in the explanation of the Bible in the modern world.

EXEMPLARISM The view that the value of the *atonement of *Christ lies in its example of suffering *love and self-surrender to *God. This approach is also often called the "subjective" or "moral" theory.

EXISTENTIALISM The philosophy that has been affected by, or is in some form of continuity with, the teaching of Søren *Kierkegaard (1813–1855), the Danish philosopher. Basic to it is an emphasis on subjectivity—the only way to *truth is through the human subject's own participation in, and experience of, reality (*being). Knowledge must begin in and with oneself. A significant recent existentialist philosopher was Martin *Heidegger (1889–1976), and through his influence on theologians such as Rudolph *Bultmann there has emerged an existentialist *theology.

EXORCISM The expulsion of *evil spirits or *demons from persons, places, and things. *Jesus and his *apostles practiced exorcism (Matt

10:1ff.; Acts 16:18), and the church has continued the practice. Because of the possibility of abuse, large *denominations and churches seek carefully to control the selection and appointment of exorcists.

EXPERIENTIAL, EXPERIMENTAL *God is not only the One in whom a person believes but also the One who provides evidence of his existence and *love to the individual believer. Thus experiential *religion is the emphasis on the experienced signs of God's blessing, guiding, and providing in the individual life. Experimental carries with it the further idea that experiences must be subjected to testing to be sure that they are from God. See also PRACTICAL SYLLOGISM.

EXPIATION Full *atonement. Either the act of making atonement for or the means by which the atonement is made. In the *NT the *blood of *Christ is the expiation for human *sin. Whether expiation is to be understood as part of the concept of *propitiation or whether it excludes propitiation is debated by scholars. This debate effects the translation of *hilasterion* (Rom 3:25)—is it "expiation" or "propitiation"?— and of *hilasmos* (1 John 2:2; 4:10). Compare the different renderings in the AV, NIV, and RSV.

EXPOSITION OF THE SACRAMENT Exhibiting or showing to the congregation the vessel that contains the consecrated bread (consecrated at an earlier *Eucharist). The idea is that *Christ is honored through the bread, which is his *body. Exposition of this kind takes place in the Benediction of the Blessed Sacrament and during *Corpus Christi.

EXTRA ECCLESIAM NULLA SALUS (Lat. "outside the church there is no *salvation"). The traditional *Christian position that salvation is in *Christ and thus in the community of Christ, the church. In recent *theology this position as understood *dogmatically has been challenged in order to allow for the possibility of sincere adherents of other faiths to enjoy or find *God's salvation. See also BAPTISM OF DESIRE.

EXTREME UNCTION The old name for the *anointing of the sick, one of the seven *sacraments of the Roman Catholic Church. It was called extreme, for it was usually administered to people who were expected to die. Now it is administered to those who are expected to be healed by *God as well as to those about to die.

FABER, FREDERICK WILLIAM (1814–1863). English devotional writer. Coming from a Calvinist background, he was influenced at Oxford by John Henry *Newman, and he collaborated with him on the *Library of the Fathers*. Ordained in 1837, he went to a Huntingdonshire *parish in 1842, but in 1845, following Newman, he became a Roman Catholic and later a *priest. In 1849 he became head of the London branch of the Oratory of St. Philip *Neri, of which Newman was the *superior. A devout man, Faber wrote many *hymns and books that furthered the Roman Catholic cause in England, expressing profound thoughts in attractive language. His hymns include "My God, How Wonderful Thou Art," "Hark, Hark My Soul," and "There's a Wideness in God's Mercy."

FABIAN (d. 250). Pope from 236. He reportedly divided Rome into seven districts assigned to seven *deacons and founded several churches in France. He encouraged the keeping of records during those persecuting times, and he himself was martyred under the emperor *Decius. *Cyprian had a high regard for Fabian's character and administrative abilities.

FAIRBAIRN, ANDREW MARTIN (1838–1912). Congregational minister. Born of poor parents in Scotland and earning his living before he was ten, he read hard and long, finally became a Congregational minister, and in 1886 was appointed the first principal of Mansfield College, Oxford. An original teacher, preacher, and writer, he published a number of theological works and was active publicly in the cause of theological education.

FAITH Trustful *obedience to *God as he is revealed in *Jesus Christ. While certain *truths must be accepted (e.g., that God exists and is *love), faith is more than acceptance of truths. It is wholehearted trust in God through *Christ and is therefore the basis of a personal relationship with God. The Holy *Spirit working in the *heart creates, inspires, and enriches faith.

In analyzing faith, theologians speak of: (1) *Infused faith*. This emphasizes that faith is a gift of God and arises through God's *grace working in the human life. (2) *Saving faith*. The wholehearted initial commitment to Jesus Christ by which the *Christian life begins and *salvation is received. (3) *Implicit faith*. In submitting wholly to God, the believer has implicit faith in that in principle he believes all that God has revealed even though he does not as yet know the full extent of this. (4) *Explicit faith*. At any period in the Christian life the believer can only believe explicitly that of which he has knowledge. As he grows in grace and understanding his explicit faith increases. Faith always exists alongside *repentance.

FAITH, THE The body of *truth that the church teaches and Christians believe. It is found in *creeds and *confessions of faith.

FAITH AND ORDER The name given to international *Christian conferences held at *Lausanne in 1927 and *Edinburgh in 1937. They reflected the growing *ecumenical movement, which had its climax in the formation of the *World Council of Churches in 1948.

FAITH HEALING Healing that comes through religious rather than medical means (e.g., after *prayer is offered) or the process of mind over matter—healing by suggestion.

FALL, THE The original act of Adam and Eve when they disobeyed *God and lost their intimate relationship with him (Gen 3). They fell from perfect communion with God to a state of imperfect communion with him. By this act *sin entered into the life of the human race in that instead of enjoying the fact of being God's creatures, human beings lacked a meaningful and loving relationship with their Creator. See also Original Sin.

FALLENNESS A technical term referring to denying oneself in order to find identity in other things or people. It is to be in flight from one's true being and identity. Some theologians have seen this aspect of human beings (as interpreted by *existentialism) as providing a modern account of what Christians mean when they talk of humans being "fallen," or having *original *sin.

FALSE DECRETALS, THE Documents attributed to *Isidore of Seville (7th century) but belonging rather to a Frankish collection made more than two centuries later. The decretals were regarded as genuine until the middle of the 16th century and were often used to advance the papal cause. Apart from a series of conciliar *canons, the material consisted of forgeries of papal letters, the earliest of them going back to before the Council of *Nicea (325).

FAREL, GUILLAUME (1489–1565). French Reformer. Educated in Paris, he became a militant Protestant after studying the *Scriptures, and at Basel in 1524 he publicly contended for *Reformed principles. After some years of moving from city to city he settled in Geneva as a leader of the *Reformation in 1533. He tried to move too fast and withdrew when feeling ran against him. Farel, who was responsible for *Calvin's coming to Geneva in 1536, left that city in 1538 and was *pastor in Neuchâtel until his death.

FARRAR, FREDERIC WILLIAM (1831–1903). Dean of Canterbury. Born in India of *missionary parents, he studied at London under J. F. D. *Maurice, was ordained, and became a schoolmaster until he was appointed *canon of Westminster in 1876. Later he was appointed dean of Canterbury (1895). He wrote the very popular *Life of Christ* (1874) but caused a stir when his *Eternal Hope* (1878) questioned the *doctrine of *eternal *punishment, a position later modified. He preached the funeral *sermon for his friend Charles Darwin in 1882.

FAST, FASTING Partial or total *abstinence from food or from particular types and forms of food. The aim in *Christianity is to increase self-discipline and the spiritual life by weakening the attractiveness of pleasures enjoyed through the senses. Some churches have elaborate rules for fasting, and some *religious orders take the *duty very seriously.

FATHERHOOD OF GOD *God's self-revelation through the image of Father. The idea that believers are "children" or "sons" of God is a development from this image. This way of thinking about God highlights that (as the father in an oriental home) he is the One who is sovereign, who provides, and who cares. To speak of God the Father is to speak in particular of the First *Person of the *Trinity. There is a sense in which God as Creator is the Father of all people and there is a further sense in which God as *Savior is the Father only of his family, those who believe.

FATHERS OF THE CHURCH *Holy men of the early centuries who were special witnesses to the *Christian *faith. Roman Catholics claim that there are thirty-nine Latin fathers, of whom the last is *Isidore of Seville

(560–636), and fifty Greek fathers, of whom the last is *John of Damascus (675–749).

FEAR OF THE LORD Usually subdivided into (1) *servile fear*—doing *God's *will because *punishment is feared unless it is done; and (2) *filial fear*—doing God's will with reverence and a desire not to offend him. The fear of the Lord is the beginning of true *wisdom.

FEASTS Days set apart by a church for giving special honor to *God, *Christ, *angels, *saints, and special events. Each *Sunday is a celebration of the *Resurrection; then there is *Christmas, *Easter, Ascension Day, and such days as St. Matthew, Mark, Luke, and John's Days. Special events include the anniversary of the dedication of a church, the *transfiguration of Christ, and the *Annunciation.

FEBRONIANISM The radical views of the Roman Catholic auxiliary *bishop of Trier, J. N. von Hontheim (1701–1790). They concerned the place of the *papacy in the church and the relations of church and state. He wished to create a German national church in communion with but not ruled from Rome. He saw the *pope as the first among equals, not as the unique *vicar of *Christ on earth.

FEDERAL THEOLOGY Another name for developed covenant *theology, which reached its mature expression in the *Calvinism of the 17th century. See also COVENANT THEOLOGY.

FELLOWSHIP *Christian unity and community, whether expressed in common *worship, *faith, *hope, mutual help, and commitment or in a lifestyle of communal living and sharing. It is based on the fact that believers are united to *Christ and to each other by the Holy *Spirit and so belong to each other.

FELLOWSHIP OF INDEPENDENT EVANGELICAL CHURCHES A group made up of autonomous *evangelical churches in Britain. Founded in 1922 with a conservative basis of *faith but laying down no rules on *sacraments or church *polity, it has welcomed those concerned that their mainline *denominations have increasingly been infected by theological liberalism. Some 450 churches are in the fellowship, and they have an annual assembly.

FEMINIST THEOLOGY Contemporary theological movement that seeks to identify and criticize the patriarchal tendencies it finds in the Judeo-Christian faith and to act as a corrective by emphasizing the positive aspects of the Christian tradition regarding women. It also challenges the sexism of the early church fathers regarding women's nature and potential. While some feminist theologians have attempted to work within a more-or-less traditional orthodoxy, others (e.g., Mary Daly), are quite willing to dispense with Christian tradition and resurrect the ancient goddesses of antiquity.

FÉNELON, FRANÇOIS DE SALIGNAC DE LA MOTHE (1651–1715). French mystic and *archbishop of Cambrai. He was ordained in 1675, and he embarked on a thirteen-year *mission to reclaim the *Huguenots. He became thereafter guardian to the duke of Burgundy, grandson of *Louis XIV, at whose court he exercised great influence. Appointed *archbishop in 1695, he was attacked for his affinity with Madame *Guyon and her associates, and despite his *orthodoxy in most things, his writings incurred papal condemnation. It seems clear that his *mysticism was imperfectly understood by his contemporaries.

FERDINAND II (1578–1637). Holy Roman emperor. One of the sponsors of the *Counter-Reformation, he supported the *Jesuits (under whom he had been educated) and moved against Protestants, particularly in Austria, of which he was archduke. His policies caused Protestant princes to rebel twice, but the military skill of his general, Wallenstein, and the timely death of his chief adversary, Gustavus Adolphus (1632), supported his plan to further Roman Catholic interests in his territories.

FERGUSON, JAMES (1621–1667). Scottish minister and scholar. Minister of Kilwinning in Ayrshire and described as one of the wisest men in the land, he declined all advancement and sought to bring moderation while the *Covenanters were increasingly becoming involved in defense of religious liberty. Ferguson was a man of notable piety whose commentaries on the Pauline Epistles were warmly commended by C. H. *Spurgeon.

FERRAR, NICHOLAS (1592–1637). Anglican clergyman. A former member of Parliament, he was ordained by William *Laud (1626) and formed an Anglican religious community at Little Gidding, Huntingdonshire. Ferrar's piety and austerity impressed *Charles I, who visited Little Gidding twice. With the Puritan influence increasing, much of Ferrar's work was undone when after his death his community was condemned as the "Arminian nunnery" and his manuscripts were destroyed in a 1646 raid that saw the end of the settlement.

FERRER, VINCENT See VINCENT FERRER.

FESTIVALS See FEASTS.

FIDEI DEFENSOR See DEFENDER OF THE FAITH.

FIDEISM Coined in the 19th century to emphasize that believers live by *faith and that therefore their position cannot be proved by *reason. It now usually has the meaning of a *theology that undervalues the place of reason and relies heavily on subjective religious experience.

FIDES HISTORICA (Lat. "historical *faith"). The traditional faith inherited from one's ancestors, family, or predecessors.

FIDES QUA CREDITUR (Lat. "the faith by which [it] is believed"). The act of *faith itself; the actual trust in *God of the believer.

FIDES QUAE INTELLECTUM (Lat. "*faith that is believed"). *Doctrines of the faith.

FIDES QUAERENS INTELLECTUM (Lat. "*faith seeking understanding"). The search for *truth within the commitment of trusting in *God.

FILIATION (Lat. *filius*, "a son"). The relation of the *eternal Son to the eternal Father within the Godhead. The Father eternally begets the Son, and thus the Son is eternally begotten; this eternal process is filiation.

FILIOQUE A phrase from the Latin version of the *Nicene Creed meaning "and the Son." The purpose of its insertion, for it is not in the original Greek version, is to teach the double procession of the Holy *Spirit. Within the *eternal Godhead the Spirit proceeds not only from the Father but also from the Son. This addition to the creed was made in the Western church in 1014 on the authority of Pope Benedict VIII. Its inclusion led to the *Schism between the Eastern and Western parts of the church, a schism that remains to this day. The *Orthodox Church insists that the Spirit proceeds from the Father only or from the Father through the Son but not from the Father and the Son. Behind the Eastern and Western *dogmas lie two different ways of explaining the *doctrine of the *Trinity.

FINAL PERSEVERANCE The *doctrine that true believers, in whom the Spirit has created *eternal life, will not die in *apostasy or unbelief but will be true believers at death. In a popular form this is sometimes stated: "Once saved, always saved." Those Christians who teach this (e.g., Calvinists) emphasize that *perseverance is only possible through the *grace of *God and that human effort alone is insufficient. Passages such as John 10:27–28 are quoted in support.

FINNEY, CHARLES GRANDISON (1792–1875). American revivalist. Employed in a New York law office, he was converted in 1821 after reading the *Bible. He entered the Presbyterian *ministry in 1824. He became a successful evangelist and continued this work even after appointment as professor of *theology at Oberlin College, Oberlin, Ohio (1835–1875; principal also from 1851 to 1866). His methods were often regarded as novel, and traditionalists criticized his modified brand of *Calvinism, but he had a profound influence on American life and thought, and it is estimated that a half million people professed *conversion through his *ministry.

FISH An early *symbol of *Christ. The Greek word is *ichthus,* and these letters become the first letters of five words: *Iesous* (*Jesus); *Christos* (Christ); *Theou* (of *God); *Uios* (Son); and *Soter* (*Savior)—*Jesus Christ, *Son of God, Savior.

FISHER, EDWARD (c. 1601–1655). Anglican theological writer. An anti-Puritan Royalist, he was the author of various works, including one that argued against *Sunday as the *Sabbath, which had some vogue in New York in the mid-19th century. Fisher has been suggested also as the author of the *Marrow of Modern Divinity* which had an influence on Thomas *Boston, but it is doubtful if he was indeed the "E. F." referred to there.

FISHER, GEOFFREY FRANCIS (1887–1972). *Archbishop of Canterbury, 1945–1961. Headmaster of Repton School (1914), he became *bishop of Chester (1932) and bishop of London (1939) before succeeding William *Temple as *primate. A shrewd administrator and ecclesiastical statesman, he encouraged *ecumenical relations, particularly with the *Eastern churches. He was president of the *World Council of Churches (1946–1954), and he created history and some controversy by his visit to Pope *John XXIII in 1960. On retirement he became Baron Fisher of Lambeth.

FISHER, JOHN (1469–1535). Roman Catholic martyr. Born in Yorkshire and ordained priest in 1491, he became the confessor of Henry VII's mother, who at his instigation founded the renowned Lady Margaret chairs of divinity at Oxford and Cambridge. As chancellor of Cambridge he encouraged Hebrew studies, oversaw the training of priests, and brought *Erasmus to teach there. Fisher, who became also *bishop of Rochester in 1504, was a strong opponent of secular interference in church affairs, including the appointment of *Henry VIII as "Supreme Head of the Church and Clergy of England." He also espoused the cause of *Catherine of Aragon against the king's quest for a *divorce. Like his friend Thomas *More, he was imprisoned for rejecting the king's pretensions. The two were subsequently executed within three weeks of each other.

FIVE MILE ACT (1665). Legislation enacted by the post-*Restoration Parliament in England against Nonconformist ministers and teachers. They were forbidden to come within five miles of a city, town, or parliamentary borough.

FIVE POINTS OF CALVINISM The five areas of *doctrine expounded by the Synod of *Dort (1618–1619). They are sometimes indicated by the mnemonic t-u-l-i-p: *total *depravity of man, unconditional divine *election, limitation of the *Atonement to the elect, irresistibility of divine *grace, and *perseverance in grace to the end. These are not the only doctrines of the *Reformed *faith (*Calvinism) but were responses to positions taken up by the Remonstrants who taught *Arminianism. See also Calvin, John; Calvinism.

FIVE WAYS, THE Five closely connected arguments or proofs used by Thomas *Aquinas (1225–1274) to argue from the world in which we live to the existence of the living *God. The facts of change, causation, and contingency represent three ways to God by *reasoning to the Origin of change, a Final Cause, and a Necessary Being. Then the reality of morality is the way of the moral argument to the Perfect One, and finally the purposiveness of the world points to the Ultimate Goal.

God is the Origin of change, the Final Cause, the Necessary Being, the Perfect One, and the Ultimate Goal. There have been many objections raised against this type of argument, but nevertheless they continue to interest philosophers. See also ARGUMENTS FOR THE EXISTENCE OF GOD.

FLACIUS, MATTHIAS ILLYRICUS (1520–1575). Lutheran Reformer. Born in Illyria (in modern Yugoslavia), he studied in Italy and Germany, and in 1544 he became professor of Hebrew at Wittenburg. Through contact with *Luther he had been converted to *evangelical *doctrine, his strict adherence to which brought him into controversy, notably with *Melanchthon, which may partly explain why his life was a succession of moves from city to city. Among his writings was a major work in church history that came to be known as the *Magdeburg Centuries*.

FLAGELLANTS The name given to a *sect which, originating in Italy in the mid-13th century, made a profession of drastic self-discipline. Within a century they had spread themselves over Europe, carrying a cross in their hands and going naked to the waist. They lashed themselves with knotted cords to which pins were attached, holding that their blood mingled with *Christ's and that it had the same virtue. They believed that remission of *sin, obtained through thirty days' whipping, made the *sacraments superfluous. The Flagellants were condemned by the Council of *Constance in the early 15th century.

FLAVEL, JOHN (c. 1630–1691). English *Presbyterian minister. Oxford-educated and ministering in Devon, his views led to his ejection in 1662 by the Act of *Uniformity. He preached secretly in Dartmouth until the *Five Mile Act forced his removal outside the limit, but even then his former parishioners journeyed to hear him. He later became a Congregational preacher. Like many fellow Puritans, his writings concerned the controversial times, but many of his works, notably *Husbandry Spiritualized* (1669), were reprinted for many years after his death.

FLAVIAN (c. 320–404). *Bishop of Antioch. A defender of orthodox *Christianity against *Arianism, he was appointed bishop in 381, but his position was challenged by those whose views adumbrated *Nestorianism (so beginning the *Meletian Schism), and Flavian's tenure was not consolidated until the intervention of John *Chrysostom about 398.

FLESH Theologically, human *nature with its *evil and sinful inclinations. To walk according to the flesh is contrasted with walking according to the *Spirit (Rom 8:4–8; Gal 5:16ff.).

FLETCHER, JOHN WILLIAM (1729–1785). Methodist clergyman. Swiss by birth, he came to England about 1750, was episcopally ordained in 1757, and three years later became *vicar of Madeley, a mining town in Shropshire, which post he held until his death. His sanctity of life and devotion to duty endeared him to the rough colliers. For a time he collaborated with the *Countess of Huntingdon's Connexion, but his closest affinity was with John *Wesley, who wanted him as his successor as Methodist leader. Though necessarily a controversialist through upholding *Arminianism against *Calvinism, he was courteous and irenic in temperament.

FLORENCE, COUNCIL OF (1438–1445). An *ecumenical council of the Roman Catholic Church, held successively in three Italian cities: Ferrara (1438–1439), Florence (1439–1442), and Rome (1442–1445). A continuation of the Council of *Basel, it first discussed *purgatory, the *doctrine of the Holy *Spirit, the *Eucharist, and papal primacy—the Roman views on which the seven-hundred-strong Greek delegation accepted. But the most significant move was the reunion of Greek and Latin churches, in which the threat from the Turks was an issue. The union was, however, repudiated swiftly by the Greek church.

FLORENTIUS, RADEWIJNS (1350–1400). Leader of the *Brethren of the Common Life. Converted through the *preaching of Gerhard *Groote, whom he encouraged to found the Brethren, Florentius became a *canon of Utrecht, and in 1384 he succeeded Groote as leader of the movement. He gave the Brethren a settled establishment and made it a center of spiritual life and scholarly study.

FONT (Lat. *fons*, "a spring of water"). A receptacle for water used in *baptism inside churches. They have differed in size over the centuries. As baptism by pouring became the rule in the West, fonts became smaller than earlier ones (which had been big enough to immerse a child in). Traditionally the font is placed near the entrance of the church and thus symbolizes that baptism is the entry into the *Christian life.

FOOTWASHING A practice based on the example of *Jesus (John 13:4–20; cf. 1 Tim 5:10), it is a religious ordinance for *Mennonites and a symbolic act once a year (*Maundy Thursday) in some Roman Catholic and *Eastern churches.

FORBES, JOHN (1593–1648). Professor of divinity at Aberdeen from 1620, he was a prominent theologian who, on grounds of conscience, differed from the *Covenanters and suffered the fate of many moderate men in an intolerant age. He lost his chair and his home in 1639, and from 1644 he was in exile for two years in Holland.

FOREKNOWLEDGE
Either (1) God's knowledge of things before they occur (knowledge that things will certainly occur) or (2) *predestination. Thus its meaning is determined by the theological system using it (e.g., in *Calvinism and *Arminianism). In some modern theologies (e.g., *process *theology) God's foreknowledge is his knowledge of all the possibilities of what may happen, not his knowledge of what will surely happen.

FORENSIC By a legal act or by a legal declaration. It is often placed alongside the word "*righteousness" or "*justification" in Protestant *theology to emphasize that a sinner is *declared* righteous (as opposed to *made* righteous) by *God on the basis of the righteousness of *Christ.

FOREORDINATION *God not only sees what will happen; he actually ordains and causes to happen. See also PREDESTINATION.

FORGIVENESS *Pardon or *remission of an offense. *God pardons sinners for the sake of *Jesus Christ. Thus God's forgiveness is unmerited and undeserved. However it can be received only by those who are penitent, who see their need of it. There is a sense in which God's forgiveness is conditional on the person to be forgiven showing a forgiving *spirit to others ("Forgive us our trespasses as we forgive those who trespass against us"). See also PENITENCE, REPENTANCE.

FORM CRITICISM (Ger. *formsgeschichte*, "history of the forms"). It has been used by scholars in studies of the *OT (e.g., of the *Pentateuch and Psalms) and of the *NT (especially the first three *Gospels) as a technical method. It assumes that the earlier use of the material in the community of *faith (*Israel or the church) shaped it and caused a variety of oral forms, which became, when written down, a variety of literary forms. In other words, the community in which the stories and sayings were remembered and told before being written down gave particular shape to them. In the case of the Gospels this method often assumes that it is impossible to recover the original words of *Jesus, for what we possess are his words adapted and molded in the life of the primitive churches.

FORMAL CAUSE One of Aristotle's four causes (material, formal, efficient, and final) taken over and used in the *theology of both Roman Catholic and Protestant churches. The formal cause is the account of what anything is; it is that which it is, in actuality. So in the *doctrine of the *justification of sinners the formal cause is *righteousness, the righteousness of *Christ.

FORMAL PRINCIPLE The source and criterion accepted by a church for its teaching. At the *Reformation the Reformers claimed that the *Bible alone was the formal principle. See also MATERIAL PRINCIPLE.

FORMOSUS (c. 816–896). Pope from 891. *Bishop of Porto, Italy, from 864, he carried out diplomatic *missions for successive popes and made powerful political enemies. These were augmented during his *pontificate by his opposition to the *patriarch *Photius of Constantinople. Stephen VI, who succeeded him as pope, had his corpse exhumed, propped up on a throne, and given a posthumous trial. The election of Formosus was declared invalid, his body mutilated and later thrown into the Tiber—proceedings annulled after Stephen was imprisoned and strangled.

FORMULA OF CONCORD See CONCORD, FORMULA OF.

FORNICATION Sexual intercourse between a man and woman who are not married but who are free to marry. This is contrary to biblical and *Christian teaching (Gal 5:19; Eph 5:3). See also ADULTERY.

FORSYTH, PETER TAYLOR (1848–1921). Congregational theologian. Educated at Aberdeen and Göttingen, he served Congregational pastorates until appointment in 1901 as principal of Hackney College in London. A liberal *Evangelical, he was concerned to relate *Christianity in terms of personal experience and events of the day. It is said that Forsyth, whose works have been rediscovered in recent years, anticipated many of the issues raised by Karl *Barth. His best-known work is *The Person and Place of Jesus Christ* (1909).

FORTITUDE A traditional *Christian *virtue linked with the fourth *Beatitude (Matt 5:6). A firmness of *spirit and endurance in the pursuit of *righteousness. It finds its distinctive expression in martyrdom.

FORTY MARTYRS OF SEBASTE See SEBASTE, FORTY MARTYRS OF.

FOSDICK, HARRY EMERSON (1878–1969). American Baptist minister. Ordained in 1903, he ministered in Montclair, New Jersey (1904–1915), during which time he began a long association as teacher of *practical *theology at Union Theological Seminary in New York (1908–1946). In 1919 he became associate *pastor at First Presbyterian Church in that city, but his anti-Fundamentalist views led to his resignation in 1925. He was called to Park Avenue Baptist Church, which soon developed into the interdenominational Riverside Church, where he ministered until retirement in 1946. His books include *The Manhood of the Master* (1913) and his autobiography, *The Living of These Days* (1956).

FOUR SPIRITUAL LAWS The means by which members of the Campus Crusade for Christ (founded in 1951 by W. R. Bright) present the *gospel. They are: (1) *God *loves you and created you to have a personal relationship with him. (2) Man is sinful and guilty before God, who is perfect and just. Sin has separated man from God, and the relationship between them is broken. (3) *Jesus Christ is God's solution for man's *sin. Through him alone you can have a personal relationship with God. (4) We must each respond by asking Jesus Christ into our lives as *Savior and *Lord. In this way we can know God personally.

FOURSQUARE GOSPEL Term used by the International Church of the Foursquare Gospel to describe their theological (Pentecostal) doctrines. For them the *gospel has four main parts: *justification by *faith, entire *sanctification through the *Spirit, divine *healing, and the *second coming of *Christ after the *Millennium. *Jesus is thus presented as *Savior, Sanctifier, Healer, and Coming King. The International Church of the Foursquare Gospel was begun by Aimee Semple *McPherson in the 1920s. See also McPherson, Aimee Semple.

FOX, GEORGE (1624–1691). Founder of the *Society of Friends, or *Quakers. Apprenticed to a shoemaker, he left his Leicestershire home in 1643 to seek religious enlightenment. After painful experiences he spoke of having found One who spoke to his condition, and in 1646 he came to rely on the "inner light of the living *Christ." He forsook church attendance, rejected outward *sacraments and paid *clergy, and taught that *truth is to be found primarily in *God's voice speaking to the *soul. So emerged the "Friends of Truth." Fox taught the *priesthood of all believers and urged a simple lifestyle on his colleagues, who later included William *Penn. He established a base at Swarthmore Hall in northwest England but traveled widely at home and abroad. Eight times he saw the inside of prisons, serving terms totaling six years. He fought prison conditions and other social *evils and sought to establish religious *toleration in an intolerant age. Fox could show a mean *spirit on occasion toward opponents, but he was a true pacifist, whose use of group silence was a brake on impetuous conduct.

FOXE, JOHN (1516–1587). Author of the 16th-century best seller now known as *Foxe's Book of Martyrs* (referring to Protestant victims during Mary *Tudor's reign). Exiled on the Continent while Protestants were being persecuted in England, he became a strong Puritan but later sought to intercede with Queen *Elizabeth on behalf of *Anabaptists and *Jesuits condemned to death. His book was widely acclaimed even in his own day and provides valuable material on the English Reformation.

FRACTION The breaking of the bread in Holy *Communion and done in such a way that the worshipers can see. It is based on what *Christ did in the sight of his *disciples at the *Last Supper (Matt 26:26). In different *liturgies and churches the moment when fraction takes place varies as also does the number of pieces into which the bread is first broken.

FRANCIS XAVIER See Xavier, Francis.

FRANCIS DE SALES (1567–1622). *Counter-Reformation leader. Having abandoned legal studies for the *priesthood, he was ordained in 1593 and embarked on a *mission to bring the erring Swiss back to the fold. In 1599 he became *bishop-coadjutor of Geneva, where he declared that *love alone could break down the barriers of distrust. A tireless worker, he is credited with eight thousand *conversions in two years. He became *patron *saint of Roman Catholic journalists in 1923.

FRANCIS OF ASSISI (1182–1226). Founder of the *Franciscans. *Son of a prosperous merchant, he turned in 1205 to a life of *prayer and *poverty, renouncing his worldly possessions. He began to preach in 1208, and in 1209 he received papal approval for the establishing of his *order. Francis resigned the leadership in 1223, disliking internal disputes about administration. He spent his last three years in solitude and prayer and in occasional writing. He is the first known stigmatist; he received the *stigmata in 1224 while praying on Monte La Verna. He composed the *Canticle of the Sun* and the very familiar prayer beginning, "Make me an instrument of thy peace."

FRANCISCANS *Religious *order founded by *Francis of Assisi in Italy in 1209. His *friars, who had no possessions, made an immediate impact as street preachers, and within a decade the order numbered five thousand. At first they had no *rule but the example of Francis, but he reluctantly cooperated in the preparation of one that reached its final form in 1223. The friars penetrated into all of Europe, into Morocco, and as far east as Syria. The Franciscans knew decline and division, but many famous men have been associated with them, among them John *Duns Scotus, Bernardino of Siena, and *John of Capistrano.* Five popes have been Franciscans.

FRANCK, SEBASTIAN (c. 1499–1542). German Protestant. Born in Bavaria and ordained as a *priest in 1524, he converted to *Lutheranism in 1525. Finding that both Lutheranism and Anabaptism were too *dogmatic, he came to regard the *Scriptures as full of contradictions and to hold that the only *doctrines necessary were the *Ten Commandments and the *Apostles' Creed.

FRANCKE, AUGUST HERMANN (1663–1727). German Lutheran minister and Pietist. Three years after becoming professor of Hebrew at Leipzig he was converted. The *Bible classes he thereafter conducted led to a *revival but brought opposition from his academic colleagues. From 1692 he taught Oriental languages and from 1698 *theology at the University of Halle. Francke worked tirelessly for the social, economic, and spiritual welfare of poor children.

FRANSON, FREDRIK (1852–1908). Founder of The Evangelical Alliance Mission (TEAM). Born in Sweden, he went to America in 1869, was converted in 1872, and was ordained in 1881 in the *Evangelical Free Church. His largely itinerant *ministry produced spiritual reawakening in many countries and led to the appointment of scores of *missionaries. His message stressed the urgency of the harvest in view of *Christ's *second coming. He founded the Scandinavian Alliance Mission (1890); it assumed its present name in 1949.

FRATICELLI The name originally described members of the *Mendicant Orders, but since the early 14th century it has been applied especially to the "Spiritual" branch of the *Franciscans.

FREDERICK I (BARBAROSSA) (c. 1123–90). Holy Roman emperor from 1155. From the time he was crowned by the English pope *Adrian IV in 1155, his reign was a succession of challenges to the *papacy and to curb the growing power of princes in his empire and maintain the unity of Germany. In view of his opposition to papal authority, it seems ironic that he should have died while engaged in the Third *Crusade to the Holy Land.

FREDERICK II (1194–1250). Holy Roman emperor from 1220. Regarded as the last of the great medieval emperors, he emulated his grandfather, *Frederick I, in battling against papal pretensions to superiority over the emperor. He too embarked on a crusade and had himself crowned king of Jerusalem in 1229. Eleven years before Frederick II's death, *Gregory IX excommunicated him, which sentence was repeated by *Innocent IV in 1245 with no effect.

FREDERICK III (THE PIOUS) (1515–1576). Elector Palatine of the Rhine and prominent Protestant. A Roman Catholic converted to *Lutheranism in 1548, he was elected eleven years later to the Palatinate, where both the main forms of *Protestantism had made significant impact. Frederick finally decided to support *Calvinism and sponsored production of the *Heidelberg Catechism (1563). Despite the opposition of both *Roman Catholicism and Lutheranism, he introduced *presbyterian polity into the Palatinate in 1570. Frederick also gave aid to Protestants in France and the Netherlands.

FREDERICK III (THE WISE) (1463–1525). Elector of Saxony. A critic of imperial power, he declined to be a candidate for the crown himself but helped to secure the election of *Charles V in 1519. Frederick was a patron of the arts, founded the University of Wittenberg (1502), and supported Albrecht *Dürer and Lucas *Cranach. Though a devout Roman Catholic, he protected *Luther from papal wrath and the imperial ban. Luther gave his funeral address.

FREE CHURCH OF ENGLAND A body that describes itself as "a Protestant Episcopal church adopting outside the Church of *England the standpoint of the Evangelical Party within it." It originated in 1844 in protest against the *Oxford Movement's influence on the national church. Formally constituted in 1863, it united in 1926 with the *Reformed Episcopal Church, retaining both names. Democratic in church government, it gives prominent place to the *laity and practices open *Communion and pulpit exchange with other churches. It has never, however, had a popular appeal in England. With steady losses in recent years, it is doubtful if membership now exceeds 1,800.

FREE CHURCH OF SCOTLAND A name assumed originally by those who left the Church of *Scotland at the *Disruption in 1843 in protest against state interference in church matters. It nonetheless approved (and still does) the principle of an established church. In 1900 the majority in the Free Church joined with the *United Presbyterians to form the *United Free Church, but a minority stayed out. The Free Church of *Scotland holds strongly to the *Westminster Confession in its unmodified form and uses only metrical psalms in church *worship, without instrumental accompaniment. Strongest in north and northwest Scotland, it has some 20,000 members and adherents.

FREE OFFER OF THE GOSPEL A phrase used by Calvinists in order to emphasize that their *doctrine of divine *election does not prohibit them from *preaching the *gospel everywhere and offering *Christ to the whole world. Since *God alone knows who the elect are, then the gospel is to be offered to all; however, only the elect will truly receive it.

FREE METHODIST CHURCH OF NORTH AMERICA Group founded by B. T. Roberts in Pekin, N.Y., in 1860 because of objections to "new school" *Methodism. Free Methodists call for a return to primitive Wesleyan *doctrine, stressing the *deity of *Christ, the necessity of *conversion, and entire *sanctification, along with strict adherence to the general rules of *Methodism. Currently there is a worldwide membership of about 155,000.

FREE PRESBYTERIAN CHURCH OF SCOTLAND This group was formed by those in the Free Church of *Scotland who felt that acceptance of the *Westminster Confession had been qualified by a Declaratory Act of 1892. Though the act was repealed in 1900, the smaller church, more rigid in its interpretation of *Calvinism, has continued its independent existence and has about six thousand members and adherents.

FREE WILL BAPTISTS Group of Arminian Baptists in the U.S. dating back to colonial times, which after several mergers and changes became the National Association of Free Will Baptists in 1935. There are currently about 250,000 members in 2,500 churches.

FREEDOM, CHRISTIAN Freedom from *selfishness and freedom to practice self-forgetful and self-sacrificing *love. Only *Jesus was truly free. By the help of the Holy *Spirit the *Christian is enabled to be free to love *God and man with a pure *heart. Thus Christian freedom can be known even by those who lack various types of human freedom.

FREEDOM OF THE WILL, FREE WILL The ability to act in one way or another without compulsion or coercion from within or without. Theologians have argued whether a human being has the free *will to choose the *gospel. Some claim that because of *sin the will is no longer free in its own power to choose *Christ; thus it can only choose him with the special and particular help of the Holy *Spirit. Others claim that the will is free to choose Christ with the general help of the Spirit. In fact, the way in which the freedom or bondage of the will is understood is usually related to other aspects of a theological system—the *nature of sin and *grace, the work of the Spirit, etc.

FREEMASONRY The principles, usages, and *rites of the Freemasons (or Masons). Their origins are with the stonemasons of medieval Europe. They worked on free stone and had their own lodges and guilds. After the *Reformation, when the building of churches (the main task of these masons) ceased, the lodges and guilds continued but were made up primarily of men who did not work in stone. However, they continued the rites and *ritual of the guilds, treating these as symbolic. The Grand Lodge of England was formed in 1717, and the movement spread to Europe and North America. It is powerful today among members of the professional classes in much of Western society. There is disagreement among Christians whether membership is compatible with church membership.

FREEMASONS An international organization of men whose principles are embodied in symbols and allegories connected with the art of building. Some trace the origins of *freemasonry back to the 12th century, when English masons formed a religious fraternity to guard the secrets of their craft. In its elaborate *ritual Freemasonry omits the name of *Christ, gives no preeminent place to the *Bible, claims that initiation gives illumination unattainable elsewhere, and implies that good works will enable a man to "ascent to the Grand Lodge Above." Critics have pointed out that the initiate is "required to commit himself to Freemasonry in the way that a *Christian should only commit himself to Christ."

FREETHINKERS A term that originated in the late 17th century, used of those who opposed the exclusive claims of *Christianity. They questioned the subordination of *reason in matters of religious belief and disputed the authority of the *Bible. From being a reaction against orthodox Christianity, freethinking developed into a rejection of the *supernatural and is now generally regarded as synonymous with *agnosticism and *atheism.

FREYLINGHUYSEN, THEODORE JACOBUS (1691–1747). Dutch *Reformed revivalist. Born in Prussia and ordained as a Pietist minister, he served in the Netherlands, then emigrated to New Jersey in 1720. His *preaching brought numerous *conversions and contributed to the *Great Awakening in the Colonies, in which *revival he collaborated with Gilbert *Tennent, George *Whitefield, and Jonathan *Edwards. Freylinghuysen was a prime mover in the organization of Dutch Calvinist churches in America.

FRIAR A member of one of the *Mendicant Orders in *Roman Catholicism. Friars take a *vow of *poverty, and their *rule of life combines *contemplation with activity.

FRIENDS, SOCIETY OF See QUAKERS.

FRIENDS OF *GOD (GOTTESFREUNDE) A 14th-century movement in Germany and the Netherlands that took its name from John 15:14–15. A reaction to the widespread corruption and abuse in the medieval church, this lay movement, which attracted all classes of society, stressed *prayer and piety, *love and self-discipline. Among those identified with the movement were Johann *Tauler, Henry *Suso and Jan van Ruysbroeck.

FRONTIER RELIGION A term used to describe the type of *Christianity associated with the Western expansion of the United States (1790–1890). It featured *circuit riders, *camp meetings, emphasis on an intensely personal *faith, and a sense of *fellowship often found among those in isolated areas who face common physical hardships. Among the churches, the Methodists and *Baptists adapted their outreach most effectively to frontier conditions.

FROUDE, RICHARD HURRELL (1803–1836). Prominent *Tractarian. He was ordained in 1829 and, with John Henry *Newman and John *Keble (whom he introduced to each other), led the *Oxford Movement within the Church of *England. The extended illness that led to his early death may have contributed to his melancholy temperament and to his savage attacks on *Protestantism.

FRUIT OF THE SPIRIT The nine *graces or *virtues listed by Paul in Galatians 5:22–23 that contrast with the twelve "*works of the *flesh." The image of fruit suggests that the *Spirit who lives in the human *heart cultivates these virtues that grow from the new principle and power he implants within the heart.

FRUMENTIUS (4th century). "*Apostle of the Abyssinians." He and Edesius of Tyre (Rufinus calls them brothers) were reportedly taken as prisoners to Abyssinia but gained favor with the emperor. Set free, they began to evangelize the country. About 340, Frumentius was consecrated *bishop of Ethiopia by *Athanasius in Alexandria. He is said to have originated the title of *Abuna ("Our Father"), which is still held by the head of the *Ethiopian church.

FRY, ELIZABETH (1780–1845). *Quaker prison reformer. Daughter of a wealthy Norwich banker, she was an indefatigable worker for the welfare of prisoners and the physically and mentally ill. She taught women prisoners how to sew, and she read the *Bible to them. Her special *ministry was recognized by the Quakers in 1811, and her views influenced legislation in Parliament. The bankruptcy of her merchant husband in 1828 limited her philanthropic work to some extent. Elizabeth Fry's motto was "*Charity to the *soul is the soul of charity."

FULFILLMENT OF PROPHECY The actual occurrence of that which has been promised earlier by *God. Thus the life and *work of *Christ fulfilled *prophecies concerning the *Messiah made by God to *Israel and recorded in the *OT. This principle is revealed in the *NT by the frequent citation of texts from the OT (e.g., those in Matt 1–2). There are yet prophecies to be fulfilled concerning the end of this age, the *second coming of Christ, and the arrival in fullness of the *kingdom of God.

FULLER, ANDREW (1754–1815). Baptist minister. Born in Cambridgeshire, he was minister successively in nearby Shoam (1775–1782), then in Kettering (1782–1815). Largely a self-taught man, he read widely and was particularly influenced by John *Owen and Jonathan *Edwards. From the monthly *prayer meeting he held to intercede for the *conversion of the world came the Baptist Foreign Mission Society, which sent William *Carey to India and appointed Fuller as its first secretary. A man of original mind who rejected extremes, whether hyper-*Calvinism or *Arminianism, Unitarianism or *Deism, he wrote various works, notably *The Gospel Worthy of All Acceptation* (1785) and *The Gospel Its Own Witness* (1799).

FUNDAMENTAL THEOLOGY The study of what is basic to *theology. It therefore majors on the questions: What is divine *revelation? How is revelation received? What effects does it have? The term is used more frequently by Roman Catholics than by Protestants.

FUNDAMENTALISM A term coined around 1920 to describe conservative Evangelicalism, found particularly in the U.S. Taking its name from a series of booklets entitled *The Fundamentals* (1910–1915), it is an attempt to preserve traditional Protestant *doctrines and values—especially the belief in the *inerrancy and literal interpretation of *Scripture—from the eroding effects of *rationalism and *modernism.

FUNDAMENTALS, THE A series of booklets (some large) published between 1910 and 1915 in the U.S. They defended the verbal *inspiration of the *Bible, the *deity of *Christ, the *Virgin Birth, the penal substitutionary *atonement of Christ, the bodily *resurrection of Christ, and his literal *second coming. The three million copies printed were paid for by two wealthy Californians and sent free to theological students and *Christian workers on both sides of the Atlantic. The pamphlets themselves were the work of sixty-four writers under an editorial committee that included R. A. *Torrey.

G

GAEBELEIN, ARNO CLEMENS (1861–1945). American *Fundamentalist leader and writer. With a special interest in *evangelism of the Jews, he directed a Jewish *mission in New York City (1894–1899) and kept involved in Jewish work, the struggles of the emerging *Israel, and the *dispensationalist interpretation of *prophecy. He wrote (more than forty books) and lectured about prophecy for most of his adult career. He was the founder and editor of *Our Hope* magazine (1894–1945), in which he promulgated his views in convincing yet irenic fashion.

GAEBELEIN, FRANK ELY (1899–1983). Educator and biblical scholar. The son of Arno C. *Gaebelein, a well-known writer on *prophecy, he graduated from New York and Harvard Universities. In 1921 he organized Stony Brook School on Long Island and was its headmaster from 1922 to 1963. Then he coedited *Christianity Today* for three years and took part in the 1965 Selma march for civil rights. In addition to writing numerous books, he played a key part in preparing the New International Version and was general editor of *The Expositor's Bible Commentary*, the work he was engaged in up to the week of his death.

GALERIUS (c. 250–311). Roman emperor. Nominated as his colleague by *Diocletian in 293, he commanded the Roman armies victoriously over the Persian invaders in 297. A fanatical pagan, Galerius was probably responsible for initiating the persecution against Christians in 303. Some time after he succeeded Diocletian in 305 he felt forced to issue an edict granting *toleration to the Christians—some say because, dying of a dreadful disease, he regarded this as the vengeance of the Christians' *God.

GALESBURG RULE A statement on *pulpit and *altar *fellowship accepted by the Lutheran General Council meeting at Galesburg, Illinois, in 1875. The wording, at the instigation of C. P. *Krauth, was: "Lutheran pulpits are for Lutheran ministers only; Lutheran altars are for Lutheran communicants only."

GALILEO GALILEI (1564–1642). Italian scientist. Teacher successively at Siena, Florence, Pisa, and Padua, he came to support the explanation of the solar system advanced by *Copernicus but fell foul of the *Inquisition and was forbidden in 1616 to teach the Copernican theory. The Inquisition brought him to trial later because of his *Dialogue Concerning the Two Chief Systems of the World* (1632). The work was condemned, and Galileo recanted and was sentenced to life imprisonment but was allowed to live under house arrest until his death.

GALLICAN ARTICLES, THE FOUR (1682). A statement adopted by the French *clergy about their church's relationship to the *papacy, which said, in brief: the *pope is supreme in spiritual but not secular matters; he is subordinate to *ecumenical councils; he must accept certain rights and customs traditional in the French church; and while acknowledging his special position in doctrinal matters, the pope's judgments may be questioned. Not surprisingly, the articles were condemned by Rome and were revoked in France by *Louis XIV in 1693, but they are characteristic of the historic assertiveness of the French church.

GALLICAN CONFESSION (1559). French *Reformed *confession of *faith. Drafted initially by John *Calvin, it was accepted with some revisions by the *synod in Paris. After further revision by Theodore *Beza, Calvin's successor, it was ratified finally by the synod at La Rochelle in 1571 and was not superseded until 1872.

GALLICANISM The view that claimed for the French church autonomy from Rome and that held the *pope to be subordinate to general councils of the church. Gallicanism was popularized by the late 14th-century scholars Pierre *d'Aille and Jean Charlier de *Gerson, though *Philip IV had pursued a similar policy a century earlier. The view was embodied in the *Gallican Articles sponsored by *Louis XIV in 1682, but thereafter it declined and finally disappeared after *Vatican Council I had (not without opposition) agreed on the *dogma of papal *infallibility.

GANSFORT, JOHANN See Wessel, Johann.

GATHERED CHURCH The meeting of Christians in a locality for *worship and *fellowship in a self-conscious attempt to be a pure church—an independent, self-governing, visible church of obvious *saints. The worship of the *parish, or traditional, church is rejected as being impure or compromised. This idea of a church was found in English *Separatism and *Puritanism in the 17th century, and it has continued as an idealistic option in *Protestantism since.

GAVAZZI, ALESSANDRO (1809–1899). Italian religious reformer. A school teacher in the Barnabite Order, he espoused the cause of Italian freedom against ecclesiastical authority and attacked the *papacy for its neglect of social problems, for which attitudes *Pius IX dubbed him heretical. Gavazzi continued his criticism during ten years in England (1849–1859). He served as chaplain with Garibaldi's army and founded a new Italian Free church (1870).

GEDDES, JENNY Said to have cast her folding stool at the Bishop of Edinburgh in St. Giles's church in Edinburgh when the attempt was made in 1637 to introduce a new *liturgy into Scotland, she is part of the folklore of the Covenanting period. Though a memorial to her is preserved in St. Giles's, there are different views as to whether history has handed down an authentic account.

GEHENNA See Hell.

GELASIUS I (d. 496). Pope from 492. Probably a Roman citizen in Africa, he stood out even in a century of able popes. Living in a controversial age, he upheld the Roman primacy against Constantinople and wrote against *Monophysitism, *Arianism, *Pelagianism, and *Manichaeism. He held that the world was chiefly ruled by the sacred authority of the priesthood and the authority of kings, each divine in origin, each independent in its own sphere. His writings had a profound influence on later generations.

GENERAL ASSEMBLY The highest court in churches with a *presbyterian form of government. Presided over by a *moderator elected by the assembly itself, the assembly is made up of equal numbers of ministers and *elders from each *presbytery. In the case of the established Church of *Scotland, decisions of the general assembly are final, not subject to review by any civil court.

GENERAL ASSOCIATION OF REGULAR BAPTIST CHURCHES An association of autonomous *evangelical churches in the U.S. It originated in 1932 when twenty-two congregations withdrew from the Northern Baptist

Convention as a protest against modernist teaching and against the threat to local independence. In 1978 the GARBC listed some 236,000 members in 1,544 churches.

GENERAL SYNOD The central legislative body of the Church of *England, known until 1969 as the Church Assembly. The *synod comprises three houses: *bishops, *clergy, and *laity. All diocesan bishops are automatically members; clergy and laity are elected by each *diocese on a basis of proportional representation. Meeting three times a year at Westminster, the synod aims to give a larger say in church government to the laity.

GENERATION OF THE WORD/SON The manner in which the *eternal Son proceeds from the eternal Father within the eternal Godhead. It is an eternal generation, for the Father did not exist before the Son. It is the theological exposition of the biblical phrase "only begotten" (John 1:14, 18; 3:16, 18).

GENERATIONISM See Traducianism.

GENEVAN ACADEMY A *Reformed institution founded in Geneva at the instigation of John *Calvin in 1559. It trained Christians for the *ministry and for other professions, offering courses, for example, in mathematics and physical science. Theodore *Beza was the first rector of the academy.

GENUFLECTION The causing of the right knee to touch the floor (sometimes while bowing) as a sign of *ritual reverence. It is used, especially by Roman Catholics, when passing in front of the reserved *sacrament and when the *pope, a *cardinal, or a *bishop is passing in front of the faithful.

GERHOH OF REICHERSBERG (1093–1169). German Roman Catholic reformer. A critic of disorderliness in ecclesiastical matters, he tried unsuccessfully to have a reform program adopted by the First Lateran Council (1123). He joined the *Augustinian canons in 1124, reorganized their rule, and became their provost at Reichersberg in 1132. An orthodox theologian who was a supporter of the reforms advanced in the previous century by Gregory VII, he was exiled from his *monastery in 1166 for refusal to support the *antipope set up by *Frederick I. His many letters throw valuable light on contemporary church-state relations.

GERMAN-CHRISTIANS Protestants who conformed to the church policies of the Nazis. Organized in 1932, the so-called German-Christians incorporated the nationalist and racist tendencies that had disfigured German *Protestantism in the country's recent past and held Hitler to be a divine agent. In 1933 the German-Christians acquired in Ludwig Müller a *reichsbischof, but they were opposed by the *Confessing church, of which Martin *Niemöller was a leader. The German-Christian church was banned after World War II.

GERSON, JEAN CHARLIER DE (1363–1429). French theologian and church reformer. Much of his energies and writings were absorbed by controversies arising out of the *Great Schism. Holding that a general council was superior to any pope, he supported the Council of *Pisa (1409) in its unsuccessful attempt to resolve the *Schism. With greater success he played a leading part in the Council of *Constance (1414–1418); the schism ended in 1417. Gerson's views are highly significant in the history of *Christian political thought.

GESCHICHTE (Ger. "history"). Another German word is **historie*. Theologians use these two words to denote different ideas of history. *Historie* is the "objective" study of history of the past in order to ascertain what truly happened. *Geschichte* is the study of the past in order to see its significance so that the past may benefit the present. Thus the *Gospels are said to be not mere historical records of *Jesus—*historie*—but records that present the *truth of Jesus for today (as for yesterday and tomorrow)—*geschichte*.

GIDEONS INTERNATIONAL An association of *Christian business and professional men who took their name from Gideon, whose small band triumphed over the Midianite host (Judg 6–7). Founded in the U.S. in 1899 to promote the *gospel and supported by freewill offerings, it places *Bibles in hotel rooms, prisons, schools, hospitals, and other institutions where there are large groups of people. Its activities extend to about ninety countries.

GIFTS OF THE SPIRIT See SPIRITUAL GIFTS.

GILLESPIE, GEORGE (1613–1649). Scottish *Covenanter. A strong opponent of royal attempts to force *episcopacy on Scotland, he became the youngest commissioner at the *Westminster Assembly, where his debating skills made him influential beyond his years. His chief book, *Aaron's Rod Blossoming* (1646), was hailed as a masterpiece in its closely argued dismissal of state influence in church affairs. He died early, but his works greatly encouraged fellow Covenanters during the ensuing times of persecution.

GILMOUR, JAMES (1843–1891). Scottish *missionary to China. Educated at Glasgow University and at Congregational colleges, he was sent to China in 1870 by the London Missionary Society at a time when anti-Western feeling was rising. He developed a special *ministry among nomad Mongolians, learning their language and lifestyle by sharing their tents. The English weekly *Spectator* found his *Among the Mongols* (1883) as fascinating as *Robinson Crusoe*. His diary for 1886 exemplifies the lack of response in a predominately Buddhist area. He wrote that he preached to 24,000 people, treated more than 5,700 patients, distributed 10,000 books and tracts—"and out of all this there are only two men who have openly confessed Christ."

GILPIN, BERNARD (1517–1583). Anglican minister, often called the "*Apostle of the North." An Oxford graduate ordained in 1542, he was not happy about *Henry VIII's brand of reformation of the church but found Mary *Tudor's reversion to *Roman Catholicism even more odious and said so at great risk to his life. Even under *Elizabeth I, by whom he was offered (and declined) high preferment, he continued to express his independent mind on abuses. This, along with his *missionary tours in the North, his special concern for the unreached masses, and his own ascetic way of life, brought him respect even from those of different views.

GLADDEN, WASHINGTON (1836–1918). American Congregational *pastor. He served churches in Massachusetts, New York, and Ohio, and liked to speak of a practical *gospel that had liberated him from "the bondage of an immoral *theology." He wrote twelve books and was a leader in formulating and popularizing the so-called *social gospel. He was also the author of the well-known *hymn "O Master, Let Me Walk With Thee."

GLADSTONE, WILLIAM EWART (1809–1898). British prime minister. He wanted to be ordained in the Church of *England, but his father persuaded him to take up politics. He entered Parliament in 1832 and was a member nearly all his life, serving four times as prime minister. A *High Churchman who wrote extensively on ecclesiastical matters, he abolished church rates, disestablished the Church of *Ireland, and often attacked the Roman Catholic Church, notably over the decrees of *Vatican Council I.

GLAS, JOHN (1695–1773). Founder of the *sect known as Glasites and later as Sandemanians. Minister of Tealing, near Dundee in Scotland, his unorthodox views brought him before the ecclesiastical courts. He argued that the *NT offered no warrant for a national church, that the civil arm had no right to punish heretics, that the *National Covenant and the *Solemn League and Covenant lacked biblical authority, and that the true church was to be sustained only by the *Word and

*Spirit of *Jesus Christ. Suspended and deposed for *heresy, he began his independent movement, which did not cooperate with other churches, imposed uniformity, cared for the poor, and held that *Scripture did not command continuance of the *missionary task. Control of the Glasites gradually passed to his son-in-law Robert Sandeman.

GLASITES See SANDEMANIANISM.

GLEGG, ALEXANDER LINDSAY (1882–1975). British lay *evangelist. Born in London of Scottish parents, he was converted at *Keswick in 1905 shortly after graduating in electrical engineering. He continued in business but spent all of his free time in *mission work among London slum dwellers. He traveled thereafter all over the country, taking the *gospel to businessmen and students, prisoners and vacationers, and even making a successful appeal for decisions during a *sermon in Westminster Abbey. Glegg was a great encourager and supporter of young evangelists, many of them now known worldwide. He preached until nearly the end of his long life.

GLORIFICATION The final act of *God's *salvation and *redemption of the believer. In the future *kingdom of God each person will have a *resurrection *body of glory (1 Cor 15:42–44), for it will reflect the glory of God in *Jesus Christ (2 Cor 3:18; 4:6; Phil 3:21).

GLOSSOLALIA (Gk. *glossa*, "tongue"; *lalia*, "speaking"). The word was coined in the 19th century and refers to the Holy *Spirit's gift of *speaking in *tongues. Some identify this with human languages (Acts 2:4, 6); others say that it refers to angelic language (1 Cor 13:1) or something else that needs spiritual interpretation (1 Cor 14); and some see both in *Scripture.

GLOVER, TERROT REAVELEY (1869–1943). English Baptist scholar. He taught classics at Queen's University, Kingston, Ontario (1896–1901), and at Cambridge. His teaching and writing contributed greatly to the understanding of the *NT world. His most famous work is *The Jesus of History* (1917). Glover was president of the Baptist Union in 1924.

GNESIO-LUTHERANISM (Gk. *gnesios*, "true, genuine"). That part of *Lutheranism, led by M. Falcius Illyricus (1520–1575), that claimed to defend true Lutheranism against compromise with either *Calvinism or *Roman Catholicism.

GNOSTICISM (Gk. *gnosis*, "knowledge"). Salvation through special knowledge. The word covers a wide variety of 1st- and 2d-century teachings, some of which may be called *Christian Gnosticism. All have the essential ingredient that *salvation is by enlightenment and by possession of special knowledge. Famous teachers were Valentinus (2d century), Basilides (2d century), and *Marcion (d. 160). Christian authors who attacked Gnosticism as being pagan in origin and for misusing the *Bible were *Irenaeus (d. 200), *Tertullian (d. 225), and *Hippolytus (d. 236). Modern knowledge of Gnosticism has been greatly supplemented by archaeological findings, notably at Nag-Hammadi in 1945.

GOD The *Christian view of God is based on the record of God's self-revelation recorded in the *Bible. This teaching may be received either in its basic biblical form as dynamic images and ideas (*biblical *theology) or in its developed and processed form (*dogmatic theology). The Bible presents God under various images—Father, Shepherd, King, Rock, Holy One of *Israel, etc.—and he is also described as righteous, wise, and faithful. In particular, he is made known in the life, teaching, and activity of *Jesus of Nazareth, who is God made man. By the power of the Holy *Spirit, God is a reality for the people who trust and obey him. They know him as *Yahweh and *Elohim—their Creator, Sustainer, and *Savior—and they recognize that he is both transcendent and immanent.

In the teaching of the church the

dynamic ideas of the Bible are given *dogmatic and precise form. Thus there is the *doctrine of the *Trinity, that God is one, yet three in one. There is one Godhead but three Persons: Father, Son, and Holy Spirit. Then there are attempts to define God such as this: "There is one, true, living God, the Creator and *Lord of *heaven and earth. He is almighty, *eternal, beyond measure, incomprehensible, and infinite in intellect, *will, and very perfection. Since he is one unique spiritual Being, entirely simple and unchangeable, he must be really and essentially distinct from the world, perfectly happy in himself and by his very *nature, and inexpressibly exalted over all things that exist or can be conceived other than himself."

For Christians, *knowing* God is more than *knowing about* God. It is to have a spiritual relationship with him; it is to be united to *Jesus Christ by the Holy Spirit and experiencing God as Father.

See also CREATION, IMMANENCE, NATURAL THEOLOGY, PREDESTINATION, PROVIDENCE, THEISM, TRANSCENDENCE.

GODET, FREDERIC LOUIS (1812–1900). Swiss *Reformed theologian. *Pastor and professor in Neuchâtel, he was an influential champion of *orthodoxy against encroaching liberalism in *theology. Many of his commentaries on *NT books have been translated into other languages, including English.

GODPARENT A sponsor who makes a profession of *faith for the person (child) being baptized. In the event of the death or neglect of the parents, he or she has an obligation to see that the promises made at *baptism are fulfilled.

GOLDEN RULE, THE The teaching of *Jesus in Matthew 7:12 concerning treatment of others. The principle of doing to others what you would have them do to you.

GOMAR, FRANCIS (1563–1641). Dutch *Reformed theologian. Named professor of *theology at Leiden in 1594, his rigid *Calvinism was opposed by Jacobus *Arminius. Gomar later taught at Saumur and Groningen, helped to revise the Dutch *OT, and was a leader of the strict Calvinists at the Synod of *Dort (1618–1619).

GOOD FRIDAY The Friday immediately before *Easter on which the death of *Jesus is commemorated. It is one of the rare days when Roman Catholics do not celebrate the *Eucharist but partake of the *Mass of the Presanctified. A popular act of *worship on this day is the Three Hours' Service from 12:00 to 3:00 P.M.

GOOD WORKS The actions of a person that are designed for the good of the recipient—e.g., visiting the sick. *Christian teaching insists that while good works cannot of themselves merit God's *salvation, they ought to be top priority for Christians out of their *love for *God and humankind (Matt 25:31ff.). Salvation is not *by* good works but *for* them (James 2:17).

GOODALL, NORMAN (1896–1985). English Congregational minister and pioneer in the modern *ecumenical movement. Birmingham born, he served the London Missionary Society before appointment as secretary of the *International Missionary Council in 1944. He oversaw the IMC's union with the *World Council of Churches in 1955 and was prominent in the 1972 Congregational-Presbyterian union that formed the *United Reformed Church. He was an occasional lecturer in many educational institutions, including the Gregorian University in Rome.

GOODSPEED, EDGAR JOHNSON (1871–1962). American *NT scholar. After study and extensive travel at home and abroad, he taught in the New Testament department at the University of Chicago (1900–1937), specializing in biblical and patristic Greek. He was a member of the RSV NT committee (having himself produced in 1923 a significant translation of the NT), and he wrote more than sixty books. After retirement from Chicago he taught history at the University of California until he was eighty.

GORDON, ADONIRAN JUDSON (1836–1895). Leading Fundamentalist and Baptist *pastor. Besides ministering in two churches in Massachusetts (one for over twenty-five years), he was an author and also wrote the *hymn "My Jesus, I Love Thee." He founded the Boston Missionary Training School (now Gordon College and Gordon-Conwell Divinity School) and the Boston Industrial Home and was one of the founders of the early prophetic conferences.

GORDON, SAMUEL DICKEY (1859–1936). American devotional writer. After ten years with the *Young Men's Christian Association, he began a career of speaking; he traveled much, including four years in Asia. An *Evangelical with a persuasive style, he is best remembered for his more than twenty "Quiet Talk" books.

GORE, CHARLES (1853–1932). Anglican *bishop. Oxford don and theological college principal, he was an Anglo-Catholic of irenic spirit and strong social concern. He was bishop successively of Worcester (1902), Birmingham (1905; a newly established *diocese), and Oxford (1911–1919). Author of many books, including *The Sermon on the Mount* (1896) and *Christ and Society* (1928), he was the most versatile churchman of his age.

GOSPEL (Gk. *euangelion*, "good news"). A word with several meanings: (1) the central content of the proclamation of the church concerning *Jesus and aimed at the world; (2) the four books, Matthew, Mark, Luke, and John, which describe what Jesus said and did; (3) the portion of one of these books read on *Sunday at the *Eucharist in church. See also SYNOPTIC GOSPELS.

GOTTESFREUNDE See FRIENDS OF GOD.

GOTTSCHALK (c. 803–c. 869). German theologian and monk, born of noble Saxon birth, he was put into the *Benedictine abbey of Fulda by his parents but released from his *vows by a church *synod in 829, despite the protest of his *abbot, *Rabanus Maurus, who then enlisted the civil arm to get him back into a French *monastery. Gottschalk's *doctrine of *double *predestination, which he based on the teaching of *Augustine of Hippo, incurred the enmity of the powerful *Hincmar of Reims and the condemnation of two church synods (848–49). Then he was imprisoned in a *monastery for the rest of his life. Gottschalk wrote poetry that is still highly regarded.

GOVERNMENT, DIVINE *God's rule of the universe as he executes his plan for it. See also PROVIDENCE.

GRACE The favor of *God freely shown and given to human beings, especially in and through the life, death, and exaltation of *Jesus Christ, *Son of God. It is *love which, as sinners, human beings do not merit, but it is freely given by God. It is love over and above that displayed in the normal *blessing and benefits of life. Protestants and Roman Catholics have differed in their statements of how God communicates his grace to sinners. Protestants have especially emphasized the *ministry of *preaching and the receiving of *forgiveness through *faith (itself a gift of God), while Roman Catholics have emphasized grace as a renewing and cleansing power, experienced especially through the *sacraments. Both agree that the source of grace is God in *Christ by and through the Holy *Spirit. For the sake of clarity theologians have described grace under different aspects: (1) *actual grace*—the work of the Spirit that helps a person respond to the *gospel and become a *Christian and further assists the believer in remaining faithful to God; (2) *baptismal grace*—the placing by God of a new principle of life in the *heart of the one who is baptized (see also BAPTISMAL REGENERATION); (3) *common grace*—the kindness of God commonly experienced by human beings of all types and thus distinguished from special grace; (4) *efficacious grace*—the work of the Spirit that achieves in an individual the end that God had in view (thus, e.g., grace makes the heart and *will of man ready to respond to God's will and word); (5) *habitual grace*—the presence of a new habit of life in the heart of man that leads to love of God and to *good works (also called sanctifying grace); (6) *illuminating grace*—the work of the Spirit illuminating the *mind of the sinner so that he recognizes his *sin and what God has provided for him in Christ; (7) *imputed grace*—the *merit (*righteousness) of Christ that the Father reckons, counts, or imputes to the sinner who believes on Christ (also known as imputed righteousness); (8) *irresistible grace*—the work of the Spirit that makes an individual desire and then accept the gospel (similar to efficacious grace but emphasizing that the sinner had no choice but to be made willing and responsive); (9) *prevenient grace*—the preparatory work of the Spirit in the heart of the sinner, making him interested in and ready to hear the gospel; (10) *sacramental grace*—the work of the Spirit bringing the blessing and love of God to the faithful as they receive the *sacraments of the church; (11) *sanctifying grace*—the presence of the Spirit in the life of the believer, making him holy; (12) *special grace*—the particular love of God for sinners revealed in Jesus Christ and the offer of *salvation in and through him (in contrast to common grace); (13) *substantial grace*—God's self-communication in Jesus Christ, Son of God made man (God himself coming to the aid of man and giving himself wholly to man); (14) *sufficient grace*—the particular help provided by the Spirit to perform a special task or specific act.

GRAHAM, WILLIAM FRANKLIN ("BILLY") (1918–). American *evangelist. He became a Southern Baptist minister, moving into full-time *evangelism in 1943, first with *Youth for Christ, then with the Billy Graham Evangelistic Association. Since then he has conducted crusades all over the world, and has perhaps preached to more people than anyone else in history. Subsidiary ministries include the weekly "Hour of Decision" radio broadcast, the California-based Worldwide Films, *Decision* magazine, and a weekly syndicated newspaper column. His books include *Peace with God* (1952), *World Aflame* (1965), and *Angels* (1975).

GRAY, JAMES MARTIN (1851–1935). Educator and *pastor. He was rector of the First Reformed Episcopal Church (Boston, 1879–1894), lecturer at Reformed Episcopal Seminary, and an editor of the Scofield Reference *Bible. In 1893 he began lecturing at Moody Bible Institute, in 1904 he became dean, and from 1925 to 1934 he served as its president. He developed and popularized the synthetic approach to Bible study and wrote many books and a number of popular *hymns.

GREAT AWAKENING, THE A religious *revival in the American colonies between 1725 and 1760. A stark contrast to *rationalism, formalism, and pastoral neglect in different areas, the awakening was experienced mostly among churches with Calvinistic links, including *Reformed churches, *Congregationalists, *Baptists and, to a lesser extent, Anglicans. Among the more prominent revivalists were George *Whitefield, Jonathan *Edwards, and Samuel *Davies. A notable opponent of the movement was Charles *Chauncy of Boston, who rejected it as an outbreak of extravagant emotion. While it split some of the *denominations, the revival encouraged *missions to the Indians; led to the founding of what are now well-known universities, such as Princeton, Dartmouth, and Brown; contributed much to church growth; and fostered a greater *toleration in doctrinal matters and a greater democracy in church government. The *Second Great Awakening began at the end of the 18th century.

GREAT SCHISM The term is applied to two different events in church history: (1) the division between East and West in 1054, when Pope *Leo IX and Michael *Cerularius, *patriarch of Constantinople, led their churches into a breach that became permanent. It was no new argument that had blown up but the culmination of centuries of wrangling, chiefly about the *nature and practice of papal authority. (2) The so-called *Western Schism (1378–1417) was a matter of different papal claimants. European countries lined up over rivals at Rome and Avignon, and the Council of *Pisa (1409), far from solving the problem, contrived to raise up a third candidate. This *schism officially ended with the Council of *Constance's election of *Martin V in 1417.

GREBEL, CONRAD (c. 1498–1526). Founder of the Swiss Brethren Movement, elsewhere called *Anabaptists. Having broken with *Zwingli in 1524, Grebel organized the Brethren as an independent Anabaptist church in Zürich. An able humanist and biblical scholar, he defied the city council's ban on his activities, and performed the first adult *baptism in modern history. He served two prison terms, totaling six months, before his early death.

GREENE, OLIVER B. (1915–). *Evangelist, radio broadcaster, and author. A tent preacher for twenty-five years—one of the best-known evangelists of the Southeast—his radio program, "The Gospel Hour," is carried nationwide on 150 stations, and he has written many books and pamphlets.

GREENHILL, WILLIAM (1591–1671). English nonconformist minister. Formerly incumbent of a Sussex *parish (1613–1631), he became preacher to a congregation in London and at the *Westminster Assembly opposed the *Presbyterian party. He ministered in a Congregational church, became one of the Triers under Oliver *Cromwell, and was ejected from a London vicarage in 1660 for *Nonconformity. His five-volume commentary on Ezekiel was highly regarded.

GREGORIAN CALENDAR The calendar as reformed in 1582 by Pope *Gregory XIII and now used by most churches and nations. It superseded the Julian Calendar (46 B.C.), which had by 1582 accumulated an error of ten days in terms of the earth's revolution round the sun. Gregory decreed simply that October 4 be followed by October 15. The new calendar was not adopted in England until 1752; most *Eastern Orthodox churches began to accept it only in 1924.

GREGORY I (c. 540–604). Pope from 590. One of the most important of medieval popes, he brought to the task personal piety, business acumen, reforming zeal, and the experience gained during a five-year nunciature in Constantinople (579–584). He did much to establish the temporal power of the *papacy, consolidated the position of the church in various countries, encouraged *monasticism, and in 596 sent *Augustine to England.

GREGORY II (669–731). Pope from 715. A noble Roman by birth, his *pontificate saw (1) *Boniface become the "*apostle of Germany"; (2) the dispute with the *Byzantine emperor *Leo III over the respective status of each, which developed into the *Iconoclastic Controversy; (3) and the threat to the West through the advance of Islam. Gregory also improved papal relations with some of the remoter branches of the church within Europe itself.

GREGORY VII (HILDEBRAND) (c. 1023–1085). Pope from 1073. After a comprehensive education and having served several popes in very different circumstances, Gregory was well equipped for the task when he was elected by acclamation in 1073. Seeking to remedy church abuses, he became involved in the controversy over lay *investiture with the emperor *Henry IV, who was excommunicated, humbled himself to receive absolution at Canossa in 1077, and was excommunicated again and declared deposed by Gregory. After a lengthy siege the imperial troops took Rome in 1084, and

Gregory died in Salerno the following year. Autocratic in temperament, he was jealous in upholding the rights and dignity of church and *papacy.

GREGORY IX (1170?–1241). Pope from 1227. A former papal legate in Germany and a friend of emperor *Frederick II, he had to contend just after his election with imperial designs on papal territory and with Frederick's prevarication over launching a long-promised crusade. Open *war erupted between the two forces on two occasions during Gregory's reign, resulting in two sentences of *excommunication on the emperor, whose army was advancing on Rome as Gregory lay dying. Gregory encouraged *Franciscans and *Dominicans and showed a degree of enlightenment in his attitude to controversial scholarship.

GREGORY XI (1329–1378). Pope from 1370. The last French pope and the last to have his papal base at Avignon, it was he who ended the so-called *Babylonian Captivity of the church by returning to Rome in 1377—despite the protests of French *cardinals but with the encouragement of *Catherine of Siena. Gregory had earlier failed to mediate in the longstanding *war between France and England. While Gregory's death in 1378 was the beginning of a series of *antipopes, it left the significant papal connection with Rome restored.

GREGORY XII (c. 1325–1417). Pope from 1406 to 1415. He was the last of the Rome-based popes during the *Great Schism in the Western church. Opposed by the Avignon-based *Benedict XIII, Gregory protested when both were pronounced deposed by the Council of *Pisa in 1409. With neither willing to relinquish his claim, Gregory finally had the good sense to resign in 1415 and to approve the Council of *Constance, which elected *Martin V as pope. Gregory survived for two more years with the title of *cardinal *bishop of Porto.

GREGORY XIII (1502–1585). Pope from 1572. A former lecturer in law who had participated in the Council of *Trent, he promoted church reform, founded colleges and *seminaries, issued the *Gregorian Calendar, and carried out an extensive building program that emptied the *Vatican coffers. He championed the Irish rebels against *Elizabeth I of England and celebrated the Massacre of St. *Bartholomew's Day with a *Te Deum* in Rome.

GREGORY OF NAZIANZUS (330–389). *Christian apologist. Brought up in Cappadocia where his father was *bishop of Nazianzus, he chose the monastic life, but family pressure led to his *ordination as *priest in 362 and his *consecration some ten years later as bishop of Sasima. He withdrew from diocesan work in Nazianzus, where he had been helping his father until the latter's death in 374, but in 379 he was called to Constantinople to battle for the orthodox *faith against *Arianism, a battle won at the First Council of *Constantinople in 381. He was appointed bishop of the city but resigned within a few months when his election was questioned. His five *Theological Addresses* reflect the significant part he played in upholding the Nicene faith.

GREGORY OF NYSSA (c. 335–c. 394). *Bishop of Nyssa. Brother of *Basil the Great, he became bishop about 371, lost his see for two years because of Arian influence (376–378), and at the First Council of *Constantinople (381) showed himself to be a leader of the orthodox party. Subsequently, he became the leading orthodox theologian of Asia Minor. He was recognized four centuries after his death when the Second Council of *Nicea (787) called him "Father of Fathers."

GREGORY OF TOURS (c. 540–594). *Bishop of Tours. Born of a noble Roman family, he became bishop in 573, remedied the disorder in his *diocese, and defended *orthodoxy against *Arianism. He was the author of a multivolume *History of the Franks,* a valuable record that told the story down to 591.

GREGORY THAUMATURGUS (c. 213–c. 270). *Bishop of Neo-Caesarea. A lawyer converted through the testimony of *Origen, he later returned to his native city and was made its bishop. He reportedly changed it from a pagan to a *Christian place. Many miracles were traditionally associated with him, hence his name, which means "wonder-worker."

GREGORY THE ILLUMINATOR (c. 240–332). "*Apostle of Armenia." Little is known for certain about his life, but he may have been brought up as a *Christian in Cappadocia. On returning to his native Armenia he reportedly was responsible for the *conversion of the king, after which the whole nation followed suit about 303.

GREGORY THE GREAT He ordered the training of singers of plainchant and arranged the ordering of the chants used in the Roman Catholic Church.

GRENFELL, SIR WILFRED THOMASON (1865–1940). *Missionary to Labrador. While a medical student at London University, he was converted at a D. L. *Moody *mission service. After qualifying, he joined the Royal National Mission to Deep Sea Fishermen. In 1892 he went to Labrador, where he labored until retirement in 1935, when, because of his efforts, Labrador was equipped with hospitals, nursing stations, orphanages, schools, and industrial centers. Grenfell, who tells his story in *Forty Years for Labrador* (1932), was knighted by George V in 1927.

GREY FRIARS See FRANCISCANS.

GRINDAL, EDMUND (1519?–1583). *Archbishop of Canterbury from 1575. A moderate Calvinist, he helped to revise the *liturgy, became *bishop of London in 1559 and archbishop of York in 1570. Because he was regarded as being too soft on *Puritanism, *Elizabeth I regretted having appointed him to Canterbury and virtually suspended him for several years.

GROOTE, GERHARD (1340–1384). Founder of the *Brethren of the Common Life. A wealthy Dutch scholar who held benefices in Aachen and Utrecht, he was converted about 1374 and subsequently preached in the Utrecht *diocese with great success among the people but not among those *clergy whose abuses he criticized. His Brethren of the Common Life originated about 1380. His license to preach was withdrawn in 1383, and he died of plague the following year.

GROSSETESTE, ROBERT (c. 1168–1253). *Bishop of Lincoln. Previously *chancellor of Oxford University and then lecturer in *theology to the *Franciscans, he was appointed to Lincoln (England's largest *diocese) in 1235. A diligent and faithful *pastor who championed the superiority of church over state, he nonetheless spoke out valiantly against abuses and corruption in both spheres. Grosseteste was also a versatile and imaginative scholar who made more widely known in the West scientific and philosophical writings from Greek and Arab sources.

GROTIUS, HUGO (1583–1645). Dutch jurist and theologian. Educated at Leyden and supporting the Arminian party in *theology, his tendency toward *toleration in an intolerant age incurred the opposition of powerful Calvinists, and this led to a sentence of life imprisonment in 1618. He escaped in 1621, settled in Paris, and there published his renowned work *On the Law of War and Peace* (1625), which with other writings established him as a pioneer in the field of international law. His *De veritate religionis Christianae* (1627), a guide for *missionaries, reflects his convictions about the essential orderliness of *God's world. He regarded the *Atonement as an act by which God and the sovereignty of law are satisfied.

GRUNDTVIG, NIKOLAI FREDERIK SEVERIN (1783–1872). Danish *bishop and *hymn writer. Educated in *theology at Copenhagen, he lived largely as a writer, except for brief periods in the Lutheran *ministry until 1825 when, beginning with a published pamphlet, he started a reform movement within the *state church on the basis of the *Apostles' Creed. In 1839 he became chaplain at the Vartov Foundation (home for the aged) in Copenhagen, where he remained until his death. He was given the rank of bishop in 1861. A tireless champion of liberty in church and state, an imaginative sponsor of education, a sacramental theologian and a prolific hymn writer, his name has been linked with that of *Kierkegaard as the most prominent religious figure in 19th-century Denmark.

GUILT This has different meanings in psychology, jurisprudence, and *theology. In the latter there is the basic idea of guilt that arises from a lack of a loving relationship with *God and makes a person feel unworthy before God and alienated from him. Also there is the guilt that arises from the belief that one has broken a commandment of God, and this leads to a sense of shame. Such guilt is cancelled by divine *forgiveness, but sometimes the results of guilty actions have still to be set right.

GUNPOWDER PLOT (1605). A conspiracy to blow up *James I and the Parliament at Westminster, said to have been part of a plan to restore Roman Catholic supremacy in England. Thirteen men were involved, including Robert Catesby and Guy Fawkes, and all variously paid the supreme penalty (including one who died in prison). The gunpowder had been deposited in the palace of Westminster some months before the opening of Parliament on November 5, but at the end of October the plot was revealed by an anonymous letter.

GUSTAVUS VASA (1496–1560). King of Sweden. Previously active in *war against the Danish overlordship of his country, he led the independence movement from 1520, after the success of which he was elected king in 1523. He broke with Rome and established *Lutheranism as the *state church, partly because Roman Catholic authority had allied itself with Denmark, partly because he needed money and the old church controlled much of the country's wealth. He confiscated much church property, ordered *Protestantism to be taught in schools, and persuaded Parliament to make the monarchy hereditary in 1544.

GUTENBERG BIBLE Printed by Johann Gutenberg (c. 1397–1468), it was the first Bible printed in movable type. It was actually the Mazarin Bible, printed in 1455. The Mazarin Bible was discovered in the library of Cardinal Mazarin in Paris.

GUTHRIE, JAMES (c. 1612–1661). Scottish *Covenanter. As minister of Stirling, he was suspicious of the ecclesiastical policies of the new king, *Charles II, but under *Cromwell upheld the principle of monarchy. Continuing his independence of mind after the *Restoration, he reminded Charles of his obligation to the *Solemn League and Covenant. Charged with disputing the king's authority over the church, he was found guilty and hanged in Edinburgh. Guthrie was author of *Causes of God's Wrath Against Scotland* (1653), which provided guidelines for later Covenanters.

GUTZLAFF, KARL FRIEDRICH AUGUST (1803–1851). German *missionary to China. He went to the Far East in 1823, serving successively in Singapore and Batavia before beginning work in China. His work, plans, and inspiration laid the basis for later evangelistic work by Timothy *Richard and J. H. *Taylor, among others.

GUYON, MADAME (JEANNE-MARIE DE LA MOTTE) (1648–1717). French mystic. Forced by her mother into marriage at sixteen to an invalid who died twelve years later, she left her children after claiming to have received visions and *revelations. With François Lacombe, a Barnabite *friar, she spent several years wandering through France, Switzerland, and

Italy, incurring charges of *heresy and immorality. Both were imprisoned (Lacombe for twelve years), but Madame Guyon was soon released through royal intervention. Her writings and letters brought her an influential *disciple in François Fénelon,* and greatly encouraged his Quietist* tendencies. A theological commission condemned her in 1695 for such teaching as the uselessness of petitionary *prayer and the need to suppress all explicit acts of *faith. She was jailed for eight years and thereafter lived and wrote quietly until her death.

H

HABIT Used in Medieval and Roman Catholic *theology to describe a permanent quality possessed by the *soul (*heart) which affects the whole person. E.g., sanctifying *grace is a habit, and so are *faith and *hope.

HADES The place of departed human *spirits. In Greek mythology, Hades is the name of a grim and pitiless deity, lord of the lower world; thus it came to be used of the shadowy underworld or the state of death. The term is used in the *Septuagint to translate the Hebrew **sheol*. See also DESCENT INTO HELL (HADES), THE.

HADRIAN (76–138). Roman emperor. Succeeding Trajan in 117, he embarked on a series of journeys to consolidate his empire. On his instructions a 73½-mile wall, which still bears his name, was constructed from the Tyne to the Solway, as a protection against Picts and Scots. He suppressed a Jewish revolt against the Roman presence in Jerusalem but was a protector rather than a persecutor of Christians. Hadrian was a cultured scholar who sponsored the erection of many fine buildings in his domains.

HADRIAN, POPES See ADRIAN.

HADRIAN THE AFRICAN (c. 709). Formerly an *abbot near Naples, he was sent by Pope *Vitalian to England with the newly appointed *archbishop of Canterbury, *Theodore, reportedly to ensure that the latter did not introduce any Greek customs into the English church. He helped Theodore raise the level of education of church music throughout the land.

HAGIOGRAPHY The literature on the *saints and the *cults associated with them. Hagiology is the study of the saints and their *veneration/cults.

HAILE SELASSIE (1892–1975). Emperor of Ethiopia. Formerly called Ras Tafari (hence *Rastafarians, who were named after him), he became emperor in 1930, taking a name that means "Might of the Trinity" and assuming that his was a divinely ordained task. Forced into exile during the Italian occupation (1936–1941), he thereafter resumed his grip on the country. While restrictions remained on foreign *missionaries, he participated in the *World Congress on Evangelism at Berlin in 1966 and was host to the *World Council of Churches central committee meeting in Addis Ababa in 1971. He was deposed in 1974.

HALDANE, JAMES ALEXANDER (1768–1851). Scottish *evangelist. A former East Indiaman captain converted soon after he left the navy in 1794, he helped found the Society for Propagating the Gospel at Home (1797) at a time when liberalism dominated the Church of *Scotland. He embarked on a series of *preaching tours throughout Scotland and met with great response despite opposition from *parish ministers and local lairds. In 1799 he was ordained as the first Congregational minister in Scotland and established preaching tabernacles in Scottish cities. It was said that no other since *Whitefield had been used of *God in the *conversion of sinners.

HALDANE, ROBERT (1764–1842). Scottish *evangelist, philanthropist, and writer. A wealthy landowner in Stirlingshire, he held after his *conversion in 1795 that "*Christianity is everything or nothing. If it be true, it warrants and commands every sacrifice to promote its influence." He sold his estate in order to start a *mission in Bengal; but thwarted by the opposition of the East India Company, he devoted himself, like his brother James, to home missions. His evangelistic work took him to Switzerland and France, where his *ministry contributed much to revival of the flagging Protestant cause. He criticized the British and Foreign Bible Society for circulating the *Apocrypha with the *Bible. Haldane's social standing gave him unique opportunities among all classes. His written works include a commentary on Romans (1834).

HALFWAY COVENANT (1662) A modified form of church membership in New England Congregational churches. By a Massachusetts synodical decision, baptized adults who had no *conversion experience but who professed *faith and lived uprightly would be regarded as "half-way" church members and could present their children for *baptism, but neither children nor parents could participate in the *Lord's Supper or vote in church business. This form of two-tier membership did not survive the 17th century.

HALL, ROBERT (1764–1831). English Baptist preacher. A graduate of Aberdeen, he ministered in Bristol (1785–1790) and Cambridge (1791–1806), where his brilliant oratory and liberal outlook attracted many. When ill health forced his resignation and a year's rest, he had what he called a *conversion experience, and for nearly twenty years thereafter he exercised a fruitful *ministry in Leicester (until 1825). Hall was a champion of freedom of the press, a zealous social reformer, and a writer whose six-volume *Works* (1832) were published in Britain and America.

HALLELUJAH (Lat. *alleluia*). Hebrew for "Praise the *Lord," it is found especially in Psalms 111–117.

HALLESBY, OLE KRISTIAN (1879–1961). Norwegian theologian. As chairman of the Norwegian Lutheran Home Mission and professor of *dogmatics at the Free Faculty of Theology in Oslo, he greatly influenced Norway's *clergy and *laity. He cooperated with neither liberal theologians nor Nazi occupiers during World War II (he spent two years in a concentration camp). He became internationally known for work among students and for (in English translation) *Prayer* (1948) and *Why I Am a Christian* (1950).

HALLOWEEN See ALL SAINTS' DAY.

HAMILTON, PATRICK (c. 1503–1528). Protomartyr of the Scottish Reformation. Of noble birth, he studied in Paris, where he embraced Lutheran views. These he spread on his return to St. Andrews University in 1523, but he was soon forced into exile in Germany. Conscience having called him home to preach the *gospel, he was arrested, condemned for *heresy, and died at the stake fearlessly professing his *faith in Christ. A servant of the *archbishop unwittingly spoke his epitaph: "The reek of Mr. Patrick Hamilton has infected as many as it did blow upon."

HAMPTON COURT CONFERENCE (1604). An assembly called by *James I at the instigation of the Puritans to discuss ecclesiastical reforms suggested by the *Millenary Petition. The four-day conference, with James as chairman and with strong representation from the side of the *bishops, achieved no more than a few minor reforms.

HANDEL, GEORGE FREDERICK (1685–1759). Music composer. Born in Germany and educated there and in Italy, he settled in England in 1712 and became a naturalized British subject in

1726. His many Italian operatic works have been little performed in recent times, and he is now known best for his oratorios and odes, usually on biblical themes. Among his works are **Israel in Egypt* (1739); *Messiah* (1742), the most popular oratorio in history; and *Belshazzar* (1744).

HARDENBERG, F. L. F. VON See NOVALIS.

HARDENING OF THE HEART A biblical metaphor (Isa 6:10; Matt 19:8). If understood as a *sin, it carries the general idea of malice. If understood as a *punishment from *God, it is the deprivation of his *grace so that it is impossible to respond to his *revelation and *salvation.

HARDING, STEPHEN (c. 1060–1134). *Cistercian *abbot. Born in Dorset, he studied in Paris and entered a Cluniac *monastery. Its loose observance of the *Benedictine *rule made him and others leave. They founded a monastery at Citeaux, and this was the beginning of the Cistercian *order, which was greatly boosted by the support of *Bernard of Clairvaux. Stephen, who became the third abbot in 1109, combined an ascetic life with great administrative abilities.

HARMONY SOCIETY A Protestant community set up in Pennsylvania in 1805 by five hundred German Pietists. The moving spirit was George *Rapp, who with his son John and a few others had emigrated to America in 1803 after years of persecution by the (Lutheran) *state church. Once established, they sent for their followers, most of whom became founding members of the *Harmony Society—a communistic *theocracy with Rapp as a very autocratic leader. Despite defections and litigation they prospered economically, relocated in Indiana in 1815, then returned to Pennsylvania in 1824. Rapp held some bizarre *doctrines, especially on Christ's return. He taught perfectionism, but it was teaching on *celibacy and the lack of converts that finally resulted in the group's disbandment in 1906.

HARNACK, ADOLF (1851–1930). German theologian and church historian. Having taught at Leipzig, Giessen, and Marburg, Harnack became professor of church history at Berlin (1889–1921) despite powerful Lutheran opposition. He was probably the outstanding *patristics scholar of his age. His best-known work, translated into English as *History of Dogma* (7 vols., 1894–1899), suggested that early *Christianity was so mixed with Greek thought that much extraneous matter crept into the church's belief and practice—a theory strongly denied by conservative Lutheran scholars. His other works include *What Is Christianity?* (1901) and *New Testament Studies* (1907–1912).

HARRIS, HOWEL (1714–1773). Welsh preacher. A lifelong Anglican who was nonetheless one of the chief founders of *Calvinistic Methodism, he had been converted in 1735 and traveled throughout Wales *preaching the *gospel. He established a center for revivalist activities and from 1768 helped to train there the *ministers of the *Countess of Huntingdon's Connexion. Harris was also the author of a number of Welsh *hymns that became very popular.

HARROWING OF HELL The defeat of the *Devil and *evil forces by Christ as he descended into *hell (*Hades) between his *death and *resurrection. This is a medieval English term and provided the subject for some powerful religious drama. See also DESCENT INTO HELL (HADES), THE.

HASTINGS, JAMES (1852–1922). Scottish theological editor. After ministering in various congregations of the *Free and *United Free Church of Scotland, he retired to Aberdeen, there to complete his monumental *Encyclopaedia of Religion and Ethics* (1908–1922). He had earlier published his *Dictionary of the Bible* (1898–1904) and founded the *Expository Times*, which he edited from 1889 to 1922.

HAUGE, HANS NIELSEN (1771–1824). Norwegian preacher. Feeling himself called to an itinerant *ministry, this layman went around the country with the *gospel for eight years, stressing the need for *conversion and *sanctification. At the same time he founded various industrial businesses. Such *preaching was illegal, and Hauge spent seven years in prison from 1804, and in 1814 he was fined for this offense and for criticizing the *clergy. He was the founder of the *Christian laymen's movement in Norway.

HAVERGAL, FRANCES RIDLEY (1838–1879). English *hymn writer. Daughter of a Worcestershire rector, she began writing verse at seven, was converted at fifteen, and became a proficient linguist. She published a number of prose writings but is best known for her *hymns (e.g., "Take My Life and Let It Be").

HEADLAM, ARTHUR CAYLEY (1862–1947). *Bishop of Gloucester (1923–1945). Previously professor of *theology at London (1903–1917) and Oxford (1918–1923), he collaborated with William *Sanday in writing a commentary on Romans (1895) that is still used. Headlam, an influential churchman, disliked extremes. He wrote many books on *NT themes and on church reunion, including *Christian Unity* (1930) and *Christian Theology* (1934).

HEALING The cure of bodily and mental illness by the power of *God connected with the use of religious means. *Jesus and the *apostles healed the sick (Matt 10:1; Acts 3:1–16). Christians were told to pray for healing (James 5:14–16). Throughout church history the idea that God heals both via natural (medicines, human skills, etc.) and supernatural means (the power of the Holy *Spirit in connection with *prayer, *laying on of hands, *anointing with oil, etc.) has always been present. At some periods it has been more prominent and pronounced. For example, in recent times there are many, both in and out of the major denominations, who believe that the gift of healing (1 Cor 12:19) has been given to various people and that they have exercised it for the healing of the sick.

HEALING, SACRAMENT OF The seventh of the Roman Catholic *sacraments and otherwise known as either the *anointing of the sick or the sacrament of *unction.

HEART Used in the *Bible of the center of human spiritual and mental activity. *God sees the heart (1 Sam 16:7) and sends his *Spirit into the heart (Gal 4:6; Rom 5:5). The heart can be wicked through *sin (Jer 17:9) or pure through the *love of God (Matt 5:8). See also SOUL.

HEAVEN Used in the *Bible in two ways—of the skies above the earth and of the sphere in which *God, the *angels, and ultimately all the redeemed live for eternity. The latter is the theological sense and thus the sense intended by the church over the centuries. Since human language is fitted for finite experience, the only way heaven can be described is in picture language, metaphor, and symbolism (cf. 1 Kings 8:27 and Eph 4:10). So *Christ is presented as sitting at the right hand of the Father, and the whole is seen as a city of gold (Rev 22). Heaven is the goal of God's work of human *salvation, and it is the sphere where his creatures perfectly enjoy his friendship and *fellowship. As concerns the redeemed, it may be said that heaven was constituted for them by the ascension of Christ, for he went to prepare a place for his *disciples.

HEBER, REGINALD (1783–1826). *Bishop of Calcutta, and *hymn writer. A Shropshire *vicar for sixteen years, he was consecrated and went to India in 1823. He was a diligent *pastor who died at forty-three and was the biographer of Jeremy *Taylor, but he is best remembered for his *hymns, which include "Holy, Holy, Holy," "From Greenland's Icy Mountains," and "Hosanna to the Living Lord."

HECKER, ISAAC THOMAS (1819–1888). Founder of the *Paulists. Born in New York City and converted from

*Methodism to *Roman Catholicism (1844), he was educated and ordained in England and worked as a *Redemptorist among American immigrants in New York. An individualist, he was released from his *vows and was allowed to establish his new *order in New York in 1858. He made full use of press and platform in his work among non-Catholics, and in 1865 he founded the *Catholic World,* which he edited until his death.

HEFELE, KARL JOSEPH (1809–1893). Roman Catholic *bishop and historian. Born in Germany, he was ordained in 1833 and taught church history at Tübingen (1836–1869) until consecrated as bishop of Rottenburg. At *Vatican Council I he opposed the decree on papal *infallibility but finally submitted. He wrote a multivolume history of church councils (1855–1874).

HEGEL, GEORG WILHELM FRIEDRICH (1770–1831). German philosopher. Born in Stuttgart and educated at Tübingen (1788–1793), he taught at various universities until his 1818 appointment to the chair of philosophy at Berlin, a post he held until 1830. During his early career he wrote a life of *Jesus that rejected miracles and took Jesus to be the son of Joseph and *Mary. For Hegel the world was created by a philosophical evolution, with the meaning of life discernible in the history of the human race. *Christianity was the highest manifestation of *religion, which came through tension between man and his world.

HEGELIANISM The philosophy of G. W. F. Hegel (1770–1831), which had a tremendous effect on 19th-century thought, including Marxism and certain types of *theology. Hegel held that there is in the universe an "Absolute Spirit," which is achieving self-realization in and through matter, mind, and action. The process of realization is dialectic—thesis, antithesis, and synthesis. Opposites in conflict produce a higher unity, which then becomes the source of further conflict. So the process goes on and on. The influence of Hegelianism on theology was varied but is possibly best known in the writings of D. F. Strauss, especially *The Life of Jesus* (1846).

HEIDELBERG CATECHISM A Protestant *confession of *faith published in Germany in 1563 and associated chiefly with two Heidelberg theologians, Zacharias *Ursinus and Kaspar *Olevianus. It may have tried to pacify the Lutherans by not stressing overmuch certain distinctively Calvinist elements in *Reformation *doctrine. Biblical and practical, the *catechism was approved by the Synod of *Dort in 1619 and has always been highly regarded by Dutch and German *Reformed churches. It has been described as combining the intimacy of *Luther, the *charity of *Melanchthon, and the fire of *Calvin.

HEILSGESCHICHTE (Ger. "*salvation history"). *God's activity in human history, the means of his self-revelation and of his bringing salvation to men—e.g., the Exodus, the settlement in Canaan, the exile in Babylon, the restoration of the Jews to Jerusalem, and the life and *work of *Jesus.

HEIM, KARL (1874–1958). German Lutheran theologian. From a Pietist background in Swabia, he was concerned to stress the *transcendence of *God, but he sought also to relate *faith to modern society. In his presentation he never lost sight of his *evangelical origins, and he stoutly defended *orthodoxy against *atheism and Nazi deviations.

HELL The sphere where fallen *angels and sinful human beings who reject *God's *love exist everlastingly, deprived of God's *grace and thus under his *wrath. The idea of *punishment in hell is based on such passages as Matthew 25:46. As with *heaven, the problem facing the church is how to interpret the picture language of the *NT in its description of life after death. See also GEHENNA, HADES, SHEOL.

HELLENISM Various ideas, ideals, and practices associated with ancient, classical Greece that became part of the *culture of the Roman Empire. As *Christianity expanded within this empire, Hellenism was an important factor in the way in which the church expressed its *faith. The language of the *NT is *koine,* the common Greek of the time, and several important Greek words were used to convey with accuracy the content of *Christian *doctrine (e.g., *ousia, logos*).

HELVETIC CONFESSIONS Two Protestant *confessions of *faith. The First Helvetic Confession was compiled in Basel in 1536 by Johann Heinrich *Bullinger and other Swiss theologians. It became a standard for Swiss Protestant cantons. Its mingling of *Lutheranism and *Zwinglianism reflected contemporary hopes of union between *Reformed and Lutheran churches. Bullinger, in 1562, drafted the Second Helvetic Confession, which was published four years later. It reflected fewer Zwinglian elements than did the First Confession and more *Calvinism. It was soon accepted in the Reformed churches of Europe.

HELWYS, THOMAS (c. 1550–c. 1616). Baptist minister. One of an English *Separatist group that emigrated to Holland in 1608, he helped to organize the first Baptist church in Amsterdam and became its *pastor briefly in succession to John *Smyth. In 1611 Helwys and his followers returned to London and practiced a form of believers' *baptism in a congregation he set up there.

HENDERSON, ALEXANDER (c. 1583–1646). Scottish *Covenanter. Originally an Episcopalian, he was among those who stoutly resisted the efforts of *Charles I and William *Laud to impose further Anglican practices on Scotland. He played a large part in drafting the famous *National Covenant of 1638, and at the crucial general assembly at Glasgow that year, he was chosen as *moderator ("incomparably the ablest man of us all"). His was a key role in *Presbyterian resistance against the Stuart theory of the *divine right of kings.

HENDERSON, IAN (1910–1969). Scottish theologian. An admirer of Rudolph *Bultmann, he became professor of *systematic *theology at Glasgow in 1948 and was a prolific writer. In 1967 he became more widely known through his book *Power Without Glory: A Study in Ecumenical Politics,* a sardonic attack on the *World Council of Churches. He felt that failure to recognize institutional churches as power structures was leading to mass delusion and that "One Churchness" was "the greatest thing we have to repent of." He accused the WCC of making a false distinction between ecclesiastic and theologian, to the detriment of the latter.

HENGSTENBERG, ERNST WILHELM (1802–1869). German theologian. Westphalian by birth, he taught at Berlin University from 1824 and increasingly defended orthodox *Lutheranism against contemporary German *rationalism. He founded and edited the *Evangelische Kirchenzeitung,* a journal that became a rallying point for conservatives. He wrote many biblical commentaries, most of which were translated into English and became known in Britain and the U.S.

HENOTHEISM The *worship of one *god in preference to others, while not denying the existence of other gods. It is a stage between polytheism and monotheism.

HENRY II (973–1024). German king and Holy Roman emperor. The last of the Saxon rulers of Germany, he was crowned king in 1002 and became emperor at Benedict VIII's instigation in 1014. He was often accused of interference in church matters but was usually supported by the *papacy, which he defended against Greeks and Lombards. He founded the new bishopric of Bamberg, which became famous for its support of the arts.

HENRY III (c. 1017–1056). German king and Holy Roman emperor. King from 1039, emperor from 1046, he announced his intention of thoroughly reforming the church. His policy of religious strictness was coupled with one of political leniency, and both provoked adverse reaction. Henry was a builder of schools and *cathedrals and a patron of the arts. He was also instrumental in ending the scandal of three competing popes.

HENRY IV (1050–1106). German king and Holy Roman emperor. His reign was taken up with a bitter feud with the reforming pope Gregory VII as church and state jockeyed for supremacy. The emperor deposed the *pope, and the pope excommunicated the emperor before the latter found it politic to make his dramatic submission at Canossa in 1077. Peace did not last long, for Gregory supported a rival king and Henry set up an *antipope. Gregory died in exile; Henry died before he could successfully unite the warring factions in Germany.

HENRY IV (1553–1610). King of France. He became king of Navarre in 1572 and supported the Protestant cause against *Roman Catholicism, but he himself converted before acceding to the French throne in 1589. By the *Edict of Nantes, Henry ensured a degree of religious freedom for Protestants. Henry was assassinated by a fanatic in 1610.

HENRY VIII (1491–1547). King of England. No friend of the Reformers on the Continent, he produced in 1521 his *Defence of the Seven Sacraments,* for which Pope *Leo X conferred on him the title "Defender of the Faith." The new pope, *Clement VII, clashed with the king over Henry's desire to have his marriage to Catherine of Aragon annulled, and this led up to the repudiation of papal authority, Henry's *excommunication in 1534, and the *Dissolution of the Monasteries. Though his reign saw the beginning of the *Reformation in England, Henry remained Roman Catholic in many things. He could be ruthless with those who incurred his displeasure. Among those he had executed for different reasons were Thomas *More, Anne Boleyn, and Thomas *Cromwell.

HENRY, MATTHEW (1662–1714). Nonconformist minister. Son of an Anglican clergyman ejected for *nonconformity after the *Restoration, he was ordained as a *Presbyterian minister and served a pastorate in Chester (1687–1712). His great *love was practical and devotional biblical exposition. His multivolume *Commentary on the Bible* is still used.

HENRY SUSO See Suso, Henry.

HENSON, HERBERT HENSLEY (1863–1947). *Bishop of Durham. Fellow of All Souls, Oxford, he was briefly *bishop of Hereford before going to Durham in 1920, a see he held for nearly two decades, during which he was involved in numerous controversies. He was attacked for theological unorthodoxy and later for urging the disestablishment of the Church of *England after Parliament had rejected the *Prayer Book revisions in 1927—1928.

HEPBURN, JOHN (c. 1649–1723). Scottish minister. Ordained by exiled Scots ministers in London in 1678, he returned to Scotland as a field preacher of whom other *Covenanters remained suspicious. He was imprisoned at least twice, mysteriously freed, and then became a fugitive again. Yet for over three decades he served as *parish minister of Urr without having been legally settled. In 1690 he and his followers (Hebronites), evidently numbering four thousand, complained that the kirk had been insufficiently purged of *episcopalian features. They opposed the 1707 Act of Union with England and the 1712 *Toleration Act and showed *Jacobite sympathies in 1715. Though suspended and deposed, Hepburn continued to minister in Urr, with people walking more than twenty miles to hear him.

HERACLAS (d. c. 247). *Bishop of Alexandria. Called by *Eusebius of Caesarea "an outstanding exponent of philosophy and other secular studies," he succeeded *Origen as head of the catechetical school in Alexandria in

215 and became bishop of that *diocese in 232.

HERACLIUS (575–641). *Byzantine emperor. Reigning from 610, he is credited with having laid the foundations of the medieval Byzantine state despite the continual hostility of the Persians and the loss of Syria and Egypt to the Arabs. In an attempt to resolve differences between *orthodoxy and *Monophysitism, Heraclius proposed the compromise of Monothelitism, which held that *Christ had two *natures but only one *will.

HERBERT, GEORGE (1593–1633). Poet. Born in Wales and educated at Cambridge, he was elected public orator there in 1620, was ordained, and from 1629 ministered in a Wiltshire *parish until the end of his short life. His deep piety is reflected in his poetry, notably in his *hymns, which include "The King of Love My Shepherd Is" and "Teach Me, My God and King."

HERESY (Gk. *hairesis*, "what is chosen"). A *doctrine that is chosen in preference to the official teaching of the church. Thus heresy is false doctrine consciously held, and a heretic is a *Christian who holds erroneous views. It is used particularly of the major doctrines, such as the *Trinity and the *person of Christ.

HERMANN VON REICHENAU (HERMANN THE LAME) (1013–1054). *Christian poet and historian. He took monastic *vows at Reichenau (Lake Constance) in 1043 and proved to be such a gifted and versatile scholar that students flocked to him. He wrote a chronicle that covers *Christianity until the mid-11th century. His secondary name came because of a severe physical disability.

HERMANN VON WIED (1477–1552). Church reformer. As *archbishop-elector of Cologne from 1515, he at first opposed *Protestantism, but in setting out to reform his own *diocese (1541), he invited advice from Martin *Bucer, Philip *Melanchthon, and others. He became more and more Protestant until in 1546 he was excommunicated by Pope *Paul III and deposed by emperor *Charles V.

HERMAS (2d century). Regarded as one of the *apostolic fathers, he is known only through his work *The Shepherd*. He was a freed slave in Rome who claimed to be a contemporary of Clement of Rome (*Clement I), and his book was written as a result of a series of visions. Its chief significance is the information it supplies on Jewish *Christian beliefs.

HERMENEUTICS (Gk. *hermeneuo*, "to interpret"). The science of interpreting (especially) ancient literature. It covers both the analysis of the text in its context and presuppositions of the interpreter who lives in a different context from the original author. As a subject it has become of great importance in recent times to theologians who are particularly conscious that the horizon of understanding of biblical and ancient writers and their own are widely different. *Exegesis can proceed with profit only in the context of a theory of hermeneutics.

HERMIT One who withdraws from the world, chiefly for religious reasons, and lives in solitude. There were *Christian *hermits, such as *Antony during the latter 3d century, some of them as a result of persecution that erupted under *Decius. They gradually came together in communities, paving the way for the rise of *monasticism. Hermits disappeared completely from the Western church in the 16th century, but some remain in *Eastern Orthodoxy.

HERRNHUT See ZINZENDORF, N. L. VON.

HERTFORD, COUNCIL OF (673). A council of *bishops convened by *Archbishop *Theodore of Canterbury to discuss the reorganization of the English church. Among its decisions were reaffirmation of the Roman dating for *Easter; a ban on *clergy leaving their places without permission and on bishops interfering in the affairs of other *dioceses; and the recognition of *adultery as the only ground for *divorce. It was the first time the English church had met together in such a council.

HERZOG, JOHANN JAKOB (1805–1882). Swiss-German *Reformed theologian. Professor successively at Lausanne, Halle, and Erlangen, he wrote extensively on the Waldensians but is best known for his editing of, and substantial contributions to, a multivolume work, an abridged version of which was published in English as *The New Schaff-Herzog Encyclopedia of Religious Knowledge* (15 vols., 1951–1955).

HESYCHASM Spiritual movement in the *Eastern church stressing an inner, mystical form of *prayer. Its aim was the attainment of divine quietness so as to achieve full unity with *God. Hesychasm (*tranquility, solitude*) flourished in the monasteries of Eastern Orthodoxy especially from the 6th to 14th centuries. Gregory Palamas (1296–1359) was its principal theologian. Other masters of the prayer were Macarius of Egypt (d. c. 400), John Climacus (c. 580–650), Simeon the New Theologian (949–1022), and Gregory of Sinai (1255–1346).

Nicodemus the Hagiorite (1748–1809) published a collection of Eastern writings on "pure prayer" and the "mysticism of the Name" in 1782 in the **Philokalia*.

Theophan the Recluse (1815–1894) of Russia expanded the *Philokalia*. The anonymous diary *Way of a Pilgrim* of 1860 and reprinted in the 20th century has introduced this Eastern way of prayer to many in the West and made the *Jesus Prayer accessible to practice by laypeople. Hesychasm provoked great controversy but was pronounced orthodox at a council at Constantinople in 1341.

Hesychasm provoked great controversy but was pronounced orthodox at a council at Constantinople in 1341.

HESYCHIUS OF JERUSALEM (d. c. 450). Greek theologian. The most eminent biblical scholar of his region, he wrote *OT commentaries that followed the allegorical method of *Origen and so rejected a literal interpretation of the whole *Bible. More Monophysite than Arian, he is said to have annotated the entire *Scriptures.

HETERODOXY (Gk. *heteros*, "other"; *doxa*, "word, *doctrine"). A position that is doctrinally contrary to, or at least different from, the standard or traditional position of the church on one or more doctrines.

HETERONOMY (Gk. *heteros*, "other"; *nomos*, "law"). The view that man is subject to moral laws that are not created by himself but by others and ultimately by *God. It is the opposite of *autonomy.

HETZER, LUDWIG (c. 1500–1529). Swiss *Anabaptist. Having been expelled from Zurich and Augsburg for anti-Lutheran tendencies, he also alienated *Zwingli but in 1526 found a more congenial associate in Hans *Denck, who collaborated with him in a translation of the Hebrew *prophets. Arrested on a dubious charge of immorality in Constance, it is said to have been rather his theological unorthodoxy that led to his execution by beheading.

HEYLYN, PETER (1600–1662). Anglican controversialist and historian. A royal chaplain who gained favor with William *Laud, he worked strongly against the Puritans, became subdean of Westminster, suffered heavily during the Parliamentary ascendancy in England, but did not live long to enjoy the rehabilitation brought by the *Restoration. He wrote extensively, notably on the English Reformation, the life of Laud, and a history of the Presbyterians.

HICKSITES The name given by opponents to an American liberal *Quaker group that broke away from the orthodox main body and established its own yearly meetings in 1827–1828. The new group, which took its name from Elias Hicks (1748–1830), a strong abolitionist, stood against the proposal to have a written constitution, was anti-evangelical, and stressed social activity.

HIERARCHY (Gk. *hieros,* "sacred"; *aiche,* "rule"). The *clergy of the church as they exist as an ordered body—*bishops, *priests, and *deacons—and as they rule the church in the name of *Christ. The word is commonly used of the Orthodox and Roman Catholic churches, and in the latter it is often particularly associated with the *papacy and the jurisdiction connected with it.

HIGH CHURCH EVANGELICALS Those who wish to hold together the basic emphases of Evangelicalism in the context of the historical church and its traditions. Thus such people can only exist in the older Protestant churches (e.g., Anglican, Lutheran, *Reformed).

HIGH CHURCHMEN Those members of the Church of *England (in particular but not exclusively) who have a high view of the reality of the visible church. Thus they emphasize the importance of historical continuity, the value of the *sacraments, and the place of *bishops. They are not necessarily Anglo-Catholics.

HIGH COMMISSION, COURT OF See Court of High Commission.

HIGH MASS A traditional term used in *Roman Catholicism and *Lutheranism to describe a *Eucharist that was sung (not recited) by a *priest and choir. A low mass, by contrast, is a recited Eucharist.

HIGHER CRITICISM An expression used since 1881 to describe the scientific and technical (critical) study of the *Bible. It is distinguished from *Lower Criticism, which attempts only to determine the exact original text of the *Bible. See also Biblical Criticism.

HILARION (c. 291–c. 371). Founder of *Christian *monasticism in Palestine. Born into a pagan family, he became a Christian in Alexandria and was influenced toward the eremitic life by *Antony. According to *Jerome, Hilarion returned to Palestine when he was fifteen, erected a hut in the wilderness near Gaza, supported himself by weaving baskets of rushes, evangelized the nomad tribes, and was credited with wonder-working. In 329 he went in search of greater solitude and finally settled in Cyprus, where he died.

HILARY OF ARLES (401–449). *Bishop of Arles. After spending some time as a monk, he assisted the *bishop of Arles then succeeded to that French see in 429. As a reformer who was sometimes overzealous in not confining himself to his own metropolitical jurisdiction, he was deprived of those powers (but not of his see) by Pope *Leo I. It seems clear from his views on *predestination and from other evidence that Hilary was semi-Pelagian.

HILARY OF POITIERS (c. 315–c. 367). *Bishop of Poitiers. Sometimes called the "*Athanasius of the West," he was the champion of *orthodoxy against *Arianism, for which defense of Christ's divinity he, like Athanasius, spent some years in exile. He wrote the first work in Latin to deal with the controversies over the *Trinity, and he introduced into Western Christendom the theological works of the Greek fathers. Hilary returned from exile in 361 and spent his closing years still combating *heresy while few others were doing so in the West.

HILDA (614–680). *Abbess of Whitby. Great-niece of King Edin of Northumbria, she was given land on which she founded, in about 657, a double *monastery of monks and *nuns at Streaneschalch (now Whitby), which became one of the great spiritual centers of the region. It was at her abbey that the Synod of *Whitby was held (664) to settle the dispute over the date of *Easter. She and some others supported the *Celtic church in this, but the Roman church supporters won the day, and Hilda loyally accepted the decision.

HILDEBRAND See Gregory VII.

HILL, ROWLAND (1744–1833). English *evangelist. A graduate of Cambridge at a time when there were few

*Evangelicals there, he became a preacher in Kingston. After he had inherited money he built Surrey Chapel, Blackfriars, where he had a powerful *ministry. He developed an extensive program of religious education and was a prime mover in the establishment of the Religious Tract Society, the British and Foreign *Bible Society, and the London Missionary Society. He also encouraged advances in science and personally vaccinated the children of his congregation.

HINCMAR OF REIMS (c. 806–882). *Archbishop of Reims. One of the most powerful men of his time in church and state, he defended the independence of the French church against papal claims and was a notable champion of *orthodoxy. In his actions and in his writings he thought nothing of confronting emperor, pope, or fellow *bishops. He wrote much, notably on the *Christian argument against *divorce, on *predestination, and on the *Trinity.

HIPPOLYTUS (c. 170–c. 235). Roman *antipope and *martyr. Having criticized Pope *Zephyrinus for being soft on heretics, he was disappointed not to succeed him when the church chose *Callistus I in 217. Hippolytus became head of a dissident group that consecrated him as the church's first antipope, a position he retained under the next two *pontificates. With the second of these incumbents, Pontianus, he became reconciled when both were exiled to the Sardinian mines during the persecution under Maximinus. Before dying as *martyrs, the two resigned so that the new pope would head an undivided church. Hippolytus was the first Roman *priest to produce a work on *dogma.

HISTORICAL THEOLOGY The study of the teaching of the church and of individual theologians in its historical context. It is closely linked with church history but separable from it.

HISTORIE See GESCHICHTE.

HODGE, ARCHIBALD ALEXANDER (1823–1886). American *Presbyterian theologian. *Son of Charles *Hodge, he was educated at Princeton, served as a *missionary in India (1847–1850), returned to minister in Presbyterian congregations, then taught at Western Theological Seminary in Pennsylvania (1864–1877). For his last eight years he was his father's successor in the chair of didactic *theology at Princeton. A less creative mind than his father, whose biography he wrote, and more flexible on certain issues, he published *Outlines of Theology,* a useful volume revised in 1878.

HODGE, CHARLES (1797–1878). American *Presbyterian theologian. Educated at Princeton, he joined the *seminary faculty there in 1820 and held the chairs of Oriental and biblical literature (1822–1840) and *theology (1840–1878). A Calvinist of the old school in an age when liberalism was rising, he presented his position lucidly in his three-volume *Systematic Theology* (1872–1873) and was thus established to be America's leading theologian of the century. He had earlier written *A Commentary on the Epistle to the Romans* (1835), which went through many editions and had founded (1825) and edited for more than four decades the *Biblical Repository,* later known as the *Princeton Review.*

HOFBAUER, CLEMENT MARY (1751–1820). *Redemptorist *priest and, since 1914, *patron *saint of Vienna. Moravian by birth, he became a Redemptorist in Rome in 1784 and, after ordination, worked chiefly in Warsaw (1787–1808). As Redemptorist *vicar-general north of the Alps from 1793, he founded new houses in that region. When Napoleon ordered the disbandment of the Redemptorists in Warsaw, Hofbauer returned to Vienna, where his *ministry won many from all classes of society.

HOFMANN, JOHANN CHRISTIAN KONRAD VON (1810–1877). German theologian. Professor at Erlangen from 1845, he was active in the 19th-century *revival of *Lutheranism but caused controversy through his rejection of the substitutionary view of the *Atonement. Among his more significant books was *Interpreting the Bible* (Eng. Trans. 1880).

HOFMANN, MELCHIOR (c. 1495–1544). German *Anabaptist. By trade a furrier, he coupled business with *preaching in Baltic countries and was forced out of Latvia and Estonia because of his zeal. He was *pastor to German Lutherans in Stockholm (1526–1528) and then moved to Kiel. Shortly afterwards he was converted to *Anabaptist views and did some extravagant prophesying about the end of the world and about his own unique participation in it. He won some converts in the Netherlands, and these "Melchiorites" survived for some years after Hofmann's arrest and death in prison in Strasbourg.

HOLINESS MOVEMENT A religious movement dating from the mid-nineteenth century that tried to preserve the original thrust of the Methodist teachings on entire *sanctification and Christian *perfection as taught by John *Wesley. The influence of American *revivalism and the camp meeting added an emphasis on individualism, emotionalism, and the crisis experience. The movement became fragmented at the end of the nineteenth century but has had an influence well beyond *Methodism. The Holiness movement, though it has many similarities and historical connections with the *Pentecostal movement, should be distinguished from the latter.

HOLISTIC SALVATION A modern phrase used to promote the idea that *God's *salvation is to be seen its totality, not as the sum of fragmented parts. Thus the individual and corporate, the spiritual and material, and the temporal and *eternal aspects are seen as belonging together, to one gift of God's *grace. This view has been contrasted with *Fundamentalism's separation of *evangelism and social responsibility and service. See also NEW EVANGELICALISM.

HOLLAND, HENRY SCOTT (1847–1918). Anglican theologian. Educated at Oxford, he was *canon of St. Paul's Cathedral (1884–1910) and then regius professor of divinity at Oxford. He was a notable contributor to *Lux Mundi* (1889), showed a marked social concern, wrote a number of books, and was author also of the *hymn "Judge Eternal, Throned in Splendor."

HOLTZMANN, HEINRICH JULIUS (1832–1910). German theologian. Briefly a *pastor in Baden, he taught at Heidelberg (1858–1874) and Strasbourg (1874–1904). A moderate liberal, he was reportedly the pioneer of modern study of the *Synoptic gospels.

HOLY, HOLINESS, THE HOLY The holy is that which creates a sense of awe and wonder. In being absolutely pure and totally different from and apart from the created order, *God awakens a sense of awe, wonder, and reverence in his creatures. However, holiness is also understood, as a development from purity, in moral terms as morally pure and thus righteous. As applied to Christians, holiness is that purity created in the *heart by the presence of the Holy *Spirit. Isaiah 6, the vision of Isaiah, reveals both sides of holiness—God's purity and *perfection on the one side, and the lack of it, on the other, in human beings. The need for moral purity is emphasized throughout *Scripture (e.g., 1 Peter 1:15–16).

HOLY ALLIANCE (1815). A declaration signed in Paris by most European monarchs after the final defeat of Napoleon, stating that international relations thereafter would be based on "the sublime *truths which the Holy Religion teaches." Russia, Austria, and Prussia were the chief signatories of a document signed by all European sovereigns except the British prince regent, the sultan, and the *pope. It came to be regarded as a triumph for reactionary forces. One English statesman called it "a piece of sublime *mysticism and nonsense."

HOLY CLUB The popular name given to a group of Oxford students organized about 1730 to study the *Scriptures and the classics. Prominent among them were John and Charles *Wesley and George *Whitefield. They had also a great social concern, working among prisoners and poor. The club ceased to exist after the Wesleys left Oxford, but some of its practices were adopted by Methodist societies.

HOLY COMMUNION See Communion, Holy.

HOLY CROSS DAY The feast known also as the Exaltation of the Holy Cross, kept on September 14 in honor of the *Cross of *Jesus.

HOLY GHOST See Spirit, Holy.

HOLY ROMAN EMPIRE The title of Holy Roman emperor was given by Pope *Leo III to *Charlemagne in 800, and from the mid-10th century until its dissolution in 1806, it was held almost continuously by successive lines of German kings. Originally a symbol of the happy union between church and state, the Holy Roman Empire was all too often involved in conflict with the *papacy for the leadership of *Christian Europe and was, in Voltaire's words, "neither holy, nor Roman, nor an empire." The emperor Francis II relinquished the title in 1806 at a time when Napoleon set himself up as a parallel emperor.

HOLY SCRIPTURE(S) See Scripture(s), Holy.

HOLY SPIRIT See Spirit, Holy.

HOLY SYNOD The supreme authority in the Russian Orthodox Church from 1721 until 1917. Established by the emperor Peter the Great as second only to himself, it was a committee of the higher *clergy, replacing the former patriarchate of Moscow. The Holy Synod survived until the restoration of the patriarchate. Two months later legislation separated church and state.

HOLY TABLE See Altar.

HOLY WEEK The week immediately before *Easter *Sunday, the most important week in the church year. Beginning with *Palm Sunday, it includes *Maundy Thursday, *Good Friday and Holy Saturday. It is a time for special services and *fasting. The term was used in the 4th century by *Bishop *Athanasius of Alexandria.

HOMILY, HOMILETICS (Gk. *familia*, "familiar conversation"). The homily was originally the exposition in a conversational style of a passage of *Scripture to a congregation. It contrasted with the *sermon, which was a more polished, rhetorical performance and not an exposition. However, the two words homily and sermon became synonyms and referred to any address given inside *worship. Homiletics is the branch of *theology that suggests rules for the construction and delivery of homilies/sermons.

HOMOEANS (Gk. *homoios*, "like"). Members of the church in the 4th century who asserted that *Christ is like the Father and denied that he is of the same *being or *substance (*ousia*) as the Father.

HOMOIOUSIOS (Gk. *homoios*, "like"; *ousia*, "substance, essence, being"). The word used by those in the 4th century who wanted to affirm that the Son is like but not identical to the Father in essence (i.e., Godhead).

HOMOOUSIOS (Gk. *homos*, "one"; *ousia*, "substance, essence, being"). The word used by those in the 4th century and since who wish to affirm that the Son is of one substance in Godhead with the Father. In whatever sense the Father is *God, so is the Son. They share the one Godhead with the Holy *Spirit. This is the teaching of the *Nicene Creed.

HOMOSEXUALITY Preferential sexual behavior between members of the same sex. It is primarily a condition, not behavior; its cause is not known, and it varies in intensity in different individuals. The *Bible condemns homosexual practice (Rom 1:26–27), but the *condition* of homosexuality as such is not sinful.

HONORIUS I (d. 638). Pope from 625. He took a special interest in the evangelization of the Anglo-Saxons and approved metropolitan status for the *archbishop of Canterbury and the *bishop of York. While he was diligent also in Italy itself, he is chiefly remembered for some unguarded words to the *patriarch of Constantinople in 634 when he seemed to be supporting the *Monothelite *heresy. In 680 a council at Constantinople rejected Monothelitism and condemned Honorius as "a favorer of heretics," a condemnation endorsed by Pope Leo II in 682. The matter is questionable, but Honorius was cited at *Vatican Council I to counter the claim of papal *infallibility.

HONORIUS III (d. 1227). Pope from 1216. One of the *papacy's great administrators, he was also a church reformer and a promoter of the *Crusades. The latter project was hampered when pope and emperor clashed over the question of Sicily. Honorius launched his own crusade in the West—against the Moors in Spain. He settled an uprising in England after the death of King John, interceded in a Danish-German dispute, encouraged a campaign against the *Albigensians in France and approved the establishment of the *Dominican, *Franciscan, and *Carmelite *orders.

HOOKER, RICHARD (c. 1554–1600). Anglican theologian. In the latter 16th century he was the greatest champion of the Church of *England, particularly against the Puritans but also against *Roman Catholicism. He embodied his views in the multivolume classic *Treatise on the Laws of Ecclesiastical Polity* (1593–97). He described the Anglican tradition in terms of a threefold cord not quickly broken: *Bible, church, and *reason.

HOOKER, THOMAS (1586–1647). Puritan minister described as the "father of American democracy." A Cambridge graduate who later became an Evangelical preacher in Essex at a time when William *Laud was rising to power, he fled to Holland in 1630 to escape appearance before the *Court of High Commission and subsequently settled in Massachusetts (1633) as *pastor to a band of English immigrants. They went as a body to Hartford in 1636 and in 1638 declared publicly that it was a God-given right for people to choose their magistrates. Influential in church and state in Connecticut, Hooker championed the congregational over the *presbyterian system of church government.

HOOPER, JOHN (d. 1555). English Protestant *martyr. An Oxford graduate converted to *Protestantism, he twice fled from England to the Continent, where he supported the Swiss Reformed church. Later *bishop of Gloucester (1550), then also of Worcester (1552), due to his strongly Puritan views he was arrested on Mary *Tudor's accession in 1553, convicted of *heresy and burned at the stake.

HOPE A looking to *God as the Fulfiller and Fulfillment of life. It is a confident desire for the completion of *salvation in the age to come. In particular it involves the expectant belief in the *second coming of *Christ, the *resurrection of the dead, and the abundant life of the future *kingdom of God. It is rooted in Christ's resurrection and God's faithfulness, and it is possible only through the work of the *Spirit in the *heart (Rom 5:1–5; 8:20–24; 1 Peter 1:3).

HOPKINS, GERARD MANLEY (1844–1889). Priest and poet. Under the inspiration of J. H. Newman and the revival of doctrine and devotion in the Oxford Movement, Hopkins became a Roman Catholic in 1866 and joined the Society of Jesus in 1868, becoming ordained in 1877. From his years of deep depression, which others knew to be the "dark night of the soul," and periods of elation over the world of natural beauty, he composed a body of poetry that has profoundly influenced the course of 20th-century poetry. His poetry is noted for its brilliant imagery, intense awareness of spiritual conflict, God and nature, and experiments in diction that included "sprung rhythm," which seeks to approximate natural speech intonation.

HOPKINS, SAMUEL (1721–1803). American Congregational minister. A close friend of Jonathan *Edwards, he was ordained in 1743, served a country congregation in Massachusetts until 1769, then was *pastor of the Congregational church at Newport, Rhode Island, until his death. In that busy seaport he actively opposed slave trade and helped to expand the cause of *missions at home and overseas. His modified *Calvinism, which came to be known as Hopkinsianism, held that man's egocentricity must be conquered by "disinterested benevolence" and even a willingness "to be damned for the glory of *God."

HORMISDAS (d. 523). Pope from 514. His *pontificate is noteworthy because in 519 he resolved the thirty-five-year-old *Acacian Schism between Eastern and Western churches. After protracted negotiations he persuaded Emperor Justin I and *Patriarch John of Cappadocia to sign a statement accepting the findings of the Council of *Chalcedon (451), including the *Nicene Creed and the Tome of Leo.

HORNE, THOMAS HARTWELL (1780–1862). English biblical scholar. Born in London, he was a barrister's clerk and a Wesleyan Methodist when he decided to give his whole time to bibliographical projects. In 1818 he published his three-volume *Critical Study of the Holy Scriptures,* which was for many years a handbook for theological students. Horne was ordained in the Church of *England in 1819 and held various minor church posts in the London *diocese.

HORNER, RALPH (1853–1921). Founder of the *Holiness Movement Church in Canada. Born in Quebec, converted in 1876, and ordained as a Methodist, in 1886 he began work as an independent *evangelist. In 1895 he was expelled by the Methodist conference for his independence and for teaching a view of entire *sanctification unacceptable to the *denomination at that time, one which was in danger of creating a *sect within the church. He founded his Holiness Movement Church and was elected its *bishop (1895), but he withdrew in 1916 over a difference in church government and formed the Standard Church of America.

HORT, FENTON JOHN ANTHONY (1828–1892). Anglican *NT scholar. He is chiefly remembered for his famous collaboration with B. F. *Westcott on the Greek text of the NT, but he was no narrow specialist, evidenced by his last two works: *Judaistic Christianity* (1894) and *The Christian Ecclesia* (1897).

HOSIUS (OSSIUS) (c. 256–c. 357). *Bishop of Cordoba. Consecrated to that Spanish see about 295, he was ecclesiastical adviser to the emperor *Constantine (312–326) and was one of the upholders of *orthodoxy against *Donatism and *Arianism. At his instigation the emperor summoned the Council of *Nicea (325) at which Hosius may have presided for part of the time. He did preside at the Council of *Sardica in 342, boycotted by Eastern bishops because of the presence of *Athanasius. He rebuked the emperor Constantius II for interfering in church affairs but was detained at court and intimidated into signing an Arian formula which, however, he retracted before his death.

HOSIUS, STANISLAUS (1504–1579). Polish *cardinal and leader in the *Counter-Reformation. Born in Cracow and holder of a doctorate in law from Bologna, he became *bishop in 1549 and carried on such a relentless campaign against *Protestantism that he was dubbed the "hammer of the heretics." Brought to Rome by Paul IV in 1558 to join the curial staff, he was made cardinal in 1561 and appointed presiding papal legate to the Council of *Trent.

HOSKYNS, SIR EDWYN CLEMENT (1884–1937). Anglican biblical scholar. Cambridge graduate ordained in 1908, he had experience of ministering in industrial areas and in army chaplaincy work before returning to Cambridge in 1919. He became progressively less liberal in outlook, and this was reflected in *The Riddle of the New Testament* (1931), a work written in conjunction with F. N. Davey, and also in his unfinished volume, *The Fourth Gospel* (1940), in which he argued for the unity of John's *Gospel. A former colleague pays tribute to Hoskyns's profound personal influence on successive generations of Cambridge theological students.

HOSPITALLERS The usual name for a religious military *order founded in the 11th century. The order originated in a hospital for sick pilgrims in Jerusalem. After the city had been captured by Crusaders in 1099, the Hospitallers extended their functions to the protection of pilgrims and became in time a formidable force that acquired extensive lands on the route to Jerusalem. After the *Crusades were abandoned in 1291, the order withdrew successively to Cyprus (until 1308), Rhodes (until 1522), and Malta, on which latter island they remained until suppressed by Napoleon in 1798.

HOST (Lat. *hostia*, "a victim"). The bread of Holy *Communion. It is so named because in the traditional Latin *Mass it was thought of as being the *body of Christ, the victim who died on the *cross.

HOWARD, JOHN (1726–1790). Prison reformer and philanthropist. An *Evangelical of *Calvinist tendencies, he became high sheriff of Bedfordshire in 1773 and there encountered the appalling prison conditions, which, for the rest of his life, he sought to improve. At his instigation a 1774 Act of Parliament corrected some of the abuses. His *State of the Prisons* made the English situation widely known, but he also toured Continental and Near Eastern prisons and wrote about them. It was on one such journey when he traveled into Russia that he caught camp fever and died.

HOWE, JOHN (1630–1705). English Puritan minister and writer. A *nonconformist who had been a chaplain to Oliver *Cromwell, he was ejected from his Devon *parish after the *Restoration, was an itinerant preacher, and from 1670 spent six years in Ireland. From 1676 he was copastor of a London *Presbyterian congregation but later had to spend some time on the Continent (1685–1687). Under the more relaxed reign of *William III he fought for religious *liberty for nonconformists and tried to unite Presbyterians and *Congregationalists. His works include *The Living Temple of God* (1675).

HROMADKA, JOSEF LUKI (1889–1969). Czech *Reformed theologian. Born in Moravia, he was ordained by the Czech Brethren in 1912 and was later *theology professor at the Jan *Hus Theological Faculty in Prague. After lecturing at Princeton during World War II, he chose to return to Czechoslovakia in 1947. He founded and was chairman of the Christian Peace Conference, which sought to reconcile Christians and communists. He was greatly disillusioned when the Soviet Union invaded his homeland (1968), an event that he protested at the cost of losing his headship of the Christian Peace Conference. He died six weeks later.

HUBERT, WALTER (d. 1205). *Archbishop of Canterbury from 1193. One of the great medieval administrators in church and state, he served three English kings, traveled to the Holy Land on the Third Crusade, and raised the ransom for Richard I's release from his Austrian captivity. As both lord *chancellor and *primate he held court in such splendor that some were said to have considered him the real ruler of England. He was accused of neglecting church duties, but he did institute some reforms.

HUBMAIER, BALTHASAR (c. 1485–1528). German *Anabaptist leader. A doctor of *theology appointed *cathedral preacher at Regensburg (1516), he crossed into Switzerland in 1521 to become *parish *priest at Waldshut, where he was influenced by *Zwingli toward the *Reformation. Soon, however, he joined those of Anabaptist tendencies and rose to prominence among them, spreading their views in Germany and Moravia. Pursued by imperial authority, he was captured and burned at the stake for *heresy in Vienna.

HÜGEL, FRIEDRICH VON See VON HÜGEL, FRIEDRICH.

HUGH OF CLUNY (1024–1109). *Abbot of Cluny. A distinguished *Benedictine, the trusted adviser of nine popes, he was active in all of the pressing issues of his age. He influenced church councils, attacked clerical abuses, combated heretics, helped to organize the First Crusade (1095), and all the time governed his *abbey for sixty years and extended the *order in other countries.

HUGH OF LINCOLN (1135–1200). Bishop of Lincoln. Born in France, he became a *Carthusian and about 1175 was appointed by *Henry II of England as the first *prior of a Carthusian house founded by the king at Witham in Somerset. Henry in 1186 persuaded this pious and fearless monk to accept the see of Lincoln, which had been vacant for eighteen years. He defended the church's rights before three kings and defended the cause of peasants, Jews, and lepers. Every year he retreated for a time to the priory at Witham.

HUGH OF ST.-VICTOR (c. 1096–1141). Theologian and mystic. Of noble Saxon birth, he joined the *Augustinian *Canons. In about 1115 he settled in the *monastery of St.-Victor in Paris, where he spent the rest of his life. He became known for his *exegesis and interpretation of *Scripture. A student of the writings of *Augustine and earlier church *fathers, he evolved a theological system that included both the mystical and the practical, *faith and *reason. "Learn everything," he urged, "and you will see afterward that nothing is useless."

HUGUENOTS A name given in the 16th century to French Protestants. The energies of church and state were taken up by the *doctrines of the Reformers that had spread across the border from Germany. Huguenots were placed under penal disabilities and subjected to violence by their opponents, but even that was little compared with the officially inspired Massacre of St. *Bartholomew's Day in 1572. Freedom of *worship was granted by the Edict of *Nantes (1598), but this was revoked in 1685 at the instigation of *Cardinal *Mazarin, at which time a half million of the persecuted took refuge in neighboring Protestant states. Those who remained were hunted down like the *Camisards when they rebelled, and their Calvinist doctrines were condemned as illegal. When captured they were imprisoned and killed. The Protestants survived to be given full *toleration at the French Revolution. Over the whole period some two million Huguenots left France, but unlike other national groups, they merged with the cultural and economic life of their newly adopted lands, notably in Canada and the U.S. It is probably to the Huguenots that we owe the origins of benefit societies such as Foresters and Odd Fellows.

HUMANAE VITAE (Lat. "human lives"). A famous *encyclical of Pope *Paul VI (1968). It was subtitled "The right order to be followed in the propagation of human offspring." As a prohibition of most forms of *birth control, it has caused much debate and dissent.

HUMANISM, CHRISTIAN The conviction that there is a positive relationship between true human values and concerns and the true *Christian life guided by the Holy *Spirit. Thus the capacities for goodness and wholeness in human *nature are only realized in the life of *grace.

Secular humanism today usually involves the assertion of the self-sufficiency of man, although it also is often concerned to establish the rights and dignity of man. Classical humanism flourished from the 14th century to the 16th century and meant an education based on the Greek and Latin classics in a Christian setting.

HUMANITY OF CHRIST, THE Either the *dogma that *Jesus Christ was completely human, having a full human *nature (as taught by the Definition of *Chalcedon) or the example of the life of *Christ as a model of how to live as *God wishes.

HUMILIATION OF CHRIST The act of the *eternal *Son of *God in becoming man, assuming the role of a servant of humankind, and dying in the most degrading way on the *cross. The theme is developed from Philippians 2:6–8 and is contrasted with the *exaltation of *Christ.

HUNDRED YEARS' WAR The name given to the series of conflicts that flared up sporadically between England and France between 1337 and 1453. The period, which, near the end, saw the appearance of *Joan of Arc, led to the expulsion of the English from France, where their territorial possessions had long been an affront to French pride.

HUNT, JOHN (1812–1848). English *missionary to Fiji. Son of a farmer near Lincoln, he was converted at seventeen, ordained to the Wesleyan *ministry in 1838, and arrived in Fiji in 1839. He and his wife worked in isolated places but were used in the *conversion of "one of the most barbarous races of cannibals on the face of the earth." The hardships he endured led to his early death, not, however, before he had completed a translation of the *Bible.

HUNT, WILLIAM HOLMAN (1827–1910). English painter. He became known in 1854 for *The Light of the World,* a work that John Ruskin helped to popularize. To paint biblical scenes more authentically he spent two years in Palestine, Syria, and Egypt (returning to Palestine several times). His other works include *The Shadow of the Cross* (1869) and *The Triumph of the Innocents* (1885). A repainting of *The Light of the World* (1904) is in St. Paul's Cathedral, London. The original hangs in Keble College, Oxford.

HUNTINGDON, COUNTESS OF See COUNTESS OF HUNTINGDON'S CONNEXION.

HUS, JAN (1373–1415). Bohemian reformer. After graduating from Prague University in 1394 he taught in the faculty of arts, continuing there after *ordination and appointment (1402) as rector and preacher of the Bethlehem Chapel, a center of the Czech reform movement. Meanwhile he had become acquainted with the theological works of John *Wycliffe. The reform party grew in strength, but Hus's attitude had alienated the Roman church, and when the city was put under *interdict because of his presence, he left for two years and preached widely elsewhere. When the Council of *Constance met in 1414 to resolve the *Great Schism in the Western church, the emperor *Sigismund invited Hus to attend, promising his safe conduct. He went, and within a month he was arrested and tried for Wycliffism. He refused to recant views he did not hold and finally was turned over to the civil authorities and burned at the stake.

HUTCHINSON, ANNE (1591–1643). Religious liberal and a founder of Rhode Island. Born in Lincolnshire, she married a merchant in 1612, and they migrated to Massachusetts in 1634. In Boston she organized meetings at which the women discussed *sermons, and she allegedly held that *God's *grace made observance of moral precepts unnecessary for believers. Puritan Massachusetts tried her in 1637 and, despite her claims of divine *revelations, banished her. She and others established a settlement in what is now Rhode Island, but after her husband's death in 1642 she moved to Long Island. Indians killed her the next year, an end her former Puritan colleagues hailed as a divine judgment.

HUTTEN, ULRICH VON (1488–1523). German humanist and poet. He fled a *Benedictine *monastery at seventeen, studied in Germany, Austria, and Italy, then joined the court of *Albert of

Brandenburg in 1517. He aimed at the unity of Germany against the Roman church, not only for religious motives, and enthusiastically supported *Luther in speech and in writings. Assailed by the old church and badly let down (he felt betrayed) by his friend *Erasmus, in 1522 he fled in failing health to Switzerland, where *Zwingli found him refuge.

HUTTERITES *Anabaptist *sect. They were named for Jakob Hutter, an Austrian minister who joined the community-of-goods section of *Anabaptists and in 1535 became their chief *pastor. He was tortured and burned as a heretic in 1536 at Innsbruck. With able administrators during the 16th century, the Hutterites increased in numbers, set up communities, and sent out *missionaries. Later they declined through persecution and civil penalties but established themselves in Hungary and the Ukraine. Finally in the 1870s, like other Anabaptists, they found a home in North America, first in South Dakota, then in 1918 in Canada. Their refusal to conform or participate in local government and their insistence on maintaining their communal life has made things difficult at times for the estimated 20,000 Hutterites in North America.

HYMN (Gk. *hymnos*, a song in praise of gods or heroes). Throughout the history of the church hymns (sacred poetry set to music) have been part of *worship. Most used have been the hymns of the *Bible (e.g., the Psalms and the songs in Luke 1; Rev 5:12, 13b; 15:3–4). Nonbiblical hymns have increased in numbers and usage particularly since the 18th century and the contributions of such men as Isaac *Watts and Charles *Wesley.

HYMNOLOGY The technical study of *hymns, including the history of the evolution of hymns, their use in *worship, their content, and their *music.

HYPERDULIA (Lat. "*virtue of deep submission" [based on Gk. *hyper*, "more than"; *douleia*, "*veneration"]). The special regard paid to *Mary, the mother of *Jesus, because her Son is *God made man. This is a greater veneration than shown to the *saints (*douleia, dulia*) but is not the same in essence as *latria, *worship offered to God himself.

HYPOSTASIS (Gk. "individual reality, a mode of being, person"). Used in the classic statement of the *Trinity—three hypostases (persons) in one *ousia (Godhead). See also PERSON; TRINITY, DOCTRINE OF THE.

HYPOSTATIC UNION The union of the divine and human *natures in the person of *Jesus Christ as described in the Definition of *Chalcedon (451).

I

I–THOU From the book, *I and Thou* (1923) by the Jewish philosopher Martin Buber. It has been used by *Christian theologians as a shorthand for emphasizing the personal *nature of *God's self-revelation. We know God not as "I–It" but as a personal reality, a "Thou."

ICON (Gk. *eikon*). A flat picture used as a basic aid to devotion in the *Orthodox Church. Traditionally icons are painted in egg tempera on wood, but they are also made of metal, ivory, and other materials. They represent *Jesus, the Virgin *Mary, or a *saint, or combinations of these.

ICONOCLASM The policy of breaking *icons (whether painted or carved) or forbidding their use in *Christian *worship and devotion. There was fierce debate especially in the Greek church in the *Iconoclastic Controversy.

ICONOCLASTIC CONTROVERSY A dispute concerning the presence of *icons (religious *images) in church. The pioneer iconoclast ("image-breaker") was Emperor *Leo III, who in 726 issued an *edict banning the use of images on pain of severe punishment; that edict greatly antagonized the people of Constantinople and was rejected by successive popes. A council called by the next emperor, Constantine V, at Hieria in 753 confirmed the condemnation of images. The Second Council of *Nicea (787) decreed that *icons should be used, and it defined the type of *veneration due to them. Leo III's policies were confirmed in 815, but in 843 icons returned to stay in the *Eastern Church.

ICONOSTASIS The screen, usually of wood, that separates the *sanctuary from the main part of the church within the Orthodox churches. It is covered with *icons from which its name comes. It has three doors, the central one known as the royal door. This has the effect of shutting off the *altar from the lay worshipers, since only the *priests and *deacons go through the doors to the altar. The Western name for the screen is the *reredos.

IDEALISM A term used in a variety of ways by philosophers and theologians, but these are different from the popular use of the word as "possessing high ideals." For scholars idealism may be "idea-ism," the priority of idea (*mind/*spirit) over matter in explaining reality. Or idealism may be the belief that the world we see and know depends for its existence on its being perceived by mind (be that mind the mind of *God or the minds of men).

IDIOMATUM (Lat. "an attribute or property of a thing"). Used in *Christology in the phrase **communicatio idiomatum* (communication of attributes), where it refers not only to the natural properties of each of the *natures (human and divine) of *Christ but also what they do and suffer.

IDOLATRY The *worship of a god created by man rather than of the *God who created man. It is contrary to a basic commandment of God (Exod 20:4–5). Protestants have often asserted that the devotion paid to statues of *Christ, the Virgin, or *saints in the Roman Catholic Church and to *icons in the *Orthodox Church is idolatry. In fact, in both churches different words are used to describe the worship of God and the *veneration of saints (*dulia, *latria), and there is a close relation claimed between the *images and the reality symbolized.

IFCA See INDEPENDENT FUNDAMENTAL CHURCHES OF AMERICA.

IGNATIUS (d. c. 110). *Bishop of Antioch (Syria) and *martyr. All we know about him comes from seven of his letters that tell how he was tried and condemned at Antioch by the governor and was escorted across Asia Minor by ten guards and thrown to the wild beasts in Rome. On the way they stopped at Smyrna and Troas, at which times Ignatius took the opportunity to write his letters to the churches at Ephesus, Magnesia, Tralles, Rome, Philadelphia, and Smyrna, and also to *Polycarp. Two heretical groups were particularly attacked in the letters: the Judaizers, who rejected the authority of the *NT; and the Docetists, who regarded Christ's sufferings and death as only apparent. His letter to the Romans asks them not to take steps to prevent the martyrdom by which he will "attain to *God."

IGNATIUS OF LOYOLA (c. 1491–1556). Founder of the *Jesuits. Born into a noble Spanish family, he became a soldier, read religious works while convalescing from a wound, and turned in 1522 to the ascetic life. He studied in Spain and France, worked on his famous *Spiritual Exercises,* and gathered around him in Paris a group of *disciples. The Society of Jesus was formed there in 1534, and Ignatius and most of his colleagues were ordained in 1537. Ignatius became the first general when the *order received papal approval in 1540. Probably the most influential figure of the *Counter-Reformation, he sought to reform the church from within, to battle against *heresy, and to take the *gospel throughout the world.

ILLUMINATI See ALUMBRADOS.

ILLUMINATION The work of the Holy *Spirit bringing light and understanding to the human *mind in its search for *God's *truth. In particular, the light shining from the truth of the *Bible is intended.

IMAGE OF GOD (Lat. *imago dei*). A theological evaluation of the true *nature of man based on Genesis 1:26, the claim that *God created human beings in his own image and likeness. Nowhere in the *OT is the image defined, but it relates to the way in which humans are different from animals and how they have the capacity to have *fellowship with God. The *NT calls *Christ the image of God (2 Cor 4:4), for he had a perfect relationship with God and in his pure life reflected the character of God. There has been much discussion concerning to what extent human *sin has affected the image in man. While answers vary, there is agreement that in Christ, by the work of the Holy *Spirit, a believer is restored to the position of living as one made in God's image. He relates to his Creator in a way that reflects the kind of creature he is. Western theologians tend to equate "image" and "likeness" (Gen 1:26), but Eastern theologians see a difference, holding that the two words convey two different aspects of the special relationship of man to God.

IMAGES, VENERATION OF The giving of honor to representations of *Christ, the Virgin *Mary and the *saints. This includes the kissing and incensation of them as well as placing candles before them. Although this practice is widespread in the Roman Catholic and *Orthodox churches, and although it was sanctioned by the seventh *ecumenical council, Protestants have always found it difficult to accept, thinking that it is condemned by Exodus 20:4–5.

IMITATION OF CHRIST This has two meanings: (1) the title of a famous book that appeared anonymously in c. 1418 but is probably by Thomas à *Kempis and (2) a *Christian ideal for life. *Jesus as portrayed in the *Gospels is seen as the ideal, and the aim is to imitate him by the help of the *Spirit and to cultivate the *mind of *Christ.

IMMACULATE CONCEPTION OF THE BLESSED VIRGIN MARY A belief of the Roman Catholic Church defined by Pope Pius IX in 1854: "The Blessed Virgin *Mary, in the first moment of her conception, by a singular *grace and privilege of Almighty *God, in *virtue of the *merits of *Jesus Christ the *Savior of the human race, was preserved immune from every stain of original *sin." So Roman Catholics believe that Mary was sinless from her birth. Never officially declared as a Roman Catholic *dogma by an *ecumenical council, though it is widely regarded as such, it is a view that Protestants have always rejected. See also ASSUMPTION (OF THE BLESSED VIRGIN MARY).

IMMANENCE OF GOD The presence of *God in and through his creation. The Holy *Spirit is the *omnipresence of God in the *universe. This idea is in contrast to the *transcendence of God, his presence outside creation.

IMMANUEL (Heb. "*God with us"). The name of the *Messiah as given in Isaiah 7:14 and Matthew 1:23. It is a description of *Jesus as God incarnate.

IMMENSITY The quality of not being measurable. Applied to *God alone, it means that he is immeasurable and boundless.

IMMERSION A form of *baptism in which the candidate is submerged in water. It is used for infants in the *Orthodox churches and for adults in Baptist and many independent churches. The symbolism of immersion is provided by Paul in Romans 6:1–11—union with *Christ in death, *burial, and *resurrection. Other modes of baptism are *affusion and *aspersion.

IMMINENCE OF THE END The belief that the present age could end at any moment. Usually such a view is a part of a millenarian *doctrine that teaches that *Christ may return at any time and that his *saints will be caught up to meet him in the air (1 Thess. 4:16–17) before the actual *Millennium starts.

IMMOLATION An act of sacrificial offering. Roman Catholics have traditionally spoken of "the immolation of *Christ in the *Mass." Protestants agree with Roman Catholics that the sacrifice of Christ on the *cross may be called an immolation; however, they claim that it is misleading to talk of the offering of the Christ in the *Eucharist as an immolation. See also SACRIFICE.

IMMORTALITY Life that is exempt from death and decay. Only the *eternal *God is absolutely immortal. He always has been and always will be. *Angels and humans have immortality in that once created they are intended to live forever. The immortality of the *soul is not a specifically *Christian *doctrine, but it becomes so when it is integrated into the doctrine of the *resurrection of the *body (1 Cor 15). Thus immortality is a gift of God and not an essential aspect of human beings.

IMPANATION (Lat. *panis*, "bread"). Similar to *consubstantiation and differing from *transubstantiation, a way of understanding how the presence of *Christ is in the Holy *Communion. The bread and wine remain bread and wine, but they include within themselves, in a marvelous and mysterious way, the spiritual *body and *blood of Christ. As a theory of the real presence of Christ, it is associated with the name of Andreas *Osiander (d. 1552).

IMPASSIBILITY Incapable of experiencing *suffering and pain: freedom from every kind of *evil and suffering. As applied to *God, it cannot be used in the strong sense that God is incapable of feelings of pleasure and pain in respect of human actions.

IMPECCABILITY The impossibility of committing *sin or the inability to sin.

*God alone is ultimately impeccable. A question in *Christology is: was *Christ impeccable? If he were truly man, than the possibility of sin must always have been there, even though in practice he did not sin. In the future life of the *kingdom of God the glorified *saints and *angels will be impeccable.

IMPRECATORY PSALMS Those psalms in which a curse is pronounced over the enemies of *God or of *Israel–e.g., 35, 59, and 109. There is constant discussion as to whether such psalms are suitable for use in *Christian *worship.

IMPRIMATUR (Lat. "Let it be printed"). The permission by a church authority for a book on *faith or morals to printed. In most cases in *Roman Catholicism this authority is the diocesan *bishop. The permission means that there is no fundamental objection to the book's contents (*nihil obstat*).

IMPUTATION The reckoning or counting something for or against a person. It is often used in the Protestant *doctrine of *justification (e.g., that *God reckons to the believing sinner the *righteousness of *Christ while the sinner is in actual fact still sinful). That is, God does not reckon the sinner's *sins but rather the perfect righteousness of *Christ to the sinner's account. Such a *doctrine is supplemented by another—*sanctification.

INCARNATION (Lat. *caro*, "flesh"). The act by which the *eternal *Son of *God became man and was known as *Jesus of Nazareth. He was born of the Virgin *Mary and received from her his human *nature. Thus he was the *Word made flesh (John 1:14). As the incarnate Son he became the *Messiah (*Christ) of *Israel.

INCOMMUNICABLE ATTRIBUTE A *perfection of *God that he cannot give to another–relationships of the Holy *Trinity in the one Godhead.

INDEFECTIBILITY Used of the church to claim that, from its apostolic beginnings to the *Second Coming, through *Christ's power it will be faithful to its calling. Because of the Holy *Spirit's presence, the church will confess the true *faith until the end of the age. This is a general claim and does not exclude the possibility of error and decay in parts of the one church.

INDEPENDENCY A form of church government based on the autonomy of each local church. Each congregation chooses its own officers and *pastor and is responsible only to itself (under *God). Those who practice this may be called by a variety of names (e.g., *Congregationalists, *Baptists, *Independents) and may also have different ways of expressing the congregation's autonomy.

INDEPENDENT FUNDAMENTAL CHURCHES OF AMERICA This group of independent churches began with a February 1930 meeting in the study of Rev. William McCarrell, *pastor of Cicero Bible Church, of a number of *Presbyterian, Congregational, and *Independent leaders. It has emphasized *Bible teaching of the *Scriptures, separation from *heresy and compromise, and dispensational *eschatology. It has come to include about 1,000 churches that are directly or indirectly affiliated. More than 1,450 ministers, missionaries, evangelists, and Christian workers are members and represent a total memebership of more than 125,000.

INDEPENDENTS A name given to exponents of Congregationalism in 17th-century England. Though the Independents as such originated in Holland about 1610, the Brownists had earlier professed similar tenets. Independents formed the hard core of Oliver *Cromwell's army, and after his triumph they acquired great influence in the land. At the *Westminster Assembly they played a prominent part and, formally rejecting "the proud and insolent title of Independency," were tolerant in an intolerant age. In 1658 they expressed their *doctrines in the *Savoy Declaration. Like other *nonconformists, they suffered persecution during the reigns of *Charles II and *James II.

INDEX, THE The commonly used abbreviation for Index Librorum Prohibitorum ("list of forbidden books"), containing works proscribed by ecclesiastical authority as dangerous to Roman Catholics' *faith or morals. The Index was initiated by Paul IV in 1557 and remained obligatory for the faithful until 1966 when the *Vatican announced it would no longer be published.

INDULGENCE, DECLARATIONS OF A series of nine declarations on religious matters in England and Scotland, made between 1660 and 1688 by *Charles II and *James II. These were concerned generally with the position of *Nonconformist ministers, and the conditions under which they might hold, or be restored to, their livings, or might conduct public *worship. The last declarations concerned also Roman Catholics and *Quakers.

INDULGENCES The remission of temporal *punishment for *sin. This is done by the hierarchy of the Roman Catholic Church (and especially by the *pope) in virtue of the *merits of *Christ and the *saints. It is much less common and much more carefully controlled now than it was when attacked by *Luther in 1517. Even so, the *theology of merit on which it is based is complex and difficult for modern people to appreciate.

INERRANCY The quality of truthfulness with the absence of error. Both Roman Catholics and conservative *Evangelicals use the term of the *Bible as the revealed and written *Word of *God. There is, however, debate concerning whether the inerrancy covers only *faith and morals or whether it extends to matters of history, cosmology, and geography.

INFALLIBILITY Inability to err or free from error. It is used in four ways: (1) of the universal church in creating *dogma at *ecumenical councils, (2) of the *pope when defining *doctrine for the Roman Catholic Church, (3) of the actual doctrine defined by the pope, and (4) of the contents of the *Bible concerning *faith and morals. Traditional Roman Catholics would accept all four meanings, while traditional Protestants would accept only the fourth.

INFANT BAPTISM See BAPTISM, INFANT.

INFANT COMMUNION The practice of giving the bread and wine of Holy *Communion to the children who are baptized and who attend the *Eucharist with their parents or *godparents. This is the universal practice in the *Orthodox Church and is becoming increasingly common in *Roman Catholicism and *Anglicanism. Those who oppose it usually argue that it should only be given after *confirmation.

INFANT SALVATION The belief that if a child dies before having reached an age when he can positively reject *God he will go to *heaven. The *atonement of *Christ is seen as covering all such children. However, some theologians have argued that a child must be baptized for the removal of *original *sin. Some believe in the medieval *doctrine of *limbo (*limbus infantium*), a permanent abode of the unbaptized. Theologians who have a strong doctrine of *election state that if a child is of the elect he will go to *heaven; if he is not he will go to *hell.

INFINITE, INFINITY That which has no bounds or limits. Only *God is actually and absolutely infinite, for he alone is infinitely perfect.

INFRALAPSARIANISM See PREDESTINATION.

INFUSION Used of the work of the Holy *Spirit, who pours divine *grace into the *heart and *soul of a sinner so that he may have *eternal life and divine *forgiveness. This process begins with *regeneration and continues in *sanctification.

INGE, WILLIAM RALPH (1860–1954). Dean of St. Paul's. Successively Oxford don, London clergyman, and professor at Cambridge, Inge was an influential churchman who was articulate and at times provocative. He expressed unorthodox views on the *Incarnation and was universally known as "the gloomy dean" because of his criticism of the secular gospel of inevitable progress. He wrote widely on theological and philosophical subjects, notably in his *Outspoken Essays* (1919, 1922), and *Christian Ethics and Modern Problems* (1930).

INGENERACY Also called the *paternity of the First *Person, it is the particularizing characteristic that *God the Father, as First Person of the Holy *Trinity, possesses. Ingeneracy was widely used in discussion of the nature of the Triune *God from the 4th century and contrasts the Father with the Son (who is eternally generated) and the Holy *Spirit (who eternally proceeds).

INITIATION, CHRISTIAN The means of entry into the *Christian church. It usually involves *baptism but may also include *confirmation or another particular ceremony for reception into the congregation (e.g., handshakes from members). Often it may include the first reception of Holy *Communion. Anthropologists refer to the initiation *rites of different tribes and *religions, and the use of the term in the modern church appears to have been affected by this usage in anthropology.

INNER LIGHT Used by *Quakers (*Society of Friends) to express their claim to an internal, personal experience of *God, by which they are led. It can also mean the assurance in the *heart of God's *love for the individual and God's acceptance of him as his child.

INNERE MISSION The agency through which all the charitable activities of the German Protestant churches are coordinated. The concept was originally that of J. H. *Wichern, who engaged in work among underprivileged children in Hamburg in the 1830s and founded a school and later a training institute. Wichern pointed out the need for the Innere Mission at the 1848 congress of the German Evangelical churches at Wittenberg. The work has greatly expanded but has never lost sight of its *evangelical aims to reach the lost.

INNOCENT I (d. 417). Pope from 401. A strong upholder of the Roman Catholic primacy yet tactful in his dealings with the *Eastern Church, he defended *orthodoxy in the persons of *Chrysostom and *Jerome, condemned *Pelagians and *Donatists, ended the *Melitian Schism, and acted as mediator between the emperor Flavius Honorius and the invading Visigothic chief Alaric.

INNOCENT III (1160–1216). Pope from 1198. One of the greatest of medieval popes, he defended his office ably against the claims of emperors and other rulers. He supported the Fourth Crusade, encouraged the beginnings of the *Franciscan and *Dominican *orders, summoned the *Lateran Council of 1215, and launched a campaign in France against the *Albigensians. He was a shrewd organizer and statesman, and under him the *Papal States were expanded.

INNOCENT IV (d. 1254). Pope from 1243. The greater part of his *pontificate was taken up with the battle against the emperor *Frederick II about superiority in church and state. Like *Gregory IX, Innocent excommunicated Frederick and laid charges against him at the Council of *Lyons in 1245. The council declared the emperor deposed. Innocent is regarded as one of the more prominent popes of his time but not for the best reasons. Not only did he become embroiled in political entanglements, he allowed the *Inquisition to further its purposes by the use of torture.

INNOCENT X (1574–1655). Pope from 1644. A Roman by birth, he served several popes and gained political experience that he did not always use wisely. He supported the Spanish against Portuguese claims to independence, then clashed with France, where *Cardinal *Mazarin had given refuge to some of Innocent's Roman enemies, bringing Italy close to invasion. He condemned the Jansenists, thus initiating a century of controversy, and diminished the papal prestige through his nepotism.

INNOCENT XI (1611–1689). Pope from 1676. Elected against the wishes of *Louis XIV of France, he took steps to remedy the *Vatican's shaky financial position and strongly supported the campaign to repel the encroaching Turks. As the result of differences with Louis over the French church, the king issued the *Gallican Articles (1682), which widened the breach between the two. A man of integrity, Innocent showed sympathy for the sufferings of *Huguenots and Jansenists.

INNOCENT XII (1615–1700). Pope from 1691. Born in Naples, he entered *Vatican service at age twenty, became *cardinal in 1681, and was *archbishop of Naples when elected pope, as a compromise between French and Spanish factions. He proved himself to be both peacemaker and reformer, ending the long confrontation with the French church when *Louis XIV conceded the *pope's right to fill French bishoprics. He was firm in his condemnation of *Quietism and *Jansenism, sought to rid the church of nepotism, built hospitals and schools, and showed a notable pastoral concern.

INQUISITION, THE An ecclesiastical tribunal set up in the 13th century by Gregory IX with a threefold aim: to investigate the spread of *heresy; to summon before it all Roman Catholics suspected of heresy; and to show them their errors, punish them, and call them to *repentance. It was not intended for the *conversion of Jews, Muslims, and other non-Roman Catholics. The power of the inquisitors, most of them *Dominicans or *Franciscans, was great, and some were notorious for their cruelty. The use of torture was sanctioned by *Innocent IV in 1252. The Inquisition waned for a time, but in 1542 *Paul III established the Roman Inquisition. In Spain in the latter 15th century the Spanish Inquisition sought to counter apostate former Jews and Muslims, heretics such as the *Alumbrados, and those accused of sorcery or *witchcraft. The Spanish Inquisition lasted until 1808, was restored briefly twice, and was finally suppressed in 1834.

INSPIRATION OF THE BIBLE The belief that the Holy *Spirit so guided the authors (and editors) of the books of the *Bible that what they wrote was what *God wanted written (2 Tim 3:16). This has been the traditional *Christian view, and many would include in their *doctrine of inspiration the concepts of the *inerrancy and *infallibility of *Scripture. In much modern *theology this traditional view has been modified or even denied.

INSTITUTES OF THE CHRISTIAN RELIGION The textbook of *Reformed *theology, composed by John *Calvin and first published in 1536 in Latin. Divided into four main sections, these deal respectively with *God the Creator, the *Trinity, *revelation, man's first estate and original *righteousness; the *fall of Adam and a discourse on *Christ the Redeemer; justifying *faith, *election, and reprobation; and the *presbyterian idea of the church. The work is based on *Scripture, the authority of which rests not upon fallible human reasoning, but upon the internal persuasion of the Holy *Spirit.

INSTRUMENTAL CAUSE That which serves as a subordinate cause. The phrase was much used by Protestants in their statement of *justification to describe the place of *faith. The meritorious cause is the *work of *Christ, for this is the only basis on which *God justifies. Yet since faith is a divinely appointed means of receiving justification and is the gift of God, it is a subordinate or instrumental cause, which is efficient. The expression can be used in other areas of *doctrine as well.

INSUFFLATION Blowing or breathing upon a person or thing in order to symbolize the giving of or the influence of the Holy *Spirit for the expulsion of an *evil *spirit. As a ceremony it is still retained in the *Eastern churches in *baptism.

INTENTION Used in several ways. (1) In *sacraments the intention is the purpose and aim of doing what the church intends by means of the appointed *rite and *liturgy. (2) In morality the intention is the purpose of an action. Thus a good intention can make a "neutral" action into a good action. (3) In the *liturgy of the *Eucharist there is sometimes an intention to say it for a particular stated purpose (e.g., to pray for rain, for a sick person, or for relief from problems).

INTER-VARSITY CHRISTIAN FELLOWSHIP OF THE U.S.A. Inter-Varsity Christian Fellowship is a non-profit, interdenominational student movement that ministers to college and university students. It was begun in Britain in 1928 and in Canada in 1929. Inter-Varsity began in the United States in 1939, when students at the University of Michigan invited C. Stacey Woods, then General Secretary of the Canadian movement, to help establish an Inter-Varsity chapter on their campus. Inter-Varsity Christian Fellowship of the U.S.A. was incorporated two years later. Inter-Varsity's various chapters are student-initiated and student-led. Inter-Varsity strives to build collegiate fellowships that engage their campus with the gospel of Jesus Christ and develop disciples who live out biblical values. Inter-Varsity students are encouraged to be actively concerned with evangelism, spiritual discipleship, serving the church, human relationships, righteousness, vocational stewardship, and world evangelization. The Inter-Varsity triennial missions conference held in Urbana, Illinois, and jointly sponsored by the Canadian and U.S.A. Fellowships, has long been a launching point for missionary service. See also Universities and Colleges Christian Fellowship.

INTERCESSION *Prayers of petition on behalf of others. They are an expression of *love for the true good of our neighbor. Thus intercession is a common element in public *worship. *Jesus himself practiced it (e.g., John 17) and still continues it (Rom 8:34).

INTERCOMMUNION A relationship between churches or *denominations in which each accepts members of the other(s) for the purpose of receiving Holy *Communion and allows its members to receive the same from the other(s).

INTERDICT An ecclesiastical penalty barring church members from specified spiritual benefits but not excommunicating them from membership. The use of this is much less common now than it was in medieval times.

INTERMEDIATE STATE The sphere of existence for those who die before the end of the age. The nature of this state is not clear, and it varies in different *theologies (*purgatory, *limbo, *sleep of the *soul). The *NT has little teaching on what happens at death and before the *Second Coming, for its emphasis is upon the end of the age and the glorious life of the age to come. Thus various theories have arisen.

INTERNATIONAL BIBLE STUDENTS' ASSOCIATION See Jehovah's Witnesses.

INTERNATIONAL COUNCIL OF CHRISTIAN CHURCHES A strongly *Fundamentalist interdenominational body set up in Amsterdam in 1948 as a witness against the inadequate theological basis of the *World Council of Churches. The moving spirit behind it was Dr. Carl *McIntire.

INTERNATIONAL MISSIONARY COUNCIL A body set up in 1921 to promote greater cooperation among Protestant *missions. It arranged conferences, published from 1912 *The International Review of Missions,* helped missions "orphaned" by *war, and set up in 1957 a fund for theological schools in mission lands. In 1961, not without opposition, it merged with the *World Council of Churches as the latter's mission and *evangelism department.

INTERNATIONAL PENTECOSTAL HOLINESS CHURCH. One of the oldest and largest Pentecostal denominations in the U.S. With roots in the *Holiness Movement, it was formed before the advent of the Pentecostal movement. Under the influence of the *Azusa Street Revival, it was one of the first organized denominations to adopt a Pentecostal statement of faith. Its present membership is in excess of 110,000.

INTERTESTAMENTAL PERIOD The period between the writing of the last book of the *OT and the *ministry of *Jesus Christ, leading to the writing of the *NT. Scholars differ on the dating of this period because some believe that the Book of Daniel was written in the 2d, not in the 5th, century. There is the further problem as to whether the *Apocrypha (*Deuterocanonical books) is treated as part of the OT.

INTINCTION (Lat. *intingere*, "to dip in"). The method of receiving Holy *Communion in both kinds by dipping the bread into the wine or sprinkling the bread with wine. The former is the common way in the *Eastern churches and is also used in the Roman Catholic Church. It is particularly useful when giving Holy Communion to the sick.

INTROIT (Lat. *introitus,* "opening"). The opening act of *worship in the *Eucharist, usually a congregational *hymn.

INTUITION Insight into the meaning of something and knowledge of it that is arrived at without the use of the senses. Being made in *God's *image, it is possible for human beings to know God and to know deep truths about him by intuition. To claim this ability does not necessarily include the further claim that such knowledge could be adequately or accurately expressed in verbal form.

INVESTITURE CONTROVERSY (1075–1122). Part of the general conflict during medieval times, concerned largely with whether pope or emperor should control the church. Investiture meant giving the new holder of an ecclesiastical post the *symbols of his authority (i.e., ring, staff, and keys). The practice of lay rulers conferring bishoprics, abbacies, and other offices was condemned by Pope *Gregory VII in 1075, and this led to the celebrated confrontation with the emperor *Henry IV, a struggle that continued under their successors, and ended only in a compromise effected in 1122 at the Concordat of *Worms. The matter had been resolved more peaceably in France in 1080 and in England in 1107.

INVINCIBLE IGNORANCE A lack of knowledge for which a person is not morally responsible. For example, a member of a remote tribe could not be held morally responsible for making alcohol if he had not been told of the decision of the central government that making alcohol was illegal and if he had not seen the results of drinking too much alcohol.

INVISIBLE CHURCH The true church as *God alone sees it, invisible to human eyes. This expression has been much used in *Protestantism, especially in controversy with *Roman Catholicism and as a justification for the existence of both *separatist churches and *parachurch organizations. The relation of an individual *Christian to *God is seen as of paramount importance; he must be born again. In visible churches only God knows who is truly born again and who is only a nominal Christian; the totality of all those who are born again is the invisible church. Certainly, where the emphasis is on the invisible rather than the visible, it is much easier to take church membership lightly and to form new and separated congregations.

INVOCATION OF SAINTS Asking those who have attained *eternal life in *heaven for assistance. The idea is that since the *saints in *heaven are near to *God, they have special powers of *intercession. To ask for their help in *prayer is not different in essence from asking a friend to pray for you. Most Protestants reject this practice because they believe that it obscures the *truth that *Jesus Christ is the only true heavenly Intercessor and *Mediator.

IONA COMMUNITY A group within the Church of *Scotland concerned that *worship be related to daily life. It was founded by George MacLeod on the island of Iona where *Columba had built a *monastery in the 6th century. MacLeod and his craftsmen and minister colleagues began to restore the ruins, sharing the *fellowship of work and worship, "to find a new community for men in the world today." A threefold rule bound the members, most of whom could spend only a small part of the year on Iona, to regular *prayer, *Bible reading, and tithing. The community, membership of which is open to all Christians, saw the church as committed to *mission. It trained parishioners to take responsible political action; it stressed the church's *healing *ministry; and it established links with the pacifist movement. The community carries on work on the mainland, and its ministerial members are traditionally in the forefront of the church's witness in industrial areas and in home missions.

IPSISSIMA VERBA OF JESUS The precise words that *Jesus spoke. Scholars raise the question whether the *Gospels contain the original words of Jesus. The reason for doubting that some or all of the words of Jesus have been edited or developed is twofold: first, the same saying appears in two or three Gospels in slightly different forms (e.g., Mark 5:1–12; Luke 6:17, 20–23), and second, there was a long period between the *ministry of Jesus and the actual writing of the Gospels.

IRELAND, CHURCH OF A member body of the *Anglican Communion, extending over both Northern Ireland and the Republic of Ireland and tracing its origins from the beginning of *Christianity on the island. It accepted *obedience to Rome only in the 12th century, after which English influence became stronger. An *Act of 1537 declared *Henry VIII's supremacy over the Church of Ireland, but most of the population remained Roman Catholic—a fact that led finally to the Church of Ireland's disestablishment in 1871. It maintains two provinces (Armagh and Dublin), elects its *bishops, and in 1980 had some 164,000 members.

IRENAEUS (c. 130–c. 200). *Bishop of Lyons. Born in Asia Minor, he had known *Polycarp who, he wrote, "had intercourse with John and with the rest of those who had seen the *Lord." Irenaeus probably studied in Rome, and he became bishop about 178. His defense of *orthodoxy, *Against Heresies* (c. 180), took issue with *Gnosticism and *Montanism and underlined his claim to be the first great Western theologian. He contributed toward the development of the *canon of *Scripture.

IRISH ARTICLES (1615). Doctrinal statement of the Irish Episcopal Church, numbering 104 and largely the work of James *Ussher. They incorporated the 1595 Lambeth Articles and reflected an Irish-flavored *Puritanism, with strong Calvinist emphases. They were superseded in 1635 by the *Thirty-Nine Articles.

IRRESISTIBLE GRACE See Grace.

IRVING, EDWARD (1792–1834). Scottish minister. An Edinburgh graduate, he taught school (1810–1819), then in 1820 became assistant to Thomas *Chalmers in Glasgow. In 1822 he was inducted to the rundown Caledonian Chapel in London, where his oratory attracted all classes as he attacked the *evils of the age and championed the *poor. He more and more stressed *prophecy and *eschatology, and he reluctantly allowed *tongues-speaking in his church in 1831. His trustees deserted him, his *presbytery deposed him, but most members left with him to form a separate congregation. In 1833 he was deprived of ministerial status, ostensibly for heretical writings on the *Incarnation. He submitted to a form of *ordination in the emerging *Catholic Apostolic Church but with modest status as one who had neither spoken in tongues nor prophesied. His health deteriorated, and he died at age forty-two and was buried in Glasgow Cathedral. Irving has been largely rehabilitated in recent years.

ISIDORE OF SEVILLE (c. 560–636). *Archbishop of Seville. Having succeeded his brother as *archbishop about 600, he continued the battle against *Arianism and influenced several church councils. A versatile scholar, Isidore produced many useful writings for his age and for posterity. These included the first manual of *Christian *doctrine in the *Latin church and a comprehensive encyclopedia used by students throughout the Middle Ages.

ISRAEL Used in several ways: (1) of Jacob, who became Israel (Gen 32:28); (2) of the descendants of Jacob/Israel; (3) of those descendants of Jacob who possessed true *faith and were faithful (Rom 9:6ff.); (4) of the modern state of Israel; (5) of those of Jewish stock who will accept *Jesus as the *Messiah before his *second coming (Rom 11:26); (6) with the adjective "new," of the church.

J

J The supposed source of the *Pentateuch that uses the name (Y)Jahweh. See also Documentary Hypothesis.

JACKSON, SAMUEL MACAULAY (1851–1912). American *Presbyterian scholar and philanthropist. Born in New York City and educated in the U.S. and Germany, he was a *pastor in New Jersey before devoting himself from 1880 to literary and philanthropic work. Even later when he taught church history at New York University (1895–1912) he took no salary. His many works include a biography of *Zwingli and the editorship of the *New Schaff-Herzog Encyclopaedia of Religious Knowledge* from 1908.

JACKSON, SHELDON (1834–1909). American *Presbyterian *missionary. Born in New York, he was ordained after graduating from Princeton Seminary (1858). He served his church in frontier areas from Minnesota to Arizona (1859–1882) and subsequently worked in Alaska (1884–1907), where the government appointed him the first superintendent of public instruction. He introduced reindeer from Siberia into Alaska to help the Eskimos. For his pioneer work he was nicknamed the "*Bishop of All Beyond."

JACOB OF NISIBIS (4th century). *Bishop of Nisibis, sometimes called the "Moses of Mesopotamia." He was found among the orthodox supporters at the Council of *Nicea (325) and is said to have organized a week of public *prayer which was answered by the death of *Arius. He successfully led the defense of Nisibis against the Persians at least twice (338, 350).

JACOBINS A name given originally to *Dominican *friars in Paris because their first house was located on Rue St. Jacques (1219). The house became in the late 18th century the meeting place for the more radical politicians who kept the old name associated with the place.

JACOBITES The Monophysites of Syria who take their name reportedly from Jacob Baradaeus (c. 500–578), *bishop of Edessa, but not described as Jacobites until the Second Council of *Nicea in 787. Attempts to bring them back to *orthodoxy failed. Many became Muslims when the Arabs occupied Syria in the 7th century; others joined the Roman Catholic Church in the 17th century. In recent times the *patriarch is based in Kurdistan (Iran). Jacobite *Monophysitism is reflected in their making the *sign of the *cross with one finger, indicating belief in the one *nature of *Christ.

JAMES I See James VI (of Scotland) and I (of England).

JAMES II (OF ENGLAND) AND VII (OF SCOTLAND) (1633–1701). King of Great Britain from 1685 to 1688. His promotion of *Roman Catholicism was to topple the Stuart dynasty. His views on *toleration were changeable, and in Scotland he outdid even his brother (*Charles II) in persecuting the *Covenanters. His downfall in 1688 was hastened by the birth of a son who would presumably have ensured the Roman Catholic succession. He was, in the event, succeeded by his daughter Mary, ruling jointly with her husband, *William III (William of Orange).

JAMES VI (OF SCOTLAND) AND I (OF ENGLAND) (1566–1625). Son of *Mary, Queen of Scots, and Lord Darnley, he became king of Scotland in 1567. He had George *Buchanan as tutor and also had a series of regents before he came of age. His view of the *divine right of kings caused a clash with Andrew *Melville, but he had imposed on Scotland a modified *episcopacy when he inherited the English throne also in 1603. There his religious measures satisfied no one, and he diminished his position through indiscrete liaisons. He took the lead in settling Protestants in Ulster and is perhaps chiefly remembered for having planned the *King James Version (1611).

JANSEN, CORNELIUS OTTO (1585–1638). Initiator of *Jansenism. Born in Holland, he was still in his twenties when he saw the need for a Roman Catholic *revival movement to offset Protestant advances. He encountered opposition from his coreligionists but encouraged a reexamination of the church *fathers, especially *Augustine of Hippo. Jansen became *bishop of Ypres in 1636.

JANSENISM A theological movement within *Roman Catholicism that took its name from Cornelius O. *Jansen (1585–1638), bishop of Ypres, and was expounded in his work *Augustinus* (1640). The teaching emphasized the irresistibility of the grace of God in baptism and conversion and advocated a harsh or rigorous approach to morality. In *Augustinus* Jansen attacked the tendency of *Counter-Reformation supporters, notably *Jesuits, to overstress human responsibility and so to relapse into *Pelagianism, playing down *original *sin and the *grace available through *Christ. Jansenism had powerful followers in France but even more powerful enemies. Condemned by the *papacy in 1653, it survived as a force in France until 1730 and had some impact on Italy. A Jansenist church was formed in Holland in 1723, known as the Little Church of Utrecht. Traces of the movement can still be found today in Holland.

JEHOVAH A common rendering of the Hebrew letters JHVH (YHWH), the *OT name of *God. It has been in use since 1520 and is found in the *King James Version and the American Standard Version. Today it is more common to see the *Tetragrammaton rendered as *Yahweh or as LORD.

JEHOVAH'S WITNESSES Also known as the *International Bible Students' Association, Millennial Dawnists, Russellites, and the Watch Tower Bible and Tract Society. It is a *sect founded by C. T. *Russell (1852–1916) in 1872 and given the name of Jehovah's Witnesses in 1931 by J. F. *Rutherford (1869–1942), who also gave it a worldwide *mission from its American base. Members meet in Kingdom Halls and are required to do at least ten hours of door-to-door visiting per month. They announce *Christ's *second coming and the great battle of *Armageddon. However, they appear to be modifying the claim that only 144,000 people will finally attain to *everlasting life. They deny the *doctrine of the *Trinity and the *deity of Christ. They do not allow alcohol, tobacco, *divorce, blood transfusions, military service, do not vote or salute the flag.

JEROME (c. 347–c. 419). Biblical scholar. Born in Dalmatia, he studied in Rome, and in 375 he began a two-year search for peace as a Syrian desert *hermit, during which time he learned the biblical languages. Ordained in Antioch in 378, he returned to Rome in 382 as secretary to Pope *Damasus, after whose death he went back to Palestine and later established a *monastery at Bethlehem. One of the early church's greatest scholars, he published many works. His *Vulgate

(Latin translation of the *Bible) had a great influence on the Middle Ages.

JEROME OF PRAGUE (c. 1365–1416). Bohemian Reformer. Having studied at the Charles University of Prague and at Oxford, where he was influenced by John *Wycliffe, he returned to Prague as professor in 1401. With Jan *Hus he advocated reformist views, notably that *Christ's laws override papal decrees. Having gone to the Council of *Constance to defend Hus, he was taken prisoner and was later burned as a heretic.

JERUSALEM CONFERENCE (1928). A meeting convened by the *International Missionary Council and held on the Mount of Olives. Its purpose was to look again at the *Christian *mission in the light of the growth of secularism. For fifteen days 231 representatives from fifty-one countries dealt with a wide-ranging agenda. While some *Evangelicals objected to an emphasis on the *social *gospel, the conference affirmed: "Christ is our motive and Christ our end. We must give nothing less, and we can give nothing more."

JERUSALEM, SYNOD OF (1672). A council of the *Eastern Orthodox church. Its purpose was to reject the Calvinist *doctrine of Cyril *Lucar, as expressed in his *Confession of Orthodox Faith* (1629). The council confirmed the statement of *orthodox *doctrine produced by Peter *Mogila and affirmed also that the Holy *Spirit proceeds from the Father alone, that church and *Scripture are equally infallible, that there are seven *sacraments, and that the books of Tobit, Judith, Ecclesiasticus, and Wisdom of Solomon are part of canonical Scripture.

JESUITS (SOCIETY OF JESUS) Roman Catholic *religious *order founded by *Ignatius of Loyola and officially established in 1540. It had originated six years earlier when six young men in Paris joined Ignatius in *vows of *poverty, *chastity, and acceptance of any apostolic task on instructions from the *pope. Such *obedience was to become a hallmark of the Jesuits, as was a concentration on education. They were a potent force in the *Counter-Reformation, but opposition grew in and out of the church. Political pressure led to the abolition of the order in 1773, but it was reestablished in 1814. It is now the largest religious order for men and has a wide variety of ministries throughout the world.

JESUS CHRIST I.e., Jesus, *the *Christ*. Jesus received his name from his Father on the command of an *angel (Matt 1:20). It is a Greek form of the Hebrew name Joshua meaning "The *Lord is *salvation." Jesus was called the *Messiah (Christ) when it was recognized that he was fulfilling the prophecies concerning the King and *Savior of *Israel (Matt. 16:16).

JESUS OF HISTORY, THE A scholarly way of referring to the historical portrait of Jesus that may be constructed from the *Gospels by the use of modern methods of historical study. Those who use the phrase assume that the Gospels are not simple history but interpretation of Jesus made in the light of his *resurrection. Thus a scholar's task is to reconstruct the history of Jesus, and this becomes a "quest for the historical Jesus," leading to a distinction being made between the Jesus of history and the *Christ of *faith.

JESUS PRAYER The Jesus Prayer is the center of *hesychasm, the "prayer of the heart" developed and practiced by monks and laypeople of Eastern *Orthodoxy. The first explicit use of the form "Lord Jesus Christ, Son of God, have mercy upon me" is found in the 6th-century Eastern authors. It is a *prayer that comprises *worship of *Jesus, sorrow for *sin, and confidence in his *mercy and the power of his Name to deliver.

JEWEL, JOHN (1522–1571). *Bishop of Salisbury. An Oxford graduate whose support of the *Reformation wavered under Mary *Tudor, he was appointed bishop by *Elizabeth I in 1560 and carried out his duties diligently. He taught something akin to the *divine right of kings, and his *Apology of the Church of England* was later acclaimed as the best defense of *Anglicanism.

JIMENES DE CISNEROS, FRANCISCO See XIMENEZ DE CISNEROS, FRANCISCO.

JOACHIM OF FIORE (c. 1135–1202). Italian mystic and scholar. Reportedly converted during a *pilgrimage to the Holy Land, he joined the *Cistercians and became *abbot of Corazzo in 1177. In 1191 he resigned and withdrew for *contemplation to a mountain retreat. In 1196 he founded the Order of San Giovanni in Fiore. His philosophy of history had a great influence on the latter Middle Ages.

JOAN, POPE Apocryphal female *pontiff said to have reigned during twenty-five months from 855; another account places her accession about 1100. The story was evidently believed and used as an argument at the 15th-century Council of *Constance, and ironically it was a Protestant, David Blondel, who in 1647 made the first serious attempt to discredit the myth.

JOAN OF ARC (c. 1412–1431). French national heroine. A peasant's daughter from Champagne, she was told in visions of her mission to save France during the *Hundred Years' War. Having convinced King Charles VII, she led the relief of Orleans but was captured by the English in 1430. Charged with *witchcraft and *heresy before an ecclesiastical court at Rouen, she was condemned and burned. *Callistus III declared her innocent in 1456, and she was canonized in 1920.

JOHN VIII (d. 882). Pope from 872. He encouraged the evangelization of the Slavs, took a firm line against the Saracens, and resolved a bitter controversy over *orthodoxy between Eastern and Western churches. He was a shrewd diplomat but was bedeviled by problems within Rome, including the pretensions of his successor, *Formosus. He was murdered by his enemies.

JOHN XII (c. 937–964). Pope from 955. His election was contrived by his father Alberic II of Spoleto, the *secular ruler of Rome. Pope at eighteen, he was the first to assume a new name on his election (he was formerly Octavius). He crowned *Otto I as Holy Roman emperor in 962, but refusing to take an *oath of *obedience to the emperor, John was deposed on justifiable grounds of gross immorality (963). Two months after Otto left Rome, John had Leo VIII deposed. Death ended his scandalous reign the following year.

JOHN XXII (d. 1334). Pope from 1316. The second Avignon-based *pontiff during the *Great Schism, John was a good administrator, but his reign was disrupted by controversies. He was at odds with a large segment of the *Franciscans, whose cause was espoused by Louis of Bavaria, no friend of the *papacy. In 1327 John anathematized Marsilius of Padua, who argued for imperial supremacy over the papacy. Louis set up an *antipope in Rome.

JOHN XXIII (d. 1419). *Antipope. Born in Naples, he was reportedly a pirate captain before *ordination. Elected in 1410 by a group of *cardinals, he found himself one of three rival claimants to the *papacy. The Council of *Constance decided that the *Great Schism could be ended by the abdication of all three so-called popes, so the self-seeking worldly John was formally deposed in 1415. Detained by a political enemy until 1418, he was reconciled finally to *Martin V but died a few months later.

JOHN XXIII (1881–1963). Pope from 1958. Coming from a poor family, he was ordained in 1904 and served in various positions overseas, notably in the *Vatican diplomatic corps, before becoming *cardinal and *patriarch of Venice in 1953. The five-year reign of this warm-hearted old man revitalized the church, particularly in his summoning of *Vatican Council II in 1962. Zealous for *Christian unity, John nonetheless remained thoroughly conservative in upholding his church's *dogmas.

JOHN CLIMACUS (c. 580–650). Orthodox mystic and theologian. He wrote *Ladder to Paradise,* a manual on moral and spiritual *perfection. His book, which describes the thirty steps of the spiritual life, was well known in the Middle Ags. Its focus is the *Jesus Prayer. The symbol of the ladder (*klimax*) created a new symbol for Byzantine painting, the ladder to *heaven. *Abbot of Mount Sinai 639–649.

JOHN FREDERICK (THE MAGNANIMOUS) (1503–1554). Elector of Saxony. A warm supporter of the Protestant cause, he became elector in 1532 and headed the *Smalcald League of Lutheran princes. When the battle against *Charles V was finally lost in 1547, John Frederick was imprisoned for five years and regarded as suffering for *Protestantism. He founded the University of Jena.

JOHN OF AVILA (1500–1569). Spanish Reformer, preacher, and mystic. Jewish by birth, he was ordained in 1525 and thereafter gave his inherited *wealth to *charity. So successful was his *mission work in Andalusia that the *Inquisition, suspicious where there was enthusiasm, investigated and exonerated him. He won fame also as a spiritual director, founded educational institutions, encouraged the *Jesuits, and produced devotional works that are still read.

JOHN OF CAPISTRANO (1386–1456). *Franciscan preacher. Born in Italy and converted while in prison for a civil offense, he joined the Franciscans in 1426 and became prominent in their more ascetic wing. Sent by *Nicholas V to Austria to bring back the erring Hussites to the church, he went on to lead an army to relieve Belgrade from the Turks, but he soon died of plague in Austria.

JOHN OF DAMASCUS (c. 675–749). Greek Orthodox monk and scholar. Born in Damascus, he was the chief *Christian representative at the caliph's court, but he resigned in middle age and became a monk. He wrote in defense of the *veneration of sacred *images during the *Iconoclastic Controversy, but is best known for his *Source of Knowledge,* which became a standard textbook of Greek Orthodox *theology, establishing his place as the last of the great Eastern *fathers.

JOHN OF GOD (1495–1550). Founder of the *Hospitallers. Born in Portugal, he was successively shepherd and soldier but was converted through the *preaching of *John of Avila and began work in Spain among the *poor and sick in 1538.

JOHN OF LEYDEN (c. 1509–1536). Dutch *Anabaptist. A tailor by trade, he became so-called king of "New Zion" soon after Protestant rebels took over the German city of Münster. The bizarre and intolerant regime he initiated discredited the Anabaptist movement. Catholic and mainline Protestant forces combined to retake the city, and John was among the victims of the slaughter that ensued.

JOHN OF PARIS (c. 1255–1306). *Dominican monk and scholar. Born in Paris, he remained there and lectured at the university. He expressed independent theological ideas that brought him into conflict with ecclesiastical authority, notably on the topic of *transubstantiation. Against the autocratic tendencies of Pope *Boniface VIII (1294–1303), moreover, John published a work that limited papal intervention in secular matters to cases involving moral or theological order.

JOHN OF SALISBURY (c. 1115–1180). English philosopher. Born in Salisbury and educated in Paris under Peter *Abelard and other distinguished teachers, he entered papal service and later was secretary to *archbishops *Theobald and Thomas *Becket at Canterbury. He became *bishop of Chartres in 1176. One of the best Latin scholars of his age, he left valuable works on philosophy and *theology and showed himself an astute commentator on contemporary affairs.

JOHN OF THE CROSS (1542–1591). Spanish mystic. He joined the *Carmelites in 1563 and collaborated with *Teresa of Avila (1568) in introducing some much-needed reforms. This tendency led to two brief terms of imprisonment. In his writings and poetry he stressed the experience of the mystical union between the *soul and *Christ.

JOHN OF WESEL (c. 1400–1481). German ecclesiastical Reformer. Professor and preacher, he was charged with teaching Hussite *doctrines, and when nearly eighty he was summoned before the *Inquisition. He recanted, was sentenced to confinement in a *monastery, and died two years later. His works adumbrate Protestant views in their rejection of *indulgences, *transubstantiation, and *extreme *unction, and in their acceptance of *Scripture as the final authority.

JOHN PAUL I (1912–1978). Pope for thirty-four days in 1978. Ordained in 1935, he became a *bishop in 1958 and the *archbishop of Venice in 1969. For his installation as pope he declined to be carried by throne-bearers to and from the ceremony. This first pope to choose a double name was beloved for his piety and friendliness.

JOHN PAUL II (1920–). Pope from 1978. The first non-Italian pope since *Adrian VI (d. 1523), he was born in Poland, was ordained in 1946, was consecrated *bishop in 1958, and became *cardinal in 1967. By the end of his first twelve months in office he had visited Mexico, Poland, Ireland, the U.S., and Turkey, and since then he has traveled all over the world—farther than any of his predecessors. As popular and essentially as theologically conservative as *John XXIII, he has been described as the most interesting and the most unpredictable of popes, with strong conservative tendencies.

JONAS, JUSTUS (1493–1555). German Reformer. Professor at Wittenberg and a supporter of *Luther, he took part in early *Reformation conferences such as Marburg in 1529 and Augsburg in 1530. He translated the Latin writings of *Melanchthon and Luther and preached the latter's funeral *sermon.

JONES, BOB (1883–1968). American *evangelist and founder in 1924 of Bob Jones University, Greenville, South Carolina. Born in Alabama, he became a Methodist preacher at fifteen and studied at Southern University, but he realized that his Fundamentalist *religion and conservative politics would best be promoted by founding his own institution. It is estimated that he preached 12,000 *sermons to 15 million people in his evangelistic *ministry.

JONES, ELI STANLEY (1884–1973). American *missionary to India. A Methodist minister, he went first to Lucknow in 1907 and later ministered also to the educated Indians. So identified was he with the cause of Indian independence that the British kept him out of India for a time. Of his many books, the most widely used is his *Christ of the Indian Road* (1925).

JONES, GRIFFITH (1683–1761). Welsh preacher. Ordained as an Anglican *priest in 1709, he served various parishes in Wales, though his Calvinist tendencies were not acceptable to many. He was fervent in teaching people to read the *Bible in Welsh, opened his first *charity school for this purpose in 1730, and saw the system extended over the principality in thirty years.

JONES, RUFUS MATTHEW (1863–1948). American *Quaker scholar. Teacher of philosophy at Haverford College, Pennsylvania, for forty years, he was one of the founders of the American Friends Service Committee in 1917 and wrote extensively on the history of *mysticism and Quakerism.

JOSEPH CALASANCTIUS (1556–1648). Founder of the *Piarists and "heavenly *patron of all *Christian schools" (*Pius XII). Born in Spain, he engaged in pastoral work after *ordination until he went to Rome in 1592. There he became involved in education and in 1597 opened Europe's first free school for poor children. In 1621 his community was papally authorized as a *religious *order. Joseph, who patiently endured misunderstanding and dissension that led to the order's status being reduced in 1646 (it was restored in 1669), was canonized in 1767.

JOSEPHINISM The exercise by the state of complete control over the church, especially in 18th-century Austria. Empress Maria Theresa (1717–1780) was influenced by her *chancellor, Prince A. W. von Kaunitz, to take totalitarian control over the Roman Catholic Church in Austria. The policy came to fruition under her son, Joseph II (1741–1790). His primary aim was the reform of the Austrian church. He created more *parishes, established hospitals and poorhouses, and organized church finances. More than eight hundred cloisters were closed and the money given to care for the *poor. State-controlled *seminaries robbed the *Vatican of influence over the education of *priests.

JOWETT, JOHN HENRY (1864–1923). English Congregational minister. Born in Yorkshire, he was educated at Edinburgh University and at Congregational colleges. He was ordained in 1889. He ministered in Newcastle-upon-Tyne, Birmingham, New York's Fifth Avenue *Presbyterian Church, and London's Westminster Chapel. One of the most notable preachers of his day, he wrote many books, had a highly developed social conscience, and in addition to many university honors, was made a Companion of Honour by George V in 1922.

JUBILEE YEAR Each fiftieth year in the *OT (Lev 25:8–55; 27:17–21; Num 36:4). A year of release and liberty proclaiming *God as the owner of the world. Hebrew slaves were set free and debts cancelled. It has been an important concept in recent *liberation *theology, and some think that *Jesus spoke of a Jubilee Year when he preached in Nazareth (Luke 4:19).

JUDAISM The *religion and *culture of the Jewish people. Used particularly of the period from the captivity in Babylon/Persia (586–333 B.C.) to modern times. On account of the *Diaspora and other factors, Judaism is not uniform but exists in a variety of forms from Eastern to Western, from orthodox to liberal, from support of the State of *Israel to opposition to it, and from cultural to religious. A sense of being "Jewish" is the uniting factor.

JUDGMENT, THE LAST Seen by most theologians as the judgment that will fix the *eternal destiny of all human beings (Matt 10:15; 11:22; 12:36; 2 Tim 4:1; 2 Peter 2:3,9). Premillennial theologians recognize a judgment of believers (Rom 14:10; 2 Cor 5:10) and one of unbelievers (Rev 20:11–15).

JUDSON, ADONIRAM (1788–1850). American Baptist *missionary to Burma. Born in Massachusetts and educated at Brown University and Andover Theological Seminary, he was ordained as a *Congregationalist minister and appointed to India. On the voyage, however, he decided to become a Baptist, settled later (1813) in Rangoon, and endured incredible hardships in Burma (including a seventeen-month term of imprisonment) for the rest of his life, taking only one furlough. He translated the *Bible into Burmese, established congregations and schools, trained preachers, and always pressed local customs into the service of the *gospel.

JULIAN OF NORWICH (c. 1342–c. 1416). English mystic. Personal details about her are sparse. She was an *anchoress, known almost entirely for her *Revelations of Divine Love,* produced twenty years after she claimed to have had a series of sixteen *revelations. Her book deals with the most fundamental mysteries of the *Christian *faith in a remarkably lucid way.

JULIAN THE APOSTATE (332–363). Roman emperor from 361. He was the last of the emperors who sought to replace *Christianity by paganism. His reign was notable for its harassment of Christians. Struck by an arrow in battle, he died, reportedly acknowledging that the "Galilean" had conquered, but the account has been disproved.

JULIUS I (d. 352). Pope from 337. Roman born, he showed himself a champion of *orthodoxy in 339 when he gave shelter to *Athanasius of Alexandria, who had been deposed through *Arian influence. Julius mustered the Western *bishops against the *heresy at the Council of *Sardica, was responsible for the restoration of Athanasius to his see, and in the process advanced the power of the *papacy.

JULIUS II (1443–1513). Pope from 1503. Coming from a noble family, he was made *cardinal before he was thirty by his uncle, Sixtus IV. Under successive popes he was involved in intrigue and was himself elected on giving to his fellow cardinals promises he did not in fact carry out because they would have weakened his position. Aggressive and frequently caught up in political battles, he was nonetheless generous in his patronage of the arts.

JULIUS III (1487–1555). Pope from 1550. A lawyer by training, he had presided at the opening of the Council of *Trent in 1545. He was a *patron of the *Jesuits and of the arts but gradually became disillusioned about reforming the church. He sent Reginald *Pole to England with far-reaching powers on the accession of Mary *Tudor in 1553.

JULIUS AFRICANUS, SEXTUS (d. c. 240). *Christian writer. Born probably in Palestine, he enjoyed royal patronage, met many scholars during his travels, and was commissioned by the emperor Severus to erect the public library in Rome. He wrote a five-volume world history and a twenty-four-volume encyclopedia, but only fragments of both projects survive. He is known to have corresponded with *Origen.

JUSTICE The biblical idea is to be understood in terms of the obligations that arise from personal relationships—with *God and with people. There is a debt of personal loyalty, faithfulness, and devotion to be fulfilled to the Creator and to his creatures. In practical terms this means obeying the revealed laws of God. But justice is not in the keeping of laws but in the development of true, personal relationships. In the *OT God's justice is his maintenance of the *covenant that he made with Moses and *Israel, while in the *NT it is his faithfulness to that covenant he made with Christ and all who are *Christ's people. It is loyal fulfillment of obligations. What justice is may be seen in what Christ did and was. He became the *righteousness of the people of God. See also JUSTIFICATION, RIGHTEOUSNESS.

JUSTIFICATION *God's act of declaring, or making, or both declaring and making, a sinner righteous (just) through the *righteousness (*merits) of *Christ. From the human viewpoint it is the finding of *pardon and acceptance with God by a believing sinner; it is the beginning of a personal and meaningful relationship with the God of all *grace. Protestants and Roman Catholics have disagreed as to how the sinner receives pardon and acceptance. This is best seen in the way they have understood the following traditional headings of the *doctrine. (1) *The meritorious cause*. Here there is agreement. It is the perfect life, the sacrificial death, and the *resurrection of *Jesus Christ. (2) *The formal cause*. This is that by which God actually pronounces and accepts the sinner as righteous. The Roman Catholic position has been that God infuses his own righteousness into the *soul at *baptism (through the work of the Holy *Spirit) and then justifies that person on the basis of what he now sees within him—his own gift. The Protestant position has been to point away from this internal righteousness (which they say becomes human when possessed by a human being) to an external righteousness, the presence of the exalted, perfectly righteous Christ at the Father's right hand in *heaven. (3) *The instrumental cause*. This is the means by which, or the channel through which, God actually achieves the justification of a sinner. Roman Catholics have emphasized the priority of the *sacrament of baptism, while Protestants have pointed to the priority of *faith.

There is evidence in modern times that the traditional positions are being reexamined as further study of such biblical words (ideas) as faith (faithfulness), justice, and righteousness proceed and as the historical contexts of disagreements are carefully examined.

Traditionally, justification by faith alone has been seen as the primary emphasis of *Protestantism, the article of faith by which the church stands or falls. Yet it has always been seen as requiring an emphasis on *sanctification in order to give a full view of the nature of God's gracious *salvation.

JUSTIN MARTYR (c. 100–165). *Christian apologist. Born of pagan parents in Samaria, he was converted about 132. A few years later he went to Rome and stoutly declared his Christian *faith to the highest in the land, trying to show how it went beyond even the noblest aspects of Greek philosophy. Finally, with some fellow believers he was denounced as a Christian and subversive and was condemned to be beheaded. Justin is held to have been the first Christian apologist to bring together the claims of faith and *reason. His *First Apology* (c. 155) and *Dialogue with Trypho* (c. 160) both emphasize that Christians are the inheritors, the heirs of Israel and its promises.

JUSTINIAN I (483–565). Roman emperor from 527. Born in modern Yugoslavia, he was educated in Constantinople, was legally adopted by his uncle Justin (emperor from 518), and became successively caesar and coemperor. He continued the old struggle with Persia and sought to regain Roman provinces in the West lost to the barbarian invaders. He established many churches and *monasteries, closed pagan schools of philosophy in Athens, and was ambivalent in his attitude to *Monophysitism, but he took strong steps against Arians and Manichaens. He is chiefly remembered, however, for the Justinian Code, which in 529 brought order into the Roman law by which the empire was governed.

K

KAGAWA, TOYOHIKO (1888–1960). Japanese *Christian leader. Disinherited when he became a Christian in his teens, he studied in Japan and in the U.S. Devotion to the improvement of appalling living and labor conditions resulted in two brief imprisonments. He was *evangelist, organizer of trade unions, pacifist, and church leader. Having gained suffrage for men in 1925, he led a similar movement on behalf of women after World War II.

KAIROS (Gk. "time, a point in time"). Used by theologians of the unique time for humankind caused by Christ's first *advent (see Mark 1:15, Rom 3:26; 1 Peter 1:10ff.). See also AEON.

KANT, IMMANUEL (1724–1804). German Idealist philosopher. Kant was the embodiment of the *Enlightenment period, a time when thinkers were struggling to free themselves from what they perceived as the bondage of authoritarian thinking, especially ecclesiastical. His three great critiques—*Critique of Pure Reason* (1781), *Critique of Practical Reason* (1788), and *Critique of Judgment* (1790)—were designed to destroy false dependence upon unknowable absolutes and force man back on himself as the source of authority. Metaphysical realities cannot be known; we have only our subjective apprehensions of things. Although Kant rejected traditional arguments for *God, he did not reject the idea. He wanted to have "*religion within the limits of *reason alone," and he wrote a book by that title in 1793. Kant's influence has been immense, and a major branch of *liberal *theology followed his lead in denying the possibility of *supernatural *revelation and the knowability of God.

KARLSTADT (CARLSTADT) (c. 1480–1541). German Reformer. Born Andreas Rudolf Bodenstein at Karlstadt, he was a teacher and upholder of traditional *doctrine at Wittenberg from 1505 but changed his views after a visit to Rome. He espoused *Augustinianism and an extreme *Protestantism, which he upheld publicly against Johann *Eck (1518–1519). On *Christmas Day, 1521, he celebrated the first Protestant *Communion service. Differing from *Luther, whom he accused of compromising, he left Wittenberg and eventually became in 1534 professor at Basel.

KASATKIN, IVAN See NICOLAI (IVAN KASATKIN).

KEBLE, JOHN (1792–1866). A leader of the *Oxford Movement and author of the *Christian Year* (1827). He became professor of poetry at Oxford in 1831 and was one of a group concerned to defend the national church against liberal and reforming influences. He cooperated with J. H. *Newman to produce *Tracts of the Times* and edited Richard *Hooker's *Works* and the *Library of the Fathers* (1838, with Newman and E. B. *Pusey). Deeply pious, Keble was commemorated in 1870 by the founding of Keble College, Oxford.

KEITH, GEORGE (1638–1716). "*Christian *Quaker." Born in Aberdeen, he was trained there for the Church of *Scotland *ministry, but two years after the *Restoration he became a Quaker. He worked with Robert *Barclay, George *Fox, and William *Penn, and he suffered several terms of imprisonment. Arriving in Philadelphia in 1689, he soon found his views suspect among his coreligionists, was prevented from *preaching, and set up a group known as the Christian Quakers. He returned to England in 1694, was later ordained in the Church of *England, and subsequently served the Society for the Propagation of the Gospel in America (1702–1704) before becoming a rector in Sussex.

KEITH-FALCONER, ION GRANT NEVILLE (1856–1887). Arabic scholar and *missionary. Born in Edinburgh, son of an *evangelical Scottish earl, he distinguished himself at Cambridge, where he taught Hebrew and was later appointed to a nominal chair of Arabic. He worked also among the *poor, was a cycling champion, and wrote for *Encyclopaedia Britannica* the article on shorthand. His attention directed to Africa by David *Livingstone, he visited Aden and saw its strategic position as a point of communication with the interior. In 1886 at his own expense but recognized by the *Free Church of Scotland, he and his wife established a *mission hospital at Sheikh Othman. Only a few weeks later he was struck down with Aden fever, which recurred and was exacerbated by primitive living conditions. He died the following spring.

KELLS, BOOK OF An illuminated copy of the *Gospels in *Jerome's Latin version, with various notes and local Irish records. The work took its name from the *monastery in County Meath, where it was completed probably about the beginning of the 9th century (one suggestion is that it was begun at Iona). The book is in the library of Trinity College, Dublin.

KELLY, THOMAS (1769–1854). Irish *hymn writer. Born in Dublin and converted in 1792, a minister briefly in the Church of Ireland, he became an independent *evangelist and writer of several hundred *hymns (including "Look, Ye Saints, The Sight Is Glorious" and "We Sing the Praise of Him Who Died."

KELLY, WILLIAM (1821–1906). *Plymouth Brethren scholar. Born in Ulster and educated at Trinity College, Dublin, he was converted at twenty and joined the J. N. *Darby group of Brethren. From 1856 he edited the **Bible Treasury,* a project that gave scope to his scholarly talents. He also edited Darby's works (34 vols., 1867–1883), wrote a number of books, and stood for a more moderate viewpoint than most of the *Exclusive Brethren.

KEMPIS, THOMAS À (c. 1380–1471). German mystic and probably the author of the classic *The *Imitation of Christ*. Educated by the *Brethren of the Common Life, he entered an *Augustinian *monastery near Zwolle in the Netherlands and remained there for the rest of his life. Well known as a copyist and as a spiritual counselor, he produced works that were devotional, intelligible, and relevant to his age.

KEMPE, MARGERY (c. 1373–c. 1440). English visionary and author. In her *Book of Margery Kempe,* she composed what may be the first English autobiography. It is composed of prayers, visions, devotions, and chronicles of her many pilgrimages to holy places. It was composed between 1432 and 1436. She married John Kempe, a burgess, when she was twenty and had fourteen children. She is known to have had lengthy conversations with *Julian of Norwich around 1413.

KENOSIS (Gk. "emptying"). Kenotic *Christology is an attempt to explain how the *eternal *Son of *God was able to become incarnate as *Jesus of Nazareth. The word is used concerning *Christ in Philippians 2:7, where the words "he emptied himself" occur. Some German 19th-century theologians claimed that the Son of God abandoned (in becoming man) certain attributes of *deity—total knowledge, power, and *sovereignty. Embarrassed by such a claim, other theologians taught that he simply concealed or did not make use of these attributes.

KENOTIC CHRISTOLOGY See KENOSIS.

KENSIT, JOHN (1853–1902). Protestant preacher. Born in London, he spent his life after *conversion in trying to counter what he saw as the Romeward drift of the Church of *England. He founded a Protestant book depot (1885) and the Protestant Truth Society (1890) and demonstrated against the *consecration as *bishops of men he considered unsuitable, notably Charles *Gore. He was fatally injured by a Roman Catholic mob while conducting a crusade.

KENTIGERN (Mungo) (518?–603). *Apostle of the Strathclyde Britons. Grandson of a semipagan British prince, he, with his mother, was baptized at Culross in Fife where Kentigern trained at the monastic school. He became a *missionary to his own people, living in what is now Glasgow. Chosen as *bishop, he suffered persecution from local heathen and finally moved to Wales. There he founded a *monastery with nearly a thousand monks engaged in agriculture, education, and religious pursuits. Those more experienced accompanied Kentigern on missionary travels. When in 573 the *Christian party triumphed among North Britons, the king recalled Kentigern, who settled subsequently in Glasgow, of which he is the *patron *saint. A great church in Glasgow bears his name and houses his tomb.

KERYGMA (Gk. "*preaching, proclamation"). Often used to describe the essential content of the preaching of the *apostles as recorded in the early *sermons of the Acts of the Apostles. Thus also used of the content of *Christian proclamation in contrast to Christian teaching within the church, which is *didache.

KESWICK CONVENTION Annual *evangelical gathering in the English Lake District. Begun in 1875 after the Moody-Sankey meetings, it emphasizes *prayer and *Bible study, a deeper spiritual life, and *missions. Its motto, "All one in *Christ *Jesus," has been made more widely known through the promotion of Keswick-type meetings in many parts of the world.

KETCHUM, ROBERT T. (1889–1978). Baptist *pastor, author, and conference speaker. In addition to his thirty-five years of pastoral *ministry in Indiana, Illinois, Iowa, Ohio, and Pennsylvania, Ketchum was one of the founders of the *General Association of Regular Baptist churches, the national representative of that group, a speaker at numerous denominational and interdenominational *Bible conferences, and the author of several books.

KEYS, THE POWER OF THE A *doctrine based on the words of *Jesus to Peter in Matthew 16:19. In Roman Catholic teaching this refers to the place of Peter and his successors, the *popes, as *vicars and stewards of *Christ. It also refers to the authority of *bishops and *priests. The basic reference is to the power to forgive *sins or not forgive sins, but it also includes the power to admit into the *kingdom of *heaven and, for the pope, the power to be the vicar or representative of Christ on earth.

KHOMYAKOV, ALEKSEI STEPANOVICH (1804–1860). Russian philosopher and theologian. Born in Moscow, he had a comprehensive education completed by eighteen months in France. He had a brief but distinguished career as a soldier before devoting himself to intellectual pursuits. His practical abilities were nonetheless extensive: successful landowner, constructor of agricultural machinery, gun designer, and self-taught physician. He is best known, however, as writer, poet, lay theologian, and enthusiast for the Russian way of life. He held that the triumphant march of Western civilization carried with it certain defects, and he sought to combine the best of both traditions. In religious matters he saw the *Orthodox Church as offering a balanced presentation (both anti-Roman Catholic and anti-Protestant). He had a keen social sense, but the oppressive regime of Tsar Nicholas I prevented his using his great gifts for the public good.

KIERKEGAARD, SØREN AABYE (1813–1855). Danish philosopher. Born into an orthodox Lutheran family in Copenhagen and educated at the university there, he inherited enough money at age twenty-five to devote himself to intellectual pursuits. After a flurry of philosophical works, he felt himself divinely called to attack a national church whose *clergy, he was convinced, were more servants of the *state than of *Christ. Leaders such as J. P. *Mynster and H. L. *Martensen came especially under fierce attack. Kierkegaard's health and fortune declined after a two-year crusade, and he died when he was only forty-two.

KIKUYU CONTROVERSY A dispute within *Anglicanism arising from *missionary work in Kenya. A conference at Kikuyu in 1913 attended by representatives of various Protestant missionary bodies approved a scheme of federation. Frank *Weston, *bishop of Zanzibar, saw in it an inadequate view of church and *ministry and protested to Randall *Davidson, *archbishop of Canterbury, particularly about two fellow bishops who supported the scheme. The controversy spread throughout the *Anglican Communion. Davidson finally and with reluctance advised against Anglican participation.

KILHAM, ALEXANDER (1762–1798). Founder of *Methodist New Connexion. A weaver's son who became an itinerant Methodist preacher in 1785, he urged separation from the Church of *England and defended the legitimacy of the (non-Anglican) Methodist *ministry. Expelled by the Methodist conference in 1796, he founded the new body but died soon afterwards.

KING JAMES VERSION American name for the Authorized Version of the *Bible (1611), authorized by King *James I. See also BIBLE (ENGLISH TRANSLATIONS).

KING, MARTIN LUTHER, JR. (1929–1968). American civil rights leader. A black Baptist *pastor who received his Ph.D. at Boston University, he became leader in the struggle for racial equality, his work acknowledged by award of the Nobel peace prize in 1964. Sometimes criticized by more militant blacks, he was killed by a white man's bullet in Memphis before his fortieth birthday.

KING'S CONFESSION See SCOTS CONFESSION.

KING'S EVIL A name given to scrofula (tubercular swelling of the lymph glands), once regarded as curable at the touch of the sovereign. Known in England from the 11th century and in France perhaps only slightly later, the practice flourished in the 17th century with *Charles II. He is said to have touched more than 90,000 sufferers. Queen *Anne was the last practitioner in England, but the custom continued in France until well into the 19th century.

KINGDOM OF GOD The rule of *God or the sphere in which God rules. The phrase occurs often in the teaching of *Jesus, and many of his *parables serve to illustrate it. Its fullest meaning is as a description of the age to come when God will rule effectively and all will obey him perfectly. In the present age of *sin the rule of God is effective in individual lives and in the *fellowship of the church as people experience the *salvation of *Christ in the power of the Holy *Spirit and obey God. This present experience of the people of God in living under the rule of God and knowing his sovereign *grace is a foretaste of the future glory of the kingdom. Jesus did not merely proclaim the kingdom; he also embodied it, for his life was wholly committed to God and wholly ruled by God. Further, he established the kingdom for believers by his death and *resurrection, for on this basis they receive the gift of the Spirit and the taste of the life to come.

Only Matthew speaks of Jesus as talking about the "kingdom of *heaven," and most scholars take "heaven" as a Jewish synonym for "God." Others, especially adherents of *dispensationalism, maintain that the kingdom of heaven is different from the kingdom of God and was offered to the Jews and rejected by them; however, it will come in the Millennium. The kingdom of God will come after the Millennium and the Last *Judgment.

KINGS, DIVINE RIGHT OF The belief that the sovereignty of monarchs is derived directly from *God. Such a view was held by many Christians in Europe from the late Middle Ages until the 18th century. It is a rare belief today but is found in certain Muslim *cultures.

KINGSHIP OF CHRIST The rule that *Jesus Christ exercises as he is considered as the God-Man. *God is King, and as *eternal *Son of God, *Christ is naturally King. Yet as the vindicated *Messiah he was exalted above all human rule to become the King of Kings and Lord of Lords (Rev 2:27; 19:16). It is his kingship and rule as Messiah and *Mediator that will continue until the end of this age (1 Cor 15:24ff.).

KINGSLEY, CHARLES (1819–1875). Anglican social reformer and writer. Born in Devon, he graduated from Cambridge, was ordained in 1842, and ministered in the *parish of Eversley, Hampshire. He was a founder-member of the *Christian *Socialist movement, wrote social and historical novels, and became a royal chaplain and a not-too-highly regarded professor of modern history at Cambridge. He was also an early supporter of *Darwin's evolutionary theory. His criticism of the *Oxford Movement and his attack on J. H. *Newman led the latter to write his famous *Apologia*.

KIRK SESSION The meeting of the ordained minister and *elders of a congregation in the Church of *Scotland or other *Presbyterian churches. "Kirk" means "church."

KISS OF PEACE Also known as the *pax. The greeting of one another as a sign of *Christian *fellowship. This is a part of the *Eucharist and takes different forms usually related to the *culture in which the church lives and works.

KITTEL, RUDOLPH (1853–1929). German *OT scholar. Born in Swabia and a graduate of Tübingen, he taught successively at Breslau and Leipzig. His works included commentaries on many *OT books and an edition of the Hebrew *Bible that superseded all earlier ones. His work on Israelite history was said to have been among the first to use archaeological evidence.

KNIGHTS HOSPITALLERS See HOSPITALLERS.

KNIGHTS TEMPLAR See TEMPLARS.

KNIGHTS OF COLUMBUS Roman Catholic men's fraternal benefit society. Founded by Father Michael J. McGivney (1852–1890) in New Haven, Connecticut, in 1882, its interests include insurance, education, and social welfare. More recently it has sponsored advertising to explain Roman Catholic *doctrines. Membership is reportedly 1.5 million and extends to several other countries.

KNOWLEDGE OF GOD Knowledge of *God exists at different levels, but all knowledge of him comes through *revelation. (1) Basic information about who God is and what he has done. This is gained both from studying the *universe and from reading the *Bible. (2) *Spiritual relationship and *fellowship with God, knowing God as a living being—the knowledge of God that means *eternal life (John 17:3). (3) The special gift of the *Spirit called "a word of knowledge" (1 Cor 12:8).

KNOX, EDMUND ARBUTHNOTT (1847–1937). *Bishop of Manchester. Successively Oxford don and *parish minister, he was *suffragan bishop of Coventry (1894–1903) before translation to Manchester (1903–1921). A well-known *Evangelical, he supported beach *missions in his *diocese and wrote against the deficiencies of *liberalism and *ritualism. After retirement he campaigned against the proposed *Prayer Book revisions (1927–1928) and had the satisfaction of seeing Parliament reject them.

KNOX, JOHN (c. 1513–1572). Scottish Reformer. Born at Haddington and probably educated at Glasgow University, he was ordained as a *priest about 1539 but soon began to support the Reformer George *Wishart. He was then a tutor, minister in St. Andrews, galley slave in French bondage, and chaplain to *Edward VI, whose offer of an English bishopric he declined. After some years of exile on the Continent he returned in 1559; led the triumph of the *Reformation in Scotland; and by personality, administrative ability, and writings laid the foundations of the Church of *Scotland. He became minister of the High Kirk of Edinburgh (St. Giles) and often preached to thousands during the week. At his funeral the Regent Morton, no friend of ministers, acknowledged, "Here lies one who neither flattered nor favoured any flesh."

KNOX, RONALD ARBUTHNOTT (1888–1957). Roman Catholic scholar. Son of E. A. *Knox, he was educated at Oxford, shared his father's dislike of liberals, but was converted to *Roman Catholicism in 1917. He was ordained as a *priest, later served as chaplain at Oxford (1926–1939), then withdrew to continue his literary work. He wrote detective novels, summarized his theological position in *The Belief of Catholics* (1927), produced a number of witty and satirical works, and labored for years over a translation of the *Bible (1945, 1949).

KOIMESIS The feast of the *Dormition of *Mary (the falling asleep) in the *Orthodox Church.

KOINE The common Greek of the Roman Empire and the Greek used in the *NT. It is less pure than the classical or Attic Greek of an earlier period.

KOINONIA (Gk. "*fellowship"). Used of the local church as it is a community of *Christ in mutual sharing (2 Cor 13:4; Phil 2:1). Expressions of community vary from deep friendship to attempts to live together in a common lifestyle.

KOMVOLOGION The equivalent in the *Eastern churches of the *rosary in the Roman Catholic Church. Often used when reciting the *Jesus Prayer.

KRAEMER, HENDRIK (1888–1965). Dutch theologian. He served the *Dutch Reformed Church in Indonesia as a translator and adviser on *missions (1922–1937) and there obtained much background material for his well-known volume, *The Christian Message in a Non-Christian World,* written for the 1938 *Tambaram Conference. He was professor at Leiden from 1937 but was an internee during the German occupation of his country and thereafter was the first director of the Ecumenical Institute at Bossey (1947–1955).

KRAPF, JOHANN LUDWIG (1810–1881). *Missionary to Kenya. Born and educated in Germany, where he was briefly a Lutheran *parish minister, he served the church missionary society in Ethiopia (1838–1844) before going to Kenya. He translated the *NT into Swahili and engaged with a fellow countryman (Johannes *Rebmann) in pioneer missionary work and in exploratory travel. Ill health forced his return to Germany in 1853, but he continued translation work and paid three more short visits to Africa.

KRAUTH, CHARLES PORTERFIELD (1823–1883). American Lutheran theologian. Born in Virginia, he was ordained as a Lutheran *pastor in 1842, served several congregations under the Evangelical Lutheran General Synod, then became a professor, notably at the University of Pennsylvania. He was prominent in the movement against non-Lutheran influences in his *denomination, formulated the *Galesburg Rule, promoted a liturgical *revival in *Lutheranism, and outlined his position in *The Conservative Reformation and Its Theology* (1871).

KRUMMACHER, FRIEDRICH WILHELM (1796–1868). German *Reformed *pastor. Born in the Rhineland, he studied at Halle and Jena, was ordained, served various Reformed *pastorates, and became one of the most influential preachers of his age. A theological conservative highly regarded in Britain and the U.S., he warmly supported the *Evangelical Alliance in Germany.

KULTURKAMPF A conflict in Germany in the 1870s when nationalists became alarmed at the increasing power and claims of *Roman Catholicism. This was partly the result of *Vatican Council I's decree of papal *infallibility, partly because of local Catholic-Protestant disputes, and partly because Bismarck saw German unity in danger. Drastic legislative measures against the Roman Catholics included the expulsion of the *Jesuits, the state's domination of education, and the withdrawal of financial subsidy from the state. Diplomatic relations were broken off for some years until political discretion called for a concordat between the two sides.

KÜNG, HANS (1928–). Liberal Roman Catholic theologian. From his teaching chair on the Roman Catholic faculty at Tübingen, Küng has steadily worked to reform the traditional Roman Catholic views of apostolic succession, papal *infallibility, and the absolute normative position of *Trent. By 1975 his views had been judged too far from an acceptable position, and having refused to recant, he was deposed from his official teaching position in the church. Küng's views, though wide of Rome's contemporary conservative stance, are also wide of traditional *Protestantism as well and are far closer to liberal Protestantism than anything else.

KUYPER, ABRAHAM (1837–1920). *Dutch Reformed theologian and political leader. After some years as a *pastor, he entered politics. He formed the Anti-Revolutionary Party in 1878, attracting influential supporters by combining religious *orthodoxy and social reform. He founded the Free University of Amsterdam in 1880 and led a secession out of the established *Reformed Church in 1886. In 1901 he became prime minister in a coalition government. Even after defeat in 1905 he remained politically influential, seeing many of his reforms accomplished.

KYRIE ELEISON (Gk. "O *Lord have *mercy"). A much-used *prayer that appears in many *liturgies in its original Greek form. The response to it is another prayer, "*Christe eleison*" ("O *Christ have mercy").

KYRIOS (Gk. "*Lord"). *God's name (*Yahweh) in the *Septuagint (Gk. *OT) and the name given to the exalted *Jesus in the *NT (Phil. 2:11). He is the Lord of Lords.

L

LABADIE, JEAN DE (1610–1674). French pietist. Successively *Jesuit and French Reformed Church pastor, he founded in Middleburg, Holland, a communistic group that emphasized the Spirit's illumination in understanding *Scripture, allowed the *sacraments only to the reborn, supported themselves by manual labor, and shunned worldly contacts. Encountering great opposition, they made many unsuccessful migrations, including one to Canada. The Labadists died out soon after their leader's death.

LACORDAIRE, JEAN-BAPTISTE-HENRI (1802–1861). French preacher. Trained as a lawyer, a religious experience led him to the priesthood in 1827. Soon he joined a group including F. R. de *Lamennais in founding a journal that urged separation of church and state, but Lacordaire submitted when the pope condemned it. He became a popular preacher at Notre Dame but felt frustrated at not reaching the masses. Responsible for restoring the *Dominican *order in France, he was outspoken also in urging a republican form of government.

LACTANTIUS (c. 240–c. 320). Christian apologist. A teacher of rhetoric in Nicomedia (modern Turkey), he was converted to Christianity about 300 and resigned his post during the persecution under *Diocletian (303), on which period he wrote a valuable history. Some time later he became tutor to Crispus, son of the emperor *Constantine. Sometimes called "the Christian Cicero," his writings made wide use of pagan sources in commending the faith.

LADISLAS I (LASZLO) (1040–1095). King of Hungary. Born in exile in Poland (his mother's native country), Ladislas became king in 1077. He took the papal side in the *Investiture Controversy, acted forcefully against paganism, founded the bishopric of Zagreb, expanded his country's boundaries, was beloved by the people he ruled so wisely, and was canonized within a century of his death.

LAICIZATION The return of someone in *holy *orders (*deacon or *priest) to the status of an ordinary lay church member. The complexity of this process differs from church to church. In some (e.g., Roman Catholic) it is very difficult.

LAITY The traditional definition is all members of churches who are not *clergy, monks, or *nuns. However, in recent times many have felt that the sharp distinction between clergy and laity is unwarranted, and they prefer to speak of the laity (Gk. *laos*, people) of *God as a whole. The fundamental distinction is then between God's people (God's laity) and the rest of humanity; within God's people a secondary distinction may then be made between clergy and laity.

LAKE, KIRSOPP (1872–1946). Anglican *NT scholar and historian. After parish work in England, he taught at Leyden (1904–1913) and Harvard

(1914–1938). A versatile and prolific author, especially in NT and patristic studies, he is remembered most for *The Beginnings of Christianity* (5 vols. 1920–1933), a project he edited in association with F. J. Foakes Jackson.

LALEMANT, JEROME (1593–1673). French *Jesuit missionary to Canada. He was forty-five when he went as a missionary to the Hurons, on which work he wrote valuable accounts. Later becoming superior of the Jesuits in the region, he was highly regarded both for saintly living and inspiring leadership in a pioneering age.

LAMB, THE A *symbol of *Christ. In the *NT *Jesus is described as the Lamb of *God (John 1:29; Rev 5:12–13), and this usage has continued in *Christian *liturgies, especially in the *Eucharist, where such an image is particularly relevant. The idea is of Christ as the pure *sacrifice for the *sins of the world but who is now alive and victorious in *heaven. Also the lamb became a Christian art form (e.g., a lamb with a wound in its chest from which blood pours into the *chalice of the Eucharist).

LAMBETH ARTICLES (1595). Nine theological statements on the doctrine of *predestination produced by *Archbishop John *Whitgift and his advisers. The influential Calvinist wing of the Church of *England had considered that treatment of the subject in the *Thirty-Nine Articles needed to be supplemented, hence the Lambeth Articles asserted double predestination. *Elizabeth I refused to authorize them, but they were included in the *Irish Articles of 1615.

LAMBETH CONFERENCES Meetings of the *bishops of the *Anglican Communion usually held in London every ten years, with the *archbishop of Canterbury as chairman. The first assembly was in 1867, with seventy-six bishops attending over the four days. The 1978 gathering, held for the first time in Canterbury and lasting nearly a month, saw 440 bishops in attendance. The Lambeth Conference has no legislative powers.

LAMBETH QUADRILATERAL (1888). An Anglican statement of *faith agreed upon at the *Lambeth Conference of Anglican *bishops. It has four articles concerning Holy *Scripture, the *Apostles' and *Nicene Creeds, the two *sacraments of *baptism and *Eucharist, and the historic episcopate. It is a supplement to the *Thirty-Nine Articles.

LAMENNAIS, FÉLICITÉ ROBERT DE (1782–1854). French Roman Catholic *priest and writer. Born in Saint-Malo and ordained in 1816, he sought in his writings to link the church with political liberalism, in which quest he founded with *Lacordaire and others a short-lived journal that advocated church-state separation. When *Gregory XVI rejected its policies Lamennais lost confidence in the church as an instrument of reform, finally devoted himself to writing and politics, and was buried in a pauper's grave.

LANDMARKISM A Baptist view of the church common in the U.S. Its name is derived from a book by one of its creators, J. M. Pendleton, *An Old Landmark Reset* (1854). There is a strong emphasis on the independence of the local church and the particular claim of an unbroken succession of true Baptist churches practicing *believers' *baptism by *immersion from the apostolic age to the present.

LANFRANC (c. 1005–1089). *Archbishop of Canterbury from 1070. An Italian Benedictine who had started schools in Europe, he was an adviser to William of Normandy, after whose conquest of England he became primate. He brought order into the English churches and monasteries at a critical period and exercised when necessary a sturdy independence toward both king and *pope. His writings include a defense of the traditional view of *transubstantiation.

LANG, COSMO GORDON (1864–1945). *Archbishop of Canterbury from 1928 to 1942. Son of a Scottish

Presbyterian minister, he studied at Glasgow and Oxford, was ordained in the Church of *England (1890) and subsequently became *bishop of Stepney (1902) and archbishop of York (1908). As primate he played a controversial part in connection with the abdication of Edward VIII (1936). His last three years in office were during World War II.

LANGTON, STEPHEN (c. 1155–1228). *Archbishop of Canterbury from 1207. Born in Sussex, he studied and taught in Paris, was made *cardinal in 1206, then was named and consecrated archbishop of Canterbury by *Innocent III in 1207. The English King John's subsequent quarrel with the *pope meant that Langton could not take up office until 1213, in time to play a significant though subdued role in the signing of Magna Carta (1215). Disputes with the papacy eventually strengthened the position of the English primacy.

LANGUAGE, RELIGIOUS The words that Christians use in *worship, *prayer, and speaking of their *faith one to another. To them it is meaningful because of their confident faith that *God is alive and that he *loves them. However, philosophers find religious language rather odd (e.g., the claim is made that "God is my Father," but this does not mean the same as "Jack is my father," for there is no procreation intended in the first claim). Believers speak of God as if he is Someone we know through our five senses, but in fact he is not. Thus various explanations have been offered to this problem, the best known being *analogy. So when it is said that God is Father, the believer does not mean that God is the begetter of humankind by procreation. What he does mean is that there is a genuinely analogical relationship between God's Fatherhood and true human fatherhood. The theological basis for this claim is that God is Creator and all are made in his *image.

LAPSARIAN CONTROVERSY The debate among high Calvinists in the 17th and 18th centuries concerning a logical point in the *doctrine of *predestination. What was the order of *God's thoughts as he contemplated within *eternity his elect (yet unborn)? This type of enquiry led to various positions given such names as *supralapsarianism and *infralapsarianism.

LAPSI The name given to early Christians who lapsed from the *faith during times of persecution. Such practice was not common until the mid-third century when measures taken against the church of the emperor *Decius resulted in thousands of executions. Guided largely by *Cyprian, the church tempered its previously strict attitude with *mercy, and discipline was administered according to individual circumstances. Clerical offfenders were reduced to lay status on restoration.

LAS CASAS, BARTOLOMÉ DE (1474–1566). "The Apostle of the Indies." Born in Spain and trained in law, he went to Hispaniola in colonial service (1502), was ordained priest there (15510), and campaigned for better treatment for the oppressed Indians, in which cause he was partially successful. Briefly a *bishop in Mexico (1544–1547), he spent his last years in Spain still working and writing to improve the lot of the Indians.

LASKI, JAN (1499–1560). Polish nobleman and Protestant Reformer. Nephew of the Polish primate, he was ordained and looked set for high preferment. Travel had allowed him to meet various Reformers, however, and he subsequently left Poland and served in Western Europe as a Reformed pastor. On Thomas *Cranmer's invitation he visited England (1548), where he was later to spend two years ministering to foreign Protestants.

LAST SUPPER The last meal *Jesus ate with his *disciples before the Crucifixion and at which he instituted the *Lord's Supper (Matt 26:26ff.; Mark 14:22ff.; Luke 22:17ff.).

LAST THINGS The events that will occur at the end of this age—the *Second Coming, the *resurrection of the dead, the judgment of the nations, and the birth of the new age. The study of the last things is *eschatology.

LATERAN COUNCILS Five ecumenical councils held in the Lateran Palace in Rome between the 12th and 16th centuries. The first, in 1123, under *Callistus II, was concerned largely with detail related to the recently-ended *Investiture Controversy. The second, in 1139, under Innocent II, condemned various heresies, confirmed Innocent as valid *pope against a rival, and pronounced clerical marriages illegal. The third, in 1179, under *Alexander III, laid down regulations for papal elections, established cathedral schools, and declared against the *Albigensians. The fourth, in 1215, under *Innocent III, brought together an impressive array of church and state dignataries. It was concerned with church reform, the definition of *transubstantiation, annual confession, *Easter *Communion, recovery of the Holy Land, and condemnation of heretics. The fifth, in 1512–1517 under *Julius II, called as a riposte to the Council of *Pisa, was concerned with church reform and international peacemaking, and it rejected the view that councils were superior to the pope.

LATIMER, HUGH (c. 1485–1555). English Protestant *martyr and *bishop of Worcester. Ordained in 1522, his Lutheran sympathies soon emerged, and after *Henry VIII's break with Rome (1534), Latimer became a royal adviser. As bishop from 1535 he denounced social injustices and Roman teaching on *purgatory and *images but resigned his see in 1539 when Henry showed disapproval of the *Reformed teaching. Twice imprisoned, Latimer became a court preacher under *Edward VI, but under Mary *Tudor he was condemned for repudiating Roman doctrine. Led to the stake at Oxford with Nicholas *Ridley, Latimer encouraged his friend with the immortal words: "Be of good comfort Master Ridley, and play the man. We shall this day light such a candle by God's *grace in England, as I trust shall never be put out."

LATIN CHURCH That part of the universal church that has traditionally used the Latin language and that is subject to the *pope in Rome. Sometimes, however, the expression is used to contrast the Western church and the *Eastern church so that Latin is a synonym for Western. When so used, all the continuations of the medieval church are intended (e.g., Swiss Protestant, German Lutheran, Scandinavian Lutheran, and English Anglican).

LATITUDINARIANISM An approach to *theology that allows a latitude of interpretation in *doctrine, ecclesiastical organization, and forms of *worship. It is an antidogmatic approach to *Christianity. Those who hold it may be called *broad church or broad churchmen.

LATOURETTE, KENNETH SCOTT (1884–1968). Church historian. Born into a Baptist family in Oregon, he graduated from Yale, worked for the Student Volunteer Movement, then taught in China until he fell ill and had to return home in 1912. Later he taught at Yale (1921–1953), encouraged the work of *evangelism, and produced a series of remarkably useful works on history and *missions, including *History of the Expansion of Christianity* (7 vols., 1937–1945).

LATRIA (Lat. "*worship," from Gk. *latreia*). Used to describe the particular *worship and *adoration offered to *God alone. It is an interior reverence and submission to God as the *Lord. Thus it is to be distinguished from *hyperdulia (*veneration offered to *Mary) and *dulia (honor paid to the *saints).

LATTER RAIN MOVEMENT *Pentecostal movement of the mid-twentieth century that became an important component in the post–World War II evangelical awakening and a catalyst for the *charismatic movement of the 1960s and 1970s. The movement was characterized by many reports of healing and other miraculous phenomena, which had been absent in the preceding decade. It stressed the imminent return of Christ, which would be preceded by an outpouring of the Holy Spirit (the "latter rain" of Joel 2:28 KJV). In many ways the Latter Rain Movement paralleled the early Pentecostal movement that originated in the *Azusa Street Revival.

LATTER-DAY SAINTS See MORMONISM.

LAUBACH, FRANK CHARLES (1884–1970). American Congregational *missionary and "*apostle of literacy." Born in Pennsylvania, he was ordained in 1914 and went to work in the Philippines for nearly forty years, developing his "each one teach one" Laubach Method in literacy. He wrote extensively in that field and also produced devotional works.

LAUD, WILLIAM (1573–1645). *Archbishop of Canterbury from 1633. An early champion of *Anglo-Catholicism, he rejected Rome's claims and held that the Church of *England was in the *apostolic succession. Initially supported by *Charles I, Laud went too far in his views on the *divine right of kings, in his repressive measures against Romans and Puritans, and in his attempt to enforce *ritualism on Scotland. With dubious legality he was executed for treason. He was an enthusiastic patron of learning.

LAUSANNE CONFERENCE (1927). A conference organized by the *Faith and Order Movement for the purpose of discussing church unity and kindred topics. Some ninety Protestant churches were represented, as were several branches of Eastern Orthodoxy (notably not the Russian). Under the chairmanship of C. H. *Brent, the meeting was a significant step toward the formation of a world council of churches.

LAUSANNE CONGRESS ON WORLD EVANGELIZATION (1974). An assembly called by an international group of *evangelical leaders, with Billy *Graham as honorary chairman. With nearly three thousand participants from 150 countries, the congress discussed the biblical principles and the practical outworking of world evangelization, issued the *Lausanne Covenant, which has been warmly welcomed by the church worldwide, and set up a continuation committee "to further the total biblical *mission of the Church." The official conference volume was *Let the Earth Hear His Voice* (1975).

LAUSANNE COVENANT A binding contract and commitment to world evangelization agreed upon by the International Congress on World Evangelization at Lausanne, Switzerland, July 16–25, 1974. It is distinctly *evangelical in tone, affirming the *inspiration of the *Bible, the *deity and universality of *Christ, and other basic *doctrines. *Evangelism is defined, and alongside it is placed social responsibility. The existence of *parachurch agencies is not taken for granted, but they are called to self-examination. The necessity of the church in *God's purposes is affirmed, and its need to be related to the *culture in which it is found is emphasized. This *covenant represents one of the most important statements of *faith produced within evangelicalism in recent times.

LAVIGERIE, CHARLES-MARTIAL-ALLEMAND (1825–1892). French *archbishop and founder of the *White Fathers. Ordained in 1849 and consecrated *bishop of Nancy in 1863, he went to Algiers as archbishop in 1867 and subsequently became *primate of Africa and archbishop of Carthage. A man of vision and tireless energy, he founded the White Fathers in 1868, encouraged their outreach to equatorial Africa, and later crusaded against the slave traffic.

LAW, WILLIAM (1686–1761). Anglican religious writer. Deprived of a fellowship at Cambridge for refusing to take the *oath of allegiance to George I, Law later devoted his time to charitable and literary work. Author of several Puritan publications, including the classic *A Serious Call to a Devout* *and Holy Life* (1728), he was greatly influenced by the German mystic, Jacob *Boehme.

LAW AND GOSPEL The two principal ways in which *God relates to humankind. In the law God's *will is revealed in terms of commandments; in the *gospel God's will is revealed in terms of his free gift of *salvation in *Christ. One shows what men are to do for God; the other shows what God has done for men. One demands *perfection and pronounces judgment, while the other offers *assurance and *pardon. This distinction is made with greatest emphasis in Lutheran *theology and is found in the Formula of *Concord (1577).

LAW OF GOD The *will of *God expressed in commandments of a positive and negative kind. This includes the requirement to *love God and neighbor (Mark 12:29ff.), the need to keep the *Ten Commandments (Exod 20), and the acceptance of the fulfillment of the law as provided by *Jesus (Matt 5–7; John 13:34; 15:12–13). Since *Christ fulfilled the law for his people, he is the end of the law for them (Rom 10:4). Thus they obey him (and thus the law) not to earn *salvation but out of gratitude and love for him.

LAWRENCE, BROTHER. See BROTHER LAWRENCE.

LAWRENCE OF THE RESURRECTION. See BROTHER LAWRENCE.

LAWS, ROBERT (1851–1934). Scottish *missionary to Central Africa. Born in Aberdeen and early resolved to follow in David *Livingstone's footsteps, he was ordained in 1875 and joined a *Free Church of Scotland expedition charged to found a *mission in Central Africa to be named Livingstonia. In charge from 1877, Laws planned a series of mission stations at strategic lakeside and interior sites. When he left Africa in 1927 there were over seven hundred primary schools, facilities for further education, and a Christian community of 60,000 with thirteen ordained African pastors. He served on the legislative council of Nyasaland (now Malawi).

LAY INVESTITURE See INVESTITURE CONTROVERSY.

LAYING ON OF HANDS The placing of the hands of one or more persons on the head of another person. It occurs in services of *healing, *confirmation, *exorcism, and *ordination. The practice may be traced to the *OT (Num 27:18) and to the *NT (Acts 6:1–6; 8:15–17). The symbolism varies according to the purpose of the *act (e.g., in ordination there is the idea of transmission of authority).

LAYNEZ, JAMES (1512–1565). *Jesuit general and theologian. Born Diego Lainez in Spain, he was one of *Ignatius of Loyola's colleagues in Paris founding the Society of Jesus, and succeeded him as general in 1558. A leading theologian of the *Counter-Reformation and one of Rome's most able and uncompromising champions, he took a prominent part at the Council of *Trent.

LAZARISTS See VINCENTIANS.

LECLERC, JEAN (1657–1736). French Protestant theologian. Formerly Calvinist, he renounced this view for that of *Arminianism, became professor in the Remonstrant College, Amsterdam, and opposed all forms of dogmatism. An extreme biblical critic, he denied the Mosaic authorship of the *Pentateuch, wrote a series of commentaries, and edited three influential encyclopedias.

LECTIONARY An ordered system of selected readings from the *Bible appointed for use in services of *worship throughout the ecclesiastical year. Different churches have different lectionaries, and some churches have several.

LEE, ANN (1736–1784). Founder of the *Shakers in America. Born in Manchester, she joined in 1758 the "Shaking Quakers," and in 1774 she sought freedom from persecution by emigrating to New York State with her husband and a small group. Though abandoned by her husband soon after, the so-called "Mother Ann" saw her movement grow. She stressed *pacifism, communistic living, *celibacy, and *spiritual healing and claimed to have been guided by visions.

LEFEBVRE, MARCEL (1906–). Roman Catholic archbishop. Instigator of the first split within the Roman Catholic Church since the *Old Catholic Church was founded in protest over the doctrine of *infallibility in 1870. He and his followers uphold the anti-Modernism of *Pius X and reject the renewal of Catholic life and *liturgy begun by *Vatican II (1962–1965). He founded the St. *Pius X Fraternity in 1970 in Econe, Switzerland, which has trained *priests in line with Pius X's condemnation of *modernism in 1907. Though Pope *Paul VI deprived him of his priestly role, he has ordained more than two hundred priests since 1976.

LEGALISM A relationship that is governed primarily by rules or by law. It is used in *ethics (a person's relationship to another is governed by rules) and in *theology (a person's relationship to *God is governed by law). Legalism can lead to the negation of *compassion and *love.

LEGATE See NUNCIO AND LEGATE, PAPAL.

LEIBNITZ, GOTTFRIED WILHELM (1646–1716). German rationalist philosopher and mathematician. Liebnitz was probably the most brilliant German thinker of the 17th century and is best remembered in religious studies for his defense of *God in *Theodic* (1710), inventing the term. He is also known for his attempt to go beyond *Newton's mechanistic views, *Descartes's *dualism, and Spinoza's *pantheism, with his own view of monads, which postulated an atomic theory with an underlying metaphysical realm consisting of spiritual entities (monads) structured in a preestablished harmony (*Monadology*, 1720). His view that we live in the best of all possible worlds was caricatured by Voltaire in his *Candide*.

LEIGHTON, ROBERT (1611–1684). *Archbishop of Glasgow. Minister of Newbattle from 1641, he became principal of Edinburgh University in 1653 and *bishop of Dunblane in 1661 under the restored *episcopacy in Scotland. He was a saintly and scholarly man who sought to bring peace to church squabbles and never quite understood either the cause of the *Covenanters or the persecution against them. He became archbishop reluctantly in 1670 but withdrew disillusioned to England in 1674. His commentary on 1 Peter is still regarded as a classic.

LEIPZIG, DISPUTATION OF (1519). A debate on *Reformation issues involving Johann *Eck, *Karlstadt, and Martin *Luther. Extending over some eighteen days, it highlighted the real issues and differences between Rome and *Protestantism. On the matter of ecclesiastical authority, Luther gave ammunition to his opponents by conceding that church councils had in fact been in error.

LENT The period of forty days from *Ash Wednesday until Holy Saturday. As a preparation for *Easter, the celebration of the *Resurrection, it has traditionally been a period for *fasting, self-examination, and extra compassionate activities.

LEO I (THE GREAT) (d. 461). Pope from 440. During his reign the primacy of the *bishop of Rome was forcefully asserted and extended also in the East. This was seen notably at the Council of *Chalcedon (451), when the so-called Tome of Leo was declared to be definitive on the *nature of *Christ. Many of Leo's letters and *sermons have survived.

LEO III (THE ISAURIAN) (c. 680–741). *Byzantine emperor from 717. A successful soldier, he used the Arabs to help him seize the throne but then discarded and defeated them when he achieved that aim. Decisive in religious policies, he had Jews and Montanists forcibly baptized, and by banning the use of *images in public *worship he initiated the *Iconclastic Controversy, for opposition to which he took strong measures against the *papacy.

LEO III (d. 816). Pope from 795. Under pressure from fellow Romans, he enlisted the aid of *Charlemagne, whom he crowned as emperor in Rome on *Christmas Day, 800. This was an opportunistic gesture and one of dubious legality, especially in the eyes of Eastern Christendom. That attempt to enchance the *papacy was prudently offset by some concessions to the Greeks. While he lived at peace with the strong-minded emperor, Leo never solved his domestic problems and finally had some of his enemies executed.

LEO IX (1002–1054). Pope from 1049. Born in Alsace, he became *bishop of Toul (France) in 1026, and in 1048 he was nominated as pope by the reforming emperor *Henry III. Leo stipulated, however, that the *clergy and people of Rome should agree—and they did. He gathered around him a number of able men who helped him in carrying out reforms and in changing the *papacy from a local institution into an international power. It was ironic, then, that it was during the reign of such an able *pontiff that an ill-judged action in Sicily (the excommunication of Patriarch Michael *Cerularius), should have outraged the *Eastern church and led to the *Great Schism in 1054.

LEO X (1475–1521). Pope from 1513. Born into the famous de' Medici family in Florence, he became a *cardinal at sixteen and pope at thirty-seven. A typical *Renaissance pope accustomed to living in great style, he continued the sale of *indulgences (a fruitful source of revenue), underestimated *Luther's protest against the practice, and so helped open the door to the *Reformation.

LEO XIII (1810–1903). Pope from 1878. Elected after long experience in the *Vatican diplomatic service and as a *bishop of Perugia, he was forced into policies of political reconciliation and compromise that his predecessor *Pius IX would have abhorred. Toward France particularly he made overtures, but he insisted on the independence of the church. Sometimes called the working man's pope, with advanced views on industrial relations, Leo welcomed historians into the Vatican archives. He also made normative the teaching of *Aquinas.

LEONARDO DA VINCI See Vinci, Leonardo da.

LEONTIUS OF BYZANTIUM (c. 485–c. 543). *Byzantine monk and theologian. Little is known about his life, but from his works he is seen to have been a staunch upholder of *orthodoxy against *Monophysitism, in accordance with declarations made at the councils of *Ephesus (431) and *Chalcedon (451).

LEWIS, CLIVE STAPLES (1898–1963). Christian apologist. Born in Belfast, he served in World War I, distinguished himself as a student, classical scholar, and teacher at Oxford (1918–1954). Later he was professor of medieval and *Renaissance English at Cambridge (1954–1963). Best know for his *Screwtape Letters* (1942), his writings ranged from children's stories to Christian *apologetics and from religious *allegories to the autobiographical *Surprised by Joy*. Lewis often caught attention through coming at matters of *faith from unusual angles; it was said of him that he made *righteousness readable.

LEX ORANDI, LEX CREDENDI (Lat. "the rule of *prayer is the rule of *faith"). The church that is engaged in true prayer and *worship will not be a church that falsifies its God-given faith. Thus true faith is to be found in the context of worship and prayer.

LIBERAL THEOLOGY, LIBERALISM A form of *theology that flourished in the Western church from the mid-19th to the early 20th century. Found primarily in *Protestantism, it also had supporters in *Roman Catholicism. The key themes were freedom and progress—freedom from old *dogmas and freedom to investigate new ideas, progress in collaboration with the new confident sciences. Important thinkers who set the stage for this type of theology were F. D. E. *Schleiermacher (1768–1834) and Albrecht *Ritschl (1822–1889). The result was a theology that had few points of contact left with the traditional view of the *Bible and *Christian *faith. Two world *wars and the massive influence of Karl *Barth caused the demise of the old liberal theology as a major movement. It still lives on in a new dress in modern forms of theology that deny the *deity of *Jesus Christ and allow belief only in what is said to be rational.

LIBERATION THEOLOGY A modern, essentially Latin American way of stating the relationship of *God—*Savior and Redeemer—to his world. It is both reactionary—against traditional Roman Catholic *theology, which appeared to support the status quo—and revolutionary—offering new ways of understanding what *salvation in the real world means. It is *doctrine that is inspired by a certain German *political theology but that has its roots in the context of *ministry to the millions of poor people who live in the cities of Central and South America. It is a theological cry that God is concerned with the whole person and the whole society. It calls for a salvation that is meaningful to the *poor and needy, here and now. Throughout the 1960s and 1970s this theology has not been static, and as it gains more adherents it is changing and developing in its understanding of salvation and its plans to bring salvation (liberation) to the poor.

LIBERIUS (d. 366). Pope from 352. His *pontificate was marked by the controversy over the rise of *Arianism, wherein he upheld the orthodox *Athanasius against the Arian tendencies of emperor Constantius II. The latter sent Liberius into exile in Greece and installed an *antipope as Felix II, but after Liberius had made some concessions (the details of which are unknown) he returned to Rome in 358 when Constantius decreed that he co-rule with Felix. After Constantius died in 361 Liberius reasserted that the Nicene faith was still the test of orthodoxy.

LIBERTY, CHRISTIAN See Freedom, Christian.

LIBERTY, RELIGIOUS The right to hold and practice a specific *religion and the right to change that belief and observance. It is included in the Universal Declaration of Human Rights of the United Nations. The church has held different views of religious liberty during its history. At first it desired the right to exist as an accepted religion. When it became the dominant religion in the Roman Empire it often persecuted minorities. The Protestant *Reformation led to Protestants and Roman Catholics persecuting one another. Religious liberty in most European countries and in North America came slowly, and though technically guaranteed in communist countries, it hardly exists in practice.

LICENTIATE In *Presbyterianism, one who is fully trained, licensed to preach the *gospel by a *presbytery but is not yet ordained to the ministry. Under normal circumstances *ordination follows after a probationary period, but some devote themselves to other forms of Christian service while retaining the status of licentiate. As such, however, they are not permitted to administer the *sacraments.

LIDDELL, ERIC (1902–1945). Scottish athlete and *missionary to China. An all-around sportsman, he became an Olympic champion and world record-breaker and would have won more laurels had he not steadfastly refused to run on *Sunday. He returned to China (he had been born there) in 1925, worked at Tientsin until interned by the Japanese in 1942, continued his witness in prison camp, and died there of a brain tumor at the end of the *war.

LIDDON, HENRY PARRY (1829–1890). Anglican theologian. Born in Hampshire, he graduated from Oxford, was ordained in 1852, and from 1870 held simultaneously a theological chair at Oxford and a canonry of St. Paul's Cathedral, London. From these strategic posts he warmly supported the *Oxford Movement and was a friend and biographer of E. B. *Pusey. Later in life he traveled extensively and promoted contact with the *Old Catholic and *Eastern Orthodox churches.

LIFE AND WORK That section of the *ecumenical movement concerned with Christianity's relation to the contemporary world. It organized conferences at Stockholm in 1925 and at Oxford in 1937 and became the responsibility of the *World Council of Churches from 1948.

LIGHTFOOT, JOHN (1602–1675). English clergyman and biblical scholar. A Cambridge graduate ordained in the Church of *England, he supported the parliamentary forces in the Civil War and was a member of the *Westminster Assembly. He returned to Cambridge in 1650 as master of Catharine Hall and became university vice-chancellor in 1654. All the time he was producing erudite works of Old Testament and Jewish studies, notably *Horae Hebraicae et Talmudicae* (6 vols., 1658–1678).

LIGHTFOOT, JOSEPH BARBER (1828–1889). *Bishop of Durham and biblical scholar. Professor at Cambridge (1861–1879) before *consecration, he was a popular lecturer and preacher and an industrious and far-sighted bishop. His best-known books are his commentaries on Galatians (1865), Philippians (1868), and *Colossians with Philemon* (1875). He was also an accomplished *patristics scholar, producing works on *Clement of Rome (1869) and *Ignatius (1885).

LIGHTFOOT, ROBERT HENRY (1883–1953). Anglican biblical scholar. Oxford graduate, he spent most of his working life there, notably as professor of the *exegesis of Holy *Scripture (1934–1949). His 1934 Bampton Lectures, published as *History and Interpretation in the Gospels* (1935), reflected his indebtedness to German radical theology. He edited the influential *Journal of Theological Studies* (1941–1953).

LILJE, JOHANNES ERNST RICHARD (1899–1977). German Lutheran *bishop. Born in Hanover, he was ordained in 1926 and suffered a year's imprisonment for opposition to the Nazi supremacy. Later, because of his links with a group that was planning to assassinate Hitler, he was sentenced to death but was saved by the advancing Allied Forces "and the *grace of God." A noted linguist and writer, Lilje was understanding about *Christian leaders in communist countries where lines were not easily drawn, holding that even a totalitarian state has its authority from God. He was president of the Lutheran World Federation (1952–1957) and presiding bishop of the United Evangelical Lutheran Church of Germany (1955–1969).

LIMBO (Lat. *limbus*, "border, edge"). There are two kinds: (1) The limbo of the *fathers is the concept of the waiting place or condition in which the *righteous who had died before the death of *Christ remained until he opened the gates of *heaven to them. (2) The limbo of infants is the concept of the permanent state of those who die in *original *sin (unbaptized) but who are innocent of personal *guilt. They are neither in *heaven nor in *hell. This topic was much discussed in the medieval church.

LIMITED ATONEMENT Also called particular redemption. The view that the *Atonement was restricted to those whom *God, before Creation, specially chose for *salvation; *Christ died for the elect, not for the whole world.

LINDSAY, THOMAS MARTIN (1843–1914). Scottish church historian. Professor (1872) and principal (1902) of the Free Church College, Glasgow, he was an unsuccessful defender of W. Robertson *Smith in the *general assembly (1877–1881). Lindsay was a contributor to the *Cambridge Modern History* and, like

Smith, to the *Encyclopaedia Britannica*. Two of his highly regarded works are *Luther and the German Reformation*, and *A History of the Reformation in Europe* (2 vols., 1906–1907).

LITANY (Gk. *litaneia*, "a supplication"). A form of public *prayer used in *worship. A leader says or sings a series of petitions, and the congregation replies with set responses.

LITURGICAL MOVEMENT A reforming and renewing movement since 1903 (when Pius X instituted a new breviary) to make the *liturgy more meaningful for the congregation. The aim is to involve the people in an intelligent way in the act of *worship and to get away from the position of the congregation being onlookers on a drama acted out by the *priest and his helpers. The movement began in *Roman Catholicism, especially following *Vatican II, but has affected other churches as well. Perhaps the most obvious ways in which the effect of the movement is seen is in the giving of the kiss of peace (the *pax) and in the arrival of new forms of services in churches that have used the same ones for centuries.

LITURGY The written and prescribed services of *worship in a church and usually printed in a service book. The chief of these is the *Eucharist; in the *Eastern churches, liturgy is sometimes reserved for the Eucharistic service alone. Not a few Protestants have objected to liturgy, for they have felt that a set form of words does not allow for the leading of the *Spirit and may well quench the Spirit. In defense those who use liturgy have claimed that it is better to have a set form of excellent words than to rely on the uncertain and unpredictable words of a preacher each week.

LIVINGSTONE, DAVID (1813–1873). Scottish *missionary and explorer. A former mill worker who studied Greek, theology, and medicine at Glasgow, he went to South Africa in 1840. He preached against white exploitation of blacks, criticized the concentration of missionaries in more developed areas, and urged greater use of indigenous workers. He moved ever further north and found himself *evangelist, doctor, teacher, builder, and gardener. He embarked on long journeys, preparing scientific reports and studying languages. His address at Cambridge in 1857 led to the founding of the Universities' Mission to Central Africa. He discovered the Victoria Falls and raised such an outcry against slave trading that his expedition was recalled. He dropped from sight and was found in 1871 by H. M. Stanley of the *New York Herald*. When Livingstone died, his native assistants bore his body fifteen hundred miles to the coast, and one of them was among the huge crowd at the subsequent funeral in Westminster Abbey.

LLOYD-JONES, DAVID MARTYN (1900–1981). Minister and author. Regarded by some as the greatest *Bible expositor in the English-speaking world, he wrote numerous books and ministered at Westminster Chapel, London (1938–1968).

LOCI THEOLOGICI (Lat. "fundamental theological *truths"). Used by Lutheran theologians of the major headings in a system of *theology but also used of a book on theology.

LOEHE, JOHANNES KONRAD WILHELM (1808–1872). Lutheran theologian and philanthropist. Born in Germany, he served pastorates there, and in 1841 founded a *mission society to train pastors to serve Germans overseas. By 1853 settlements had been established in Michigan and Iowa, and some of those sent by Loehe formed the Lutheran Church, Missouri Synod. He also engaged in home missions work and in social, medical, and educational welfare.

LOGIC The study of the structure and principles of reasoning or of sound argument. Thus it has great relevance to the *Christian apologist and theologian.

LOGICAL POSITIVISM One form of modern philosophy developed by the

Vienna circle of thinkers in the 1920s. It posed a threat to *Christianity by its insistence that metaphysical statements are nonsensical for they cannot be verified. Because much of the language of *faith is about *God (and thus above and beyond nature), there is no means of verifying it. From it developed logical *empiricism, which accepts that each area of life has its own language; and thus it asks what is the logic of the language of *religion.

LOGOS (Gk. "word, reason"). Used by John to describe the Second *Person of the *Trinity in the prologue of his *Gospel (1:1ff.). The word was much in use in contemporary Stoic philosophy and referred to the universal "*mind" and "*reason" that gave coherence to the *universe. It had also been used in the Greek *OT of the *wisdom of *God, a wisdom that is sometimes personified (Prov 8:22ff.). It is not clear whether John was relying on Greek or Hebrew thought, but whatever his source, he was presenting the *eternal Son of *God in a way that would have meaning to both educated Greeks (Gentiles) and Hellenistic Jews. Thus it is not surprising that the word *Logos* was much used by the Greek theologians of the church in their efforts to understand and state the *doctrine of the *Incarnation. The only satisfactory way to translate it into English is "Word," and this is used by most translations of John 1.

LOGOS SPERMATIKOS (Gk. "the germinal word"). The *reason possessed by each human being is a means of uniting him to *God when he does not possess special *revelation. Used by Justin *Martyr (c. 100–c. 165) to suggest that some men before *Christ truly knew *God.

LOISY, ALFRED FIRMIN (1857–1940). Usually considered the father of Roman Catholic *modernism in France. Ordained in 1879, he taught Hebrew and *OT, but his radical approach to * Scripture and his increasing uneasiness with Roman Catholic *dogma made him suspect in orthodox circles and finally led to his *excommunication in 1908. He became professor of the history of *religions at the Collège de France (1909–1930), and in his many writings he cast doubt on the historicity of the *Gospels.

LOLLARDS A term applied originally to followers of John *Wycliffe. The word is said to have derived from an old Dutch word meaning "mumbler." The Lollards originated in Oxford about 1380. They questioned the office of the *papacy, denied transubstantiation, and urged the importance of *preaching and the primacy of * Scripture. The movement spread to other places despite repressive action by church authorities, and Norfolk *priest William *Sawtrey was, in 1401, the movement's first *martyr. An uprising under Sir John *Oldcastle in 1414 was suppressed, and those involved were harshly dealt with. The movement was thereafter fairly quiescent until the start of the following century, and subsequently it merged in the new Protestant movement.

LOMBARD, PETER (c. 1100–1160). *Bishop of Paris and theologian. Born in Italy, he studied in France and then taught in the Notre Dame school in Paris (1148–1150). Bishop of Paris from the year before his death, he is best known for his *Book of Sentences* (1148–1150), a collection of the teachings of church *fathers and later scholars. Its four volumes cover the whole range of *Christian *doctrines and were for long regarded as a standard work.

LORD The name of *God. When printed as Lord in most translations of the *OT it is rendering the Hebrew *adonai* (e.g., Exod 4:10). However, when printed as LORD, it represents the Hebrew *Tetragrammaton YHWH (e.g., Exod 3:15). It is used in the *NT (translating **kyrios*) of the *God of *Israel (e.g., Matt 1:20, 22, 24) and of the exalted *Jesus (Acts 2:36; Rom 10:9). Thus in *Christian usage it may refer to God in general or Jesus in particular.

LORD HIGH COMMISSIONER The monarch's representative at the Church of *Scotland *general assembly. Addressing the assembly by invitation, he traditionally assures it of the sovereign's intention to maintain *presbyterian church government in Scotland. In his official capacity he is not a member of the assembly and does not participate in its debates unless (as sometimes happens) he is also a *kirk *elder duly appointed as a commissioner by his home *presbytery.

LORD'S DAY, THE The first day of the week on which Christians *worship. It is the Lord's Day because *Jesus, the *Lord, arose from death on the first day (Rev 1:10).

LORD'S PRAYER, THE The form of words that *Jesus gave to his *disciples to teach them how to pray (Matt 6:9ff.; Luke 11:2ff.).

LORD'S SUPPER, THE The name of the *Eucharist used most by Protestants and taken from 1 Corinthians 11:20.

LOUIS IX (ST. LOUIS) (1214–1270). King of France. A pious man of austere lifestyle and given to good works and the impartial dispensing of justice, he was considered the personification of a *Christian monarch. During his long reign (he acceded at thirteen) he dealt firmly with rebellion, led one crusade during which he was captured and held for ransom, but undaunted led another during which he died of fever near Tunis.

LOUIS XIV (1638–1715). King of France. He was four years old at the time of his accession, and power was therefore in the hands of Jules *Mazarin, prime minister and *cardinal, who sustained his position against the rebellious French nobility and others until his death in 1661. The insecurity of those early years Louis never forgot; it undoubtedly encouraged his view of absolute monarchy by divine right, a role he sustained unflaggingly for fifty-four years. French Protestants, resisting forcible *conversion, were savagely suppressed, and many of France's ablest citizens were for conscience' sake driven into exile during his reign.

LOUIS THE PIOUS (778–840). Frankish emperor. Son of *Charlemagne and appointed by him king of Aquitaine in 781 and coemperor in 813, he became sole ruler in 814 and divided the empire among his sons, thus beginning a turbulent period in its history. Louis encouraged *Anskar and others in *missionary outreach and sponsored monastic reform.

LOVE An essential characteristic of *God's *nature (1 John 4:8, 16). The primary Greek word is *agape,* which is a word *Christianity made particularly its own; it means pure, *holy love flowing toward those who deserve no love. From God's love for his people, *Christian love for others and for God is derived (1 John 4:19; Rom 5:5). Paul provides a description of love in action in the believer's life in 1 Corinthians 13:4ff.: "Love is patient and kind; love is not jealous or boastful; it is not arrogant or rude; it is not irritable or resentful; it does not rejoice at wrong, but rejoices in the right. Love bears all things, believes all things, hopes all things, endures all things."

LOW CHURCH A description used especially in *Anglicanism of a way of *worship and an attitude in *theology that takes a low view of the usefulness of *ritual, the *sacraments, and historical tradition. At different times both Latitudinarians and *Evangelicals have been called Low Church.

LOW MASS See HIGH MASS.

LOWER CRITICISM The scholarly work on the *Bible that attempts to produce from the manuscripts available the best text of the Bible in the original languages. See CRITICISM, BIBLICAL.

LUCAR (LUCARIS), CYRIL (1572–1638). *Patriarch of Constantinople. Born in Crete, he studied at European universities and was particularly impressed by the work of John *Calvin. He served the *Orthodox Church in Poland and later became patriarch first of Alexandria (1602), then of Constantinople (1620). His attempts to introduce Protestant *theology and reforms drove him from office five times, and it was the Ottoman Turk authorities who had him restored each time. It was they, however, who had him strangled for supposedly stirring up dissension against them. Lucar is remembered also for having sent the famous *Codex Alexandrinus to *Archbishop *Abbot of Canterbury about 1625.

LUCIAN OF ANTIOCH (c. 240–312). *Christian theologian and *martyr. Born in Samosata (Turkey), he became head of the theological school at Antioch, where he stressed the literal sense of *Scripture in contrast to the allegorical interpretations popularized by *Origen in Alexandria. Such was his view of the *doctrine of *Christ that he was been regarded as the father of *Arianism. A saintly man, Lucian produced revisions of the *Septuagint and the *Gospels. He was tortured and martyred at Nicomedia for refusing to eat meat offered to idols.

LUCIFER (Lat. "light-bearer"). Another name for *Satan. In the Latin of Isaiah 14:12 the "Day Star" is rendered as Lucifer. This was taken to mean the *Devil/Satan, and this meaning has passed into general usage.

LULL, RAMON (c. 1235–1316). *Franciscan *missionary, scholar, and mystic. He served *James I of Aragon until converted at thirty, when he became a *Franciscan and dedicated his life to reaching Muslims. He learned Arabic and traveled widely, arguing the case for *Christianity. He held that its mysteries could be rationally explained (a view that was later to be condemned by *Gregory XI). He was reportedly stoned to death by Muslims in Tunisia, but the authenticity of this account has been questioned.

LUND CONFERENCE (1952). Convened by the *World Council of Church's *Faith and Order commission, it followed up topics cited at the 1937 Edinburgh Conference, notably "The Church, Ways of Worship and Intercommunion." The two-week conference in the Swedish university town brought 225 delegates from 114 countries and included Roman Catholic observers.

LUNETTE, LUNA (Lat. "moon"). A circular receptacle with glass sides to hold the consecrated bread (*host) upright in the *monstrance.

LUTHARDT, CHRISTOPH ERNST (1823–1902). Lutheran scholar. He taught *theology at Marburg and Leipzig and produced works that defended *Christianity against the claims of modern natural science. As president of the Leipzig Mission Society he resisted when Saxon religious institutions were threatened in measures that aimed toward the unification of Germany.

LUTHER, MARTIN (1483–1546). Leader of the *Reformation in Germany. Son of a Saxon miner, he graduated in arts at Erfurt, then in 1505 forsook further studies in law to become an *Augustinian. He was ordained in 1507, and from 1508 taught theology at Wittenberg. There his lectures began to reflect his growing belief that *justification by *faith rather than by *works expressed the church's true faith. He grew increasingly uneasy about the sale of papal *indulgences as a means of boosting church revenue, but his demand for a theological examination of the practice brought only a trial for *heresy. Others who saw the need for reforms in *Roman Catholicism gathered around him and protested that the *gospel of *Jesus Christ had become obscured in the church by worldly accretions. Excommunicated by the *pope and outlawed by the emperor, Luther nonetheless found powerful protectors and sympathizers, and soon the cause of the Reformation was irreversible. Luther rejected on one hand various kinds of religious extremists within *Protestantism, and on the other such humanists as *Erasmus, who sought reform from within the old church. Luther's fear of anarchy led him to side with authority against the *Peasants' Revolt in 1525, an action that alienated some of the common people. And he differed also with the Swiss Reformer Ulrich *Zwingli over the meaning of the *Lord's Supper. Luther was a prolific writer, issuing pamphlets to combat the *evils of the time and doctrinal works that would set Protestantism on a sound theological foundation. His greatness can be seen, suggests one scholar, in that more books have been written about him than about anyone else in history except Jesus of Nazareth.

LUTHERAN CHURCH–MISSOURI SYNOD Church founded by German emigrants in 1847 under the name German Evangelical Lutheran Synod of Missouri, Ohio, and Other States. It requires strict adherence to the *Bible as interpreted by the Book of *Concord, the three ecumenical *creeds, and the six Lutheran *confessions. Recent years have been bitter controversy over the issue of the Bible's infallibility. Currently it has more than 1.9 million members in almost 6,000 churches.

LUTHERANISM The *doctrines and practice of those churches that take their name from Martin *Luther, the Reformer. Either they originated in the 16th century or they are developments from or separations from churches that began in the 16th century. They are found in Germany (where they are known as *Evangelical), in Scandinavia (where they have *dioceses and *bishops), and in the U.S. A major merger occurred in 1987 when three American Lutheran groups—the American Lutheran Church, the Lutheran Church in America, and the American Evangelical Lutheran Church—merged to form the Evangelical Lutheran Church in America. Another major Lutheran *denomination is the Lutheran Church, Missouri Synod. From the European and American churches other Lutheran churches have been planted throughout the world. The Lutheran World Federation seeks to cultivate unity in Lutheranism. Lutherans are known for their great emphasis on *justification by *faith and their particular way of stating the relation of *law and *gospel. See also AUGSBURG, CONFESSION of; FORMULA OF CONCORD.

LUWUM, JANANI (1922–1977). *Archbishop of Uganda, Rwanda, Burundi, and Boga-Zaire. Born the son of a church teacher in East Acholi, bordering on Sudan, he was converted in 1948 and ordained in 1956 as an Anglican priest. After independence in 1962, Uganda relapsed into dictatorship, and Luwum, who was to become *bishop of Northern Uganda, became a champion of human rights amid tyranny and intertribal warfare. He was elected archbishop in 1974, but such a man could not long survive under President Idi Amin, and he was murdered in 1977 after having been arrested on a false charge.

LUX MUNDI A book published in 1889, edited by Charles *Gore and purporting to be "A Series of Studies in the Religion of the Incarnation." It was in part a reaction against the alleged shallowness of the *Oxford Movement, and it set out to "put the Catholic *faith into its right relation to modern intellectual and moral problems." In doing so, however, the conservatives were upset, not least by Gore's own liberal approach to the *OT.

LYONS, COUNCILS OF Two general church councils were held in the French city. The first was convened in 1245 by *Innocent IV, much of whose *pontificate was taken up by a battle with the emperor *Frederick II. This council, attended largely by western European *bishops, declared Frederick deposed and recommended a renewal of the *Crusades (this came to nothing). The Second Council of Lyons, called by Gregory X in 1274, made more practical crusading arrangements and effected a reunion between Eastern and Western churches, which, however, lasted no longer than fifteen years.

LYTE, HENRY FRANCIS (1793–1847). Anglican *hymn writer. Born in Scotland and educated in Ireland, he was ordained in 1815 and served various curacies, chiefly in southwest England. He was the author of many poems and hymns, among them ''Praise, My Soul, the King of Heaven,'' and ''Abide With Me.''

M

MACARIUS (c. 1482–1564). Metropolitan of Moscow from 1542. Originally a monk who became *archbishop of Novgorod in 1526, he held that the leadership of Christendom had been divinely bestowed upon the Russian Empire. He set up the first printing press in Russia, canonized more than forty *saints, carried out far-reaching ecclesiastical reforms, and supported Ivan the Terrible in order to advance church-state unity.

McCHEYNE, ROBERT MURRAY (1813–1843). Scottish minister. Despite severe illnesses and the brevity of his *ministry (1836–1843) in St. Peter's, Dundee, his impact on Scotland was like that of Samuel *Rutherford. He had the same self-discipline, fervent *prayer, emphasis on *Bible study, assiduous preparation for the *pulpit, and sense of urgency. He wrote letters, tracts, and poems; encouraged a Scottish *mission to the Jews; and preached all over Scotland. It was said of him, "He cared for no question unless his Master cared for it; and his main anxiety was to know the *mind of *Christ."

MacDONALD, GEORGE (1824–1905). Scottish writer. Born in Aberdeenshire, he became a Congregational minister in Sussex, but having his *orthodoxy questioned, he took to literature from 1855. He wrote children's stories, poetry, and *allegories about man's spiritual *pilgrimage. His writing influenced later writers, among them C. S. *Lewis.

MACEDONIANISM A form of *doctrine that denies the full deity of the Holy *Spirit. The name comes from *Bishop Macedonius of Constantinople (d. 362), believed to have been a leader of those who taught this doctrine.

McGREADY, JAMES (c. 1758–1817). American *Presbyterian revivalist. Born in Pennsylvania, he ministered with remarkable success in North Carolina and Kentucky. He made a significant contribution to the *Second Great Awakening and to the founding of the *Cumberland Presbyterian Church, and he is said to have originated the *camp meeting.

MACHEN, JOHN GRESHAM (1881–1937). American *Presbyterian theologian. Born in Baltimore, he studied at American and German universities and taught *New Testament at Princeton Theological Seminary (1906–1929). In the tradition of the earlier *Princeton theology, he finally left because of encroaching *modernism and helped found an independent *mission board and Westminster Theological Seminary (1929), where he taught until his death. Censured for this by the Presbyterian Church, U.S.A., he withdrew and helped form what later was called the *Orthodox Presbyterian Church (1936). His many works include *Christianity and Liberalism* (1923) and *The Virgin Birth of Christ* (1930).

McINTIRE, CARL (1906–). *Presbyterian minister, educator, and author.

He has pastored three churches—since 1938, the *Bible Presbyterian Church of Collingswood, N.J. (which he organized). He has edited *The Christian Beacon* and has founded Faith Theological Seminary (1937), Shelton College (1941), the American Council of Christian Churches (1941), "The Twentieth Century Reformation Hour," and the *International Council of Christian Churches (1948). He also became widely known through his demonstrations against such things as *abortion, communism, *Roman Catholicism, and theological *liberalism.

MACK, ALEXANDER (1679–1735). Founder of the New Baptists (1708), known from 1871 as German Baptist Brethren and now represented largely by the *Church of the Brethren. Born in Germany, Mack early adopted Pietist views, which brought persecution to his congregation in Schwarzenau. They moved to Holland in 1720 and to Pennsylvania in 1729.

MacKAY, ALEXANDER MURDOCH (1849–1890). Scottish *missionary to Uganda. Trained as an engineer, he went to Uganda in 1876. He constructed roads, printed part of the *Bible in Swahili, then translated all of it into the native vernacular. He never returned home, and he died of malaria after laying the foundation for the Church Missionary Society's work in Uganda.

MACKINTOSH, HUGH ROSS (1870–1936). Scottish theologian. A brilliant student at Edinburgh and at German universities, he was ordained in the *Free Church and ministered in Tayport and Aberdeen. In 1904 he became professor of *systematic *theology in New College, Edinburgh. Critics accused him of preoccupation with German theology but, said one of his students, "Step by step he led us into the great deeps where we knew the abasement of our *sin, and thought of the *love of *God that could reach even deeper than our sin." Among his still-used works are *The Christian Experience of Forgiveness* (1927) and *Types of Modern Theology* (1937).

MACLAREN, ALEXANDER (1826–1910). British Baptist *pastor. He ministered in Southampton (1846–1858) and then began a forty-five year pastorate of Union Chapel, Manchester, where a larger building had to be built to accommodate the crowds who wanted to hear "the prince of expository preachers." An *Evangelical sympathetic to other views, he attacked *Roman Catholicism but conceded that it contained "true and devout *souls" and maintained good relations with Roman Catholic and Anglican *bishops. He warmly advocated union of *Baptists and *Congregationalists and was the first president of the *Baptist World Alliance. He sponsored *preaching stations to evangelize the *poor.

McPHERSON, AIMEE SEMPLE (1890–1944). Controversial *evangelist. Born in Ontario, she married a *Pentecostal *pastor who died soon afterwards. Her second husband left her when she began a career as an evangelist. She opened Angelus Temple in Los Angeles, operated a radio station, published various works, founded the *International Church of the Foursquare Gospel and LIFE Bible College, and had an extensive social program. She acquired fame and money, but her reputation was further tarnished when her third marriage also ended in *divorce. Her personal life was not above suspicion, and in her later years she constantly was entangled in lawsuits.

MAGI The name given the Eastern experts in astrology who visited the baby *Jesus (Matt 2:12). Tradition says that there were three, and gives their names as Gaspar, Melchior, and Balthasar. In *Christian *art the *adoration of the Magi became a popular subject.

MAGISTERIUM (Lat. *magister*, "master"). The teaching authority of the church. Roman Catholics claim that this is vested by *God's appointment in the *pope and *bishops. Extraordinary magisterium is exercised when the pope makes a declaration alone or with *bishops, and ordinary magisterium is exercised when a *bishop teaches his *diocese.

MAGNIFICAT The first word ("My *soul magnifies") in the Latin version of *Mary's song in Luke 1:46–55. Mary sung it after Elizabeth had greeted her as the mother of the *Messiah. The song is widely used in the *liturgy of *vespers as a *canticle.

MAIER, WALTER ARTHUR (1893–1950). Lutheran professor and broadcaster. Maier was professor of Semitic languages at Concordia Seminary (St. Louis) for many years but is best remembered as the speaker on the "Lutheran Hour" from its inception in 1930 on CBS until his death in 1950. He offered "a confidence that banishes all reliance on human attainments, and instead points sin-stained man to Christ's atonement."

MAJOR, JOHN (1469–1550). Scottish historian and theologian. Born near Edinburgh, he taught in Paris, Glasgow, and St. Andrews. His works, written in Latin, include the *History of Greater Britain* (1521) and a famous commentary on Peter Lombard's *Sentences* (1509–1517). He wrote against tyranny, called for church reform, defended *transubstantiation, and endorsed religions of persecution. His students at St. Andrews included Patrick *Hamilton and George *Buchanan. Major died ten years before the *Reformation triumphed in Scotland.

MAJORISTIC CONTROVERSY A 17th-century controversy among German Protestants concerning the relation of *good works to *salvation. It took its name from Wittenberg professor Georg Major (1502–1574), who stressed the necessity of good works while holding to *justification by *faith. He was opposed by N. von *Amsdorf and M. I. *Flacius. The Lutheran *Formula of Concord in 1577 took a middle view, declaring that regenerate man is bound to do good works.

MAKARIOS III (1913–1977). *Archbishop and president of Cyprus. Born Michael Mouskos, he was ordained in the *Orthodox Church, studied in Athens and Boston, and returned to Cyprus in 1948 as *bishop of Kition. Prominent in the island's struggle against British rule, he was elected archbishop in 1950, was exiled for three years by the British, but became president on his independence in 1960. From 1963 he was accused by the Turkish minority of repressive measures, and by his own right wing and his fellow bishops he was charged with cooling toward the idea of union with Greece to which he had committed himself. He was overthrown briefly in a misguided coup that provoked Turkey to occupy 37 percent of Cyprus in 1974. With Makarios died also the dual role of church and state leader.

MAKEMIE, FRANCIS (1658–1708). Regarded as the chief founder of *Presbyterianism in America. Born in County Donegal and educated at Glasgow University, he was ordained in Ireland as a *missionary to America and arrived there in 1683. He organized *Presbyterian congregations, joined with two other ministers in forming the first *presbytery in America at Philadelphia in 1706, and became its first *moderator.

MALABAR CHRISTIANS A group of Christians living in Kerala, South India, who claim that their church was founded by the *apostle Thomas. Certainly there were Christians in Kerala in the 6th century who used a Syriac *liturgy and were connected to the Nestorian *patriarch of Baghdad. During the period of Portuguese colonialism, some, under pressure, converted to *Roman Catholicism. Today they are divided into various churches—the Malakarase Uniat church (in communion with Rome), the Mar Thoma church (which maintains cordial relations with the Church of South India), and the Syrian Orthodox Jacobite church (an *Eastern Church).

MALINES CONVERSATIONS Meetings between Roman Catholics and Anglicans in the Belgian town of Malines between 1921 and 1925. *Cardinal

Mercier and Lord Halifax were the respective leaders. Various areas of agreement were found, but nothing came of the exchanges, partly because Mercier was more ecumenically minded than many of his coreligionists and partly because Halifax was a *high churchman whose views were more sympathetic to Rome than those of Anglicans whose traditions were different.

MAMMON (Aram. "riches"). Used in the *Gospels of riches/possessions that can take the place of *God in the human life (Matt 6:24; Luke 16:9, 11, 13).

MAN, CHRISTIAN VIEW OF Although creatures and thus related biologically to the animal world, man and woman are more than mere creatures. They are made in the *image of *God (Gen 1:26), which at least means that they are made to have meaningful friendship and *fellowship with God. But *sin has separated humans from God. Though possessing the potentiality to *love God, sinful man is unable to do so in and of himself and by his own power. He is a captive of sin. *Salvation is *God's activity in restoring sinful man to a right relationship with himself. He does this through *Jesus Christ, who is the *Second Adam, the head of the new humanity that God is creating. Where the first Adam went wrong and where the Israelites went astray was in their failure to obey, trust, and love the *Lord God. But where they failed, Jesus Christ was successful, for he loved God perfectly. He was truly the image of God (Col 1:15). Thus sinful man becomes saved, justified, and forgiven man in *Christ (Rom 5). Also by the Holy *Spirit what sinful man is declared to be in Christ he gradually becomes in reality. This process of *sanctification is concluded at death and with the resurrection *body for the life of the age to come.

Each human being is a unity that may be viewed under different aspects—e.g., as body and *soul (dichotomy) or as body, soul, and *spirit (trichotomy). In the body he lives and loves; on earth he has a physical body, but in *heaven he has a *spiritual, heavenly body (1 Cor 15:35ff.). The idea of an immortal soul is more a Greek philosophical *doctrine than a biblical one.

From the belief in the essential unity of the human race (all stemming from one couple, Adam and Eve) and in all humans being made in God's image, Christians teach that individual personhood is to be respected and honored. Thus all human beings are to be treated with true dignity—whatever their age, race, or class. This also has implications for such ethical decisions as whether to allow *abortion and *euthanasia, especially since most Christians hold that the fetus in the womb is truly a living being with a body and soul. See also CREATIONISM, TRADUCIANISM.

MANICHAEISM A dualistic religious movement founded in Persia by Mani (c. 216–c. 276), who was said to have been of royal Parthian birth. He held that there were two principles, producing respectively the good and bad *souls of man, and that there would be an ongoing struggle between the kingdom of light and the kingdom of darkness, with the latter being destroyed by fire after 1468 years. Mani's teaching is a bizarre mixture of many different *religions and philosophies, including elements of *Gnosticism, Zoroastrianism, Buddhism, and *Christianity. Pope *Leo I declared that the *Devil reigned in all other heresies but that he had built a fortress and raised his throne in that of the Manichaeans.

MANNING, HENRY EDWARD (1808–1892). *Cardinal and *archbishop of Westminster. Ordained (1833) and made an *archdeacon (1840) in the Church of *England, he was a supporter of the *Oxford Movement who converted to Rome in 1851 and, after a meteoric rise, went to the chief English Roman Catholic see in 1865. At *Vatican Council I Manning upheld papal *infallibility, and in England he was a champion of the *poor and of working men during industrial disputes.

MANSON, THOMAS WALTER (1893–1958). British *NT scholar and Rylands professor of *biblical *criticism and *exegesis (Manchester, 1936–1958). Manson's major contribution was in the area of the life and teaching of *Jesus, writing works of enduring worth, such as *The Teaching of Jesus* (1931), *The Sayings of Jesus* (1949), and *The Servant-Messiah* (1953). He was critical of *liberalism's easy optimism and took a conservative stance on the question of the quest for the *historical Jesus. Rejecting both radical and traditional views of the "*Son of Man" question, Manson postulated a corporate Son of Man theory whereby Jesus was the only embodiment of the idea, and after his death and *resurrection fills out his corporate *nature in the church, which is his body here on earth.

MANTON, THOMAS (1620–1677). English minister. As a London clergyman he often preached before Parliament (1647–1658) and generally supported Oliver *Cromwell's regime while disapproving of the execution of *Charles I. The *Restoration church was too liturgical for him; he resigned his living and preached privately. In 1670 he served a six-month jail term for declining to take an *oath against attempting any change in church and state. A Puritan concerned with *religion, not politics, he used his influence "for the public tranquillity." His many works include very useful commentaries on James (1651) and Jude (1658).

MAR THOMA CHURCH See MALABAR CHRISTIANS.

MARANATHA (Aram. "Our *Lord, come" or "Our Lord has come"). A primitive *Christian *prayer or exclamation that is kept in its original Palestinian form in 1 Corinthians 16:22.

MARBURG, COLLOQUY OF (1529) A debate aimed at achieving unity between German and Swiss Reformers, especially on the question of the *Eucharist. The crucial issue was whether *Christ was literally or symbolically present in the elements. The leading participants—*Luther, *Melanchthon, *Oecolampadius, *Zwingli, and *Bucer, agreed in other areas, but on that vital point the colloquy broke down.

MARCELLUS OF ANCYRA (d. c. 374). *Bishop of Ancyra (Turkey). Like *Athanasius, a supporter of the orthodox position decreed by the Council of *Nicea in 325, he was accused by fellow *bishops in the East of going to the other extreme and embracing a form of *Sabellianism. More than once deposed and restored to his see, he was pronounced heretical by the First Council of *Constantinople in 381.

MARCION (2d century). *Christian heretic from Asia Minor. Born in Pontus, he went to Rome about the mid-2d century. He held that there were two Gods: the just God of the Jewish *Scriptures, and the good *God as revealed in *Christ. Marcion rejected the *OT and accepted as canonical *Scripture only ten Pauline Epistles (he excluded the Pastorals) and an edited version of Luke's *Gospel. Marcion has some affinities with *Gnosticism, but the precise link has been much debated. Many Marcionites were killed, and with the 4th-century triumph of *orthodoxy many others became Manichaeans.

MARGARET (c. 1045–1093). Queen of Scotland. Brought up in exile at the Hungarian court, she married the Scottish king Malcolm III about 1070. Of saintly character (she was canonized in 1250), she championed the cause of women, orphans, lepers, prisoners, and beggers and brought Scotland into the mainstream of the Roman Catholic *obedience.

MARGARET OF NAVARRE (1492–1549). French Protestant. Sister of Francis I of France and wife of Henry, king of Navarre, she used her influence to help the *Reformation cause, especially in giving refuge to persecuted Protestants.

MARIOLATRY The giving of *worship (*latria) to *Mary, a charge that Protestants have often brought against *Roman Catholicism. Yet, according to Roman Catholic *theology, latria is given only to *God, while *hyperdulia (*veneration) is given to Mary.

MARIOLOGY The study of *Mary, mother of *Jesus in her role as the *theotokos (God-bearer). Such study involves the material on Mary in the *Gospels, as seen in the context of the *Incarnation, and the teaching and practice of the church over the centuries. The latter includes the two *dogmas of the *Immaculate Conception and the *Assumption and the important document produced by the Second *Vatican Council on the church (chap. 8).

MARIST BROTHERS A teaching *order founded in France in 1817 for the *Christian education of youth in the generation after many had been lost through the French Revolution. The work spread overseas from 1836, and there are now some one hundred schools in twenty-three *mission areas.

MARITAIN, JACQUES (1882–1973). French Roman Catholic philosopher. Maritain was the leading exponent of *Neo-Thomism in the 20th century and as such has ensured himself a place in the history of *theology and philosophy. His numerous volumes build upon the work of *Aquinas but bring him up to date in striking and original ways. Maritain's mind ranged widely, covering *art, politics, *ethics, philosophy, *epistemology, and *metaphysics. Some of his best-known works are *True Humanism* (1938), *Moral Philosophy* (1964), *The Range of Reason* (1942), and *The Degrees of Knowledge: A New Translation* (1959). He called his autobiography *The Peasant of the Garonne*. See also NEO-THOMISM.

MARIUS MERCATOR (5th century). *Christian writer. Probably North African by birth, he lived in Constantinople from about 429. Evidently a *disciple and friend of *Augustine of Hippo, he wrote against *Pelagianism and *Nestorianism. A collection of his writings is still extant in the *Vatican.

MARKS OF THE CHURCH Known also as the Notes of the Church: the description of the church as one, *holy, catholic, and apostolic as found in the *Nicene Creed. The church is one in that it has one *Lord, one *baptism, and one *faith; the one *Spirit works within it. It is holy because the same Spirit indwells it and gives it his holiness. It is catholic because, as the word suggests, it is found in all parts of the world. And it is apostolic because it is based on the teaching and the apostolic *faith recorded in the *NT. In the context of the division of the one church into many subdivisions, many Protestants interpret these marks with the idea of the *invisible church primarily in mind.

MARONITES A *Christian community found primarily in Lebanon. It is about a million strong and is led by the *patriarch of Antioch. There are *dioceses in Lebanon, Syria, Egypt, Australia, Brazil, and the U.S. The history of the church began in the 5th century (if Maro, who died in 407, is seen as the founder), but since the 13th century it has been subject to the influence of the Church of Rome. In recent decades there have been attempts to shed aspects of the Latin, Western influence within the church and its *liturgy in order to enable the church to be a genuinely *Eastern church. As a *Uniate church they have their own Syriac liturgy but maintain communion with Rome.

MARPRELATE TRACTS A series of violent tracts in 1588–1589 by a Puritan writer with the pseudonym Martin Marprelate, attacking *episcopacy and certain *bishops. Seven tracts have survived, but their authorship is still unknown. Probably the most brilliant prose satire of the period, the tracts through their virulence aroused hostility rather than sympathy for the Puritan cause, and replies came from several Anglican writers.

MARRIAGE, INDISSOLUBILITY OF The view that lawful and valid marriage consummated by sexual intercourse can be dissolved only by the death of one partner. Thus, *divorce given by a secular law court cannot change the true situation as *God sees it. It is usually set in the context of marriage as a *sacrament and is thus the teaching of the Church of Rome. Some Protestants, however, hold to it solely on the basis of *NT teaching (Mark 10:2–12; Luke 16:18).

MARROW CONTROVERSY, THE An 18th-century religious division in Scotland between those who stressed *legalism and *merit and those for whom the *grace of *God in *Christ was at the heart of sound *doctrine. The name had originated from Thomas *Boston's publicizing of an earlier Puritan work entitled *The Marrow of Modern Divinity* (authorship uncertain) that now spoke to the condition of a land that reportedly had replaced *evangelical fervor by "mere morality without *religion." The so-called Marrowmen, who included Ebenezer *Erskine, were condemned in the *general assembly of 1720, but it was they whom the people flocked to hear.

MARSILIUS OF PADUA (c. 1275–1342). Italian scholar. Born in Padua, where he studied medicine, he became rector of Paris University in 1313 but was forced to flee the city in 1326 when he was found to have been the main author of an antipapal work called *Defensor pacis* ("Defender of Peace"). He held that the church should concentrate on its spiritual function and not cause trouble by dabbling in politics and that the supreme authority in church matters should be vested in a general council composed of both *clergy and *laity. Predictably such views were regarded as heretical by the *papacy. Two centuries later, however, they provided useful ammunition for the Reformers against *Roman Catholicism.

MARTENSEN, HANS LASSEN (1808–1884). Danish Lutheran theologian. Philosophy professor and champion of conservative *theology against *Kierkegaard, he had an influential academic and pastoral career. He became *bishop of Zealand in 1854 and, unusual among his church contemporaries, showed a degree of social concern. Translations of Martensen's *Christian Dogmatics* (1866) and *Christian Ethics* (1881–1882) are available in English.

MARTIN I (d. 655). Pope from 649. Born in Italy, he called soon after his accession the *Lateran Council that condemned Monothelitism. Because of a dispute with the emperor Constans II, Martin ended his days in exile in the Crimea at the imperial instigation and is regarded as the last papal *martyr.

MARTIN IV (c. 1210–1285). Pope from 1281. Of noble French birth, he saw union between East and West as being dependent on the conquest of the *Byzantine Empire. This policy led to worsening relations between Constantinople and Rome. His unpopularity with the Romans and a series of disastrous political involvements provoked an uprising that led to his flight from Rome to Perugia, where he died.

MARTIN V (1368–1431). Pope from 1417. Elected during the Council of *Constance as the first pope after the ending of the *Great Schism in the Western church, he faced formidable difficulties. He rejected the conciliar theory that the *pope was subordinate to a general council, suppressed the followers of Jan *Hus, defended the church's prerogatives against the rulers of Spain and England, was lukewarm toward badly needed church reform, and increased the power and property of his own influential family.

MARTIN OF TOURS (c. 316–397). *Bishop of Tours and pioneer of Western *monasticism. Born of pagan parents in what is now Hungary, he was a soldier and traveler before joining *Hilary of Poitiers in 360 and taking to the monastic life. In 372 he became bishop of Tours and began an evangelistic outreach to rural districts where the *gospel was scarcely known. A great encourager of monasticism, he spoke out strongly against civil interference in church affairs.

MARTYN, HENRY (1781–1812). Anglican *missionary to India. Cambridge graduate ordained in 1803, he was *curate to Charles *Simeon before going to Calcutta in 1805 as chaplain to the East India Company. His evangelistic *preaching and zeal displeased the British authorities, but he found freer scope for his talents in translating the *NT and *The Book of *Common Prayer* into Hindustani. Failing health in 1810 led to a sea voyage and a stay in Persia, where he finished an Arabic and Persian translation of the NT in 1812. He died in Armenia on the way home.

MARTYR (Gk. "witness"). The early Christians were seen as witnesses (martyrs) of *Jesus Christ (Acts 1:8, 22). Gradually the word came to be used specifically of those who bore witness as Christians in death. Thus in the persecutions of the church by the Roman government in the 2d and 3d centuries there were many martyrs. These men and women were highly regarded by the church, and special services were held annually in their honor. *Tertullian (d. 220) said of martyrdom: "The more you cut us down, the more we grow; the seed is the blood of Christians." This is often paraphrased as "the blood of the martyrs is the seed of the church."

MARTYR, PETER (c. 1205–1252). *Dominican reformer. Born in Italy to parents of a *Cathari *sect, he nonetheless studied at Bologna and became a Dominican about 1221. So successful was he in *preaching and in combating *heresy that he was appointed papal inquisitor in 1232. That very sucess against the Cathari proved fatal when some of its members attacked and killed him while he was returning from a preaching *mission in northern Italy.

MARTYR, PETER (Pietro Martire Vermigli) (1491–1562). Born in Florence, he became an *Augustinian and subsequently *prior of a *monastery in Naples. Becoming a Protestant through studying the writings of *Bucer and *Zwingli, he taught *theology at Strasbourg and in 1548 became regius professor at Oxford. He returned to the Continent on the accession of Mary *Tudor in England.

MARY, QUEEN OF SCOTS (1542–1587). Six days old when she became queen, she was brought up in France, where she was briefly queen consort, and returned to Scotland only in 1561, one year after the *Reformation had triumphed. She was involved in religious controversy with John *Knox for her Roman Catholic practices, in political intrigue because of her claim to be lawful queen of England, and in scandal because of a marriage to her second husband's alleged murderer. Deposed in 1567, she fled to England, was imprisoned by her cousin *Elizabeth I, and finally was executed for reportedly plotting to replace Elizabeth on the English throne.

MARY, THE BLESSED VIRGIN The mother of *Jesus, who is specially regarded by many Christians because she is the mother of the Redeemer of the world. The first important title given her by theologians was **theotokos* (God-bearer, mother of *God). Other important privileges claimed for Mary—mainly in Roman Catholic *theology and devotion—are *Immaculate Conception (preserved free from *original *sin), *Perpetual Virginity (a virgin before and after the birth of Jesus), and *Assumption (her *body and *soul assumed into *heaven when she died). See also MARIOLOGY.

MARY TUDOR See TUDOR, MARY.

MASON, CHARLES HARRISON (1866–1961). Founder of the *Church of God in Christ (COGIC). In 1893 Mason was brought into the Holiness movement after reading the autobiography of Amanda Smith, an influential black Holiness evangelist of the nineteenth century. In 1906 Mason received the baptism of the Holy Spirit under the ministry of William J. *Seymour at the *Azusa Street Revival. Initially, Mason ordained ministers of all races. The barrier of segregation fell back into place by 1913, however, and the COGIC became a primarily Black church, even though Mason himself maintained fellowship with the white Pentecostals. He led the COGIC until his death at age ninety-five.

MASS (Lat. *missa*). The Roman Catholic name (and medieval name) for the *Eucharist. "Missa" is found in the words of the dismissal at the end of the Latin service: *Ite, missa est* (Go, you are dismissed). Since the Latin Mass contains certain theological ideas unacceptable to Protestants (e.g., the mass as a propitiatory *sacrifice), the use of "Mass" for the *Lord's Supper/-Eucharist has made little headway in *Protestantism. It is used by some Lutherans and some Anglicans.

MATERIAL PRINCIPLE Use of the central *doctrine of a church. Thus the 16th-century Reformers claimed that *justification by *faith was the material principle of *Christianity and the *Scriptures were the *formal principle.

MATHER, COTTON (1663–1729). American Puritan minister. Grandson of John *Cotton and son of Increase Mather, he did more than any of his contemporaries to perpetuate the vision of the founding fathers. During his forty-seven-year *ministry in Boston this champion of *Reformed *doctrine produced a valuable church history of New England, 1620–1698 (reprinted in two volumes in 1979).

MATHESON, GEORGE (1842–1906). Scottish minister and writer. Born in Glasgow and almost blind by age twenty, he surmounted that obstacle, became a minister, and served the *parishes of Innellan (1868–1886) and St. Bernard's, Edinburgh (1886–1899). Great crowds flocked to hear the blind preacher with a rare gift of language. Alexander *Whyte hailed Matheson's *Studies of the Portrait of Christ* (1899, 1900) as a work of genius. His verse is haunting and winsome. His *Sacred Songs* (1890) includes "O Love That Wilt Not Let Me Go," written, he explained, out of "the most severe mental suffering."

MATHEWS, SHAILER (1863–1941). Liberal Baptist theologian and educator. Mathews was a member of the University of Chicago Divinity School from 1894–1933, where he became the dean in 1908. Heavily into a sociological approach to *religion and *theology, he saw religious *faith as a functional, not absolute, value. He was a leading spokesman for radical *liberalism and the *social *gospel during the so-called Fundamentalist-Modernist controversy and was an advocate for the *Chicago School of theology. His social views may be found in his *The Social Teachings of Jesus* (1897) and in his autobiography, which he tellingly called *New Faith of Old* (1936). See also CHICAGO SCHOOL OF THEOLOGY.

MATINS Either (1) the traditional office said in the night by Roman Catholics (at 2 A.M.), now called "Office of Readings" and said at night before sleep, or (2) the Anglican daily service of *morning prayer, the structure of which is similar to *evening prayer.

MAUNDY THURSDAY (HOLY THURSDAY) The Thursday before *Easter. It commemorates *Christ's institution of the *Eucharist, taking its name from "*Mandatum novum do vobis*" ("A new commandment I give to you"), a Latin *anthem based on John 13:34. On Maundy Thursday *alms are distributed to the *poor at a ceremony in Westminster Abbey by, or on behalf of, the sovereign (in earlier centuries the sovereign washed the feet of the poor on that day).

MAURIAC, FRANCOIS (1885–1970). French Roman Catholic writer. Born into a religious family in Bordeaux, he early preferred writing to academic studies, first publishing poetry (1909) then from 1913 a remarkable series of novels which, it was said, examined "the ugly realities of modern life in the light of *eternity." Mauriac condemned totalitarianism, supported the resistance movement during World War II, and was awarded the Nobel prize for literature in 1952.

MAURICE, JOHN FREDERICK DENISON (1805–1872). Anglican theologian. Born in Suffolk, he became professor at King's College, London, but resigned after his *Theological Essays* (1853) denying *eternal punishment created a controversy. He was concerned about applying *Christian principles to social reform, and he founded a "working men's college" to further such views. An original and profound thinker and writer, Maurice, who was professor of moral philosophy at Cambridge from 1866, wrote many works, including *The Kingdom of Christ* (1838) and *The Conscience* (1868).

MAXIMUS THE CONFESSOR (c. 580–662). *Byzantine theologian. Secretary to the emperor *Heraclius, he forsook the civil service for *monasticism about 613, later became *abbot of the *monastery of Chrysopolis, and finally after 626 settled in Carthage. His championship of *orthodoxy against the Monothelites and his subsequent support for Pope *Martin I led to the arrest of both by the emperor Constans II in 655. After internment in Thrace until 661, Maximus was tried for treason, had his tongue and right hand cut off, and was banished to the Caucasus, where he died the following year.

MAY LAWS (1873). Legislation passed in Prussia at the instigation of Bismarck as part of his *Kulturkampf policy against *Roman Catholicism. The new laws imposed political restrictions on the church and insisted that the training and licensing of *priests should be under state control. Nonconforming *bishops and *clergy were imprisoned. *Pius IX protested, and generally the harassment united the church. By 1880 Bismarck found it politic to modify the laws, and by 1887 they were no longer in force.

MAYFLOWER COMPACT (1620). A document that male passengers on the *Mayflower* signed before landing at Cape Cod. It bound the signatories to stay together, form "a civil body politic," and obey any laws that might be established by that body. It is regarded as the forerunner of the American constitution.

MAZARIN, JULES (1602–1661). French statesman and *cardinal. Born Guilio Mazarini in Italy, he was educated in Rome and Madrid, entered the *Vatican diplomatic service, but due largely to the influence of Cardinal *Richelieu, he transferred to French government service in 1640 and became naturalized there. Appointed cardinal in 1641 and first minister of France in 1642, he controlled the country and greatly enhanced French influence during the long minority of *Louis XIV.

MAZZARELLA, BONAVENTURA (1818–1882). Italian patriot and preacher. Legally trained, he was active in the Italian liberation movement when he was converted and founded a spiritual home in the Free Italian church in Genoa. A highly regarded scholar who occupied chairs at Bologna and Genoa, he became a member of Parliament and strove for religious liberty and humanitarian reform.

MEDE, JOSEPH (1586–1638). A Cambridge graduate who remained there for the rest of his life as professor of Greek, he was one of the Church of *England's most versatile biblical scholars. He is regarded also as the pioneer of so-called progressive *millennialism, which ignored the allegorical interpretation traditionally associated with the Book of Revelation and saw in it the promise of a literal *kingdom of *God, with the redemptive work fulfilled in human history and in this world.

MEDIATOR One who stands between two parties in order to reconcile them. Thus *Jesus, who is both *God and Man and exists as one *Person, is the only Mediator between God and man (1 Tim 2:5). Particularly by his sacrificial death and glorious exaltation Jesus has achieved *reconciliation. However, his continuing work as Mediator in *heaven (as *Prophet, *Priest, and King) is necessary for the results of the achieved reconciliation to be received, known, and experienced by sinners. See also CHRIST.

MEDIATRIX OF ALL GRACES A title once given to *Mary, mother of *Jesus, and also a feast once celebrated in the Roman Catholic Church. The Second *Vatican Council declared that Mary may be called by this title as long as it is understood in such a way that it does not take away from or add to the role of *Christ as sole *Mediator.

MEDITATION Devout reflection on a chosen passage or theme as a means of gleaning topics for praise and *intercession, thus to strengthen the resolve to live the *Christian life. See also CONTEMPLATION.

MELANCHTHON, PHILIP (1497–1560). German Reformer. A classicist by training, he was professor of Greek at Wittenberg when he became friendly with *Luther (1518), whose views he soon espoused. In 1521 Melanchthon produced *Loci Communes,* the first comprehensive book on Lutheran *theology; subsequently he wrote various confessions and defenses of the Lutheran position. He organized school and university education, participated in the Colloquy of *Marburg (1529), and had a major part in the Concord of *Wittenberg (1536). As a humanist his irenic attitudes were sometimes misunderstood, but the consensus of modern Lutheran scholarship seems to have reasserted Melanchthon's integrity.

MELCHITES A name applied originally to Syrian and Egyptian Christians who accepted the pronouncements of the Council of *Chalcedon (451) against *Monophysitism. Since this orthodox position was held by the emperor, the term Melchites or "royalists" (from a Syrian word meaning "king") was scornfully applied to the orthodox by those who held a different view.

MELITIAN SCHISMS Two 4th-century divisions in the *Eastern church. The first arose in Egypt when Melitius, *bishop of Lycopolis, ordained some of his supporters while Peter, bishop of Alexandria, was imprisoned during the persecution under *Diocletian (305). Peter excommunicated Melitius, who later set up a schismatic church (he apparently ordained *Arius). Their situation was briefly regularized by the Council of *Nicea (325), but when *Athanasius became bishop of Alexandria (328), the Melitians again became schismatics. They survived as a *sect into the 8th century.

The second Melitian Schism concerned Melitius, bishop of Antioch (d. 381), who in 360 was sent into exile by the emperor Constantius II for *preaching a *sermon displeasing to the influential Arians there. An Arian sympathizer was appointed in his place. Even when Melitius returned in 362 the position was not clear-cut, for he failed to command the allegiance of all the orthodox because Athanasius held him to be doctrinally suspect. The *Schism in this case was therefore primarily between groups claiming to be orthodox.

MELVILLE, ANDREW (1545–1622). Scottish Reformer, often called "the Father of *Presbyterianism." Born in Angus and educated in Scotland, France, and Switzerland, he became professor of humanity in Geneva in 1569 but returned to Scotland in 1574 to fill the vacuum left by John *Knox's death. Principal first of Glasgow University, then of St. Andrews, he championed the Reformed Kirk against the efforts of *James VI, who sought to impose *episcopacy on the country. He rejected both threats and bribes, even the archbishopric of St. Andrews, and stood out against the royal claim to supremacy over the church. He led the *general assembly in ratifying the 1578 Second Book of *Discipline, a work that has been called the Magna Carta of Presbyterianism. After a defiant speech in 1607 Melville was consigned to the Tower of London for four years and released into exile in 1611. He became professor of *biblical *theology at Sedan University, France, and was never again allowed to return home. Amid all the controversy Melville's chief aim was to make *Christianity a matter of popular concern. It is questionable whether his attempt to transplant Genevan thinking into the political circumstances of Scotland was practicable, but it was Presbyterianism of Melville's type that ultimately triumphed in Scotland in 1690.

MENDICANT ORDERS Dating from the 13th century, these Roman Catholic *orders emphasized apostolic *poverty, renouncing personal and community property, and working or begging for their living. Originally associated only with the *Franciscans and *Dominicans, they came later in the century to include *Carmelites and *Augustinian *hermits.

MENNONITES An *evangelical group descended from the 16th-century *Anabaptists, founded by Conrad *Grebel, and named after Menno *Simons. Early emphases were on separation from the world and on rigid discipline for both community and individual. Because of persecution and restrictions placed on them, particularly in Switzerland, Anabaptists sought refuge in other lands. They settled and prospered in Poland, southern Germany, the Netherlands, North America, and (later) the Ukraine. A major controversy among them marked the origins of the *Amish church. Most Mennonites have four ordinances—*believers' *baptism, the *Lord's Supper, *footwashing, and the kiss of *charity—and emphasize *pacifism, independent local churches, and the importance of practical holiness. Numbering now some 550,000 worldwide, they operate a comprehensive social, humanitarian, and *missions program.

MERCEDARIANS Founded in 1218 by Peter Nolasco (c. 1189–c. 1256) in Barcelona, these were members of a *mendicant *order of men dedicated to caring for the sick and rescuing *Christian captives from the Moors. Their rule was written by Raymond of Penafort. They spread to the New World by the start of the 16th century.

MERCERSBURG THEOLOGY A form of *Reformed (Calvinist) *theology developed at the German Reformed Seminary at Mercersburg, Pennsylvania, in the 1840s. Its leaders were Philip *Schaff (1819–1893) and William Nevin (1803–1886). It was in part a reaction against *revivalism, then popular in America, and in part an attempt to discover the true principles of the Protestant *Reformation.

MERCY *Compassion and *love for those in need or who suffer and the readiness to do what is possible to help them. Applied to *God, it refers to his *love and practical activity for *Israel (Hos 11:8) but particularly for the *redemption of the world through *Jesus Christ. *God is the Father of all mercies (2 Cor 1:3). Traditionally mercy is described in terms of what it achieves in human lives through *love for others. Thus there are seven corporal works of mercy—to feed the hungry, to give drink to the thirsty, to clothe the naked, to give hospitality to the stranger, to care for prisoners, and to bury the dead (cf. Matt 25:31ff.). Also there are seven spiritual works of mercy—to convert the sinner, to instruct the ignorant, to counsel the doubtful, to comfort the sorrowful, to bear wrongs patiently, to forgive injuries, and to pray for others.

MERIT Roman Catholic teaching concerning the right of a *Christian to be rewarded by *God with *salvation and *eternal life for *good *works done in the power of the Holy *Spirit. It claims a basis in the *NT teaching about *rewards (see Matt 5:3–12; 6:4; 6:19ff.; 7:21). Developed in the Latin church by *Tertullian, *Cyprian, and *Augustine, it was elaborated by medieval theologians and defined by the Roman Catholic Council of *Trent (1545–1563). It is claimed that when a Christian does more than God expects of him, he acquires more merit than is needed for his own salvation. This extra or surplus merit then becomes part of the Treasury of Merit on which the church can draw for the benefit of those who are deficient in merit. This is how *indulgences could be justified.

In Protestant teaching the idea of merit making a contribution to one's salvation has no place. There is, however, discussion of what precisely "rewards in *heaven" really means, for it suggests that there is some special reward to those who unreservedly and freely give themselves wholly to God in the service of *Christ.

MERTON, THOMAS (1915–1968). Roman Catholic author, poet, and monastic. Merton was a world citizen, well traveled and well educated, earning degrees from Cambridge University and Columbia. After a time of spiritual trial and conflict, the worldly Merton converted to Roman Catholicism and in 1941 became a Trappist. Ordained as a *priest as Father M. Louis, he lived many years in a hermitage from which he wrote many works on the contemplative life, the evils of war, books of meditations, a journal of his visit to Asia, and volumes of poetry. To the general reader his most well-known work was the chronicle of his early life through his *conversion entitled *The Seven Storey Mountain* (1948). He died from an electrical accident during a conference of Catholic and Buddhist monks in Thailand.

MESSIAH (Heb. "The Anointed One"). It became *Christos* in Greek (from *chrio,* "to anoint"). Thus Messiah and *Christ are the same. It is the word used to summarize the *hope of the Israelites/Jews for a deliverer; it is the word that unites the prophetic promises of a Son of David, a *Savior, and a *Servant (cf. Pss 2, 110; Isa 9:1–7; 11:1–10; Jer 23:5–6; Mic 5:2–5). Because it had acquired political overtones in the *Judaism of his day, *Jesus rarely used the word, but he did believe he was the Messiah (Matt 16:16), and his *disciples did call him Messiah after his *resurrection (Acts 2:36). See also CHRIST.

METANOIA (Gk. "change of mind or view"). The *NT word for repentance, used often in the Gospels and Acts (Mark 1:15; Acts 2:38). It involves a turning from one direction to another, from self-centered to God-centered living.

METAPHYSICS That which is beyond physics and thus the study of first principles of *being. There have been many systems of metaphysics presenting a "vision" of the *universe as a whole. Since *Christian *faith includes a view of the world that goes beyond appearances to the reality of the invisible *God, it often makes use of the terms derived from metaphysics to express its understanding of the *supernatural and transcendent. An example is *ontology.

METEMPSYCHOSIS (Gk. *meta,* "change"; *empsychos,* "animate"). The teaching that *souls migrate from one *body to another. It is found in Hinduism, *spiritualism, and *theosophy. It is in contrast to the *Christian *doctrine of the raising of the immortal *spiritual body. See also REINCARNATION, RESURRECTION OF THE DEAD, and TRANSMIGRATION OF SOULS.

METHODISM The teaching, organization, and *discipline of those *denominations that see themselves following the idea of *Christianity originally supplied by John and Charles *Wesley in the 18th century. The word "Methodists" came into use in Oxford in the 1720s as a description of a group of serious-minded young men who were methodical in their devotions and *good *works. Out of this group came the leaders of the evangelical *revival of the 18th century, and out of the revival came the societies of the people called Methodists. They have spread to many countries and, because of divisions, comprise various Methodist and Holiness *denominations—of which twenty are found in the U.S. Virtually all Methodist bodies are Arminian in *doctrine (the exception is the Welsh Methodists [Presbyterians who are Calvinist]). The World Methodist Council has delegates from over forty countries representing over 45 million members, and this does not account for all Methodists. Modern Methodism *worship varies from a strong liturgical emphasis on the one side to an emphasis on freedom on the other. This in turn reflects the origins of Methodism—converts from the Church of *England made by Church of England *priests (therefore liturgical) and the pursuit of "scriptural holiness" and the fullness of the *Spirit by the membership of the societies (therefore freedom). In terms of church polity it is *connectional.

METHODIST NEW CONNEXION A breakaway group in British *Methodism. It was founded in 1797 by Alexander *Kilham and others concerned to put a greater distance between Methodists and the Church of *England and to make greater use of the *laity. The Methodist New Connexion survived until 1907, when it joined with two other groups to form the *United Methodist Church.

METHODIUS See CYRIL AND METHODIUS.

METROPOLITAN A *bishop who exercises provincial jurisdiction. In the early church he was the bishop of a province's principal city (hence, metropolis), but this is no longer necessarily so. The *archbishops of Canterbury and York are metropolitans, each with provincial and diocesan jurisdiction.

MEYER, FREDERICK BROTHERTON (1847–1929). English *Evangelical. Ordained in 1870, he ministered in Baptist and independent Evangelical churches in Liverpool, York, Leicester, and London until 1921. A preacher who attracted great crowds, he had a special affinity with, and concern for, working-class people. His devotional works on biblical themes are still highly regarded.

MICHAEL CERULARIUS See CERULARIUS, MICHAEL.

MICHELANGELO BUONARROTI (1475–1564). Sculptor, painter, and architect. Stellar Renaissance master, he was patronized by *Julius II. His depiction of biblical events and characters have indelibly influenced Western consciousness. His sculptures include two *Pietas, David, Moses*. Julius II commissioned him to paint frescoes on the ceiling of the Sistine Chapel from 1508 to 1512. Between 1535 and 1541 he worked on the chapel's *Last Judgment*. He was the primary architect for the planning of St. Peter's in Rome.

MIDTRIBULATION RAPTURE The belief that the *rapture of the church will occur in the middle of the *Tribulation that will come on the earth.

MILAN, EDICT OF (313). A political agreement between the emperors *Constantine and Licinius establishing equal *toleration for all *religions, including *Christianity, within the Roman Empire.

MILIC, JAN (d. 1374). Bohemian Reformer. In 1358 he entered the imperial service. Dissatisfied by the church's low spiritual state, he relinquished his property and appointment in 1363 and began *preaching reform and the simple lifestyle. His messages and his calls for renewal were popular, but ecclesiastical authority twice indicted him for *heresy. Urban V and *Gregory XI exonerated him, and the latter even invited him to preach before the College of *Cardinals. He had a formative influence on the later Reformer Jan *Hus.

MILLENARIANISM, MILLENNIALISM The *doctrine that a thousand-year reign of *Christ and the *saints on earth will end this present age and come prior to the new age. Based primarily on Revelation 20:1–5, it takes two main forms: (1) postmillennialism (Christ will return to earth after the millennium) and (2) premillennialism (Christ will come to earth to inaugurate and reign during the millennium). *Amillennialism denies a literal millennium.

MILLENARY PETITION (1603) A request for changes in certain Church of *England practices made by Puritan ministers to *James I in 1603. The name came from *millenarius* (Lat. "of a thousand"), reportedly denoting the number of signatures. The king called the *Hampton Court Conference, which rejected most of the requested changes.

MILLER, WILLIAM (1782–1849). Often regarded as the founder of the *Adventist movement. Born in Massachusetts, he was a farmer and a magistrate when converted in 1816. He became a Baptist preacher, took to *Bible study, and prophesied that *Christ's return would be in 1843 or 1844. More than 50,000 people awaited the day, disposed of their property in many cases—and then suffered great disappointment. Miller himself soon withdrew from the movement he had initiated, but others continued it and subsequently claimed that Christ had indeed come in 1843 but to a heavenly rather than an earthly *sanctuary.

MILLIGAN, GEORGE (1860–1934). Scottish *NT scholar. Minister in Perthshire, he developed an interest in Greek papyri, lectured on the subject at Oxford, Cambridge, and in the U.S., and used this expertise in a highly praised commentary on Paul's Epistles to the Thessalonians. He became professor in Glasgow in 1910 and is best remembered for his remarkable *Vocabulary of the Greek New Testament* (1914–1929).

MILMAN, HENRY HART (1791–1868). Anglican historian. A versatile scholar who held the chair of poetry at Oxford (1821–1831), he went to St. Paul's in 1849 and held the deanery until his death. A theological liberal who wanted to abolish the practice of requiring *clergy to subscribe to the *Thirty-Nine Articles, he wrote the highly regarded *History of Latin Christianity* (1855).

MILTON, JOHN (1608–1674). English poet. Born in London and educated at Cambridge, where he wrote *Ode on the Morning of Christ's Nativity* (1629). Expressing his concern for religious and political liberty by supporting the Puritans, he produced many tracts for the times in addition to poetry of the highest rank. Among the most noble of the former was *Areopagitica* (1644), an eloquent and impressive argument against restriction of freedom of the press. By 1652 he was blind, but he continued to write and to actively assist the cause of Oliver *Cromwell, although he disagreed with some aspects of Cromwell's policies. Briefly imprisoned after the *Restoration, Milton completed his famous work *Paradise Lost* in 1665 and published its sequel, *Paradise Regained,* in 1671.

MIND-BODY The spiritual and physical aspects of the one person. Philosophers have suggested various ways in which mind and *body relate to each other. What is important for *Christian theologians is to use the best suggestions available to illuminate the biblical *doctrine of man in order to deal with such problems as moral freedom (*freedom of the *will) and personal *immortality.

MINDSZENTY, JOSEF (1892–1975). Hungarian *cardinal. He became *primate of Hungary in 1945 but was arrested by the communist government in 1948 on charges of treason and espionage and was sentenced to life imprisonment. Released briefly by freedom fighters during the 1956 uprising, he was given asylum by the American Embassy in Budapest. Until 1971 he refused *Vatican appeals to leave the country (he wanted the government to acknowledge his innocence of the charges on which he had been convicted) but finally went to Vienna, where he made no secret of his disapproval of Vatican dealings with communist rulers. In 1974 *Paul VI took away his title as primate of Hungary.

MINISTRY The service that the church renders to *God for the sake of *Jesus Christ. Each member has a ministry to perform. Specialized ministries often can only be undertaken after *ordination—e.g., those of *pastor, *bishop, *deaconess, etc. But each member, on the *analogy of the church as a body, has a function to perform for the right ordering and function of the whole. And the whole works efficiently only when each part performs that function.

MINISTRY OF THE WORD Used either to describe the task of *preaching from the *Bible to the congregation each Sunday (and as such a Protestant expression) or of the first part of the *Eucharist (*Scripture readings, *creed, and *sermon).

MIRACLE An event that is contrary to what is known of nature and that is the means of revealing the character or purpose of *God. *Jesus' miracles were part of his *ministry and inseparably linked with God's kingly and saving purposes and with the proclamation of the *kingdom of God. Scientific laws will never explain the miracle at the center of *Christianity—the bodily *resurrection of Jesus; it was a unique *revelation of *God's *grace and power. In the context of modern science, miracle is a word to be used with care.

MISSAL The book in which everything is contained for the celebration of the Roman Catholic *Mass throughout the ecclesiastical year—*prayers, *liturgy, directions for ceremonial (*rubrics) and all other needful instructions.

MISSIOLOGY (Lat. *missio,* "a sending"; *logos,* "study"). The branch of *theology that studies the principles and practice of the church's *mission in the world. At one time seen primarily as the work of the Western church in the developing world, it is now seen as the study of the mission of the whole church in all the world.

MISSION The task of the church in the world. It is, however, only the task of the church because first it is the work and activity of the Holy *Trinity. The Father sent the Son into the world as the *Savior; the Father sent the Holy *Spirit into the world in the name of the Son to continue the work of the incarnate Son (*Jesus of Nazareth); and the Son sends his church into the world, filled the Spirit, to do the *will of the Father (even as he did). Mission is both *evangelism and *social service—the sharing of *God's concern for his world and for all people in their total situation.

MISSIONARY One who is sent by the church (usually to another country) in order to lead the work of *mission or to serve a strategic place in mission. At one time the missionary from the West was seen as a servant of both *Christ and Western *culture and capitalism, but now he/she is seen as a servant of the local churches to which he/she is sent.

MODALISM An erroneous *doctrine of the Holy *Trinity. *God manifests himself at different times as Father or Son or Holy *Spirit. He is not three *Persons but has three modes of appearance. Here the unity of the Godhead is emphasized at the expense of the Trinity. Modalism was an early *Christian *heresy, which reappears from time to time in the history of the church.

MODEL An image or picture used to convey the reality of a thing. The *Bible has many models—e.g., *kingdom of *God, *redemption, *salvation, *reconciliation—and *theology has many more—e.g., models of the *Atonement (e.g., *penal substitution) and of the church (e.g., *mystical body of *Christ). The word has come into theological language from the human and behavioral sciences. See RELIGIOUS LANGUAGE.

MODERATES The name given to the dominant party in the Church of *Scotland for about a century before the 1843 *Disruption. The Moderates approved of patronage in church appointments and conceded ultimate authority in church affairs to the civil courts. Moderatism was better known for *culture and morality than for those matters of sound *doctrine that exercised the *Evangelicals. At its worst, Moderatism reflected a spiritual deadness and neglect of pastoral care that led to many parishioners joining one or other of the *secession bodies.

MODERATOR The chairman of the various courts of *Presbyterianism. Apart from the *kirk session, of which the minister normally retains the moderatorship during his incumbency, the appointment is for one year only. Moderators of *presbytery, *synod, and *general assembly are merely presidents or representatives of the courts and have no enhanced status over fellow ministers.

MODERNISM The accommodation of *Christianity to modern knowledge. Originally it was used of a movement in the Roman Catholic Church associated with the teaching of Alfred Loisy (1857–1940) and George *Tyrrell (1861–1909). This was firmly condemned by *Pius X in 1907. Then it was used of the new theological attitude in *Protestantism known as *Liberalism or *liberal *theology. In the U.S., Modernism and *Fundamentalism were often contrasted (and still are), for they represented liberal *Protestantism on the one side and conservative Evangelicalism on the other. Modernism involves a critical approach to the *Bible, a readiness to believe what "modern science says" when that apparently is different from biblical teaching, and a general unreadiness to take the idea of *God's self-revelation seriously.

MODES OF BEING (Ger. *Seinwesen*). The expression used by Karl *Barth and others as a modern equivalent of *Persons within the *Trinity. It represents an alternative translation of *hypostasis, since it is held that in modern Western languages "Person" no longer conveys the accurate meaning that it did when classical *culture dominated education. Thus in the Godhead there are three Modes of Being. The weakness of such a translation is that it lacks the personal ring of *truth.

MOFFAT, ROBERT (1795–1883). Scottish *missionary to Africa. Born in East Lothian, he went to South Africa in 1816 and moved to Bechuanaland in 1825. He was there until 1870, except for an extended furlough when he inspired David *Livingstone (who married Moffat's daughter) to join him in Africa. Moffat encouraged an indigenous *ministry, translated the *Bible into Sechuana, used exploration as a means to extend *missions, and introduced new methods of agriculture. Most of all he was an outstanding *Christian leader who thought of himself as one who "simply did the work of the day in the day."

MOFFATT, JAMES (1870–1944). Scottish biblical scholar. A minister of the *United Free Church, he was church history professor in his church's Glasgow college (1915–1927), then in Union Theological Seminary, New York (1927–1940). Ranging over a wide field of scholarship, he is best known for his translation of the *Bible (1922–1926). Other works include *Introduction to the Literature of the New Testament* (1911), the International Critical Commentary on *Hebrews* (1924), and **Presbyterianism* (1928).

MOGILA, PETER (1596–1646). *Metropolitan of Kiev. From an aristocratic family, he studied in Europe. In 1627 he became *superior of Kiev Monastery, which he made a center of *culture, and in 1633 he was appointed metropolitan with jurisdiction over Orthodox Christians in Poland. He supplied some much-needed intellectual muscle against both *Roman Catholicism and *Protestantism by his *Orthodox Confession of Faith* (1645). With only minor amendments, this was later adopted as orthodox *doctrine by the Synod of Jerusalem in 1572.

MOLINOS, MIGUEL DE (c. 1627–1696). Spanish Quietist. Educated in Spain and ordained in 1652, he went in 1663 to Rome, where he became highly regarded as a spiritual director. In 1675 he published his *Spiritual Guide,* which held that *Christian *perfection was attainable through annihilation of the individual *will and by combining *contemplation and divine help. This caused a sensation and disrupted traditional patterns of *worship, but Molinos had a powerful ally in Pope *Innocent XI. Suddenly in 1685 the scene changed. He was arrested, charged with *heresy, and subsequently sentenced to life imprisonment. He died in prison. The savage sentence was caused by the discovery of unspecified personal immorality.

MONARCHIANISM (Gk. *monarchia,* "one origin, rule"). A 2d- and 3d-century *doctrine concerning *God as one Sovereign. So much emphasis was placed on the unity and oneness of God that no room was left for the existence of three *Persons in the oneness. It came in two types. (1) That God is one and thus *Jesus was not God made man but only a creature whom God adopted as his Son. (2) That God is one and appears as either Father or Son or Holy *Spirit. See also SABELLIANISM.

MONASTERY A residence built for those who live in a community under *religious *vows. It could house men or women (or sometimes both in "double monasteries"), though the term has come in modern times to denote men only. Monasteries are common in other *religions, such as Buddhism and Hinduism.

MONASTICISM (MONACHISM) A way of *Christian life involving *asceticism, self-denial, and *obedience to a superior, followed in whole or partial seclusion from the secular world. Usually it is according to a fixed rule of life and under lifelong *vows of *poverty, *chastity and *obedience. The purpose is to seek *God and to gain *perfection; this pursuit may involve service to human beings or commitment to a life of *prayer.

Christian monasticism began in Egypt and was introduced into the West in the 4th century. A *rule was provided by St. Benedict (480–543) that was used as the basis of many communities of monks and *nuns. In the East the great center of monasticism has been Mount *Athos in Greece. Protestants have criticized monasticism on the basis that it encourages the idea of *salvation by *works and that it elevates the idea of *celibacy over that of the married state.

MONERGISM (Gk. *monos,* "alone"; *ergon,* "work"). The teaching that *God is the only efficient cause of *salvation. It is the opposite of *synergism and has been used to describe the idea of *grace taught in *Gnesio-Lutheranism and in developed *Calvinism. It is a view that leaves no place for the cooperation of the human *will.

MONICA (MONNICA) (c. 331–387). Mother of *Augustine of Hippo. Left a widow at forty, she prayed for the *conversion of her son through his wayward years, followed him from North Africa to Italy, and rejoiced at his *conversion in Milan. The influence on him of this deeply pious woman continued until her death near Rome.

MONOD, ADOLPHE THEODORE (1802–1856). Probably the greatest Protestant preacher in 19th-century France. Born in Copenhagen and educated in Paris and Geneva, he was converted about 1825 and was *pastor of Protestant congregations in Naples and Lyons, was dismissed because of conservative *theology in 1831, and ministered in a Free Church until called to teach theology at Montauban in 1836. He succeeded his brother Frederic in 1847 as pastor of the most prestigious Protestant congregation in Paris and became widely known as a preacher, writer, and champion of the *Reformed cause.

MONOGAMY The institution of marriage in which husband and wife may have only one marital partner. Thus it contrasts with *polygamy (a man having several wives) and polyandry (a woman having several husbands). Monogamy is what *Christ and his church teach as *God's *will.

MONOLATRY (Gk. *monos,* "single"; *latreia,* "*worship"). The restriction of worship to one *god even though it may be allowed that other gods exist. This was the position of the Israelites at least in part of their history as recorded in the *OT. From monolatry developed *monotheism, which insists there is only one true God.

MONOPHYSITISM (Gk. *monos,* "single"; *phusis,* "*nature"). Originating in the 5th century, the belief that *Christ has only a divine nature. The human nature is either absorbed by the divine or is said never to have existed. The classic position adopted by the Council of *Chalcedon in 451 is that Christ has two natures, human and divine. Some Monophysites rejected the council's decision; others took their own interpretation from it. The situation was further complicated by political and religious controversies between East and West, but the Third Council of *Constantinople (680–681) finally condemned Monophysitism, though it is the official *doctrine in certain *Eastern churches—*Coptic, Syrian, *Jacobite, and *Armenian.

MONOTHEISM Belief in one *God who is personal and distinct from the *universe. The three great monotheistic *religions are Islam, *Judaism, and *Christianity. The Christian monotheism is distinctive in that while insisting on the unity and oneness of God it affirms that God exists in three *Persons.

MONOTHELITES Those who held that *Christ had only one *will. *Heraclius (7th-century emperor) and *Sergius (*patriarch of Constantinople), concerned to unify the empire that had been badly split by the Monophysite controversy and threatened with foreign invasion, began this new debate in 738. An imperial statement declared that Christ's divine and human *natures, while distinct in his one *Person, had only one will. A storm broke and the new emperor Constans II in 648 forbade discussion of the subject, but it was revived with Constantine IV's accession in 668. He summoned the Third Council of *Constantinople in 680, which asserted two wills, a view that had been taken by a Roman *synod earlier that same year.

MONSTRANCE The *vessel in which the consecrated bread (*host) is carried in procession or exposed during the service of *Benediction.

MONTANISM A 2d-century *Christian *heresy. It originated in Montanus, a Christian who, in a Phrygian village about 156, fell into a trance and reportedly began to "prophesy under the influence of the *Spirit." Two young women also prophesied, and the movement quickly spread through Asia Minor. Montanus claimed to have a new and final *revelation, foretold the return of *Christ and the establishment of the New Jerusalem on a Phrygian plain, encouraged *fasting, and welcomed persecution. The Asia Minor *bishops finally excommunicated the Montanists about 177, but the *sect survived until the 6th century (remnants of it into the 9th century). *Tertullian was its most famous adherent.

MOODY, DWIGHT LYMAN (1837–1899). American *evangelist. Born in Massachusetts, he was converted at age eighteen in Boston and later became a successful shoe salesman in Chicago. At age twenty-three he gave up his lucrative employment for full-time service in *YMCA and *Sunday school work at a meager salary. He built churches, schools, and YMCA buildings; organized conferences; and in 1886 founded what came to be known later as Moody Bible Institute. His remarkable gifts as an *evangelist were acknowledged in the meetings he held all over the world. It was said that he traveled a million miles and preached to more than a hundred million people.

MOON, SUN MYUNG See Unification Church.

MORAL ARGUMENT An argument for the existence of *God. Since human beings have a *conscience and feel the sense that they ought to do something (or not do something), it is argued that there is a moral law operative in the *universe and that God is both the author of this law and the One who planted the moral sense within human beings. See Arguments for the Existence of God.

MORAL RE-ARMAMENT See Oxford Group.

MORAL THEOLOGY The branch of *theology that considers human conduct in relation to *God. Often it is called *Christian *ethics. However, moral theology may be defined as the study to establish the minimum standard to which conduct must attain if it is to be worthy of the name of Christian; this then contrasts with Christian ethics, which seeks to establish what is true Christian conduct.

MORAVIAN BRETHREN Known by this name since the early 18th century, they are the direct descendants of the *Bohemian Brethren, to whom the name *Unitas Fratrum (Unity of Brethren) is also given. In 1722 refugees from Moravia were made welcome at *Herrnhut, the Saxon estate of Count *Zinzendorf. The settlement there became a center of religious *revival, followed by an outreach that pioneered the modern Protestant *missionary movement. The Moravian Church, which has always been reluctant to adopt formal *creeds, retains its European bases, but more than half of its 400,000 membership is now found in the North American settlements. *Worship is basically liturgical, the *theology is related to *Lutheranism and *Pietism, and the office bearers are called *bishops, *presbyters, and *deacons.

MORE, HANNAH (1745–1833). English writer and philanthropist. With some talent as a playwright and acceptable in London's social and literary circles, she was increasingly drawn to *evangelical beliefs, in which she was encouraged by William *Wilberforce and John *Newton. She wrote a series of treatises in support of traditional values, established schools in the West Country, and sponsored a number of schemes for poor relief.

MORE, HENRY (1614–1687). Best-known member of the *Cambridge Platonists. A graduate of Cambridge, he lived almost all of his life in Christ's College there, rejecting preferment in university and church, and devoting himself to writing against materialism and other dangers of the age. Among his books were *Antidote Against Atheism* (1653) and *Divine Dialogues* (1668).

MORE, SIR THOMAS (1478–1535). English statesman and writer. A lawyer and briefly *Henry VIII's lord *chancellor (1529–1532), he was beheaded for refusing to acknowledge the king as head of the Church of *England and died loyal to Rome. More's great work *Utopia* (1516) satirically attacked the acquisitive society and discussed the nature and function of an ideal community.

MORGAN, GEORGE CAMPBELL (1863–1945). English Congregational minister. Son of a Baptist preacher in Gloucestershire, he ministered in various Congregational churches, notably in Westminster Chapel, London, over two different periods (1904–1917, 1933–1945). His evangelistic *preaching and *Bible studies always attracted large crowds, and his many writings are still popular. He was a close friend and collaborator of D. L. *Moody and made many trips to America.

MORGAN, WILLIAM (c. 1545–1604). Welsh *bishop and *Bible translator. Born in Caernavonshire and ordained in 1568, he was a *parish *priest before becoming successively bishop of Llandaff (1595) and of St Asaph (1601). Champion of the church against secular interests and an encourager of *preaching, he is remembered for a translation of the *Bible into Welsh that helped to standardize the literary language of the principality and to lay the foundation for modern Welsh *Protestantism.

MORISON, JAMES (1816–1893). Scottish minister. Educated at Edinburgh University, in 1839 he became minister of the United Secession Church in Kilmarnock, where people flocked to hear him. His *preaching tours were accompanied by spiritual *revival. Suspended by his own *denomination for *preaching the universal nature of the *Atonement, he was the chief mover, with his father and two other ministers, in founding the

Evangelical Union in 1843 and in establishing a theological college headed by himself. Widely acclaimed as a biblical commentator, he found great affinity in America with the *Cumberland Presbyterians. The Evangelical Union united with Scottish *Congregationalism in 1896.

MORMONISM The *religion of the Church of Jesus Christ of Latter-Day Saints, founded by Joseph *Smith in 1830. He claimed to have received the *Book of Mormon* from an *angel and to have been given the priestly powers of both Aaron and Melchizedek from the *OT. He claimed to have founded the true church because all others had become apostate.

Mormons have a tritheistic concept of *God. They believe that the creator of this world is a supremely evolved human being who lives in a physical body. A favorite saying is, "As man is, God once was; as God is, man may be." They identify the Yahweh of the Old Testament with *Jesus, not God the Father.

Mormonism is now centered in Utah. It is led by a president or high *priest to whom, it is held, God still speaks. He is assisted by twelve *apostles. Almost all males are recognized as holding some rank of priesthood. Faithful Mormons *tithe their income; do not use tobacco, alcohol, coffee, or tea; and they fully participate in the life of the congregation. They await the millennium. *Baptism is by *immersion, and baptism for the dead is practiced. The *Lord's Supper is held weekly, but water instead of wine is used. Their interpretation of *God is tritheistic. They believe that the creator of this world is a supreme evolved human being who lives in a physical body. A favorite saying is, "As man is, God once was; as God is, man may be." They identify the Yahweh of the Old Testament with *Jesus, not God the Father.

MORNAY, PHILIPPE DE (1549–1623). French *Huguenot leader. Norman by birth, he became a Protestant as a boy, was educated at Paris and foreign universities, then returned to France and barely escaped being a victim of the Massacre of St. *Bartholomew's Day in 1572. He entered the service of *Henry IV, drafted the Edict of *Nantes in 1598, and took part in the *synods of the *Reformed churches. He wrote much in defense of *Protestantism.

MORNING PRAYER The Anglican daily service of morning *worship and sometimes called *matins. It was derived in the 16th century from the medieval services of matins and *prime. It is made up of *Scripture readings, psalms, the *creed, and *intercessions.

MORRISON, ROBERT (1782–1834). Often described as the father of Protestant *missions in China. Born in Northumbria of Scottish parents, he was converted as an apprentice shoemaker, and after improving his scanty education, went to China in 1807 under the London Missionary Society. In the most unhelpful circumstances he translated the *Bible into Chinese and helped to found in 1818 the Anglo-Chinese college at Malacca for "the cultivation of English and Chinese literature in order to encourage the spread of the *Gospel of *Jesus Christ." On furlough, Morrison promoted the understanding of China and its evangelization, but he soon returned to lay the foundations of much future *missionary work.

MORTAL SIN A *sin of such gravity that if the sinner dies before *penance he will receive *eternal *damnation. Roman Catholic teaching distinguishes between *mortal and *venial sins. Mortal sins separate a man from *God and cause him to lose his state of *grace. Venial sins offend God but do not cause the loss of the state of grace.

MORTIFICATION The effort to put to death sinful and selfish tendencies (Rom 8:13; Gal 5:24; Col 3:5). Traditionally this is done through self-denial, *asceticism, and *fasting. Yet unless it is done in the power of the *Spirit in union with *Christ, it is of little avail in terms of producing true holiness (Rom 6:1–11).

MOTHER OF *GOD A translation of **theotokos*, a title given to *Mary by the Council of *Ephesus.

MOTT, JOHN RALEIGH (1865–1955). American ecumenist and Methodist layman. After graduation from Cornell, he joined the *YMCA staff for work among students, and in 1895 he helped to found the *World Student Christian Federation. A powerful speaker and a persuasive promoter of *missions, he made an extraordinary impact on religious movements at home and abroad. He consistently refused high political office, convinced that his place was in *Christian work. His best-known book reflected a popular contemporary slogan: *The Evangelization of the World in this Generation* (1900).

MOULE, HANDLEY CARR GLYN (1841–1920). *Bishop of Durham. A Cambridge graduate ordained in 1867, he became successively principal of Ridley Hall, Cambridge (1881); Norris professor of divinity (1899); and bishop of Durham (1901). For many years a *Keswick speaker and a great influence on the national *evangelical scene, he was the author of many devotional and expository works.

MOULTON, JAMES HOPE (1863–1917). *New Testament scholar. Entering the Methodist *ministry in 1886, he later taught New Testament at his church's Manchester college before his appointment to the chair of Hellenistic Greek at Manchester University. He collaborated with George *Milligan in demonstrating the link between NT Greek and the language of newly discovered papyri. He died after his ship was torpedoed during World War I.

MOULTON, WILLIAM FIDDIAN (1835–1898). Methodist scholar. He taught at Richmond (Methodist) College from 1858 until appointment as the first headmaster of the Leys School, Cambridge. One of the leading biblical scholars of his day, he was closely involved in the production of the Revised Version of the *Bible (*NT 1881). He was the father of J. H. *Moulton.

MOWLL, HOWARD WEST KILVINTON (1890–1958). *Archbishop of Sydney. Cambridge graduate, he was tutor in Canada and army chaplain in France before becoming an Anglican *bishop in China, where he served for ten years, furthering the movement toward indigenous Chinese bishops. In 1933 he was elected archbishop of Sydney and also became *primate of Australia in 1947. A warm *Evangelical, he could work happily with those of different church traditions.

MUGGLETONIANS An English *sect that took its name from Lodowicke Muggleton (1609–1698). He and his cousin John Reeve (1608–1658) presented themselves as the two prophetic witnesses of Revelation 11:3 and declared that failure to believe in them was the unforgivable *sin. Even his followers were alienated at times by their leader's extremism, but the sect survived until the early 20th century.

MÜHLENBERG, HENRY MELCHIOR (1711–1787). Father of American *Lutheranism. Born and ordained in Germany, he went to Pennsylvania in 1742 to supervise the scattered Lutheran congregations, and in 1748 he organized the first Lutheran *synod in America. Scholar, administrator, and *evangelist, he planted churches from New York to Georgia. Three of his sons became nationally known public figures.

MÜLLER, GEORGE (1805–1898). Pastor, philanthropist, and prominent member of the *Plymouth Brethren. Born in Germany and converted in 1825, he worked briefly among the Jews in England before becoming *pastor of Ebenezer Chapel, Teignmouth. Concerned for poor children, he opened an orphanage in Bristol in 1836, depending on *prayer and *faith, and *God supplied every need as the work expanded. When he was seventy, Müller and his wife undertook a seventeen-year tour in which they visited forty-two countries and preached to some three million hearers. His *Narration of Some of the Lord's Dealings with George Müller* had a wide circulation and influenced many in their *Christian faith and work.

MULLINS, EDGAR YOUNG (1860–1928). American Baptist scholar. Born in Mississippi, he served various pastorates until appointment in 1899 as professor (and later principal) at Southern Baptist Theological Seminary. He served a three-year term as his *denomination's president (1921–1924) at the height of the Fundamentalist controversy in the U.S. and was also president of the *Baptist World Alliance (1923–1928). His many works include *The Axioms of Religion* (1908) and *Christianity at the Crossroads* (1924).

MUNGO See KENTIGERN.

MÜNSTER, SEBASTIAN (1489–1552). German biblical scholar. A remarkable Semitic linguist, he was a *Franciscan until won to the Protestant cause about 1529. Thereafter he taught at Basel, where he produced an edition of the Hebrew *Bible from which Miles *Coverdale greatly benefited.

MÜNZER, THOMAS (c. 1490–1525). German Anabaptist. An ordained *priest, in 1520 he became a Protestant preacher at Zwickau but was soon expelled for contentious *preaching and bizarre views. Moving from place to place, he advocated open rebellion, joined the so-called *Peasants' Revolt in 1524, and was captured and executed.

MURILLO, BARTOLOME ESTEBAN (1617–1682). Spanish painter described as "the most popular Baroque religious artist of 17th-century Spain." Born in Seville, where he spent most of his life, he was an austere man whose works appealed to traditional piety and contributed to the *Counter-Reformation. His best-known painting is *The Immaculate Conception*. He died of injuries sustained when he fell while working in a Cadiz church.

MURRAY, ANDREW (1828–1917). South African minister. Educated at Aberdeen and Utrecht, he returned to South Africa and served various pastorates (1850–1906), during which time he was six times *moderator of the *Dutch *Reformed Church in Cape Colony. He maintained a wide *preaching and writing *ministry, introduced the Keswick movement into South Africa, and even after retirement conducted evangelistic meetings at home and abroad.

MUSIC IN CHURCH In the early centuries musical instruments were not used. Singing the psalms to monody and *chant was the rule. In the Middle Ages polyphony (two or more voices singing individual parts simultaneously) was introduced and so were musical instruments (e.g., harp and organ). Thus both chanting and music developed. This was maintained in *Roman Catholicism after the *Reformation, while in much of *Protestantism congregational *hymns and chorales became means whereby the whole congregation could join in *worship. The organ played an important part in *Lutheranism and *Anglicanism (as in Roman Catholicism), but in the *Reformed churches there was opposition to it. Metrical psalms were much used in the latter churches. In modern times congregational singing has become a part of Roman Catholic worship, and a variety of musical instruments are being used in services, especially the guitar in services involving young people. See also ANTHEM, CANTICLE, CHANT, CHOIR, HYMN.

MYCONIUS, FRIEDRICH (c. 1490–1546). German Reformer. A *Franciscan from 1510, he was ordained in 1516 but soon was caught up in the *Reformation movement and became a friend of *Luther and *Melanchthon and a persuasive preacher of the Protestant cause. He wrote a history of the Reformation that is a valuable contemporary record.

MYCONIUS, OSWALD (1488–1552). Swiss Reformer. Born in Lucerne, he was forced to leave that city later because he preached *Reformation *doctrines. A warm supporter of *Zwingli, whose biographer he became, he was latter a *pastor and professor at Basel.

MYNSTER, JAKOB PIER (1775–1854). Danish *bishop. Born in Copenhagen, he was at first a radical young *pastor but was converted in 1803 and became a staunch upholder of *evangelical *doctrines. Royal chaplain from 1828 and bishop of Zealand from 1834, he was, says a modern Danish minister, "the great central figure in Danish church life, standing between rationalists on one side, revivalists on the other." With other national church supporters he was bitterly attacked by Søren *Kierkegaard.

MYSTERY (Gk. *mysterion*, "a secret"). The fullness of *God's redemptive purpose in *Jesus Christ was kept secret by God until the *Incarnation and the sending of the *Spirit to the church (Eph 1:9; 3:3). Now by the Spirit the secret or mystery is revealed. In *theology mystery is used of the depth, width, height, and breadth of the inner life of God as Holy *Trinity and his *eternal purposes; it is also used of the Incarnation and especially of the union of the human and divine *natures in the one *Person. What we know of God and of *Christ is meaningful, but the more we know, the more we recognize that there is more to know; God is always a mystery in that there is much more of him that we can reverently know.

MYSTERY RELIGIONS Ancient Oriental *worship that flourished for centuries before and after the time of *Christ. There were numerous varieties of these mystery religions, some of the most popular centering around Eleusis, Mithras, Orpheus, Cybele, and Isis. They had in common their appeal to silence; stress on emotion and *ecstasy; promise of *eternal life; close connection to life, death, and reproduction; use of *symbols, *rituals, and sometimes drugs as intoxicants; religious frenzy and sexual license; and strong general appeal, being open to all, including women, slaves, and outcasts. Paul borrowed some of the terminology of the mystics, but a fundamental difference exists between the *NT and the mysteries. The mysteries are based upon an elaborate mythology and a sympathetic magical relation to the elemental forces of nature, whereas the NT is based upon a historical person, *Jesus of Nazareth.

MYSTICAL BODY A description or model of the church once popular in *Roman Catholicism. It is based on two considerations: (1) Paul's image of the church as the body (Rom 12:12ff.; 1 Cor 12:27) and (2) the church as a *mystery (*sacrament) in the sense that *God's secret of *redemption in *Christ is being worked out by the power of the *Spirit within the church. Thus mystical body as a description of the church emphasizes the spiritual essence of the church and suggests that each member has a position to maintain and a part to perform. To some it also highlights the sacramental character of the church—God's *grace revealed in and conveyed by the sacraments.

MYSTICAL THEOLOGY The branch of *theology that provides an analysis and systematic presentation of mystical experience of *God (*mysticism). It is related to, but not the same as, *ascetical *theology.

MYSTICISM The experience in which the believer arrives at a special union of *love with *God. It transcends knowledge of God achieved through the normal powers of mind and *reason. There is a loss of the sense of time with great feelings of joy and exultation. God is felt to be extremely near. It is *fellowship with God known through the embrace of a unifying love. To know what mysticism is requires a personal knowledge of mystical experience or the reading of books by those known as mystics (e.g., *Teresa of Avila, John of the Cross, Julian of Norwich, and *Eckhart). A classic treatment of the subject is found in *Mysticism* (1911) by Evelyn Underhill.

N

NAIROBI ASSEMBLY (1975). Fifth assembly of the *World Council of Churches. Meeting in the Kenyan capital, it had as its theme "*Jesus Christ liberates and unites." It was studied in six sections, dealing respectively with confessing *Christ today, unity of the church, search for community, education for liberation, structures of injustice and the fight for liberation, and human development. During the eighteen-day meetings, discussion of current issues by the seven hundred delegates took up a substantial amount of time. The alleged denial of religious freedom in the Soviet Union was aired more candidly than in most conciliar gatherings. The Programme to Combat Racism still drew fierce criticism, but South Africa was the only nation singled out (as an aggressor in Angola). Fifteen more churches were admitted to WCC membership at Nairobi, making the total 286 member and associate member churches.

NANTES, EDICT OF (1598). An agreement between *Henry IV and the *Huguenots intended to define the position of French Protestants. It gave them freedom of *worship in certain defined areas but modified other liberties. It remained in force until revoked by *Louis XIV in 1685.

NATIONAL ASSOCIATION OF EVANGELICALS (U.S.) Tracing its descent from the *Evangelical Alliance formed in 1867, the NAE was organized in St. Louis, Missouri, in 1942. All *denominations, congregations, and individuals willing to sign its credal statement are welcome to join the organization. At present it consists of 50,000 local churches representing seventy denominations, serving approximately 10 million people.

NATIONAL COVENANT (1638). The Scottish document that gives its name to the *Covenanters. A protest against *Charles I's attempt to impose a more rigid *episcopacy on Scotland, the Covenant was based on the 1580 Negative Confession, which condemned *Roman Catholicism. In addition, it defended the *Reformed *faith, ecclesiastical freedom, and *presbyterian polity.

NATIVITY OF JOHN THE BAPTIST, FEAST OF THE The commemoration of the miraculous birth of John (Luke 1) kept on June 24.

NATIVITY OF OUR LORD, FEAST OF THE Another way of describing *Christmas.

NATIVITY OF THE BLESSED VIRGIN MARY, FEAST OF THE The commemoration of the birth of *Mary, mother of *Jesus, kept on September 8.

NATURAL LAW (Lat. *lex naturalis*). The knowledge of what is ethically good derived from use of human *reason alone. It can be defined as the knowledge of the good placed in human beings by *God and discerned through their reason. Possibly Paul referred to this in Romans 2:14–16.

Some theologians hold that because of *original *sin, knowledge of what God requires is only possible through his *revelation, for all other knowledge is marred and twisted by the sinfulness of humankind and is therefore not reliable.

NATURAL MAN A human being considered as a sinner living by his sinful tendencies and habits and outside of a relationship of submission to and *love of *God. In contrast spiritual man is man considered as being in spiritual communion with God.

NATURAL THEOLOGY The knowledge of *God and of God's relationship to the world that is acquired without reference to special *revelation but based wholly on natural revelation. It is reflection upon the evidence provided by the *universe and the *nature of human beings. The great exponent of natural theology was Thomas *Aquinas (c. 1225–1274), but its possibility as a viable enterprise has been denied by others—notably by Karl *Barth. See also THEISM, CHRISTIAN.

NATURE (Lat. *natura,* "the internal principle and unity of a thing"). As a technical term it has been used in the classic *theology of both the *Trinity and the *Incarnation. Thus it is used of the one Godhead, the nature of *God, which is shared by each of the three *Persons. In Greek the usual word is **ousia*. Each Person is said to have the divine nature in fullness, that is as his true internal principle and unity. When used of the Incarnation it is claimed that in the one *Jesus Christ there are two natures, a human and a divine. One is perfectly human and the other perfectly divine. The Greek word for nature as applied to the Incarnation is **phusis*.

NATURE AND GRACE This phrase highlights the two major realities of human existence as lived in *God's world. Nature points to what a human being is by birth, a sinful creature whom God wishes to make his child. *Grace is what God offers and what the human being needs in order to achieve his destiny and to be a child of *God. Grace supplies what nature lacks and corrects what nature has got wrong. There is also a sense in which grace perfects nature, in that the grace of God working in a human life renews and refreshes natural talents and graces so that they function as part of the life of *love and service to God.

NAUMBURG CONVENTION (1561). This gathering in the Saxon town of Naumburg brought together Protestant rulers and others holding *Reformed views in an attempt to achieve unity on doctrinal matters. The occasion served chiefly to highlight disagreements, particularly regarding the different versions of the *Augsburg Confession. There was greater consensus about rejecting a papal invitation to send representatives to the Council of *Trent.

NAYLOR, JAMES (1618–1660). English *Quaker. After a nine-year term in the parliamentary army during which he was also an *Independent preacher, he met George *Fox and became a Quaker. Influenced by some extremist elements, Naylor and some followers in 1656 entered Bristol in procession, after the manner of *Christ's entry into Jerusalem. For this he was tried before a parliamentary committee, found guilty of *blasphemy, and was whipped and imprisoned. But in 1659 he was released and was reconciled to Fox and orthodox Quakerism.

NAZARENE, CHURCH OF THE An international Protestant body that is largely in the 19th-century Wesleyan tradition in its emphasis on personal holiness. It developed from the merging of three U.S. Holiness groups: the Association of Pentecostal Churches in America, the Church of the Nazarene, and the Holiness Church of Christ. In 1919 it took the name Church of the Nazarene. It has an extensive *missionary program, puts great stress on *Christian education and on the giving of *tithes, and enjoins members to shun all forms of worldly activity. Its chief governing body is the church assembly, which meets every fourth year in the U.S. Worldwide it has a membership of almost 600,000 in more than 6,900 churches.

NEAL, DANIEL (1678–1743). Historian of the Puritans. Born in London, he trained for the *ministry at a *Dissenting academy, studied further in Holland, and after *ordination in 1703 ministered in a London Congregational church until his death. He was a splendid preacher, but it was his writing that brought him renown. Harvard gave him an honorary M.A. for his *History of New England* (1720), but his best-known work is the *History of the Puritans* (1732–1738), four volumes covering the period from the *Reformation down to 1689.

NEALE, JOHN MASON (1818–1866). Anglican *hymn writer. Born in London of *Evangelical parents, he graduated at Cambridge, where he became a *High churchman. Ordained in 1843, he was prevented by chronic ill health from assuming parochial responsibilities, and he gave himself to charitable work. His many hymns, some of them translations from Greek and Latin, include "All Glory, Laud, and Honor" and "Of the Father's Love Begotten."

NEANDER, JOACHIM (1650–1680). German *hymn writer. Born and educated at Bremen, he was converted in 1670 and became a Pietist, which led to the promulgation of views that prevented his advancement as teacher and preacher. He made a lasting contribution to the *Christian church through his hymns, which include "Praise to the Lord, the Almighty" and "All My Hope on *God Is Founded."

NEANDER, JOHANN AUGUST WILHELM (1789–1850). German church historian. Born a Jew and called David Mendel, he was influenced by F. D. E. *Schleiermacher, became a *Christian in 1806, and changed his name. His great work, *General Church History* (6 vols., 1826–1852), covered the period up to 1450. His aim throughout this project was to trace *God's dealings with the human race.

NECROMANCY (Gk. *nekros,* "a corpse"; *manteia,* "*divination"). A way of telling the future through supposed communication with the *souls of the dead. It is condemned by the law of Moses (Lev 19:31; 20:6; Deut 18:11–12) and by *Christian churches.

NEESHIMA, YUZURU (1843–1890). Japanese *Christian leader. Born into a Buddhist family, he fled to America in 1864, became a *Christian, graduated from Andover Theological Seminary, was ordained as a Congregational minister, and in 1875 returned to Japan. In Kyoto he founded Doshisha ("One Purpose Society"), the first Christian school in Japan.

NEGATION, WAY OF (Lat. *via negativa*). The way of understanding *God in which all imperfections in God are denied so that all perfections that admit of no defect may be affirmed. It proceeds by saying that God is not spatial, finite, etc., in order to be able to say that God is *eternal and *infinite, etc. It was much used in the medieval church.

NEO-EVANGELICALISM See New Evangelicalism.

NEOLOGY New teaching. New *doctrines, contrary to received *orthodoxy but expressed in traditional terminology. Often used by British theologians of the mid-19th century to refer to German rationalistic *theology.

NEOORTHODOXY A type of Protestant and *Reformed *theology of the 20th century, the name of Karl *Barth (*Barthianism) is especially associated with it. It is neo (new) in that it opposes the dominant *Liberalism of the day; it is orthodox in that it attempts to recover the major theological themes of the *Reformation and the *Patristic period. This approach involves the use of higher critical methods in the interpretation of the *Bible. They do not regard the Scripture to be inerrant but believe that God speaks through Scripture and his Son to obligate humankind to obedience and faithfulness to God.

NEO-PENTECOSTALISM The cultivation of the "*Pentecostal" experience (especially speaking in *tongues) outside the Pentecostal *denominations (e.g., *Assemblies of God) by members of traditional churches and *denominations. It is the old Pentecostal experience but in new structures. Neo-Pentecostalism is also called the *charismatic movement.

NEOPHYTE A new convert who has not yet become a *catechumen and who has not received *baptism. It is also used today of entrants into the monastic life who aspire to be *nuns and monks. The Greek word is used once in the *NT at 1 Timothy 3:6, where a new convert is said not to be eligible for *ordination.

NEOPLATONISM The recasting of the philosophy of Plato by Plotinus (205–270) and others. Some *Christian theologians used it to expound the *truths of *Christianity, and its influence lasted into the medieval period.

NEOSCHOLASTICISM Also known as Neo-Thomism. A study of philosophy modeled on that of Thomas *Aquinas (c. 1225–1274). It began as a movement in the late 18th century. Although it has been mainly a Roman Catholic phenomenon, it has attracted certain Anglican theologians as well.

NEO-THOMISM Contemporary movement basically in Roman Catholic philosophy, updating Thomas *Aquinas. Pope *Leo XIII virtually canonized the thought of Aquinas in 1880, and from that time readjustments began to be made. Several changes have been attempted, but the branch associated with Etienne Gilson and Jacques *Maritain became known as Neo-Thomism. Beginning with the premise that *Being is primary, the Neo-Thomists proceed to develop a complex rational system that includes proof of *God's existence (by traditional arguments); an extensive natural *theology; an analogical approach to talking about God; defense of human dignity and ethical absolutes; and essentially orthodox theological formulations. Neo-Thomism has also had an appeal to some Protestant theologians such as E. L. Mascall and Austin Farrer.

NERI, PHILIP (1515–1595). Known as the "*Apostle of Rome." Born in Florence and educated by *Dominicans, he was an ascetic given to charitable *works. After *ordination in 1551 he became renowned as a spiritual director in Rome. He established the Congregation of the Oratory (which added social and artistic dimensions to religious exercises), was an adviser to all classes, and was known for compassion and cheerfulness.

NESTORIANISM The *doctrine that holds that *Christ combined in himself two *persons as well as two *natures. It took its name from Nestorius (d. c. 451), *bishop of Constantinople from 428, who advised against use of the term "*Mother of God" for the Virgin *Mary. The Council of *Ephesus (431) declared him deposed, but it seems clear that Nestorius's stance originated in a distrust of *Monophysitism, and that it was distorted by his ecclesiastical enemies. A Nestorian church arose, based in Persia, with modern descendants (now known as the Assyrian Christians) found also in Iraq, India, and the United States.

NETTLETON, ASAHEL (1783–1843). American *evangelist. Converted at sixteen, he trained at Yale and became an itinerant evangelist among the churches. Instrumental in the spiritual *awakening of many, he strongly opposed the methods of Charles *Finney, notably the practice of calling for an immediate public profession of commitment to *Christ. He saw his task as *preaching the claims of *God, the duties of sinners, and the necessity of possessing the distinguishing evidences of *regeneration.

NEUMANN, JOHN (1811–1860). Catholic *priest and *saint. John Neumann was ordained a priest in 1836 in New York and joined the *Redemptorist *order in 1840. *Pius IX named him *bishop of Philadelphia, Pennsylvania, in 1852. He was the first Roman Catholic churchman to organize the Roman Catholic diocesan school system in America. Canonized in 1977, he thus became the first male saint of the U.S.

NEVIUS, JOHN LIVINGSTON (1829–1893). American *missionary to China. Born in Ohio and trained at Princeton for the *Presbyterian *ministry, he arrived in China in 1854. His "Nevius method" of a self-supporting national *Christian work was widely and effectively applied, notably in Korea. A translator of the *Bible, he also wrote a remarkable book on *demon possession and allied themes.

NEW APOSTOLIC CHURCH Until 1906 known as the Universal Catholic Church, it was an 1863 offshoot from the *Catholic Apostolic Church. It was formed in Germany by those who believed that the Catholic Apostolic Church should appoint new *apostles in place of those who had died. With headquarters in West Germany, where most of its estimated 600,000 members live, the New Apostolic Church is less liturgical than the parent body but has largely the same *doctrines.

NEW CHURCH See NEW JERUSALEM, CHURCH OF THE.

NEW DELHI ASSEMBLY (1961). Third assembly of the *World Council of Churches. In addition to some 580 voting delegates, there were more than 1,000 others, including Roman Catholic observers, at the meetings. The theme was "Jesus Christ, the Light of the World." Approval was given to membership applications from twenty-three churches, including the Russian Orthodox; to a merger between the WCC and the *International Missionary Council; and to the formula: "The WCC is a *fellowship of churches which confess the *Lord *Jesus Christ as *God and *Saviour according to the *Scriptures, and therefore seek to fulfil together their common calling to the glory of the one God, Father, Son and Holy *Spirit."

NEW ENGLAND THEOLOGY A Calvinist movement originating in Jonathan *Edwards, which during the latter 18th and early 19th centuries sought to harmonize traditional *Puritanism with distinctively American trends. Among later leaders of the movement, which dominated Congregational *seminaries for more than a century, were Timothy *Dwight, Samuel *Hopkins, and Nathaniel *Taylor.

NEW ENGLISH BIBLE See BIBLE (ENGLISH VERSIONS).

NEW EVANGELICALISM Term used in the U.S. to describe the modified form of traditional, conservative Evangelicalism (or *Fundamentalism) that manifests a greater emphasis on social concern and responsibility. Basic *doctrines are not changed, but they are related to concern for the external as well as internal lives of human beings. The idea of *holistic *salvation represents a further development.

NEW HAMPSHIRE CONFESSION (1833). Moderate Calvinist Baptist *confession of *faith. *Baptists traditionally defend a "no *creed but the *Bible" position, but in America the New Hampshire Confession has served as a nonbinding standard for a large majority of Baptists for over a century and a half. It has been reissued and revised over the years, but its fundamentally orthodox and Baptistic formulations have remained unchanged. Its strong emphasis on *Scripture ("It has *God for its author, *salvation for its end, and *truth, without any mixture of error, for its matter") and its moderate *Calvinism have made it attractive to Fundamentalists, *Moderates, Calvinists, and Arminians alike. The *Southern Baptist Convention (1925) followed its intent closely when they wrote their own Statement of Baptist Faith and Message.

NEW HAVEN THEOLOGY An approach to *theology developed at Yale Divinity School under the leadership of N. W. *Taylor (1786–1858). It opposed traditional *Calvinism, encouraged the *revival movement (and the work and teaching of Charles *Finney, the revivalist), and helped to inspire various charitable and social reform movements.

NEW HEAVEN AND EARTH One aspect of the biblical portrayal of the age to come (2 Peter 3:13; Rev 21:1). It suggests a totally restored and renewed sphere in which the *saints will dwell. See also ESCHATOLOGY.

NEW HERMENEUTIC, THE Recent hermeneutical position based on Rudolf *Bultmann and Martin *Heidegger's stressing of the normative nature of language. Bultmann and his successors (the "post-Bultmannians"), following Heidegger, have argued that the world cannot be understood in the mythological terms of the *NT but must be demythologized for the modern man. To do this we must drop to the level of existential awareness present in the *kerygma (preached message) and confront people with the possibility of a new self-understanding. This is what *salvation means. The new hermeneutic explores the relation of language to event, meaning, and depth as opposed to the "old" hermeneutic that sought to understand the *Bible as text and *revelation. In essence, the new hermeneutic is concerned to exegete the reader of the text and his existential state rather than the text itself except insofar as the text gives rise to a new state of being in the reader. See also BULTMANN, RUDOLF.

NEW INTERNATIONAL VERSION See BIBLE (ENGLISH VERSIONS).

NEW JERUSALEM, CHURCH OF THE A body dating from about 1788 based on the writings of Emanuel Swedenborg, hence the alternative name *Swedenborgians. The American branch began about four years after its British counterpart. They emphasize liturgical *worship, interpret *Scripture spiritually, and believe in a new *dispensation revealed through Swedenborg, whereby believers passed into the New Jerusalem. Swedenborgians are divided into three different groups, but total membership (apart from *missionary statistics) is unlikely to be much over 10,000.

NEW LIGHT SCHISM Conflicts within the Congregational and *Presbyterian churches in the mid-18th century over the relation of *faith to life. The Old Side argued that *God's unconditional *election took precedence over everything, thus correct belief rather than correct life was primary. They were strongly opposed to the *Great Awakenings, *revivalism, the idea of *conversion, and pietistic forms of life. Charles *Chauncy is a good representative of this point of view. George *Whitefield, Jonathan *Edwards, and Gilbert *Tennent represented the New Light and defended the newer stress on experience. Eventually their views prevailed, with a reunion being effected in 1758. Hardline Old Siders eventually drifted into Unitarianism.

NEW TESTAMENT The books of *Scripture belonging exclusively to the *Christian church and not read in the Jewish synagogues. There are twenty-seven books—four *Gospels, the Acts of the Apostles, the Pauline and General Epistles, and the Book of Revelation. They were written in koine Greek some twenty-five or more years after *Jesus' *resurrection. They arose out of the new *covenant (testament) that *God made in *Christ with all who believe on his name.

NEW AND OLD SCHOOL PRESBYTERIANS A division within American *Presbyterianism in the mid-19th century. The "New" wanted a liberal interpretation of the *confession of *faith, was opposed to *slavery, and wanted a union with *Congregationalists. The "Old" was the conservative, traditionalist group.

NEWMAN, JOHN HENRY (1801–1890). English *cardinal. A leading figure in the *Oxford Movement, he preached highly influential *sermons as *vicar of St. Mary's, Oxford. In 1845 he was received into the Roman Catholic Church and was subsequently ordained in Rome. He was rector of Dublin University (1854–1858) and was made cardinal in 1879. Newman, who was involved in a number of painful controversies, made notable literary contributions, among them the autobiographical *Apologia Pro Vita Sua* (1864) and *Grammar of Assent* (1870).

NEWTON, JOHN (1725–1807). Anglican clergyman and *hymn writer. Involved in slave trading even after *conversion in 1747, he was ordained in 1764 and became *curate of Olney. In 1779 he moved to London as *vicar of St. Mary, Woolnoth, and was later an adviser of the young William *Wilberforce. Newton is remembered chiefly as coproducer with the poet William Cowper of the famous *Olney Hymns,* which included "Glorious Things of Thee Are Spoken," "How Sweet the Name of Jesus Sounds," and "Amazing Grace."

NIAGARA CONFERENCES Bible Conferences held in Niagara-on-the-Lake, Ontario (Canada), from 1883–1901. Originally designed to unite *Evangelicals in the study of *Scripture, the Niagara Conferences came increasingly under the influence of pretribulational, dispensational *premillennialism, which eventually brought about the dissolution of the meetings after unresolvable conflict over the timing of the *rapture of the church. These conferences were of great significance, giving rise to numerous premillennial prophetic conferences over the entire North American continent that continue to this day. They helped to spread the dispensationalist message at the popular level and made it a part of *Fundamentalism as it took shape following World War I.

NICEA, COUNCIL OF (325). First *ecumenical church council. Summoned by Emperor *Constantine, it dealt with controversy in the church, especially *Arianism. It was the young *deacon *Athanasius who saw the real danger to *orthodoxy and contended successfully for the *Christian *doctrine of *God and of *Creation. Largely through the intervention of Athanasius the council affirmed that the Son was "out of the *being of the Father," was "begotten, not made," and was of "the same *nature with the Father." Some other matters decided at Nicea were that all churches should observe *Easter on the same *Sunday, that *bishops and *priests who had been ordained while unmarried should remain unmarried, and that bishops and *clergy should not move from one church to another.

NICEA, SECOND COUNCIL OF (787). Seventh *ecumenical council of the *Christian church. Called by the Empress Irene to deal with the *Iconoclastic Controversy, the largely Western assembly condemned the iconoclasts and decreed that the persons represented by the *images might receive *veneration but not *adoration. In 794 *Charlemagne rejected this decision, and even in the East the iconoclasts found influential support for a half century more.

NICENE CREED Technically it is the *creed produced by the Council of *Nicea (325), but in general usage it is the Nicene-Constantinopolitan Creed produced by the Council of *Constantinople (381). This latter creed, which is a revised version of the original one, is widely used in churches as a *confession of *faith to be recited in the *liturgy. In origin the creed was a way of excluding the *heresy of *Arianism and affirming that *Jesus Christ is truly *God made man. The Eastern and Western versions of this creed differ in that the latter contains the famous *filioque clause.

NICHOLAS I (THE GREAT) (d. 867). Pope from 858. A great upholder of *Christian unity and Christian marriage, he imperfectly understood developments in the *Eastern church, where he precipitated a *Schism. He had a high view of his office and tended toward a theocratic rule, but he was hailed as an impartial dispenser of justice and the friend of the *poor.

NICHOLAS II (d. 1061). Pope from 1058. French by birth, he is remembered chiefly for having brought at the 1059 Lateran Council orderliness to papal elections. He assigned responsibility to the leading *cardinals and precluded any imperial part in the proceedings. This precipitated conflict between empire and *papacy.

NICHOLAS V (1397–1455). Pope from 1447. Elected after wide experience of diplomatic service, he quickly brought peace to warring factions in church and state. He embarked on an imaginative rebuilding program in Rome and patronized the *arts, but his failure to remedy religious ills contributed to the success of the 16th-century *Reformation.

NICHOLAS OF CUSA (1401–1464). German *cardinal and scholar. A versatile man, he argued for the supremacy of general councils over the *pope but changed his mind when he considered the Council of *Basel ineffectual. He was ordained in 1440 and became *bishop of Brixen in 1450. He was adept also at mathematics, philosophy, and science, and he anticipated some of the findings of *Copernicus.

NICHOLAS OF HEREFORD (d. c. 1420). English *Lollard. An Oxford scholar, he was influenced by the teachings of John *Wycliffe, defended that position publicly, narrowly escaped execution, was imprisoned twice, and finally renounced Lollard *doctrines and helped to suppress the dissidents. He reportedly became a *Carthusian monk shortly before his death. He collaborated with Wycliffe in the first complete English translation of the *Bible.

NICHOLAS OF LYRA (c. 1270–1349). *Franciscan scholar. He joined the Franciscans about 1300 and subsequently taught for many years at the Sorbonne. His famous fifty-volume commentary on the *Bible emphasizes a literal interpretation. In 1325 Nicholas founded the College of Burgundy in Paris.

NICHOLAS OF MYRA (4th century). Also known as Saint Nicholas. *Bishop of Myra in Asia Minor. Feast Day December 6. Saint of sailors, children, and pawnbrokers. He was loved by the Dutch, who called Saint Nicholas "Sint Nikolaas." From this name came Santa Claus.

NICHOLSON, WILLIAM PATTESON (1876–1959). Irish *evangelist. Converted in 1899 after a wild career as seaman and railroad laborer in South Africa, he became a *Presbyterian minister, worked in America for a time, then returned to Ireland for a remarkably fruitful series of *missions. A speaker of colorful language and imaginative approach, he was an unlikely candidate for conducting a university *mission in sophisticated Cambridge. Nevertheless, when he did so, about one hundred students professed *conversion, and one observer described that mission as a landmark in the history of the Christian Union there.

NICOLAI (IVAN KASATKIN) (c. 1835–1912). Russian *missionary to Japan. A *priest of the *Orthodox church, he went to Japan in 1861, and in 1872 he organized a church in Tokyo. He was a great believer in delegating responsibility to nationals, and at his death (by which time he was an *archbishop) there were more than 30,000 converts.

NICOLL, SIR WILLIAM ROBERTSON (1851–1923). Scottish editor. A *Free Church of Scotland minister who resigned because of ill health, he edited the *Expositor* from 1885 and the *British Weekly* from 1886. Contributors to each included many leading scholars. He also edited *The Expositor's Greek Testament,* was knighted in 1909 and was made a Companion of Honour in 1921.

NIEBUHR, HELMUT RICHARD (1894–1962). American theologian. He was born in Missouri and was professor of *Christian *ethics at Yale (1931–1962). In teaching and writing he always tried to apply *Christianity to contemporary social issues and modern scholarship. A minister of the *Evangelical and Reformed church, he wrote much, including *The Meaning of Revelation* (1941) and *Christ and Cul-*

ture (1951). He was a brother of Reinhold *Niebuhr.

NIEBUHR, REINHOLD (1892–1971). American theologian. Born in Missouri, he was a *pastor in Detroit (1915–1928) and professor at Union Theological Seminary, New York (1928–1960). Formerly a pacifist, he supported the *war against Hitler. His many books included *The Nature and Destiny of Man* (1941, 1943) and *Christian Realism and Social Problems* (1953). He founded the journal *Christianity and Crisis* in 1941.

NIEMÖLLER, MARTIN (1892–1984). German theologian and ecumenist. After naval service in World War I he began theological studies, and in 1931 he became *pastor in a fashionable Berlin suburb. He protested and acted against Nazi policies, founded the *Confessing church, and was imprisoned (1938–1945) until freed by Allied forces. He helped reorganize the postwar church in Germany, became an outspoken pacifist, and in 1961 was elected one of the presidents of the *World Council of Churches. His writings include an autobiographical work translated into English in 1939 as *From U-Boat to Concentration Camp*.

NIHIL OBSTAT The Latin formula by which an ecclesiastical censor expresses the judgment that a book contains nothing that would harm the *faith and morals of the faithful. It was once a common formula in books by Roman Catholics.

NIHILISM A social and political philosophy of the 19th century that rejected religious and moral values. Basically a Russian phenomenon, it advocated belief only in science, materialism, revolution, and "the People."

NIKON (1605–1681). *Patriarch of Moscow. A friend of Czar Alexis and the spokesman for a reform group within the *Orthodox Church, he became patriarch in 1652 and tried to establish the supremacy of church over state. He pushed his reforms so insensitively that a *Schism was caused from which the *Old Believers emerged. Despite this and the alienation of the czar, the reforms were consolidated. Nikon was deposed in 1660, exiled to a remote area, and pardoned just before his death.

NINETY-FIVE THESES, THE (1517). The famous document that, nailed by *Luther to a Wittenberg church door in 1517, sought to draw the *pope's attention to the scandal of *indulgences. Although Luther's points were put in a comparatively restrained way—statements proposed for theological debate—the angry reaction of church authorities transformed a protest into the first blow struck for the Protestant *Reformation.

NINIAN (c. 360–c. 432). Scottish *missionary and first *bishop of Galloway. Details of his career are uncertain. He is said to have trained and been consecrated in Rome, to have established his see at Whithorn about 397, and to have used his see as a base from which he and his monks went out to evangelize Britons and Picts and so laid the foundation for the work of *Columba and *Kentigern.

NITSCHMANN, DAVID (1696–1772). First *bishop of the Reorganized Moravian church. Having joined Count *Zinzendorf at *Herrnhut, he was consecrated in 1735 and immediately led a group of *missionaries to Georgia. On the ship were John and Charles *Wesley, of whom Nitschmann made a profound impression. His missionary and episcopal work involved him in constant travel in Europe and in the New World.

NOETICS (Gk. *noetikos,* "intellectual"). The name given to a group of teachers in Oriel College, Oxford, in the early 19th century. They wanted great intellectual freedom and theological comprehensiveness within their university and the Church of *England.

NOLASCO, PETER (c. 1189–1256). A founder of the *Mercedarians. Born in France, he used his inheritance to ransom *Christian slaves of the Moors in Spain and subsequently helped to found the Mercedarians in Barcelona in 1218. He redeemed other slaves in Africa before relinquishing leadership of his *order about 1249.

NOMINALISM (Lat. *nominalis,* "belonging to a name"). The medieval theory that universal ideas such as *truth and goodness are only names. Only individual things exist. Abstract ideas are merely useful labels used by the mind and do not correspond to any objective reality. Nominalism began at the end of the 11th century as the opposite of *Realism. It was revived in a more sophisticated form by *William of Occam (c. 1280–1349). It is an important background study for students of *Luther and the *Reformation of the 16th century.

NONCONFORMITY The principle of not conforming to the established church. Used particularly in English history of those who on grounds of *conscience left the national church rather than conforming to *theology and ceremonies that they found objectionable. Thus that part of the Puritan and *Separatist movement in England that did not conform between 1660–1662 became Nonconformity. It included *Baptists, *Congregationalists, Presbyterians, and *Quakers, and as such is known as Protestant Nonconformity or Protestant *Dissenters. Roman Catholics who did not conform were also Nonconformists.

NONJURORS Members of the Church of *England who would not take the *oath of loyalty to William and Mary after 1688 because they believed that the deposed *James II was the true king. They became a schismatic party within the church but had little influence after 1715.

NORBERT (c. 1080–1134). Founder of the *Premonstratensians. German by birth, he gave up a comfortable *clerical position in 1115 along with all his possessions, and in 1120, at the suggestion of Callistus II, he founded his *order at Premontre, France. Norbert became *archbishop of Magdeburg in 1126, defended Pope Innocent II against a rival, and established friendly relations between the *papacy and the church in Germany.

NORMA NORMANS (Lat. "the ruling *rule"). Use of *Scripture by Protestants (especially Lutherans) to indicate that it is the only rule and norm by which all *doctrine and teachers are to be judged.

NORMA NORMATA (Lat. "the *rule having been ruled"). Use of *confessions of *faith that have been tested by *Scripture and are thus acceptable.

NORRIS, JOHN FRANK (1877–1952). Fundamentalist *pastor and editor. Illustrious pastor in Fort Worth (First Baptist, 1909–1952) and Detroit (Temple Baptist, 1934–1947)—the combined membership of his two congregations being 25,000 in 1946—he was famous for his *preaching, *Sunday school work, training of *pastors, and work as editor of *The Fundamentalist*.

NORTH END A position adopted by the president of the *Eucharist as he stands or kneels at the *holy table. As the congregation views him, he is on the lefthand side of the table facing the wall on the right of the congregation. Many *Evangelicals in the Church of *England have held this position to be the right one, especially in opposition to the eastward position (the president having his back to the congregation). In recent days the westward position (the president facing the congregation from behind the table) has become increasingly popular.

NORTH INDIA, CHURCH OF A union of six *denominations effected at Nagpur in 1970. The participating bodies were Anglicans, United Church of Northern India (Presbyterians and *Congregationalists), *Baptists, Methodists, *Church of the Brethren (U.S.), and *Disciples of Christ. Eight of the seventeen *bishops of the new body were Anglicans; the total membership was 569,546. In addition to the bishops, the *synod comprised equal numbers of *clerical and lay representatives. Following the custom of three of the joining churches, the new body permits believer's *baptism as well as *infant baptism.

NORTHFIELD CONFERENCES Bible Conferences held in Northfield, Massachusetts, during the latter part of the 19th century under the spiritual leadership of D. L. *Moody. Their significance lies in their *ecumenical *spirit, with Moody including such men as Henry *Drummond, William Rainey Harper, and Josiah Strong, as well as A. J. *Gordon, R. A. *Torrey, and C. I. *Scofield, and the impact of the conference for college students beginning in 1886. These meetings eventually resulted in the enlistment of over two thousand recruits for foreign *missionary service, the founding of The *Student Volunteer Movement (which played such an important part in the spread of *Christianity), and the early ecumenical movement.

NOTES OF THE CHURCH That the church is one—*holy, *catholic, and apostolic. See also MARKS OF THE CHURCH.

NOVALIS (1772–1801). Pen name of Friedrich Leopold Freiherr von Hardenberg, German poet and writer. Born of Pietist parents, he believed that man's goal was to regain a lost union with nature, wherein man had once been able to communicate directly with animals, plants, and things. He rejected the *Reformation as having disrupted the spiritual unity of medieval times. His poetry influenced the later so-called Romantics in Germany, France, and England.

NOVATIANISM A 3d-century *separatist movement within the church. Its name came from Novatian (c. 200–c. 258), a prominent Roman *priest and theologian who took up a severe attitude toward the Lapsi Christians who had renounced their *faith in time of persecution. When Cornelius was elected pope in 251 a minority adhered to Novatian as *antipope. Though excommunicated, the Novatianists expanded, established their own church throughout the empire, and survived for several centuries. Novatianism was not only doctrinally orthodox; Novatian himself defended *orthodoxy in a treatise on the *Trinity.

NOVICE The name given to one who is a candidate or probationer for the religious life, prior to the profession of *vows. The noviciate usually lasts for at least one year, during which time the novice is free to leave or may be requested to do so.

NOYES, JOHN HUMPHREY (1811–1886). American social reformer. He trained for the Congregational *ministry at Andover and Yale, but views on *perfectionism and his own *sinlessness, coupled with personal irregularities, led him to establish the *Oneida Community in 1848. Public opinion caused him to spend his last ten years in Canada. He wrote a useful book called *History of American Socialism* (1870).

NUMINOUS A word coined by Rudolf Otto and used in his *Idea of the Holy* (1923) to describe the experience of encountering the *holy, whether it be of the living *God or of the mystery of nature or natural events. In this experience there is both a fascination and a self-abasement, a feeling of attraction and of being repelled—as a great fire both attracts and repels.

NUN A woman who, by taking *vows of *poverty, *chastity, and *obedience, has become a member of a *religious *order or group. In *Roman Catholicism nuns are strictly those who live a cloistered life (as distinct from sisters). A similar situation obtains generally in *Eastern Orthodox churches. In Protestant churches, notably Lutheran and Anglican, where religious communities of women were revived in the 19th century, sisters or *deaconesses is the normal description for those who combine the active with the contemplative life.

NUNCIO AND LEGATE, PAPAL A *nuncio represents the *holy see to both civil and religious authority in a country or region. A legate is usually the papal representative on a particular occasion, such as a king's coronation or a Eucharistic congress over which he would preside.

NUREMBERG DECLARATION (1870). *Old Catholic Church theological statement. Drawn up by fourteen German professors in Nuremberg, it rejected *Vatican Council I as not being a true *ecumenical council, rejected papal *infallibility as *dogma and asserted that it could cause trouble between church and state, and called for an unrestricted general council to meet in Germany.

NYGREN, ANDERS THEODOR SAMUEL (1890–1978). Swedish theologian and ecumenist. Professor of *systematic *theology at Lund (1924–1949) and *bishop of Lund (1949–1958), he supported *ecumenical enterprises and was active in the formation of the *World Council of Churches in 1948. His many writings include *Agape and Eros* (Eng. trans. 1953), *Christ and His Church* (Eng. Trans. 1957), and a commentary on Romans (1941).

O

OAK, SYNOD OF THE (403). A church gathering in a suburb of Chalcedon ("The Oak") convened by imperial command, in which John *Chrysostom's ecclesiastical enemies contrived to condemn him on a number of bogus charges. He was duly condemned and sentenced to exile, but popular opinion, combined with the guilty *conscience of the empress Eudoxia, resulted in his reinstatement within a few days.

OATH A formal affirmation in which *God is called upon as witness that one is speaking the *truth. On the basis of Matthew 5:33–37 some Christians (e.g., *Quakers and *Mennonites) have refused to take oaths. Other Christians believe that what *Jesus forbade was careless and uncontrolled use of the name of God, not the solemn taking of an oath.

OBEDIENCE The moral *virtue that inclines the *will to do what a lawful superior or authority requires. As there is only one perfect *Lord, the *God and Father of our Lord *Jesus Christ, then absolute obedience can only be given to him. This does not exclude the rightful obedience due from children in the home, church members in church, and citizens in a country. Without the principle of obedience in the world there would be chaos. God's law and sound reason both point to the need for obedience in all human societies and relationships. A *Christian is one who becomes by *grace a slave of *righteousness (Rom 6:12ff.) and a servant of Jesus Christ, obedient to God.

OBEDIENCE, VOW OF The promise made by one who enters the *religious life to obey his/her *superior and to obey *God. Other *vows are of *chastity and *poverty.

OBEDIENCE OF CHRIST The total obedience which *Christ offered to the Father, and usually described under two aspects: (1) The active obedience whereby he joyfully obeyed the *will of the Father in all his life and submitted to the law of Moses and (2) The passive obedience whereby he was ready to suffer and die in order to bring *salvation to the world (passive is from Lat. *passio,* *suffering.).

OBERAMMERGAU The village in Bavaria which every ten years produces the famous Passion play. Started in 1634, it reportedly owes its continuance to a *vow made by the villagers when they were spared during an outbreak of plague the previous year.

OBERLIN THEOLOGY A form of Protestant *theology taught at Oberlin College, Ohio, under the leadership of Asa Mahan (1799–1889), Charles *Finney (1792–1875) and James H. Fairchild (1817–1902). It involved the rejection of traditional *Calvinism, an emphasis on seeking for *Christian *perfection and the encouragement of *revivalism.

OBLATIONS (Lat. *oblatio,* "offering"). The gifts of bread and wine that are offered to the president of the *Eucharist for *consecration as the *body and *blood of *Christ. See also OFFERTORY.

O'BRYAN, WILLIAM See BIBLE CHRISTIANS.

OCCAM, WILLIAM OF See WILLIAM OF OCCAM.

OCCAM'S RAZOR The law of parsimony. In any given enterprise (physical or mental) only that should be used which the purpose requires. For example, no excess time, no unnecessary development of of ideas or energy should be expended. *William of Occam (d. 1349) actually said, "Beings should not be multiplied unnecessarily." Thus, simplicity is the idea.

OCCASIONALISM The view that *God's direct intervention causes every single change in the *universe. The emphasis is on "direct." Creatures do not exercise true causality but are merely the means and occasions for God's causal actions in their relations with one another. A famous exponent of this view was Arnold Geulinex (1624–1669), a Dutch Roman Catholic who joined the *Reformed church. It is rejected by most theologians because it undermines the belief that man is responsible for what he does.

OCCULT, OCCULTISM Belief in, or practice of, such things as *astrology, magic, *theosophy, *witchcraft, and *spiritualism (spiritism). The aim is to get into contact with invisible powers (good, bad, or neutral) for the purpose of using them for a specific end. Christians condemn such practice because it runs the danger of allowing *Satan and satanic forces to affect human personality and relationships.

OCHINO, BERNARDINO (1487–1564). Italian Reformer. Born in Siena, he became first a *Franciscan, then joined the stricter *Capuchins, whose *vicar general he became (1538–1542). In 1536 he had been converted to *Protestantism, but he kept that secret until a *sermon criticizing the *Inquisition brought a summons to Rome. He fled to Geneva, was warmly welcomed by *Calvin, and was later welcomed just as warmly by Thomas *Cranmer in England (1547–1553), where he preached to the Italians. After Mary *Tudor's accession he settled successively in Zurich and Cracow before dying of the plague in Moravia. He wrote a number of highly regarded theological works.

OCKHAM, WILLIAM OF See WILLIAM OF OCCAM.

O'CONNOR, MARY FLANNERY (1925–1964). Writer of finely crafted, macabre tales of Southern rural life. Her writing brings a disguised but strongly Roman Catholic perspective to the quest for spiritual meaning in a world of meaningless mayhem. Her novels and stories often bizarrely portray the self-absorbed and encapsulated souls who live without a sense of the divine which surrounds them. Into these lives she weaves the offer and invitation of God's *grace and *redemption, clothed in dense *epiphanies. A volume of her complete stories received a posthumous National Book Award in 1972. Her letters have been collected in the volume *The Habit of Being* (1979).

ODENSE, DIET OF (1527). A meeting between Roman Catholics and Lutherans in Denmark at which king Frederik I decreed religious *liberty for the latter. Nine years later the old *religion was toppled and *Lutheranism became the official *state church.

OECOLAMPADIUS (1482–1531). German Reformer. Born Johannes Huszgen in Weinsberg, he was adept in the ancient languages, published translations of the Greek fathers, and helped *Erasmus produce his Greek *NT. Becoming a Protestant about 1522 and subsequently professor and preacher in Basel, he supported *Zwingli, particularly in his view of the *Eucharist.

OECUMENICAL COUNCILS See ECUMENICAL COUNCILS.

OESTERLEY, WILLIAM OSCAR EMIL (1866–1950). English *OT scholar. Educated at Cambridge and ordained in the Church of *England, he served *parishes and a Jewish *missions society until appointment to the chair of Hebrew and Old Testament in London University. His writings included commentaries on Proverbs and the Psalms and *The Background of Christianity* (1941). T. H. *Robinson—with whom he engaged in a famous writing partnership that produced many works on *OT themes—called him "thoroughly *evangelical in outlook."

OFFERTORY Used both of the presentation of gifts of money to *God in *worship and of the presentation of bread and wine to the president of the *Eucharist for *consecration as the *body and *blood of *Christ.

OFFICE, DIVINE Also called *canonical hours, the regular services of *worship held each day in religious communities and said privately by other *clergy and *laity. The revised *breviary prescribes these: office of readings, *morning *prayer, daytime prayer, *evening prayer, and night prayer.

OFFICES OF CHRIST The titles—*Prophet, *Priest, and King—that state the present position and role of *Christ in *heaven. He rules the world as coregent with the Father; he has presented himself as the perfect *sacrifice for our *sins, and he now prays for us; and he speaks to the world through the *Spirit and through the gifts that the Spirit gives to the church.

OIL, HOLY The (olive) oil consecrated by a *bishop, usually on Holy Thursday, for use in *parishes throughout the year. It is used in many churches for *anointing the sick and in others as part of the ceremony of *baptism, *confirmation, and *ordination. See also CHRISM.

OLD BELIEVERS Russian Orthodox groups who would not accept reforms imposed during the patriarchate of *Nikon (1652–1658). Many of those who protested against the innovations were exiled, executed, or treated brutally. After a period of *toleration the persecution was renewed under Nicholas I (1825–1855) and was alleviated only in 1903. The Old Believers still survive in two main groups that reflect traditional Russian *Christian piety.

OLD CATHOLICS A name given to those who hold orthodox *Christian *doctrine but who are not in communion with Rome because they reject certain decisions made at the Council of *Trent or on later occasions. Those dissidents who associated themselves with what became known as the Old Catholic church trace their origin to 1724, when a dispute over *Jansenism, leading to the *consecration of an *archbishop unacceptable to Rome, saw the *diocese of Utrecht beginning a tradition of electing its own archbishop. The name became more widely known in 1889 when the Declaration of *Utrecht brought together many who had rejected the 1870 declaration of papal *infallibility. Old Catholics, who are in communion with most Anglican provinces, are found mostly in western and northern Europe and in North America. See also NUREMBERG DECLARATION.

OLD SCHOOL PRESBYTERIANS See NEW AND OLD SCHOOL PRESBYTERIANS.

OLD TESTAMENT The *Christian title for the Jewish *Bible. It was first used by Melito of Sardis (c. 170 A.D.). There are two canons of the OT—one Hebrew (which Protestants and Jews accept) and one Greek (which Roman Catholic and *Orthodox churches accept). The latter has what is known as the *Deuteroncanonical books. In the earliest decades of the history of the church the OT was the only *Bible that the church possessed.

OLDCASTLE, SIR JOHN (c. 1378–1417). English *Lollard. Soldier, member of Parliament, and a baron from 1409 as *Lord Cobham, he was arrested for Lollard sympathies. Many of his beliefs (e.g., rejection of *transubstantiation and *confession) anticipated the Reformers. He was sentenced to death, escaped, tried to organize the Lollards, but was eventually captured and hanged.

OLDHAM, JOSEPH HOULDSWORTH (1874–1969). British ecumenist. Born in Scotland, he graduated at Oxford and became secretary of the *Student Christian Movement (1896). He played a key role with John *Mott in the *Edinburgh Conference of 1910 and thereafter in its continuation committee until 1921, when he began service with the *International Missionary Council. He founded and edited the *International Review of Missions* (1931–1938).

OLEVIANUS, KASPAR (1536–1587). German Reformer. A convinced Calvinist, he taught and preached *evangelical *sermons at Treves despite civil and ecclesiastical opposition. Arrested but released after ten weeks, he went to Heidelberg, where in 1561 he became professor of *dogmatics. He contributed largely to the revision of the *Heidelberg Catechism.

OLIER, JEAN-JACQUES (1608–1657). Founder of the *seminary and Society of Priests of St.-Sulpice. Born in Paris and educated by *Jesuits, he was ordained in 1633, worked with *Vincent de Paul, and in 1641 became *priest of the large *parish of St.-Sulpice. At the seminary there he trained priests to work among all classes in society in the promotion of spiritual *revival. He was also a champion of *orthodoxy against *Jansenism.

OLIVETAN (c. 1506–1538). French Protestant Reformer. Born Pierre Robert in Picardy, he was converted in 1528 and subsequently worked in Italy among the *Waldensians. He taught briefly in Geneva (1533–1535), where he had a great influence on his cousin John *Calvin. Olivetan's translation of the *Bible into French (1535) was widely used when Reformers sought to carry the *gospel into France.

OLOPUN (7th century). First known *Christian *missionary to China. Evidently a native of Syria, he is known through a monument set up in 781 in what is now the city of Hsianfu. According to this so-called "Nestorian Tablet," Olopun had come in 635 from the Near East and was welcomed by the emperor. The *Scriptures were translated and propagated by imperial command, and *monasteries were founded. Two centuries later *Christianity was proscribed by a Taoist emperor.

OMAN, JOHN WOOD (1860–1939). *Presbyterian theologian. Born in Orkney, he served a Presbyterian congregation in Northumberland before becoming professor (1907) and principal (1925) of Westminster College, Cambridge. His many works include *The Natural and the Supernatural* (1931), in which he argues that man's *religious experience is normal and independent of true religious knowledge and feeling.

OMNIPOTENCE The possession of all power by *God.

OMNIPRESENCE The presence of *God outside and inside the *universe.

OMNISCIENCE The knowledge of all things by *God.

ONEIDA COMMUNITY A communistic society organized by J. H. *Noyes, it had its origins in Putney, Vermont, in 1835; but is associated chiefly with Oneida, New York, where it relocated in 1848. Noyes taught a perfectionist *doctrine, holding that the *soul becomes free from *sin only when *selfishness is destroyed. Strong discipline was exercised and a system of mutual *criticism operated. The original community was dissolved, or changed its character, in 1880.

ONENESS PENTECOSTALISM A religious movement that emerged in 1914 in early *Pentecostalism. It is an expression of Christianity on the fringe of the evangelical-Pentecostal movement that shares much of its *theology but stands outside the accepted canons of orthodoxy by its rejection of the *doctrine of the *Trinity and Trinitarian *baptism. These are replaced with a modalistic view of *God, a revelational theory of the name of *Jesus, and an insistence on rebaptism in the name of the Lord Jesus Christ only. The largest organization that embraces Oneness Pentecostalism is the United Pentecostal Church International, with a membership of 350,000 in the U.S. and Canada and a foreign membership of 680,000. It is also known as the "Jesus Only" movement.

ONTOLOGICAL ARGUMENT A way of reasoning concerning *God's existence. It was first advanced by *Anselm of Canterbury (d. 1109). God is said to be a *being such that a greater being cannot be thought of. Anyone having such an idea of God and accepting what it means cannot deny that God truly and necessarily exists. This is an *a priori form of augumentation and is still debated by modern philosophers. See also ARGUMENTS FOR THE EXISTENCE OF GOD.

ONTOLOGY The science of *being. In traditional scholastic philosophy it is much the same as *metaphysics, the study of being in general. In existentialist *theology there is much emphasis on being, which is the reality we encounter in special moments of *religious experience or of knowledge of ourselves.

OOSTERZEE, JAN JAKOB VAN (1817–1882). Dutch *Reformed minister and theologian. Born in Rotterdam and educated at Utrecht, he gained a great reputation as a preacher, notably in the chief church of Rotterdam, before appointment in 1863 as a theological professor at Utrecht. Moderate Calvinist and *evangelical leader, he wrote a number of books, including several *NT commentaries and *The Image of Christ As Presented in Scripture* (1874).

OPEN BRETHREN See PLYMOUTH BRETHREN.

OPHITES *Gnostic *sect. Taking their name from a Greek word meaning "followers of the serpent," they regarded the serpent held up by Moses in the wilderness as a mediator, symbolic of the supreme emanation of the Godhead.

OPUS DEI (Lat. "the work of *God"). A *Benedictine name for the fixed form of liturgical services of *religious communities. The idea is that *prayer and *worship are the primary responsibility of human beings.

OPUS OPERATUM (Lat. "an act that automatically achieves its end"). The claim that a *sacrament is valid and efficacious because it is of *God, guaranteed by him. Men may provide obstacles to God's *grace (e.g., stubbornness of *heart), but unless they do they will receive grace in the sacraments as they receive them. This is essentially a Roman Catholic way of looking at the sacraments and is not used by Protestants, because they wish to highlight the necessity of active *faith in the *hearts of those who receive the sacraments in order to receive aright.

ORANGE, COUNCIL OF (529). A gathering of thirteen *bishops under the presidency of *Caesarius of Arles, it upheld the *Augustinian view of *grace against *semi-Pelagianism. Caesarius had evidently taken advice from Rome in advance, and in 531 Pope *Boniface II duly ratified the council's declarations.

ORANGEMEN Members of the Orange Order, founded in Ireland in 1795 as a body pledged to mutual protection and the defense of *Protestantism. The name comes from William of Orange (*William III), whose victory over the Roman Catholic *James II in 1690 is still commemorated in annual processions in Northern Ireland and in some other British cities where the Irish Protestants have sizable numbers.

ORATORY A term used in *Roman Catholicism, deriving from a Latin word meaning "place of *prayer." An oratory may be public in the sense of being open to all worshipers in addition to a community; semipublic, in which case a community may admit or exclude others; or private, as part of a family home. Members of two associations of secular *priests, founded respectively in Rome (1564) and Paris (1611) were called Oratorians.

ORDER (Lat. *ordo,* "rank"). Used with reference to the church's organization, especially the hierarchy of church government and ordained *clergy (e.g., in the *Faith and Order Movement that was absorbed into the *World Council of Churches).

ORDERS, HOLY The offices or ranks of the ordained ministry—*bishop, *priest, and *deacon. For Orthodox and Roman Catholic, the receiving of holy orders through *ordination is a *sacrament.

ORDERS, RELIGIOUS Communities, societies, and fraternities living under a *rule and under authority. They are of both sexes and of the active and contemplative types.

ORDINAL The book that contains the services (with details of *ritual and ceremonial) in which candidates are admitted to the holy *orders of *deacon, *priest, and *bishop.

ORDINATION The act by which a candidate is admitted to holy *orders or into the ordained pastoral *ministry of the church. The essential parts of an ordination are the *prayer to *God for his *blessing and the *laying on of hands by the *bishop (sometimes assisted by *presbyters/*priests) or by the officiating *clergy (in non-Episcopalian churches). Some see ordination as the receiving from God of a special *gift of the Holy *Spirit for the performance of the duties of the *ministry, while others see it only as the authorization to perform specific tasks and responsibilities. In most churches it is preceded by long training and testing so that the candidate has time to master the *Scriptures and such other knowledge as will serve him in ministry. For the Roman Catholic and *Orthodox churches it is a *sacrament.

ORDINATION OF WOMEN See WOMEN IN THE CHURCH.

ORDO SALUTIS (Lat. "order of *salvation"). The acts and processes by which an individual passes from a state of sinfulness to that of full and perfect *redemption. Here the different *Christian traditions teach different orders—e.g., some place *regeneration before true *faith, while others reckon that by true faith regeneration comes. In the 17th century such matters were keenly debated.

ORIGEN (c. 185–c. 254). *Christian theologian and writer. Born of Christian parents in Egypt, he was educated in the famous catechetical school in Alexandria under *Clement, whom he succeeded as head. An original and speculative thinker whose works later were often regarded with suspicion in orthodox circles (he was never canonized), Origen upheld the authority and integrity of *Scripture against heretics who sought to undermine it. He died from torture inflicted during the persecution of Christians under *Decius. Origen is criticized for having failed to stress the importance of our *Lord's humanity, but he is remembered as the pioneer of *textual criticism. He compiled the *Hexapla,* six texts of the *OT in parallel columns. According to the historian *Eusebius, Origen took Christ's observation in Matthew 19:12 so seriously that he castrated himself. Much of his theology was condemned by the Second Council of *Constantinople (553). His theological system was enunciated in *De Principiis* (c. 230). He interpreted biblical texts on the literal, ethical, and allegorical levels. He was a versatile man who gained a great reputation among the Greeks and notably at the imperial court.

ORIGENISM The teaching of *Origen of Alexandria (185–254), the great theologian, or of his *disciples. Some of this teaching was condemned by the Council of *Constantinople (553). This included the preexistence of *souls and the inferiority of the Son to the Father (*subordinationism). It is not clear whether Origen himself was a heretic and whether the views of his disciples were the same as his own. He certainly was one of the great intellectuals of the early church.

ORIGINAL RIGHTEOUSNESS The morally and spiritually perfect state in which Adam and Eve were made by *God before they disobeyed him to become sinners (Gen 2–3). Thus since this first couple no one has had original *righteousness.

ORIGINAL SECESSION CHURCH The name given to an 1842 union of various Scottish groups that traced their origins to the initial secession of Ebenezer *Erskine and others from the Church of *Scotland in 1733. The united body, which regarded itself as a *synod rather than as a separate church, survived in a much diminished form until 1956, when it merged with the Church of Scotland.

ORIGINAL SIN A sinful condition common to every member of the human race since the *sin of Adam. It is contrasted with actual sin, which is self-conscious rejection of *God's *will. There are different theories concerning the nature of original sin. (1) Some hold that when Adam sinned he sinned as the federal head of the human race and therefore all sinned in him. Thus all are guilty of his sin and all are born as sinners (out of *fellowship with God). (2) Others accept that all are born with a sinful *heart but reject the idea of *guilt for the sin of another. Here original sin is a bias toward *evil. (3) When the historicity of Adam is denied, original sin becomes a way of expressing the fact of corporate sin, failure, and evil in the human race. Many hold that original sin is forgiven at *baptism and that its effects are removed through *regeneration and *sanctification. Roman Catholics hold that *Mary, mother of *Jesus, was preserved from original sin.

ORR, JAMES (1844–1913). Scottish theologian. Born in Glasgow, he became a *United Presbyterian church minister. From 1891 he taught church history and then *theology after the union that formed the *United Free church in 1901. He had four lecture tours in North America and became one of the best-known theologians in the English-speaking world. His many books include *The Virgin Birth of Christ* (1907) and *The Resurrection of Jesus* (1908). He was general editor of *The International Standard Bible Encyclopedia*.

ORTHODOX CHURCH, THE The churches that accept the teaching of the first seven *ecumenical councils and that allow an honorary primacy to the *patriarch of Constantinople. They are found primarily in Eastern Europe and the Middle East. They are sometimes called Eastern (but this is misleading; see EASTERN CHURCHES) in contrast to Western. One way to identify them is in terms of patriarchates, central bishoprics. The oldest are Constantinople, Alexandria, Antioch, and Jerusalem; then there are those of Russia, Serbia, Rumania, Bulgaria, and Georgia. But to these must be added the churches in Greece, Cyprus, Albania, Czechoslovakia, and Poland with smaller ones in Finland, Hungary, and Japan. The congregations in Britain, Western Europe, North and South America, and Australasia are under general direction of the patriarch of Constantinople.

The *Byzantine *liturgy is used in the Orthodox churches. It has three forms: the Liturgy of St. James the Brother of the Lord (used only on the feast of that *saint), the Liturgy of St. *Basil the Great (used on several specific days—e.g., *Sundays of *Lent and Feast of Basil), and the Liturgy of St. John *Chrysostom (used most of the year). It is a dramatic and colorful way of *worship and is supplemented by the use of *icons, which allow the *laity to venerate *Christ and the saints in an open way during the liturgy. Worship is led by and dominated by *clergy (with some lay assistants) who may be married or celibate. All *bishops are unmarried, but *parish *priests may marry if they do so before *ordination. The monastic ideal is still cherished, and the great center of *monasticism is Mount *Athos in Greece.

ORTHODOX CHURCHES See Eastern Orthodox Churches.

ORTHODOX PRESBYTERIAN CHURCH An American Protestant body so called from 1938. It had been founded two years earlier as the *Presbyterian Church in America by J. G. *Machen and several other ministers who had with him been suspended from the *Presbyterian Church in the U.S. for actions taken because of their concern about that *denomination's increasing *modernism. Orthodox Presbyterian church students are usually trained at Westminster Theological Seminary, founded by Machen in 1929. The church holds to the *infallibility of *Scripture and to the *Westminster Confession as a subordinate standard. It currently has approximately 16,000 members.

ORTHODOXY (Gk. *orthos,* "right"; *doksa,* "opinion"). Used in several ways: (1) of the teaching of the *ecumenical councils from Nicea to Chalcedon on the *doctrines of the *Trinity and *Person of *Christ; (2) of the *worship, doctrine, and organization of the so-called *Orthodox churches that submit to the teaching of the seven *ecumenical councils; (3) by North American Evangelicals to describe basic *evangelical doctrine, which adds to the Trinity and Person of Christ views about the *Atonement, the *Bible, and personal *faith.

ORTHODOXY, FEAST OF The festival begun in 842 to celebrate the downfall of those in the Roman Empire who wanted to remove *icons from churches. It has since been expanded to include a victory for the right *faith. It is kept by the *Orthodox churches on the first *Sunday in *Lent.

ORTHOPRAXIS (Gk. *orthos,* "right"; *praxis,* "action"). As there is *orthodoxy in *doctrine (rightness in what is believed), so there is orthodoxy in *Christian action (rightness in what is done and how it is done). However, it is more difficult to gain agreement as to what is right action (especially in a complicated, developed, and secularized world) than it is to gain agreement as to what is right doctrine.

OSIANDER, ANDREAS (1498–1552). German Reformer. Born in Brandenburg and ordained in 1520, he espoused Lutheran views and introduced the *Reformation to Nuremberg. He was involved in many of the public debates of the day and in 1549 became *pastor and professor at Koenigsberg. His unorthodox views on *justification and the *Atonement, combined with his aggressive manner, involved him in a succession of controversies.

OTTERBEIN, PHILIP WILLIAM (1726–1813). Cofounder of the Church of the *United Brethren in Christ. Born in Germany and ordained in the *Reformed church there, he went to America in 1752, ministering in Pennsylvania and Maryland. Then he joined with Martin Boehm, a Mennonite preacher, in a long series of evangelistic meetings that brought thousands of converts. He founded the United Brethren in Christ in 1800 with Boehm, and they were elected joint *bishops.

OTTO I (THE GREAT) (912–973). Holy Roman emperor and German king. Claiming to be the head of the church in Germany as well as of the state, Otto followed *Charlemagne in his claim to supremacy over spiritual and temporal. He suppressed rebellions at home, encouraged *monasticism, and defeated the encroaching Magyars (955). In 962 Pope *John XII crowned him Holy Roman emperor.

OTTO, RUDOLF (1869–1937). German theologian. For twenty years professor at Marburg, he was a strong Lutheran concerned to deepen public *worship. His best-known work is *Das Heilige,* translated into English in 1923 as *The Idea of the Holy,* which greatly influenced contemporary thinking.

OUSIA (Gk. "*substance, *essence, *being"). Used by the *bishops at the Council of *Nicea to establish that the Father and the Son shared the one, identical Godhead; they had the same *ousia*. Thus the Son is **homoousios* (of the same substance, essence, or being) as the Father. Later it was stated that the Holy *Spirit also shares the one *ousia* with Father and Son, and thus the *doctrine of the *Trinity emerges, three *Persons in one *ousia* of Godhead.

OWEN, JOHN (1616–1683). English theologian. Ordained at Oxford, he dissented from the *High Church policies of William *Laud and subsequently approved of the Congregational form of church government. Under his friend Oliver *Cromwell he became dean of Christ Church and vice-chancellor of Oxford University. Ejected at the *Restoration, he became *pastor of a London church in 1673. A Calvinist, he wrote many highly regarded books on biblical and devotional themes.

OXFORD CONFERENCE (1937). Second conference of the *ecumenical Life and Work movement. Directed by J. H. *Oldham, who had played a key role in the 1910 *Edinburgh Conference, it had as its theme "Church, Community and State." Most mainline Protestant churches were represented among the 425 delegates. The conference, which was under the chairmanship of John R. *Mott, approved the formation of a *World Council of Churches, a development that, because of World War II, was not fulfilled until 1948.

OXFORD GROUP Known also as *Moral Re-Armament, this was a nondenominational movement found by F. N. D. *Buchman. Convinced of the need for *God's guidance and moral absolutes, he had been engaged on his campaign of "life-changing" for some years before the name "Oxford Group" was in 1928 applied to him and his colleagues in South Africa by the press. In 1938 the movement became known as Moral Re-armament. It stresses four absolute standards: purity, unselfishness, honesty, and *love. Many thousands, some in high places, have been helped by the worldwide movement.

OXFORD MOVEMENT A renewal movement in the Church of *England (1833–1845) and then in *Anglicanism, led originally by John *Keble (1792–1866), E. B. *Pusey (1800–1882), and J. H. *Newman (1801–1890). It attempted to recover those "Catholic" aspects of *doctrine and piety that it believed were eclipsed by *Protestantism and Nationalism. It opposed *Erastianism, encouraged a revival of liturgical usages, and stressed the apostolic authority of the Church of England. In support of these ideals came a great volume of literature, notably *Tracts for the Times*, the first of these produced by Newman in 1833. The Oxford Movement began as the Tractarian Movement (*Tractarianism) in 1833 and gradually became a movement that not only had new doctrines of the *Eucharist, *salvation, and the church but also wished to introduce new *vestments and *ritual into the services of the church together with new designs for churches as places of *worship. In most cases the "new" was in fact a *revival of the patristic or the medieval. As such it was known as *Anglo-Catholicism, and it still remains a major force in Anglicanism.

OZANAM, ANTOINE FRÉDERIC (1813–1853). French writer and founder of the Society of St. *Vincent de Paul. He was a leader in the 19th-century Roman Catholic *revival in France. His society, formed in 1833, sought to carry out spiritual as well as charitable work among the *poor. His status as a literary historian was acknowledged by appointment to a professorship in foreign literature at the Sorbonne (1844).

P

P A supposed literary source of the *Pentateuch designated *P* because it was thought to have been produced by *priests. See also DOCUMENTARY HYPOTHESIS.

PACHOMIUS (c. 290–346). Founder of cenobitic *Christian *monasticism. Born in Upper Egypt, he served in the imperial army in North Africa (evidently against his *will) until about 314 and soon afterwards was converted and baptized. He drew together the scattered *hermits into one place, providing for them shelter and a daily program of work and *prayer. Pachomius founded eleven such *monasteries.

PACIFISM, CHRISTIAN A dedication to peace as the implication of discipleship that makes *love the principle of life. This means refusal to kill and thus to fight in *war. German Brethren, Grace Brethren, *Mennonites, *Quakers, and other *Christian groups make pacifism one of their basic tenets. The *Bible stresses peacemaking as a mark of believers, and *Jesus exalted the meek, but the *NT generally leaves practical implications to the believer. There is sympathetic reference to the centurion Cornelius (Acts 10:47), and military allusions elsewhere suggest warfare to have been a normal feature of life. The early church fathers were divided on the subject, and *Augustine declared that while war was *evil it was justifiable as a last resort. *Luther, *Calvin, and *Zwingli saw it as a necessity on occasion, but others (e.g., *Anabaptists and *Waldensians) condemned war on principle. The frightfulness of modern war has added a new dimension to the controversy. The *World Council of Churches in its Program to Combat Racism has given support to those it regards as freedom fighters for national liberation, but the dissension caused by this policy is a measure of Christian differences on this subject.

PAEDOBAPTISTS (Gk. *pais,* "child"; *baptizein,* "to baptize"). A 17th-century description of Christians who baptized the infants of *Christian parents.

PALAMAS, GREGORY (c. 1296–1359). *Saint of the *Orthodox Church, canonized in 1368. Foremost practitioner and theologian of *hesychasm. Rejecting a promising career at the court of Emperor Andronicus II, he entered the monastic life of Mount *Athos around 1316 and remained there for twenty years. He went on a *pilgrimage to Thessalonica, where he became a *priest by 1325. He returned to Athos in 1331 and remained in the hermitage of St. Sabbas through 1335. Palamas was excommunicated by *Patriarch Calecas in 1344 for his support of the empress regent Anne. A council convened by Anne deposed the patriarch in 1347. A later council made Palamas *archbisiop of Thessalonica in 1347, where he died in 1359. His teachings were declared orthodox by an Orthodox council in 1351.

PALESTRINA, GIOVANNI PIERLUIGI DA (1525–1594). Italian composer.

Holding a number of posts in Rome under papal patronage, he was regarded as supreme in the composition of *Masses. These, with the beautiful motets based on words taken from the Song of Solomon, have not only been rightly acclaimed down the centuries—they made a significant contribution to the *Counter-Reformation.

PALEY, WILLIAM (1743–1805). Anglican clergyman and philosopher. He lectured in philosophy at Cambridge (1766–1776), ministered in northern England *parishes (1776–1792), and became subdean of Lincoln (1795). His most famous work is *View of the Evidences of Christianity* (1794), an attack on 18th-century *Deism.

PALINGENESIS (Gk. *palin,* "again"; *genesis,* "birth"). *Rebirth, new birth, *regeneration. The work of the Holy *Spirit in *Christian initiation into the *kingdom of *God and the church.

PALLADIUS (c. 364–c. 431). *Bishop and writer on *monasticism. Born in modern Ankara, he was a monk in Palestine and Egypt before becoming bishop of Helenopolis in Bithynia about 400. For supporting John *Chrysostom against charges of *heresy he was exiled by the emperor for six years. He became bishop of Aspuna in Galatia about 413 and some years later wrote a valuable account of early Egyptian and Middle Eastern *Christian monasticism.

PALLADIUS (5th century). *Missionary to Ireland. A native of Gaul, he was sent by Pope *Celestine I as the first *bishop to the Irish, charged especially to counter the spread of *Pelagianism. Not much is known about his *mission or about his subsequent career; one account says he continued his *ministry in Scotland, where he died.

PALM SUNDAY The *Sunday before *Easter and the sixth and last Sunday of *Lent. It is the celebration by the church of the triumphal entry of *Jesus into Jerusalem on a donkey when palms and olive branches were placed in his path (Matt 21:1–9; Mark 11:1–10; Luke 19:29–38; John 12:12–18). In many *parish churches there is a procession on this day when *clergy, *choir, and congregation carry palms and sing appropriate songs. The day is now also called Passion Sunday in the new Roman Catholic calendar.

PANENTHEISM (Gk. "everything exists in *God"). The belief that the *universe exists in God but is not identical with God—that God's being includes and penetrates the universe but is not exhausted by it. Thus it differs from *pantheism, which identifies the world with God. A modern form of panentheism is *process *theology.

PANTAENUS (d. c. 190). First known head of the catechetical school at Alexandria. Perhaps Sicilian by birth, he was an itinerant preacher of the *gospel before taking up the Alexandria post, where he taught *Clement (who was to be his successor) and *Bishop *Alexander.

PANTHEISM (Gk. "*God is all there is," "all is God"). God and the *universe are identical. Few have defended a literal pantheism, but many overemphasize God's presence within creation. See also IMMANENCE OF GOD.

PANTOCRATOR, PANTOKRATOR (Gk. "ruler of all"). *Christ is often presented as *Lord of all in the picture in the dome of *Byzantine churches. One hand holds the roll of the law, and the other is raised in a gesture of command.

PAPACY (Lat. *papa,* "father"). The system of ecclesiastical government in the Roman Catholic church headed by the *pope. It is sometimes claimed that since the pope is the *vicar of *Christ on earth the papacy has universal spiritual authority and jurisdiction over all churches and Christians. Since the *Reformation many Protestants have believed that the papacy is the (or an) *antichrist, and they have seen some of the prophecies of the Book of Revelation (e.g., Rev 17) as referring to God's judgment on it.

PAPAL STATES The area of central Italy ruled by the *pope from 756 until the unification of Italy was completed in 1870. The possession of these lands, the extent of which varied with political developments, involved the *papacy in much strife down the centuries and necessarily diluted concentration on spiritual matters. In 1871 the *Vatican, Lateran, and Castel Gandolfo were declared to be papal territory, and the pope is still regarded as a secular head of state in addition to his ecclesiastical responsibilities.

PAPIAS (c. 60–c. 130). *Bishop of Hierapolis in Phrygia. Nothing is known of his life except that *Irenaeus said that he was "a hearer" of the *apostle John and "a companion of *Polycarp." Only quotations in Irenaeus and in *Eusebius of Caesarea survive of Papias's great work, *Expositions of the Oracles of the Lord*. Even in fragments this provides a valuable account of the origins of the *Gospels and of the history of the early church.

PARABLES OF JESUS Short stories or sayings based on familiar life experience used by *Jesus in his public teaching. They were intended to illustrate and illumine the nature of the *kingdom of *God (God's kingly, saving *rule). Jewish rabbis used them extensively, but Jesus apparently used them much more effectively (see, e.g., Matt 13; Mark 4; Luke 14–15). There are no parables in John's *Gospel, but there are sayings of a similar character (e.g., "I am the good shepherd . . ."). Scholars have debated whether some parables are in fact allegories, each part of a parable having a specific meaning (see Mark 4:14–20), or whether the early church made parables into allegories and thus allegories were recorded by the *evangelists.

PARACHURCH GROUPS/ORGANIZATIONS Used mostly by Evangelicals to describe *Christian organizations that, though not under the control of any church or *denomination, perform functions normally associated with the organized church (e.g., Campus Crusade, Navigators, *Inter-Varsity Fellowship). Keen supporters of these usually have a strong belief in the *invisible church.

PARACLETE (Gk. "advocate"). A word used by *Jesus to refer to the Holy *Spirit whom the Father would send at his request to the *disciples and to the world (see John 14–16). The word may also be used of *Christ himself as in 1 John 2:1. See also SPIRIT, HOLY.

PARADISE (Gk. *paradeisos,* "a park, the Garden of Eden"). *Heaven, the abode of the blessed. In *Judaism, by the time of *Jesus, it referred to the place or sphere where the righteous dead awaited their *resurrection. Its opposite was Gehenna. In *theology it came to be a synonym for heaven. Jesus spoke of it to the thief on the *cross (Luke 23:43), and Paul referred to it in terms of his own experience in 2 Corinthians 12:3–4.

PARADOX An apparently contradictory statement that is really true. In *Christianity many claims are of this kind, e.g., *God suffered and died on the *cross. In fact, paradox arises where human *reason cannot fully penetrate the *truth of the matter and thus has to make a statement that is true but contradictory. E.g., God who is *eternal and *infinite cannot die; but the eternal Son of God as man did die on a cross.

PARDON An act of clemency to a guilty person. It can refer to *God's giving *forgiveness to repentant sinners or to the action of one man cancelling the debt of another man. Until modern times it was used as a synonym for *indulgence.

PARENESIS (Gk. moral exhortation and/or instruction). Used to describe such passages in the *NT as Romans 12; Colossians 3:18ff.; 1 Peter 2:1ff.

PARIS, MATTHEW (c. 1200–1259). English *Benedictine historian. A monk in St. Albans from about 1217, he is remembered for his *Chronica Majora,* a voluminous account of world history up to 1259. The latter two or three decades of this detailed work are regarded as especially valuable for the light they throw on European events of that period.

PARISH A territorial or geographical division belonging to a church. This may be part of a *diocese, or it may be the sphere of activity of a particular denominational church. The word is also used of the membership of a church or that over which the *pastor has the pastoral charge.

PARKER, JOSEPH (1830–1902). English Congregational minister. Born into a poor family in Northumberland, he augmented his scanty education by reading and attending public lectures. He entered the *ministry in 1853. He served pastorates in Banbury, Manchester, and in London, where the City Temple was constructed in 1874 to accommodate all who wished to hear him. There he ministered until his death, gaining in the process a worldwide reputation as an *Evangelical preacher and as a champion of the deprived.

PARKER, MATTHEW (1504–1575). *Archbishop of Canterbury from 1559. Of moderate *Reformed sympathies, he was deprived during the reign of Mary *Tudor but was later chosen for Canterbury by *Elizabeth. He participated in the issue of the *Thirty-Nine Articles and, perhaps because of his tolerance, incurred the opposition of Puritans.

PAROUSIA (Gk. "arrival"). The word used in the *NT and in *theology to describe the coming of *Christ to earth at the end of this age in order to judge the living and the dead (Matt 24:27–39). See also SECOND COMING.

PARTHENOGENESIS (Gk. "birth from a virgin"). The term originates in entomology (the study of insects). In *theology it describes the belief that *Jesus had no human father but was born of a virgin. See also VIRGIN BIRTH.

PARTICULAR BAPTISTS A group originating in London about 1638 and holding to believer's *baptism, it took its name from the belief that *Christ died only for the elect (particular *atonement). This *doctrine did not encourage proselytism and gradually numbers tapered off until the latter 18th century, when *Methodism brought an emphasis on *evangelism and *missions. Not exclusively strict Calvinists, Particular Baptists were the ones who organized the Baptist Union of Great Britain and Ireland in 1813.

PASCAL, BLAISE (1623–1662). French mathematician, scientist, and religious writer. Having shown brilliance in mathematics and in scientific inventions, he was converted in 1654. He retired into the convent of Port-Royal for most of his last eight years, there producing notes that were gathered together to form the famous *Pensees,* a brilliant literary and *apologetic work upholding *Christianity. Pascal also defended the Jansenists against the *Jesuits in *Provincial Letters* (1657). See also JANSENISM.

PASCH (Aram. "Passover"). In its Greek form as *pascha* it came to be used of *Easter, since the dates of the Passover and Easter are linked and *Christ is the *Christian Passover (1 Cor 5:7).

PASCHAL CONTROVERSIES Church disputes about the correct date for observing *Easter (Gk. *pascha*). The earliest of these concerned the problem of whether Easter should always be celebrated on a *Sunday or on a fixed day of the lunar month (the Jewish custom). The former was preferred by the end of the 2d century. A subsequent controversy over different ways to calculate the paschal moon was settled at the Council of *Nicea in 325 in favor of putting Easter after the vernal equinox. The issue was not clear-cut, however, because of different calendars and different methods of computation. This led, for example, to a long wrangle with the *Celtic churches, which was not settled until the 7th century. The *Eastern Orthodox churches still observe Easter on a later Sunday than those of the West.

*Vatican Council II agreed in principle that Easter might be observed on a fixed Sunday.

PASCHAL II (d. 1118). Pope from 1099. His *pontificate was dominated by wrangles over the *Investiture Controversy with the kings of England and France and more seriously with holy Roman emperors *Henry IV and Henry V. The latter subjected the *pope to two months' harsh captivity until he submitted to the imperial demands. The problem was not solved until four years after Paschal's death.

PASCHASIUS RADBERTUS (c. 785–c. 860). *Benedictine theologian. Born in Soissons, France, and adopted as an abandoned infant by the monks there, he later became a Benedictine at Corbie, near Amiens, and was elected *abbot of that famous institution about 843. He resigned after ten years to devote himself to writing. His works include a commentary on Matthew's *Gospel and the first doctrinal treatise on the *Eucharist.

PASSAVANT, WILLIAM ALFRED (1821–1894). Lutheran *pastor and philanthropist. Born in Pennsylvania, he was ordained in 1842 and withdrew from the *parish *ministry in 1855 to devote himself to *mission, editorial, and philanthropic work. He founded and edited *The Missionary* (1848) and *The Workman* (1881) and had a part in the establishment of the general council of the Evangelical Lutheran Church (1867). He also established a number of hospitals and orphanages from New York to Minnesota.

PASSION, THE (Lat. *passio,* "*suffering"). The suffering of *Jesus both on the *cross and in the days leading up to *Good Friday. This suffering is not merely physical but is spiritual, for in his purity he encountered the depth and power of human *sin with *God's judgment on it.

PASSIONISTS Roman Catholic *religious *order for men founded in Italy by *Paul of the Cross in 1720. Members promise to further the memory of *Christ's *Passion in the *souls of the faithful. They follow an austere *rule of life and engage chiefly in *missions and retreats. A women's branch of the order was established in 1852.

PASSIONTIDE Traditionally the two weeks before *Easter when the *suffering of *Christ is remembered by the church. Recently the period has been reduced to one week in *Roman Catholicism and so *Palm Sunday is now also called Passion Sunday; formerly it was the *Sunday before Palm Sunday.

PASTOR (Lat. "shepherd"). Commonly used to describe a clergyman in charge of a congregation. It is one of the gifts to the church (Eph 4:11).

PASTORAL EPISTLES The name used for three *NT books (1 and 2 Timothy and Titus). As the work of being a *pastor figures prominently in their contents, they are given this title.

PATEN A saucerlike dish or plate (usually of silver) used to hold the bread of Holy *Communion. It is normally large enough to cover the top of a *chalice.

PATER NOSTER (Lat. "Our Father"). The opening words in Latin of the *Lord's Prayer (Matt 6:9–13; Luke 11:2–4) and thus a title for that *prayer.

PATERNITY, DIVINE The Fatherhood that exists in the First *Person of the Holy *Trinity. As Father, the First Person eternally begets the Son. In a secondary sense this expression may refer to the fact that *God the Father adopts believing sinners into his family (Rom 8:15–16).

PATON, JOHN GIBSON (1824–1907). Scottish *missionary to the New Hebrides. Born in Dumfriesshire, he was a city missionary in Glasgow for ten years. He went to the New Hebrides under the *Reformed Presbyterian church in 1857. He endured incredible hardships and dangers for many years but saw many islanders converted. Later he traveled much to promote *missions, but he never forgot his New Hebrideans, whom he last visited in his eightieth year.

PATON, WILLIAM (1886–1943). *Missionary and *ecumenist. Born in London of Scottish parents, he was educated at Oxford and Cambridge, ordained to the *Presbyterian *ministry, served the *Student Christian Movement as missionary secretary (1911–1921), then worked in India for seven years before returning to Britain as secretary of the *International Missionary Council and editor of the *International Review of Missions*.

PATRIARCH A title used since the 6th century of the five most important bishoprics in the ancient church—Rome, Alexandria, Antioch, Constantinople, and Jerusalem. More recently the title has been used by various *Orthodox and *Eastern churches of their senior *bishop, and thus patriarchs are found in the Bulgarian, Serbian Russian, Romanian, Armenian, Nestorian, and Ethiopian churches. In terms of the *Bible, the leaders of *God's people in the *OT are also called patriarchs—Abraham, Isaac, Jacob, and the twelve sons of Jacob, with king David (Acts 2:29; 7:8ff.; Heb 7:4).

PATRICK (c. 390–c. 461). *Patron *saint of Ireland. Born of *Christian parents probably in Roman Britain, he was taken as a slave to Ireland by raiders when he was sixteen. He escaped after six years and returned home. In obedience to a *revelation he returned to Ireland about 432 and began an *evangelical *ministry that broke the power of heathenism in that land. Many of the accounts that have sprung up around his career cannot be substantiated.

PATRIMONY OF ST. PETER A name given the material possessions of the Roman Catholic church, particularly the lands later known as the *Papal States.

PATRIPASSIONISM (Lat. *pater*, "father"; *passus*, "having suffered"). The *doctrine that *God the Father actively suffered on the *cross of *Jesus. The word was used by critics of those who taught *Modalism or *Sabellianism and who believed that God is One who appears in three forms (Father, Son, and Spirit) but is not really three Persons.

PATRISTIC, PATRISTICS (Lat. *patres*, "fathers"). The study of the *fathers of the church of the first seven or eight centuries—their lives, *doctrines, and writings. Patrology is also used of the study of the fathers but can also refer to a textbook listing the fathers and their writings.

PATRON SAINT A *saint whose protection and *prayers are requested by people in a particular place, church, institution, or profession, e.g., St. Patrick of Ireland.

PATTESON, JOHN COLERIDGE (1827–1871). *Bishop of Melanesia. Educated at Oxford, he was ordained in 1853 and two years later went to join G. A. *Selwyn in his South Sea islands work. A brilliant linguist and translator, he conducted remarkably fruitful *missions among the pagan islanders and was consecrated bishop in 1861. He was killed by the inhabitants as he landed on an island previously exploited by unscrupulous white traders.

PAUL III (1468–1549). Pope from 1534. Although made *cardinal when only twenty-five, he was the father of four illegitimate children before his *ordination in 1519. He was a patron of the *arts, whose relatives benefited from his bounty. He nonetheless became a church reformer who recognized the *Jesuits (1540). He was the first pope of the *Counter-Reformation inasmuch as he convened the Council of *Trent in 1545.

PAUL IV (1476–1559). Pope from 1555. Neapolitan by birth, he early entered papal service that engaged him in much travel. He was a cofounder of the *Theatines (1524) and strongly supported the *Counter-Reformation and the *Inquisition. His reforming zeal, with his anti-imperial and anti-Spanish policies, were marks of his *pontificate.

PAUL V (1552–1621). Pope from 1605. A lawyer by training, he was elected at a time when Naples and Venice were encroaching upon papal prerogatives. While he took a strong stand on this, as he did in forbidding English Roman Catholics to take an *oath of allegiance to *James I, he was forced to compromise, and even more so in his attitude to the *Thirty Years' War that broke out in 1618. He encouraged *missions, favored the *Jesuits* in a doctrinal dispute, condemned *Galileo, and was a patron of the *arts.

PAUL VI (1897–1978). Pope from 1963. Formerly *archbishop of Milan (1954), he inherited *Vatican Council II with all its implications as the successor of *John XXIII. His *pontificate saw abolition of the regular abstention from meat on Fridays, Latin replaced by vernacular tongues in the *Mass, and the establishment of an international *synod of *bishops to advise the pope. The first pope to leave Italy since 1809 and the first to travel by air, Paul traveled widely and was always conspicuous for a notable social concern. He did not shrink from hard decisions (e.g., the reaffirmation of priestly *celibacy and the ban on artificial *birth control). He ruled that *cardinals could not participate in papal elections after reaching the age of eighty and that *bishops should retire at age seventy-five.

PAUL OF CONSTANTINOPLE (d. c. 351). *Bishop of Constantinople. Appointed to the see about 335 he was deposed for a time by the Arian party, which had imperial support. Twice more he recovered the see, twice more he was exiled, and he died out of office (some say he was strangled). In an age when *heresy had champions in high places, he was a staunch defender of *orthodoxy.

PAUL OF SAMOSATA (3d century). *Bishop of Antioch. A wealthy man who previously held high civil office, he became bishop through the in- fluence of the Syrian queen Zenobia. He introduced odd liturgical practices, but it was his *doctrine that diminished the *Person of *Christ that led to his undoing. A provincial council at Antioch in 268 pronounced Paul heretical for refusing to put Christ on the same level as *God, and he was subsequently deposed.

PAUL OF THE CROSS (1694–1775). Founder of the *Passionists. Born in Italy, he dedicated his life to *God in 1720. He claimed that the Virgin *Mary appeared to him in a vision, and from this came the impetus for the new *order, which received papal approval in 1746. In 1770 he founded a similar order for women.

PAULICIANS A *sect that originated in mid-7th-century Armenia. Its dualistic tendencies suggest the influence of *Marcion and of *Manichaeism. The founder seems to have been an Armenian called Constantine, who took the additional name of Silvanus, a companion of the *apostle Paul, after whom the group was said to have been named. Some scholars think, however, that the link went no further back than *Paul of Samosata. The Paulicians believed in an *evil *God and a good *God; denied the humanity of *Jesus; rejected the *OT and the Petrine Epistles; and rejected the *sacraments, *worship, and hierarchy of the Orthodox Church. Constantine and his successor both died violently, but the sect expanded, flourished for a time, and survived until at least the end of the 11th century

PAULINUS (353–431). *Bishop of Nola (Italy) and poet. Born in Bordeaux, he spent some years in imperial service. Then he sold his possessions and was ordained in 395, becoming bishop ten years later. Paulinus carried on an extensive correspondence with famous contemporaries, such as *Augustine of Hippo and *Jerome (about fifty of the letters have survived), and he was among the most important *Christian Latin poets of his age.

PAULINUS (c. 584–644). First *bishop of York. Roman by birth, he was among the *missionary contingent sent to England by *Gregory I to help

*Augustine of Canterbury in the *conversion of England. He was made bishop of York by the Northumbrian king, Edwin, whom he had converted and baptized, and he soon spread his work throughout that kingdom. When Edwin was killed in battle against the Anglo-Saxons (632), Paulinius fled to Kent, where he became bishop of Rochester (*archbishop from 634).

PAULISTS American Roman Catholic society. This community of *priests (officially The Missionary Society of St. Paul the Apostle) was founded in 1858 by I. T. *Hecker and others. They dedicate themselves to the pursuit of Christian *perfection and to the apostolic *ministry, particularly in the outreach to non-Catholics. They also publish the *Catholic World*.

PAX See Kiss of Peace.

PEAKE, ARTHUR SAMUEL (1865–1929). English Methodist scholar. Son of a *Primitive Methodist minister, he graduated from Oxford but gave up opportunities there as a don to be tutor in his *denomination's Manchester College (1892), a post he combined from 1904 with the Rylands chair of biblical *exegesis at the university. The *Bible commentary he edited (1919) was widely used.

PEARSON, JOHN (1613–1686). *Bishop of Chester. A Cambridge graduate ordained in 1639, he was a Royalist denied preferment until after the *Restoration in 1660, when he held key academic posts at Cambridge. He was the champion of the Church of *England against Rome and *Nonconformity alike, but he is remembered best for his masterly work, *Exposition of the Creed* (1659).

PEASANTS' REVOLT (1524–1525). A German uprising soon after the start of the *Reformation. Sparked off by their economic plight, the repression of their princes, and some inflammatory Protestant literature, the peasants demanded certain civil and religious rights, setting out their grievances in the *Twelve Articles. The movement developed into mob violence and pillaging, and Lutheran and Roman Catholic civil leaders joined forces to crush the rebellion. Its leader Thomas *Münzer was executed. After initial sympathies with the revolt, *Luther lost much popular support by siding with the authorities.

PECULIAR PEOPLE A phrase in *Scripture that several religious groups have applied to themselves. It is especially associated with the "Plumstead Peculiars," who were organized in London in 1838 and practiced *faith healing.

PEGUY, CHARLES PIERRE (1873—1914). French Roman Catholic writer. Son of a poor widow in Orleans, he became a socialist and early protested the miscarriage of justice in the Dreyfus case. He ran a bookshop, published a prestigious fortnightly journal, and wrote plays and poems that sought to combine *Christianity and socialism. His strange and brilliant writings have been rediscovered in recent decades; he was killed in action in World War I.

PELAGIANISM A theological system that stresses the primacy of the human *will in achieving *salvation. It took its name from Pelagius (c. 354–c. 420), a British lay monk who, arriving in Rome about 380, became highly regarded as a spiritual director. He taught that people were responsible for their deeds and that divine *grace was bestowed in proportion to human merits. He saw the church as a community of baptized believers committed to strive toward *perfection. Much of this was designed to improve the low moral standards of *Christian Rome, but *Augustine took issue with Pelagianism because it denied man's total dependence on the grace of *God. Pelagius and his colleague *Celestius were banished from Rome because of the violence they had stirred up. In 418 they were condemned by pope *Zosimus and later more strongly by the North African *bishops meeting in Carthage. Pelagianism found supporters in Gaul, Britain, and among the *Eastern churches. It was further condemned by the Council of *Ephesus in 431.

PENAL SUBSTITUTION A theory of the meaning of *Jesus' death, it has been central in Protestant *theology since the 16th century and is zealously held by Evangelicals. It assumes that each person is under *God's moral law and has failed to keep that law. Thus, all are guilty. *Christ, who was true man, also lived under law but perfectly obeyed it. Then he offered himself as a pure *sacrifice in the place of human beings and took what they deserve—death and God's *wrath and *punishment. Because he was not only pure man but also perfect *God, that which he suffered and bore has validity for all those to whom God wills to apply it. Thus he was the *Substitute for sinners (some would say only for the elect), and because of what he has done, it is possible to have *forgiveness from God. See also ATONEMENT.

PENANCE, SACRAMENT OF One of the seven *sacraments of *Roman Catholicism and also accepted as a sacrament by the *Orthodox Church and by some Lutherans and Anglicans. It comprises three acts of the penitent sinner—*contrition, confession of *sin, and *satisfaction (doing penance)—together with the words of the *priest (normally said before satisfaction), giving *absolution. Older teaching on satisfaction was linked with a *theology of *merit, but modern teaching emphasizes the need to show true contrition and *repentance in acts of *love and concern for others. A new *rite of penance has also been available in Roman Catholicism since 1973.

PENINGTON, ISAAC (1616–1679). English *Quaker leader. Son of a lord mayor of London, he was educated at Cambridge and associated with the *Seekers, but after hearing George *Fox speak in 1657, he joined the Quakers. After the *Restoration he was jailed six times for refusing to take an oath of allegiance to *Charles II. His house and property were confiscated, but his saintly character and his irenic writings greatly advanced the development of Quakerism in England.

PENITENCE The state of being repentant for having sinned against *God. It may involve a sense of deserving some form of *punishment, and it certainly involves a desire to do better for God.

PENITENTIAL PSALMS
Seven psalms have traditionally been used as ways of confessing *sins: 6, 32, 38, 51, 102, 130, and 143.

PENN, WILLIAM
(1644–1718). *Quaker leader and founder of Pennsylvania. An admiral's son, he became a Quaker at age twenty-one, and in those immediate post-Restoration years he was jailed four times for *nonconformity of writings and practices. In 1682 he founded the "Free Society of Traders of Pennsylvania," whose constitution stressed freedom of religious *worship. He spent two two-year periods in the colony. Among his writings was *Primitive Christianity* (1696).

PENTATEUCH (Gk. "five-roll") The first five books of the *Bible (Genesis, Exodus, Leviticus, Numbers, and Deuteronomy). The name was provided by *Origen (c. 254). The author of these is traditionally given as Moses.

PENTECOST (Gk. "fiftieth day"). The Greek name for the Jewish Feast of Weeks when the first fruits of the harvest were presented to *God. It was fifty days after Passover. On the Feast of Pentecost ten days after the *ascension of *Christ, the Holy *Spirit came in his fullness to the church (Acts 2). Pentecost is often called *Whitsuntide by English-speaking people.

PENTECOSTALISM Either a movement in which the *gifts of the Holy *Spirit are said to be experienced or several *denominations that emphasize the possession and exercise of the gifts of the Spirit. The name arises since the Spirit (and thus the gifts of the Spirit) were first given to the church at the Feast of Pentecost (Acts 2). As a movement in modern times it began with the Topeka Revival of 1901 and the *Azusa Street Revival of Los Angeles in 1906, with claims to certain gifts of the Spirit, especially speaking in *tongues. Similar events took place in other places, and thus the movement to encourage *prayer for and receipt of the gifts began. It occurred outside the mainline denominations and churches and led ultimately to the formation of various new groups—*Assemblies of God, Pentecostal Assemblies of the World, Pentecostal Church of God, and *United Pentecostal Church International. These denominations, with others, have continued; but since World War II a new form of the Pentecostal movement has arisen and has deeply affected most of the traditional churches and denominations. It is known as the *Charismatic movement or *Neo-Pentecostalism and is best described as a renewal movement in which the gifts of the Spirit are emphasized in the context of each church being seen as a body of *Christ.

PEOPLE OF GOD An image of the church (based on 1 Peter 2:9–10) often used as a major theological model/construct by theologians. The people of God know *Jesus as *Savior and *Lord, and among them there is *fellowship and *love.

PEPIN III (THE SHORT) (714–768). King of the Franks. Son of Charles Martel and father of *Charlemagne, he was elected by the nobles (751) and anointed thereafter by Pope Stephen in 754—the first Frankish king to be so approved. The mutual support between church and state during his reign anticipated the *Holy Roman Empire that was to emerge under Charlemagne.

PERDITION (Lat. *perdere*, "to destroy"). A way of describing the result of *God's condemnation at the Last *Judgment of those who have been disobedient to him. It is the nature of a future life of everlasting pain and *punishment (Matt 3:12; 8:12; Mark 9:43; Rev 17:8, 11).

PERFECTION The ideal and goal of the *Christian life is to imitate the perfection of *God. *Jesus Christ did this and showed how a human being can be morally and spiritually perfect in *love of God and human beings. He called his *disciples to perfection (Matt 5:48; 19:21) in their discipleship. Some Christians have held that perfection in love to God and man is possible on earth by the committed believer. Thus they use such terms as entire *sanctification* and *Christian perfection. Usually, however, they mean a relative perfection rather than an absolute one. The majority believe that perfection is the goal to which discipleship moves and that, because of *sin, the goal is never realized on earth but comes with the *resurrection and *redemption of the *body. Jesus reached it on earth because he was without *original sin from the beginning and because he lived in perfect communion with the Father all the time.

PERICHORESIS
(Gk. "surrounding"). An intimate union, communion, and interpenetration. It has been used by theologians to describe the relation of the human and divine *natures in the one *Christ. Also it has been used of the intimate relation of the three *Persons in the one Godhead. The Latin equivalent is *circumincession.

PERICOPE (Gk. "a section"). A distinct section or paragraph containing one story, *parable, or event found in the *synoptic *Gospels (Matthew, Mark, and Luke). It is a technical term used by scholars in their analysis of the text.

PERKINS, WILLIAM (1558–1602). Puritan scholar. Born in Warwickshire and educated at Cambridge, he taught and preached there all his life. His versatile scholarship coupled with a rare gift of lucidity in writing and a pastoral *heart gave him an influence far beyond Cambridge and the Church of *England.

PEROWNE, JOHN JAMES STEWART (1823–1904). *Bishop of Worcester. Born a *missionary's son in Bengal, he was educated at Cambridge and ordained in 1847. He held various teaching posts, including a divinity chair at Cambridge. He was appointed dean of Peterborough in 1878 and held the see of Worcester for ten years from 1891. An eminent preacher and *OT scholar who helped produce the Revised Version of the *Bible, he wrote extensively and was general editor of *The Cambridge Bible for Schools*.

PERPETUA (d. 203). *Christian *martyr. From a noble family in Carthage, she was arrested with four other believers and condemned to die in the amphitheater. A fellow Montanist (some say it was *Tertullian) has given, in the *Passion of Perpetua,* insights into the contemporary scene and has included Perpetua's account of her prison ordeal and of her visions.

PERPETUAL VIRGINITY OF MARY The Roman Catholic belief that *Mary had no sexual intercourse before or after the birth of *Jesus. Thus the brothers of Jesus (Matt 12:46) are usually explained not as blood brothers but as the sons of Joseph by a previous marriage.

PERSEVERANCE The continuance to the end of life in a state of *grace and as an active *Christian despite temptations, testings, and difficulties. Final perseverance is to arrive at death and face it as a Christian. As to whether a true believer can ever fall completely away from *God's grace and be lost forever, various answers are given. Those who believe that God's elect will certainly persevere to the end maintain that true Christians will always repent, even if on a deathbed; this is the position of orthodox *Calvinism. Those who hold to *Arminianism and other theologies that emphasize human freedom cannot affirm the certainty of final perseverance.

PERSON A technical word when used of the Holy *Trinity or of the *Lord *Jesus Christ. Translating **hypostasis*, it is used of the modes of *being of the one *God as Father, Son, and Holy *Spirit—thus the First Person, Second Person, and Third Person of the Godhead. It is also used of the one *Christ who has two *natures—one Person with two natures. The idea it conveys is not that of personality in the modern sense but concrete objectivity, genuine individual entity.

PERSON OF CHRIST The theological study of the true identity and essence of *Jesus of Nazareth, called *Lord and *Christ by his *disciples. It answers the question, "Who is he?" while the further question, "What did he achieve for us?" is the study of the *work of Christ. See also CHRIST.

PERSONALISM A philosophy that has had an important impact on *theology in recent times. It takes as its starting point human personality, which it affirms to be much more important than systems of thought or theories about humanity. It represents an antidote to the general impersonalism of modern society and thought. Theologically *God is seen as the primary manifestation of personality. An example of this type of thinking is in E. S. Brightman, *The Problem of God* (1930).

PERTH, FIVE ARTICLES OF (1618). Measures passed by the general assembly of the Church of *Scotland as part of *James VI's policy of bringing his northern kingdom more into line with the Church of *England. The articles decreed kneeling at *Communion, private Communion in cases of necessity, private *baptism in similar circumstances, observance of the great annual festivals of the church, and episcopal *confirmation. The decision to accept these, under direct royal coercion, was reversed by the Covenanting assembly of 1638, but *Charles II reimposed these as part of an even more stringent episcopal system after the *Restoration.

PESSIMISM At a practical level it is the depressive view that the world and human existence are essentially *evil, painful, and hopeless. As an intellectual system it is the belief that evil will overcome the good. Various theologies have been termed pessimistic due to their emphasis on the *depravity of man (e.g., forms of *Calvinism and *Jansenism).

PETER Simon, called Peter. He was the leader of *Jesus' apostolic band (Matt 10:2; Mark 3:16; Luke 6:14; Acts 1:13). He was called the "rock" on which the church was to be built (Matt 16:16–18) and was given a special commission by the resurrected *Lord to care for the church (John 21:15–19). According to the best tradition, he visited the church in Rome and was martyred there (perhaps writing 1 Peter from Rome [cf. 1 Peter 5:13, where Babylon may mean Rome]). Roman Catholics regard him as the first *bishop of Rome and believe that his leadership of the *apostles is passed on to the bishops of Rome so that they are *vicars (*Christ's representatives on earth, head of the visible church).

PETER I (1672–1725). Emperor of Russia. He acceded at ten, took control at seventeen, and embarked on expansionist policies. He established closer links with Europe, reformed his country's government, and greatly increased his own power by downgrading the nobility and the *Orthodox church.

PETER CLAVER See CLAVER, PETER.

PETER DE BRUYS See DE BRUYS, PETER.

PETER LOMBARD See LOMBARD, PETER.

PETER MARTYR See MARTYR, PETER (PIETRO MARTIRE VERMIGLI).

PETER MARTYR (PIETRO MARTIRE VERMIGLI) See MARTYR, PETER.

PETER NOLASCO See NOLASCO, PETER.

PETER THE HERMIT (c. 1050–1115). Preacher of the First Crusade (1095). After *Urban II had proclaimed the crusade, Peter preached extensively over Europe, then led his followers—a motley and ill-disciplined band of some thousands—to Constantinople, where they arrived the following summer. During Peter's absence they were decimated by the Turks at Civitot. He behaved less than valiantly at the siege of Antioch, but in 1099 he was appointed almoner of the *Christian army in Jerusalem. He returned to Europe in 1100 and became *prior of an *Augustinian* *monastery at Huy (now in Belgium).

PETER THE VENERABLE (c. 1092–1156). *Abbot of Cluny. Born into a noble French family, at age thirty he became abbot of Cluny, a foundation that exercised a remarkable influence on the church generally, though *Bernard of Clairvaux criticized it for departing from the strict *Benedictine *rule. Himself an ascetic and a peacemaker, Peter was also a moderate reformer who traveled much, supported the *papacy against an *antipope, and championed *orthodoxy against Peter de *Bruys and against the Jews.

PETER'S PENCE A church tax raised in England for the *pope. It seems to have originated in the 8th century but to have been paid only fitfully. In the 12th century the sum was fixed at just under 200 pounds. Peter's Pence was abolished under *Henry VIII in 1534.

PETRARCH (1304–1374). Italian scholar. Educated largely in France, he took minor *orders in the church but devoted his life to literature and poetry and is regarded as one of the pioneers of the *Renaissance. He wrote much on religious themes, notably on the conflicting demands of the temporal and the *eternal, and is said to have been the greatest scholar of his age.

PETRI, LAURENTIUS (1499–1573). *Archbishop of Uppsala. The first Protestant to hold that position, he advanced the *Reformed cause in Sweden by making a major contribution to the first complete Swedish *Bible (1541), and he fought for the church's independence from the *state.

PETRI, OLAVUS (1493–1552). Swedish Reformer. Brother of Laurentius, he studied at Wittenberg during 1516–1518—decisive years for the *Reformation. He eagerly took the new teaching back to Sweden and found a warm supporter in King *Gustavus Vasa, whose coronation *sermon he preached but with whom he later lost favor for a time. Petri wrote much, including the first vernacular service-book of the Reformation and a hymn-book.

PHARISEES A party within *Judaism at the time of *Jesus. Their aim was to obey not only the written law of Moses but also the unwritten interpretation of it known as the tradition of the elders. Extremely pious, they separated from anyone or anything they regarded as impure. They often displayed spiritual superiority, without humility or modesty. Jesus came into conflict with them because his example and teaching challenged their whole approach to *religion and to the place of law in human relationship with *God. Paul had been a Pharisee before he became a *Christian (Phil 3:5). Sometimes the word Pharisee is used today to describe overly legalistic Christians.

PHENOMENOLOGY OF RELIGION A method of study developed from the philosophical approach of E. Husserl (1859–1938). The student of a specific *religion attempts to suspend his own views and presuppositions in order to observe fully that which he sees in any given religious practice. He seeks to see the world or *God as a devout member of that *religion would. So, in theory, he is able to describe the religious consciousness he studies. It is debated to what extent a committed *Christian can adopt this approach.

PHILARET, DROZDOV (1782–1867). *Metropolitan of Moscow. A monk who in 1808 became professor of philosophy and *theology at St. Petersburg Ecclesiastical Academy, he was *archbishop of Tver before going to Moscow in 1821. He soon showed himself to be his country's leading churchman of the age, one who also had considerable influence in state affairs. He oversaw translation of the *Bible into modern Russian and produced a *catechism that profoundly influenced Russian *theology.

PHILARET, THEODORE NIKITECH (c. 1553–1633). *Patriarch of Moscow. Cousin of Czar Theodore I, he served as soldier and diplomat, was banished to a *monastery under Theodore's successor (1598–1605), then became *archbishop of Rostov. He was imprisoned by the Poles (1610–1619), saw his own son Michael become czar, and was made patriarch of Moscow. Having a great influence in church and state, he encouraged theological scholarship and made fiscal and agricultural reforms.

PHILIP II (1527–1598). King of Spain from 1556. Son of *Charles V and a champion of the *Counter-Reformation, he was Europe's most powerful king, ruling over an extensive empire. He won battles against the French (1557) and the Turks (1571) but had to concede independence to the Netherlands (1579) and failed miserably in his onslaught on England (1588). Philip strongly supported the *Inquisition.

PHILIP IV (THE FAIR) (1268–1314). King of France from 1285. One of the most important reigns in France's history, Philip's rule saw the monarchy changing its feudal and ecclesiastical character for a legal constitution. His victory over *Boniface VIII brought about the *Babylonian Captivity of the church and was the first step in the evolution of the secular state in Europe.

PHILIP, JOHN (1775–1851). Scottish *missionary to South Africa. He was a Congregational minister in Aberdeen (1804–1819) before going to South Africa as the London Missionary Society's field director. He sturdily and effectively championed the rights of native peoples against unjust colonist policies. During his thirty years in the field he aimed to visit each of his far-flung *mission stations at least every second year.

PHILIP NERI See NERI, PHILIP.

PHILIP OF HESSE (1504–1567). Landgrave of Hesse. He was won for *Protestantism in 1524, took part in the Diet of *Speyer (1526), and founded the University of Marburg (1527). He sought to promote unity between Lutheran and *Reformed churches and helped to organize the *Smalcald League, but he became a prisoner of *Charles V for five years when its forces were defeated. After his release in 1552 he still strove for the unity of Protestantism.

PHILIP THE ARABIAN (d. 249). Roman emperor from 244. While he is often regarded as the first *Christian emperor (notably by *Eusebius of Caesarea), the facts are unclear. It can at least be said that he was no persecutor of Christians. In 248 he took part in the one thousandth anniversary celebration of the founding of the city of Rome, but he was killed by *Decius soon afterwards, an event quickly followed by severe persecution of the church.

PHILIPS, DIRK (1502–1568). Dutch Anabaptist theologian. Previously a *Franciscan, he joined the *Anabaptists in 1533, about the same time as his brother Obbe. While he disapproved of the excesses of the movement such as had earlier been found in Thomas *Münzer, he was less flexible than others such as Menno *Simons, and he contributed to division in the Mennonite ranks.

PHILIPS, OBBE (c. 1500–1568). Dutch Anabaptist preacher. Converted through the *preaching of Melchior *Hofmann in 1533, he organized an independent Anabaptist congregation, ordained Menno *Simons to the *ministry (1537), and relinquished to him leadership of the group that took Menno's name. It was said that Philips subsequently returned to *Roman Catholicism.

PHILOCALIA, PHILOKALIA (Gk. "*love of spiritual beauty"). An anthology of writings by thirty authors (4th–14th century) on the spiritual life of members of *Eastern churches. It first appeared in Venice in 1782 and has had an important part in the *revival of *spirituality in the *Orthodox church in the last century. It is a collection devoted to the practice of *hesychasm and its focus on the *Jesus Prayer.

PHILOSOPHICAL THEOLOGY The expression of *faith in search of a rational explanation and articulation. It is the effort to explain how a rational person, being true to the search for *wisdom, can believe in *Christianity and the *Christian chain of *revelation from *God as true. It is similar to *philosophy of religion but unlike this always starts from the commitment of faith and within this searches for rationality.

PHILOSOPHY OF RELIGION The critical study of religious belief, claims, and language. It may be undertaken by believers or nonbelievers, for it is a rational enquiry. Such concepts as *faith, religious experience, *miracles, good and *evil, and life are death are studied. There are various types of philosophy of *religion depending on the position and tradition from which the study begins. That which begins within British *empiricism is not the same as that which begins within German *existentialism. One type may appear to be *Christian *apologetics while another may appear to be *agnosticism.

PHOTIUS (c. 810–891). *Patriarch of Constantinople and the most versatile scholar of his age. A philosophy professor in Constantinople, he was chosen as patriarch despite opposition from local dissidents and from Pope *Nicholas I, whose claim to supremacy over the whole of Christendom widened the breach between East and West. A new emperor deposed Photius (867–877), but his successor reinstated him, and meanwhile Pope *John VIII did not press controversial issues. Photius was again deposed, or perhaps he resigned, on Leo VI's accession as emperor in 886, and he died in an Armenian *monastery.

PHUSIS, PHYSIS (Gk. "nature"). The intrinsic principle of a reality. As a technical term the word is used in definitions of the *Trinity and *Person of *Christ. (1) The one Godhead is one *phusis*, one *nature, but three Persons exist within the one nature. Another technical word used is **ousia* (*substance, *essence, *being). (2) There is one *Lord, but he has two natures, one human and the other divine.

PIARISTS A Roman Catholic *order founded in 1597 by *Joseph Calasanctius. Its members added to the usual *vows a vow to devote themselves to the education of the young. The order spread throughout Europe and the New World and gave valuable educational contributions during the period (1773–1814) when the *Jesuits were suppressed.

PIERSON, AUTHUR TAPPAN (1837–1911). American *Presbyterian minister and writer. Born in New York City, he was ordained in 1860; served pastorates in New York, Detroit, Indianapolis, and Philadelphia; and thereafter served for two years during C. H. *Spurgeon's illness as minister of the Metropolitan Tabernacle, London (1891–1893). In 1896, when he was nearly sixty, he was baptized by *immersion. A great promotor of *missions by the spoken and written word, Pierson also wrote a number of expository and devotional works.

PIETISM A renewal movement among German Lutherans that began in the 17th century. In origin it is associated with the names of P. J. *Spener (1635–1705) and A. H. *Francke (1663–1727). It emphasized the need for genuine communion with *God, pointed out that dead *orthodoxy was of no use, and called for *missions to the heathen.

Pietism is also used in a wider sense, often pejoratively, to designate an overemphasis on *religious experience and claims to be led by the Holy *Spirit.

PIGHI, ALBERT (c. 1490–1542). Dutch Roman Catholic theologian. Born in Kampen, he graduated from Louvain University in 1509, spent some time in Cologne and Paris, then in 1522 went to Rome at the invitation of a fellow countryman who that year became pope as *Adrian VI. He became one of the chief apologists for the Roman Catholic Church against *Luther, *Calvin, and *Bucer.

PILGRIM FATHERS The English *Separatists who sailed from England in 1620 on the *Mayflower* to Massachusetts in order to enjoy religious freedom.

PILGRIM'S PROGRESS The title of John Bunyan's famous book, published in 1676 and based on Matthew 7:13. Describing the *Christian life from a Calvinist position, it has great artistic and literary merit.

PILGRIMAGE OF GRACE (1536–1537). A revolt led by a number of aristocrats in the north of England against *Henry VIII's policies in church affairs and reflecting a large measure of social discontent in the region. The rebels, who disapproved of Protestant tendencies and the *dissolution of the monasteries, were put down by Henry, and two hundred of them were executed.

PILGRIMAGES Journeys made to *shrines or *sanctuaries that are regarded as particularly *holy. Motivation for the journey could vary (e.g., *duty, *repentance, petition, thanksgiving, or curiosity). The most frequented places of pilgrimages have been shrines of the Virgin *Mary (e.g., at Lourdes in France. With modern forms of travel the "Holy Land" is becoming a place of pilgrimage for thousands of people.

PILKINGTON, GEORGE LAWRENCE (1865–1897). *Missionary to Uganda. Born in Ireland and a graduate of Cambridge, he went to Uganda under the Church Missionary Society in 1890. He began work on a translation of the *Bible into Luganda, was involved in a great *revival that broke out in 1893, but four years later was killed by rebellious Sudanese militiamen.

PISA, COUNCIL OF (1409). A church assembly called by the *cardinals with the aim of ending the *Great Schism in the Western church. Both claimants to the *papacy, *Gregory XII and *Benedict XIII (*antipope), were declared deposed and a new pope elected as *Alexander V. This council, which the Roman Catholic Church does not regard as *ecumenical, did not heal the *Schism and left the church with three popes.

PIUS IV (1499–1565). Pope from 1559. He ended the nepotistic tendencies of his predecessor with the single exception of making his own nephew, Charles *Borromeo, a *cardinal at age twenty-two (an action for which his church has had reason to be grateful). Pius reconvened the Council of *Trent for 1562 and directed it to a successful conclusion.

PIUS V (1504–1572). Pope from 1566. A *Dominican who served the *Inquisition for two spells before becoming pope, he was a reformer who strenuously sought implementation of recommendations made by the Council of *Trent. He stamped out *Protestantism in Italy, but the result of his excommunication of *Elizabeth I of England was less beneficial to his church's cause and certainly to its English adherents.

PIUS VII (1740–1823). Pope from 1800. A *Benedictine who inherited the *papacy at a low ebb after Pius VI, he made the famous *Concordat of 1801 with Napoleon. The agreement was short-lived; French troops occupied Rome in 1808 and claimed the *Papal States for France, and Pius, who excommunicated the invaders, was subsequently held prisoner until 1814. After the French had been defeated Pius revived the *Jesuit *order, condemned *Freemasons and other secret societies, made concordats with various states, and encouraged orthodox *doctrine and the *arts.

PIUS IX (1792–1878). Pope from 1846, his *pontificate was the longest in history. It saw the unification of Italy, the proclamation of the *Immaculate Conception, the convocation of *Vatican Council I with its definition of papal *infallibility, the issuing of the *Syllabus of Errors, and the incorporation of Rome into the Italian *kingdom, which left Pius virtually a prisoner in the Vatican.

PIUS X (1835–1914). Pope from 1903. Conservative by nature, he clamped down on what he saw as *modernism within the church, objected to Roman Catholics operating independently in social and political matters, and rejected the compromise offered when church and state were formally separated in France in 1905. He did mend some fences with the Italian government, reorganized the church's administration, and encouraged *clerical education.

PIUS XI (1857–1939). Pope from 1922. A notable scholar who disliked Mussolini and was disliked by him, he entered into agreement with the dictator. The *pope gave up his temporal dreams, recognized the kingdom of Italy, and promised political neutrality. Roman Catholic chaplains were appointed to the army, masons and *Freethinkers were banned, *priests' salaries were increased, religious education was taught in elementary schools, and the church received 750 million lire in cash and one billion in government stock. *Roman Catholicism was declared to be the national *religion. Pius won independence for the *Vatican, and Mussolini won support for his regime. Pius remained silent over the Italian invasion of Ethiopia, but he did speak out when fascism made demands on children that contradicted Catholic teaching.

PIUS XII (1876–1958). Pope from 1939. Papal secretary to *Pius XI, whose choice as successor he was, he was a shrewd diplomat and militant anticommunist who faced the enormous problem of steering his church through World War II. Two particularly controversial issues marked his *pontificate: his silence when Hitler embarked on a policy of genocide toward the Jews and his 1950 proclamation of the *Assumption of the Virgin Mary.

PLATONISM The teaching of Plato (427–347 B.C.) as adapted and taught by his *disciples. It was found attractive by *Christian thinkers especially after it had been recast by Plotinus (c. 205–270). Platonism had confidence in the human mind to find absolute *truth; also it made people long for a better world and encouraged a high view of morality. Throughout the history of the church up to modern times there have always been some who saw in Platonism (either as taught by Plato or by Plotinus) a fine philosophy in which to set a rational presentation of the Christian *faith.

PLINY'S LETTER TO TRAJAN The report to the emperor of a Roman administrator sent to investigate corruption in Bithynia. It throws light on the spread and practice of *Christianity in the province, seeks advice on how to handle the situation, and shows the author to have been a fair-minded and loyal public servant.

PLURALISM This has a religious and a theological meaning. Religious pluralism is the recognition of the right of various religious groups (e.g., Jews, Muslims, and *Christians) to be allowed to function lawfully in a society. Theological pluralism is the acceptance or encouragement of various interpretations of the *faith within a church. Theological pluralism is also found in such bodies as the *World Council of Churches.

PLYMOUTH BRETHREN So called because its first congregation was formed in Plymouth in 1831, this Protestant body (which prefers the name *Christian Brethren) sought to return to the simplicity of the apostolic church. Among its earliest members were A. N. Groves and J. N. *Darby. They met to break bread, with the accompanying *worship service led by members according to the *Spirit's guidance (having no ordained *clergy). The meetings stressed *Bible study, *evangelism, and *prophecy. The movement spread but subsequently divided into *Open Brethren and Closed or *Exclusive Brethren (the latter body then split into several groups). The majority of the Brethren are Open and cooperate with other *evangelical *Christian bodies. Evangelical in their *theology, they usually emphasize *eschatology, being premillennialist or dispensationalist. There are currently about 1,000 Open assemblies, with more than 750,000 communicants in the U.S. and Canada, and about 300 Closed assemblies, numbering less than 10,000.

PNEUMATOLOGY (Gk. *pneuma,* "spirit"; *logos,* "study"). The branch of *theology that studies the Holy *Spirit, who he is and what he does. See also SPIRIT, HOLY.

POLE, REGINALD (1500–1558). *Archbishop of Canterbury from 1556. A relative of *Henry VIII, he was educated at Oxford and in Italy but disagreed with the king over the *divorce he sought from Catherine of Aragon and over the king's claim to supremacy over the church. He found it politic to remain in Italy; he was a presiding legate when the Council of *Trent opened in 1545, and he was nearly elected pope in 1549. On the accession of Mary *Tudor, Pole returned to England and formally received the country back into the Roman Catholic fold. He became *archbishop of Canterbury two days after *ordination as *priest, but internal and foreign developments (hardly of his making) led to papal denunciation, and the shattered archbishop died just a few hours after his queen.

POLITICAL THEOLOGY Either a *theology that supports a particular political party or political order (as some German theologians supported Nazi ideas in the 1930s), or a theology that states the need for revolutionary change in society and provides a theological rationale for such change. As such it seeks to interpret the world in the light of *God's *revelation and *Gospel. It served as one source of the development of modern *liberation theology. The two names usually associated with it are J. B. Metz (the Roman Catholic theologian) and J. Moltmann (the Protestant theologian), both Germans.

POLITY, ECCLESIASTICAL The form of government and organization of a church. There are three basic types—congregational, *presbyterian, and episcopal—and many variations of these or combinations of them.

POLYCARP (c. 70–c. 155). *Bishop of Smyrna. According to *Irenaeus, Polycarp was a *disciple of the *apostle John, and thus his long life was a significant link with the earliest days of the church. A champion of *orthodoxy against *heresy, notably against *Gnosticism, he was burned to death for refusing to recant his *faith. Because he said that he had been a *Christian for eighty-six years, some scholars place his martyrdom as late as the 160s.

POLYGAMY The marriage of one man to several wives simultaneously. Allowed in the *OT, it has usually been rejected by Christians. How to treat converts who are involved in polygamy is a major pastoral problem in *missions.

POLYTHEISM The belief in at least several and possibly many deities (gods). *Christianity, affirming belief in one true *God, often has claimed that the deities of paganism represent the presence and work of *devils or *demons.

PONTIFEX MAXIMUS (Lat. "supreme *pontiff"). A title used of the popes since the *pontificate of *Leo the Great (440–461). Originally it was used of the head of the college of *priests in charge of the pagan *religion of Rome.

PONTIFF (Lat. *pontifex,* "high *priest"). A Roman Catholic description of the *pope but originally used of any *bishop.

PONTIFICAL (ROMAN) A liturgical book containing the *prayers and ceremonies reserved to a *bishop in all church services, except the *Eucharist.

PONTIFICATE The period in which a man is the *pontiff (*pope) of the Roman Catholic Church.

POOR CLARES An *order for women founded about 1213 by *Francis of Assisi and Clare, a *nun whose profession he had received. Briefly placed under a modified form of *Benedictine *rule, it received its own rule from Francis in 1224, with *vows of complete *poverty added by 1253. The Poor Clares, who are divided into the Urbanists and the Colettines, is said to be the most austere order for women in *Roman Catholicism.

POOR, THE Used in the *Bible of both the economically poor and the poor in *spirit (humble). In the *OT, *God is often presented as on the side of those who are poor through no fault of their own (Deut 23:24–5; 24:19–21; Lev. 19:1–10; 23:22; Isa 1:23; 10:2), and gracious promises are made to the pious poor (Pss. 9:18; 10:14; 12:5; 34:6). *Jesus referred both to the "poor in spirit" (Matt 5:3) and "poor" (Luke 6:20) as blessed by God. In recent years theologians have debated whether the *gospel that Jesus said was addressed to the poor (Luke 4:18) means the literally poor of this world or the poor in spirit (whether rich or poor in worldly goods). One of the tenets of *liberation *theology is that the gospel is primarily addressed to the literally poor.

POPE, THE (Gk. *pappas;* Lat. *papa,* "father"). Once a title used of any *bishop as "a father in *God" to his flock, it is now usually restricted to the bishop of Rome. A more formal title is "The Holy Father." However, the *patriarch of Alexandria is also styled "the pope."

POPISH PLOT Said to have been a *Jesuit conspiracy in 1678 to replace *Charles II by the Roman Catholic *James II on the English throne, the story caused panic and a witchhunt, in which thirty-five suspects were executed before it was found to have been the invention of Titus Oates, a rejected seminarian.

PORPHYRY (c. 232–303). Philosopher and historian. Perhaps once a professing *Christian, his sustained attack on *Christianity was serious enough to be condemned by the Council of *Ephesus in 431. The work itself has not survived, but he evidently held that the *Gospels contradicted themselves, and he rejected *Christ's divinity because of the supposed failure of his *mission.

POSITIVISM The view that only facts can certainly be affirmed—only what is personally experienced is true. Associated with the name of Auguste Comte (1798–1857), its emphasis on the supremacy of the sciences leaves no room for *God or for belief in him as a reasonable activity of mind.

POSSESSION, DEMON The control of the human *body by an *evil *spirit. The presence of the *demon may be intermittent or continual. The casting out of such an evil force is known as *exorcism, an activity practiced by *Jesus and the *apostles. Usually, those who attribute a problem to a demon or evil spirit try to exclude all physical and mental explanations first.

POSTLAPSARIANISM The view that *God's *eternal decree to save the elect logically followed his decree to create humankind and to allow the entrance of *sin into the world. See also PREDESTINATION.

POSTMILLENNIALISM Also known as postmillenarianism and *theology of the latter-day glory. The teaching that *Christ will return to earth after the Millennium. The thousand years may be understood literally or as a long period in which, through the power of the *Spirit, there will be a great time of *revival and expansion of the church.

POSTTRIBULATION RAPTURE The belief that the *rapture of the church will occur at the end of the Great *Tribulation that will come on the earth.

POSTULANT A person who lives in a religious house under supervision for a period before officially becoming a *novice.

POVERTY, VOW OF This has two Roman Catholic forms. The solemn *vow is the renunciation of the right of ownership; the simple vow is the surrender of the right to dispose of and to acquire material possessions. Poverty is seen as part of the demands of the *gospel (Matt 6:5, 20, 25; 8:20; 19:21; 2 Cor 8:9), especially for monks and *nuns and generally for *priests and all *Christians. The two other vows are of *chastity and *obedience. See also POOR, THE.

POWELL, VAVASOR (1617–1670). Welsh Puritan minister. Born in Radnorshire, he became an itinerant *evangelist about 1639, but with the progress of the parliamentary cause in the Civil War, he became *vicar of Dartford in Kent (1644). He returned to Wales in 1646, formed a band of *missionary preachers, and was known as the "*metropolitan of the itinerants." His millenarian views made him clash with Oliver *Cromwell, and his *Puritanism led to his arrest at the *Restoration in 1660. He refused to abstain from *preaching and was imprisoned for most of the remainder of his life.

PRACTICAL SYLLOGISM Used in English *Puritanism, especially by William *Perkins (1558–1602), of the method by which a regenerate man or committed *Christian may discern that he has the *assurance of being one of the elect of *God. It has three parts: (1) The *Bible states that everyone who believes in *Christ is a child of God; (2) I do so believe; (3) therefore I am one of the elect children of God. See also EXPERIENTIAL, EXPERIMENTAL.

PRACTICAL THEOLOGY Theological reflection upon the internal and external life of the church. Thus it covers such areas as religious education, *homiletics, *liturgy, church *music, and church organization. It may mean the same as *pastoralia*, and it is often a compulsory part of training for *ordination or leadership within the churches.

PRAEMUNIRE, STATUTES OF Fourteenth-century legislation in England, the intention of which was to protect the crown against papal encroachment. The three statutes in question (those of 1353, 1365, and 1393), forbade appeal to Rome in cases that could be decided in England, banned the use of papal *bulls and *excommunications in the country, and prescribed penalties for offenders.

PRAGMATIC SANCTION OF BOURGES (1438). An edict issued by Charles VII of France, designed to reduce papal power in his kingdom. It held that councils were superior to popes and that French ecclesiastical affairs, including appointment to vacant benefices, should be the responsibility of the French. The sanction was not withdrawn until 1516.

PRAGMATISM The view that the meaning of an idea is perfectly expressed in the way in which it affects human lifestyle and behavior. In religious terms, unless an article of a *creed or a theological idea generates something useful for the individual and society, it is without value. Two well-known exponents of pragmatism were William James (1842–1910), who wrote on religious experience, and John Dewey (1859–1952), the educator.

PRAYER The approach of human beings to *God. It can involve praise, *adoration, and thanksgiving, for God alone is worthy to be worshiped; it can include *confession of *sin, for before God sinners stand guilty; and it involves petition (asking for personal needs) and *intercession (asking for the needs of others). It is an act to be learned, and so *Christ provided a model prayer (Matt 6:9ff.). Sometimes prayer is classified in stages—discursive (arising from initial *meditation), affective (arising from experienced meditation), and contemplative (arising from a deep sense of union in *love with God).

PRAYER BOOKS Either the books containing the official services of *worship for a church (e.g., the Book of *Common Prayer of *Anglicanism) or printed collections of prayers for public and private use.

PRAYER, THE LORD'S See LORD'S PRAYER, THE.

PRAYERS FOR THE DEAD See DEAD, PRAYERS FOR THE.

PREACHING For the primitive church, to preach was to address non-Christians with the good news of *Christ's death and *resurrection so that they would have opportunity to believe on his name. In modern times, to preach is more often that which is done within the *Christian congregation, the delivery of a *sermon in a service of *worship. Textbooks on preaching classify sermons—expository, thematic, exhortatory, and *evangelistic. For *Protestantism, preaching has always been seen as a major means of *God's *grace, and this is why a *pastor or clergyman is often call "a preacher."

PREBENDARY The holder of a prebend (a *cathedral benefice). The name is retained in the older Church of *England cathedrals but usually the office is honorary, with the original income going now to the ecclesiastical commissioners.

PRECENTOR The person responsible in a church for congregational or choral singing. In the Church of *England's older *cathedrals he is a member of the *chapter next in rank after the dean and normally delegates his duties to a deputy (the *succentor). In Scottish *Presbyterian churches the precentor led the singing where there was no musical accompaniment. This lay office is still found in parts of Scotland and in the Church of *Scotland *general assembly.

PRECEPTS A matter of obligation. Either a commandment of *God or the commandment of a *superior in a religious community to one who has taken a *vow of *obedience. Precepts are often contrasted with *evangelical *counsels, which are matters of persuasion rather than obligation.

PRECIOUS BLOOD The *blood of *Jesus, an essential part of his human *nature. That which remained in his *body at death was marvelously transformed with the body into his *resurrection body, a *spiritual and heavenly body. His blood has always been seen as a powerful *symbol of his atoning, sacrificial death; it gains its meaning from the *OT sacrificial system (Heb 9:22; 1 Peter 1:2; 1 John 1:7; Rev 1:5). It is precious because it is that of the Man who is also the God-Man, the *Mediator. In the Middle Ages, special devotion to the "precious blood" arose, and in *Roman Catholicism there are societies and fraternities that give themselves particularly to *meditation on the "precious blood." It is also an expression found in Protestant *hymns and devotional language.

PREDESTINATION (Lat. *praedestinare,* "to foreordain"). The divine plan concerning human *salvation, it existed in *God's mind before *Creation (Rom 8:28–30; Eph 1:3–15; 2 Tim 1:9). *Augustine of Hippo (354–430) provided the first formal statement of this *doctrine. He claimed that God, not dependent on his foreknowledge of the reaction of these people to the *preaching of the *gospel, in *eternity chose some people to be saved; then in time his *irresistible *grace brought them to *salvation. The rest of humankind was justly left in their *sins to receive *damnation.

In the 16th century Augustine's teaching was accepted by *Luther and *Calvin, and it became important because of the emphasis on the sovereignty of divine grace. However, in later Protestant teaching various schools of thought developed that represented either clarifications of the *Augustinian position or reactions against it. One group, which came to be called *Arminians, rejected predestination, claiming that God's decrees were based on his foreknowledge of human response to the offer of grace. Meanwhile those who held to the Augustinian doctrine were divided in various ways. First, some claimed that God made two decrees—one of *election unto salvation and one of *reprobation to damnation—while others affirmed only the positive decree of election. Second, there were differences as to the logical order of God's decrees in his *eternal mind. Did God take into account the *fall of man into sin before he decreed the salvation of the elect? Those who claimed that he did not but rather chose them out of pure good pleasure, without respect to being sinners, were seen as teaching *supralapsarianism or *antelapsarianism (above or before the Fall). Those who claimed that God did take into account the reality of the Fall were seen as teaching *infralapsarianism or *postlapsarianism (below or after the Fall). Despite all this theological activity, the church has always confessed that predestination is essentially a *mystery. See also *ARMINIANISM; DORT, SYNOD OF; ELECTION.

PREEVANGELIZATION That which precedes *evangelism. The process or method of preparing a situation for the direct *preaching of the *Gospel. This may include a variety of activities from teaching to social work, depending on a particular *culture and local needs.

PREEXISTENCE Used especially of the *eternal *Son of *God before he became incarnate of the Virgin *Mary. He preexisted before he lived as *Jesus of Nazareth, but he preexisted only in his divine *nature, not in his human, which he took from Mary. The view that the human *soul exists and enters the human fetus is also another form of preexistence, and it was part of *Origenism, which the church condemned.

PRELATE, PRELACY An ecclesiastical official of high rank. In the Church of *England it refers to a diocesan *bishop, whereas in the Church of

Rome it refers to a senior official in the *Vatican. Prelacy describes a system of church organization and *polity in which bishops rule as lords.

PREMILLENNIALISM The view that *Antichrist and a period of especially intense *evil and tribulation will come before *Christ returns to earth to destroy Antichrist and resurrect believers. This will be followed by a thousand years of peace when Christ will reign on the earth. After this time the wicked will be raised for the final judgment and the forces of evil will be consigned to *eternal *punishment. Dispensational premillennialists teach that the church will be removed (raptured) from the earth before the Great *Tribulation.

PREMONSTRATENSIANS A Roman Catholic *religious *order that, sometimes known also as White Canons, was founded by *Norbert in France in 1120. Based on the *Augustinian *rule supplemented by *Cistercian ideals, it combines the contemplative and the active life. It is still strong in Belgium.

PREMUNDANE FALL Before the disobedience of Adam and Eve (and thus their *fall from purity into *sin) and even before the *Creation, there was a rebellion against *God (and thus a fall into sin) by some of the angels. They disobeyed God to do their own *will. One such angel became known as *Satan. Biblical texts dealing with this include Genesis 6:1–4; Isaiah 14:12; and 2 Peter 2:4.

PRESBYTER (Gk. "elder"). Leaders of the early *Christian communities were called presbyters (Acts 11:30; 14:23; 15:2; 1 Tim 5:17, 19). In terms of their function as shepherds and *pastors they were also known as *bishops (Acts 20:17–18; Phil 1:1; Titus 1:5, 7). Later the three *orders of ordained *ministry developed—bishop, presbyter (*priest), and *deacon. So from the 2d to the 16th century the presbyters were shepherds or pastors of congregations or *parishes while bishops were shepherds of *dioceses. At the *Reformation, in the attempt to restore primitive church organization, "presbyter" was used especially by Calvinists (*Reformed churches) of the ordained and lay *elder, and "bishop" became a functional word meaning "pastor." Thus the ordained elder was the pastor or bishop of the congregation. See also ELDER; PRIEST.

PRESBYTERIAN The form of church *polity directed by *elders (*presbyters). It developed in the 16th century in the Calvinistic *Reformation. There is one *order of presbyters that is divided into *preaching elders, ministers of *Word and *sacraments (*pastors), and ruling elders, who assist the pastor in the leadership and *discipline of the congregation. Presbyters of churches in a particular district form the *presbytery, from which representatives go to the local *synod and the *general assembly.

PRESBYTERIAN CHURCH (U.S.A.) A 1983 union of the *United Presbyterian Church in the U.S.A. and the *Presbyterian Church in the U.S. While both bodies had declined markedly during the 1970s, the new *denomination's 3.2 million members made it the fourth largest in the country. *The Plan for Reunion,* outlined in a 288-page report, was accepted 571–18 in the United Presbyterian Church and 344–30 in the Presbyterian Church in the U.S. The latter majority surprised many observers. Many fears were apparently allayed because the plan made provision for any congregation's withdrawal from the union "to another *Reformed body of its choice" after eighteen months, taking its property with it.

PRESBYTERIAN CHURCH IN AMERICA Conservative Calvinistic *denomination founded in 1973 as a protest to growing liberalism within the Presbyerian Church in the U.S. and its movement toward union with the *United Presbyterian Church in the U.S.A. It stresses adherence to the historic Westminster standards of faith. There are currently about 165,000 members in more than 950 churches.

PRESBYTERIAN CHURCH IN CANADA In modern times, the successors of the Presbyterian minority that stayed out of the 1925 union of Methodists, *Congregationalists, and three-fifths of the Presbyterians, to form the *United Church of Canada. The continuing Presbyterians, some 150,000 at that time, now have about 190,000 members.

PRESBYTERIAN CHURCH IN THE U.S. (SOUTHERN PRESBYTERIAN CHURCH) A body that originated in various Presbyterian groups that came together prior to and during the American Civil War. Concerned chiefly with the southern states, the church reflected in many ways the conservatism and traditions often found in those of Scottish and Ulster ancestry. It rejected attempts made in the 1950s to merge it with the larger *United Presbyterian Church in the U.S.A., but the two finally came together in 1983 to form the *Presbyterian Church (U.S.A.). At that time the Southern Presbyterian membership was 840,000.

PRESBYTERIAN CHURCH IN THE U.S.A. See UNITED PRESBYTERIAN CHURCH IN THE U.S.A.

PRESBYTERIAN CHURCH OF ENGLAND See UNITED REFORMED CHURCH.

PRESBYTERIAN WORLD ALLIANCE See WORLD ALLIANCE OF REFORMED CHURCHES.

PRESBYTERIANISM The *doctrine, ethos, polity, and *worship of the churches that developed from (or from churches related to) the Church of *Scotland. This church adopted a Calvinistic *faith, *worship, and polity during the 16th and 17th centuries, clearly expressed in the *Westminster Confession of Faith, Catechisms, and Directory for Public Worship (*Westminster Standards) adopted in Scotland in 1648. The *Presbyterian Church U.S.A. is the major expression of Presbyterianism in the U.S. Normally Presbyterianism is used of the movement that had its origin in the English-speaking world. Other churches that have a *presbyterian* polity but originated in Germany, Switzerland, and France are called *Reformed, or Calvinistic, churches.

PRESBYTERY In *Presbyterian churches, the court between the *kirk session and the *synod. Composed of equal numbers of ministers and *elders from churches within its bounds, it exercises oversight, ordains, inducts, is an appeals court for decisions of kirk sessions, and sends a representative number of its members to meetings of synod and *general assembly.

PRESCIENCE, DIVINE *God's foreknowledge of all what will occur.

PRESENTATION OF CHRIST IN THE TEMPLE, THE Anglican name for the feast on February 2 of the *Purification of the Blessed Virgin Mary. Also known as the Presentation of the Lord by Roman Catholics. See also CANDLEMAS.

PRESENTATION OF THE BLESSED VIRGIN MARY The Orthodox and Roman Catholic feast on November 21 commemorating the presentation of *Mary in the temple when she was three years old (based on the apocryphal Protevangelium of James [c. 150]).

PRESENTATION OF THE LORD, THE The new Roman Catholic name for *Candlemas or the *Purification of the Blessed Virgin Mary.

PRETERITION The passing over of the nonelect by *God. The nonelection to *salvation. A term used by Calvinist theologians in their exposition of the *doctrine of *predestination.

PRETRIBULATION RAPTURE The belief that the *rapture of the church will occur before the Great *Tribulation that will come on the earth.

PREUNDERSTANDING (Ger. *Vorverstandnis*). In interpreting the *Bible it is claimed by some that there must be a preunderstanding—that is, there must be knowledge of the original situation in which the author of that part of the Bible lived. By this a relationship with the author is developed, and then understanding of what he wrote is possible. See also HERMENEUTICS.

PREVENIENT GRACE The work of the Holy *Spirit in preparing a sinner to receive divine *illumination and *grace. See also GRACE.

PRIDE The first of the seven (traditional) deadly *sins. It involves a total reliance on personal ability and power and a refusal to submit to *God. It is the expression of a self-centered existence. This is the sin of *Lucifer and Adam and is condemned often in the *Bible (Prov 16:18; 1 Peter 5:5; et al.).

PRIEST Technically, in etymological terms this is a contraction of "*presbyter." It has this meaning of presbyter in the Church of *England's description of its *clergy as *bishops, priests, and *deacons. The term "priest" was preferred in England to that of "presbyter" (which was used in Scotland) to emphasize that the English church was not *presbyterian in *polity. Problems arise, however, because "priest" in the *OT and in the medieval and Roman Catholic churches has the association of offering *sacrifice (either animal or of the *Mass). Further, the *NT uses "priest" only in the plural to describe Christians (Rev 1:6; 5:10; 20:6), who are a royal *priesthood (1 Peter 2:9).

PRIEST, CHRIST AS *Jesus never called himself a *priest and never worked in the temple as a priest. However, in the Letter to the Hebrews he is presented as the unique High Priest. He is the perfect High Priest of the *order of Aaron; he offered a perfect *sacrifice (himself) and then presented it (himself) to the Father in his *ascension. Then having fulfilled the Aaronic priesthood, he became a high priest of the order of Melchizedek, a perfect Priest-King. Thus he rules and is the *Mediator of the *people of *God.

PRIESTHOOD OF ALL BELIEVERS The whole church is a priesthood (1 Peter 2:5–9; Rev 1:6; 5:10). The idea develops one already in the *OT, where *Israel is described in this way (Exod 19:5ff.). Believers offer the *sacrifice of praise to *God and also intercede for human needs. The church in service of God in the world offers further spiritual sacrifice of *obedience to God's *will in the *love of the neighbor. A *Christian is not a *priest individually but only in so far as he is a member of the *people of God.

PRIMATE In episcopal churches in modern times the title given to the chief *bishop of a region. Since 1354 the *archbishop of Canterbury has been known as "Primate of All England," and the archbishop of York is the "Primate of England."

PRIMITIVE CHURCH The church of the Apostles and thus also called the Apostolic church. Usually the primitive church is seen as being the church from A.D. 30 to 100. After this point it is usual to refer to the early church and the patristic period.

PRIMITIVE METHODIST CHURCH This was founded in 1811 by the union of groups led respectively by Hugh *Bourne and William *Clowes. By mid-century they had established *missions in Australasia. The body stressed *evangelism and lay participation in church government. In 1932 it joined with two other groups (Wesleyan and United Methodists) to form the present Methodist church.

PRIMORDIAL SACRAMENT Used especially by Roman Catholic theologians to describe *Jesus Christ and, by derivation, his church. Jesus, as the personal, visible expression and realization of *God's *grace in *redemption is the *sacrament (*mystery), the first and fundamental sacrament. To meet Jesus was to have an opportunity of encounter with God. Today Jesus is present on earth by the *Spirit in the church. Jesus can be met within the church, his body, through the power of the Spirit. So, as indwelt by *Christ through the Spirit, the church is a primordial sacrament, giving a basis for *baptism and *Eucharist.

PRIMUS The name given to the presiding *bishop of the Episcopal Church in

Scotland. He is elected by the seven-strong college of bishops; his office is not linked to any particular *diocese.

PRIMUS INTER PARES (Lat. "first among equals"). A primacy of honor not of jurisdiction. The expression is normally used of a *bishop, and many non-Roman Catholics who want the reunion of the churches are willing to think of the *pope as the first among equals.

PRINCETON THEOLOGY The Calvinist and *Presbyterian theology at Princeton Theological Seminary, New Jersey, from 1812 to 1921, especially that associated with the names of A. *Alexander, C. *Hodge, A. A. *Hodge, and B. B. *Warfield. It was a combination of *orthodoxy based on the *Westminster Standards and explained with the help of Scottish *common sense philosophy. It contained a new emphasis on the *infallibility of the *Bible, especially in the latter part. From 1921 its main emphases were continued in the new *seminary, Westminster Theological Seminary in Philadelphia.

PRINCIPALITIES AND POWERS *Evil forces in the *universe often associated with fallen *angels (Rom 8:38; 1 Cor 15:24; Eph 1:21; 3:10; 6:12; Col 16). Although defeated in *Jesus' death and *resurrection, they are permitted by *God to remain with influence until the end of the age. This is why Christians still have to face them (Eph 6:12–18).

PRIOR, PRIORESS, PRIORY (Lat. *prior,* "first, *superior"). A prior is the head or assistant to the *abbot of a monastic community of men; a prioress is either the head or assistant to the *abbess in a monastic community of women; and a priory is a small *monastery governed by a prior or prioress and dependent on an *abbey.

PRISCILLIANISM A *heresy associated with Priscillian, *bishop of Avila (380–381). A mixture of false teaching—e.g., a denial of the *Trinity and of *Christ's *deity—and ascetic practices—e.g., *fasting on *Sundays and *Christmas Day. It was condemned by various church councils from the 4th to the 6th century.

PRIVATE JUDGMENT The right of the individual *Christian to decide for himself the meaning of the *Bible and how it relates to his own life. This principle is often asserted by Protestants and seen by many as an emphasis of the Protestant *Reformation. When properly understood it does not deny the use of lexicons, commentaries, and other aids. Rather it claims that in the last analysis an individual is personally responsible to *God. Roman Catholics see it as one of the factors in *Protestantism that has led to the many divisions and *schisms of the Protestants.

PROBABILIORISM (Lat. *probabilior,* "more likely, credible"). A theory used in Roman Catholic moral *theology for resolving doubts about the morality of a particular action. It is right only to favor liberty only when that proposed action is more probably correct than the opinion favoring the obeying of a received or respected interpretation of a law or rule.

PROBABILISM (Lat. *probabilis,* "likely, credible"). A theory used in Roman Catholic moral *theology that is opposed to *probabiliorism. When there is a genuine conscientious doubt about the morality of a particular action, one may follow a likely or probable opinion concerning the application of a law or rule. It is based on the assumption that a doubtful rule does not bind the *conscience. See also EQUIPROBABILISM.

PROBATIONER The name given to a person between completion of training and full acceptance into a vocation. Many Protestant churches use the term; it is especially common among Scottish Presbyterians. The probationer is licensed to preach the *gospel but is not yet ordained.

PROBLEM OF EVIL See EVIL.

PRO-CATHEDRAL A church used by a *bishop as his temporary *cathedral until the proper, permanent cathedral is built or available.

PROCESS THEOLOGY A modern type of *theology that accents that the *universe and man are in a process of evolution and that also claims that *God himself is in a process of change and development through his involvement in the universe. Its philosophical background is in the teaching of A. N. Whitehead (1861–1947) and Charles Hartshorne (b. 1897). Classic theology is criticized for being static while process theology claims to do justice to the dynamic images of God given in *Bible. The claim is made that God is related to everything through an immediate, sympathetic participation. See also PANENTHEISM.

PROCESSIONS, LITURGICAL Solemn, *ritual actions in which people go from one place to another. Many church services begin with a procession of *choir and *clergy through the church to the *chancel. Likewise, funerals and weddings usually have simple processions. They also occur in special services, especially at festivals when they symbolize or dramatize aspects of that which is being celebrated or remembered (e.g., the carrying of palm branches in procession on *Palm Sunday).

PROCESSION(S), TRINITARIAN The internal, immanent operations of the Holy *Trinity that give rise to the distinct, three *Persons in the one Godhead. Thus the Son eternally proceeds from the Father, and the Holy *Spirit proceeds from the Father through the Son.

PROHIBITED DEGREES The relationships by blood or marriage that prohibit the marriage of a man and woman. Obvious prohibitions are a mother and her son and a man and his mother-in-law. Some of these prohibitions are written into the law of countries, while others are contained in church law (e.g., the prohibited degrees listed in the Anglican Book of *Common Prayer).

PROLEGOMENA (Gk. "the things said beforehand"). Usually the preliminaries to a *systematic *theology. These may include the nature of systematics, the relationship to philosophy, and the methodology to be used.

PROOFS OF THE EXISTENCE OF GOD Rational argument demonstrating the probability of the existence of one supreme *Being. They fall into two kinds: (1) The *a priori kind. Here there is no appeal to human experience. The classic example is the *ontological argument first stated by *Anselm (1033–1109). (2) The *a posteriori kind. This makes use of experience. The classic example is the *Five Ways of Thomas *Aquinas (c. 1225–1274). See also ARGUMENTS FOR THE EXISTENCE OF GOD.

PROPAGANDA The deliberate and systematic effort to change the beliefs of others. It is used by Roman Catholics of the work of the Congregation for the Evangelization of Peoples or for Propagation of the Faith (founded in 1622 by Gregory XV), as well as for the College of Propaganda, founded by the Congregation. Here the propaganda is the teaching of the church. In general usage it refers to the careful and systematic dissemination of religious or political views.

PROPASSIONS OF CHRIST The physical and psychological passions (e.g., hunger and sorrow) of the sinless *Christ. They are passions possessed and used in a perfect manner. To distinguish them from their existence in sinful human beings, his are called propassions.

PROPER Those parts of a fixed liturgical service that vary according to the day or season of the ecclesiastical year. E.g., the set *prayer (*collect) and *Bible readings change.

PROPERTIES IN THE TRINITY The Holy *Trinity is Three in terms of personal properties. These are the *paternity of the Father, the *filiation of the Son, and the *spiration of the Holy *Spirit.

PROPHECY *God's word or verdict upon a situation and/or God's word about what will happen. *Old Testament *prophets spoke to the *people of God of the past, present, and future, though their major emphasis was on God's word for the contemporary situation. They helped the people to form clear ideas as to the *nature and character of God as well as of the *duty of men to God. The prophets who were active in the church (Eph 4:11; 1 Cor 12:28–29) appear to have had a greater role than is suggested by the *NT, for Paul describes the church as being built upon both *apostles and prophets (Eph 2:20). They spoke God's word for both the present and the immediate future (Acts 21:10ff.).

Prophecy was one of the *gifts of the *Spirit (Rom 12:6; 1 Cor 12:10) that a prophet possessed in fullness and that many ordinary Christians possessed as a gift that they exercised from time to time. As a gift of the Spirit (1 Cor 14:1ff.), it appears to have been the speaking of a timely and beneficial word from God to the congregation. Pentecostal Christians believe that the gift of prophecy is given to believers to guide the church today.

PROPHET A person who spoke, acted, and wrote under the Holy *Spirit's direct influence in order to declare *God's word. The *OT contains accounts of the work and words of many prophets—Elijah to Malachi. John the Baptist may be seen as the last of the line of these important messengers. *Christ himself was a prophet, for in his *ministry he declared and expounded God's word. The prophets of the *NT era (Eph 4:11), of whom Agabus was one (Acts 21:9–10), were part of the church's foundation (Eph 2:20) in that their prophetic word was its foundational teaching.

PROPHET, CHRIST AS While on earth, *Jesus declared *God's *truth. In *heaven, as the exalted *Messiah (*Christ), he continues to declare it through the Holy *Spirit's work in the lives of the *apostles and *prophets, as he had predicted (John 14:26). Jesus is also *Priest and King.

PROPITIATION To make *atonement by appeasing *God's *wrath through the offering of of an acceptable *sacrifice. The word appears in some translations at Romans 3:25; 1 John 2:2; 4:10; and Hebrews 2:17. Other translations use *expiation. Considered as a propitiation, *Christ in his death satisfied God's wrath against human *sin by himself bearing that wrath for sinners. See also PENAL SUBSTITUTION.

PROSELYTE (Gk. *proselytos,* "one who has approached, newcomer"). A convert to *Judaism who had been circumcised and was a member of a *synagogue (Acts 2:11; 6:5; cf. Matt 23:15). This full acceptance of *Judaism by a convert meant that he was a proselyte of *righteousness; a lesser commitment that did not involve *circumcision was that of a proselyte of the gate.

PROSOPON (Gk. "person"). Used as a synonym for **hypostasis*, but the latter was preferred in discussions of the *Person of *Christ. It does, however, occur in the Definition of *Chalcedon (451) alongside *hypostasis* and is usually translated "person." In secular Greek it meant an actor's role or mask and thus lacked the idea of concrete individuality that was needed to express the oneness of Christ's Person.

PROSPER OF AQUITAINE (c. 390–c. 463). *Christian apologist. A lay theologian who championed *Augustine of Hippo and orthodox *Christianity against *Semi-Pelagianism, he continued the fight after Augustine's death with works written against Cassian and *Vincent of Lerins. He seems to have modified his position somewhat after 440, on becoming secretary to Pope *Leo I.

PROSPHORA The bread used in the *Eucharist by the *Eastern churches. A part is used for Holy *Communion and is consecrated. The rest becomes the *antidoron and is distributed at the end of the Eucharist as blessed but not consecrated food. There is an elaborate *ritual for the actual cutting of the bread before the beginning of the Eucharist.

PROTESTANT EPISCOPAL CHURCH An American church, part of the *Anglican Communion. Colonists built its first church in Virginia in 1607, but its first *bishop, Samuel *Seabury, was not consecrated until 1784. A constitution and *canons were drawn up five years later. The governing body is the general convention. It meets every three years and elects the presiding bishop. U.S. membership is approximately 3 million.

PROTESTANT ETHIC The moral values associated with Anglo-Saxon *Protestantism. They were developed in 17th-century Britain. They are said to include the right to religious and personal freedom, six days hard work each week, integrity, faithfulness, and the profit motive. Many have held that modern capitalism is a development of the Protestant ethic.

PROTESTANT PRINCIPLE Normally this refers to the *doctrine of *justification by *faith alone, as expounded by Martin *Luther.

PROTESTANTISM A form of Western *Christianity rooted in the *Reformation. "Protestant" was first used in 1529 and referred to a Protest of Lutherans (reforming party) at the Diet of *Speyer (1529) in Germany. Thus, in origin the word referred to something different from and, in some ways, opposed to *Roman Catholicism. This protest movement took shape in Lutheran (Germany and Scandinavia), Calvinist (Switzerland, France, and Scotland), and Anglican (England) churches, alongside of which was a small but potentially powerful radical movement known as the Anabaptist or *Radical *Reformation. What unites orthodox Protestantism, apart from the protest against Rome, is an insistence on the priority of the *Bible as the final authority on *faith and morals. To this may perhaps be added the common emphasis on the *doctrine of *justification by faith and the right of *private judgment.

PROTO-EVANGELIUM (Lat. "first good news"). A way of describing *God's promise in Genesis 3:15 concerning the coming *Savior: "I will put enmity between you and the woman, and between your seed and her seed; he shall bruise your head and you shall bruise his heel."

PROVIDENCE *God's purpose and plan for the *universe and the carrying out of them by his almighty power and *holy *love. This includes the certainty of the triumph of God's purpose at the end of the age and his use now (without their actual knowing or realizing it) of human intentions and activities in history. God's ultimate purpose centers in *Jesus Christ, and God's ways cannot be understood apart from him (John 1:3; Heb 1:1). God acts in human history secretly and mysteriously for the good of his elect people, using the free decisions and sinful activities of men for his own ends (Rom 8:28). See also God.

PROVINCE The territorial jurisdiction of an *archbishop or *metropolitan. The regional heads of certain Roman Catholic *religious *orders are known as "provincials."

PRYNNE, WILLIAM (1600–1669). Puritan writer. Trained as a lawyer, he soon started to attack *High Church tendencies in England and the frivolities of the age, particularly stage plays. A book regarded as an oblique attack on *Charles I and his queen led to prison, deprivation of status, and the loss of both ears. For a later offense he was jailed from 1637 to 1640. He thereafter defended the lawfulness of taking up arms against the king, denounced William *Laud, supported *Erastianism, attacked *Independents, and welcomed the *Restoration, when *Charles II appointed him keeper of the tower records.

PSALMODY The chanting of psalms in divine *worship. The practice of using the Book of Psalms was taken over from the *synagogue by the church.

PSALTER Either an ancient stringed instrument or the Book of Psalms translated into the vernacular and often set as poetry. Metrical psalms used much in the Calvinist and *Reformed churches are biblical psalms paraphrased into metered verse.

PSEUDEPIGRAPHA Writings attributed to those who are not their genuine authors, usually with the intention of giving a greater authority to what is written. It is used particularly of Jewish writings that were not included in the Greek version of the *OT (e.g., the Assumption of Moses and the Psalms of Solomon).

PSILANTHROPISM (Gk. "a mere man"). The *doctrine that *Christ was a mere man and nothing more.

PSYCHOLOGICAL ANALOGY The attempt to highlight *God's *nature as *Trinity by providing an *analogy from the human mind or *soul. *Augustine of Hippo developed several of these (e.g., *esse, nosse*, "*being, knowledge, *love"), and they are still in use by theologians. D. Sayers suggests creative idea, creative energy, and creative power. See also SOCIAL ANALOGY.

PSYCHOLOGY OF RELIGION The application of the ideas and methods of psychology (the study of mind and behavior) to *religious experience, behavior, and activity. Different schools of psychology have produced different types of psychology of *religion. Fruitful investigations have been done of such things as *conversions to *Christianity, speaking in *tongues, the nature of *guilt feelings in religious people, and the nature of mystical experience.

PSYCHOSOMATIC (Gk. *psyche*, "*soul"; *soma*, "*body"). The way in which mind (soul) and body are interrelated. It is used of illness that has no obvious physical cause. Sometimes *psychophysiological* is preferred or used as a synonym. The interrelatedness of mind and body accords well with the *Christian view of the unity of a human being.

PULPIT (Lat. *pulpitum*, "platform"). An elevated wooden or marble stand for preachers. It is usually situated in the north side of the nave near the *chancel steps in medieval churches. Originally *bishops preached from their chairs, but in the Middle Ages it became common for all to preach from the pulpit. In modern Protestant churches the pulpit is often in the center to emphasize the priority of the *preaching of the *Word.

PUNISHMENT The infliction of pain or penalty because of wrongdoing. *God punishes human beings for their *sin, and humans punish humans for their crimes against society. God punishes men in his *holy *love and *wrath, always acting justly (Matt 10:28; Luke 12:4; Rom 12:19). His punishment can be called chastisement (Heb 12:6; Rev 3:19) if it is corrective, intending to teach a lesson. At the end of the age God will justly punish those who deserve his wrath (Matt 25:46; 2 Thess 1:9). Punishment in society, inflicted by appropriate authority, may be retributive (justly paying back the offender), corrective (intended to keep the criminal from committing further crime), or deterrent (warning others not to offend). See also CAPITAL PUNISHMENT.

PURGATORY (Lat. *purgatio*, "cleansing"). The Roman Catholic and medieval *doctrine of the place or sphere in which the *souls of the faithful are purified after death and before they enter into the fullness of the divine presence or enjoy the *beatific vision. It is based on 2 Maccabees 12:39–45, with reference also to 1 Corinthians 3:11–15. The individual soul (person) is purified of *venial *sins and accepts *suffering imposed by *God as punishment for sins already forgiven. These sufferings can be lessened through the *prayers of the faithful on earth. Immediately after purification the soul is received into *heaven. Purgatory ceases when *Christ returns to earth and the Last *Judgment occurs. See also HADES, HELL, INTERMEDIATE STATE.

PURIFICATION OF THE BLESSED VIRGIN MARY The celebration of the ceremony in which Mary obeyed the Mosaic law (Num 18:15) to present *Jesus in the temple at Jerusalem (Lev 12:2–8; Luke 2:22–24). The feast is on February 2. It has been called *Candlemas because of the custom of *blessing and distributing candles to symbolize *Christ, the light of the world (Luke 2:32). In recent times the emphasis in both the *Orthodox and Roman Catholic churches has been on Christ rather than *Mary, and so Roman Catholics now call the feast The *Presentation of the Lord.

PURIFICATOR A folded piece of white linen used in Holy *Communion to wipe the *chalice. It functions as a small towel.

PURITANISM The movement in the Church of *England in the late 16th and 17th centuries to introduce further Protestant (Calvinist) reforms. The *Elizabethan Settlement of Religion (1559) was seen as a move in the right direction but one that did not go far enough. Puritans, tending to divide over matters of church *polity, became *Baptists, *Independents, *Quakers, Presbyterians, and other types of Protestants. In the period 1660–1662, after the return of *Charles II as king, Puritanism was only an ethos, an attitude, and a hope. In reality it was what became Protestant *nonconformity or dissent from 1662.

Puritanism is sometimes also used to describe the Calvinist *theology held by the major Puritans or Nonconformists of the 17th century and those in the 18th and 19th centuries who saw themselves as following in the same doctrinal *tradition.

PUSEY, EDWARD BOUVERIE (1800–1882). Anglican theologian. Professor of Hebrew at Oxford from 1828, he issued tracts on *fasting and *baptism in support of the *Oxford Movement. He became its sole leader when J. H. *Newman withdrew. Advocating confession and the *doctrine of the *Real Presence of *Christ in the *Eucharist brought the displeasure of university authorities, but his austere *preaching won much support. He also edited *Augustine's *Confessions* (1838) and wrote *Is Healthful Reunion Impossible?* (1870).

PUSEYISM Another name for *Tractarianism and *Anglo-Catholicism, of which E. B. *Pusey was a leader.

PUTATIVE MARRIAGE An invalid marriage that was, however, contracted in good faith by at least one of the two involved.

PYRRHONISM Any skeptical system of thought. Pyrrho (c. 360–270 B.C.) was a Greek philosopher and the founder of systematic skepticism—the view that there is no possibility of attaining absolute knowledge or certain *truth.

PYX (Gk. "a box"). The small container in which the consecrated bread of Holy *Communion is carried to the sick.

Q

Q (Ger. *quelle*, "source"). Used by some *NT scholars to describe the source for material common to Matthew and Luke but not found in Mark (see *synoptic *Gospels). They presuppose a definite literary relationship between the synoptic Gospels in which Matthew and Luke used Mark and this further source, Q.

QUADRAGESIMA The forty days of Lent from Ash Wednesday to Holy Week.

QUAKERS (SOCIETY OF FRIENDS) A *Christian body that originated in mid-17th-century England, chiefly through the activities of George *Fox. Their popular name dates from 1650 when a Derby judge "first called us Quakers because we bid him tremble at the word of *God." In their meetings members waited for the *Spirit to speak in and through them; they emphasized this *doctrine of the *Inner Light and rejected *clergy and *sacraments. Harassed at home, the Quakers spread their activities to North America; one of their leaders, William *Penn, founded Pennsylvania. Their *theology was outlined in Robert *Barclay's *Apology for the True Christian Divinity* (1678). Quakers refuse military service and *oaths and are involved in social and international relief work. With an estimated 200,000 Quakers throughout the world, their influence is out of proportion to their modest numbers.

QUARRIER, WILLIAM (1829–1903). Founder of the Orphan Homes of Scotland. Born in the Glasgow slums and converted at seventeen, he prospered in business and began work for destitute and orphan children. His Orphan Homes opened in 1874, followed by a tuberculosis sanatorium, a colony for epileptics, a huge night shelter in Glasgow, and an evangelistic center. He arranged for many orphans to be settled in Canada. The Homes have never appealed for money, and the work still continues as an enterprise of *faith.

QUARTODECIMANISM (Lat. *quartodecimum,* "fourteenth"). The early custom in the churches of Asia Minor of observing *Easter on the 14th day of the Jewish month Nisan, the day on which *Christ was crucified. This meant that the celebration of the death and *resurrection of *Jesus did not necessarily take place on a Friday and *Sunday each year. The Jewish date was fixed with reference to the moon and thus Passover and the Nisan 14 did not occur on the same day of the week each year. The custom was eventually abandoned.

QUESNELLIANISM A rigid *doctrine of *grace taught by Pasquier Quesnel (1634–1719), similar to that of Cornelius *Jansen (1585–1638). He emphasized the irresistibility of *grace and the fact that it was not found outside the church. It was condemned by Pope *Clement XI in 1713. See also JANSENISM.

QUICUNQUE VULT (Lat. "whosoever wishes"). The opening words of the *Athanasian Creed and an alternative name for it.

QUIETISM (1) A form of *Christian *mysticism involving passive devotional *contemplation, the extinction of the *will, and withdrawal of everything connected to the senses. It appeared most prominently in the 17th century in the teaching of Miguel de *Molinos and became more widely known through Madame *Guyon and F. *Fénelon. It was condemned by Pope *Innocent XI in 1687, and de Molinos was sentenced to life imprisonment. Some aspects of Quietism have been found in Pietists and *Quakers. (2) The practice of Christians abstaining from worldly (social and political) affairs that they may cultivate their interior, spiritual lives.

QUINQUAGESIMA The fifty days before *Easter beginning on the *Sunday before Ash Wednesday. Therefore used to describe this particular Sunday.

QUMRAN The place at the northwest end of the Dead Sea, thirteen kilometers from Jericho, where the Dead Sea Scrolls were found in 1947. A Jewish religious community lived near Qumran from c. 150 B.C. to A.D. 70. They were probably Essenes, and from them came the scrolls.

QUO VADIS? (Lat. "Where are you going?"). Words of the *apostle Peter, said to *Christ, whom he met near Rome as he fled the city around A.D. 64. Christ responded, "To Rome to be crucified again." This story is found in the apocryphal *Acts of Peter,* written about A.D. 200. According to the narrative the encounter caused Peter to return to face persecution and martyrdom.

R

RABANUS MAURUS (c. 776–856). *Benedictine *abbot and *archbishop of Mainz. Born in Mainz and educated under *Alciun, he became a Benedictine and a notable educator at Fulda, where he was later elected abbot (822-842). For five years thereafter he gave himself to *prayer, study, and writing, then he reluctantly became *archbishop. He was a renowned biblical commentator and theologian and a champion of *orthodoxy, especially against *Gottschalk.

RABAUT, PAUL (1718–1794). French *Huguenot leader. Born into a Protestant family, he was ordained *pastor in the *Reformed Church at a time of severe persecution. He was pastor at Nimes from 1744 but soon had to go into hiding. He succeeded Antoine *Court as unofficial Huguenot leader in 1760. When *toleration finally came in 1787 it was a landmark in French *Protestantism.

RABBULA (c. 350–c. 435). *Bishop of Edessa. Born near Aleppo in Syria, he was a government official but after *conversion became a monk. Consecrated as bishop about 411, he set about improving *clerical standards. He defended the *faith against pagans, Jews, and Gnostics, supported *Cyril of Alexandria against *Nestorianism, and produced a Syriac version of the *Gospels.

RACISM Prejudice against members of a race or races other than one's own and a readiness to treat them unjustly, usually by discrimination in social and economic matters. It is often difficult to identify and prove, and even more difficult to remove. Since all men are made in *God's image and are precious to God, racism is opposed to *Christianity and is thus particularly reprehensible when practiced by Christians or by a church.

RACOVIAN CATECHISM The statement of Socinian *doctrines published first in Poland in 1605. *Christ is presented as *Prophet, *Priest, and King but yet not in a form that accords with orthodox *Protestantism or *Roman Catholicism. He is not the *eternal *Son of *God who became incarnate, and there is no doctrine of the *Trinity. See also SOCINIANISM.

RADBERTUS, PASCHASIUS See PASCHASIUS RADBERTUS.

RADER, DANIEL PAUL (1879–1938). Pastor and *evangelist. Well-known *pastor of Congregational, *Christian and Missionary Alliance (C&MA), and Independent churches (including Moody Memorial Church, Chicago), he succeeded A. B. *Simpson as president of the C&MA (1921–1923) but left that group in 1924.

RADICAL REFORMATION That part of the Protestant *Reformation that rejected the idea of national/state churches and worked for a radical approach to the nature and *polity of the church. Radical reformers were once called *Anabaptists, but it is now recognized that the Anabaptists and

*Mennonites were only one aspect of the movement for radical solutions to the church's problems.

RADICAL THEOLOGY An attempt to explain the *Christian *faith in modern terms. It is controlled by modern scientific assumptions, and therefore, traditional ideas that do not match these are rejected. Where *God is believed to exist he is described in ways that bear little resemblance to received *orthodoxy. The *deity of *Christ is rejected, and the value of *religion is seen in what it does for humankind, rather than what it does for the glory of God. Recent English examples are J. A. T. *Robinson's *Honest to God* (1963) and *The Myth of God Incarnate* (ed. J. Hick, 1978); even more radical is Don Cupitt, *Taking Leave of God* (1980).

RAHNER, KARL (1904–1984). Roman Catholic theologian. One of the most significant theologians of the 20th century, his writings fall within the Thomist tradition but outside the *Neo-Thomism of *Maritain and Mascall. His *Thomism is informed by the Kantian, Hegelian, and phenomenological traditions that stress immediacy, interiority, and subjectivity. To know myself is to know *God as part of that self-knowledge. This insight causes Rahner to seek beyond the *eternal structure of the church for authenticity; anyone who validates himself thereby knows God, whether or not God is named differently or at all. Even *atheism can be a valid form of belief. Rahner's influence was most significantly felt in the reform efforts of *Vatican II.

RAIKES, ROBERT (1735–1811). Pioneer of the *Sunday school movement. Born in Gloucester, he became a successful businessman, worked among prisoners, then arranged for neglected children to be taught reading and the *catechism on Sundays. By 1786 about 200,000 English children were being taught in this way.

RAINY, ROBERT (1826–1906). Scottish theologian. Born in Glasgow and serving as a *Free Church of Scotland minister from 1851, in 1862 he became professor at New College, Edinburgh, where he taught church history (and from 1874 was also principal) until his death. He was one of the architects of the 1900 union with the *United Presbyterian Church and was *moderator of its first assembly. Prime Minister Gladstone called him "the greatest of living Scotsmen."

RAMABAI, PANDITA SARASVATI (1858–1922). Indian *Christian reformer. Born the daughter of a Brahman in southern India, she early spoke out for female emancipation and broke caste by marrying a man of lower rank (he died two years later). Helped by Anglicans, she furthered her education in Britain and was baptized there. She was converted in 1891, began *missionary work near Poona that led to a *revival, and made a Marathi translation of the *Bible.

RAMSAY, SIR WILLIAM MITCHELL (1851–1939). *New Testament scholar. Born in Glasgow, he held various posts at Oxford before becoming a professor of humanity at Aberdeen (1886–1911). A versatile and well-traveled scholar, he contributed much original work in the fields of classical archaeology, geography, and NT. His many volumes include *The Historical Geography of Asia Minor* (1890), *St. Paul the Traveller and Roman Citizen* (1895), and *Letters to the Seven Churches of Asia* (1904).

RAMSEY, ARTHUR MICHAEL (1904–1988). *Archbishop of Canterbury, 1961–1974. He was professor of divinity at Durham (1940–1950), regius professor of divinity at Cambridge (1950–1952), *bishop of Durham (1952–1956), and archbishop of York (1956–1961). He visited Pope *Paul VI in Rome, but he also worked for union of the Church of *England and the Methodist Church. Two of his highly acclaimed works are *The Resurrection of Christ* (1945) and *The Glory of God and the Trans- figuration of Christ* (1949). He became a baron upon retirement.

RANCÉ, ARMAND-JEAN LE BOUTHILLIER DE See DE RANCÉ, ARMAND-JEAN LE BOUTHILLIER.

RANDALL, BENJAMIN (1749–1808). Founder of the Freewill *Baptists. Converted through the *ministry of George *Whitefield, he subsequently joined with some *Arminian *Baptists, and in 1780 formed the New England Freewill Baptist Church, which by the time of his death had some six thousand members.

RANKE, LEOPOLD VON (1795–1886). Lutheran historian. He was professor of history at Berlin (1825–1871) and highly regarded as a meticulous researcher. Official historian of Prussia from 1841, his most famous work, which has gone through many editions, is the *History of the Popes* (1834).

RANTERS A satirical name given to a disorganized and ill-defined 17th-century movement in England. Lacking central leadership and claiming to restore the principles and practices of the primitive church, they appealed to inward experience of *Christ and rejected * Scripture as the highest authority.

RAPHAEL, SANZIO (1483–1520). *Renaissance painter. Born in Italy, he studied and worked successively in Perugia, Siena, and Florence before Pope *Julius II called him to work in Rome, where he spent the last twelve years of his short life. Among his many productions were his Madonna altar panels (1505–1507) and a remarkable series of paintings in the *Vatican.

RAPP, GEORGE (1757–1847). Founder of the *Harmony Society. Having been linen weaver and lay preacher, he emigrated from Germany, to America in 1803. He, his son, and some six hundred followers established a community at Harmony, Pennsylvania; moved to Indiana in 1814; and returned to Pennsylvania in 1825. Rapp rejected the *sacraments and school attendance, was universalist in *theology, and approved of *celibacy and community of goods.

RAPTURE A sudden experience or form of ecstasy. It is used in two ways: (1) of an intense mystical union with *God in which the external senses of the person appear not to be operating; (2) of the future event in which *Christ will lift his *saints from earth to meet him in the air (1 Thess 4:17). See also MIDTRIBULATION RAPTURE, POSTTRIBULATION RAPTURE, and PRETRIBULATION RAPTURE.

RASHDALL, HASTINGS (1858–1924). Anglican theologian and historian. A scholar in the tradition of the *Cambridge Platonists, he taught philosophy at Oxford (1888-1917), then was dean of Carlisle. He published historical and philosophical works, but in church circles he is best remembered for *The Idea of Atonement in Christian Theology* (1919).

RASKOLNIKI See OLD BELIEVERS.

RASPUTIN, GRIGORY YEFIMOVICH (c. 1872–1916). Russian "sinless" monk. Of Siberian peasant stock, he early acquired the surname Rasputin, which means "debauchee," but even after a visit to Mount *Athos, he held that sinning was necessary for *salvation. In St. Petersburg a gullible society hailed his healing talents, which he coupled with a scandalous life. He exercised a baneful influence over the empress, was said to have a damaging effect on the *war effort, and finally died violently through a conspiracy involving court and royal officials.

RASTAFARIANS Jamaican politico-religious movement. Beginning soon after 1930 when Ras Tafari was crowned as the Emperor Haile *Selassie of Ethiopia, it considered him to be the champion of the black race and a divine being who would redeem them by repatriation to Africa, the only *heaven. Because this did not take place, the movement took on elements of black militancy. Among Rastafarian emphases are a rejection of Western-oriented *culture and the eating of pork, a somewhat Puritan ethic, and approval of the use of marijuana.

RATIONALISM A system of thought or a method of thinking that supposes that human reason is self-sufficient for all purposes. It does not need the light of divine *revelation and denies that there is valid knowledge in supposed *revelation. Some forms of rationalism accept the existence of *God (proved by reason) while others do not.

RATISBON (REGENSBURG), COLLOQUY OF (1541). An attempt by *Charles V to reconcile Roman Catholics and Lutherans. Among those participating were *Eck, *Melanchthon, and *Bucer. While a substantial area of agreement was found, discussions reached an impasse over church authority and the *Eucharist. Both the *pope and *Luther later rejected such agreement as had been effected.

RAUSCHENBUSCH, WALTER (1861–1918). American theologian. Baptist minister in New York City (1886–1897) and professor at Rochester Theological Seminary (1897–1918), he is regarded as the most successful exponent of the *social gospel movement. With theological *liberalism he combined biblical piety and the insistence on "social *redemption of the race through *Christ." His impact on church and state was reflected in the success of his books, which included *Christianity and the Social Crisis* (1907) and *A Theology for the Social Gospel* (1917).

READER A man or woman who is not ordained but who assists in the *liturgy either by reading or *preaching. Normally a reader is given a license by a *bishop to assist in a *parish or in the whole *diocese.

REAL PRESENCE A true presence of *Christ (by the Holy *Spirit) in the *Eucharist, which is specifically connected with the consecrated bread and wine. This means that he is truly present and not merely figuratively or symbolically present. Precisely how he is present in connection with the bread and the wine is difficult to determine; there are various theories. See also Consubstantiation, Realism, Transignification, Transubstantiation, and Virtualism.

REALIZED ESCHATOLOGY An expression coined by C. H. *Dodd (1884–1973) in the 1930s with reference to his belief that the *kingdom of *God (which truly belongs to the age to come) entered this present *evil age in the *Person and activity of *Jesus; thus, in a real sense, the end had already arrived in and with Jesus. There is much *truth in this position if it does not deny the personal return of Jesus at the end of the age.

REALISM The view that the human mind actually knows reality, that is, knows the objective existence of the world and of *God himself, not simply its own ideas and mental images. In the Middle Ages realism was in dispute with *nominalism over the relation of *universals (i.e., general categories such as fish and bird) to particulars (a specific fish or bird).

REASON The function and process of the human mind in reaching *truth. The *Christian uses reason within his acceptance of the truths of *revelation. Having believed in *God he then uses his reason within the context of his belief in God. *Theology is reasoning upon the basis of what the *Scriptures and the *tradition of the church teach.

REBAPTISM The practice of repeating *baptism. There was a controversy in the 3d century involving *Cyprian of Carthage (d. 258) as to whether *baptism administered by heretics and schismatics was valid. The view that prevailed was that baptism in the name of the Holy *Trinity is valid, whoever performs it. And this is the common view in the church. When it is probable but not certain that a person has been baptized, then a form of baptism is used known as conditional baptism. In modern times the form of rebaptism that is most common is that of those who, having been baptized as infants, decide as adults to receive believers' baptism.

REBIRTH Born again (or from above) into new life in *Christ. *Spiritual birth into the *kingdom of of *God (John 3:3). See also BAPTISMAL REGENERATION, REGENERATION.

REBMANN, JOHANNES (1819–1876). German *missionary to East Africa. Appointed in 1846 to assist J. L. *Krapf in Kenya, he became one of the great missionary-explorers and translators of African languages, in addition to conducting a notable evangelistic work. He was the first European to see Kilimanjaro (1848). He became totally blind, and after twenty-nine years on the field without a furlough, he returned to Germany in 1875 and spent the last year of his life with his old colleague Krapf.

RECAPITULATION (Lat. *recapitulatio*; Gk. *ancephalaiosis*; "summing up," "a summary"). A *doctrine expanding the idea that *God will sum up all things in *Christ (Eph 1:10). *Irenaeus (c.130–200) first provided a theological description of all fallen creation being taken up, restored, renewed, and reorganized in Christ. Also all previous *revelation under the old *covenant was summed up in Christ. These basic ideas were developed by the Greek fathers into a comprehensive explanation of the purpose of the *Incarnation.

RECEPTIONISM The teaching that while the bread and wine remain unchanged after *consecration, the faithful communicant receives with them *Christ's *spiritual *body and *blood. This is the most widely held view in the Anglican and Methodist churches of the *Real Presence of Christ and is well presented in the Holy *Communion *hymns of Charles *Wesley (1707–1788).

RECIDIVISM (Lat. *recidivus,* "relapsing"). The habit of some people continually to fall back into their particular and besetting *sins. Also the apparent inability or unwillingness to overcome *temptation.

RECOLLECTION The concentration of the *heart and mind on realizing the presence of *God. It is used by writers on the spiritual life to cover both the elimination of distractions to true *prayer and the determination to give continual attention to *God.

RECONCILIATION The *restoration of sinful humankind, who are enemies of *God, to a state of friendship and *fellowship with him. This image was a favorite one of Paul's (2 Cor 5:19). He emphasized that reconciliation was what God did in *Christ (Rom 5:10; Eph 2:13; Col 1:19–20) to form a new humanity in communion with himself (Eph 2:15–16). God's reconciliation also has reference to the creation of harmony among human beings (Eph 2:11–18; Col 1:20–22). Thus, the church has a *ministry of reconciliation in that it calls people into friendship with *God and into friendship with others who believe (Christ having brought together Jew and Gentile). See also ATONEMENT, SALVATION.

RECUSANTS, RECUSANCY A term applied to those who refused to obey the Act of *Uniformity of 1559. This required attendance at Church of *England services and acknowledgment of *Elizabeth I as supreme governor of the church. In the 16th and 17th centuries they were subject to *punishment under the penal laws. The crime of recusancy was abolished in 1791.

REDACTION CRITICISM (Ger. *Redaktiongeschichte*). A term used by *NT scholars of the study of the way in which certain NT writers (e.g., Matthew and Luke) edited the material that they took from other sources (e.g., from Mark). Cf. FORM CRITICISM.

REDEMPTION *God's saving and liberating activity on behalf of his people. The *OT presents God as the Redeemer of *Israel, the One who delivered from Egypt and *slavery and who will deliver from future bondage. He who redeems is the Deliverer (Isa 49:26; 60:16; 63:16). The *NT presents God in *Christ as liberating men from the bondage of *sin through what is done in the *Cross and *Resurrection (Rom 3:24; Eph 1:7). By this act of God, sinners become the children of God, knowing him as *Savior and

Father (Gal 4:5ff.). The completion of redemption, the full experience of the glory of the *kingdom of God and the possession of a heavenly *body, will occur after the *second coming of Christ (Rom 8:23; Eph 4:30). See also SALVATION.

REDEMPTORISTS Otherwise known as the Congregation of the Most Holy Redeemer, this community of *priests and lay brothers originated in Scala, Italy, in 1732. Engaging in *mission work among the *poor, it extended into northern Europe in 1785, to America in 1832, and to England in 1843. The congregation specializes in *parish missions and retreats, works in foreign missions and in military chaplaincy, and encourages theological scholarship.

REDUCTIONIST, REDUCTIONISM The attempt to reduce the essentials of *Christian *faith to a bare minimum or into an acceptable form. Thus, some modern religious literature denies the *deity of *Christ, reinterprets the idea of the *supernatural to conform to modern scientific views of the natural, and minimizes the difference between *Christianity and other *religions.

REES, THOMAS BONNER (1911–1970). English *evangelist. An Anglican layman, he early became involved in youth and in general *mission work all over Britain. He became better known after World War II through more than fifty mass rallies held in the Royal Albert Hall, London, and in other British cities, and through his addresses at the *Keswick and Portstewart conventions. He also founded the well-known Hildenborough Hall conference center, where his son Justyn continues his work.

REFORMATION, THE A term chiefly applied to the religious revolution in the Western church in the 16th century. The Reformation originated in Germany with the inability of *Roman Catholicism to cope with Martin *Luther's protest against the sale of *indulgences in 1517. This shortsightedness on the part of long-entrenched authority opened the door to demand for the renewal of biblically based *Christianity—primitive purity in *doctrine, *worship, and organization. Progress was helped in those early years by political squabbling between *Charles V and the *papacy and by several influential German rulers throwing in their lot with the Protestants. The movement was introduced into Switzerland by Ulrich *Zwingli and continued by John *Calvin. It was *Calvinism that spread more readily to other parts of Europe, notably to the Netherlands and Scotland. Calvinism fathered what became known as the *Reformed churches. Alongside the two main groupings—respectively following *Luther and Calvin and becoming Protestant state churches (or national churches)—and often opposed to and by them were the extreme Protestants who worked for a *radical Reformation; they included *Anabaptists, *Mennonites, and *Separatists, all of whom rejected the idea of a close relation between church and state and called for religious liberty. The two great doctrinal emphases of the Reformation as confessed by the Protestants were the final authority of the *Bible in matters of *faith and conduct (the *formal principle) and the doctrine of *justification by faith (the *material principle). The *Counter-Reformation was Roman Catholicism's belated reaction to the Reformation.

REFORMED The name for the Calvinist tradition/churches in contrast to the Lutheran. Reformed churches have Calvinist *doctrine and *presbyterian *polity. The name is usually given to the Calvinist churches in Europe and those in the U.S. and elsewhere that were founded from and by them.

REFORMED CHURCH IN AMERICA Originating in the *Dutch Reformed Church settlements in New York early in the 17th century, it became autonomous after the American Revolution and took its present name in 1867. Further immigration in that century concentrated in the Midwest, notably Michigan, which was much more conservative than the older section of the church along the eastern seaboard and voted against a projected union with the *Presbyterian Church in the U.S. in 1969. The membership of the Reformed Church in America is 375,000 in more than 900 churches.

REFORMED CHURCHES A blanket description, covering one of the two major Protestant divisions stemming from the *Reformation. In 1529 at the famous *Marburg Colloquy the breach between Lutheran and Reformed became irreparable when *Luther and *Zwingli disagreed on the *sacraments. From Switzerland the Reformed Church spread, generally retaining that name in some form. In Scotland, however, it was styled "*Presbyterian" after the form of church government found in all churches of this tradition; in France it was represented by the *Huguenots. In 1628 the *Dutch Reformed Church was established in what became New York, to be followed by other immigrants, including Scottish Presbyterians. American Reformed churches have developed in their own way, showing greater willingness to cooperate with other churches.

REFORMED CONFESSION OF FAITH (1530–1647). See CONFESSION OF FAITH.

REFORMED EPISCOPAL CHURCH A division from the *Protestant Episcopal Church in America. It was founded in 1873 by G. D. *Cummins, assistant *bishop of Kentucky, who had been censured for officiating at a *Communion service open to non-Anglican Christians at a time when the *Oxford Movement had profoundly affected his church. Cummins resigned and, with seven other ministers and a number of laymen, formed the new group with himself as the first bishop (regarded as first among equals). *Evangelical in *doctrine, the church has about 7,000 members and is associated with the *Free Church of England.

REFORMED PRESBYTERIAN CHURCH (CAMERONIANS) Tracing its history to 1681, it would not enter the Church of *Scotland at the Revolution Settlement because some of the principles of the *Covenanters had not been recognized. The church still holds to the *National Covenant of 1638 and the *Solemn League and Covenant of 1643, refuses to exercise the political franchise, and regards much of political life as anti-Christian. There are sister churches in Ireland and in North America, and all adhere to the *Westminster Confession of Faith and the Larger and Shorter Catechisms. Total membership plus adherents stands at less than 20,000.

REGENERATION (Gk. *paliggenesia*). Renewal through new birth. In Matthew 19:28 regeneration is used of the *universe renewed and restored, while in Titus 3:5 it refers to the spiritual birth that accompanies *baptism. In *theology regeneration is normally used in the sense of the impartation of a principle of new life, through the Holy *Spirit in the *heart of a sinner. It is often called the "new birth" or the state of being "born again." This is what *Jesus explained to Nicodemus (John 3:3). See also BAPTISMAL REGENERATION.

REGENSBURG, COLLOQUY OF See RATISBON.

REGINA COELI (Lat. "Queen of *heaven"). The opening lines of a 12th-century *Easter anthem addressed to the Virgin *Mary. She is called upon to rejoice and to celebrate the *resurrection of her Son. It is recited or sung in Roman Catholic churches between Easter and *Whitsuntide.

REGULAR The name given to *clergy who are bound by *vows and live in a community that follows a *rule. *Priests who live in the world are known as "*secular."

REGULARS (REGULAR CLERGY) Ordained *priests who are full members of a *religious *order and who live under *vows and a *rule (Lat. *regula*, "rule"). They are contrasted with diocesan and "secular" *clergy.

REICHSBISCHOF
A Protestant church office in Nazi Germany. When a united German Evangelical Church superseded the many provincial churches after Hitler's accession, the office of reichsbischof was created as its head. The *German-Christians sponsored Ludwig Müller (1883–1945) for the post, but Friedrich von *Bodelschwing was elected in 1933. Within months, however, the Nazis forced him to resign, and Müller replaced him. The post ceased to have significance in 1935, when the Nazis created the Ministry of Church Affairs.

REIGN OF GOD See KINGDOM OF GOD.

REIMARUS, HERMANN SAMUEL
(1694–1768). German Deist. Born in Hamburg, he was appointed to the chair of Hebrew and Oriental languages there at the Gymnasium in 1727. In a series of essays he dismissed the *Gospels as fraudulent, rejected *revelation and *miracles, and regarded *Jesus as an ambitious but misguided human.

REINCARNATION The belief that the *soul leaves the *body at death to enter another body. It is the *transmigration of souls and is widely believed in the East, especially by Hindus. *Christianity teaches that a person has one life only in this world, and this is a preparation for life with *God eternally. See also METEMPSYCHOSIS.

RELICS The material remains of a *saint now dead and all *holy things that were intimately connected with him or her. These are venerated because of their association with a *body that has been the temple of the Holy *Spirit. A few verses are used to justify the practice (2 Kings 2:14; 13:21; Acts 19:12), which began early in the history of the church and continues in the *Eastern and Roman Catholic churches. Protestants have rejected such *veneration because it detracts from the centrality of *Jesus Christ and *worship of him.

RELIEF CHURCH Scottish *Presbyterian body formed in 1761. Thomas *Gillespie had been deposed from the Church of *Scotland for supporting a protest against patronage in the appointment of ministers. With two colleagues, he founded the new body that survived until an 1847 union, when it helped to form the *United Presbyterian Church.

RELIGION Used in a variety of ways that often appear contradictory. To say "the *Christian religion" is a means of distinguishing *Christianity from other religions. Religion here means "belief, way of *worship, and morality." However, the *OT contrasts the *faith of *Israel with "religions" of the surrounding peoples. Religion is human effort, human *justification, and human attempts to please *God. In this sense religion is opposed also to Christianity, which is centered on the *revelation and *grace of God in Christ.

RELIGIONS, COMPARATIVE STUDY OF The scientific investigation and assessment of religious phenomena as found in any or all of the religions of the world. It began as a recognized study in the late 19th century, principally in Germany, where it often went under the title of "history of religion," *Religionsgeschichte*. Though seen only as an adjunct to *Christian *theology, it stands as a subject in its own right.

RELIGIONSGESCHICHTLICHE SCHULE (Ger. "the history of religions school"). A school of thought and an academic methodology in German universities at the close of the 19th and beginning of the 20th centuries. It studied and emphasized common themes, *doctrines and developments in *Christianity and *Judaism as well as in other Middle Eastern forms of *religion.

RELIGIOUS (Lat. *religiosus*). A technical term for a member of a *religious *order or congregation bound by solemn *vows.

RELIGIOUS A PRIORI The awareness of the *holy or the divine as a basic aspect of a human person. On this assumption *religion is the expression in word, *symbol, and ceremonial of this fundamental consciousness of the divine.

RELIGIOUS EXPERIENCE An awareness of nearness to the *holy or divine or a relationship with the holy or divine. It is basic to all forms of *religion. Psychologists differ as to whether there is an objective Reality that causes the subjective experience. Christians believe in the objective existence of *God and thus claim that they experience him in *worship, in *prayer, and in everyday life. They experience more than the mere projection of personal imagination or feelings, for it occurs only because God takes the initiative in making himself known.

REMARRIAGE The taking of a marriage partner for a second time. This may be possible because of the death of the first partner or through *annulment or *divorce. Remarriage in church services is possible in most *denominations if the first partner has died or if the first marriage has been declared not a marriage; but when a divorced person is involved, some churches, especially the Roman Catholic, find it impossible to allow.

REMBRANDT VAN RIJN (1606–1669). Dutch painter. Born in Leiden, he studied at the university there and then lived in Amsterdam from 1631. He knew great *suffering—some of it self-inflicted through incompetence and immorality—but this gave new depth to his work. Among the more religious subjects of this greatest of Dutch painters were *Saul and David,* the *Last Supper,* and the *Return of the Prodigal Son.*

REMI (REMIGIUS) (d. c. 533). "*Apostle of the Franks." *Archbishop of Reims from 459, he founded several bishoprics, made efforts to restore Arians to *orthodoxy, and was successful in converting *Clovis, pagan king of the Franks, to *Christianity.

REMISSION OF SINS *God's *pardon and *forgiveness for offenses against his *holy law, both of omission and commission. The *Nicene Creed speaks of one "*baptism for the remission of *sins," thereby making a close link between God's forgiveness and the *sacrament of baptism. This is because of the nature of baptism, the sign of entry into the new *covenant, when what *Christ achieved for man in his *atonement is made over to the one baptized. See also Forgiveness.

REMONSTRANCE, THE (1610). The classic statement of Arminian teaching produced at Gouda in 1610 by forty-six *pastors who had rejected orthodox *Calvinism in favor of the teaching of Jacobus *Arminius (1560–1609). The document had five sections, each of which denied an aspect of orthodox Calvinism (e.g., *irresistible *grace in *conversion). The teaching of the Synod of *Dort (1618–1619) was a response to this Remonstrance (whose authors and supporters were called Remonstrants). *Arminianism, as an alternative interpretation of biblical *theology, gained many supporters and over the centuries has become the basic theology of many Protestants.

RENAISSANCE, THE The complex period of transition in European *culture from medieval to modern times (c. 1300–c. 1600). It was in two parts, the Italian (beginning c. 1300–1350) and the Northern Renaissance (beginning c. 1450). The latter was more religious in character. In terms of *Christianity two aspects of it are worthy of mention: (1) the study of the Greek classics, which led to the study of the *NT in Greek (rather than Latin) and then the *OT in Hebrew; (2) the call for reform of church and society. This had its effects on many men who turned from humanism to reform of the church. If one man is to be singled out as embodying the spirit of the northern Renaissance, it must be Erasmus of Rotterdam (c. 1466–1536). As not a few leaders of the Protestant *Reformation had a training in the new humanism of the Renaissance, the general relationship of the Reformation to the Renaissance is clear. However, scholars still debate the precise relationship.

RENAN, JOSEPH ERNST (1823–1892). French historian and philosopher. He began studies for the priesthood, but plagued by religious doubts he left the Roman Catholic Church in 1845. He wrote a life of *Jesus, whom he did not regard as divine, and this work caused his temporary removal from the chair of Hebrew at the Collège de France, to which he had been appointed in 1862 (he was reinstated in 1870). Renan also wrote *History of Christian Origins* (1863–1883).

RENWICK, JAMES (1662–1688). Scottish *Covenanter. Sent to Holland for theological training during the time of persecution in Scotland, he returned in the summer of 1683. He and his followers claimed the rights of people to rise up against a tyrannical ruler and denounced *James II as an enemy of true *religion. He was hunted but continued *preaching until captured and executed. He was the last of the Covenanting *martyrs.

REORDINATION The act of ordaining someone who already has experienced an *ordination. This happens when someone ordained in an Independent or Free church becomes a clergyman in one of the Episcopalian churches (e.g., Anglican or Roman Catholic). It also sometimes happens when a Roman Catholic *priest leaves his church and seeks to minister among *evangelical churches.

REPARATION The act or fact of making amends. It is sometimes used of the *sacrifice of *Christ; it was an act of reparation in that it restored the relationship between *God and man. It is also used in certain Roman Catholic communities to describe the *prayers, acts of self-denial, and *good *works offered to God in order to make amends for offenses against the blessed "*sacrament of Christ's *body and *blood."

REPENTANCE A change of mind leading to a change of direction in life. A turning from a self-centered existence to a God-centered existence. When such a change occurs it is intimately connected with *faith and constitutes what may be called *conversion. Thus there is the initial act of repentance that leads to the beginning of the *Christian life. There is also the continuing repentance within the Christian life that represents a recognition of failure and disobedience and the determination to keep moving in the direction of *obedience to *God.

REPRESENTATIVE, CHRIST AS By becoming a true man, the *eternal *Son of *God became the representative Man. He lived, suffered, died, rose again, and ascended into *heaven as representative Man. By him humankind can have access to God and enjoy *fellowship with him. This idea is presented in the *NT through *Christ being the new and *Second Adam (Rom 5:12ff.; 1 Cor 15:45) and the One in whom all things and people are completed and fulfilled (Eph 1:10). Cf. RECAPITULATION. Theologians differ as to whether Christ may also be presented as our *Substitute, and thus there are learned discussions as to the precise difference between representation and substitution.

REPROBATION The decision made by *God before the creation of the *universe to condemn sinners not saved by *Christ to *eternal *punishment in *hell. Such a view of the activity of God's eternal mind has been held by high Calvinists who have thought of God as making a decree of *election and a decree of reprobation. This is known as *double predestination. See also PREDESTINATION.

REQUIEM A *Mass (*Eucharist) in the Roman Catholic Church offered for those who have died. The old Latin service began, "Requiem aeternam donam eis, Domine" ("Give them *eternal rest, O *Lord"). Thus the name.

REREDOS From a French origin, this word refers either to decoration placed over and behind the *Lord's table (*altar) or to painted wooden panels fixed to the back of the altar. Thus another expression used is altar-piece.

RESCISSORY ACT (1661). A piece of legislation passed by the Scottish Parliament after the *Restoration. It repealed the Acts that, in the last year of *Charles I's reign, had reestablished *Presbyterianism as the *religion of Scotland, and followed this by rescinding all the statutes passed since 1633 (the year of Charles's coronation as Scottish king). The ruling junta were said to have discussed this legislation over their cups and "when they had drunk higher, they resolved to venture on it."

RESERVATION OF THE SACRAMENT The practice of keeping consecrated bread (rarely wine) from a *Eucharist for later purposes. These would include giving Holy *Communion to the sick and (for Roman Catholics) the devotional practice of *Benediction and processions at *Corpus Christi.

RESERVE The withholding of deep teaching about the *Christian *faith from converts until they are spiritually able to receive it. The biblical basis is the idea of not casting pearls before swine (Matt 7:6). As a principle it was utilized by the *Tractarians of the mid-19th century, and they criticized careless use by Christians of such phrases as "saved by the *blood of *Christ." With the idea of withholding *doctrine there went the further idea of reverence when talking about precious matters.

RESTORATION, THE (1660). The return of the Stuart Dynasty, in the person of *Charles II, to the throne of England and the restoration of the Church of *England to its former position after the Cromwellian era. Charles was duly crowned king; he had theoretically been king of Scotland since 1649.

RESTORATION OF ISRAEL The belief that before the end of the age the Jewish people will not only return to the land of Palestine but also turn to *Jesus as *Messiah. The military triumphs of the state of *Israel have helped to popularize this view, especially among conservative Evangelicals. A biblical basis is sought in the *OT *prophecies of the restoration of Israel (e.g., Jer 33; Isa 60) that are connected with such passages as Romans 11:25ff. and Luke 21:24. Before the actual appearance of modern Israel and the Zionist movement, the *doctrine of the restoration of Israel was stated in the form of a great *conversion to *Christ of Jews in all parts of the world and then their return to Palestine.

RESURRECTION OF CHRIST The *Gospels describe the empty tomb and the appearances of *Christ to his *disciples, not his actual rising from the dead. His resurrection was resuscitation with transformation; the whole physical *body was transformed into the whole *spiritual body, so that there was an identity-in-transformation. This spiritual body, normally invisible and immaterial, could assume a form similar to the previous physical form. Thus *Jesus appeared to his disciples, and they were able to recognize him.

The Resurrection occurred within history and thus may be fixed in time, yet aspects of it are beyond history. There is historical evidence—the empty tomb, the experience of the disciples, and the claims of Christians to know the living Christ now. Yet, in that it was a special (uniquely so) act of *God, a true *miracle, some aspects of it can be known only through *revelation, through God himself giving the interpretation and meaning. So it is beyond history in that it signifies the coming of the *kingdom of God, the appearance of the new creation, and the promise of the resurrection of believers. The primary material in the *NT is Matthew 28; Mark 16; Luke 24; John 20–21; and 1 Corinthians 15.

RESURRECTION OF THE DEAD The belief that at the end of the age, when *Christ returns to earth in power and glory as Judge, those who have died will be given new bodies. The faithful will live in these bodies in the *kingdom of *God, enjoying his *holy presence. The resurrection *body will not be a physical body, but as Paul states in 1 Corinthians 15, a *spiritual body, the perfect embodiment of the sanctified human *spirit and personality. The identity between the physical body that dies and the spiritual body that is everlasting is probably to be sought in the continuance of the identical human spirit and personality.

Apart from the resurrection of believers there will also be a resurrection of unbelievers and the disobedient (John 5:29). Their destiny will not be the kingdom of God but separation from God. This topic is, however, not so clearly stated in the *NT as is the destiny of believers. See also Hope.

RETREAT A period of time, normally several days, spent in silence, *meditation, and other religious exercises. *Ignatius Loyola developed the practice in *Roman Catholicism, and retreat houses have been established throughout the world. In England the custom was introduced widely to Anglicans through the *Oxford Movement.

RETZ, CARDINAL DE (1614–1679). *Archbishop of Paris. Ordained and consecrated (1643) despite a lack of *faith and morals, he involved himself in politics, opposing *Richelieu and then *Mazarin. It was for political reasons also that he was nominated and made *cardinal in 1652. Having backed the wrong side, he was imprisoned later that year, escaped into exile in 1654, and agreed to resign his archbishopric in 1662 in return for money and an abbacy.

REUCHLIN, JOHANNES (1455–1522). German humanist. One of the most versatile men of his time, he included an intimate knowledge of Hebrew, Greek, and Latin among his achievements. His Hebrew grammar and lexicon greatly encouraged study of the *OT, and his love of scholarship was seen also when he contested an imperial order for the destruction of all Jewish books. Reuchlin was summoned to appear before an inquisitorial court on a charge of *heresy. A long drawn-out controversy ended with the condemnation of Reuchlin's writings by *Leo X. Though he intervened to save the burning of *Luther's books at one point, he never joined the *Reformed cause.

REUNION OF CHURCHES Since the 16th century—and especially in the 19th and 20th centuries—the Protestant part of the church has become divided into many *denominations. This process is now challenged by another process, the move to unite those who are separated from each other. The merging process is a slow and painful one, but there have been some notable successes—e.g., the union of the United Free Church and the Church of *Scotland in 1929, the union of the Methodist groups into the Methodist Church of Great Britain in 1932, the union of the Methodist Church and the *Evangelical United Brethren to form the *United Methodist Church of U.S. and Canada in 1968, and the formation of the Lutheran Church in America from various Lutheran groups in 1987. Those who advocate reunion claim that that is what *Christ prayed for (John 17) and that it will promote a richer experience of *God and each other.

REUSCH, FRANZ HEINRICH (1825–1900). *Old Catholic theologian. Westphalian by birth, he was ordained in 1849 and from 1854 taught in the *Old Testament department at Bonn, later becoming rector of the university (1873). At *Vatican Council I he joined his friend J. J. I. von *Döllinger in opposing the declaration of papal *infallibility, was excommunicated, and helped to organize the Old Catholic Church. He moved out of prominence in 1878, disagreeing with that body's abolition of *clerical *celibacy.

REVEALED THEOLOGY A system of *theology based mainly on *revelation of *God recorded in the *Bible. It is contrasted with *natural theology.

REVELATION *God's disclosure of himself and the communication of his word and *will to humankind. This is often divided into two types. (1) General revelation. This is what God makes known of himself in and through the *universe and the human *conscience (Rom 1:19ff.; 2:14ff.), its true significance being seen only in the light of special revelation (Acts 17:22ff.), because human beings are sinful and do not see nature through pure eyes. (2) Special revelation. This is what God made known in his dealings with the *patriarchs and the people of *Israel, in and through *Jesus Christ and by the *apostles. Here God's disclosure is both in word and event and in word and personal *Being (Jesus). The record of this revelation is found in the *Bible. However, there is more revelation to come, and this will occur at the end of the age with the personal return of the *Lord Jesus (1 Cor 13:12; 1 John 3:2; Rev 1:7).

REVEREND (Lat. *reverendus,* "worthy of being honored"). Though used of *clergy since the 15th century, only in the 17th century did it become a formal title. In *Anglicanism, senior clergy are called "Most Reverend" if an *archbishop, "Right Reverend" if a *bishop, and "Very Reverend" if a dean.

REVIVAL, REVIVALISM Used in two ways. (1) Of a tremendous outpouring of the Holy *Spirit on a church or churches in a specific area. The results are felt both in terms of the internal life of the people and in their *mission to the world. Revivalism then is the way in which the *grace of *God is channeled and managed by leaders in the churches. (2) Of evangelistic meetings held over a short period of time with the aim of making converts. Thus revival is a synonym for evangelistic campaign, and revivalism refers to the techniques used in the campaign.

REWARD A term used in Roman Catholic *moral *theology to refer to the attainment of happiness and blessedness in the presence of *God in *heaven. It is to be understood as a correlative of *merit. The faithful are rewarded because they freely cooperated with God in his *grace. In doing so they gained merit, and, having merit, they will receive the reward of *eternal life.

REWARDS There is no uniformity in the biblical teaching on rewards in *heaven for serving *God on earth. Biblical support for receiving rewards or greater *blessings can be found in the teaching of *Jesus (Matt 6:20; Mark 10:21) and Paul (1 Tim 6:18–19; 2 Tim 4:6–8). The idea of special rewards does not fit easily into the Protestant understanding of *grace unmerited and free.

RHODES, KNIGHTS OF See HOSPITALLERS.

RICCI, MATTEO (1552–1610). *Jesuit *missionary to China. Born in Italy, he became a Jesuit in 1571 and went to China in 1582, learning the language and adopting the local *culture. His knowledge and his sympathetic approach to Confucianism (which was criticized by fellow Christians in the Chinese Rites Controversy) opened doors in high places, and many were converted under his *ministry.

RICE, JOHN R. (1896–1980). American author, conference speaker, educator, *pastor, radio preacher, and revivalist. He began *The Sword of the Lord* in 1934, and its circulation reached over a quarter of a million. He wrote more than 125 books (with a circulation of over 40 million).

RICE, LUTHER (1783–1836). American Baptist minister. Ordained to the Congregational *ministry in 1812, he was one of the group (Adoniram *Judson was another) that sailed for India under the new *American Board of Commissioners for Foreign Missions. En route, Rice and Judson adopted Baptist principles, and Rice returned to the U.S. in 1813 to organize a Baptist foreign *missionary society, with special reference initially to the work established by Judson in Burma. Rice tirelessly promoted *missions at home and abroad.

RICHARD, TIMOTHY (1845–1919). *Missionary to China. Born in Wales and ordained as a Baptist minister in 1869, he at once sailed for China. Like the 16th-century Matteo *Ricci, he believed in making Chinese *culture serve *Christian ends, and, like Ricci, he was criticized for such policies. He worked as an *evangelist, relief worker, healer, colporteur, and educator.

RICHARD OF CHICHESTER (c. 1198–1253). *Bishop of Chichester. After studies at Oxford and on the Continent, he was chancellor of Oxford University and later *chancellor to Edmund of Abingdon (1236–1240). He was then ordained and subsequently named bishop of Chichester, thus earning the enmity of *Henry III, whose own nominee had been rejected by the *pope. A pious man, Richard was active in church reform, notably in the welfare of his *clergy.

RICHARD OF ST.-VICTOR (d. 1173). Theologian and mystic. Born probably in Scotland and educated in Paris, he became prior of the Abbey of St.-Victor there in 1162. He wrote much on the *Trinity and on the *exegesis of *Scripture, but he is remembered most for works that greatly influenced medieval *mysticism. Dante regarded Richard as one of the church's greatest teachers.

RICHELIEU, ARMAND-JEAN DUPLESSIS, DUC DE (1585–1642). French *cardinal and statesman. Through family influence he was nominated as *bishop of Lucon at age twenty-one, gained favor at court, became cardinal in 1622, and from 1629 was chief minister and virtually ruler of France. In his aim to establish the royal supremacy he dealt mercilessly with the dissident nobility and with the *Huguenots. In foreign policy, on the other hand, he supported German Protestant princes against the Hapsburg Empire. He distrusted the *Jesuits, encouraged the independence of the French church from Rome, opposed *Jansenism, and was a patron of the arts.

RIDLEY, NICHOLAS (c. 1500–1555). *Bishop of London. A versatile scholar, he held academic and church posts before becoming bishop of Rochester in 1547. Gradually coming to accept *Reformed *doctrine, he helped compile the 1549 Book of *Common Prayer, furthered the Protestant cause at Cambridge, and showed great social concern. Appointed *bishop of London in 1550, he subsequently supported the claim to the throne of Lady Grey (1553), was deprived, later condemned for *heresy, and burned at Oxford with Hugh *Latimer.

RIGHTEOUSNESS A word with several meanings in the *Bible and in *theology. (1) Biblical usage (Heb. *tsedaqah*; Gk. *dikaiosune*) is mainly for *God's activity in creating and maintaining right relationships between human beings and himself and between human beings and other human beings (Isa 46:13; 51:5–7; Rom 1:16). People are righteous when they have a right relationship with God (i.e., they are justified) through *Christ, the Righteous One, who has a perfectly right relationship with God himself. (2) Righteousness is also used of an ethical quality that may or may not be commendable. *Jesus condemned the righteousness of the scribes and *Pharisees (Matt 5:20; 6:33) as Paul condemned the righteousness of the law (Phil 3:19; Rom 10:3). James looked for ethical righteousness in those who claimed to be in a right relationship with God (2:18–26; 5:16). The presence of the Holy *Spirit in the *heart of the believer means that God, the Righteous One, is present, and so the believer is being renewed in righteousness. See also JUSTIFICATION.

RIGORISM In moral *theology, rigor is the insistence that the law or a rule must be kept, however probable are the doubts that it is no longer in force or is invalid. Extreme rigorism is known as *tutiorism. Less technically, rigorism is the opposite of laxity in regard to moral questions.

RILEY, WILLIAM BELL (1861–1947). Gifted debater, expositor, and *pastor. A pastor for more than fifty years (forty-five at the more-than-2,600-seat First Baptist Church in Minneapolis), he was also the founder and president of Northwestern Schools. The leader in founding the *World's Christian Fundamentals Association, he led in its work for eleven years, speaking out against—and debating the ablest defenders of—evolution and *modernism.

RITE A distinctive liturgical form and style related in origin to specific linguistic, geographical, historical, and cultural factors. The Roman rite, originating in Latin *culture, is the rite of *Roman Catholicism, and to a lesser extent of *Lutheranism and *Anglicanism. In the *Eastern and *Orthodox churches there are other ancient rites (e.g., the *Byzantine rite, whose origins are in the Greek culture and *theology of Constantinople).

RITSCHL, ALBRECHT (1822–1889). German Protestant theologian. He taught *theology at Bonn (1846–1864) and Göttingen (1864–1889). He emphasized the uniqueness of *Christ but denied his propitiatory death. He was concerned with the ethical implications of *Christianity and applying these to the church in contemporary society. Much of Ritschl's thinking is incorporated in his three-volume *Christian Doctrine of Justification and Reconciliation*.

RITSCHLIANISM The teaching of Albrecht Ritschl (1822–1889) and of his *disciples—e.g., J. Kaftan (1848–1926), W. Herrmann (1846–1922), and F. Loofs (1858–1928). It steered a middle path between *metaphysics and subjective piety and emphasized the moral value of *God's *revelation to man. Thus it was known for its exposition of *ethics and the community of the church/society.

RITUAL Technically the prescribed form of words that constitutes a service of *worship. However, in ordinary usage ritual covers both the prescribed form of words and prescribed actions (ceremonial). The book known as the *Roman Ritual* contains the liturgies that the Roman Catholic *priest reads.

RITUALISM Based on their understanding of medieval Catholic *worship, the attempts by Anglo-Catholic *priests of the Church of *England during the late 19th century to introduce new ceremonies and customs into the services of the church. Thus they were accused of ritualism and called ritualists.

RIVER BRETHREN See BRETHREN IN CHRIST.

ROBBER SYNOD OF EPHESUS See EPHESUS, ROBBER SYNOD OF.

ROBERSON, LEE (1909–). Pastor, *evangelist, and educator. He is the founder and *chancellor of Tennessee Temple University and the *pastor emeritus of the 45,000-member Highland Park Baptist Church of Chattanooga, Tennessee. He has been a radio and TV evangelist and has written more than twenty books.

ROBERT OF JUMIÈGES (d. c. 1055). *Archbishop of Canterbury, 1051–1052. He became a *Benedictine *abbot at Jumièges (1037). Edward the Confessor brought him to England and made him *bishop of London (1042). Later appointed to Canterbury, he soon fled to the Continent because of the enmity of Godwin, earl of Wessex, leader of the English party. Robert spent his last years at Jumièges; the treatment he underwent was a chief factor in the *pope's support for the Norman invasion of England in 1066.

ROBERT OF MOLESME (c. 1027–1111). French *Benedictine *abbot. Born in Troyes, be became a Benedictine as a youth, became *prior and abbot, but found resistance to reforms he wished to initiate. With others of similar outlook he established a community at Molesme in 1075, but this too proved unsatisfactory in the end, and in 1098 he founded Citeaux Abbey, which saw the beginning of the *Cistercian *order. The monks of Molesme, however, requested that Robert return the following year, and he continued as their abbot until his death.

ROBERTSON, FREDERICK WILLIAM (1816–1853). English preacher. Ordained in 1840 in the Church of *England, he ministered briefly in various places before becoming incumbent of Trinity Chapel, Brighton, in 1847. There for six years, still dogged by illness, he made a remarkable impact, especially on otherwise unreached working-class people. His profound social concern was matched by spiritual insight. He belonged to no school, which fact may account for the carping opposition he faced. No greater testimony to his *preaching can be made than the fact that he is still sufficiently identified as Robertson of Brighton.

ROBINSON, HENRY WHEELER (1872–1945). English Baptist scholar. Born in Northampton, he had a wide-ranging education, served as *pastor and lecturer, then became principal of Regent's Park College, which moved to Oxford during his incumbency (1920–1942). A specialist in *OT and widely known in university circles, Wheeler wrote works that included *The Religious Ideas of the Old Testament* (1913) and *Redemption and Revelation* (1938).

ROBINSON, JOHN (c. 1575–1625). *Pastor to the *Pilgrim Fathers. Ordained as an Anglican, he joined some *Separatists near Nottingham and became their pastor when persecution forced their withdrawal to Holland. A section of his congregation sailed in the *Mayflower*. He died before he and the majority who remained could join them in America.

ROBINSON, JOHN ARTHUR THOMAS (1919–1983). Anglican *bishop and writer. Bishop of Woolwich (1959–1969), he initially created a stir by defending D. H. Lawrence's *Lady Chatterley's Lover* in a court trial, but in 1963 his own *Honest to God* caused a greater outcry—questioning traditional *Christian *doctrines, going over ground largely trodden by 19th-century German theologians. Robinson was more original—and more conservative—in his published works on *NT history and *theology.

ROBINSON, THEODORE HENRY (1881–1964). *Old Testament scholar. Son of a Baptist minister in Kent, he graduated at Cambridge and in 1908 went to Serampore College, Bengal, as professor of Hebrew and Syriac. He returned to Britain in 1915 to be lecturer (and later professor) in Semitic languages at University College, Cardiff (1915–1944). An internationally known scholar who often collaborated with W. O. E. *Oesterley, he wrote many books on the *OT and commentaries on Matthew and Hebrews.

RODEHEAVER, HOMER ALLAN (1880–1956). American song leader and *hymn writer. Born in Ohio, where he was educated at Wesleyan University, he is remembered as musical director and trombonist of the Billy *Sunday campaign meetings. He published music, wrote books and *hymns, and ran a ranch in Florida for deprived boys.

ROGATION DAYS Traditionally days of *prayer and *fasting when *intercession is made for a good harvest. The most important day was April 25, when processions from *parish churches to the fields were made. In recent times such days have not been kept, except by the few, and in their place have come days of *prayer not only for agriculture but also for industry and commerce.

ROGERS, JOHN (c. 1500–1555). English Protestant *martyr. He edited "Matthew's Bible," the first complete version published in English. A clergyman in London, he was arrested for *preaching *Reformed *doctrine during the reign of Mary *Tudor and was burned at Smithfield, London.

ROLLE OF HAMPOLE, RICHARD (c. 1295–1349). English *hermit and mystic. He took to the life of a wandering hermit in northern England about 1326. He gained a reputation for *asceticism and spiritual life and wrote in language people could understand, his works being read long after his death.

ROMAINE, WILLIAM (1714–1795). Anglican clergyman. He combined Hebrew scholarship with warm *evangelical zeal. Many thousands came to hear him on his *preaching tours throughout the country. From 1766 he was rector of St. Anne's, Blackfriars, during which time he wrote his famous work, *The Life, Walk, and Triumph of Faith* (3 vols., 1771–1794).

ROMAN CATHOLICISM The teaching and practice of the Roman Catholic Church. "Roman" indicates that Roman Catholics consider the *bishop of Rome, the *pope, to be the earthly head of the church. "Catholicism" indicates that the church claims to be either the one true worldwide church of *Christ or a major part of this one church. Roman Catholicism, one of the three major branches of *Christianity, is in fact the major, continuing part of the Western medieval church. Although it lost what became known as the Protestant churches in the 16th century, it has gained since then many more members, through emigration from Roman Catholic countries to the New World and through *missionary activity in Africa and Asia. So Roman Catholicism is distinguished both from the *Eastern and *Orthodox churches on the one side and from Protestant churches on the other. It is particularly strong in Italy, Spain, Portugal, Central America, and South America. The three major characteristics are (1) the hierarchical structure (pope, *cardinals, bishops, etc.) centered in the *Vatican in Rome, (2) the great emphases on *dogma as defined *truth, and (3) the unity and uniformity of the *liturgy throughout the church. The many distinctives of Roman Catholicism include its view of papal *infallibility, the *doctrine of *transubstantiation, the exalted position given to the Virgin *Mary, its acceptance of uncanonical books as *Scripture and putting all on a par with *tradition, its insistence on auricular *confession, its teaching on *purgatory, and its rule of *clerical *celibacy. Everywhere the central act of *worship is the *Mass. Since the Second *Vatican Council (1962–1965) there has been an openness within Roman Catholicism for positive change (e.g., liturgy in the vernacular, not in Latin) and, in relations with other churches and *religions, a greater readiness to treat them in a humbler manner (e.g., to call other Christians "separated brethren" rather than "heretics").

ROMERO Y GALDAMES, OSCAR ARNULFO (1917–1980). Salvadoran *archbishop. Born into a village family of modest means, ordained in Rome in 1942, and made bishop in 1970, he was regarded as an establishment figure who opposed radical tendencies in the *clergy. About the time he was installed as archbishop in 1977, a tyrannical government waged a campaign of harassment and murder against *priests and people who opposed it. Against all expectation, he became champion of the *poor and of civil rights. He gained international recognition and the hatred of the ruling junta. He was shot dead, and his assassin was never found.

ROOKMAAKER, HANS (1922–1977). *Christian *art historian. Son of a Dutch colonial administrator in Sumatra, he was a student and then an underground activist after the German invasion of Holland in 1940. He read *Dooyeweerd in prisoner of war camps and found that his *faith in *Christ "acquired a firm underpinning of philosophic thought." Later professor at the Free University of Amsterdam, he declared that "*God's hand in history" had not been properly discerned by Protestants with an irrational distrust of beauty.

ROSARY A form of *prayer in *Roman Catholicism that involves the recitation of Hail Marys (*Ave Marias), preceded by the *Lord's Prayer (*Pater Noster), and followed by a *doxology (Gloria Patri). The word is applied also to the string of 165 beads, or a smaller one of 55 beads, used to help the memory in reciting the rosary. This set of devotions is said to date from at least the beginning of the 12th century. The derivation of the word (Lat. *rosarium*, a rose) indicates that it has a particular relation to *Mary, for the rose is an emblem of her, and she is known as the mystical Rose.

ROSE, MYSTICAL An emblem of *Mary, mother of *Jesus. The origin is Ecclesiasticus 24:14, "I was exalted like the rose plant in Jericho." Her rose has five or seven petals to signify her "joys"—in the *Annunciation, *Visitation, *Nativity of Jesus, *Epiphany, Finding Jesus in the Temple, *Resurrection, and *Assumption.

ROSE OF LIMA (1586–1617). Peruvian *nun, the first canonized *saint of the Western Hemisphere. She became a *Dominican tertiary in 1606. She embarked on a life of the strictest austerity despite initial disapproval from her wealthy family, and many *miracles were attributed to her. Canonized in 1671, she is the *patron saint of South America.

ROSMINIANS The Roman Catholic congregation founded in 1828 by Italian philosopher Antonio Rosmini-Serbati (1797–1855). Its members are either *presbyters (who take a special *vow of *obedience to the *pope) or coadjutors. They stress personal holiness and engage in different kinds of charitable work as necessary. It was introduced into England in 1835 soon after a women's branch, the Sisters of Providence, had been founded.

ROSSETTI, CHRISTINA GEORGINA (1830–1894). English poetess. Younger sister of D. G. *Rossetti, she was known for religious verse and prose conspicuous for symbolism and intensity of feeling. Her many *poems include "In the Bleak Mid-Winter" and "None Other Lamb, None Other Name."

ROSSETTI, DANTE GABRIEL (1828–1882). English poet and painter. A friend of W. H. *Hunt, he greatly admired Dante, whose lyrics he translated into English. Many of his early poems had religious themes, but his life was shadowed by the death of his wife after two years of marriage (1862), and he fell into sad decline. Some of his paintings had biblical subjects.

ROTHMANN, BERNT (c. 1495–1535). German Anabaptist leader. Formerly strong Lutheran preacher in his native Münster, he became an Anabaptist in 1533 and joined the extremist group that took over the city in 1534. He was court preacher to self-styled king *John of Leyden, urged the killing of the "godless," and perished when orthodox forces retook the city.

ROWLAND, DANIEL (1713–1790). Cofounder of Welsh Calvinistic *Methodism. A converted Anglican clergyman, he began a remarkable *preaching *ministry and founded societies for his converts. Though for a time he led one group of Calvinistic Methodists, he retained his curacy at Llangeitho until dispossessed in 1763, at which time he resumed preaching in a new building in the *parish.

ROWLEY, HAROLD HENRY (1890–1969). English Baptist scholar. After training at Bristol and Oxford Universities, he served a pastorate in Somerset, had a five-year term with the Baptist Missionary Society in China, then taught Hebrew in Cardiff, Bangor, and finally in Manchester University (1945–1959). Highly regarded by *OT scholars throughout the world, Rowley wrote many works including *The Faith of Israel* (1956) and *The Dead Sea Scrolls and the New Testament* (1957).

RUBRICS The directions provided in *liturgies to guide those who lead *worship services. They are of two kinds—obligatory and directive (optional).

RUFINUS, TYRANNIUS (c. 345–410). Latin theologian and translator. He became a monk and a friend of *Jerome but was suspected of *heresy because of his interest in the teachings of *Origen. He translated many Greek theological works into Latin and wrote a commentary on the *Apostles' *Creed.

RULE OF FAITH The criterion or norm upon which *faith in *God is based. All Christians claim this is the *Bible; but it has to be interpreted, and differences arise as to what precisely the Bible teaches. Thus *creeds and *confessions of faith become subordinate rules of faith, and often the Bible is interpreted in the light of these. Thus it can happen that in practice, if not in theory, the primary rule of faith is the particular teaching of a given church. Protestants often accuse Roman Catholics of allowing *tradition (accumulated teaching and practice) to be more important than the Bible itself.

RULE OF LIFE A plan of life that provides a set pattern each day for the duties of *prayer, work, recreation, and rest. It is a means to an end, glorifying *God, not an end in itself.

RUOTSALAINEN, PAAVO (1777–1852). Finnish Pietist leader. He is said to have influenced the *Christian life in Finland more than anyone else in modern times and to have popularized words once given him by a counselor: "Lacking one thing, you lack everything—the inner knowledge of *Christ."

RUSSELL, CHARLES TAZE (1852–1916). Founder of *Jehovah's Witnesses (The *International Bible Students' Association). A successful businessman in Pennsylvania, he questioned certain orthodox *Christian *doctrines and claimed to believe from *Bible study that *Christ would return in 1874 (later amended to 1914). His six-volume *Studies in the Scriptures* is still a standard work in the movement. Various unpleasant court proceedings showed him to have been guilty of questionable acts that reflect on his honesty and morality.

RUTHERFORD, JOSEPH FRANKLIN ("JUDGE") (1869–1942). Second leader of *Jehovah's Witnesses. A lawyer who had defended C. T. *Russell and in 1917 succeeded him as head of Jehovah's Witnesses, he served a prison sentence in 1918 for conduct arising out of his opposition to military service. When the *Second Coming did not take place in 1914 he argued that it had happened invisibly. He was a man who attracted charges of fraudulent conduct.

RUTHERFORD, SAMUEL (1600–1661). Scottish theologian and *Covenanter. Deprived of his *parish on the Solway for opposing *Arminian trends in the ruling Episcopalian party, he was exiled to Aberdeen (1636) but returned south to sign the *National Covenant when *Presbyterianism triumphed in 1638. He became professor of divinity at St. Andrews, attended the *Westminster Assembly, wrote *Lex Rex* (1644) in reply to the *divine right of kings theory, and would almost certainly have joined the *martyrs after the *Restoration had he not been fatally ill. Rutherford is remembered most for his *Letters,* hailed by *Spurgeon and *Baxter as the nearest thing to *inspiration after the *Bible in *evangelical literature.

RYLE, JOHN CHARLES (1816–1900). *Bishop of Liverpool. After a brilliant academic and athletic career at Oxford, he was ordained in 1642 and served rural *parishes until consecrated as the first bishop of Liverpool in 1880. A sensible *evangelical who encouraged those of like mind to take their full part in church affairs, he interested himself in pension funds and in building churches, and he had a strong appeal to working men in his *diocese.

S

SABATIER, AUGUSTE (1839–1901). French Protestant theologian. Professor at Strasbourg (1867–1873) and Paris Protestant theological faculty (1877–1901), he espoused German *biblical *criticism, particularly that of *Schleiermacher and *Ritschl. His teaching that theological *dogmas were fleeting symbolic expressions of abiding *religious experiences greatly influenced his generation.

SABATIER, PAUL (1858–1928). Calvinist *pastor and scholar. Born in Strasbourg, he studied for the Protestant ministry in Paris, served as a *pastor, but resigned in 1894 because of poor health. He gave himself to study, producing a biography of *Francis of Assisi among other works.

SABBATARIANISM The view that the fourth commandment of the *Decalogue (Exod 20:8–11), which prohibits work on the seventh day, is to be applied rigorously to the *Christian day of *worship, the first day of the week. It originated in Puritan England in the early 17th century and became a part of the British Nonconformist conscience in the 19th century.

SABBATH The seventh day of the Jewish week and set apart by divine appointment for *worship, rest, and recreation (Exod 31:13–17; Deut 5:14). It is still the *holy day for Jews and one *Christian *sect: the *Seventh-Day Adventists keep it as their day of worship. Since *Christ arose from the dead on the first day of the week and thereby hallowed that day, Christians worship on *Sundays, looking for the fulfillment of the idea of the Sabbath in the age to come (Heb 4:9).

SABBATICAL YEAR The one year in every seven in which Jews allowed their land to lie fallow (Exod 21:2–6; Deut 15:1–3; Lev 25). It had the purpose of reminding them that *God is the true owner of everything. However, its beneficial aspects have been noted, and it has been practiced by *Christian farmers for both religious and agricultural reasons.

SABELLIANISM The teaching of Sabellius (early 3d century), otherwise known as *Modalism (modalistic *Monarchianism), that *God is one *nature and one *Person but has three names and reveals himself in three forms—Father, Son, and Holy *Spirit. Yet the three names/forms are not separated or separable *Persons. In contrast, orthodox Trinitarianism teaches that God is One in Godhead but genuinely is three Persons. See also Trinity, Doctrine of the.

SACERDOTALISM (Lat. *sacerdos,* "*priest"). Used in two ways: (1) the domination of church life by the *clergy—excessive clericalization, and (2) the special priesthood of the clergy with the idea that in the *Eucharist they reoffer *Christ (in a magical or mysterious way) as a *sacrifice to *God for the *sins of the world.

SACRAMENT (Lat. *sacramentum,* "*oath, solemn obligation"). An outward and visible sign or *symbol of an inward and spiritual *grace given by *God, and ordained by *Christ. So the sacraments of *baptism (Matt 28:19) and the *Lord's Supper (Matt 26:26–29), being ordained by Christ, are accepted by virtually all churches. To these the Roman Catholic and Orthodox church add five more: *confirmation, *penance, *extreme unction, *ordination, and marriage. Protestants generally refuse to see these as sacraments because they are not necessary to *salvation and because Christ did not introduce them for the purpose of receiving salvation. In a true sacrament it is generally recognized that Christ himself, acting through the minister, is the true minister or celebrant of the sacrament. Thus it is he who really baptizes and it is he who gives from his own table his own spiritual *body and *blood in the Lord's Supper.

SACRAMENTALS Religious activities that, though similar to *sacraments, are not so. They include (in Roman Catholic thinking) such things as making the sign of the *cross, saying the *rosary, keeping the *stations of the cross, and giving the *blessing of *God to others.

SACRAMENTARIANS A term *Luther applied to those theologians, notably *Zwingli, who hold that only in a symbolic ("sacramental") sense were the *body and *blood of *Christ in the bread and wine at the *Eucharist.

SACRED HEART OF JESUS Devotion to the humanity of the Incarnate Son of *God. It is expressed in terms of the physical *heart as the center of human, biological life and as the *symbol of *love. Thus the total *Lord *Jesus, who is God made man, is approached through what he has in common with all humankind—his heart, his humanity. Though it has a long history, this type of devotion has officially been practiced in the Roman Catholic Church only since the 18th century. It can become a very subjective and individualistic form of piety.

SACRIFICE The offering to *God, in recognition of his sovereignty and of human dependence on him, of a gift, usually a living creature. The *OT provides many examples of different types of sacrifices (e.g., the four kinds of animal sacrifice: the whole burnt offering, the sin offering, the guilt offering, and the peace offering).

In the *NT the death of *Jesus on the *cross is presented as the fulfillment and culmination of all previous sacrifices of the old *covenant. He was a voluntary victim; being the *Son of God he was a victim of infinite value, and he acted also as the *Priest, presenting himself. Thus in *theology the death of *Christ has been understood as a sacrifice offered to God for the *sin of the world, and its meaning has been developed from ideas in the OT concerning the purpose of the sacrifices of Israelite *worship. See also ATONEMENT.

There has been much debate in the church over the centuries as to precisely what kind of sacrifice is offered to God in the *Eucharist. Older ideas claimed that in some mysterious way it was the reenactment or the reoffering of Christ who died on the cross at Calvary. Modern Roman Catholic ideas suggest that since in *heaven Christ as Priest is always and ever presenting himself to the Father as the perfect sacrifice, the Eucharistic *offering is the representation of this offering. That is, what is happening in *heaven is demonstrated in the Eucharist. Protestants reject both the modern and medieval ideas of a sacrificial offering of Christ and insist that the only offering is that of praise, worship, and *adoration (Heb 13:15) followed by the offering of one's whole life in service (Rom 12:1).

SACRILEGE The deliberate violation, abuse, defilement, or desecration of a sacred person, thing, or place. E.g., to maliciously dig up a graveyard or to tear up *Bibles or *prayer books.

SACRISTY A *vestry or annex of a church where *clergy and other lay ministers robe for *worship and where the *vestments/robes are kept.

SADDUCEES The *priests of the Jerusalem temple and their sympathizers. Probably Sadducee is derived from Zadok, the high priest (2 Sam 8:17). They attempted to preserve Jewish identity, *culture, and *religion at the time of Jesus through a policy of cooperation with the occupation armies of Rome. Further, they disagreed with the *Pharisees on certain doctrinal points (e.g., unlike the Pharisees they did not accept the *resurrection of the dead or the oral interpretation of the law known as the tradition of the elders). Their interests centered on the *cult of the temple and the written Law of Moses. Jesus found himself opposed by them, and he criticized their approach to religion (Matt 16:1–12; 23:23–34; cf. Acts 23:7–8).

SAINT(S) In the *NT, Christians are either "saints" or "called to be saints" (Rom 1:7; 1 Cor 1:2; Eph 1:1; Col 1:2). Because they are called to serve a *holy *God and because the Holy *Spirit indwells them, they are holy and saints (Lat. *sanctus,* "holy"). Soon after the apostolic age the word came to be used particularly for those who showed genuine *Christian character and *virtue in life and, in some cases, in death (cf. Martyr). Later the church canonized such "special" Christians, which meant that they were enjoying the full *blessings of God's presence in *heaven. This, together with the fact that they share human *nature and so still have a close relation to human beings, formed the theological basis for invoking the *prayers of such saints. So the *cult of the saints exists in both the *Eastern and Roman Catholic churches. See also Beatification, Canonization. Protestants have usually avoided these ideas and sought to preserve the original, biblical idea that all true Christians are saints—saints by *grace alone. Even so they appear quite happy to refer to St. Paul, St. John, St. Augustine, St. Patrick, etc.

SALESBURY, WILLIAM (c. 1520–c. 1584). Welsh *NT translator. Though an Oxford-educated lawyer, he early withdrew to follow scholarly pursuits in Denbighshire. He translated the NT (1567) and the Book of *Common Prayer, each with some collaborators, and produced a Welsh-English dictionary.

SALESIANS Roman Catholic congregation of men, founded by John *Bosco in Italy in 1859. Taking its name from *Francis de Sales, it is concerned with the religious education of youth and spread rapidly until it became the third largest men's *order, found in Latin America as well as in Europe.

SALT Because of its particular quality as both a preservative and seasoner of food, salt has been highly regarded in human cultures. It was used in religious ceremonial and ritual in the *OT (Num 18:19; Lev 2:13). Jesus called his disciples the salt of the earth (Matt 5:13). It has been used in the Roman Catholic Church in the service of baptism until recent times. It was placed on the tongue of the candidate before baptism with the words, "Receive the salt of wisdom. . . ." It is still used in the preparation of holy water, being blessed and put into the water.

SALVATION The activity of *God in delivering human beings from the power of *sin, death, corruption, and the *Devil and giving to them the gift of *eternal life and the joy of membership in his *kingdom of *love. God alone is the *Savior (Rev 7:10). To be "in *Christ" is Paul's way of expressing what salvation means. Through his life, death, *resurrection, and exaltation come deliverance from the *guilt and power of sin and the gift of new life through the indwelling Holy *Spirit. So the believer is saved by Christ's work on the *cross (Acts 4:12); he is being saved now by the work of the Holy *Spirit, the Sanctifier (Phil 2:12); and he looks forward to completed salvation in the life of the age to come (1 Thess 5:9; 1 Peter 1:5). The final state of salvation means living in a *spiritual/heavenly *body in the presence of God in the age to come. See also HOLISTIC SALVATION.

SALVATION ARMY An international *Christian body organized on military lines, it was founded by William *Booth in London as the Christian Mission in 1865 and took its present name in 1878. For Booth, *God required loosing the chains of injustice, freeing the captive and oppressed, sharing food and home, clothing the naked, and carrying out family responsibilities. Right from the outset his army waged war on a dual front: against the pinch of poverty and the power of *sin. Its *doctrines are Arminian (*evangelical Methodist), except that it has no *sacraments, and its services are informal. Members usually dress in a military-style uniform, and *worship is often accompanied by music provided by a brass band. Soldiers (it has officers, no clergymen) must sign the *Articles of War. The Salvation Army has work in some seventy-five countries.

SALVATION HISTORY The type of history contained in the *Bible. The record of what *God has done for humanity in revealing his *will and purpose in and through historical events and people. While such history has similarities to ordinary history, it is special because it tells how God brought *salvation to humankind in and through *Israel's calling and history, the *Messiah (*Jesus), and the first *apostles and *disciples. See also HEILSGESCHICHTE, HISTORIE.

SALVIFIC WILL OF GOD A phrase based on 1 Timothy 2:4, it expresses the idea that God desires and wills that all human beings come to know and *love him, thus receiving his *salvation—not that all will in fact be saved.

SANCTIFICATION (Lat. *sanctificare,* "to make *holy"). The process of either making or being made pure and holy. *God is holy in the sense of being utterly pure—without any *sin, *evil, or corruption. His people are holy because they belong to him, the Holy One (Exod 19:6; 1 Peter 2:9). Yet they are also called to become holy in practice, in reality (1 Thess 4:3; 5:23–24). *Jesus is the pattern and example of this holiness (Rom 8:29), but the *apostles also provide examples (1 Thess 2:10). The Holy *Spirit's presence in believers' lives guarantees the possibility and direction of progress toward holiness.

Entire sanctification, as taught by John *Wesley and some Methodists, is a relative not an absolute *perfection. It is the state of having knowingly committed oneself wholly to the *love and *will of God and of growing in holiness within that love and will.

Traditionally, Protestant *theology has carefully distinguished between what God declared to be true in *Christ of the believer (*justification) and what God achieves within the life of the believer (sanctification). Protestants accuse Roman Catholics of confusing justification and sanctification.

SANCTUARY The part of a church containing the *altar. If there are several altars, it is the area where the high altar is located. In *Orthodox churches the sanctuary is enclosed by the *iconostasis.

SANCTUARY, RIGHT OF The protection claimed by criminals in a sacred place. While *sanctuaries had earlier been known in the Jewish and other *religions, they were a feature of the *Christian scene by the end of the 4th century, recognized by Roman law. The 6th-century emperor *Justinian restricted the privilege of sanctuary to those not guilty of major crimes. Steps were taken against the practice in England by *Henry VIII and *James I, but it continued there and in mainland Europe until about the end of the 18th century.

SANCTUS (Lat. "*holy"). The *hymn "Holy, Holy, Holy" is sung in Protestant churches and is said in the *Eucharist in Roman Catholic churches. The hymn was composed by Reginald Heber and taken from Isaiah 6:3 and Matthew 21:9.

SANDAY, WILLIAM (1843–1920). *New Testament scholar. Holder of theological chairs at Oxford for thirty-seven years from 1882, he was unusually knowledgeable about the work of continental biblical scholars. Sanday, who belonged to the liberal school of *theology, was a copious writer, notably on John's *Gospel, but he is best remembered for his collaboration with A. C. *Headlam on a commentary on *Romans* (1895).

SANDEMAN, ROBERT (1718–1771). Leader of the *Glasites, or Sandemanians. Son-in-law of John *Glas, whose religious views he adopted, he exercised a *ministry in Scotland and then founded congregations in England and in New England (where his Royalist views were unpopular). For the Sandemanians, *faith was an intellectual assent to the *work of *Christ, discipline was necessary to maintain church purity, and the church could control a member's finances.

SANDEMANIANISM A small Protestant movement taking its name from Robert Sandeman (1718–1771). The group was first known as *Glasites, after its first leader, John *Glas (1695–1773). Two *doctrines attracted the attention of others. First, the doctrine of saving *faith was so presented as to leave the impression that it was merely a bare acceptance that "*Christ died for me" and that living a *holy life did not really matter (a charge of *antinomianism). Second, they practiced foot-washing as an ordinance. The *sect had disappeared by 1940.

SANDERS, NICHOLAS (c. 1530–1581). English Roman Catholic scholar. Born in Surrey and educated at Oxford, where he lectured in *canon law, he left England on the accession of *Elizabeth I and was ordained in Rome. He took a prominent part at the Council of *Trent, then became professor of *theology at Louvain. Subsequently he tried to conspire toward a military invasion to overthrow Elizabeth, but neither pope nor *Philip II of Spain was as enthusiastic as he. In 1579 he landed in Ireland as a papal agent but failed to stir up trouble there and died in Ireland.

SANDYS, EDWIN (c. 1516–1588). *Archbishop of York. An enthusiastic supporter of the *Reformation, he was imprisoned by Mary *Tudor but later escaped to the Continent. Moderate Puritan and a translator of the Bishops' *Bible, he became under *Elizabeth I *bishop of Worcester (1559), London (1570), and York (1575).

SANGSTER, WILLIAM EDWYN ROBERT (1900–1960). Methodist minister. Ordained in 1926, he ministered in various circuits before going to Westminster Central Hall, London, where he attracted crowds even in an age of scholarly preachers. His many books include a study of John *Wesley's *doctrine, *The Path to Perfection* (1943), which earned him a London University doctor's degree.

SANHEDRIN The supreme council or senate (as well as court of *justice) at Jerusalem in the time of *Jesus. Its president was the high priest (Matt 26:3ff.; Acts 4:5; 6:12: 22:30). It had seventy-one members, both *priests and laymen.

SANKEY, IRA DAVID (1840–1908). Singing *evangelist and *hymn composer. Born in Pennsylvania, he joined D. L. *Moody in evangelistic work in 1870, and their two names became inseparably linked in Britain and America. His own *hymn tunes included the famous "Ninety and Nine." He compiled *hymnbooks, of which more than fifty million were sold, all the profits going to *Christian work. Sankey was blind from 1903.

SANQUHAR DECLARATION (1680). Scottish *Covenanter declaration. Posted up in Sanquhar, Dumfriesshire, it attacked *Charles II for civil and ecclesiastical tyranny and renounced allegiance to him because of his claim to supremacy over the church. It uttered a warning also over the fact that the duke of York (the future *James VII/II) was heir-presumptive to the throne. It was an audacious document, but it expressed the mind of the country eight years later when the Stuart Dynasty was toppled.

SANTA CLAUS See Nicholas of Myra.

SANTA SOPHIA The famous church in Istanbul (Constantinople) dedicated to *Christ as the Holy Wisdom in 538. Since 1453 it has been either an Islamic mosque or a museum.

SAPHIR, ADOLPH
(1831–1891). *Presbyterian minister and writer. Son of a Hungarian Jew, he and his father were converted to *Christianity in 1843. He trained as a *Free Church of Scotland minister and served Presbyterian churches in England. His intimate knowledge of *Judaism counteracted in pamphlets and lectures the rationalistic theologians of Germany.

SARAVIA, HADRIAN (1531–1613). Anglican scholar. Born in France, he was a pastor in Antwerp and helped to draft the 1561 *Belgic Confession. He subsequently became divinity professor at Leyden (1582), but those were troubled times for Protestants in the Low Countries, and finally he settled in England as rector of Tattenhill (1588). A moderate Calvinist, he became also a staunch champion of episcopacy, a rejector or *predestination, an early promoter of foreign missions, and a translator of the King James Version of the *Bible.

SARDICA, COUNCIL OF (342). This church council in modern Sofia was convened jointly by the emperors Constantius II and Constans I. The purpose was to settle the Arian controversy, but it merely widened the gap between Eastern and Western sections of the church. The pro-Nicene *Athanasius, who had been deposed by the pro-Arian Eastern *bishops, was declared restored by the Western bishops. This council is significant in formally acknowledging the bishop of Rome's jurisdiction over other sees.

SÄRKILAX, PETER (d. 1529). Finnish Reformer. He went to Germany for studies in 1516, and so was there when the *Reformation began. He eagerly espoused its *doctrines. He returned in 1523 to Finland and greatly influenced Mikael *Agricola, who was to become the prime mover in the Finnish Reformation.

SATAN A *supernatural being who is the supreme enemy of God and chief of the rebellious (fallen) *angels. Also known as the *Devil. As *Jesus proclaimed and embodied the *kingdom of *God, he did battle with Satan (Matt 4:1–11). He called him Beelzebul, prince of the *demons (Matt 12:24). In his *resurrection from the dead *Christ defeated him, for Satan's plan was to prevent his bodily resurrection. However, Satan is still free to do his work on earth until the end of the age and thus, though victorious in Christ, believers still have to face his *temptations and trials (2 Cor 2:11; Eph 6:10ff.; 1 Peter 5:8). In modern *theology it is common to see "Satan" as a pictorial representation of the powers of *evil in the world, and thus his personal nature is denied.

SATISFACTION (Lat. *satis-facere,* "to do enough"). The paying of a price for wrongdoing. Used in explanations of the death of *Christ and in moral *theology. (1) The sacrificial death of Christ was understood by *Anselm (d. 1109) as a satisfaction made to the honor of *God for the *sins of humankind. It was acceptable as satisfaction because he who offered himself was not merely a man but the God-Man. (2) After *confession of sin for wrongdoing, it was required in the early and medieval church that satisfaction in terms of some good deed or activity—almsgiving, *prayer, etc., be made. At first the satisfaction preceded the words of *forgiveness and *absolution but in later period and certainly in the modern period it has followed absolution. In Roman Catholic theology satisfaction made on earth means less *punishment/chastisement in *purgatory.

SAVIOR A biblical title for *God depicting his activity as the Deliverer of his people and their Protector from enemies and harm (Isa 43:3, 11; 45:15, 21; 49:26). In the *NT it is used of both

God the Father (1 Tim 1:1; 4:10; and the *Lord *Jesus Christ (2 Tim 1:10). See also SALVATION.

SAVONAROLA, GIROLAMO (1452–1498). Italian Reformer. Born in Ferrara, he became a *Dominican in 1475. Ten years later he began to preach the need for church reform, winning such popular support in Florence that he set up a democratic republic there in 1494. Pope *Alexander VI excommunicated Savonarola, who had preached against the corruptions of the *papacy, and after the "meddlesome *friar" continued his defiance, took advantage of a setback in the latter's popularity to have him tried for *heresy and subsequently executed.

SAVOY CONFERENCE (1661). A formal meeting between Church of *England *bishops and Puritans after the *Restoration to discuss differences in church *worship. The bishops would offer few concessions and were supported by Parliament. More than two thousand Puritans lost their livings through the 1662 Act of *Uniformity.

SAVOY DECLARATION (1658). A statement of *doctrine and *polity issued by *Independents (*Congregationalists) of 120 churches. It discusses divisions and appeals for *toleration, accepts a variation of the *Westminster Confession, and vests disciplinary powers in individual congregations, denying that Jesus' teaching warrants any wider organization.

SAWTREY, WILLIAM (d. 1401). *Lollard *martyr. A *priest in Norfolk, he was charged before his *bishop with *heresy in 1399. He was soon again in trouble after having moved to London and made no secret of his Lollard views, notably his objection to *transubstantiation. He stood firm against *Archbishop *Arundel and was finally burned as a heretic.

SAXON CONFESSION (1551). Protestant *confession of *faith. A less conciliatory document than the 1530 *Augsburg Confession, it was prepared by *Melanchthon for the Council of *Trent at the request of *Charles V. It stressed *Scripture as the only authority, set forth *justification by *faith, and defined the church as a spiritual (though visible) *fellowship of believers.

SAYBROOK PLATFORM (1708). Attempt by Connecticut *Congregationalists to shore up church discipline. Following the call of the Connecticut General Court, laymen and ministers meeting in Saybrook, Connecticut, drew up a fifteen-point "Articles for the Administration of Church Discipline." It was essentially a moderately Calvinistic statement, based largely on the *Westminster Confession as modified by the English Congregationalists in 1658. This platform gave the American Calvinists in Connecticut the basis for resolution of church disputes.

SAYERS, DOROTHY LEIGH (1893–1957). English writer. Born in Oxford, where she was later one of the first women graduates, she produced a steady stream of detective novels from 1923. She was also teacher, medieval historian, and translator of *Dante, but she became even more widely known through her wartime radio series on Jesus, *The Man Born to Be King* (1941). She later showed herself to be a competent theologian by books such as *Creed or Chaos?* (1947).

SCHAFF, PHILIP (1819–1893). Church historian and ecumenist. Born in Switzerland and educated in Germany, he went to America in 1843 and taught church history at the German Reformed church seminary at Mercersburg. From 1870 until his death he was on the faculty of Union Theological Seminary, New York. His *ecumenical outlook sometimes gained the disapproval of his more conservative colleagues of German descent. He was one of the founders of the *Evangelical Alliance and was involved in many literary projects, but his most notable work is his *History of the Christian Church* (1858–1892).

SCHISM (Gk. *schisma,* "tear" or "rent"). A division between two groups of people. Thus a separation by church members from the original body in order to form another, schismatic body. The departure of Methodists from the Church of *England in the late 18th century was a schism. The most famous schism is that called the East-West Schism (11th century), the division of the Orthodox and Roman Catholic churches, but here it is not clear which is the schismatic body, for each side blames the other. See also Great Schism.

SCHLEIERMACHER, FRIEDRICH DANIEL ERNST (1768–1834). German theologian and philosopher. He received a Pietistic education at Moravian institutions before entering Halle University. Ordained as a *Reformed *pastor in 1794, he later occupied theological chairs at Halle (1804) and Berlin (1810). He held that *religion was based on intuition and feeling and that religious language is merely an expression of religious self-consciousness, humans being absolutely dependent on God. A versatile scholar, he profoundly affected Protestant *theology. His 1821 work, *The Christian Faith* (English title), is still widely used.

SCHMALKALDIC ARTICLES (1537). A *confession of *faith written by Martin *Luther and incorporated into the Book of *Concord (1580). The articles were to be presented to the council of the church called by the *pope to meet at Mantua in May 1537. (In fact, the council did not meet until 1545 and then at Trent.) Luther attacked what he saw as abuses in the Roman Church, affirmed what Protestants and Roman Catholics had in common, and noted where Protestants disagreed among themselves. See also Saxon Confession.

SCHMALCALD LEAGUE An alliance of German Protestant princes formed in 1531 for mutual protection against Emperor *Charles V. Others joined the league later. A significant factor in European politics, it was dissolved in 1547 when the Protestants were defeated and its leaders, *Philip of Hesse and John Frederick of Saxony, were imprisoned.

SCHMUCKER, SAMUEL SIMON (1799–1873). American Lutheran minister. Ordained in 1821, he helped found the Lutheran Theological Seminary at Gettysburg, was its first theological professor, and taught there until 1864. He was deeply involved in *ecumenical projects and warmly supported the *Evangelical Alliance, even when his readiness to depart from traditional Lutheran concepts brought opposition.

SCHOLASTICISM (Lat. *schola,* "place of learning"). The system and method of philosophy and *theology developed in the academic centers of medieval Europe. It has a technical (scholastic) language and method. Much material was derived from the early *fathers, especially *Augustine of Hippo, and it made use of the philosophy of Aristotle. The most famous exponent of scholasticism was Thomas *Aquinas (1225–1274). As Protestant theologians of the late 16th and 17th centuries used a technical method and vocabulary to produce Protestant *doctrine, what they produced in their learned tomes is often called "Protestant scholasticism."

SCHWABACH, ARTICLES OF (1529). Lutheran *confession of *faith. Written by Luther, perhaps assisted by other theologians, they were intended to unite the Lutherans against Roman Catholics, *Anabaptists, and Zwinglians. The seventeen articles formed the basis for the opening section of the *Augsburg Confession of 1530.

SCHWARTZ, CHRISTIAN FREDERICK (1726–1798). German *missionary to India. A Prussian by birth, he was ordained in Copenhagen and went to India in 1750 under the Danish Halle Mission (he never returned home). He worked successively at Tranquebar, Trichniopoly, and Tanjore and was a remarkably successful peacemaker between political foes, but he never allowed such involvement to deflect him from his task as a missionary.

SCHWEITZER, ALBERT (1875–1965). German theologian, medical *missionary, and musician. Son of a Lutheran *pastor in Alsace, he studied at Strasbourg, earning not only doctorates in philosophy and *theology but a reputation as an accomplished organist. In 1913 he became a medical doctor and went to French Equatorial Africa. In Lambarene (now in Gabon) he built and maintained a hospital and spent most of his time there, apart from disruption caused by *war, until his death. His earliest book, *The Quest of the Historical Jesus* (Eng. trans. 1910), is probably the best known. He won the Nobel peace prize in 1952.

SCHWENKFELDERS, SCHWENKFELDIANS Followers of German lay theologian Kaspar von Schwenkfeld (c. 1489–1561). They objected to the Lutheran church-state link and to the view of the *sacraments as vehicles of *grace, and held that *Scripture must be supplemented by an inner witness. Forty families settled in 1734 in Pennsylvania, where their descendants are still found today.

SCIENCE AND HEALTH, WITH A KEY TO THE SCRIPTURES The basic statement of the teaching of the Church of Christ, Scientist, and written by Mary Baker *Eddy. The authoritative 91st edition appeared in 1907. This teaching is used as the means of interpreting the *Bible, and thus the Bible appears to teach different *doctrine for this *sect than for the orthodox *denominations and churches. See also Christian Science.

SCILLITAN MARTYRS A group of twelve North African Christians (five of them women) beheaded at Carthage by the Roman governor after refusing to renounce *Christianity. The account of their trial is the earliest evidence of Christianity in North Africa.

SCOFIELD, CYRUS INGERSON (1843–1921). American biblical scholar. Born in Michigan, he served in the Confederate Army, qualified as a lawyer, and after *conversion was ordained to the Congregational *ministry in 1882. He served pastorates in Massachusetts, Chicago (Moody Memorial Church), and Texas (First Congregational, now Scofield Memorial Church of Dallas) but is best known for *The Scofield Reference Bible* (1909), which stressed *premillennialism (more particularly, *dispensationalism).

SCOPES TRIAL (1925). Trial in Dayton, Tennessee, testing the state's new antievolution legislation. John T. Scopes was indicted for teaching evolution after a law passed in March 1925 forbade such teaching in public schools. He was defended by Clarence Darrow and, in effect, prosecuted by William Jennings *Bryan. Scopes was found guilty and fined by the state in a technical, temporal victory for *Fundamentalism.

SCOTISM The teaching of the *Franciscan philosopher *Duns Scotus (1264–1308). It gave primacy to *love and to the *will in both *God and man. So it contrasted with the teaching of Thomas *Aquinas (1225–1274), in which a primary place is given to knowledge and reason. Scotism was particularly influential in Roman Catholic *theology in the 17th century.

SCOTLAND, CHURCH OF Scotland's national church has been *Presbyterian since the *Reformation (1560), apart from two periods of modified *episcopacy that ended with the Revolution Settlement (1690). Successive monarchs since then have sworn to maintain Presbyterian *polity in Scotland, and the church is free from state control. It is organized in fifty *presbyteries in which ministers and *laity are equally represented; the supreme court is the *general assembly, which meets in Edinburgh each May. The church bases its *doctrine on the *Bible, with the *Westminster Confession as a subordinate standard. It maintains an extensive overseas work and has some 800,000 communicant members.

SCOTS CONFESSION (1560). A statement prepared by leading Scottish Reformers, chiefly John Knox, and approved by the parliament as "wholesome and sound *doctrine grounded upon the infallible *truth of *God's *Word." It is a compendium of Calvinistic *theology designed to consolidate the faithful, exclude unbelievers, answer criticism, and declare the truth. It sees the true church as having three features: the true *preaching of the Word of God, the right administration of the *sacraments, and scriptural administration of church discipline. In 1648 this confession was replaced by the *Westminster Confession. See also WESTMINSTER STANDARDS.

SCRIPTURE, DOCTRINE OF HOLY The main ideas that the majority of churches hold regarding Scripture are as follows: (1) The human authors were so guided in their writing by the Holy *Spirit that what they produced pleased *God and carries his authority. (2.) The books contain all—clearly set forth or necessarily required by deduction from their clear teaching—that is necessary for *salvation and *Christian living and that God requires us to believe. (3) The books contain the record of God's unique, saving activity in human history—especially in *Israel and in *Jesus—and God's explanations of this activity. (4) The books are to be interpreted within the context of *faith—i.e., by believers. (5) The books are to be translated into the various languages of the world (from the original Hebrew, Aramaic, and Greek) so that all the world may have the *truth. See also BIBLE (ENGLISH VERSIONS), EXEGESIS, HERMENEUTICS, INERRANCY, INFALLIBILITY, INSPIRATION OF THE BIBLE.

SCRIPTURE(S), HOLY (Lat. *scriptura,* "act of writing"). The collection of books inspired by *God and known as the *Bible.

SCRIPTURE UNION An interdenominational *Bible-reading movement founded in England as the Children's Special Service Mission in 1867. As well as providing *Bible-reading aids used by more than one million readers throughout the world, it engages in children's *evangelism and youth work, notably through school groups and camps.

SCROGGIE, WILLIAM GRAHAM (1877–1959). Baptist minister and writer. Trained at Spurgeon's College, London, he served various pastorates, notably that of Charlotte Chapel, Edinburgh (1913–1933), where he attracted large crowds to his *Bible expositions. The city's university recognized his eminence by awarding him a D.D. degree. Thereafter he traveled widely (1933–1937) before becoming *pastor of London's Metropolitan Tabernacle until 1944. He wrote many expository and devotional books.

SCRUPLE, SCRUPULOSITY Technically in moral *theology an exaggerated doubt about the morality of an act done or to be done. Thus the abnormal condition of a *conscience obsessed by *guilt when such guilt is not necessary or justified. In popular usage it refers to the excessive attention to detail in moral matters.

SCUDDER, IDA SOPHIA (1870–1960). Founder of the Christian Medical College at Vellore, South India. Daughter of a medical *missionary to India from the Dutch Reformed Church in America, she went to America to qualify in medicine and devoted herself to the service of Indian women. At Vellore she first opened a hospital, then a nursing school, and finally in 1918 a medical college, which from 1947 accepted men students also and from 1950 has been affiliated with Madras University.

SEABURY, SAMUEL (1729–1796). First *bishop of the *Protestant Episcopal Church in America. Born in Connecticut and a graduate of Yale, he then studied *theology and medicine in Edinburgh and after *ordination ministered in North America, serving also as teacher and doctor. Briefly imprisoned for Royalist sympathies during the Revolution, he was elected bishop of Connecticut in 1783 and consecrated by Scottish bishops in Aberdeen. He helped make his church autonomous in 1789 and was its first presiding bishop.

SEBASTE, FORTY MARTYRS OF Roman soldiers of the so-called Thundering Legion put to death about 320 because of their *Christian profession. Left naked on a frozen pond in Armenia within sight of hot baths for those who renounced their *faith, they stood firm except for one man, and his place was taken by one of the pagan guards converted at the spectacle.

SECESSION The act of leaving a church to form another church or congregation and thus to create a *schism.

SECESSION CHURCH Scottish *Presbyterian body formed after a dispute in the Church of *Scotland. Its leader was Ebenezer *Erskine, who protested against patronage and argued for the right of a *Christian congregation to choose its own minister according to what was stated in the Books of *Discipline. The *general assembly suspended Erskine and three colleagues but later tried to make amends after the latter had constituted an "Associate Presbytery." Even so it was 1740 before Erskine and seven others were deposed by the national church.

SECOND ADAM A title of *Christ as the head of a redeemed humanity. It is based on Paul's teaching in Romans 5:11ff. and 1 Corinthians 15:45–47 and contrasts Christ with the first Adam (Gen 2–3).

SECOND BLESSING A second work of *God's *grace in the believer's *heart. It is second because it follows *regeneration (the new birth) and is distinct from it. Its purpose is to deliver the believer from the power and dominion of sinful habits and tendencies. It is taught by the Holiness groups (e.g., Church of the Nazarene, Pilgrim Holiness, and certain Methodist *denominations). It is similar to the teaching of John *Wesley on entire *sanctification.

SECOND COMING The visible return to earth of *Jesus Christ, the *Lord, as King and Judge, at the end of the age. His first coming as a babe in Bethlehem was in lowliness and obscurity, but his second will be in glory and power (Matt 24:29ff.; 1 Thess 1:10; 2:19). Also called the *Parousia.

SECOND GREAT AWAKENING A *revival of religious interest in America. It did not reflect some of the more extreme features of the earlier *Great Awakening, and was not linked with the names of only a few prominent leaders. Beginning in 1787 in the East, it soon spread to Yale and to other colleges. Much less restrained was the movement that began in Kentucky under James *McGready, a revival that saw many thousands come to *camp meetings throughout the state. The Second Great Awakening is credited with having checked the spread of unbelief, boosted church membership, led to the founding of *seminaries and *Christian colleges, and encouraged interest in the *missionary enterprise.

SECOND HELVETIC CONFESSION See HELVETIC CONFESSIONS.

SECOND VATICAN COUNCIL See VATICAN COUNCIL, SECOND.

SECT(S) Religious groups outside the main *Christian churches and *denominations that teach *doctrines different from traditional *orthodoxy. They may be divided into established sects (e.g., Mormons and *Jehovah's Witnesses) and nonestablished sects (those that are new or short-lived and have not built up a permanent organization and tradition). The difference between a *cult and a sect is not clearly defined.

SECTARY A somewhat derogatory term applied usually by Anglicans to Nonconformists in England during the 17th and 18th centuries.

SECULAR In *Roman Catholicism a member of the *clergy who is living "in the world" and not subject to a *religious *rule, unlike a "regular."

SECULAR CHRISTIANITY An understanding and practice of *Christianity in the modern secular world that is far removed from traditional "churchy" and "pietistic" Christianity as practiced by most who attend churches. It is one form of *liberalism.

SECULARIZATION The process—evident in Europe since the 15th century—by which religious (church) control and influence over political, social, and educational institutions have been removed. In many cases it has been replaced by anti-Christian forces and ideologies. Secularization can also refer to the seizure of church property by the *state.

SECURITY OF THE BELIEVER The view that once a person receives *God's *salvation he will certainly keep it and die as a *Christian. He will have *perseverance.

SEEKERS A term from early 17th-century England applied to those unattached to any church but, in William *Penn's words, wandering shepherdless, "seeking their beloved but could not find Him . . . whom their *souls loved above their chiefest joy." Because of their Quietistic inclinations, many became *Quakers and during the Cromwellian period enjoyed a brief respite from persecution.

SEGREGATION The policy of separating people into classifications based on race or sex. In churches in Asia men and women sit on different sides of the church building; in South Africa most *worship is segregated in that the different racial groups worship in different buildings. Segregation is a *sin when it contradicts the teaching that all the baptized are one in *Christ.

SELFISHNESS The attitude of mind and activity that causes a person to always think first of himself and to always act in his own interest. The command to *love your neighbor as yourself is a challenge to selfishness, and the command of *Christ to love others as he loved his *disciples is a way of life that is the opposite of selfishness.

SELWYN, GEORGE AUGUSTUS (1809–1878). First Anglican *bishop of New Zealand. Ordained in 1833 and consecrated in 1841, he traveled extensively in his own *diocese and beyond, ministering to white settlers and Maoris alike and helping to establish *mission stations in Melanesia. Selwyn was a *High Churchman of robust constitution and boundless energy who helped his adopted country through difficult times before returning to spend the last ten years of his life as bishop of Lichfield.

SEMANTICS The study of meaning in language. This is of great importance to the theologian who is seeking to interpret ancient books (language). He faces such questions as, Does the *NT, though written in Greek, have basically Hebrew meanings for its words and sentences rather than Greek ones? Is meaning to be sought in words or in whole sentences and paragraphs? What are the principles that should guide the translation of the *Bible into modern languages?

SEMI-ARIANISM A *doctrine of the relation of *Jesus Christ to the Father that took a middle path between the *heresy of *Arianism and the *orthodoxy of the Creed of Nicea (325). Instead of *Christ being identical (*homoousios*, "of the same *being") with the Father (*Nicene Creed), semi-Arians preferred to say he is essentially like (*homoiousios*, "of like being").

SEMI-PELAGIANISM A *doctrine concerning the *grace of *God and sinful man that took a middle path between the teaching of Pelagius (*Pelagianism) and *Augustine (*Augustinianism). It claimed that human beings made the first step toward God out of their sinfulness, and then God assisted them toward true *repentance and living *faith. Though common in the 5th and 6th centuries, this teaching was condemned at the Council of *Orange in 529.

SEMINARY A school or college in which *theology is taught and people are prepared for *Christian *ministry. Virtually all theological colleges in the U.S. are called seminaries, but in the U.K. seminary is used only by the Roman Catholics.

SENS, COUNCIL OF (1141). A council called to consider charges of *heresy against *Abelard. *Bernard of Clairvaux was chief prosecutor in the case, which involved alleged erroneous *doctrine, particularly on the *Trinity and on the *grace of *God in man's *redemption. Abelard refused to defend himself, appealed to the *pope, but was found guilty and sentenced to banishment and perpetual silence.

SENSES OF SCRIPTURE The various meanings that can be gained from the words of the *Bible. There is the plain, literal sense that always has been seen as primary. In the Middle Ages the allegorical/typological sense, the anagogical/eschatological sense, and the tropological/moral sense were discerned. These related to deeper meaning in the text than the literal and were attempts to recognize *God as the true author of *Scripture.

SENSUS PLENIOR (Lat. "the fuller sense"). The view that *God intends a meaning greater than the literal meaning in the text of *Scripture. Believer and unbeliever alike can discern the literal meaning, but only those led by the *Spirit can discern the fuller meaning. See also SENSES OF SCRIPTURE.

SENTENCES Theological books of the 12th and 13th centuries. They provided a systematic account of *Christian *doctrine by the following method. First a question was raised. Second, this question was answered by quotations from *Scripture, *creeds, and the *Fathers. Third, arguments were provided for the *truth of the orthodox answer. The most famous presentation was the *Book of Sentences* (1148–1150) by Peter *Lombard (1100–1160). Such treatments of *doctrine were later replaced by other methods in *summae, of which the most famous was the *Summa Theologiae* of Thomas *Aquinas.

SEPARATISM Those who—in pursuit of purity of *doctrine, *worship, or *polity—leave an established church or *denomination to form an independent congregation. See also SEPARATISTS.

SEPARATISTS Seventeenth-century forerunners of those later called *Nonconformists. They believed it to be their duty to separate from the Church of *England if they saw in it anything that displeased them, and they tended to put the *Spirit's guidance before the *Bible, *tradition, or church law. Making an appeal to simple folk and popular during the rule of *Cromwell, *Separatism was one of the early forms of Congregationalism.

SEPTUAGESIMA (Lat. "the seventieth"). The ninth *Sunday before *Easter and the third before *Lent. Though not exactly seventy days before Easter, tradition still dictates its use in certain churches—e.g., in the Church of *England.

SEPTUAGINT The famous translation into Greek of the Hebrew *Bible. Because seventy (or seventy-two) men were involved in the work, it was called the Septuagint, or the LXX. It was completed a century before *Christ and was the Bible widely used in the primitive church. Besides the translations of the Hebrew books, it also contains the *Apocrypha, books written originally in Greek.

SERGIUS I (d. 701). Pope from 687. Born in Sicily of Syrian parents. Elected as a compromise candidate in an election of dubious regularity because of corrupt practices, Sergius upheld the primacy of Rome against threats from the emperor Justinian II, supported *Wilfrid of York in an English dispute, and consecrated *Willibrord as *bishop of the Friscians (695). He also brought peace after an era of unseemly squabbles in the church in Italy itself.

SERIPANDO (1493–1563). Italian *cardinal and *archbishop of Salerno. An *Augustinian from an early age, he taught at Siena and Bologna and subsequently became *superior general of his *order in 1539, a post he held for twelve years. Meanwhile his contributions at the Council of *Trent (1546–1547) showed him to be one of the most effective theologians of the *Counter-Reformation. Later to be president of the council, as well as cardinal and archbishop from 1553, he wrote commentaries on Romans and Galatians.

SERMON An address or *homily as part of an act of *worship. At the *Eucharist it is normally based on the reading from the *Gospel. The purpose of a sermon is to deepen commitment to *Jesus Christ and so may take various forms—e.g., words of rebuke, comfort, *faith, and *hope.

SERMON ON THE MOUNT, THE *Jesus' teaching in Matthew 5–7, delivered "up on a mountainside"—the great statement of *Christian ethics. A shorter, similar address is found in Luke 6:20–49, sometimes called "The Sermon on the Plain."

SERVANT OF THE LORD The person who is described in four poems in Isaiah (42:1–4; 49:1–6; 50:4–9; 52:13–53:12). In the last one the Servant suffers on behalf of the people whom he represents. The claim of the *NT is that *Jesus fulfilled these prophecies. Therefore they have been expounded in the church as description of the role and task of the *Messiah.

SERVETUS, MICHAEL (1511–1553). Spanish physician and theologian. He rejected the *dogma of the *Trinity and the divinity of *Christ and was denounced to the *Inquisition at Lyons, probably at the instigation of John *Calvin. He was arrested, escaped to Geneva, but was charged there with *heresy, refused to recant, and with dubious legality and Calvin's approval was burned alive.

SERVITES The usual name for the *order of the Servants of Mary, a Roman Catholic *religious order. Founded by seven Florentine businessmen in 1233, this order of *mendicant *friars engages in pastoral, *mission, and educational work. There is a parallel order of women commonly known as Mantellate Sisters.

SESSION The meeting of the ordained minister and *ruling elders of a congregation in the Church of * Scotland or in another *Presbyterian church.

SESSION OF CHRIST *Christ's present position in *heaven. He "sat down at the right hand of *God" (Heb 10:12), having ascended, triumphant over his enemies. He is there making *intercession for believers (Rom 8:34).

SETON, ELIZABETH ANN BAYLEY (1774–1821). Founder and Roman Catholic *saint. During her relatively short life, she was a wife, mother of five children, widow, convert to Roman Catholicism, founder of an order, and guiding initiator of the first Catholic parochial school system in American. *Paul VI named her the first native-born American saint in September 1975.

SEVEN COUNCILS, THE The seven *ecumenical councils, the first and last of which were held in Nicea (325 and 787).

SEVEN DEADLY SINS These are usually listed as *pride, covetousness, lust, envy, gluttony, anger, and sloth.

SEVEN GIFTS OF THE HOLY SPIRIT Based on the Latin text of Isaiah 11:2, these are *wisdom, understanding, counsel, fortitude, knowledge, piety, and fear of the *Lord.

SEVEN LAST WORDS OF JESUS That which Jesus said on the *cross before he expired (Matt 27:46; Luke 23:34, 43, 46; John 19:26–27, 28, 30). Often these are used as the basis for devotional talks on *Good Friday.

SEVEN SACRAMENTS In the Roman Catholic Church these are *baptism, *confirmation, *Eucharist (*Mass), *penance, *extreme unction, *ordination, and marriage.

SEVEN VIRTUES Traditionally, *faith, *hope, and *charity (*theological virtues), plus *justice, prudence, *temperance, and *fortitude (*cardinal virtues).

SEVENTH-DAY ADVENTISTS A Protestant group originating in the U.S. in 1863 and distinguished by its keeping of Saturday (the Jewish *Sabbath) as the day for *worship. Other emphases include the *baptism of believers by *immersion, the imminence of the *Second Coming and the Millennium, the *sleep of the *soul, tithing, and the proper care of the *body (including *abstinence from alcohol, tobacco, and certain foods). The world membership is about 3 million in nearly 20,000 churches.

SEX The aspect of human life that derives from the fact that *God originally created male and female (Gen 1:27). Sex is used in (1) a general way—a person must be either male or female, and (2) a restrictive way—of a person's need and ability to have a physical, sexual relationship with a person of the opposite sex. A *Christian approach to sex includes more than sex as a reproductive device; it also deals with what it means for both male and female to be made in *God's image and likeness (Gen 1:26).

SEXAGESIMA The second *Sunday before *Lent, and the eighth Sunday before Easter. The name derives from the fact that this Sunday is approximately sixty days before Easter.

SEYMOUR, WILLIAM J. (1870–1922). Prominent early Pentecostal leader and, as pastor of the Azusa Street Mission in Los Angeles, the leading figure in what became known as the *Azusa Street revival. He was influenced by Charles Parham, the key figure in the Topeka revival of 1901, at which a number of people had begun to speak in tongues. Seymour incorporated his ministry as the Pacific Apostolic Faith Mission and published a periodical with a circulation of 50,000. By 1913, however, others had taken off with his mailinglist, and the Azusa Street mission became once again a largely black church instead of the interracial revival center it had been for seven years.

SHAFTESBURY, ANTHONY ASHLEY COOPER, SEVENTH EARL OF (1801–1885). *Evangelical social and industrial reformer. After graduating from Oxford, he entered Parliament in 1826 and soon was working actively to improve industrial conditions, the lot of the mentally ill, and housing and education for the *poor. A prominent Evangelical in the Church of *England, Shaftesbury supported the political emancipation of Roman Catholics (1829) and the *missionary enterprises of other churches, as well as giving leadership in interdenominational bodies such as the *Bible Society.

SHAKERS A common name for the United Society of Believers in Christ's Second Appearing founded in England in the mid-18th century. Their practices, which involved shouting and dancing, soon earned for them the name of "Shaking Quakers." An early leader, Ann *Lee, migrated with a group of followers to New York in 1776, and within fifty years there were eighteen Shaker socialist communities in eight states. Criticized for *pacifism but respected for their industry, the body began to decline in the latter part of the 19th century. Only a few Shakers now remain.

SHARP, JAMES (1613–1679). *Archbishop of St. Andrews. Professor of philosophy at St. Andrews (1643) and minister of Crail (1649), he was an opportunist who betrayed his trust as *Presbyterian representative in London and ingratiated himself with the civil authorities. At the *Restoration, when *episcopacy was imposed on Scotland, he was rewarded by appointment as *primate. A merciless persecutor of *Covenanters, and a man whose personal life disgraced his high office, he was assassinated by a group of zealots, an act that precipitated the second major uprising by the Covenanters.

SHEDD, WILLIAM GREENOUGH THAYER (1820–1894). American Calvinist theologian. Shedd is best remembered for his three-volume *Dogmatic Theology,* which he wrote while professor of *Bible and *theology at Union Theological Seminary (New York), a post he held from 1863 until his death. Shedd's theological viewpoint was traditional *Calvinism informed by the *Westminster Confession. Although Shedd was not as comprehensive as others of his era, he was fully abreast of current thinking and was especially sensitive to the place of historical theology in his presentation of systematics.

SHEEN, FULTON JOHN (1895–1979). Roman Catholic *bishop and broadcaster. Ordained in 1919, he taught philosophy at America's Catholic University (1926–1950) and became known as "the finest Catholic orator since *Peter the Hermit." In 1951 he began a television program called "Life is Worth Living," which attracted an audience of 30 million. Many leading Americans became converts to *Roman Catholicism under his influence. He wrote more than sixty books.

SHEKINAH The manifestation of *God. Though not a word used in the Hebrew *Bible, Jewish rabbis used it to describe the physical signs of God's invisible but *real presence—e.g., of the cloud in the wilderness (Exod 14:19).

SHEMA, THE The ancient Jewish confession of *faith found in Deuteronomy 6:4–9; 11:12–21; and Numbers 15:37–41. It is recited privately, in the home and *synagogue by Jews and states a clear *doctrine of *monotheism. Shema is the Hebrew word in Deuteronomy 6:4 meaning "Hear thou. . . ."

SHEOL The Hebrew word for the place where the *spirits of the dead go (Gen 37:35; Ps 31:17; Isa 38:10). A dull, dark, and gloomy existence (2 Sam 22:6; Ps 6:5). Yet it was open to *God (Job 26:6; Prov 15:11; Ps 139:8). Thus it is similar to the Greek idea of *Hades. There will be a *resurrection of the dead from Sheol at the end of the age (Job 19:25–27; Ps 9:17; 16:8–11; Dan 12:2–3).

SHIELDS, THOMAS TODHUNTER (1873–1955). Fundamentalist *pastor, teacher, and writer. With no formal college or *seminary training, he was self-taught and received two honorary (D.D.) degrees—from McMaster and Temple universities. "The Canadian Spurgeon," he had several pastorates. The longest and most influential was Jarvis Street Baptist Church, Toronto (1910–1955), the leading church in the Ontario and Quebec Convention. Founder and editor of *The Gospel Witness*, he was president of the Canadian Protestant League, and he helped found and was the first president of the Baptist Bible Union.

SHRINE (Lat. *scrinium*, "a chest"). Originally a box-shaped repository in which *relics of a *saint were kept, it came to be used generally of a *holy place to which Christians go on a *pilgrimage. Usually the holy place is a saint's grave or a place where a saint had a great experience of *God.

SHROUD, HOLY The linen cloth kept in Turin Cathedral, Italy, which, it is claimed, was originally wrapped around the dead *body of *Jesus in the sepulcher. It has been subjected to many scientific tests and continues to attract further ones.

SHROVE TUESDAY The day before *Ash Wednesday, the beginning of *Lent. "Shrove" comes from "shriving," the *confession and *absolution of *sins, received by the faithful before the rigors of Lent begin.

SIGISMUND (1368–1437). Holy Roman emperor from 1410–1437. He became king of Hungary in 1387 and sought to restore the spiritual and political unity of Christendom. He led and lost the last general crusade against the Turks. He outwitted *John XXIII at the Council of *Constance (1415) but roused the hatred of his Bohemian subjects by sacrificing Jan *Hus. Though a cultured man, personal prejudice or passing whim often controlled his official policy.

SIGN OF THE CROSS The tracing with the hand of the lines of the *cross over oneself, others, or things. Done since the late 2d century, in the Western church the movement is from head to breast to left shoulder; in the *Eastern church the final movement is from right to left across the shoulders. Further, the fingers can be so arranged as to symbolize either the Holy *Trinity or the fact that *Christ has two *natures—divine and human.

SIMEON, CHARLES (1759–1836). *Evangelical leader. *Vicar of Holy *Trinity, Cambridge, for fifty-four years from 1782. He knew years of struggle, tension, and misunderstanding until town and gown accepted him and his "Methodist" ways. Regarded by a modern biographer as "the complete Anglican," he worked among *ordination candidates, encouraged *missions, was disciplined in his devotional life, and counseled the need for regular exercise. There is no evidence in him of any inclination to be a social reformer.

SIMEON STYLITES (c. 390–459). Pillar ascetic. The first-known *Christian to adopt the practice, he lived on a twelve-foot-square platform at the top of a pillar in Syria for more than thirty-five years (beginning in 423). His unusual lifestyle attracted thousands of spectators; led to the *conversion of unbelievers; and, because of the respect he gained, added an influential voice in support of *orthodoxy.

SIMEON THE NEW THEOLOGIAN (949–1022). Monk and *saint of the *Orthodox Church. Simeon wrote extensively on the tradition of *hesychasm and the practice of the *Jesus Prayer. His writings show remarkable and unusual descriptions of his own spiritual experience of *mysticism, which sometimes clashed with institutional traditions. He is closer to the Western *mystics in the degree of his self-revelation and encounter with *God. Many of his thoughts of hesychasm are preserved in the *Philocalia*.

SIMILITUDO DEI (Lat. "likeness of *God"). The belief that human beings are made in the image and likeness of God (Gen 1:26).

SIMONS, MENNO (1496–1551). Early *Mennonite leader. Ordained as a Roman Catholic *priest in the Netherlands in 1524, he had misgivings about the church's teaching on infant *baptism and the *Eucharist, and in 1536 he left the church and became prominent in the Anabaptist movement. Hunted and with a price on his head, he moved from place to place debating, encouraging, and writing extensively (he established a printing press). Each of his many works reflects his aim in the preface, quoting 1 Corinthians 3:11: "No other foundation can any one lay than that which is laid, which is *Jesus Christ."

SIMONY The attempt to buy or sell for material gain something that is spiritual. The name comes from Simon Magus (Acts 18:18–24), who tried to purchase the *gift of the *Spirit from the *apostles.

SIMPLICIANUS (d. 400). *Bishop of Milan. Responsible for the *conversion of Victorinus in Rome in the mid-4th century, he was also a tutor and spiritual guide to *Ambrose and had a significant part in the conversion of *Augustine of Hippo. He succeeded Ambrose as bishop of Milan in 397.

SIMPLICIUS (d. 483). Pope from 468. His *pontificate saw the *Eastern church disrupted by the Monophysite *heresy and the Western Roman Empire finally collapse. He nonetheless was successful both in his championing of *orthodoxy and in extending the influence of the Roman see.

SIMPSON, ALBERT BENJAMIN (1844–1919). Founder of the *Christian and Missionary Alliance. Canadian by birth, he served *Presbyterian churches in Ontario, Kentucky, and New York City. After a serious breakdown in health, he founded a *tabernacle in New York, opened a *Bible and *missionary training school (now Nyack College), organized two societies that merged in 1897 to form the C&MA, and edited *The Alliance Weekly*. His *preaching of *Christ as "*Savior, Sanctifier, Healer, and Coming King" led to that motto for the C&MA.

SIMUL JUSTUS ET PECCATOR (Lat. "both righteous and a sinner"). A description by Martin *Luther of a man who is justified by *faith alone. As seen in *Christ by *God he is declared righteous; as seen in himself he is yet imperfect and unrighteous, even though the *Spirit dwells in him. See also JUSTIFICATION, SANCTIFICATION.

SIN A religious and theological word having meaning only in reference to *God as almighty and righteous. It is an act or state of life that is contrary to the *will of God and that breaks the *fellowship/communion of God and man. So, in a secondary sense, sin is the breaking of God's commandments. Sin is primarily against God, the *Lord of life, even when the action or thought is directed against a human being. Thus the *forgiveness and *remission of sins leads not only to the removal of *guilt but to the restoration of communion with God. Various terms have been used by theologians to clarify the complex nature of sin.

1. **Original and *actual sin*. By their first (original) sin, Adam and Eve introduced into the world the reality of sin—of broken relationships with God. In failing to trust and obey God they sinned and put all their descendants into a state at birth in which they had no natural communion with God. Actual sin is the personal activity of human beings that fails to please God. It may also be called personal sin.

2. **Mortal and *venial sin*. This distinction is used more by Roman Catholics than by Protestants. Human disobedience of God is divided into sins that cause spiritual death (mortal) and sins that do not cause a total removal of God's favor and *grace (venial).

3. *Sins of omission and commission*. This distinction clarifies different types of disobedience to God, the Lawgiver. A sin of omission is a failure to obey God's law while a sin of commission is a deliberate transgression of that law.

4. *Material and formal sin*. This distinction is based on Aristotelian philosophy and is not used much today. Something done by a person (e.g., stealing) is the matter of sin, while the culpability of that person is the form.

5. *The unpardonable sin*. That described by *Jesus in Matthew 12:31. It probably refers to a state of such hardness of *heart that even God's *grace cannot penetrate and enter.

6. *The sin against the Holy *Spirit*. Another name for the *unpardonable sin. The states of despair, presumption, impenitence, obstinacy in sin, resistance to known *truth, and envy of other's abilities or gifts illustrate what the sin is. It is one or more of them fully developed into hardness of heart.

7. *The *seven deadly sins*. A traditional list of major sins—*pride, covetousness, lust, envy, gluttony, anger, and sloth.

8. **Capital sins*. Another term for the seven deadly sins.

See also FORGIVENESS, REMISSION OF SINS.

SINGH, SADHU SUNDAR See Sundar Singh, Sadhu.

SINLESSNESS The moral and spiritual condition that proceeds from perfect communion with *God. Only of two people is this claim made. All Christians confess that *Jesus—who freely chose always to do the Father's *will—was without *sin (1 Peter 2:22). Unless he was sinless he could not be the *Second Adam and the *Messiah. Roman Catholics claim that *Mary, the mother of Jesus, was also sinless by being preserved free from *original sin (*Immaculate Conception) and *actual sin by the special *grace of God.

SIRICIUS (c. 334–399). Pope from 384. Roman-born, he made firm pronouncements on religious discipline. *Consecrations were to be conducted by several *bishops rather than one, and *celibacy was commanded for the *clergy. Siricius ended the *Melitian schisms and staunchly upheld *orthodoxy against various *heresies.

SISTERS OF PROVIDENCE See ROSMINIANS.

SITUATION ETHICS The teaching that the rightness of an action is to be judged in relation to the situation and context in which it occurs. Thus an action is not primarily to be evaluated in terms of certain universally applicable laws or rules. It emphasizes personal character and values in contrast to impersonal rules and values. This approach can be very biased and one-sided, especially as operated by an immature person. However, if used creatively, it can have a liberating effect on ethical and moral decisions.

SITZ-IM-LEBEN (Ger. "place-in-life"). An expression used by biblical scholars to refer to the original circumstances in which a part of the *Bible originated or was translated. To know this is a great help in determining the meaning of the text itself.

SIXTUS II (d. 258). Pope from 257. Possibly Greek by birth, he took a more irenic attitude toward some of the *Eastern churches' attitude to rebaptism of converted heretics than did his predecessor and so helped the cause of unity. When the Roman emperor Valerian instigated a persecution of Christians in 258, Sixtus and four *deacons were beheaded.

SIXTUS V (1521–1590). Pope from 1585. At age twelve he became a *Franciscan and later (1566) became the head of that *order. Sixtus was a stern disciplinarian when he served as inquisitor in Venice, and he showed a similar severity as pope in putting down banditry in the *Papal States. He reformed the church's central administration and finances, embarked on an impressive building program in Rome, and strongly supported the *Counter-Reformation.

SLAVERY The institution within a society by which human beings are treated as property. It existed in the *OT in a semihumane form (Exod 21:1–11; Lev 25:44ff.) and was an integral part of society in the Roman Empire. The *NT recognizes its existence, does not condemn it (but cf. 1 Cor 7:21), and sets forth principles to regulate the relationship of master and slave (e.g., Eph 6:5–9; Col 3:22–4:1) that, if carried out, changed the nature of the relationship. Today it is generally considered wrong on two counts. First, it reduces people, made in *God's image, to less than what God intended, making them mere chattel and denying human dignity. Second, it causes owners to become cruel and harsh. In the British Empire it was a group of Evangelicals led by William *Wilberforce (1759–1833) that worked for the cessation of the slave trade from Africa to America.

SLEEP OF THE SOUL The view that at death the human *soul/*spirit leaves the *body and then "sleeps." It is in a state of inactivity and nonawareness until the *second coming of *Christ. *Jesus' and Paul's references to death as "sleep" (Matt 9:24; Mark 5:39; 1 Cor 15:20, 51) are taken literally. This teaching differs from the teaching of most churches in which "sleep" is seen as only a metaphor for death, and after death there is a state of real awareness and meaningful existence. See also INTERMEDIATE STATE.

SLESSOR, MARY (1848–1915). Scottish *missionary to West Africa. Converted as a girl, she left Dundee for Nigeria in 1876 and established a remarkable rapport through a facility with local languages and "daily mixing with the people." She was peacemaker and trader, nurse and educator, and the first woman vice-counsul in the British Empire. Most of all, she was an *evangelist who gave herself selflessly in the service of her beloved Africans.

SMITH, SIR GEORGE ADAM (1858–1942). Scottish *OT scholar. *United Free Church professor in Glasgow (1892), Aberdeen University principal (1909), and royal chaplain, he traveled extensively in the Near East and America. His works include commentaries on Isaiah (1888–1890) and Jeremiah (1923) and the *Historical Geography of the Holy Land* (1894), which had gone through twenty-five editions by 1931.

SMITH, HANNAH WHITALL (1832–1911). Born in Philadelphia of *Quaker background, she was, under *Plymouth Brethren influence, converted with her husband, Robert Pearsall Smith (a *Presbyterian layman), in

1858. In 1867 she entered into a deeper experience of *faith; later, after some skepticism, Robert testified to the same experience. They conducted many meetings in America and England, with an emphasis on the victorious life. They moved to England in 1872 because of Robert's poor health, and their interdenominational meetings there led to the founding of the *Keswick Convention. She wrote *The Christian's Secret of a Happy Life* (1875).

SMITH, JOSEPH (1805–1844). Founder of the Church of Jesus Christ of Latter-Day Saints (the *Mormons). Converted at fourteen, he claimed that at age seventeen he received direct *revelation from *God through golden plates, the contents of which linked American Indians with the Hebrews. This *Book of Mormon* (1830) he purportedly translated from "Reformed Egyptian." He founded his church that year in New York State, led his adherents to Illinois in 1839, was persecuted and jailed, and was finally murdered by a mob that stormed the jail at Carthage.

SMITH, OSWALD J. (1889–1986). Author, *hymn writer, *Presbyterian minister, and *missionary statesman. He served as *pastor of seven churches, the last being The Peoples Church, Toronto, of which he was both founder and *pastor (1930–1959). He wrote about 40 books and 1,200 hymns.

SMITH, RODNEY ("GIPSY") (1860–1947). English *evangelist. Born of Gypsy parents in a tent near London, he received very little formal education, was converted in 1876, joined the *Salvation Army (1877–1882), but found the discipline irksome. Thousands were converted in his large evangelistic meetings throughout the world (including fifty trips to the U.S.). His singing was always appreciated, and he received a decoration from King George VI.

SMITH, SIR WILLIAM ALEXANDER (1854–1914). Founder of the *Boys' Brigade. Concerned about the spiritual and physical welfare of boys, he formed his movement in Glasgow in 1883. Three years later he left his business enterprises and gave his whole time to the organization.

SMITH, WILLIAM ROBERTSON (1846–1894). Scottish *OT scholar. Professor in the Free Church College, Aberdeen (1870), he wrote articles for the *Encyclopaedia Britannica* that aroused a charge of *heresy and led to his deposition (1881) for undermining belief in biblical inspiration. He was appointed joint editor of the *Encyclopaedia Britannica* and held academic posts at Cambridge. His books include *The Prophets of Israel* (1882) and *The Religion of the Semites* (1889).

SMYTH, JOHN (c. 1565–1612). English Baptist. Ordained in 1600, he was dismissed from the staff of Lincoln Cathedral for "personal *preaching" (1602). He was *pastor of a Gainsborough independent church, many members of which went with him to Amsterdam, where he founded a Baptist church in 1607. Convinced of the necessity of believer's *baptism, he baptized himself.

SOBORNOST (Russian *sobor,* "an assembly"). *Christian *fellowship, Christians freely united with *Christ and each other. The word has been used by Russian Orthodox writers (e.g., N. Berdyaev and A. *Khomyakov) to suggest a way forward in creating true community within existing and between existing churches, based upon charitable collaboration.

SOCIAL ACTION Organized effort and work to improve the social order and thus the total situation in which people live—e.g., educational work; medical work; political action to put just laws into effect; and projects in housing, sanitation, and community development. Christians differ not only on whether this should precede, accompany, or follow the *preaching of the *gospel but also on how much effort it deserves in comparison with gospel preaching.

SOCIAL ANALOGY An attempt to provide an *analogy of what "Three in One" (in terms of the *Trinity) means through the use of an illustration taken from a group of human beings. This method contrasts with the psychological analogy, which seeks an illustration from within the human mind. The social analogy was used by the *Cappadocian fathers and has been revived in recent times by L. S. Thorton and C. J. Web.

SOCIAL GOSPEL The attempt to apply the principles of *Christianity to the complex society produced by industrialization and capitalism in the U.S. between 1890 and 1940. A prominent theological idea was that of the *kingdom of *God, which was interpreted in terms of a just and free human society on earth in the present age. Great emphasis was placed on the law of *love and on the need to educate people in *truth and goodness. There was a tendency to believe that social conditions and people in them would gradually evolve into something better. The "father" of the movement was Washington *Gladden (1836–1918), and its leader was Walter *Rauschenbusch (1861–1918). It failed as a *gospel because it did not make a realistic assessment of the nature of *sin either in the individual or in organized society.

SOCIAL SERVICE See SOCIAL ACTION.

SOCIAL THEOLOGY The study of the social and community aspects of *Christian teaching and living. It arose as a reaction to excessive individualism in the understanding of the meaning and purpose of the Christian *faith. To do its task it makes special use of the social sciences, and a particular concern is to ascertain what Christian social *justice means in theory and practice.

SOCIALISM, CHRISTIAN Either the Christian Socialist Movement of the 19th century led by such men as F. D. Maurice (1805–1872), which was, by modern standards, not anything like a radical movement, or an attempt to unite the principles of socialism (whether understood as social democracy or as communism) with those of the *Christian *faith. Not a few leaders of the socialist movement in the U.K. and Sweden have been convinced Christians who have seen such things as the welfare state as an outworking of Christian principles.

SOCIETY OF FRIENDS See QUAKERS.

SOCINIANISM The teaching of F. P. Sozzini (1539–1604), known as Faustus *Socinus. He wrote several books that deny the orthodox views of the *Person and *work of *Christ as well as the *Trinity. His teaching became that of the Minor Reformed Church of Poland and was summarized in the *Racovian Catechism (1605). Though this church did not survive, the teaching did, and it spread to England and America being absorbed into *Unitarianism.

SOCINUS, FAUSTUS (1539–1604). Italian Unitarian. Despite bitter attacks from the orthodox, he taught that the only solid foundation for *Protestantism was human *reason. At the 1588 Synod of Brest he rejected such views as *Christ's divinity, the *Atonement, man's *depravity, and *justification by *faith. To him and to his uncle, Laelius Socinus, can be traced 19th-century *Christian *Rationalism, sometimes called *Socinianism.

SOCIOLOGY OF RELIGION The study of *religion in its sociocultural context. It may be studied in its institutional aspect (and compared with other institutions) or as a form of subculture within and related to a larger *culture and other subcultures. It is a relatively new discipline, having been pioneered by Max Weber (1864–1920) and Emile Durkheim (1858–1917). There are now at least six ways of viewing this subject, and each is determined by a general approach to sociology as an academic discipline.

SÖDERBLOM, NATHAN (1866–1931). *Archbishop of Uppsala (Sweden). A great admirer of *Luther, he studied and lectured in Sweden,

France, and Germany before becoming *archbishop against conservative opposition. Deeply pious and concerned to further *ecumenical relations, he gave his *clergy a notable piece of practical advice: "You must work yourselves to death—but slowly, please."

SOISSONS, COUNCIL OF (1121). This council was called to deal with *heresies taught by *Abelard, particularly on the *doctrine of the *Trinity. No defense was permitted, and his writing on the subject was ordered to be burned.

SOLA FIDE, SOLA GRATIA, SOLA SCRIPTURA (Lat. "by *faith alone," "by *grace alone," and "only the *Scriptures"). A summary of the essential teaching of the Protestant *Reformation. "By faith alone" points to the *doctrine of *justification by faith (also known as solafidianism); "by grace alone" points to the sovereignty and priority of grace in human *salvation; and "only the Scriptures" refers to the fact that all *Christian teaching on faith and morals is to be based on the *truth of the *Bible.

SOLEMN LEAGUE AND COVENANT (1643). A document drawn up by Alexander *Henderson containing the conditions set by the Scots for their supporting the parliamentary cause in the English Civil War. The English, who accepted it, undertook to secure in England and Ireland a reform in *doctrine, *worship, discipline, and government, according to the "Word of *God and the example of the best *Reformed Churches." The subscribers bound themselves also to preserve the Reformed *religion in Scotland; to wipe out popery, *prelacy, and *heresy; and to defend the privileges of Parliament and the person and authority of the king. Those throughout both kingdoms who refused to subscribe were threatened with ecclesiastical censures and civil penalties. When the parliamentary cause triumphed in England with Scottish help, the English renounced the *covenant and then executed *Charles I.

SOLOVIEV, VLADIMIR SERGEEVICH (1853–1900). Russian theologian and philosopher. Born in Moscow, he became a lecturer in philosophy and a close friend of *Dostoevsky. He angered the civil authorities (and lost his government post) by appealing for clemency for the assassins of Czar Alexander II, and he alienated *Orthodox Church authorities by advocating union with *Roman Catholicism. He became Roman Catholic in 1896 but remained an individualist. His philosophical and ethical writings, as well as those on *religion, had a deep influence on Russian life and literature.

SON OF GOD A title of the *Messiah (Ps 2:7; John 1:49) and at a deeper level, a description of the Messiah in his unique relation with the Father (John 1:14–18; 3:16ff.). Because of its usage in the *Bible, the expression has been taken up by theologians, for whom it normally is a way of speaking of the Second *Person of the *Trinity. As the Son, he is eternally generated by the Father.

SON OF MAN A title much used by *Jesus (e.g., Mark 2:10; 2:28; 13:26), apparently to avoid the use of "*Messiah," which had political overtones in *Judaism. In Daniel 7:13–14 "one like the Son of man" (KJV) is given universal dominion. Jesus used "Son of Man" and "Son of *God" interchangeably (Matt 16:13–17).

SONS OF GOD Usually a description of those who, having believed in *Christ, have become members of *God's family (John 1:12; Rom 8:23; Gal 4:5) by *adoption. It is also used of *angels (Job 1:6; 2:1; 38:7; cf. Gen 6:2, 4).

SOTERIOLOGY (Gk. *soteria,* "*salvation"). That part of *systematic *theology that presents the saving *work and *atonement of *Christ for sinners, with the results of this in terms of the *forgiveness of *sin, *justification, and *sanctification. It presupposes that man is a sinner and thus may include a preliminary study of the nature of sin.

SOUL A human being is a "living soul," or "a living being" (Gen 2:7). The *OT, followed by the *NT, does not present a human being as having a mortal *body and an immortal soul (as in some ancient philosophy). Rather a man is a unity who may, as a unity, be described from and under various aspects—body, soul, *heart, *spirit, flesh, etc. Thus existence, except in bodily form, is not contemplated, and the *Christian *hope is of the *resurrection of the body not the *immortality of the soul. However, in *theology, due to Greek influences, the soul has often been presented as either the inner, vital, and spiritual principle of man or the individual ego, personality, and mind known through the body but separable from the body. See also MAN, CHRISTIAN VIEW OF.

SOURCE CRITICISM A technical term for the study of the possible sources, oral and literary, that were used in the formation of such parts of the *Bible as the *Pentateuch and *synoptic *Gospels. As such it is a part of *higher criticism.

SOUTER, ALEXANDER (1873–1949). *New Testament and *patristics scholar. Educated at Aberdeen and Cambridge, he taught NT at Mansfield College, Oxford (1903–1911) and Latin at Aberdeen (1911–1937). His many valuable works include his *Oxford Greek Testament* (1910; rev. 1947), *The Text and Canon of the New Testament* (1913; rev. 1954), and *The Earliest Latin Commentaries on the Epistles of St. Paul* (1927).

SOUTH INDIA, CHURCH OF A 1947 union of Anglicans, Methodists, and the South India United Church (itself a merger in 1908 of Presbyterians and *Congregationalists)—the first union of Episcopal and non-Episcopal churches. Opposition from the Anglo-Catholic wing caused some delay after an early "scheme of union" had been drafted in 1929. This was largely overcome in India itself when the four *bishops of the Anglican *dioceses involved in the projected union stated that they were prepared to accept *Communion from ministers of the new body who were not episcopally ordained. (After the union all new ministers would be episcopally ordained.) In the worldwide *Anglican Communion, however, no province entered into full communion with the new church, and difficulties persisted even after the 1968 *Lambeth Conference called for a review of such a relationship. It has about a million members.

SOUTHERN BAPTIST CONVENTION Largest Baptist body in the U.S. *Baptists established themselves in America in the 17th century and gradually formed various associations with varying degrees of cooperation in matters such as *missions and religious publications. Disagreement between North and South, notably but not exclusively over *slavery, led to the establishment of the Southern Baptist Convention in 1845 with 350,000 members. Though there was an exit of black members who formed their own churches and an internal dispute when rigidly Calvinist elements failed to set the theological tone of the new group, the SBC has grown to almost 15 million members in more than 37,000 churches. They emphasize believers' *baptism, the autonomy of the local church, *evangelism, missions, and the *Bible as the sole *rule of *faith and life.

SOUTHERN CHRISTIAN LEADERSHIP CONFERENCE An Atlanta-based body founded in 1957 by Martin Luther *King and others to help local agencies that sought full equality for blacks in American society. It figured prominently in the civil rights marches of the 1960s and promoted such matters as leadership training, voter registration, and antidiscrimination. The SCLC has always stressed nonviolent social change. It lost something of its early impetus after King's assassination in 1968 and was further weakened by internal dissension and the formation of breakaway groups.

SOVEREIGNTY OF GOD The teaching that *God is the *Lord and King of the *universe (Ps 47:7; Rev 19:6). This means that his *will and purpose will triumph and at the end of the age be seen to have triumphed. It also means that God is in control at the present and is able to use all events and people for his own purposes. Finally, it means that God always takes the initiative in *salvation and *redemption and that his *grace is sovereign grace.

SPALATIN, GEORG (1484–1545). German Reformer. Born in Bavaria, he was ordained in 1508 and became tutor and then librarian in the household of *Frederick III of Saxony. It was Spalatin's influence that persuaded Frederick to protect *Luther during the critical early months of the *Reformation, and his own encouragement of Luther made a significant contribution to the Protestant cause. Spalatin was a notable humanist scholar who collaborated with *Melanchthon in preparing the *Augsburg Confession.

SPANGENBERG, AUGUST GOTTLIEB (1704–1792). Moravian *bishop. Converted while a law student at Jena (1722), he turned to *theology and joined the *Moravian church in 1733. He worked in England and Germany and spent many years in the U.S. (where he became bishop in 1744) before returning to Germany to take over the leadership from *Zinzendorf.

SPEAKING IN TONGUES
See GLOSSOLALIA.

SPENER, PHILIP JACOB (1635–1705). German *pastor and founder of *Pietism. Influenced by Johann *Arndt and Richard *Baxter and distressed by the lack of personal content in the *theology of his day, he set out to reform *Lutheranism from within. For individuals, he stressed the local church and instituted small group sessions (*collegia pietatis*) that encouraged *fellowship, *Bible study, the *priesthood of all believers, right behavior, piety, devotion, and *love instead of argument. For the church in Germany, he called for spiritual *preaching and for the reform of theological education, an emphasis that resulted in the founding of the University at Halle (1694), where *dogmatics was deemphasized and personal piety was stressed. And for the church at large, Spener emphasized *missions and *evangelism. Spener's influence was enormous in the church, and some see the roots of the later romanticism here.

SPEYER, DIETS OF Assemblies held during the *Reformation era in the Rhineland port (usually "Spires" in English). In 1526 political circumstances compelled *Charles V to agree to a resolution of the diet that permitted each ruler to act according to his *conscience. Charles cancelled this encouragement of the spread of *Lutheranism in the 1529 diet, when he insisted on implementation of the 1521 Diet of *Worms edict that condemned Lutheranism. In two further diets at Speyer the emperor made concessions in order to get Lutheran help against the Turks (1542) and the French (1544), but he again changed his attitude when he got the upper hand in 1547.

SPIRATION (Lat. *spirare*, "to breathe"). The *eternal mode of origin of the Holy *Spirit within the *Trinity, proceeding from the Father through the Son as if eternally breathed into existence. See also PROCESSION(S), TRINITARIAN.

SPIRIT A word with a variety of meanings: (1) the nature of *God (John 4:24); (2) the Holy *Spirit as the Third *Person of the *Trinity; (3) a human being—considered as intelligent and in relation to God, with whom he can have communion, Spirit with spirit; (4) a nonphysical being, e.g., a *demon or an *angel; (5) the whole order of existence outside space and time.

SPIRIT, HOLY The Third *Person of the *Trinity, sharing the one Godhead with Father and Son. He is called *holy not only because he partakes of the holiness of the Godhead but also because he is particularly presented in the *NT as the One who makes holy and sanctifies the people of *God.

In the *OT the Spirit of God was active in creation and with the people of *Israel. The Spirit is the Life-giver (Gen 2:7; Job 33:4; 34:14–15; Ps 104:29–30; Isa 42:5). He came upon selected individuals—e.g., the deliverers of Israel (Judg 3:10; 6:34) and the *prophets (Neh 9:30; Ezek 11:24).

In the NT the Spirit is intimately associated with *Jesus and his *ministry. As *Messiah, Jesus is anointed by the Holy Spirit. Jesus was led and empowered by the Spirit (Luke 4:1). His human nature was developed, enriched, and perfected by the indwelling presence of the Spirit. When anticipating his death and *resurrection, Jesus spoke of asking the Father to send to the *disciples this same Spirit, whom he called the *Paraclete (John 14-16)—the Person who would be with them, taking Jesus' place among them and also in the world, preparing people for the *gospel.

At *Pentecost the Father sent the Spirit in the name of the exalted *Lord Jesus to the waiting *disciples (Acts 2). He came to dwell not with a few but with all the disciples and believers in *Christ. So the new people of God, the church, can be called by Paul "the temple of the Holy Spirit" (1 Cor 3:16; 6:19); they should walk and live by the Spirit (Gal 5:16–25). Jesus sends the *gifts of the Spirit for the *ministry of the church (Eph 4:8ff.). Thus, in and by the Spirit's presence the church knows, loves, worships, and serves Jesus.

After the time of the *apostles the leaders of the church had to present a coherent *doctrine of the God whom they knew as Father, Son, and Holy *Spirit. This was not an easy or quick process. To present the Father as God and as a Person (**hypostasis*) was relatively easy; it was possible though less easy to to present Jesus Christ as a Person (**hypostasis*) and as sharing the same Godhead (**homoousios*) with the Father. To think of the Spirit as sharing the one Godhead and being a distinct Person within the Godhead came much less easily. Yet it did come and is found in the *Nicene Creed (381).

The *Eastern and Western churches agree on the general doctrine of the Trinity and on the deity of the Holy Spirit but disagree on the *eternal and internal relations within the Trinity. The East says that the Spirit proceeds eternally from the Father or from the Father through the Son. The West says the Spirit proceeds from the Father *and* from the Son. See also FILIOQUE, GIFTS OF THE SPIRIT.

SPIRITUAL BODY The *body given at the *resurrection of the dead and the body in which a believer will live in the future *kingdom of *God. See RESURRECTION OF THE DEAD.

SPIRITUAL DIRECTION The help given by one *Christian to another in living as a Christian and developing an awareness of *God's presence. The one who gives help is often but not necessarily a member of the clergy and is often called a spiritual director or a soul-friend.

SPIRITUAL EXERCISES The name of the masterpiece of St. *Ignatius of Loyola (published in Latin in 1548). Its series of rules and *meditations to help Christians to conquer their sinful tendencies and give themselves wholly to *God are still used by some who conduct *retreats.

SPIRITUAL GIFTS Term used in two ways. (1) Gifts given to the church by the exalted *Christ through the Holy *Spirit for the work of ministry, building up of the church, and evangelization of the world. Nineteen such gifts are listed in the *NT by the apostle Paul in Romans 12:6–8; 1 Corinthians 12:4–1, 28–30; and Ephesians 4:7–12. It is probable that Paul was being selective and that more gifts existed. Some Christians believe that the gifts ceased at the end of the Apostolic Age, but most accept that they are still operative today. (2) The seven gifts (based on the Latin text of Isa 11:2) of *wisdom, understanding, counsel, *fortitude, knowledge, piety, and fear of the Lord.

SPIRITUAL HEALING The *healing of the whole person by *Christ. This comes through the *ministry of the church in the use of *prayer and *sacraments. Some churches hold that there is a sacrament of healing (once called *extreme unction) when the head is anointed with oil and hands are laid upon the head as prayer is made; some make use of members or visitors who claim to have the spiritual gift of healing, and others have a time for prayer for healing within the context of the *Eucharist or at another convenient time.

SPIRITUAL THEOLOGY The branch of *theology that is concerned with the living of the *Christian life as an individual and as a part of a community. It involves the study of the major contributions from the past—from "*saints" and mystics such as *Francis of Assisi and *John of the Cross. Also it seeks to state and clarify the work and purpose of the Holy *Spirit in leading the Christian toward spiritual *perfection.

SPIRITUALISM (SPIRITISM) A system of beliefs and techniques whose purpose is to establish communication with the *spirits of the dead. Some justify it on the basis of 1 Samuel 28:8, but it is in fact condemned by Deuteronomy 18:11. There are small Spiritualist churches that encourage this approach; also there are Christians within orthodox *denominations who encourage it and use it as a proof of the reality of life after death.

SPIRITUALITY The living of the *Christian life with the purpose of aiming for *perfection and making particular use of *prayer. In different Christian traditions spirituality takes different forms—from the solitude of the Orthodox monks on Mount *Athos to the activism of the conservative *Evangelical. See also MEDITATION, MYSTICISM.

SPONSOR The person who represents a child at *baptism and who professes the *faith of *Christ in the name of the child. Often called *godparent, a sponsor is responsible for the *Christian education and upbringing of the child if the parents are unable or fail to provide this.

SPOON, LITURGICAL Used in the *Eucharist in most *Eastern and Orthodox churches in giving the consecrated bread (dipped in wine) to each communicant directly on the tongue.

SPRINKLING A method of *baptism in which water is sprinkled over the head of the candidate(s). It was used when large numbers of converts were being baptized so that several were baptized at one time—e.g., in medieval times when whole tribes accepted *Christianity. This symbolism of sprinkling represents the cleansing *grace of *God. See also AFFUSION, IMMERSION.

SPURGEON, CHARLES HADDON (1834–1892). English Baptist preacher. Pastor at Waterbeach when only age seventeen, he was called to London at age twenty, attracting such great crowds that the Metropolitan Tabernacle was built for him in 1859. Spurgeon disliked rigid *Calvinism as much as *Arminianism, but he loved the Puritan authors. His habit of speaking his mind landed him in many disputes, notably the *Downgrade Controversy, which caused him to withdraw from the Baptist Union, whose members censured him (1887). He was associated with a number of educational and philanthropic projects in addition to religious organizations, but he is remembered best as an incomparable preacher who left his *tabernacle with a congregation of six thousand.

STAINER, SIR JOHN (1840–1901). English composer. A former choirboy of St. Paul's Cathedral, London, he served as its organist (1872–1888) and as professor of music at Oxford from 1889. A fine organist, teacher, and writer on musical subjects, he composed the oratorio *The Crucifixion* (1887), which is still widely performed in English-speaking countries.

STALKER, JAMES (1848–1927). Scottish minister and writer. Educated at Edinburgh and in Germany, he served the *United Free Church *ministry before becoming its professor of church history in Aberdeen (1902–1926). A refreshing preacher with a keen social concern, he was also a well-known writer, whose works included popular lives of *Jesus and Paul.

STANLEY, ARTHUR PENRHYN (1815–1881). Dean of Westminster. A moderate and tolerant churchman in a partisan age, he was *canon of Canterbury and professor of ecclesiastical history at Oxford before going to Westminster in 1864. A strong Erastian, he nonetheless championed the rights of Nonconformists and invited them to the Anglican *Communion table. He caused a furor by questioning the *doctrine of *eternal *punishment. His writings were diverse enough to include a novel about school life, a commentary on Corinthians, and *Lectures on the Eastern Church*.

STARETZ (Russian, "an *elder, spiritual father"). A member of the Russian Orthodox Church (usually a monk) who gives specific guidance to individual Christians. A feature of Eastern *Christian *monasticism, this informal office came to be more widely recognized in 18th- and 19th-century Russia and was popularized by *Dostoevsky in *The Brothers Karamazov*. The individual does not work according to a prescribed *moral *theology but seeks the guidance of the Holy *Spirit in each case. In the Greek Orthodox Church such a person is known as a *geron* (an elder), and collections of the sayings of some elders have been called *Gerontikon*.

STATE, THE The expression of the sovereignty and the source of the government of a nation and country. The passages of the *NT that relate specifically are Matthew 22:21; Romans 13:1–7; 1 Peter 2:13–17; and Revelation 13. Here the Roman Empire is in view; the *Christian attitude toward this empire changed from seeing it as the basis of law and order (Rom 13) to viewing it as the embodiment of *evil forces (Rev 13) while still the basis of law and order. Over the centuries Christians have viewed the state in both negative and positive ways—negative in the sense that it had to keep the *sin of man under control for the general good; positive in the sense of encouraging community life and mutual cooperation.

STATE CHURCH A national or established church or a church that is officially recognized as the *religion of a country. There are state churches in Scandinavia (Lutheran), Greece (Orthodox), Italy (Roman Catholic), Spain (Roman Catholic), Portugal (Roman Catholic), England (Anglican), and Scotland (*Presbyterian). There are many differences between the various state churches; for example, in Scandinavia the government pays the *clergy out of the church tax, whereas in Britain there is no church tax and there is no direct financial help for the church or clergy.

STATIONS OF THE CROSS A form of devotion involving fourteen successive parts signified by pictures, carvings, or wooden crosses, usually attached to the interior walls of a church. They represent the way to Calvary and are: (1) Jesus is condemned to death; (2) Jesus bears his *cross; (3) Jesus falls; (4) Jesus meets his mother; (5) Jesus is helped by Simon; (6) Veronica wipes the face of Jesus; (7) Jesus falls a second time; (8) Jesus consoles the women of Jerusalem; (9) Jesus falls for a third time; (10) Jesus is stripped of his garments; (11) Jesus is nailed to the cross; (12) Jesus dies on the cross; (13) Jesus is taken down from the cross; (14) Jesus is laid in the tomb. The usual time for this devotion is *Holy Week.

STAUPITZ, JOHANN VON (c. 1469–1524). Roman Catholic scholar. As *vicar general of the *Augustinians in Germany, he counseled and encouraged the young Martin *Luther in Wittenberg from 1508 and spoke out against *indulgences. In 1520 he resigned his office and subsequently became a *Benedictine, gradually losing sympathy with Luther's views and finally condemning them as heretical.

STEPHEN HARDING See HARDING, STEPHEN.

STEPHEN II (III) (d. 757). Pope from 752. Having obtained the help of *Pepin III, king of the Franks, against the Lombards, he became through political circumstances the first temporal sovereign of the *Papal States (756). The succession of papal Stephens is irregular because Stephen II's predecessor, who had opted for the title of Stephen II, died before he could be consecrated; hence the uncertainty about the numbering.

STEPHEN III (IV) (c. 720–772). Pope from 768. A *Benedictine, he assumed the papacy at a troubled time when there had been two attempts to elect partisan candidates. Stephen called a *Lateran council in 769 to resolve the problem. He himself caused further disaffection by siding with the Lombards against the Franks. He also approved the worship of icons for the *Eastern church.

STEPHEN OF HUNGARY (c. 975–1038). First king of Hungary. Son of a Magyar chieftain, he was crowned king of Hungary in 1001 and set out to make his country *Christian. Bishoprics and abbeys were founded, churches built, and home *missionaries commissioned. He is regarded as the founder of the Hungarian state.

STERN, HENRY AARON (1820–1885). *Missionary to the Jews. Born and educated in Germany, he left *Judaism for *Christianity in 1840, trained for *mission work in London, was episcopally ordained, and worked among Jews and Muslims in Asia Minor (1844–1853). After a term in Constantinople, he worked and was imprisoned for some years in Ethiopia before returning to minister among Jews in London.

STERNHOLD, THOMAS (d. 1549). Versifier of the Psalms. Oxford graduate, favorite of *Henry VIII, and member of Parliament, he is remembered for his metrical version of the Psalms, especially in a third edition (1557), which, because of the additions of another versifier, became known as "Sternhold and Hopkins."

STERRY, PETER (d. 1672). Chaplain to Oliver *Cromwell. A Cambridge graduate, he was a member of the *Westminster Assembly and in 1649 became one of Cromwell's chaplains. His name was linked with the *Cambridge Platonists, but he was an individualist and, not surprisingly, a Nonconformist after the *Restoration, when he devoted himself to tutoring and to literary work. Among his books was *A Discourse of the Freedom of the Will* (1675).

STEWARDSHIP The recognition that all gifts come from *God and are to be used for his glory and for the benefit of his creatures (1 Cor 4:1–2, 9, 17). This principle has far-reaching implications for Christians, *Christian families, and churches. Sometimes organized efforts in parishes to persuade people to give money regularly are called stewardship campaigns.

STEWART, JAMES (1831–1905). Scottish *missionary to South Africa. Born in Edinburgh, he studied arts, divinity, and medicine (the latter course completed in 1866), and in 1861 he went to Africa, where he spent some time with David *Livingstone. From 1867 he was based at the Lovedale Institute in Cape Colony until his death. There thousands of African children were educated. "Stewart of Lovedale" founded a hospital for Africans and trained nurses there. He took part in Livingstone's funeral service in Westminster Abbey, advised Robert *Laws in his work in Livingstonia, and wrote several books, notably *Africa and Its Missions* (1903), which originated in lectures to students at the University of Edinburgh.

STIGMATA The marks of the wounds of *Jesus that appear suddenly on a Christian's *body. The wounds are sometimes bleeding and sometimes accompanied by paranormal phenomena. The most well-known (and perhaps first) person to have such an experience was *Francis of Assisi (September 17, 1224). Ninety percent of the more than three hundred cases reported have involved women. The wounds do not respond to normal medical treatment and can last a short or long time.

STILLINGFLEET, EDWARD (1635–1699). *Bishop of Worcester. A renowned preacher during the reign of *Charles II, he tried to unite Episcopalians and Presbyterians, the subject of his *Irenicum* (1659), wrote much on other controversial topics, and became bishop in 1689.

STOCKHOLM CONFERENCE (1925). An *ecumenical gathering on life and work. The first such meeting since World War I and the first to have official delegates from churches, the six hundred people present from thirty-seven countries discussed a wide range of subjects, including the relation between *Christianity and economics and industry. But even more significant was the opportunity to bring together those from lands so recently at enmity. Out of Stockholm and subsequent conferences came the *World Council of Churches in 1948.

STODDARD, SOLOMON (1643–1729). American Congregational minister. A graduate of Harvard, he was ordained to the pastorate in Northampton, Massachusetts, in 1672 and remained there until his death. He had a part in all the religious and political movements of that period, approved the *Halfway Covenant, even to the extent later of admitting to *Communion those who could relate no *conversion experience. Such views involved him in controversy with other leading churchmen including his grandson, Jonathan *Edwards, who became his colleague and successor in 1727.

STOICISM A popular religious philosophy in the Roman Empire when Paul evangelized (Acts 17:18). It is probable that Paul's vocabulary was affected by it (e.g., his use of the words "nature" and "*conscience"), and it is possible that John's vocabulary was also affected by it (e.g., his use of **logos* [John 1:1ff.]). It was a form of materialistic *pantheism.

STOLE A vestment worn by *bishops, *priests, and *deacons over the *alb or *surplice. In the West it is a long narrow band or strip, while in the East it is much broader, with a hole for the head, and hangs down only at the front. Different colors are used for different seasons of the year. A deacon in the West wears it over his left shoulder and crossed under his right arm, while priest and bishop wear it hanging down from the neck to the waist or the knees.

STONE, BARTON WARREN (1772–1844). American *Presbyterian *evangelist. Ordained in 1796, he ministered in Kentucky, but the great *revival soon afterwards brought to a head the criticisms he had about *Calvinism. In 1804 he and some others formed the "Christian Church," about half of whose membership he led into a union with followers of Alexander *Campbell in 1832 as *Disciples of Christ.

STONEHOUSE, NED BERNARD (1902–1962). American *NT scholar. Born in Grand Rapids, Michigan, and a member of the *Christian Reformed Church, he had an extensive education at home and abroad before beginning his teaching career at Westminster Theological Seminary (1929–1962). A meticulous scholar whose published work on the NT won high respect, he was also the founding editor of *The New International Commentary on the New Testament*.

STORCH, NICHOLAS See Abecedarians, Zwickau Prophets.

STOWE, HARRIET BEECHER (1811–1896). American writer. Daughter of Lyman *Beecher, she married a *seminary professor in Cincinnati. Living on the edge of the South for many years, she wrote *Uncle Tom's Cabin,* an effective piece of antislavery literature that had remarkable popularity in America and was translated into many languages.

STRATON, JOHN ROACH (1874–1929). Colorful pulpiteer, able debater, and editor. An outspoken *Fundamentalist leader, he taught at Mercer and

Baylor Universities, served Baptist pastorates in Chicago, Baltimore, Norfolk, and New York City, organized the Fundamentalist League of New York, and edited *The Calvary Pulpit* and *Faith-Fundamentalist*.

STRAUSS, DAVID FRIEDRICH (1808–1874). German theologian. Influenced by the increasing *rationalism in German *theology, he was deprived of his Tübingen lectureship because of his book on the life of *Christ (1835). He rejected the historicity of *supernatural elements in the *Gospels and later rejected *Christianity altogether.

STREETER, BURNETT HILLMAN (1874–1937). *New Testament scholar. Oxford University don (1899–1937), his best-known book, *The Four Gospels: A Study of Origins* (1924), became a standard work. He was concerned also with the confrontation between science and *religion and with the *Oxford Group movement.

STRONG, AUGUSTUS HOPKINS (1836–1921). American Baptist theologian. Converted as a student under the *ministry of C. G. *Finney, he served Baptist pastorates in Massachusetts and Ohio until elected president of Rochester Theological Seminary (1872–1912), where he also lectured. He never lost touch with working *pastors, and he supported *missions and wrote a number of books, including *Systematic Theology* (3 vols., 1886).

STROSSMAYER, JOSEPH GEORGE (1815–1905). Roman Catholic *bishop. Born in what is now Yugoslavia, he was ordained in 1838, served as lecturer and royal chaplain in Vienna, and in 1850 became bishop of Bosnia. He became prominent in the national movement against Hungarian interference in his native Croatia. At *Vatican Council I he was a leading critic of papal *infallibility, and he created a furor by favorable references to *Protestantism. He collaborated with V. S. *Soloviev in seeking a reunion between Roman Catholic and Russian *orthodoxy.

STUBBS, JOHN (c. 1543–1591). Puritan. Born in Norfolk, he graduated at Cambridge and subsequently opposed *Roman Catholicism to such an extent that he published a work against *Elizabeth I's proposed marriage to the duke of Anjou, for which he and the publisher had their right hands cut off and Stubbs served a prison term. He remained loyal to the crown, became member of Parliament for Great Yarmouth in 1589, but still upheld—albeit in more prudent fashion—his strong Protestant views.

STUDD, CHARLES THOMAS (1862–1931). *Missionary. Son of a wealthy planter converted under D. L. *Moody, he was educated at Cambridge, played cricket for England, and (one of the famous "Cambridge Seven") sailed for missionary service in China in 1885. An invalid at home in 1894, he later worked among students and then served as a *pastor in India for six years before he went against medical advice by sailing for Africa in 1910. In 1912 he founded the Heart of Africa Mission (later the Worldwide Evangelization Crusade) and worked in Central Africa until his death.

STUDENT CHRISTIAN MOVEMENT The British branch of the *World Student Christian Federation founded by John R. *Mott and others in 1895. Its move toward a broader doctrinal base led to the withdrawal in 1910 of the Cambridge Inter-Collegiate Christian Union. SCM membership is open to all who "desire to understand the *Christian *faith and live the Christian life." Through its well-known publishing house and its conferences, it maintains ongoing discussion of the relevance of *Christianity in the modern world.

STUDENT VOLUNTEER MOVEMENT A body originating in a gathering of students under the sponsorship of D. L. *Moody in Massachusetts in 1886. Concerned chiefly with recruitment for *Christian *mission, the movement enlisted more than two thousand volunteers in 1887. Its slogan was "the evangelization of the world in this generation," which brought a charge of "setting a timetable for *God." Prominent in the early work of the organization were R. P. *Wilder and John R. *Mott.

STUNDISTS Russian *evangelical group. It had its origins in the mid-19th century when German settlers, many of them *Mennonites, continued in their adopted land the habit of reading the *Bible during leisure hours (Ger. "Stunden"). While there was no initial break with the *Orthodox Church, the Stundists later resorted to believer's *baptism, and this led to persecution of Russians who had joined the group. By 1909 numbers were reportedly about 250,000. Some of them joined the newly founded Russian Baptist Union in 1884, others the Union of Evangelical Christians in 1909.

STURM, JAKOB (1498–1553). German Reformer. Born in Strasbourg, where he became chief magistrate in 1526, he was early won to the Reformed cause and became a warm advocate with *Bucer of a united *Protestantism. He participated in the Colloquy of *Marburg and was sponsor of the *Tetrapolitan Confession at the 1530 Diet of Augsburg.

STURM, JOHANNES (1507–1589). German Protestant educator. Educated by the *Brethren of the Common Life and at Louvain University, he lectured at Paris (1530–1536), became a Protestant under *Bucer's influence, and settled in Strasbourg. He made that city's educational system a model for other Protestant cities and founded an academy there in 1564. His liberal outlook displeased some of the more rigid Lutherans, and he was briefly expelled from Strasbourg in 1581 but later allowed to return.

STURZO, LUIGI (1871–1959). Roman Catholic *priest and political activist. Sicilian born, he was ordained in 1894 and returned to Sicily where he championed miners and peasants against repressive authority. He was mayor of his native Caltagirone (1905–1920), considerably helped the lot of the *poor, taught in the local *seminary, and founded in 1919 Italy's Popular Party that won about one-fifth of the parliamentary seats. Refusing to support Mussolini, he went into exile in 1924, returning only in 1946 when his party was revived as the Christian Democrats. His major works included *Church and State* (1939) and *Spiritual Problems of Our Times* (1945).

STYLITE An ascetic who lived on top of a pillar. The cramped area may have been enclosed by a rail, and a small roof may have protected the stylite from the worst of the elements. Not suprisingly, it was almost entirely an Eastern practice. Its most famous exponent was *Simeon Stylites.

SUAREZ, FRANCISCO DE (1548–1617). *Jesuit theologian and philosopher. Born in Spain, he joined the Jesuits in 1564 and subsequently became the *order's most prominent theologian. He taught in Rome, Alcala, and finally was professor at Coimbra (1597–1616) on the appointment of *Philip II. His writings opposed the theory of the *divine right of kings held in England by *James I and the colonial practices of the Spanish in the West Indies. Although substantially in agreement with the philosophy of Thomas *Aquinas, Suarez here as in other areas exercised a healthy independence of outlook that did not hesitate to express differences if reasoned argument called for them.

SUBDEACON An *order of the ordained *ministry introduced in the 3d century. He had a specific role in the *Eucharist assisting the *deacon. The Roman Catholic Church abolished the order in 1972, but it is still continued in the *Eastern churches.

SUBLAPSARIAN A particular view of the order of *God's *eternal decrees. The decree to save the elect follows the decree to create and allow the *Fall. See also PREDESTINATION.

SUBORDINATIONISM The *doctrine that the Son is subordinate in status and *nature to the Father and/or that the Holy *Spirit is subordinate in status and nature to the Father and to the Son. *Orthodoxy affirms the equality of the Father, Son, and Spirit in the Holy *Trinity in terms of their Godhead. However, it recognizes that in order of thought and in presentation within the *Bible the Father is placed first. A form of subordinationism is found in *Arianism, *Socinianism and *Unitarianism, as well as in the teaching of certain *sects (e.g., *Jehovah's Witnesses).

SUBSISTENCE (Lat. *subsistentia,* "a self-contained existence"). Originally used of the act of existence of the three *Persons of the *Trinity, it came to be used in the medieval and later periods of the Godhead—the existence of the one *God. Person was used along with it to indicate the mode of being of the Father, Son, and Holy *Spirit.

SUBSTANCE (Lat. *substantia,* "that which stands under"). The translation of the Greek **ousia*—traditionally used in the English version of the *Nicene Creed ("of one *substance with the Father"). As used of *God it refers to his *eternal *being, by which and in which all three *Persons are one. Cf. **homoousios*. The word "Being" is often preferred today.

SUBSTITUTE, CHRIST AS The view that in his perfect life, sacrificial death, and glorious *resurrection, *Jesus acted as the substitute for the world (or for the elect). That is, he lived a perfect life of *obedience to *God on behalf of sinners, he paid the penalty for their *sin, and then he triumphed over all the *evil forces that oppress them. This approach is part of the theory of the *Atonement known as *penal substitution. There is discussion among theologians as to the differences between *Christ as Substitute and as Representative. A substitute physically replaces those for whom he acts as substitute; a representative does not necessarily do this, but he acts always in solidarity with them.

SUCCENTOR The assistant to or deputy of the *precentor of a *cathedral. He leads the *choir in singing.

SUFFERING The conscious experience of physical and mental pain from which there is no immediate or even long-term escape. Much suffering in the world can be traced to the existence of moral *evil in the world, caused by the *sin of humans. However, some suffering has no source in evil, and this raises problems. So also does the fact that suffering does not obviously fall only on the wicked but upon the apparently innocent as well. These difficulties are often called the problem of suffering and constitute one of the great mysteries of human existence for the believer in a good *God. Christians find comfort (but no rational explanation of the problem) in the knowledge that the *eternal *Son of God became incarnate and was an innocent victim of evil forces in the world.

SUFFERING SERVANT See SERVANT, SUFFERING.

SUFFICIENT GRACE The help *God gives to perform a particular action or to pass through a specific experience. See also GRACE.

SUFFRAGAN A title used in modern times usually to describe an assistant *bishop appointed to help the diocesan. The office was known in England from the mid-13th century, lapsed by the end of the 16th century, and was restored in 1870. In the late 1970s there were about sixty suffragan bishops serving the Church of *England, but *dioceses are often served also by "assistant bishops" (normally retired bishops residing in the diocese).

SUI GENERIS (Lat. "alone of its kind"). Used particularly of *God who as Creator and Redeemer is alone of his kind, for there is only one true and living God.

SUICIDE The killing of oneself as an act of one's own *will and by one's own decision. This is different from the willing surrender of one's life—e.g., to save someone who is in great danger. The *Bible contains little information on suicide but records several examples (e.g., Abimelech [Judg 9:53–54],

Saul and his armorbearer [1 Sam 31:3–5], and Judas [Matt 25:5]). On the basis of certain general principles, the church has always condemned suicide: (1) *God is the Giver of life, and only he can take it away, (2) the *duty of a human beings is to live until God terminates life, and (3) to take one's own life is to act selfishly and to deprive the community/family of one of its members.

SULPICIANS A congregation of *secular *priests organized by J. J. Oiler in Paris in 1642, with theological education as its primary aim. While they take no *vows and are allowed to hold private property, members are expected to use possessions in the service of *Christ. They began work in Canada in 1657, and in 1791 they founded in Baltimore what is now the oldest Roman Catholic *seminary in the U.S.

SUMMA (pl. summae). Comprehensive treatises in *theology and philosophy written in the Middle Ages. Among the famous writers of these are Peter *Abelard (1079–1142), Peter *Lombard (1100–1160), and Thomas *Aquinas (1225–1274). The latter wrote *Summa contra Gentiles* and *Summa Theologiae*. See also SENTENCES.

SUMMUM BONUM (Lat. "the supreme good"). Used particularly of *God as the supreme goal to which all human *hope and activity should be directed.

SUMNER, JOHN BIRD (1780–1862). *Archbishop of Canterbury from 1848. A Cambridge graduate, he was ordained in 1803 and was *bishop of Chester from 1828. Sumner was a convinced *Evangelical who opposed the *Oxford Movement and the *doctrine of *baptismal regeneration, but he voted for the Catholic Emancipation Bill in 1829.

SUNDAR SINGH, SADHU (1889–c. 1929). Indian *Christian. A high-born Sikh, he was converted to *Christianity and baptized in 1905. He became a Christian sadhu ("*holy man") and set out to take the *gospel not only to the villages of his own Punjab, but further afield to Afghanistan and Tibet. Later he visited other Asian countries, Europe, and the U.S., helped by financial contributions from his father, who was himself converted late in life. Sundar Singh disappeared during a trip to Tibet; no trace of him was ever found.

***SUNDAY** The day of the sun. The first day of the week, called "the *Lord's Day" by the early Christians. On this day they "broke bread" (Acts 20:7) and collected for the *poor (1 Cor 16:2). As the *Christian day of *worship it has often been debated whether the basic principles of the Jewish *Sabbath should be applied to it so as to make it into a Christian Sabbath. See also SABBATH, SABBATARIANISM.

SUNDAY SCHOOLS These are generally held to have been founded in the work of Robert *Raikes in Gloucester in 1780. He began teaching *Scripture, reading, and writing to deprived children. An article he wrote about the project fired the imagination of others, and schools were started throughout the country and were found in America by about 1790. The Sunday School Union was formed in 1803. As secular education became more common, the Sunday schools concentrated on *Bible teaching.

SUNDAY, WILLIAM ASHLEY ("BILLY") (1862–1935). American *evangelist. Born in Iowa, he was a professional baseball player when converted in Chicago in 1886. He worked for the *YMCA (1891–1893), helped J. Wilbur *Chapman, then in 1896 became an independent evangelist. His campaigns were all very systematically organized. Sunday was an entertainer in order to gain attention, but one million people are said to have "hit the sawdust trail" under his *ministry. The New York *Times* called him "the greatest high-pressure and mass *conversion *Christian evangelist that America or the world has known."

SUPEREROGATION, WORKS OF An expression based on the Latin of Luke 10:35—*quodcumque supererogaveris* ("whatever you shall spend beside"), and first used in the Middle Ages. Biblical support was found in the story of the rich young ruler (Matt 19:16ff.) and in the teaching on *celibacy and virginity (1 Cor 7). In essence such works or deeds are acts performed that are above one's normal *duty (e.g., accepting the discipline and demands of celibacy and forfeiting the chance of marriage). Though Roman Catholics have used this terminology, Protestants have never been happy with the basic distinction between ordinary *works of *love and special, extra works of love. See also MERIT.

SUPERINTENDENT A biblical term that means "overseer" but is also translated in the *NT as "*bishop." After the *Reformation, *Lutheranism developed the office of superintendent, an officer with limited powers. Superintendents emerged also after the Scottish Reformation, but the role here was temporary and even more limited than in Lutheranism. As the Church of *Scotland became more properly organized into church courts, each with a *moderator with a chairman's authority during meetings only, the role of superintendent was abolished. It still exists in some Protestant churches, denoting a minister with the oversight of a district, as in British *Methodism.

SUPERIOR The head of a *religious house, *order, or congregation. See also ABBESS, ABBOT, PRIOR, PRIORESS.

SUPERNATURAL That which transcends creation, that which is above the power and claims of nature—thus, the activity of *God in revealing himself, in acting within human events and persons, and in giving *eternal *salvation. Also, the activity and power of *Satan and *evil *spirits can be called *supernatural. In both cases the spiritual activity is outside the physical *universe, though its direct effects are experienced within that universe.

SUPPER, LORD'S See LORD'S SUPPER, THE.

SUPRALAPSARIANISM A view of the *eternal decrees of *God that places his decree to choose an elect people for himself before his decree to create the world and allow *sin in it. See also PREDESTINATION.

SUPREMACY, ACTS OF The act of the English Parliament of 1534 by which *Henry VIII and each of his successors became the "only supreme head in earth of the Church of *England" and the power of the *pope was removed. It was repealed in the reign of the Roman Catholic Mary *Tudor, but under *Elizabeth I a new act (1559) declared her to be "supreme governor of this realm . . . as well as in all spiritual or ecclesiastical things or causes as temporal."

SURETY, CHRIST AS The responsibility *Christ took upon himself to pay on behalf of humankind the payment/obligation *God required of humankind. This can be seen in terms of his living a perfect life of trust and *obedience and then offering himself as a pure, unblemished *sacrifice for the *sins of the world. See also ATONEMENT.

SURPLICE A loose-fitting white liturgical garment that extends to the knees and elbows and is worn over a *cassock. Both *clergy and lay ministers wear it.

SURSUM CORDA (Lat. "lift up your *hearts"). A basic part of the early part of the *liturgy of the *Eucharist in many churches. The presiding minister calls the people to lift up their *hearts and they reply, "We lift them up to the *Lord."

SUSO, HENRY (c. 1295–1366). German mystic. Of noble birth, he studied under Meister *Eckhart and about 1326 returned to his native Constance, where he had earlier joined the *Dominicans. His profound religious awakening led to his writing *The Little Book of Eternal Wisdom* (1328), a spiritual classic. Thereafter he suffered because of his defense of Eckhart, but he became a highly respected spiritual director and a well-known preacher who became also a leader of the *Friends of God.

SVERDRUP, GEORGE (1848–1907). Lutheran theologian and church leader. Born in Norway, he was educated there and in Germany and France before going to America in 1874 as professor at Augsburg Seminary, Minneapolis, where he was soon made president (1877–1907). He was not enthusiastic about perpetuating Norwegian church traditions in an American context and in 1897 founded with others the Norwegian Lutheran Free Church, organized on congregational principles to give greater scope for lay participation. His extensive theological works were written in Norwegian.

SWAINSON, CHARLES ANTHONY (1820–1887). Anglican theologian. Born in Liverpool and educated at Cambridge, he occupied various posts including the vice chancellorship. He specialized in church *creeds and *liturgies and produced what became standard works: *The Creeds of the Church* (1858), *The Nicene and Apostles' Creed* (1875), and *The Greek Liturgies* (1884).

SWEARING See Oath.

SWEDENBORG, EMANUEL (1688–1772). Swedish scientist and religious thinker. Born in Stockholm, he graduated from Uppsala (1709) and spent five years traveling and pursuing his interest in natural science before returning to take up an appointment with the Swedish Board of Mines (1716–1747). In middle life he claimed to have visions that made him concentrate on biblical and mystical writings that after his death led to the founding of the Church of the *New Jerusalem.

SWEDENBORGIANS See New Jerusalem, Church of the.

SWEET, WILLIAM WARREN (1881–1959). American Methodist scholar. Born in Kansas, he was ordained in the Methodist Episcopal Church in 1906 and taught later at Ohio Wesleyan, DePauw, and Chicago universities. He specialized in American church history and sought to interest others in it through many popular works, including *The Story of Religion in America* (1930) and *Religion on the American Frontier* (4 vols., 1931–1946).

SWETE, HENRY BARCLAY (1835–1917). Anglican scholar. Born in Bristol and ordained in 1859, he engaged in pastoral work and held theological chairs in London (1882–1890) and Cambridge (1890–1915). Brilliant classicist and versatile theologian, he was a prime mover in the founding of the *Journal of Theological Studies* (1899) and wrote extensively on biblical and *patristic subjects.

SWIFT, JONATHAN (1667–1745). Irish writer and dean of St. Patrick's, Dublin. Born and educated in Dublin and ordained in 1695, he was soon absorbed in political and literary matters in London and reacting strongly against English policies toward his native Ireland. On Queen *Anne's death he withdrew to the Dublin deanery to which he had been appointed in 1713. An accomplished satirist, he had earlier produced his *Argument to Prove the Inconvenience of Abolishing Christianity* (1708), but he is best remembered for *Gulliver's Travels* (1726), written, he said, "to vex the world."

SWISS GUARD A corps formed in 1506 for the personal protection of the *pope. Membership is restricted to Roman Catholic Swiss nationals.

SYLLABUS OF ERRORS (1864). A collection of eighty propositions issued by *Pius IX against theological *liberalism. Pius said in effect that liberty, *toleration, secularism, and democracy were closely linked and added up to materialism and a diminution of the church's authority. Among a mixed bag of errors and institutions are socialism, communism, secret societies, *Bible societies, and groups of liberal *clergy. The syllabus asserts that the church is not bound to submit to the laws of the *state.

SYLLOGISM An argument in philosophy so arranged that if the first two propositions are true, so also is the third. This was much used by theologians in the Middle Ages. E.g., since

(1) Jesus is a true man and (2) Jesus is true *God, then (3) Jesus is true man and true *God. It is also used by Protestants. See also PRACTICAL SYLLOGISM.

SYLVESTER I (d. 335). Pope from 314. His *pontificate spanned a vital period during which the Roman Empire became at least nominally *Christian. We know remarkably little for certain about Sylvester; he is said to have baptized the emperor *Constantine. He did not attend the significant Council of *Nicea (325) but was represented by two legates. His name was associated with the so-called *Donation of Constantine.

SYLVESTER II (c. 945–1003). Pope from 999. Born in France and educated by *Benedictines, he gained a reputation for mathematical and scientific knowledge and may even have invented the pendulum clock. He was so highly regarded at the imperial court that Otto III's influence led to Sylvester's becoming the first French pope. A champion of the church against secular interference, he battled against corruption, encouraged a *missionary outreach, and promoted scholarship.

SYMBOL (Gk. *symbolon,* "a token, pledge"). That which stands for and represents something else. While a sign is generally agreed to represent something else different from it (e.g., a green light means "go"), a symbol is more closely related to the reality to which it points (e.g., the actions of the human *body point to *truth about the person whose body it is). A symbol is the proper expression of the reality it symbolizes. So at one level the *sacraments are signs, while at a deeper level they are symbols, especially as they are used by the *Lord *Christ through the Holy *Spirit. The same may be claimed of a *cross or crucifix.

SYMBOL OF FAITH A summary of the *Christian *faith may be called a *symbol since it is, as a *confession made by a person, a definite mark and sign that the person is a Christian. At *baptism in the early church converts stated their faith before being baptized, and their *creed was called a symbol of faith.

SYMBOLICS The comparative study of the different *creeds and *confessions of *faith that have been used in the church.

SYMMACHUS (d. 514). Pope from 498. The Sardinian-born *pontiff found his reign beset by disputes, false charges, intrigues, and heresies. His election was disputed by followers of a rival aspirant, the archpriest Laurentius, and the ensuing *schism was not resolved until about 506. Symmachus had to defend the orthodox *faith against *Manichaeism and Eastern concessions to *Monophysitism and against Arians in North Africa. He was also a benefactor of the *poor.

SYNAGOGUE The Jewish congregation and the building in which it meets. Jesus visited synagogues (Luke 4:16), and Paul preached in them (Acts 17:1–2). In James 2:2 synagogue is used of the *Christian congregation. However, in post-*NT times Jews and Christians were in opposition, so synagogue came to be used only of the Jewish meeting house and people. Churches preferred to call their meetings *synaxis.

SYNAXIS (Gk. "assembly, congregation"). Used by the *Orthodox Church in Greece for an assembly for *worship and *prayer. It was also used in the early church of the meeting of the *Christian congregation.

SYNCRETISM The attempt to unite different *doctrines or different types of *worship. It was used of the attempt by G. *Calixtus (1586–1656) to propose a basic creed of *doctrines on which Protestants and Catholics could agree. It is used by biblical scholars to describe the *faith of *Israel when it took to itself aspects of Canaanite and Baal worship, as the Book of Judges shows. Also, it is used of the way in which the *Christian church has fused pagan *rites and festivals with those of *Christianity in order to keep the commitment of large numbers of people—as in Latin and South America.

SYNDERESIS (Gk. *synteresis*, "spark of *conscience"). A medieval Latin word describing the knowledge in the human conscience of the basic principles of moral law or the first principles of moral action.

SYNERGISM (Gk. *syn,* "together," *ergon,* "work"). Used with reference to the work of the Holy *Spirit in bringing a sinner to *faith and *repentance. It is the view that *God expects the cooperation of the human *will to make effective his initiative and help. This teaching was advocated by *Melanchthon in the synergistic controversy within *Lutheranism, 1550–1577. It contrasts with *monergism.

SYNOD (Gk. *synodos,* "coming together"). An ecclesiastical assembly that may be of *bishops alone, of bishops, *priests, and *laity, or of *clergy and laity. It is used in different ways in different churches and may be local, national, or international.

SYNOPTIC GOSPELS The first three *Gospels, Matthew, Mark, and Luke, which have similar material and contrast with the Fourth Gospel, John.

SYNOPTIC PROBLEM The problem of the literary similarities and differences in the first three Gospels. Various solutions have been put forward. Of these the most widely accepted is that both Matthew and Luke used Mark, that Matthew and Luke also used another source *Q (Quelle), and that Matthew and Luke also had access to other material, given the code names M and L.

SYRIAN CHURCHES *Christianity in Syria was established in the 2d century, and these Syriac-speaking believers accepted the Nicene *faith in 325. In the 5th century, however, many in the old Roman Empire became *Monophysites; those in Persian territory became Nestorians. Since the late 18th century there has been a Catholic minority as well as the *Jacobite (Monophysite) church. The Syriac influence was found also among *Malabar Christians in India.

SYSTEMATIC THEOLOGY The attempt to combine all *Christian *doctrines into one massive system of doctrine. This discipline has been attempted especially by Calvinistic theologians (e.g., Charles *Hodge of Princeton in *Systematic Theology*, 3 vols., 1871–1873). It requires a method and an underlying philosophy to become a true system of *theology. See also DOGMATICS, DOGMATIC THEOLOGY; SUMMA.

T

TABERNACLE (Lat. *tabernaculum,* "a tent"). Used in two ways: (1) of the portable *shrine and tentlike *sanctuary used by the Israelites before they entered the Promised Land (Exod 25–31, 35–40) and (2) of the "*holy" cupboard, or receptacle, used for storage of the consecrated bread of Holy *Communion and of the vessels used in the celebration of the *Eucharist. It is set in the center of the *altar and is usually beautifully decorated.

TABORITES Extreme party among the *Hussites. Called thus from their headquarters at Mount Tabor, they called for strict adherence to the *Bible. They condemned belief in *purgatory; the *worship of *saints, *images, and *relics; and the practice of *penance. They claimed the right of *laity, including women, to preach wherever they wished; they showed a marked social concern; and they looked for the imminent return of *Christ. The party was destroyed in 1434 when defeated in battle by a union of moderate Hussites and Roman Catholics.

TACITUS, CORNELIUS (c. 55–117). Latin writer. From the point of view of a secular historian he provides useful commentary on the *Christian background. He recounts Nero's cruelty against believers, is critical about the procurator Felix (cf. Acts 24), and reflects Roman ignorance or misunderstanding about *Christianity.

TAIZÉ COMMUNITY A community of Protestant monks founded in Burgundy in 1944. Its *prior, Roger Schutz, gave sanctuary in his home to Jews and other refugees in wartime France. Members, who take the usual *vows of *poverty, *celibacy and *obedience, come from many different *Christian traditions, including the Roman Catholic. Many go to work in Third World countries. They pray three times a day at specific times, as do all the monks at home or abroad.

TALMUD The two books known as the Babylonian Talmud and the Jerusalem Talmud that originated around the 5th century A.D. They contain the oral teaching of earlier rabbis (Mishnah), which was an explanation of the law of Moses together with discussions of this teaching (Gemara). *Christian scholars find these helpful for knowledge of Jewish interpretations of the Hebrew *Bible.

TAMBARAM CONFERENCE (1938). A conference held near Madras, convened by the *International Missionary Council, and under the chairmanship of the veteran ecumenist John R. *Mott. More than half of the 471 participants came from the younger churches. A significant feature of the conference was its discussion of religious liberty.

TARGUM (Heb. "translation, interpretation"). Used of the paraphrases into Aramaic from Hebrew, as provided in the *synagogues of Palestine when Aramaic was the ordinary language and Hebrew only the language of *religion. Some written ones have survived.

TATIAN (c. 120–c. 172). *Christian writer and Gnostic. Born in Syria, he produced the Diatessaron, which arranged the *Gospels in a single continuous narrative. A pupil of *Justin Martyr in Rome. He later returned to Syria and founded the Encratites, a group which most scholars have regarded as Gnostic.

TAULER, JOHANN (c. 1300–1361). German mystic. He became a *Dominican in 1315, was influenced by *Eckhart and perhaps by *Suso, and became famous as a preacher in his native Strasbourg. He associated with the *Friends of God during his residence in Basel (1338–1343) and was active in caring for those afflicted by the *Black Death. He had a very practical element in his approach, not always characteristic of the mystic school.

TAUSEN, HANS (1494–1561). Danish Reformer and *bishop. A well-educated monk who completed his studies at Wittenberg, he espoused *Reformed *doctrine, and preached it after his return to Denmark in 1525, helped by the protection given him by King Frederik I. After the triumph of the *Reformation in Denmark (1536) he was active in establishing the young church through administration, speech, and writing. He became bishop of Ribe in 1541.

TAYLOR, JAMES HUDSON (1832–1905). Founder of the China Inland Mission (now the Overseas Missionary Fellowship). Son of a Methodist lay preacher in Yorkshire, he was converted in 1849, served in China for six years (1854–1860), then returned in 1866 with his family and sixteen *missionaries after founding his new missionary society. He spent most of the rest of his life there organizing, traveling, *preaching, and identifying with the people. By his death the missionary force had grown to more than eight hundred.

TAYLOR, JEREMY (1613–1667). Anglican theologian and *bishop. Cambridge graduate and friend of William *Laud, he was a Royalist chaplain in the English Civil War. During the Cromwellian era he withdrew to Ireland, where he produced his classics, *Holy Living* (1650) and *Holy Dying* (1651). In 1660 he became bishop of Down and Connor and took harsh action against Presbyterians and Roman Catholics.

TAYLOR, NATHANIEL WILLIAM (1786–1858). American scholar and preacher. Born in Connecticut, he studied *theology under Timothy *Dwight and was ordained to the Congregational *ministry. After a ten-year pastorate at New Haven he became Yale Divinity School's first professor of theology in 1822. A modified Calvinist, he continued the tradition known as *New England Theology but in such a way as to bring charges of *heresy that led to the founding of Hartford Theological Seminary.

TAYLOR, WILLIAM (1821–1902). American Methodist *missionary *bishop. Born in Virginia, he was ordained and organized the first Methodist church in San Francisco. He then embarked in 1862 on a remarkable series of worldwide tours. In 1884 he was elected missionary bishop for Africa (1884–1897), during which he established thirty-six *missions in the Congo. He wrote numerous books about his experiences of ministering in different parts of the world.

TE DEUM LAUDAMUS (Lat. "We praise you, O *God"). The opening words of a famous *hymn much used in *worship and written in the 5th century. It is addressed to the Father and Son, and many composers have set it to music.

TEILHARD DE CHARDIN, PIERRE (1881–1955). French *Jesuit and paleontologist. Ordained in 1911, he argued for evolution and began a long battle against superiors who "did not understand." A stretcher-bearer in World War I, he spent World War II in

China and refused permission to return. His attempt at opening a few windows in the church saw him debarred from academic advancement, discouraged from lecturing, and cold-shouldered by Rome in old age, which he spent in New York. His major work, *The Phenomenon of Man* (Eng. trans. 1959), was not published until after his death.

TELEOLOGY (Gk. *telos*, "end"). The study of the end or final purpose of the *universe. The view that there is design and purpose in the world and that these are directed to a final goal. Thus the teleological argument for the existence of *God presents design and purpose in the world as an argument for a Creator-God.

TEMPERANCE The restraint or moderation or regulation of the appetites and passions of the *body by *reason or religious *convictions. Sometimes temperance has meant total *abstinence and at other times moderation since circumstances and contexts differ. For Christians it is particularly associated with the idea that the body is the temple of the Holy *Spirit and that self-control is a *fruit of the Spirit (Gal 5:22). Temperance societies of the 19th century were particularly concerned with the social *evils of excessive alcoholic drinking. They sought to persuade people to abstain from all alcoholic beverages.

TEMPLARS A military religious *order founded about 1119 to help and protect pilgrims on their ways to the Holy Land. Baldwin II, king of Jerusalem, gave them premises in part of his palace known as the Temple of Solomon, hence their name, which in full was "The Poor Knights of Christ and of the Temple of Solomon." From being bodyguards they developed into an army, in the process acquiring considerable *wealth and property—so much so that *Philip IV of France cast covetous eyes on them. He pressured Pope *Clement V into suppressing the order in 1312, after bringing disputed charges of *heresy and immorality. Philip gained only partially; most of the Templars' property was transferred by the *pope to the *Hospitallers.

TEMPLE, WILLIAM (1881–1944). *Archbishop of Canterbury from 1942. Formerly *bishop of Manchester (1921) and archbishop of York (1929), he busied himself also in social, educational, and economic affairs, and enthusiastically supported the *ecumenical movement. Especially noteworthy was his collaboration with Roman Catholics and Free churchmen in stating principles on which a postwar settlement could be based. A philosopher by training, he was versatile enough to produce books as different as *Nature, Man and God* (1934), *Readings in St. John's Gospel* (2 vols., 1939–1940), and **Christianity and the Social Order* (1942).

TEMPTATION Incitement to commit *sin. The impulse may come from the *Devil, from *evil desires, or from the world, but God is never its author (James 1:13). Theologians distinguish temptation to sin from testing or proving of *faith. Also they have divided temptation into three parts–suggestion, delight, and consent. Of these, only the last constitutes sin. To be tempted as such is not to sin, for *Christ himself, who never sinned, was tempted (Heb 4:15–16).

TEN ARTICLES, THE (1536). A doctrinal statement of the Church of *England passed at the instigation of *Henry VIII after his rejection of papal supremacy. In what was manifestly a compromise between old and new, it defined what should be believed and practiced. It was superseded the following year.

TEN COMMANDMENTS See COMMANDMENTS, THE TEN.

TEN YEARS' CONFLICT The period immediately prior to the *Disruption of 1843, when a majority of the Evangelicals in the Church of *Scotland left to form the *Free Church. The trouble arose over the vexed question of patronage and the rights of congregations to choose their own ministers. A crisis came when a Perthshire parish rejected the patron's nominee by 286 votes to 2, but the civil courts upheld his right to induction. Because of this and other factors, the Evangelicals held that the kirk was no longer free to govern its own affairs and so left the national church in the hands of the Moderate majority.

TENNANT, FREDERICK ROBERT (1866–1957). British philosopher and theologian. Tennant is best remembered for his *Philosophical Theology* (2 vols., 1928, 1930) in which he argues for basically traditional beliefs within a strongly theistic framework. His scientific training led him to view *theology along empirical lines rather than along German rationalist (and liberal) lines. He contended that the existence of *God and the human *soul could be proven and that scientific *truth and theological truth did not conflict. Tennant also wrote extensively on *sin in a time when such teaching was quite unpopular. His views are somewhat Pelagian as may be seen in *The Sources of the Doctrine of the Fall and Original Sin* (1903).

TENNENT, GILBERT (1703–1764). *Presbyterian preacher. Born in Ireland he went to America with his father William in 1817, became a *Presbyterian minister in New Jersey, and enthusiastically joined George *Whitefield during his 1740–1741 visit to the Colonies. From 1743 he ministered in Philadelphia.

TENNENT, WILLIAM (1673–1746). *Presbyterian preacher. Born in Ireland, he graduated from Trinity College, Dublin, was episcopally ordained in 1704, but transferred to the *Presbyterian Church on emigrating to America in 1718. In Pennsylvania he established his famous "log college" for the training of young ordinands, including his four sons. It closed the same year as what was to be Princeton College began (1746).

TERESA, MOTHER (1910–). *Missionary to India. Born Agnes Gonxha Bojaxhiu. Her father was an Albanian grocer in Yugoslavia. She became a *nun with the Sisters of Loretto and went to India in 1928. She taught in a cloistered school until 1948, when she heard "a call within a call" to work among the poorest in Calcutta. She founded the Missionaries of Charity, and within thirty years it had nearly two hundred branches worldwide. She and her nuns cared for the chronically sick, the aged, physically disabled, and lepers. In 1971 she received the Pope *John XXIII peace prize and in 1979 the Nobel peace prize.

TERESA OF AVILA (1515–1582). Spanish *Carmelite mystic and writer. Born in Avila, she became a Carmelite about 1535, but not until twenty years later did she undergo a spiritual experience that made her resolve to restore Carmelite life to its original austerity. In 1562 she opened the first *convent of the Carmelite reform at Avila and there wrote *The Way of Perfection* to guide her *nuns. Other houses and other books followed. She influenced *John of the Cross to open a parallel house for *friars in 1568.

TERMINUS A QUO, TERMINUS AD QUEM (Lat. "the end from which and the end to which"). Terms used for the starting point and the conclusion of something under discussion. E.g., it could be said that the writing of the *NT took place between A.D. 50, the *terminus a quo*, and A.D. 100, the *terminus ad quem*.

TERRITORIALISM The view held in the 16th and 17th centuries that in a specific territory where there is a state church the civil authority has the right to determine what is the *doctrine. See also CUIUS REGIO, EIUS RELIGIO, COLLEGIALISM.

TERSTEEGEN, GERHARD (1697–1769). German *hymn writer. Born in Westphalia, he was converted at sixteen and later gave up his trade as a weaver for spiritual counseling and was supported by friends. He translated works by other mystics and wrote many hymns, including "God Reveals His Presence" and "Thou Hidden Love of God."

TERTULLIAN (c. 160–c. 220). African *Christian apologist. Born the son of a Roman official in Carthage, he had a good classical education, traveled widely, evidently became a lawyer, and was converted about 196. He was the first great writer of Christian material in Latin, though he had equal facility in Greek. By 210, disillusioned by the low quality of Christian practice, he had become a Montanist, but even the Montanists fell short of his expectations, and he reportedly founded his own *sect. He wrote apologetic, polemic, and ascetic works on a wide variety of subjects.

TEST ACT (1673). A piece of legislation passed by the English Parliament ostensibly as a safeguard against *Roman Catholicism. It required holders of public offices to swear allegiance to the king, to take *Communion according to Church of *England usage, and to declare against *transubstantiation. The act was suspended in 1829 and repealed officially in 1863.

TETRAGRAMMATON, THE The technical expression for the four Hebrew letters (consonants) that are the name of *God. In transliteration they become either YHWH (*Yahweh) or JHVH (*Jehovah).

TETRAPOLITAN CONFESSION (1530). Protestant *confession of *faith, known also as the Strasbourg Confession or the Swabian Confession. Prepared by Martin *Bucer and two colleagues for presentation to Emperor *Charles V, it was an unsuccessful attempt to reconcile Lutheran and *Reformed views, and is significant as the oldest German Reformed *confession.

TETZEL, JOHANN (c. 1465–1519). *Dominican *friar. It was his selling of *indulgences in the Wittenberg area that prompted Luther's *Ninety-Five Theses in 1517 and so precipitated the *Reformation. He had earlier been papal inquisitor in Poland, then in Saxony.

TEUTONIC KNIGHTS German religious military *order. Founded in Palestine about 1190 during the Third Crusade, it was originally a hospital brotherhood. By the close of the century, it had taken on a military character. Soon afterward it helped Hungarians and Poles against pagan neighbors. The latter alliance gave it control of Prussia. The *pope allowed the Knights to engage in trading by releasing them from their *vow of *poverty. With power came opposition and military reverses, and the order had a checkered history until its original dedication to hospital work, and now to education, was reestablished in 1929.

TEXTUAL CRITICISM The study of the Hebrew, Aramaic, and Greek texts from which *Bible translations are made. There is not one single ancient text of the Bible, and so scholars do meticulous work on the existing manuscripts to decide which reading (when there are several or none) is the original one. See also BIBLICAL CRITICISM.

TEXTUS RECEPTUS (Lat. "The Received Text"). The Greek *NT that was widely used in the *Byzantine church and that from the 16th to the end of the 19th century appeared in printed versions of the NT. The *King James Version is based primarily on this text, but the Revised Version and more recent modern versions are not.

THANKSGIVING DAY An American and Canadian holiday for harvest thanksgiving and to commemorate the first harvest of Plymouth Colony in 1621 after the arrival of the *Pilgrim Fathers. Canada observes the holiday on the second Monday of October; the U.S. observes it on on the fourth Thursday of November.

THAUMATURGUS (Lat. "*miracle worker"). A title given to certain "*saints" who were known to have performed miracles either in their own lifetime or when canonized in answer to the *prayers of the faithful (e.g., St. Anthony of Padua [1195–1231]).

THEANDRIC ACTS The activity of *Jesus as the God-Man. What he performs as man, he also performs as *God, for he is two *natures in one *Person.

THEATINES A Roman Catholic *religious *order founded in Rome in 1524 by two *priests: *Cajetan (1480–1547) and Giovanni Pietro Caraffa, later Paul IV. Originally "Clerks Regular of the Divine Providence," the Theatines aimed to reform the church from the corruption of the age just after the *Reformation.

THEISM, CHRISTIAN (Gk. *theos*, "*God"). While *Judaism and Islam teach theism, the *Christian approach is different. Christians teach that there is one *God who is the Creator of the *universe. He is self-existent, *infinite, *eternal, without *body or shape, changeless, perfect, and personal. These may be looked at separately. (1) *God is One*. There is one God and one alone: this is *monotheism. However, for the Christian who emphasizes the unity of God, there is also the *Trinity of *Persons within the unity of God. (2) *God is the Creator*. To claim this is not only to hold that God made the *universe but that he also keeps it in being as the Sustainer and Upholder. (3) *God is self-existent*. Nothing or no one is responsible for his existence. God is wholly and entirely self-sufficient. (4) *God is *infinite*. He possesses none of the space limitations of human beings. (5) *God is eternal*. God is timeless, not limited by past, present, or future. (6) *God is without *body or shape*. As infinite and eternal, God is nonspatial and bodiless—pure *Spirit. (7) *God is changeless*. To change is only possible within time; God is outside time—in *eternity. God exists in a timeless present. (8) *God is perfect*. He is perfect in holiness, *love, *righteousness, *justice, *wisdom, knowledge, and power. (9) *God is personal*. As perfect Spirit and as Creator of human beings, God has personal relationships with his creatures. Within himself as Holy Trinity, God is also personal, for he is three Persons (Father, Son, and Holy Spirit).

For the Christian, God always remains higher than our highest thoughts and is greater than the most enlightened statements. Our words and phrases are signposts pointing to the amazing Reality who is God. See also DEISM, GOD, MYSTERY, POLYTHEISM, TRINITY.

THEISTIC EVOLUTION See EVOLUTION, THEISTIC.

THEOBALD (d. 1161). *Archbishop of Canterbury from 1138. Born in Normandy, he was monk, *prior, and *abbot of the famous abbey of Bec there before going to Canterbury. Known as a gifted administrator and an encourager of learning, he trained a number of those who became prominent churchmen, notably Thomas *Becket.

THEOCRACY Government by *God. A form of government of a people in which *God is seen as the sole ruler (though acting through priestly or prophetic *mediators). *Israel, as a twelve-tribe confederacy, was originally a theocracy. Something approaching a theocracy was attempted by certain medieval popes (e.g., Gregory VII) and by the Puritans under Oliver *Cromwell in England after 1649.

THEODICY The *justification of *God. The attempt to vindicate God's *love and *providence in the context of the tremendous problem of *evil and *suffering in God's world. Sometimes theodicy is another word for *natural *theology.

THEODORE OF MOPSUESTIA (c. 350–c. 428). Biblical interpreter. Born and educated at Antioch (modern Antakya, Turkey), he became a monk, was ordained in 381, and was consecrated *bishop of Mopsuestia (Cilicia). In an age of theological controversy in the church, he anticipated modern critical methods in approaching biblical interpretation, criticized *Origen for neglecting the literal sense of *Scripture, held *doctrines of the *Incarnation condemned at the Council of *Ephesus, and is regarded as a champion of the *faith by the Nestorian churches.

THEODORE OF STUDIUM (759–826). *Abbot and reformer. He was abbot of a *monastery near Mount Olympus (modern Turkey) when he was exiled for opposing the emperor *Charlemagne's adulterous second marriage (795), but he was restored when Irene became empress. After his community transferred to Studius, Constantinople, he was involved in further controversy: first with his *patriarch Nicephorus, leading to a further two-year exile; then over his defense of *image *worship in the *Iconoclastic Controversy; and generally over his view of the church's independence of the *state.

THEODORE OF TARSUS (c. 602–690). *Archbishop of Canterbury from 669. Born in Tarsus and consecrated in Rome in 668, he was the first archbishop to take control of the whole English church. He appointed *bishops to vacant sees, called the Council of *Hertford (673), deposed *Wilfrid from the see of York but restored him in 686, and generally reorganized the church so as to pave the way for the parochial system.

THEODORET (c. 393–c. 458). *Bishop of Cyrrhus (Syria). Born in Antioch, he became a monk about 416 and, much against his will, bishop in 423. A systematic biblical expositor who cared little for the allegorical method of the Alexandrian school, he tried to exercise a moderating influence in contemporary theological disputes. Theodoret was accused of *Nestorianism, was deposed by the Robber Synod of *Ephesus (449), partly vindicated at the Council of *Chalcedon (451), but remained an individualist with a hearty distrust of *Monophysitism.

THEODOSIUS I (c. 346–395). Roman emperor from 379 and sometimes called "The Great." Born and educated in Spain, he was a soldier with Balkan experience when appointed by Gratian to bring order to the Eastern Empire, a task he carried out with considerable skill. To bring peace to warring factions, he imposed on the empire the *creed of Nicea. Then to further the use of the creed, he convened the Second Council of *Constantinople in 381.

THEODULF (c. 750–821). *Bishop of Orléans. Born probably in Spain, he became a member of the court of *Charlemagne and was consecrated in 775. In 804 he succeeded *Alcuin as the emperor's theological adviser and defended the Roman Catholic *doctrine of the Holy *Spirit against Eastern theologians. Patron of the *arts, restorer of churches, and reforming *bishop within his own *diocese, Theodulf was deposed for dubious reasons by Charlemagne's son Louis in 818, was banished to a *monastery, and died there three years later.

THEOLOGIA CRUCIS, THEOLOGIA GLORIAE (Lat. "*theology of the *cross," "theology of glory"). Two expressions used by *Luther. He emphasized that true knowledge of *God is derived not from the use of *reason (*theologia gloriae*) but from knowing the God who in humiliation and *suffering died on the cross (*theologia crucis*). In comparison with the knowledge of God derived from the Incarnate *Son of God who died for us, that knowledge derived from the use of human reason is minimal and sometimes wrong.

THEOLOGIA GERMANICA A book written in the late 14th century about spiritual union with *God. It was printed by *Luther and was later highly appreciated by both German and English Pietists. The English translation by Susanna Winkworth appeared in 1854.

THEOLOGICAL VIRTUES A medieval way of describing *faith, *hope, and *love (1 Cor 13) and means of contrasting them with the *cardinal virtues. A theological *virtue is a good habit of mind or *will and is approved by *God.

THEOLOGUMENON, THEOLOGOUMENON A theological statement by a believing theologian, not the official *dogma of a church.

THEOLOGY The science or study of *God. In traditional terminology this is divided into the following types: *apophatic theology, *biblical theology, dogmatic theology (*dogmatics), *fundamental theology, *historical theology, *natural theology, polemical theology, *revealed theology, and *systematic theology. However, in modern times the word has become a generic term for the study of a wide variety of subjects (e.g., *OT, *NT, church history, *ethics, *philosophy of religion, et al.).

THEONOMY (Gk. *theos,* "*God"; *nomos,* "law"). The teaching that the ultimate moral authority for a person is in the divine *will and law. It has been used by Paul *Tillich (1886–1965) with reference to a principle or law that fulfills a person's being by uniting it with the ground and source of all *being, God.

THEOPASCHITES Those who hold that *God suffered, inasmuch as it was *Christ's divine *nature that endured the agony at *Calvary. The *doctrine was taught by a section of the Monophysites from the early 6th century as part of their thesis that Christ had only one nature. Although it had weighty support for a time, it was soon condemned in both *Eastern and Western churches. The normal Christian teaching is that the *eternal *Son of God suffered not in his divine but in his human nature.

THEOPHANY An appearance of *God, in a visible yet temporary form as was experienced by *Israel (e.g., Exod 33:17–23). The *Incarnation was not a theophany for the *eternal *Son of God really and actually took human *nature as his own and was seen and touched as man.

THEOPHILUS (d. c. 412). *Patriarch of Alexandria. Appointed in 385, he soon showed himself the implacable enemy of non-Christian *religions by destroying the pagan temples of North Africa. At first he thought highly of *Origen, but from 401 he denounced Origen's writings, persecuting those monks who differed and ordering their *monasteries destroyed. Challenged by John *Chrysostom in Constantinople, where many of the monks had fled, Theophilus went there and, at the *Synod of the Oak (403), had John condemned and exiled—in which action he did himself irreparable harm.

THEOPNEUSTOS
(Gk. "God-breathed, inspired by *God"). The word used only in 2 Timothy 3:16 of the *inspiration of the Jewish *Scriptures by God. It has thus been subjected to careful scrutiny in order to help theologians arrive at a *doctrine of the inspiration of the *Bible.

THEOSIS (Gk. "deification, divinization"). The *doctrine taught in the *Orthodox churches that *salvation from *sin is a process of *deification through the work of the Holy *Spirit. Carelessly stated, this can sound as if a person actually becomes as *God or as a part of God. Carefully stated, it means that man, made in God's image and likeness, has developed to his full potential the *love and power of God after the model of *Christ.

THEOSOPHY An attempt to explain the meaning and purpose of life through a synthesis of information taken from such sources as *religion (especially Hinduism), philosophy, science, and the study of the *occult. The Theosophical Society was founded in New York City in 1875, and a breakaway movement, the Anthroposophical Society, was formed in 1912. It is esoteric in nature and has a limited following.

THEOTOKOS (Gk. "God-bearer"). The title given to *Mary, mother of *Jesus, because her Son is truly *God made man. It was used at the *ecumenical councils of *Ephesus (431) and *Chalcedon (451) and became a standard word within *orthodoxy. Its purpose is to ensure that Mary's Son be thought of as God made man and that Mary not be elevated.

THÉRÈSE OF LISIEUX (1873–1897). Roman Catholic nun and *saint. Known as Theresa of the Child Jesus. With two of her isters, Thérèse entered the Carmelite convent of Lisieux in Normandy, France, in 1888. Though her outward life was uneventful, her interior spiritual life was so intense that she was commanded by her superior to write her autobiography, *Story of a Soul,* which has since become a classic of the genre. She is arguably the most popular Catholic saint of the past few generations. She spoke of her "little way" of trust in and love for *God, which she said every person in any walk of life could receive and attain.

THIELICKE, HELMUT (1908–1986). Prolific and distinguished German theologian. Born in Barmen, he sided with the *Confessing church and opposed Hitler; he exercised a powerful *preaching *ministry in bomb-shattered Stuttgart. He was professor in Tübingen (1945–1954) and in Hamburg (1954–1974). His published sermons, for which he is best known in the English-speaking world, were delivered in St. Michael's Cathedral, Hamburg. One series was on the *Apostles' Creed, called in English *I Believe*. His theological works include the vast four-volume *Theological Ethics* and a three-volume *dogmatics, *The Evangelical Faith*. Not translated into English is his important *Mensch sein—Mensch werden: Entwurf einer christlichen Anthropologie*. Among modern German theologians he stood out as doctrinally conservative, affirming all the traditional credal statements with the exception of the virginal conception of *Jesus, over the historicity of which he claimed to be agnostic.

THIRD WAVE A term used to designate a movement that is similar to the *Pentecostal movement (first wave) and *charismatic movement (second wave) but is composed largely of evangelical Christians who, while applauding and supporting the work of the *Spirit in the first two waves, have chosen not to be identified with either. The third wave, which began to form in the 1980s, may be characterized by, among other things, belief that the baptism in the Spirit occurs at *conversion rather than as a second work of *grace; low-key acceptance of speaking in tongues but not as the initial validation of Spirit baptism; focus on community rather than individuals; and avoidance of divisiveness.

THIRTY YEARS' WAR (1618–1648). Originally a religious conflict between Roman Catholics and Protestants, it spread to political issues until finally most of the nations of Europe were involved. It began with a revolt of Bohemian Protestants against Austria and ended with the Peace of Westphalia by which France and Sweden gained territory, Switzerland and the Netherlands had their independence recognized, and the growth of nationalism among German states was greatly advanced.

THIRTY-NINE ARTICLES, THE The 16th-century doctrinal statement of the Church of *England. The articles evolved through a succession of statements, beginning with the *Ten Articles of 1536, but were not completed until the time of *Elizabeth, three monarchs later. In fact, it was thirteen years into her reign (1563) before a convocation finally settled on the articles as they appear now. Since 1865 *clerical subscription to the articles has been mandatory.

THOLUCK, FRIEDRICH AUGUST GOTTREU (1799–1877). German theologian. A specialist in Oriental languages, converted under the influence of Pietist friends, he was subsequently longtime professor of *theology at Halle until his death. He exercised a profound influence on generations of students and others through his theological works and biblical commentaries, not least through a pastoral *ministry in the university and a steady championing of *orthodoxy.

THOMAS À KEMPIS See KEMPIS, THOMAS À.

THOMAS AQUINAS See AQUINAS, THOMAS.

THOMAS, JOHN (1805–1871). Founder of the *Christadelphians.

Born in London, where he studied medicine, he emigrated to New York in 1832. He joined the *Disciples of Christ but soon rejected that and other *denominations and organized societies in which primitive *Christianity would be restored. Out of these came the Christadelphians ("brothers of *Christ") in 1848.

THOMAS, W. H. GRIFFITH (1861–1924). Ordained Church of *England minister. Rector (1885–1905), principal, Wycliffe Hall, Oxford University (1905–1910), and professor at Wycliffe College, University of Toronto (1910–1919), he wrote twenty-one books and helped found Dallas Theological Seminary.

THOMISM The philosophical and theological system expounded by Thomas *Aquinas and by his followers. This remains the classic expression of *faith in rational terms within the Roman Catholic Church, in which Aquinas is known as "Doctor of the Church." Much more than a *Christian use of Aristotle's philosophy and *ethics, Thomism is a system that draws its material and method from many sources of which Aristotle is a major but not only one, for the church *fathers are much used as are the *Scriptures. See also SUMMA.

THORNWELL, JAMES HENLEY (1812–1862). Southern *Presbyterian minister and educator. Born and educated in South Carolina, he was a *pastor before joining the faculty of what later became the University of South Carolina, becoming its president (1851–1855) and then serving as professor of *systematic *theology at Columbia Theological Seminary. Thornwell founded the *Southern Presbyterian Review* (1847) and, being a secessionist, helped to found the *Presbyterian Church in the Confederate States.

THURIBLE The censer (*vessel) suspended on chains in which incense is burned during liturgical services. Usually a cup-shaped metal vessel, it contains charcoal and incense. The one who carries it is called the thurifer.

TIARA The papal crown worn by the *bishop of Rome outside regular services of *worship. It is a tall, triple crown shaped like a beehive. The three crowns represent his claim to universal spiritual rule of the church, his primacy of jurisdiction in the church, and his rule of *Vatican City. Traditionally it is placed on the *pope's head at his coronation. Some modern popes have chosen not to wear it.

TIILILÄ, OSMO ANTERO (1904–1972). Finnish theologian. Ordained in 1926, he left the Lutheran *state church in 1960 as a protest against the unchecked advance of *liberalism, which neglected the *preaching of the *Word. He was an influential figure with membership in the Academy of Sciences in Finland, but very few of his many writings have been rendered into English.

TIKHON (1866–1925). *Patriarch of Moscow. Son of an Orthodox *priest, he was trained at St. Petersburg. He was a monk and a *bishop in (modern) Poland and in the U.S. before returning to Russia in 1907. He became patriarch in 1917, condemned the Bolshevik takeover of church property, and saw many of his *priests killed or jailed. He himself was imprisoned for a time but was released in 1923 because of world opinion. He recognized the legitimacy of the communist government, but his last two years saw the church seriously divided.

TILLICH, PAUL (1886–1965). American theologian and philosopher. Born in Germany, which he left because of opposition to Hitler, he taught at Union Theological Seminary (1933) and Harvard (1955) and became one of the leading theologians of the century. For Tillich, man's quest was to be reunited with *God, from whom the *Fall had estranged him. He wrote many books, notably his three-volume *Systematic Theology* (1951–1963). See also THEONOMY.

TILLOTSON, JOHN (1630–1694). *Archbishop of Canterbury from 1691. Born in Yorkshire and educated at

Cambridge, he was originally Nonconformist but accepted the Act of *Uniformity in 1661. He was later dean of Canterbury (1670), then of St. Paul's (1689) before replacing the suspended Archbishop Sancroft at Canterbury. A distinguished preacher who would have liked to see all Trinitarian non-Roman Catholics in the Church of *England, he was the first married *primate for over a century.

TIME AND ETERNITY Because the *Incarnation took place in time (Gal 4:4), the nature of time is acute for *Christian thinkers. The problem of time includes the problem of history but also relates to the *nature of *God—e.g., Is he timeless or existing in timelessness? Is *eternity the same as timelessness? The general biblical view of time is linear, and on this time line are important points at which God involves himself in time. Of these, Creation (when time began), the Incarnation, and the *Second Coming are the most important. In the light of modern science, it is necessary to link the problem of time with that of space and work toward a theological resolution of how the *eternal God relates to this space-time continuum in which we live.

TINDAL, MATTHEW (c. 1656–1733). English deist. Fellow of All Souls College, Oxford, from 1678, he briefly became a Roman Catholic under *James II, returned to the Church of *England, but was soon calling himself a "*Christian deist" and strongly advocating *Erastianism, as well as scandalizing the House of Commons. Among his works were *The Rights of the Christian Church* (1706) and *Christianity as Old as the Creation* (1730).

TINTORETTO, JACOPO (1518–1594). Italian painter. Born in Venice, he is regarded as one of the most significant of the late *Renaissance school. Largely self-taught and a man of deep *faith who worked in Venice for most of his life, he produced many masterpieces, including *Miracle of Saint Mark, Christ and the Adulteress,* and *The Last Supper*.

TISCHENDORF, KONSTANTIN VON (1815–1874). German *NT scholar. After studies at Leipzig, he traveled to libraries throughout Europe to reexamine Greek NT manuscripts and other biblical sources. In the Near East he collected material in Greek, Arabic, Hebrew, Coptic, Ethiopian, and other languages. His most notable discovery was the *Codex Sinaiticus. Nominally professor at Leipzig from 1845, Tischendorf published many editions of the Greek NT, the last of which was the standard work on the subject for many years.

TITHES The payment of a tenth part of all the produce of the lands to *God or to his cause. This is what happened in *Israel (Deut 14:22) and was in operation in the time of *Jesus (Matt 23:23). In *Christian countries in medieval and early modern times farmers commonly gave the parish church a tenth of crops. In some countries a national church tax still supports the *state church. Some Christians still tithe (give a tenth of their earnings to Christian work).

TITIAN (c. 1477–1576). Italian painter. Early encouraged by his father, he received a good training in Venice, a city in which, like his near contemporary Tintoretto, he spent a large part of his life. Titian nonetheless traveled considerably and was highly regarded by the crowned heads and aristocracy of Europe. His many beautiful works include *Tribute Money, Assumption, Ecce Homo,* and *Christ Crowned with Thorns*.

TOLAND, JOHN (1670–1722). Deist. Born into an Irish Roman Catholic family, he converted to *Protestantism at sixteen, studied at various universities (1687–1695), then wrote *Christianity Not Mysterious* (1696), in which he claimed that divine *revelation was not necessary to understand certain biblical *doctrines. The work provoked criminal proceedings against him in England and Ireland. His writings, some of them concerning the Jews, continued to arouse controversy right up until his death.

TOLERATION The official decision by government to leave undisturbed those citizens whose *faith/*religion and practice is not that accepted by the *state. Thus the Toleration Act of 1689 in England gave specific rights to Christians who were not members of the Church of *England. In modern times toleration is seen more in the idea of tolerating all religions and accepting the reality of a pluralistic society. After the Edict of *Milan (313) the church gained legal standing in the Roman Empire. Later, when dominant in society, the church was intolerant of other religions as well as of schismatic and heretical *Christian groups. Even the 16th-century Reformers did not wish to tolerate in their churches or outside them *doctrines and groups that were directly critical of the new status quo. But Protestant principles necessitate toleration of at least related Christian groups. However, the modern ideas of toleration in a pluralistic society stem not from Christian principles but from the philosophies and activities of humanists and atheists and from the need for realism in terms of the make-up of modern society.

TOLERATION ACT (1689). Parliamentary legislation that at the start of *William III's reign gave some relief to Nonconformists who had suffered under the later Stuart monarchs. They were permitted to have their own *pastors, teachers, and church buildings. Acceptance of the *Thirty-Nine Articles was the price to be paid for these concessions, but Nonconformists, like Roman Catholics, were still debarred from public office.

TOLKIEN, JOHN RONALD REUEL (1892–1973). English writer. Son of a South African bank manager, he was educated at Oxford, where he later held chairs of Anglo-Saxon (1925–1945) and English (1945–1959). Early influenced by Andrew Lang and George *MacDonald, he said that his nature "expresses itself about things deepest felt in tales and myths." He was well into middle age and was little known when he began *The Hobbit* (1937). *The Lord of the Rings* (1954–1955) took twelve years to write. A lifelong Roman Catholic, Tolkien was deeply pained at the dropping of the Latin *Mass and regretted the return of his friend C. S. *Lewis to *Anglicanism.

TOLSTOY, LEO (1828–1910). Russian novelist and social reformer. Born into a noble family in Tula Province, his experiences in the Crimea War resulted in his *Tales from Sebastopol* (1855). After demobilization he traveled in Europe and returned to start a school for peasant children. He freed his serfs, identified with the *poor, rejected orthodox *faith, and professed "*Christian anarchism." Meanwhile, he was writing his great novels, *War and Peace* (1860) and *Anna Karenina* (1877), but in *A Confession* (1882) he told something of his endless spiritual quest.

TONGUES, SPEAKING IN
See Glossolalia.

TOPLADY, AUGUSTUS MONTAGUE (1740–1778). Anglican *hymn writer. Educated at Trinity College, Dublin, and ordained in 1762, he held various incumbencies in England. He was a strong Calvinist and wrote about his views in two books, but he is better remembered for his hymns, notably "Rock of Ages," published in the *Gospel Magazine* in 1775, and "A Debtor to Mercy Alone."

TORAH (Heb. "law, teaching"). Any teaching is torah, but *God's torah, found preeminently in the books of Moses, normally came to the Israelites through *prophet or *priest. Thus these five books are often called Torah. See also Pentateuch.

TORGAU ARTICLES, THE Lutheran confessional statements of the 16th century. On three occasions (1530; 1574; 1576) articles were drawn up at Torgau, Germany, in response to crises that had arisen in the Lutheran movement. The first article dealt with the Roman Catholic question; the second dealt with the *Eucharist, and the third dealt with intramural Lutheran squabbles. These final articles, after extensive revision, were incorporated into the Formula of *Concord (1577), which became a point of reference and agreement for all Lutherans.

TORQUEMADA, TOMAS DE (1420–1498). First grand inquisitor of Spain. Of Jewish descent, he had been a *Dominican *prior and royal confessor before appointment as grand inquisitor in 1483. During his tenure some two thousand people were executed, including Jews, Muslims, witches, and heretics. So cruel was he that his name has become synonymous with that of the *Inquisition itself.

TORREY, REUBEN ARCHER (1856–1928). *Presbyterian *evangelist, educator, and writer. Born in New Jersey and educated at Yale and in Germany, he was ordained to the Congregational *ministry in 1878, and in 1889 accepted D. L. *Moody's invitation to become superintendent of what was later known as the Moody Bible Institute (he served until 1908). He was superintendent of city *missions in Minneapolis, had several world evangelistic tours, wrote numerous books, founded the Montrose Bible Conference, and ministered in Los Angeles (1912–1924), where he helped organize the Church of the Open Door and was dean of the Bible Institute of Los Angeles (now Biola University).

TOTAL DEPRAVITY The complete effect of the *Fall on human beings. As a result of the entrance of *sin into the world, each person is totally affected—every part imperfect but not necessarily totally corrupted. The "total" refers to the whole person—*body, mind, and *will—and not to the amount of depravity. This is primarily an *Augustinian, Calvinistic type of *doctrine and is not accepted by those who follow the teaching of the Greek fathers, *Pelagianism, and *Arminianism. In reference to the doctrine of *salvation, total depravity means that a person can do nothing toward salvation, for even *repentance and *faith are totally dependent upon *God.

TRACTARIANISM The first stages of what later became known as the *Oxford Movement or the *Anglo-Catholic Movement. In the period 1833–1841 J. H. *Newman wrote and edited a series of ninety tracts. Their purpose was to call the Church of *England back to its Catholic (in contrast to Protestant) roots. This activity of writing controversial tracts, which seemed to grow in length each year, was the basis of Tractarianism but not the only activity of the Oxford theologians who produced them.

TRACTARIANS See OXFORD MOVEMENT.

TRADITION The teaching and practice of the church over the centuries. This includes the interpretation of the *Bible but not the Bible itself. Tradition is handed on from generation to generation along with the Bible. At the *Reformation different attitudes to tradition emerged. Protestants rejected much of the tradition that had arisen in the medieval period and insisted that they wanted to return to the *faith and practice of the early church. Roman Catholics accepted, with some pruning and purification, the general Western tradition and so gave the impression that they gave equal weight to the Bible and tradition. No church can escape from creating a tradition in terms of a belief system, *hermeneutics, a form of *worship, type of *spirituality, and forms of *ministry.

TRADITOR A person who surrendered the *Scriptures to the persecuting civil power when possessing the *Christian *Bible was forbidden. The name was used in North Africa during the persecution in the reign of *Diocletian (284–305).

TRADUCIANISM (Lat. *tradux,* "offshoot, sprout"). The theory that the human *soul is transmitted by parents to the child—sometimes also called generationism. The theory more commonly accepted in the church is *creationism, which asserts that each soul is created by *God at conception.

TRANSCENDENCE OF GOD The presence of *God outside and beyond the created order. God outside the space-time continuum and beyond the comprehension of human minds. If God is *infinite and *eternal (see THEISM), then he is transcendent. However, if transcendence alone is emphasized, then the result is *deism—God outside but not inside the *universe. Thus the *immanence of God is usually stated along with his transcendence.

TRANSEPT Part of a church, at right angles to the nave. It normally intersects in front of the *choir, where there often is a tower or dome.

TRANSFIGURATION The appearing of *Jesus in glory (with Elijah and Moses in attendance) to his *disciples on the mountainside (Matt 17:1–13; Mark 9:2–13; Luke 9:28–36). This was an anticipation of the glory he would have after the *resurrection as the *Son of *God in glorified human nature. This event is celebrated in the East and West on August 6.

TRANSFINALIZATION The view of the presence of *Christ in the *Eucharist that assumes that the words of consecration change the purpose, or finality, of the bread and wine. They then serve a new function but are not necessarily changed into the actual *body and *blood of Christ. See also TRANSUBSTANTIATION.

TRANSGRESSION The failure to obey the law of *God and thus a manifestation of human *sin (Rom 4:15; 5:14; Heb 2:2; 9:15). See also SIN.

TRANSIGNIFICATION The view of the presence of *Christ in the *Eucharist that assumes that the meaning or significance of the bread and wine is changed by the words of *consecration. The actual substance of bread and wine remain, but they bear a higher, nobler value and significance. See also TRANSUBSTANTIATION.

TRANSMIGRATION OF SOULS The belief that at death the *soul of man will gain a new form of existence. It may be in a new baby (*reincarnation) or as an animal, bird, or reptile (*metempsychosis).

TRANSUBSTANTIATION The official teaching of the Roman Catholic Church that assumes that the bread and wine completely change into the real *body and *blood of *Christ at the *consecration. This *doctrine was first stated with clarity by Thomas *Aquinas, and the Fourth Council of the Lateran (1215) made the first official use of the term. Some modern Roman Catholics modify it by speaking in terms of either *transfinalization or *transignification (Lutherans, of *consubstantiation).

TRAPPISTS A reformed branch of the *Cistercians. Begun by A. J. *de Rancé in 1664, it took its name from the Cistercian abbey of La Trappe in Normandy. Trappists emphasize silence, manual labor, community life, liturgical *prayer and *contemplation, and abstention from meat, fish, and eggs. "Trappistines" are members of the parallel *order for women.

TRAVERS, WALTER (c. 1548–1635). Puritan minister and writer. Born in Nottingham, he graduated at Cambridge, spent four years in Geneva (where he adopted the *presbyterian *polity) and four years ministering to a Calvinist church in Antwerp. He was deputy master of the Temple Church in London (under Thomas *Hooker), but he would not take Anglican *orders and was debarred from further preferment in England. He became provost of Trinity College, Dublin (1594–1598), where he was said to have "definitely influenced the whole Irish Church in favor of Puritanism," most notably as the teacher of James *Ussher. A strong defender of the *Reformed position in his writings, he made a notable posthumous contribution to the proceedings of the *Westminster Assembly.

TREASURY OF THE CHURCH Also called the Treasury of Merit. A development of the idea of the communion of *saints, it holds that good done by some can benefit others. *Jesus Christ and many saints did more than *God expected of them in terms of good to others. Thus a kind of treasury of *merit has been built up. A tendency in medieval times to think of this treasury in a literal manner allowed the development of *indulgences. Today Roman Catholic theologians usually explain the phrase as a metaphor. The Holy *Spirit unites *Christ and all believers in *love; thus what Christ achieved in himself and in his saints benefits other Christians, who are weak in *faith and *love. So the communion of saints becomes an intercommunion of merit. See also SUPEREROGATION, WORKS OF.

TREGELLES, SAMUEL PRIDEAUX (1813–1875). English biblical scholar. Born to Quaker parents in Cornwall, he showed a facility for languages even while earning his living in an iron works, and from 1838 he devoted himself to the biblical text and allied subjects. His many valuable contributions include Greek, Hebrew, and Chaldee concordances; *An Account of the Printed Text of the Greek *NT* (1854); and many books on *Bible *prophecy. Aberdeen University gave this self-taught man an honorary doctorate.

TRENCH, RICHARD CHENEVIX (1807–1886). *Archbishop of Dublin. A Cambridge graduate ordained in 1832, divinity professor at London, and dean of Westminster before going to Dublin in 1863, he was a philological expert who influenced the *Oxford English Dictionary,* wrote authoritatively on *parables and *miracles, and strongly opposed *Gladstone's plan to disestablish the Church of Ireland.

TRENT, COUNCIL OF (1545–63). The 19th *ecumenical council of the Roman Catholic Church. Called by Pope *Paul III, the assembly in the north Italian town was faced with the task of reforming the church in the face of *Protestantism and of clarifying the church's teaching on many vexing issues. It fixed the *canon of the *OT and *NT; gave a place to *tradition in the church's teaching; accepted as the basis of *faith the version of the *Nicene Creed endorsed by the Council of *Chalcedon in 451 (somewhat ambiguously called the Niceno-Constantinopolitan Creed); and pronounced on other matters, such as the number of *sacraments, *justification by *faith, and *original *sin. The work of the council, done during three periods (1545–1547, 1551–1552, 1562–1563), was summarized in the so-called *Tridentine Creed, and led to publication of a *catechism (1566), a revised *breviary (1568), and a *missal (1570). The council forced the church to clarify its thinking and *doctrine, and while it was criticized for offering too little too late, it made a marked contribution to the *Counter-Reformation.

TRESPASS A falling from the right way (Matt 6:14–15) and thus a false step or *transgression (Col 2:13). See also SIN.

TRIBULATION, THE GREAT An expression used especially by teachers of *dispensationalism to refer to seven years of intense sorrow and persecution before the *second coming of *Christ and the inauguration by him of the Millennium (Matt 24:21–30). There is debate as to whether or not the church will pass through this tribulation; some hold that a secret *rapture of the *saints will precede it.

TRICHOTOMISM The view that there are three basic parts to a human being—*body, *soul, and *spirit. The body is the living organism, the soul is the intellect and *will, while the spirit is that by which communion with *God is possible. Two verses are usually quoted: 1 Thessalonians 5:23 and Hebrews 4:12. See also DICHOTOMISM; MAN, CHRISTIAN VIEW OF.

TRIDENTINE That which originated at or developed from the Council of *Trent (Tridentum). E.g., the Tridentine *catechism, *Mass, and *theology.

TRINITARIANS (ORDER OF THE MOST HOLY TRINITY) An *order founded in France in 1198 by John of Matha and Felix of Valois with the aim of freeing *Christian slaves from Muslim captivity. One source gives the number of those thus redeemed at about 140,000. A *discalced branch founded in 1597 survives and is devoted to teaching, *missions, and charitable work.

TRINITY, DOCTRINE OF THE The central *doctrine of *Christianity. *God is One and God is Three—One in Three and Three in One. It is based on the teaching of the whole *Bible, especially the *revelation of God in *Jesus Christ. The *apostles began with the Jewish commitment to belief in one living God (*monotheism) and they recited the *Shema. They came to recognize God in Jesus of Nazareth, and they described him in such a way as to imply that he was God (e.g., as the **Logos* [''Word''] of John 1:1ff.). Further, they came to recognize that the Holy *Spirit was more than the power of God at work in them and in the world; in a mysterious way he was personal. They worshiped God the Father through God the Son in the power of the Holy Spirit, and they preached the *love of the Father in the Son by the Spirit.

The *NT has a skeleton of the doctrine of the Trinity (e.g., Matt 28:19; 1 Cor 12:4-6; 2 Cor 13:14 Gal 1:3-4; Eph 4:4-5; 2 Thess 2:13-14; Titus 3:4-6; 1 Peter 1:2; Jude 20, 21). The early church, not the *apostles, however, clothed the skeleton. The results are to be found in the *Nicene and *Athanasian Creeds. The first move was to assert that the *Lord Jesus is truly God. In whatever sense the Father is God so also is the Son; but the Son is not the Father, and the Father is not the Son. The Father and the Son are of the same *substance or *being (**homoousios*), yet they are two *Persons. In this, *Eastern and Western church agreed. But they differed in describing the internal (and thus *eternal) relations of the three Persons within the one Godhead—seen in the question of the relation of the Holy Spirit to the Father and the Son. Western theologians said the Spirit eternally proceeded from the Father and the Son (*filioque); Eastern theologians said (as in the original Niceno-Constantinopolitan Creed of 381) that he proceeds from the Father alone (or, they would say, from the Father through the Son). Westerners began with the idea of God's unity, while Easterners began with the Father's (logical) priority. The classical doctrine as found in the ancient *creeds has remained the teaching accepted by virtually all Christian churches. For attempts to illustrate it see Psychological Analogy, Social Analogy.

TRISAGION (Gk. ''thrice *holy''). A brief *hymn within ancient liturgies: ''Holy is *God; *holy and strong; *holy and immortal; have mercy on us.''

TRITHEISM The *doctrine that the three *Persons of the *Trinity are in fact three Gods.

TRIUMPHALISM Usually a pejorative term referring to the overconfidence or superiority (cultural and ecclesiastical) of churches, *missionary societies, and other groups in their dealings with people from backgrounds, countries, and groups different from their own.

TROELTSCH, ERNST (1865–1923). German historian and social philosopher. He is best remembered for *The Social Teaching of the Christian Churches* (1912; ET 1931), in which he analyzes what is perceived to be a collection of conflicting tendencies within the *theology of the church when it comes to the relation of church and society, tendencies that have made it ultimately impossible for the church to have any lasting impact on society as a whole. What should be learned from it all is that *God, as historical process (in Hegelian fashion), is moving within the forward thrust of time to resolve all conflicts within himself. Thus we should embrace relativism as a *virtue, seeing the absolute value of the relative flow and humbly accepting our place in the overall scheme of things. Theological *liberalism in the 20th century has generally embraced his relativism.

TROPOLOGY The spiritual, moral, or ethical sense of a (biblical) passage, it is found by penetrating through the literal sense. Tropology is the figurative sense of the passage that particularly relates to moral character (Gk. *tropos*, ''figure of speech or moral character''). It was much used in the millennium after the Alexandrian church of the 3d century developed it as a method of biblical interpretation. See also SENSES OF SCRIPTURE, SENSUS PLENIOR.

TROTTER, ISABELLA LILIAS (1853–1928). *Missionary to North Africa. Born in London into comfortable circumstances, she early showed aptitude as an artist in watercolor (John Ruskin called her ''darling Saint Lilias''), but she turned from painting to *missions—the words ''North Africa,'' she said, sounded in her *soul. She arrived in Algiers in 1888 with two colleagues, worked in remote areas and in the city, established *preaching stations, translated *Scripture into the vernacular, and painted *gospel *truths as well. She died in Algeria; her Algiers Mission Band is now part of the North Africa Mission.

TRUCE OF GOD Proclaimed by the Council of Elne (1027) to stem violence, the truce involved armistice periods of varying length that were later extended and included from Wednesday night until Monday morning and during special holidays. Diocesan *bishops had power to discipline offenders.

TRUETT, GEORGE W. (1867–1944). Gifted preacher. The best-known Southern Baptist in his generation, he was *pastor of First Baptist Church in Dallas from 1899 to 1944 and was a leader in the *Baptist World Alliance.

TRUTH This has a variety of meanings. (1) For the Hebrew, the truth is that which is trustworthy and reliable. Truth is embodied in a person and preeminently in the true *God, who is wholly reliable (Deut 32:4; 2 Chron 15:3). This *OT emphasis is found in the *NT, especially in John's *Gospel, where *Christ is presented as the truth (John 14:6). (2) Also in the NT there is the view of truth commonly found in Greek *culture, where truth is the object of intellectual knowledge (see 1 Tim 2:4). However, the dominant idea of truth in the NT is the reality of God making himself known in the world. (3) The church has preserved the dynamic, biblical idea over the centuries, but in such subjects as *systematic *theology truth is seen as accurate intellectual knowledge. Truth is rational. (4) Conscious of the *Bible's dynamic quality of truth, some theologians have emphasized that only in encounter with the living God is truth known; thus *dogmatics and systematic theology are human attempts to describe the reality of Truth (which is personal *Spirit, God).

TÜBINGEN SCHOOL A group of German (especially *NT) theologians who followed in the footsteps of F. C. *Baur (1792–1860). They applied the philosophy of historical development set forth by G. W. F. *Hegel to the history of the primitive church. They presupposed a radical division between Jewish (Petrine) and Gentile (Pauline) Christians, and this thesis/antithesis led to the synthesis of ''Catholic *Christianity.'' Cf. HEGELIANISM.

TUDOR, MARY (1516–1558). Queen of England from 1553. Daughter of *Henry VIII and Catherine of Aragon, Mary showed considerable spirit amid early adversity that saw her used as a pawn in political junketing, jilted by the emperor *Charles V, and snubbed and harassed by her father's second wife, Anne Boleyn. From her accession Mary determined to restore England to *Roman Catholicism. She married *Philip II of Spain in 1554 and gained the description ''Bloody Mary'' when a relentless persecution made *martyrs of many Protestants, including Thomas *Cranmer, Hugh *Latimer, and Nicholas *Ridley. Her marriage was unhappy and childless, her foreign policy was misguided, and she alienated nobility and Parliament. Her short reign did nothing to commend Roman Catholicism in the country.

TULCHAN BISHOPS A derogatory term applied to holders of episcopal titles in Scotland under the Regent Morton (1572–1578), who wanted to be supreme ruler. He persuaded Parliament to decree uniformity of *worship under an episcopal system. The Tulchan *bishops thus appointed were often unworthy, as records indicate. A tulchan was a calf's skin stuffed with straw to make the cow give milk. The human tulchans agreed to hold a benefice nominally but to give most of the income to the regent and his colleagues.

TULIP A mnemonic to remember the *Five Points of Calvinism produced by the Synod of *Dort (1618–1619): *total depravity, unconditional *election, *limited atonement, *irresistible *grace, and *perseverance of the *saints.

TUTIORISM A system of *moral *theology sometimes called extreme rigorism. In case of doubt one must always abide by the established rule or law. There is no such thing as "doubtful freedom." Most theologians reject it as too demanding. See also RIGORISM.

TWELVE ARTICLES, THE (1525). The claims made in the charter of the *Peasants' Revolt in Germany against their feudal lords. The document dealt with such matters as the abolition of serfdom; just conditions regarding employment, rent, and taxes; and fishing and hunting rights. If, said the last article, the demands made were incompatible with *Scripture, they would be withdrawn. While expressing initial sympathy, *Luther later sided with authority in the suppression of the peasants.

TWELVE GREAT FEASTS The twelve principal feast days in the church calendar of the *Eastern church. *Epiphany (January 6), *Presentation of Christ in the Temple (February 2), *Annunciation of the Blessed Virgin Mary (March 25), *Palm Sunday, *Ascension Day, *Pentecost, *Transfiguration of Christ (August 6), *Dormition of the Blessed Virgin Mary (August 15), *Presentation of the Blessed Virgin Mary in the Temple (November 21), and *Christmas Day (December 25). Since *Easter is the "Feast of feasts" it is not in this list but stands alone.

TWO SWORDS, DOCTRINE OF THE The teaching advocated by the *papacy in the Middle Ages concerning its power in the spiritual and temporal (secular) spheres. An exposition of this *doctrine is found in the papal *bull, *Unam Sanctam,* of *Boniface VIII in 1302. The idea of the two swords comes from Luke 22:35–38. The *pope was said to be sovereign in spiritual matters, and kings were said to rule on behalf of the pope and the church. This *doctrine is now generally regarded as historically and culturally conditioned and thus invalid for modern Roman Catholics.

TYNDALE, WILLIAM (c. 1495–1536). English biblical translator and *martyr. Educated at Oxford and Cambridge and ordained about 1521, he studied further under *Luther at Wittenberg and completed his *NT translation at Worms in 1526. Copies were smuggled into England, and his life was thereafter in danger. He continually revised that work, translated also parts of the *OT, and wrote *Obedience of a Christian Man* (1528). Tyndale followed Luther on the authority of *Scripture and on *justification by *faith but tended toward the sacramental views of *Zwingli. Possibly at *Henry VIII's instigation, he was betrayed to the imperial authorities and strangled and burned at the stake near Brussels. His translations formed the bases of the Authorized and Revised Versions of the *Bible.

TYPE, TYPOLOGY The approach to the *OT that sees there, in specific persons, events, *rituals, and ceremonies a foreshadowing of *Jesus Christ and the new *covenant that he inaugurated. A type is an example or a figure. The *NT suggests this approach of typology, especially in the Letter to the Hebrews, where Jesus is seen as a new Moses (3:2–6), a new high *priest

(4:14), and a new Melchizedek (6:20) and the ritual of the Day of *Atonement is applied to the death of *Christ (9:11–14).

Typology was popular with the Alexandrian school of *theology in the 3d century, and from this base it was much used in *exegesis for many years. It is a method that is always open to the danger of being overdeveloped so that virtually everything in the OT becomes a type.

TYRRELL, GEORGE (1861–1909). Roman Catholic modernist. Born in Dublin, he was converted from *Anglicanism to *Roman Catholicism and became a *Jesuit in 1880. He was ordained in 1891 and served the *order acceptably until 1899, when his writings began to rouse the suspicion of his superiors, who transferred him from London to the provinces. His modernist views led to dismissal from the Jesuits, and his continued defiance led to his being refused the *sacraments. Tyrrell nonetheless maintained an active devotional life and was highly regarded as a spiritual counselor, notably by F. von *Hügel, whose daughter he had greatly helped. When he died at age forty-eight after a life of chronic ill health, the Roman Catholic Church refused him a Catholic burial.

U

UBIQUITARIANISM (Lat. *ubique*, "everywhere"). The teaching of Martin *Luther and his followers that *Christ in his glorified human *nature is everywhere present by the operation of the Holy *Spirit, who makes the one Christ known in the world. Glorified humanity shares in the divine *omnipresence. This *doctrine was applied particularly to the *Eucharist and understood as the background to *consubstantiation. Calvinists firmly rejected it.

UBIQUITY (Lat. *ubique*, "everywhere"). Used of *God's omnipresence.

UCHIMURA, KANZO (1861–1930). Japanese *Christian leader. Converted at agricultural college in Sapporo, he studied further in the U.S., then taught high school in Tokyo until he found his position untenable as a Christian. He took to writing, advocated nondenominational Japanese *Christianity free from *missions control, and produced an impressive twenty-two-volume *Bible commentary.

UEMURA, MASAHISA (1857–1925). Japanese *pastor and scholar. Formerly a Shintoist of high rank, he was ordained as a *Presbyterian in 1879, began the *YMCA in Japan, and helped translate the *OT into Japanese. In 1905 he founded the Japan Theological Seminary. He fearlessly spoke out against contemporary *evils, greatly encouraged an indigenous church in Japan, aroused interest abroad through visits to the U.S. and Britain, and ministered in a large Tokyo church for over thirty years.

ULFILAS (ULPHILAS) (c. 311–c. 381). Described as "*Bishop of the Christians in Gothia." He was prominent in the *conversion of the Visigoths to a kind of *Arianism, having himself come from north of the Danube, and was consecrated by *Eusebius of Nicomedia, an Arian, about 341. Ulfilas is known to have translated a large part of the *Bible into Gothic.

ULTRAMONTANISM The movement toward centralization of authority in the Roman Catholic Church. While the word was known in the Middle Ages, it became more widely known during the 19th century with the failure of movements that sought to challenge papal authority. The latter was consolidated progressively with the *revival of the *Jesuits (1814), the publishing of the *Syllabus of Errors (1864), and the declaration of papal *infallibility (1870).

UNAMUNO, MIGUEL DE (1864–1936). Spanish scholar and writer. Professor of Greek at Salamanca, he was exiled (1924–1930) for opposing the monarchists, as he was later to defy the socialists. He denounced the materialism of the age, but Roman Catholics misunderstood him and put two of his books on the *Index. He disliked things like hypocrisy, dogmatism, and complacency; and in *The Agony of Christianity* (1928) he reminded people that *Christ had come not to bring peace but a sword.

UNBAPTIZED INFANTS Babies who die without *Christian *baptism. This occurrence created a theological problem for the medieval church. Because of the *doctrine of *original *sin, even "innocent" infants in or outside the womb were seen as having sinned in Adam's sin. Some theologians believed that it is possible to reach *heaven if one's sin is only original (and not actual); others said that such babies went to *Limbo—a state between heaven and *hell. Today it is commonly agreed that the *atonement of *Christ covers all infants who die before having committed *actual sin.

UNCTION The anointing with oil as part of a religious ceremony. This occurs as a basic element in the Roman Catholic and Orthodox *sacrament of *extreme unction; it is also used in *baptism and *confirmation. Unction is used metaphorically of the Holy *Spirit (2 Cor. 1:21; 1 John 2:20, 27). It is often used today in services of *healing, when people who desire healing are anointed with oil and hands are laid upon them as *prayer is offered.

UNDERGROUND CHURCHES Groups of Christians who meet secretly either for fear of persecution by the *state or because they are out of favor with the dominant church of their land. Examples of the former are found in Communist lands and of the latter in South America. The latter are usually in touch with *liberation *theology and have deep *ecumenical and social concerns.

UNDERHILL, EVELYN (1875–1941). English mystic. A graduate of King's College, London, she was converted in 1911 and soon produced *Mysticism* (1911) and *The Mystic Way* (1913). She was attracted by the piety of *Roman Catholicism and found a congenial spiritual director in Baron von *Hügel until his death in 1925, but her commitment was to the Church of *England. She wrote many other works and was theological editor of *The Spectator* (1929–1932).

UNIATE CHURCHES, UNIATISM A somewhat derogatory description for Eastern Christians who have the same *doctrines as the Roman Catholic Church but who use a different type of *liturgy (an Eastern type) and allow their *parish *priests to marry. They are found in Eastern Europe and the Middle East. Examples are the *Armenian and *Maronite churches. See also EASTERN CHURCHES.

UNIFICATION CHURCH Religious organization founded by the Reverend Sun Myung *Moon, its full name being The Holy Spirit Association for the Unification of World Christianity. The fundamental document of the Unification Church is Moon's book *Divine Principle* (1957). In it Moon teaches a dual *fall—one spiritual and one physical. The spiritual fall was corrected by *Jesus *Messiah, who was not *God, but a perfect man. His crucifixion (a mistake) disqualified Jesus from fulfilling man's physical *redemption in marriage. We await now a second messiah who will effect this physical redemption. It is not clear whether Moon is thought to be that messiah.

UNIFORMITY, ACTS OF Legislation that sought to enforce conformity to the *rites of the Church of *England. The 1549 Act ordered that the First Book of *Common Prayer be used in English churches. The 1559 Act was concerned to implement the *Elizabethan Settlement of the Church of England. The 1662 Act, passed after the *Restoration, called on all ministers to give consent to the revised Elizabethan Prayer Book and, where lacking, to obtain episcopal *ordination. Some two thousand chose not to conform at this time.

UNION, HYPOSTATIC See HYPOSTATIC UNION.

UNION WITH CHRIST The *doctrine developed primarily from Pauline *theology that the believer is in *Christ (Rom 6) and a part of the body of Christ (Eph 5:23). See also SALVATION.

UNIPERSONALITY OF GOD The false *doctrine that *God (i.e., the Godhead) consists of one *Person only. Thus it involves the denial of the doctrine of the *Trinity.

UNITARIANS Those who reject the *doctrines of the *Trinity and of *Christ's *deity. There were some in the early church, but they became more numerous and more organized after the *Reformation, appearing under various names in Poland, Hungary, the Netherlands, and later in England and the U.S. Some suffered death for such beliefs. Not until 1813 were Unitarians legally tolerated in England, while in Massachusetts an 1818 court decision was followed by the election of Unitarian *pastors to charges or the profession of Unitarianism by congregations. Unitarians deny the need for an *atonement because of *God's goodness, stress the use of *reason in *religion, and give prominence to the Sermon on the Mount. The Unitarian Universalist Association is the North American *denomination, and the General Assembly of Unitarian and Free churches is the British *denomination that officially holds to Unitarianism.

UNITAS FRATRUM See Bohemian Brethren.

UNITED BRETHREN IN CHRIST An American Protestant body organized in 1800, notably among German settlers. Generally it followed the Methodist pattern in *polity and *doctrine. Its first *bishops were P. W. *Otterbein and Martin Boehm (1725–1812). Following developments from an 1889 division, one section of the original Brethren is now part of the *United Methodist Church.

UNITED CHURCH OF CANADA A 1925 union of Canadian Methodists, *Congregationalists, and 60 percent of Presbyterians, joined in 1968 by the *Evangelical United Brethren. In government it retains elements from the three uniting bodies. Its ruling body is the general council, which meets every second year. While its membership reflects a wide variation of theological outlook, most of its *clergy tend toward *liberalism and an *ecumenism toward union with the Anglican Church. The 1971 figures show a census constituency of some 3.75 million.

UNITED CHURCH OF CHRIST An American Protestant body formed in 1957 through a union of the *Evangelical and Reformed Church and the General Council of Congregational Christian Churches. Each congregation is autonomous in its own affairs. Representative bodies are the association, the conference, and the general *synod, which meets every second year. Currently it has 1.9 million members in 7,000 churches.

UNITED FREE CHURCH OF SCOTLAND A 1900 union between the *Free Church and the *United Presbyterian Church of Scotland. The majority in that union joined the Church of *Scotland in 1929, and the present United Free Church represents the minority that held that for the church to have formal connection with the *state was contrary to the spirit of *Christ's teaching and fatal to full spiritual freedom. The United Free Church is distinctive among Presbyterians in allowing laymen to become *moderators of *presbytery or *general assembly. It has some 18,000 communicants.

UNITED METHODIST CHURCH (U.K.) A 1907 union between the *Methodist New Connexion, the *Bible Christians, and the United Methodist Free churches. In 1932 a further merger saw the United Methodists join with Wesleyan Methodists and *Primitive Methodists to form the Methodist Church of Great Britain and Ireland, which in the mid-eighties had a membership of some 450,000.

UNITED METHODIST CHURCH (U.S.) A 1968 union of the Methodist Church and the *Evangelical United Brethren Church. The former body had previously (1939) incorporated two sections of the Methodist Episcopal Church and the Methodist Protestant Church. The 1968 union included those whose church background could be traced back to Britain and Germany. The supreme ruling body of the United Methodist Church, which has an episcopal system, is the general conference that meets every fourth year and has an equal number of ministers and laymen. In the early 1970s the church had about 9.1 million members in 37,750 churches.

UNITED PENTECOSTAL CHURCH INTERNATIONAL Group formed from the merger of the Pentecostal Assemblies of Jesus Christ and the Pentecostal Church, Inc., in 1945. The church stresses water *baptism in Christ's name, *repentance, and speaking in tongues as a sign of the baptism of the Holy *Spirit. It currently has more than 400,000 members in 2,700 churches.

UNITED PRESBYTERIAN CHURCH (SCOTLAND) A union formed in 1847 by the *United Secession Church and the *Relief Church. Largely urban, the United Presbyterian Church united with the *Free Church in 1900 to form the *United Free Church of Scotland.

UNITED PRESBYTERIAN CHURCH IN THE U.S.A A 1958 union of the *Presbyterian Church in the U.S.A. and the United Presbyterian Church of North America. This brought together those who traced their ecclesiastical ancestry to Scots, Irish, Welsh, and English immigrants. The church is active in the *ecumenical movement and has been engaged in conversations with other major American bodies. In 1983 it had 2.4 million members and joined with the Presbyterian Church in the U.S. to form the Presbyterian Church (U.S.A.).

UNITED REFORMED CHURCH (U.K.) A 1972 union between the Congregational Church in England and Wales and the *Presbyterian Church of England. With elements from both bodies in its *polity, the church had 130,000 members in the mid-eighties and is Britain's first union across denominational lines.

UNITED SECESSION CHURCH An 1820 Scottish union of groups that traced their common origin to the 1733 *Secession under Ebenezer *Erskine. In 1847 it united with the *Relief Church to form the *United Presbyterian Church.

UNIVERSAL(S) That which is common to all or to many. Thus, human *nature may be said to be common to all humans and so a universal. Different attitudes in medieval *theology and philosophy to the concept of universals underlies, in part, the controversy between *nominalism and *realism.

UNIVERSALISM This can be understood in at least two ways. (1) The belief that *God's *love and *grace extend to all parts, nations, and peoples of the world. God is God of the whole, not only of the elect or of a part of the *universe. (2) The *doctrine that ultimately all human beings and *angels (even *Satan) will enjoy *God's love and presence. Thus, if *hell exits, it is only of a limited duration. *Apocatastasis is this general belief that in the end all will be saved. Orthodox *Christianity affirms (1) and denies (2).

UNIVERSE The whole created order, totally distinct from *God himself.

UNIVERSITIES AND COLLEGES CHRISTIAN FELLOWSHIP A movement founded in 1927 as the *Inter-Varsity Fellowship to further cooperation between the *evangelical *Christian unions in British universities and colleges. The real beginnings were, however, in 1919 when the Christian Union at Cambridge declined to join the more liberal *Student Christian Movement. In the Universities and Colleges Christian Fellowship (UCCF; the name was adopted in the mid-seventies) local groups are student-led, bearing the burden of witness toward their fellows. In 1980 the UCCF was working in more than 550 universities and colleges in the British Isles. See also INTER-VARSITY CHRISTIAN FELLOWSHIP OF THE U.S.A.

UNKNOWN GOD Part of the inscription on an *altar in Athens on the Areopagus (Acts 17:23). The expression has been used by Christians of the deity whom adherents of other *religions truly seek when they perform their religious duties and offer their *worship. The idea is that, as Paul argued, there is only one true and living *God, and it is he whom the truly religious person seeks. See also ANONYMOUS CHRISTIANS, BAPTISM OF DESIRE.

UNPARDONABLE SIN That which Jesus described in Matthew 12:22ff. See also BLASPHEMY.

UPPSALA ASSEMBLY (1968). Fourth assembly of the *World Council of Churches, with the theme "Behold! I make all things new." More than seven hundred delegates, including fifteen Roman Catholic observers (one of whom addressed the assembly), attended the sixteen-day meetings. The six sections dealt with "The Holy Spirit and the Catholicity of the Church," "Renewal in Mission," "World Economic and Social Development," "Toward Justice and Peace in International Affairs," "Worship," and "Toward New Styles of Living."

URBAN II (c. 1042–1099). Pope from 1088. Born and educated in France, he supported *Gregory VII, who named him *cardinal (1079), against emperor *Henry IV. A reformist, dedicated to upholding the church's rights against the *state and to unity with the *Eastern Church, he proclaimed the first Crusade (1095).

URBAN V (c. 1310–1370). Pope from 1362. Born in France, he was a *Benedictine *abbot there when he was elected and crowned at Avignon during the *Babylonian Captivity of the church. He took steps toward the return of the papacy to Rome, but his brief sojourn there (1367–1370) was ended because of political troubles, and he returned to Avignon. A patron of learning, he worked hard for reunion with the *Eastern Church.

URBAN VI (c. 1318–1389). Pope from 1378. Neapolitan by birth, his election was welcomed in Italy after a succession of French popes, but it caused the *Great Schism. Thirteen French *cardinals, complaining that they had been coerced, elected an *antipope, *Clement VII, who settled in Avignon. The nations were divided, and *war and bloodshed resulted, with five cardinals included among the victims. It is suspected that Urban died by poisoning.

URBAN VIII (1586–1644). Pope from 1623. Educated by *Jesuits in Florence, his hometown, he had wide experience before his *pontificate during the supremacy of *Richelieu in France and during the *Thirty Years' War. A learned, nepotistic, moderate reformer, he disciplined *Galileo, moved against *Jansenism, diverted church money to warlike pursuits, and supported *missions.

URGESCHICHTE (Ger. "prehistory"). Historical events that in the light of *Christian *faith are seen as the means *God used to reveal himself to sinners (e.g., the *Resurrection). This very specialized usage is employed mainly by Karl *Barth, Emil *Brunner, and other adherents of *dialectical theology.

URSINUS, ZACHARIAS (1534–1583). German Reformed theologian. A teacher at Heidelberg, he collaborated with *Olevianus in producing the *Heidelberg Catechism, and although he disliked controversy, he undertook defense of the document against Lutheran criticisms.

URSULINES Roman Catholic *religious *order of women. Founded in Italy in 1535 by Angela Merici (1474–1540), the Ursulines were concerned initially with the education of girls, and they remained in their own families. As the movement spread through Italy and France, they began to live in communities. The order's house in Quebec was the first congregation of women in North America.

USSHER, JAMES (1581–1656). *Archbishop and scholar. Born in Dublin, where he studied and became professor at Trinity College, he became *bishop in 1621 and was promoted to Armagh in 1625. A great champion of the Calvinistic character and independence of the Irish church, he was in England when rebellion broke out in Ireland and was never able to return. A man of integrity and a highly respected theologian whom *Cromwell permitted to be buried in Westminster Abbey, his famous biblical chronology put *Creation in 4004 B.C.

USURY Taking interest on a loan, a practice the *OT forbids (Exod 22:25; Lev 25:35-37; cf. Luke 6:35). In modern times, with changes in the economic system, usury is understood as not taking excessive interest on a loan. As a moral *evil it is seen as taking advantage of someone in need.

UTILITARIANISM The theory that moral action is to be for the general good. Thus, morality depends on good achieved and *evil reduced or removed.

UTRAQUISM The *doctrine that *clergy and *laity should both (Lat. *sub utraque specie,* "under both forms") receive the bread and wine of Holy *Communion. This was argued by the followers of Jan *Hus (c. 1373–1415) against the teaching and practice of the medieval church.

UTRAQUISTS Moderates (cf. TABORITES) among followers of Jan *Hus. They had four aims: *preaching the *gospel in the Bohemian language, the *laity's right to receive *Communion in both kinds, reform of *clerical abuses, and a ban on *clergy from owning secular property and from excessive secular jurisdiction.

UTRECHT, DECLARATION OF (1889). The doctrinal basis of the *Old Catholic Church, which affirmed adherence to the Catholic *faith and rejected Roman Catholic distortions of it (e.g., papal *infallibility and *Immaculate Conception).

V

VALIDITY What is right in terms of *canon law and also produces the intended results. It is used particularly of *sacraments that meet the basic conditions to be a vehicle of *God's *grace and *blessing to the recipient.

VAN TIL, CORNELIUS (1895–1987). Educator and author. Professor at Princeton Theological Seminary (1928–1929) and Westminster Theological Seminary (1929–1978), he was a leading 20th-century apologist for *Calvinism, author of thirty books and many articles, and contributor to several others. As he saw it, *truth was based on *God's *revelation.

VANCOUVER ASSEMBLY (1983). Sixth assembly of the *World Council of Churches. The 839 delegates met for eighteen days to *worship, to plan humanitarian aid, and to discuss social issues, especially social *justice. The question of peace was ever in the forefront; some commentators saw the condemnation of nuclear weapons as a call for unilateral disarmament.

VANE, SIR HENRY (THE YOUNGER) (1613–1662). English statesman and Puritan. After serving as governor of Massachusetts (1636–1637), he returned to join the parliamentarians against *Charles I. He helped negotiate the *Solemn League and Covenant (1643); was leader of the House of Commons; disapproved of the execution of the king; and though jailed for opposing Oliver *Cromwell, was convicted of treason after the *Restoration and was executed.

VATICAN The residence of the *pope and the territory surrounding his palace and St. Peter's Church. The Vatican state, the administrative center of the Roman Catholic Church, is governed separately from Rome and the Italian state.

VATICAN COUNCIL, FIRST (1869–1870). The 20th *ecumenical council of the Roman Catholic Church. Called by Pius IX in the closing decade of his long *pontificate, it sought to combat the rising tide of *rationalism, materialism, and *liberalism. The more than seven hundred *bishops legislated on various matters, such as *clerical education, the election of bishops, and *religious *orders, but overshadowing all during the seven-month council was the proclamation of papal *infallibility "when speaking **ex cathedra* for the definition of *doctrines concerning *faith and morals." It encountered fierce resistance but was eventually passed by a large majority. With only a small part of their work done, the bishops were allowed to disperse for a few months, but political complications led to the Piedmontese occupation of Rome, and Pius suspended the council indefinitely.

VATICAN COUNCIL, SECOND (1962–1965). The 21st *ecumenical council of the Roman Catholic Church. Called by *John XXIII, it was a reforming council of more than two thousand *bishops that emphasized *spiritual renewal and the reunion of Christendom, and its views were expressed in a series of statements: Constitution on the Sacred Liturgy (*Sacrosanctum concilium*), December 4, 1963; Decree on the Instruments of Social Communication (*Inter mirifica*), December 4, 1963; Dogmatic Constitution on the Church (*Lumen gentium*), November 21, 1964; Decree on Ecumenism (*Unitatis redintegratio*), November 21, 1964; Decree on Catholic Eastern Churches (*Orientalium ecclesiarum*), November 21, 1964; Decree on the Bishop's Pastoral Office in the Church (*Christus Dominus*), October 28, 1965; Decree on Priestly Formation (*Optatam totius*), October 28, 1965; Decree on Appropriate Renewal of the Religious Life (*Perfectae caritatis*), October 28, 1965; Declaration on Christian Education (*Gravissimum educationis*), October 28, 1965; Declaration on the Relationship of the Church to Non-Christian Religions (*Nostra aetate*), October 28, 1965; Dogmatic Constitution on Divine Revelation (*Dei verbum*), November 18, 1965; Decree on the Apostolate of the Laity (*Apostolicam actuositatem*), November 18, 1965; Pastoral Constitution on the Church in the Modern World (*Gaudium et spes*), December 7, 1965; Decree on the Church's Missionary Activity (*Ad gentes divinitus*), December 7, 1965; Declaration on Religious Freedom (*Dignitatis humanae*), December 7, 1965. Decree on the Ministry and Life of Priests (*Presbyterorum ordinis*), December 7, 1965.

Vatican II had far-reaching effects especially on the *liturgy celebrated in the church. Latin was no longer the universal language of the *Mass; the *canon was said in the language of the people. The *priest faced the people, and new hymnals were introduced, often using "Protestant" hymns. A revised *breviary (Liturgy of the Hours) was introduced. After a period of instruction, laywomen and laymen became qualified to administer the elements of the *Eucharist. *Communion in both kinds was revived, but it still occurs rarely and is not the norm in most parishes. Vatican II opened the way for greater participation by the laity in the life of the church and urged them to seek holiness as the people of God. Members of the Protestant churches were no longer called "heretics" but "separated brethren." The council absolved the Jews for Christ's death, stressed the importance of Scripture and its study, reformed the Roman liturgy, and lessened the tension between Rome and other churches. *John XXIII died in 1963; *Paul VI saw the council through to its conclusion.

VEIL, RELIGIOUS The headdress worn by women to express their particular vocation, status, or role in the church. "Taking the veil" is a way of saying that a woman has entered a *religious *order. In recent times there has been a simplification of the veil for *nuns. Some *deaconesses who are not nuns sometimes wear a religious veil.

VENERATION OF RELICS Giving honor and respect through *genuflection or other means to *relics of *saints and *martyrs.

VENERATION OF THE CROSS A ceremony of the Roman Catholic Church for *Good Friday. The people kneel and kiss a *crucifix placed at the entrance to the *sanctuary. The *Orthodox churches have a similar ceremony on *Holy Cross Day (September 14).

VENERATION OF THE SAINTS In the Roman Catholic Church it is honor paid to those called *saints by the church because they are in *God's presence and make *intercession for the faithful on earth as well as for those passing through *purgatory.

VENI CREATOR (Lat. "Come, O Creator"). A *hymn addressed to the Holy *Spirit that is sung especially at *Whitsuntide (*Pentecost) and at the *ordination of *priests and *consecration of *bishops. It was composed in the 9th century and is available in several English versions. Of these the one most widely used in the *Anglican

Communion is that by Bishop J. Cosin, "Come, Holy Ghost, Our Souls Inspire."

VENIAL SIN (Lat. *venia,* "pardon"). An offense against *God that can be pardoned and that is not so serious as to cause *God to withdraw his presence from the human *heart. It contrasts with *mortal *sin.

VENN, HENRY (1724–1797). Anglican clergyman. A graduate of Cambridge ordained in 1749, he became in 1759 *vicar of Huddersfield. Twelve years later when he left the town, according to Bishop *Ryle, darkness, immorality, and ignorance had been "shaken in the center by the lever of the *gospel." From 1771 vicar of Yelling in Huntingdonshire, Venn was greatly esteemed by many prominent evangelicals and gave the funeral oration for George *Whitefield.

VENN, HENRY (1796–1873). Anglican clergyman. Born in London, the son of John *Venn, he is best remembered as a promoter of missions. He served as secretary of the Church Missionary Society from 1841 and was an advocate of "self-governing, self-supporting and self-propagating churches." His policies were in advance of his time and have been well vindicated.

VENN, JOHN (1759–1813). Anglican clergyman. Born just before his father Henry *Venn went to Huddersfield, he graduated at Cambridge and was rector of Little Dunham, Norfolk (1783), then of Clapham (1792), where he was *spiritual adviser to the *Clapham Sect. He helped to found the Church Missionary Society (1799) and was its first president.

VERBECK, GUIDO HERMAN FRIDOLIN (1830–1898). Dutch-American *missionary to Japan. A native of Zeist, he was educated by the Moravians, and trained as an engineer in Utrecht and as a Dutch Reformed minister in New York. After *ordination in 1859 he went to Japan, established a school, helped the government by training Japanese interpreters, and finally became head of what developed into the Japanese Imperial University in Tokyo. In 1879 he left government service to return to missionary work, concerned particularly with *Christian education.

VERBIEST, FERDINAND (1623–1688). *Jesuit *missionary to China. Born in the Netherlands and trained in astronomy, he replaced fellow Jesuit Adam Schall as director of the Imperial Board of Astronomy in Peking. He early advocated the training of indigenous *clergy to advance the church in China.

VERSICLE A short sentence in *liturgy often taken from a psalm that precedes a response. E.g., Versicle: "Our help is in the name of the *Lord." Response: "Who made *heaven and earth."

VESPERS In *Roman Catholicism this is the *prayer and service for early evening, and it is now often called *evening prayer. Its main feature is the *Magnificat (Luke 1:46–55).

VESSELS, SACRED The receptacles and utensils used in the celebration of the *Eucharist and *Benediction. These are: *chalice, *paten, *ciborium, *pyx, *capsula, *lunette and *monstrance. For details of these see separate entries.

VESTIARIAN CONTROVERSY An English church dispute about *clerical dress that originated about 1550 when Richard Hooper delayed his *consecration because he objected to the *vestments prescribed by the *Prayer Book. He finally compromised on the issue, and the matter did not surface again until the accession of *Elizabeth (1558), when many of the exiles returned from the Continent, some with strongly *Reformed convictions. With some encouragement from the queen, the *bishops required *clergy to wear cope and *surplice as appropriate, and *Archbishop Matthew *Parker further pressed the matter in 1566 and deprived a number of Puritan ministers who considered vestments a *relic from Roman Catholic supremacy. The controversy recurred and even in the

20th century was still a controversial subject in the Church of *England.

VESTIGIA TRINITATIS (Lat. "marks of the *Trinity"). Illustration or *analogies of the Holy Trinity taken from human experience. E.g., water as spring, stream, and lake. Some theologians, notably Karl *Barth, deny that any illustration from our experience can begin to describe the wonderful reality of *God. See also PSYCHOLOGICAL ANALOGY; SOCIAL ANALOGY.

VESTMENTS Special garments worn by the *clergy as they take part in services of *worship. They have developed either from the dress of Roman gentlemen or from the dress of medieval academics. Undergarments include *amice, *alb, *cassock, and *cincture; outergarments include *stole, *dalmatic, *cope and *chasuble. For details see separate entries.

VESTRY The place in which *parish business was carried out in the Church of *England or the collective name for the parishioners themselves meeting as a group. Sometimes the word is applied to the *clergy retiring room (as it is in Scotland), where the communion *vessels may also be kept. The word is also used collectively for those who perform church business in the Protestant Episcopal Church in the U.S.

VEUILLOT, LOUIS (1813–1883). French Roman Catholic writer. A journalist who was also a zealous Ultramontanist, he propagated his views through *L'Univers,* a newspaper that he edited from 1843. Publication was suspended (1860–1867) because Veuillot took the side of Pius IX in a dispute with Napoleon III. He rejoiced in the triumph of papal primacy at *Vatican Council I, and despite failing health remained influential in French church circles until his death.

VIA DOLOROSA (Lat. "the sorrowful way"). The possible route taken by *Jesus in Jerusalem on *Good Friday from Pilate's residence to Calvary (Golgotha). It is marked by fourteen *stations of the cross, and annually on Good Friday *Franciscan monks lead a *pilgrimage on it, with devotions at each station.

VIA EMINENTIAE (Lat. "the way of eminence"). The method of speaking about *God that uses the *doctrine of *analogy. It presupposes that because God made man in his image and likeness, it is meaningful to describe God as possessing perfectly eternally those attributes that are found in human beings (e.g., goodness, *love, and faithfulness). See also VIA POSITIVA.

VIA MEDIA (Lat. "the middle way"). Used to describe a system of *doctrine or church polity that appears to take a middle path between two extremes. The Church of *England has often been seen as providing a *via media* between *Roman Catholicism and doctrinaire *Protestantism.

VIA NEGATIVA (Lat. "the negative way"). A method of describing *God that begins by emphasizing that ordinary creaturely qualities cannot be automatically applied to him. Human languages belong to the temporal and finite and cannot easily be transferred to the description of the *infinite and *eternal. *God is transcendent, and human language is inadequate to describe him. In the *Orthodox Church this method is called the *apophatic way. When it has done its work of preparing the way, then the **via positiva* can be used.

VIA POSITIVA (Lat. "the positive way"). A method of speaking about the *eternal and *infinite *God that affirms that human qualities may be used of God. This is because God and man are linked through creation and man is made in God's image and likeness. However, when a human quality is used of God, it is said to apply to him in a preeminent way. Thus the *via positiva* is the **via eminentiae*.

VICAR (Lat. **vicarius,* "a substitute"). In the Church of *England a clergyman who is in charge of a *parish. Originally a vicar was the substitute of a rector (who employed and paid the vicar), but both words now describe a parish *priest. In the church of Rome a vicar is one who substitutes for another or who acts in another's name. Thus there are such titles as *vicar apostolic, vicar capitular, and *vicar general.

VICAR APOSTOLIC In *Roman Catholicism a papal representative sent to govern a *diocese that is either without a *bishop or where there is special difficulty. From 1685 until the restoration of the hierarchy in 1850, the Roman Catholic Church in England was governed by vicars apostolic. They are now usually titular bishops over territories not yet organized into dioceses.

VICAR GENERAL The chief Roman Catholic administrative officer of a *diocese, appointed by the *bishop, whose deputy he may be for certain purposes. The *chancellor holds a similar office in the Church of *England. The *archbishops of Canterbury and York each appoint a *clerical or lay provincial vicar general.

VICAR OF CHRIST Replacing "Vicar of Peter," a title (found from the 8th century) of the *pope, said to be from *Jesus' words to Peter (John 21:16ff.).

VICEGERENT (Lat. *vicis,* "in place of"; *gerens,* "acting"). Used in *theology of the exalted *Lord *Jesus as he sits at the Father's right hand. He rules and acts with and on behalf of the Father.

It is also used in *Roman Catholicism of a *bishop who assists and acts for the *cardinal who is in charge of the *curia in the *dioceses of Rome.

VICTOR I (d. 198). Pope from 189. Reportedly African by birth, he is remembered most for his opposition to the Quartodecimans, who celebrated *Easter on the day of the Jewish Passover instead of on the day of *resurrection. *Polycarp had been sympathetic to *Quartodecimanism, and even *Irenaeus was not happy when Victor threatened strong action against the Asian *bishops who held that view. The *pope may have seen it as a challenge to his position, but more than a century was to pass before the Council of *Nicea finally upheld the Roman position.

VIENNE, COUNCIL OF (1311–1312). The fifteenth *ecumenical council, according to *Roman Catholicism. It was called by *Clement V at the instigation of his fellow Frenchman, *Philip IV, who demanded a trial for his dead enemy *Boniface VIII and the suppression of the *Templars. The 120 *bishops present rejected the former demand but agreed to the latter.

VIGIL A period of *prayer and self-examination on the day or evening before a major feast or *holy day in the church year. Of these the *Easter vigil is the most important.

VIGILIUS (c. 500–555). Pope from 537. Born in Rome, he was sent as a papal envoy to Constantinople, where he won the friendship of the empress Theodora. This combination of ambitious Roman and Monophysite *Byzantine contrived the deposition of Pope Silverius and the accession of Vigilius. When the *Second Council of Constantinople (553) showed Monophysite tendencies, Vigilius vacillated and, perhaps weary of an enforced seven-year stay in the East, gave the impression of agreeing to these—and gave ammunition later to those who oppose the *doctrine of papal *infallibility.

VILMAR, AUGUST FRIEDRICH CHRISTIAN (1800–1860). German Lutheran theologian. Born and educated in Marburg, he taught school there and was elected to the Parliament of Hesse, making significant contributions in the educational field. Meanwhile, his early *rationalism had been dispelled through his theological and historical studies, and when he was appointed professor of *theology at Marburg (1855), he was a staunch supporter of confessional *Lutheranism, holding strictly to the view that the church is the body of *Christ. His many theological works have not yet been translated.

VINCENT FERRER (c. 1350–1419). *Dominican preacher. Born in Spain, he became a Dominican in 1367 and later professor of *theology at Valencia. Much of his latter life was occupied in *preaching *missions throughout Europe, where he attracted great crowds. He is said to have played a significant part in ending the *Great Schism in the Western church.

VINCENT DE PAUL (1581–1660). Founder of the *Vincentians, or *Lazarists. Born in France and educated by the *Franciscans, he was ordained in 1600 and engaged in pastoral work under the spiritual direction of Pierre de *Bérulle. He founded the Vincentians (officially The Congregation of the Mission) in 1625 and cofounded in 1633 the Sisters of Charity for women devoted to the care of the sick and the *poor.

VINCENT OF LERINS (d. c. 445). French monk and theologian. A semi-Pelagian who opposed the teaching of *Augustine of Hippo, he strongly upheld *Scripture as the final arbiter in *Christian *faith and conduct. About the place of *tradition he offered, in what became known as the *Vincentian Canon, a threefold test: "What has been believed everywhere, always, and by all."

VINCENTIAN CANON The criteria proposed by *Vincent of Lerins (d. c. 445) for testing the *orthodoxy of any *doctrine: *"Quod ubique, quod semper, quod ab omnibus creditum est"* ("What has been believed everywhere, always, and by all").

VINCENTIANS (LAZARISTS) A congregation founded in France in 1625 by *Vincent de Paul, for *missions to rural people and for the training of *clergy. Its headquarters were in the former Paris *priory of St. Lazare, hence the alternative name. The Vincentians spread to other countries—notably Italy, Poland, and Spain—and began work in the U.S. in 1816.

VINCI, LEONARDO DA (1452–1519). Italian artist and scientist. Born near Florence, he was a man of unparalleled versatility. His contributions and interests covered such fields as irrigation and central heating, spiral staircases and anatomy, flying machines and architecture, botany and costume designing. He was also sculptor, musician, and poet. But he is remembered preeminently as a painter whose works include *The Adoration of the Magi, The Madonna in the Grotto, La Gioconda* (*Mona Lisa*), and *The Last Supper.* He worked in Florence, Milan, and Rome but spent his last few years in France.

VINES, RICHARD (1600–1656). Puritan divine, regarded by some of his contemporaries as "the Luther of England." A Cambridge graduate ordained in the Church of *England, he served in the *Westminster Assembly, had misgivings about parliamentary tendencies, and opposed the execution of *Charles I. He ministered and lectured in London under the Commonwealth (to which he declined formal support) and was consulted on theological matters by the authorities.

VINET, ALEXANDRE RUDOLPHE (1797–1847). Swiss theologian. He taught French at Basel (1817–1837), during which time he was ordained as a *Reformed *pastor. A strong advocate of religious liberty, he played a key part in the belated establishment of the *Reformation in French-speaking Switzerland. He was professor of practical *theology at Lausanne, wrote works on church-state separation and Pascal, and helped found the *Free Church in Vaud canton.

VIRET, PIERRE (1511–1571). Protestant Reformer. Born in Switzerland, he became a *Reformed preacher through *Farel, founded the Reformed Church in Lausanne, and was a close friend of *Calvin. Regarded as the most significant French-speaking Swiss Reformer, he spent his latter years in France.

VIRGIN BIRTH The teaching that *Mary conceived *Jesus through the power of the Holy *Spirit alone (Matt 1; Luke 1–2). Apart from discussion as to how this could be and why it should be, theologians have not always been able to agree on the theological significance of the virginal conception and birth. One traditional theme has been to preserve Jesus free from *original *sin. Others are that he had to have a unique conception to be the Incarnate *Son of *God and to become the *Second Adam.

VIRGINITY The dedication to *abstinence from sexual intercourse and to sexual purity. It is now used of both male and female *celibacy and refers to an extreme form of *chastity. It is a commitment of purity of life and a giving up all thought of marriage in order to devote oneself wholly to the *love of *God. In the Roman Catholic tradition it has sometimes been presented as a superior state (in God's eyes) to marriage.

VIRTUALISM A view of the presence of *Christ in the *Eucharist especially associated with John *Calvin (1509–1564). While the bread and wine remain actually bread and wine, the *virtue of the true *spiritual *body and *blood of Christ is received by the communicant as he eats the bread and drinks the wine in *faith and *love. A dynamic, spiritual presence of Christ is presupposed. See also RECEPTIONISM.

VIRTUE A basic habit of good action: a good intention resulting in good behavior. This concept was given systematic treatment by Thomas *Aquinas (c. 1225–1274), who made use of the ethical teaching of Aristotle and earlier theologians (e.g., *Augustine). On the basis of this idea of virtue it has become common to refer to the *cardinal virtues and the *theological virtues.

VIRTUES, CARDINAL See CARDINAL VIRTUES.

VIRTUES, THEOLOGICAL See THEOLOGICAL VIRTUES.

VISION OF GOD See BEATIFIC VISION.

VISITANDINES (VISITATION NUNS) A Roman Catholic *order founded in 1610 in France by *Francis de Sales and Jane Frances de Chantal (1572–1641). Initially concerned with the care of the *poor and sick in their own homes, the order was restricted when local church authority insisted on a cloistered life for the *nuns. By the mid-17th century the nuns were involved in educational work, and this has become a feature of the order.

VISITATION OF MARY The visit of Mary to her cousin Elizabeth in Judea after she knew she would give birth to the *Messiah (Luke 1:39ff.). It has been celebrated as a feast in the West since the 14th century.

VISITATION OF THE SICK One of the basic works of *mercy laid upon the church by *Christ (Matt 25:31ff.). Also the title of a short service of *worship in the Book of *Common Prayer for use by the *priest when visiting the sick.

VISSER'T HOOFT, WILLEM ADOLF (1900–1985). Dutch *ecumenical leader. Previously associated with the *YMCA and the *World Student Christian Federation, he became general secretary (1938) of what was constituted in 1948 as the *World Council of Churches. The most distinguished ecumenical statesman since John R. *Mott, he was at the *heart of the WCC's work until his retirement in 1966, receiving many civil and ecclesiastical awards.

VITALIAN (d. 672). Pope from 657. He coped successfully with the *Monothelite *heresy, initiated a period of good (though later deteriorating) relations with Constantinople, and consecrated *Theodore of Tarsus, who was the first *archbishop of Canterbury to rule over the whole English church.

VLADIMIR I (c. 956–1015). Grand prince of Kiev, the first *Christian ruler in Russia. A pagan polygamist who consolidated his territories through military action, he was taken in marriage by the sister of *Byzantine emperor Basil II about 987 on condition that he convert to *Christianity and help Basil against rebellious subjects. Vladimir imposed Christianity on Kiev and Novgorod, and the new

Russian church began its association with Constantinople.

VOCATION The call of *God to the life of *faith and *obedience within the people of *God. In the history of the church, vocation has been specially used of the specific call to be a *pastor, *priest, monk, or *nun. It is also used of the general tasks that all God's *people daily have to perform as their regular work. In modern secular society the word is now used without reference to God—e.g., of the vocation to be a nurse, doctor, teacher, etc. See also WORK, THEOLOGY OF.

VOETIUS, GISBERT (1588–1676). Dutch Reformed theologian. An uncompromising Calvinist against *Arminianism, he became professor of *theology at Utrecht, and for forty years there until his death he resisted a wide variety of deviations from strict *orthodoxy. These included state interference in church affairs, the views of *Descartes, and *Roman Catholicism.

VOLUNTARISM (Lat. *voluntarius*, "at one's pleasure"). The *doctrine of the primacy of the *will of *God. Whatever God wills is necessarily good; when God makes commands they are to be obeyed because he is the sovereign *Lord. Sometimes it means that, in God, will takes precedence over intellect.

VOLUNTARY A piece of *music played by the organist usually at the end or beginning of a service of *worship.

VOLUNTARYISM (Lat. *voluntarius*, "at one's pleasure"). The theory and practice of church order, membership, and support that emphasizes personal choice and decision. Thus, churches should be self-supporting, free of state control and support. The principle is best seen in the voluntary societies that engage in evangelistic and philanthropic work.

VON HARDENBERG, F. L. F. See NOVALIS.

VON HÜGEL, FRIEDRICH (1852–1925). Roman Catholic scholar. Son of an Austrian diplomat who had married a Scots lady, he was born in Florence but lived in England from the age of fifteen. Linguist, philosopher, theologian, spiritual director, and refreshing writer, he was an enigma to fellow Roman Catholics who, however, had the good sense to waive his unorthodoxies because of his deep piety and practical *Christianity. His *Selected Letters* (1928) are still eminently readable.

VORSTIUS, CONRADUS (1569–1622). Dutch Reformed theologian. Educated in Heidelberg and Geneva, he sided with *Arminius at Leyden (1610) and supported the *Remonstrance. He further scandalized the strict Calvinists by writings that brought a charge of *Socinianism, and he was banned from teaching in 1612.

VOTIVE (Lat. *votum*, "a *vow"). Doing something in honor of *God or a *saint or for an aspect of the *faith—votive candles, *Masses, *offices, and offerings. Originally it meant fulfilling a private vow to honor God.

VOW A free, solemn, and deliberate promise made to *God to perform something that it is held is good and pleasing to him. There are examples of vows in the *OT (e.g., Deut 23:21–23; Judg 11:30–39; 1 Sam 1:11) and *NT (Acts 18:18; 21:23ff.). The use of vows continued into the church. Within the monastic movement the threefold vow of *poverty, *chastity, and *obedience was the most publicized. However, in *baptism and matrimony vows are also made either to God or to each other in the presence of God.

VULGATE (Lat. *vulgatus*, "common, popular"). The Latin translation of the *Bible widely used (thus the common version) in the Western church (5th to 16th century) and in *Roman Catholicism (16th to 20th centuries). Most of the translation was done by *Jerome (382–387). This *Bible was used by the Council of *Trent as well as by the first and second *Vatican Councils.

W

WACE, HENRY (1836–1924). Dean of Canterbury. Born in London, he graduated from Oxford, was ordained in 1861, and for forty years in London he was active in many areas: writer for *The Times,* *parish minister, chaplain to lawyers and to the court, church history professor and principal of King's College. He went to Canterbury in 1903. Wace was an *evangelical who defended *Reformed teaching against liberals and *high churchmen. He produced a number of works on biblical subjects but is best remembered as coeditor of the *Dictionary of Christian Biography* (1880–1886) and of the second series of *Nicene and Post-Nicene Fathers* (1890–1900).

WAKE, WILLIAM (1657–1737). *Archbishop of Canterbury from 1717. A former chaplain at the British Embassy in Paris, he received rapid promotion in the church and held the see of Lincoln from 1705. A tolerant man who explored the possibilities of union with *Roman Catholicism and yet showed a measure of sympathy toward Nonconformists, he wrote a number of books, notably on church government.

WALDENSIANS, WALDENSES Adherents of a religious movement originating in 12th-century France and said to have been founded by Peter Waldo, who preached in Lyons (1170–1176) and gathered round him a number of followers known as the "poor men," whose message stressed poverty and simplicity. Placed under papal ban in 1184, the movement spread to other countries. The Waldenses rejected such things as *purgatory, *prayers for the dead, and civil *oaths. Persecution intensified, some defected, and by the *Reformation most Waldenses were found in certain Alpine valleys. There they were contacted by Guillaume *Farel and accepted a *Reformed Church structure about 1532, but the civil authority in Savoy was Roman Catholic, and the Waldenses knew further persecution until the "Emancipation" of 1848. In 1855 a theological college was established in Italy, where the Waldensian church, with some 20,000 members, is the most prominent representative of *Protestantism.

WALDENSTRÖM, PAUL PETER (1838–1917). Swedish scholar and churchman. Ordained in the *state church in 1864, he found his *evangelical views out of step with the times. In 1882 he resigned from the pastorate and served the Evangelical National Association, which sought religious reform in Sweden. In 1878 he organized the Swedish Mission Covenant, many members of which emigrated to the U.S. and formed the *Evangelical Covenant Church.

WALTER, HUBERT Hubert Walter.

WALTHER, CARL FERDINAND WILHELM (1811–1887). American Lutheran clergyman, often regarded as the founder of the Lutheran Church, Missouri Synod. Born, educated, and ordained in Germany, he went to America in 1839 and soon established a school that developed into Concordia Theological Seminary, serving as professor of *theology from 1849. Two years earlier the Missouri Synod had been founded, with Walther as its first president. Champion of the conservative Lutherans, he was involved in many controversies, was an outstanding preacher, and was an able theologian.

WALVOORD, JOHN F. (1910–). *Presbyterian *pastor, educator, and author. A leading scholarly dispensationalist, he has been a pastor in Fort Worth, Texas (1934–1951), an active leader in the *Independent Fundamentalist Churches of America, and a professor of *theology and president of Dallas Theological Seminary (1952–1986), where he is now chancellor. The author of twenty books, he has edited several books and *Bibliotheca Sacra* (1952–). He has also written numerous articles and served on the committee of the New Scofield Reference Bible.

WAR There is no single attitude to or *doctrine of *war among Christians. In the medieval period an attempt was made to define a just war in terms of it fulfilling three conditions—that it be waged by a proper authority (e.g., a king), that it be for a just cause, and that it have the intention of establishing a good order or correcting an *evil one. These guidelines appeared to suffice until the advent of modern warfare, especially nuclear arms. However, most Christians still believe that *pacifism* is not a viable option and that to engage in war for the purpose of self-defense or to help another country that is being devastated by an evil power is right before *God. Yet because of the terrible evils caused by war, the *Christian *faith requires that all be done to prevent war and where one exists to bring it to a speedy and just solution.

WARD, NATHANIEL (c. 1578–1652). English Puritan minister and writer. Cambridge graduate and a lawyer, he was ordained in the Church of *England, but his Puritan views led to persecution, and in 1634 he went to Massachusetts where he helped draw up the first codification of law. He returned to England in 1647 and is best remembered for his satirical attack on *toleration, *The Simple Cobler of Aggawam in America* (1647).

WARFIELD, BENJAMIN BRECKINRIDGE (1851–1921). American *Presbyterian theologian. Born in Kentucky and educated at Princeton, he held the chair of *New Testament in Western Theological Seminary (1879–1887) before succeeding A. A. *Hodge as professor of *theology at Princeton. Warfield held, taught, and fought for the fundamentals of the *faith; his many writings include *Revelation and Inspiration, The Person and Work of Christ, Calvin and Calvinism,* and *Perfectionism*. Some were reprinted many times.

WARHAM, WILLIAM (c. 1450–1532). *Archbishop of Canterbury from 1504. An Oxford-educated lawyer, his diplomatic services to the crown ensured rapid promotion in church and state, climaxing in the primacy and the lord chancellorship. His lengthy leadership of the church saw many significant events: his crowning of *Henry VIII, the rise of Thomas *Wolsey, the king's *divorce petition, and the move toward the break with Rome.

WATERBUFFALO THEOLOGY An expression used by the Japanese theologian Kosuke Koyama to state that the communication of the *gospel and *Christian *faith must make sense in a local *culture. A people to whom he ministered in Thailand spent much time with their waterbuffaloes, and this is the origin of the expression. It is the title of his book published in 1974.

WATTS, ISAAC (1674–1748). English *hymn writer. Born in Southampton, he was a Nonconformist minister in London from 1702, during which time he wrote the works that made him regarded as the father of English hymnody. His *Hymns and Spiritual Songs* (1707) went through many editions, and other collections followed. His hymns—"When I Survey the Wondrous Cross," "O God, Our Help in Ages Past," and "Jesus Shall Reign"—have endured, though some were written against the background of contemporary religious events.

WEALTH The abundance of material possessions or resources. The *Bible does not condemn the acquisition of wealth. Rather, it emphasizes that to have it is to be privileged, and thus it is to be used wisely and generously for the good of others (1 Tim 6:8–9, 17–18). It can easily become an idol or demonic snare (Matt 6:24; Mark 10:23).

WEE FREES A term usually applied to the minority in the *Free Church of Scotland, who in 1900 refused to join in the union that formed the *United Free Church and continued under the old name. Found mostly in the highlands and Western Islands, the strongly Calvinist body sings only metrical psalms without musical accompaniment.

WEISS, BERNHARD (1827–1918). German *NT scholar. Professor at Kiel (1863–1877) and Berlin (1877–1908), he contributed much to NT critical studies. His most famous work appeared in English as *The Life of Christ* (1883).

WELD, THEODORE DWIGHT (1803–1895). American abolitionist. Born in Connecticut, he was theologically trained and joined Charles G. *Finney's "holy band" of preachers, but in 1830 he turned to the antislavery crusade. He was one of the chief founders of the American Anti-Slavery Society and an active promoter of the cause in Washington. He wrote works against *slavery that reportedly inspired Harriet Beecher *Stowe to write *Uncle Tom's Cabin*.

WELLHAUSEN, JULIUS (1844–1918). German biblical scholar. Professor of Semitics at Marburg (1885–1892) and Göttingen (1892–1913), he sought to outline the historical process involved in producing *Israel's *religion and literature. Conservatives opposed his analytical approach to *Scripture, but many others accepted it. He also contributed to *NT and Islamic studies.

WELTANSCHAUUNG (Ger. worldview). A comprehensive world-view. The *Christian world-view is deeply affected by belief in *God and the *gospel but will be set within or closely related to the ideas gained from *culture and education, though it is different from all other world-views.

WESEL, JOHANN See John of Wesel.

WESLEY, CHARLES (1707–1788). Methodist *hymn writer. Eighteenth child of a Lincolnshire rector, he graduated from Oxford, where he was a member of the *Holy Club and was ordained in 1735. Three years later he experienced an *evangelical *conversion and became a revivalist preacher, often in company with his brother *John. He traveled little after 1756 but preached in Bristol and (from 1771) London. He produced several thousand hymns, many of which are still regularly sung. They include "Love Divine, All Loves Excelling," "Lo! He Comes, With Clouds Descending," "Jesus, Lover of My Soul," and "Hark! The Herald Angels Sing."

WESLEY, JOHN (1703–1791). Founder of *Methodism. Fifteenth child of Samuel and Susanna *Wesley, he was educated at Oxford and ordained in the Church of *England but did not experience *conversion until 1738. Soon afterwards, he embarked on his great task: "To reform the nation, particularly the church, and to spread Scriptural holiness over the land." Before he died he had preached more than 40,000 *sermons and covered nearly 250,000 miles. He encountered opposition from hostile mobs, uncooperative *clergy, and other Evangelicals who disliked his *Arminian *theology, and he unwillingly fathered a breakaway church. When he died, however, one secular magazine hailed him as "One of the few characters who outlived enmity and prejudice."

WESLEYANISM The *doctrine, ethos, or general influence of the teaching and example of John and Charles *Wesley and their supporters. Thus it may be used of *Methodism or of what such a *denomination as the Church of the *Nazarene seeks to revive or preserve of the Wesleys' original teaching and emphases.

WESSEL, JOHANN (WESSEL OF GANSFORT) (1419–1489). Dutch theologian. Born in Groningen, he received his early education from the *Brethren of the Common Life before going on to foreign universities. Professor thereafter at Heidelberg and Paris, he has been called "a Reformer before the *Reformation," because he sought the kind of ecclesiastical reforms advocated later by *Luther and found that his theological works were put on the *Index.

WESTCOTT, BROOKE FOSS (1825–1901). *Bishop of Durham. Previously a schoolmaster at Harrow, he was appointed to the regius chair of divinity at Cambridge in 1870, where his collaboration with F. J. A. *Hort produced a famous Greek *NT (1881). Just as significant were his commentaries on John's *Gospel (1881), the Johannine Epistles (1883), and the Epistle to the Hebrews (1889). He also wrote doctrinal works and founded a theological college (later Westcott House) and the Cambridge Mission to Delhi. As bishop of an industrial *diocese from 1890, he assiduously tackled its social problems.

WESTERN SCHISM
See Great Schism.

WESTERN THEOLOGY The *theology of the Western (Latin) church in contrast to that of the *Eastern (Greek) church. With their roots in Latin *culture and thought forms, both Roman Catholic and Protestant theology have a different type of theology than that created in the Greek *culture of ancient Alexandria and Constantinople. Western theology is much more highly defined and has adapted itself much more fully to modern thought forms than has Eastern.

WESTMINSTER ASSEMBLY (1643). A Calvinistic *synod with 151 members, including 30 laymen, appointed by the Long Parliament to reform the English church at a time when *Puritanism predominated. Four parties were represented: Episcopalians (who seldom attended), Presbyterians (the largest and most influential section), *Independents, and Erastians. To these were added six commissioners from Scotland. The Westminster Assembly sanctioned the *Solemn League and Covenant, drafted the *Westminster Confession, revised the *Thirty-Nine Articles, and prepared a Directory of Public Worship and the *Westminster Catechisms. Profound differences on *sacraments, discipline, and church jurisdiction extended the program, and 1,163 sessions were held before the assembly adjourned in 1649. Though not strictly a church court, the assembly's far-reaching results place it among the most important of *Reformed synods.

WESTMINSTER CATECHISMS Two documents, known as the Larger and Shorter Catechisms, completed by the *Westminster Assembly in 1647 and soon approved by Parliament and by the Scots *kirk. The larger is a simplified version of the *Westminster Confession. The Shorter, with its famous opening question, "What is the chief end of man?" became well known to generations of Scottish school children, testifying to its lasting influence on Scottish life.

WESTMINSTER CONFESSION (1647). A closely reasoned Calvinist document drafted by the *Westminster Assembly in 1646 and still regarded as authoritative in most English-speaking *Presbyterian churches. In thirty-three chapters it expounds the fundamentals of the *Christian *faith. It holds that the *Word of *God is the only infallible rule of *faith and practice, distinguishes between the visible and the *invisible church, and identifies the Jewish *Sabbath with the Christian *Sunday. It gained only brief official acceptance in the Church of *England but was welcomed as definitive by the Church of Scotland in 1647 and is still so regarded. It has had a marked influence also on other *denominations, notably *Congregationalists in Britain and New England and the *Baptists.

WESTMINSTER STANDARDS The collective name given to the various documents produced by the *Westminster Assembly and subsequently adopted by the Church of * Scotland in 1648. Besides the *Westminster Confession and the *Westminster Catechisms, they comprised two further documents: (1) The Directory for the Public Worship of God (1644). This was intended to replace the Anglican Book of *Common Prayer. It lays down an order of service and has sections on *preaching, the *sacraments, burying the dead, visiting the sick, *fasting, and the *Lord's Day. It fell into disuse after 1690. (2) The Form of Presbyterial Church Government (1645). Here the Scots clashed with the *Independents, who opposed the idea of a national church, and with the *Erastians, who wanted to give the civil authority control of church affairs. The *Presbyterians won, but it was only halfheartedly implemented in England.

WESTON, FRANK (1871–1924). *Bishop of Zanzibar. Born into an *evangelical family, he early accepted Anglo-Catholic views, graduated from Oxford, worked in the London slums after *ordination, and in 1901 went to Zanzibar, where he was consecrated bishop in 1908. While he strongly identified with the African, he is remembered most for his opposition to a projected scheme of federation, in what became known as the *Kikuyu Controversy.

WHEATON DECLARATION A statement adopted in 1966 by the Congress on the Church's Worldwide Mission. Sponsored by *evangelical *mission agencies, the occasion brought to the campus of Wheaton College (Ill.) 938 delegates from 71 countries. The declaration dealt with the relation of mission to areas such as syncretism, proselytism, church growth, evangelical unity, and social concerns.

WHICHCOTE, BENJAMIN (1609–1683). *Cambridge Platonist. Born in Shropshire, he graduated from Cambridge, was ordained (1637), and later became provost of King's College there (1644) because of parliamentary sympathies. He was deprived at the *Restoration but subsequently ministered in London until his death. Like other Platonists, he found himself at odds with the Puritans and their *doctrine of *total depravity. Whichcote stressed the place of *reason in *religion and was tolerant in an intolerant age.

WHITBY, DANIEL (1638–1726). British theologian and churchman. Best remembered for his violent anti-Catholic polemic and his *postmillennialism. The latter is found in an appendix to *Paraphrase and Commentary on the New Testament* (2 vols., 1703). According to Whitby, *Christianity would eventually triumph in the earth, thus ushering in the thousand-year reign of peace after which *Christ would return. His *Last Thoughts* (1727) showed decided unitarian tendencies.

WHITBY, SYNOD OF (663–664). A *Christian church meeting in Northumbria to discuss points of differences between Roman and Celtic usage. Among those who participated were Colman of Lindisfarne, *Hilda, *Wilfrid, and Oswy, King of Northumbria. the decision went against the Celtic party, but it brought England into line with most of Christendom.

WHITE, ELLEN GOULD (1827–1915). *Seventh-Day Adventist leader. Born into a Methodist family in Maine, she was early influenced by the *preaching of William *Miller. She claimed to have received *revelations, and from these came the beginnings of the Seventh-Day Adventist Church. She married James White, one of the elders, in 1846, after whose death in 1881 she traveled extensively in Europe, later moving to Australia for nine years until 1900. She wrote numerous books but always stressed that she regarded herself merely as the messenger of *God.

WHITE FATHERS Officially the Society of Missionaries of Africa, it was founded in 1868 by Charles *Lavigerie for the purpose of evangelizing the so-called Dark Continent. Beginning in North Africa (Lavigerie was *archbishop of Algeria), the society moved south from 1878, establishing *mission stations eventually as far south as Mozambique and encouraging the growth of indigenous *clergy. Lavigerie founded a parallel *order for women, the White (or Missionary) Sisters, in 1869.

WHITE FRIARS See CARMELITES.

WHITEFIELD, GEORGE (1714–1770). English *evangelist. Born in Gloucester, he was a friend of Charles *Wesley's at Oxford, was ordained after graduation in 1736, and soon became prominent as a preacher in England and the U.S., which he visited several times. He was associated for some time with the work of the Countess of *Huntingdon, with whose support he opened a church in London. Calvinist in *theology, he parted company with the *Arminian John and Charles Wesley about 1743. As an itinerant preacher who contributed much to the early Methodist movement, Whitefield drew thousands to meetings he conducted throughout the whole of Britain.

WHITGIFT, JOHN (c. 1530–1604). *Archbishop of Canterbury from 1583. A strong Anglican who opposed both Rome and *Puritanism, he so reflected the position of Queen *Elizabeth that she appointed him as *primate. He was a moderate Calvinist, an encourager of *clerical scholarship, and a founder and endower of schools and almshouses.

WHITSUNDAY The Sunday seven weeks after *Easter and sometimes called *Pentecost Sunday. The use of white comes from the use of white baptismal gowns worn by candidates for *baptism. It is the celebration of the descent of the Holy *Spirit upon the *disciples (Acts 2) and the beginning of the *mission of the church in the world.

WHITTIER, JOHN GREENLEAF (1807–1892). American Quaker poet. Member of the Massachusetts state legislature and prominent abolitionist, he endured physical violence in the antislavery cause. When the battle was won he returned to his poetry, which captured the spirit of rural New England. He also wrote *hymns, and the best known of those still used is "Dear Lord and Father of Mankind."

WHITTINGHAM, WILLIAM (c. 1524–1579). Dean of Durham. He studied at Oxford, then from 1550 to 1560 he spent most of the time abroad. He helped organize the English congregation in Frankfurt. Then in Geneva he had a prominent part in the translation of the Geneva *Bible (1560). Soon after his return to England he became dean of Durham, where his extreme Protestant views incurred the hostility of *Archbishop *Sandys of York.

WHYTE, ALEXANDER (1836–1921). Scottish minister. Aberdeen graduate and minister of the *Free Church of Scotland, he occupied the pulpit of Free St. George's, Edinburgh, for nearly forty years. With an impressive presence and dramatic style, a wide *culture and deep sense of *sin, he could speak to the condition of all classes. In 1909 he became principal of New College, Edinburgh, a post he held for nine years, but it is as a preacher that his name still lives.

WICHERN, JOHANN HINRICH (1808–1881). Founder of the *Innere Mission in Germany. After studying *theology at Göttingen and Berlin, he founded a school for neglected children near his native Hamburg and called it *Rauhes Haus* ("Rough House"). Stressing both material and *spiritual needs, the work developed, and the double emphasis has been a feature of the Innere Mission, which had its beginnings in 1848. Wichern worked also on behalf of prisoners and the *war wounded.

WIDOWS *Christian women who do not marry after their husbands' death have traditionally been special recipients of the care of the churches (Acts 6:1–3; 1 Tim 5:3–16). It has often been held that older women should not remarry but give themselves to the service of the *Lord in the life of the church.

WILBERFORCE, SAMUEL (1805–1873). Anglican *bishop. Born in London and educated at Oxford (where he knew J. H. *Newman well), he was ordained in 1828 and worked in South-coast *parishes until his *consecration as bishop of Oxford in 1845 (the year Newman converted to *Roman Catholicism). Sympathetic to the *Oxford Movement, he opposed *liberalism, *Nonconformity, and *Darwinism. He was transferred to the see in Winchester in 1869 but died in 1873 when he fell from his horse.

WILBERFORCE, WILLIAM (1759–1833). English abolitionist and philanthropist. Educated at Cambridge, he represented his native Hull (1780–1784) and then Yorkshire (1784–1825) in Parliament. Converted in his mid-twenties, he soon became involved in the abolition of the slave trade. This was achieved in 1807; the abolition of *slavery itself in the British colonies was effected one month after his death. Wilberforce was involved in the work of the *Clapham Sect and took part in the founding of the Church Missionary Society (1799) and the British and Foreign Bible Society (1804).

WILDER, ROBERT PARMELEE (1863–1938). *Missionary to India and chief founder of the *Student Volunteer Movement. Born of missionary parents in India, he was educated at Princeton, where he was the prime mover in organizing a missionary society that developed into the Student Volunteer Movement. From 1891 he engaged in student work in Europe, India, the U.S., and the Middle East, each for a period of years, before dying in Norway.

WILFRID (634–709). *Bishop of York. A Northumbrian noble's son, he was educated at Lindisfarne and Canterbury and became *abbot of Ripon. At the Synod of *Whitby in 664 he successfully argued against Celtic practices; in 669 he was installed after some dispute as *bishop of York. There was further dispute when *Archbishop *Theodore of Canterbury, to counter Wilfrid's love of power, split the York *diocese into four and appointed other bishops. Wilfrid went to Rome to appeal to the *pope, and though successful, was prevented from returning to York for some years. Political events forced Wilfrid's flight from York in 691, and he spent his last years as bishop of Hexham, a less important post.

WILKES, PAGET (1871–1934). *Missionary to Japan. Oxford educated, he went to Japan under the Church Missionary Society in 1897. There he spent most of his life serving the Japan Evangelistic Band, which he had founded as an interdenominational body, teaching scriptural holiness and writing books that included *The Dynamic of Service* (1920), *The Dynamic of Faith* (1921), and *The Dynamic of Redemption* (1923).

WILL The inner self-conscious source of the power to perform voluntary activity. The internal faculty that tends toward the good or away from the *evil (or the opposite) upon the basis of information in the mind. Theologians have often discussed whether the will of a sinful human being is free to choose the *Gospel without spiritual help from *God. It has been held by some that such is the bondage of the will to *sin that only with divine help can it choose what *God considers to be the good. Theologians separate mind and will, but many modern psychologists do not. See also FREEDOM OF THE WILL, FREE WILL.

WILL OF GOD The intention and purpose of *God. This may be deduced only from what he has revealed, from what he has said and done. So it can be said that it is his *will to be Creator, Sustainer, and Redeemer of the *universe. Also, Father, Son and *Holy Spirit, one Godhead, have the same will. However, it can be added that Jesus *Christ as God-made-Man has two wills, human and divine, and they work perfectly in harmony. To bring clarity into discussion of God's will, various distinctions are made, e.g.: (1) *The will of God's good pleasure and the signed will of God.* This is a traditional Roman Catholic distinction. The first is the secret will of God, hidden within him and known only by him. The second (which really means "signs of God's will"—*voluntas signi*) refers to what we know of God's will in terms of his revealed commandments, plans, and purposes. (2) *The secret and revealed will of God.* This is based on Deuteronomy 29:29 and is used by Protestant theologians. While the first is hidden in God, the latter is revealed in the *Law and *Gospel of the *OT and *NT. (3) *The decretive and preceptive will of God.* The former is the content of the decrees of the *eternal mind of God concerning *creation and *redemption. The latter is the rule of life God has laid upon human beings as his will for them. (4) *The perfect and permissive will of God.* The former relates to what God has planned for the individual *Christian and the latter to what God allows the individual Christian to do when he does not fulfill the perfect plan. This is a distinction often made in *Pietism and Evangelicalism.

WILLIAM III (1650–1702). King of Great Britain from 1689. Born at The Hague, he ruled the United Provinces of the Netherlands from 1672, using military action against both French and British opponents of the Roman Catholic *James II, and landed in England and became king the following year, with his wife Mary (daughter of James) as joint monarch. After thirty years of religious troubles, William helped to settle the country, notably reversing government policy by restoring *Presbyterianism in Scotland.

WILLIAM OF OCCAM (c. 1280–c. 1349). English theologian and philosopher. A pupil of John *Duns Scotus, he was the last great philosopher of the Middle Ages, a *Franciscan who studied and taught at Oxford. He opposed Pope *John XXII for his lax interpretation of *Christian poverty, was expelled from the Franciscans, and took refuge in Bavaria to avoid implementation of a sentence of perpetual imprisonment. Thereafter the emperor Louis had a powerful defender against the *papacy. Ockham produced works on the relation between church and state and held that *God could be apprehended only by *faith—not by *reason on one hand or *illumination on the other.

WILLIAMS, SIR GEORGE (1821–1905). Founder of the *Young Men's Christian Association. Son of a Somerset farmer, he was converted through the writings of C. G. *Finney, became a successful businessman in London, and was knighted in 1894. He established the YMCA in 1844, saw it grow to an international movement, and was at its diamond jubilee in Paris just before he died.

WILLIAMS, JOHN (1796–1839). "*Apostle of Polynesia." Born in London and converted at age eighteen, he was sent by the London Missionary Society to the Society Islands (near Tahiti) in 1817. The first *baptisms came thirty months later. Williams worked tirelessly for the spiritual and physical welfare of the island people, reaching them by a ship, *The Messenger of Peace,* which he himself helped to build. In 1834 he embarked on a four-year tour of the British Isles to awaken interest in the South Seas, but soon after returning there he was killed by cannibals in the New Hebrides, an event that advanced the *Christian cause as much as his words and testimony had done.

WILLIAMS, ROGER (c. 1603–1684). Founder of Rhode Island. Born in London and educated at Cambridge, he was ordained in the Church of *England, but his Puritan views led him to New England in 1631. His *separatism and championship of the Indians forced him successively out of Boston, Plymouth, and Salem. Finally, he purchased from the Indians land on which he founded the town of Providence and the colony of Rhode Island, of which he was the first president. Though a Calvinist, he gave refuge to those of other religious views, teaching liberty of *conscience in an intolerant age.

WILLIBRORD (658–739). "*Apostle to the Frisians." Born in Northumbria and influenced by *Wilfrid and Egbert, he went with eleven companions in 690 to evangelize Frankish-occupied Frisia (the Netherlands), and in 695 was made *archbishop of the province, with his base in Utrecht. In 714 he baptized *Pepin III (714), after whose death he was banished for a time. He returned in 719 and was assisted by *Boniface (Wynfrith), who was later to succeed him. He died at the Echternach *monastery in Luxembourg, which he had set up as a second *missionary base in 698.

WILSON, DANIEL (1778–1858). *Bishop of Calcutta. Educated at Oxford, he was ordained and ministered in England until appointed *bishop of Calcutta in 1832. Until his death there, he combated the caste system and secular control of *missionaries, oversaw the establishment of Anglican *dioceses in Madras and Bombay, and built churches, including a *cathedral in Calcutta.

WILSON, JOHN (1804–1875). Scholar and *missionary to India. Born in Scotland and educated at Edinburgh, he was ordained in 1828 and went to India. He and his wife established schools and built a college in Bombay (1832) that still bears his name. A brilliant linguist and public debater, he declined high government office lest it hinder his missionary usefulness. He was the first missionary to cross Sind. When Bombay University was founded in 1857, he became dean of *arts and examiner in six Eastern languages. He wrote extensively, had an influence that extended throughout India, and was elected fellow of the Royal Society in London.

WILSON, ROBERT DICK (1856–1930). *Presbyterian minister and renowned *OT scholar. Professor at three theological seminaries—Pittsburgh (1880–1900), Princeton (1900–1929), and Westminster (1929–1930)—he was a learned linguist (fluent in forty-five languages and dialects) and supporter of J. Gresham *Machen in fighting *liberalism in the *Presbyterian Church, U.S.

WINSLOW, EDWARD (1595–1655). American Pilgrim leader. Born in England, he became a *Separatist and joined the Pilgrims sailing on the *Mayflower* for the New World in 1620. He served three times as governor of the Plymouth Colony, negotiated with the Indians and with the government in England, where he served for a time under Oliver *Cromwell, and was the inspiration behind the founding of the Society for the Propagation of the Gospel in New England.

WINTHROP, JOHN (1588–1649). First governor of Massachusetts Bay Colony. Born in Suffolk and trained as a lawyer, he was elected governor of the new colony before he led a group of Puritans from England to Massachusetts in 1630. His *A Model of Christian Charity* (1630) and *History of New England* give valuable insights into contemporary aims, attitudes, and government in the early colonial era.

WISDOM *Christ is the Wisdom of *God (1 Cor 1:24; Col 2:3). In his *ministry, what he said and did proceeded from wisdom (Matt 11:19; Luke 7:35; 21:15). Wisdom is knowledge of God and of his purposes for the world. Christ had this knowledge and embodied it. The background of this idea of wisdom is the *OT and other Jewish literature. Parts of this wisdom is personalized, as in Proverbs 8:22ff. (and the Book of Wisdom 7:22ff.; cf. John 1:1ff., where **Logos* = Wisdom).

As a *virtue true human wisdom is practical knowledge based on "the fear of the *Lord'' (Ps 111:10; Prov 1:7; 9:10) and is commended by *Jesus to his *disciples (Matt 10:16). As such it has its effects on the whole of life and the judgments made in life. While it can be developed in a human person it is in origin a gift of God (James 1:5). As an occasional special insight into the meaning of life, it is also a gift of the Spirit (1 Cor 12:8).

WISDOM LITERATURE The *OT books that provide practical wisdom on everyday life and perennial problems: Job, Proverbs, and Ecclesiastes from the Jewish/Protestant *canon, and Ecclesiasticus and Wisdom from the Roman Catholic canon.

WISEMAN, NICHOLAS PATRICK STEPHEN (1802–1865). English *cardinal and first *archbishop of Westminster. Born in Spain of Irish parents, he was professor of Oriental languages at Rome University (1828) before dedicating his life to the restoration of *Roman Catholicism in England. In 1850 the hierarchy was reestablished, an event that, with Wiseman's appointment to Westminster, caused a furor in more Protestant circles. Wiseman, who influenced J. H. *Newman and H. E. *Manning when they converted to Rome, was a man of *culture but was much criticized for *Ultramontanism.

WISHART, GEORGE (c. 1513–1546). Scottish Reformer and *martyr. Schoolmaster at Montrose and *NT Greek scholar, he fearlessly denounced the corruption of the Roman Catholic Church in Scotland and spread Lutheran views. He greatly influenced John *Knox, translated a *Helvetic Confession into English, and was burned for *heresy at St. Andrews—an event that provoked the murder of *Cardinal Beaton.

WITCHCRAFT The exercise of human powers in league with demonic forces to produce extraordinary or *evil results. A female is called a witch, and a male is called a wizard, warlock, sorceror, or witch doctor. This practice is condemned in the *Bible (Exod 22:18; Deut 18:10; Acts 8:9; 13:8 19:9; Gal 5:20). Sometimes today witchcraft is mere superstition, sometimes it has demonic aspects, and sometimes (in primitive societies) it has complex cultural roots and connections. While the church has generally condemned the practice, it has insisted on examining each local manifestation carefully.

WITHERSPOON, JOHN (1723–1794). *Presbyterian minister. Born in Scotland, a descendant of John *Knox, he graduated from Edinburgh, ministered in Beith and Paisley (1745–1768), then went to America as president of the College of New Jersey (later Princeton University). As representative of New Jersey in Congress (1776–1782), he was the only clergyman to sign the Declaration of Independence.

WITNESS OF THE SPIRIT The Holy *Spirit's work of testifying that a believer is a child of *God (Rom 8:16; Gal 4:6).

WITTENBERG, CONCORD OF (1536). An agreement between Lutheran and *Zwinglian parties on the *doctrine of the *Eucharist. After *Bucer and *Melanchthon had done the preliminary work in 1534, a much larger group of theologians, including *Luther, met to discuss a doctrinal statement drafted by Melanchthon. The result was a largely Lutheran emphasis. What Bucer had conceded, however, was too much for his Swiss colleagues, and the reunion effected at Wittenberg was short-lived.

WOLSEY, THOMAS (c. 1474–1530). English *cardinal. He was ordained in 1498 and found royal chaplaincies the way to preferment and profit. By the time he was forty he was *bishop of Lincoln, *archbishop of York, *cardinal, and lord *chancellor of England. Wolsey's dual success in church and state was shattered by the break between *Henry VIII and the *pope. His customary opportunism failed to obtain the necessary papal dispensation for the king's *divorce. The king blamed him, and only Wolsey's death saved him from execution for high treason.

WOMEN IN THE CHURCH That all women who believe and are baptized are to be church members is not in question. Neither is the fact that the exalted *Lord by the Holy *Spirit gives gifts of *ministry to women so that they may serve their fellow Christians and the world in the name of *Christ. What primarily is in question is whether they should be appointed to positions of ordained leadership in churches. Here the churches are divided. The Roman Catholic Church, the *Orthodox Church, the Church of *England, and some Lutheran and Presbyerian churches (and others) refuse to ordain women as *pastors (*priests) either on the grounds of biblical teaching or *tradition or both. On the other hand, some Protestant *denominations do ordain women as pastors. The *bishops of the *Protestant Episcopal Church ordained eleven women to the priesthood on July 29, 1974. In September 1976 the Sixty-fifth General Convention of the Episcopal Church in the U.S. approved the practice of women's ordination. For those who take the *Bible seriously in terms of authority the basic questions are: Did *Jesus choose only male *apostles because he wanted to show that pastoral leadership was to be in the hands of males? Were the first apostles (and Jesus) so culturally conditioned by Jewish and Greek views of their time that they thought only in terms of male pastors in the congregations?

WOODBRIDGE, CHARLES J. (1902–). *Presbyterian *pastor, *missionary, conference speaker, author, and educator. Born of missionary parents in China, he served in Africa, helped found the Independent Board of Presbyterian Foreign Missions, and was elected its first secretary. He, Carl *McIntire, J. Gresham *Machen, and others, "unfrocked" in 1936 by the Presbyterian Church in the U.S.A., organized the *Orthodox Presbyterian Church. After being a pastor in Flushing, New York; Savannah, Georgia; and Salisbury, North Carolina, he has been a professor at Fuller Theological Seminary (1950–1957), has served on the staff of Word of Life Fellowship (1957–1964), and has spoken at numerous *Bible conferences.

WOOLMAN, JOHN (1720–1772). American social reformer. Woolman, a Quaker, beginning with a profound sense of the dignity of all human beings, preached and wrote against the *evils of *slavery and *war. His influence was such that the Philadelphia Annual Meeting rejected slaveholding in 1776 and Pennsylvania *Quakers withdrew their support for the French and Indian War. Woolman's oft-reprinted *Journal* (1774) embodies his ideas, reflections, and meditations, and is a fascinating account of colonial America. See also QUAKERS.

WORD OF GOD An expression with several meanings. (1) The **Logos* (John 1:1ff.), the *eternal *Son of *God, through whom the *universe was created and by whom *salvation comes. (2) The self-revelation of God as the words of God (in the words of the *Law, *Prophets, *Christ, *apostles, etc.). (3) The original Hebrew (with Aramaic) and Greek versions of the *OT and *NT, as well as faithful translations of these. (4) The *preaching of the *gospel of Jesus *Christ by the church and becoming in the power of the Holy *Spirit the living Word of God to man. (5) The *theology of Karl *Barth, sometimes called "a theology of the Word of God." He does not equate the words of God with the words of the *Bible. Rather he sees the Word of God as the living Christ, who in the proclamation of the gospel from the Bible becomes for people today God's living Word of *love and judgment.

WORK, THEOLOGY OF Daily work is a reality for most people. Normally it has the aspects of joy and drudgery in it, as Genesis 3 indicates. These are more or less in each situation—e.g., the worker on the production line has more drudgery than joy. Work is a necessary means of pleasing *God, the Creator and Sustainer of life, by meeting and serving human needs. From a *Christian viewpoint, the work of the doctor, lawyer, and professor is not qualitatively different from that of the unskilled laborer. Neither is the work of the *clergy more pleasing to God than the work of others. *Vocation in its basic meaning relates to doing as well as possible that which God has given a person to do. In modern industrialized society the practicalities of a theology of work are often difficult to clarify and state.

WORK OF CHRIST That which *Jesus did (and does now in *heaven) as *Messiah for the *salvation of the world. This specifically refers to his death, *resurrection, and present threefold office of *Prophet, *Priest, and King. But the work of *Christ cannot be separated from the *Person of Christ, for who he is determines what he is able to do, and only as the Incarnate *Son of God could he be the *Messiah who saved his people.

WORKS *Christian activity done for the good of others and for the glory of *God (Matt 5:16). *Salvation is by God's *grace, not by works. Yet works are the natural result and outcome of grace. Without them it is impossible to say that a person has received God's salvation (James 2:17). Protestant theologians distinguish works done before *conversion to God and those done after conversion. Neither can contribute to salvation, for that is a gift, but those performed after conversion should proceed from a different principle, the *love of God and man. Roman Catholic theologians also refer to works of *supererogation.

WORLD ALLIANCE OF REFORMED CHURCHES Founded in 1875, it is comprised of churches organized on *Presbyterian principles that hold to "the supreme authority of the *Scriptures . . . in matters of *faith and morals, and whose *creed is in harmony with the consensus of the Reformed Confessions." The function of the World Alliance of Reformed Churches is wholly advisory.

WORLD CONGRESS ON EVANGELISM (1966). Sponsored by the American Protestant magazine *Christianity Today,* it was attended by 1,200 participants from over a hundred countries and seventy-six *denominations. Presided over by Carl F. H. Henry, it discussed such matters as *evangelism and communication, the use of modern technology, religious persecution, the *cults, and work among minority groups. The ten-day meetings also featured reports from many parts of the world. In its closing statement the congress affirmed that members entered the closing third of the 20th century "with greater confidence than ever in the *God of our fathers who reveals himself in *creation, in judgment, and in *redemption," and that their goal was "the evangelization of the human race in this generation, by every means God has given to the mind and *will of men."

W.C.C. See World Council of Churches.

WORLD COUNCIL OF CHURCHES A body founded in Amsterdam in 1948, with a membership in the mid-eighties of three hundred churches in more than one hundred countries. The American Southern Baptist Convention is an exception, but the council involves nearly all of the major non-Roman Catholic *denominations. The WCC's beginnings can be traced to the famous 1910 *Edinburgh Missionary Conference, which led on to the establishment of the *Faith and Order and *Life and Work movements. Since Amsterdam, the WCC has held assemblies at *Evanston (1954), *New Delhi (1961), *Uppsala, (1968), *Nairobi (1975), and *Vancouver (1983). The WCC basis of membership is "a *fellowship of churches that confess the *Lord Jesus *Christ as *God the *Savior according to the *Scriptures and therefore seek to fulfill together their common calling to the glory of the one God, Father, Son and Holy *Spirit." There is opposition to this Council by many Evangelicals on two basic grounds—its apparent support for *liberal *theology and its leftist political stance.

WORLD EVANGELICAL FELLOWSHIP A body founded in Holland in 1951 but whose spiritual origins were in the establishment of the *Evangelical Alliance in 1846. Membership is open to national *evangelical *fellowships who subscribe to a conservative basis of *faith. The World Evangelical Fellowship operates three associated programs: theological assistance, international aid, and *Bible and evangelistic *ministries.

WORLD STUDENT CHRISTIAN FEDERATION Organized in Sweden in 1895 by John R. *Mott and others, its aim is "to lead students to accept the *Christian *faith in *God—Father, Son, and Holy *Spirit—according to the *Scriptures, and to live together as true *disciples of Jesus *Christ." About forty national bodies developed under World Student Christian Federation auspices, and it reportedly was the first to obtain the participation of Eastern *Orthodoxy.

WORLDLINESS Conforming to the lifestyle of a given *culture or subculture and thus avoiding the challenge of *Christ to be like him (Rom 12:2). The "world" here is opposition to *God and purity that exists in the human race and is manifested in different ways in different *cultures and ways of life (1 John 5:20). There is always a tension in the *Christian life between world rejection (i.e., no worldliness) and world acceptance (i.e., enjoying the world as God's creation).

WORLD'S CHRISTIAN FUNDAMENTALS ASSOCIATION Organized in Philadelphia in May of 1919 under the leadership of L. S. *Chafer, G. E. Guille, I. M. Haldeman, George McNeeley, J. C. Massee, L. W. Munhall, W. L. Pettingill, P. W. Philpott, W. B. *Riley, W. W. Rugh, J. R. *Straton, W. H. Griffith *Thomas, R. A. *Torrey, and A. B. Winchester, this *Fundamentalist group combated *evolution and *modernism for more than thirty years.

WORMS, COLLOQUY OF (1540–1541). Standing between the colloquies of Hagenau and *Ratisbon, this brief meeting in which *Eck and *Melanchthon represented *Roman Catholicism and *Protestantism, respectively, did at least find common ground in their conclusions on *original *sin.

WORMS, CONCORDAT OF (1122). The agreement between Pope *Callistus II and Henry V that ended the *Investiture Controversy. The *papacy won the long dispute, but the election of *bishops and *abbots in Germany was to take place in the king's presence, and he was to present them with the scepter.

WORMS, DIET OF (1521). The meeting of the German Diet at which Martin *Luther, called to recant, uttered the historic words, "Here I stand. I cannot do otherwise. *God help me."

WORSHIP The acknowledgement of the supreme worth and dignity of *God, Creator and Redeemer. Thus worship of God is expressed in terms of *adoration, praise, and thanksgiving because of who he is and what he has done. Also there is *prayer for God's help, for God is known as merciful. In many churches the forms of worship are based on written forms (*liturgy), while in others they are flexible. The central act of *Christian worship quickly became the *Eucharist (Acts 20:7–12; 1 Cor 11:17ff.). "Worship" of the *saints and of the Blessed Virgin *Mary is of a different order (see DULIA, HYPERDULIA, LATRIA).

WRATH OF GOD The anger of *God; the expression of the *holy, *eternal *love of God against *sin. The God who loves the right must also hate the wrong (Rom 1:18ff.). So wrath is more than a description of the working out in history of the consequences of sin; it is more than the result of the working of impersonal laws. Rather, it is the personal attitude of God to that which is the complete opposite of *righteousness and holy love. This attitude will be particularly evident at the end of the age in the Last *Judgment, which will be a day of wrath (Rom 2:5; Rev 19:5).

WREN, CHRISTOPHER (1632–1723). English architect. Born in Wiltshire, he graduated from Oxford, where he subsequently held a chair of astronomy. After the Great Fire of London (1666) he was a member of the rebuilding commission and the principal architect. He rebuilt more than fifty churches, but his masterpiece was St. Paul's Cathedral (1675–1716). His many other works include the Chelsea Hospital and Trinity College Library, Cambridge. One of the founders of the Royal Society, he was its president for two years.

WULFSTAN (c. 1010–1095). *Bishop of Worcester. A monk before his *consecration (1062) and a friend of King Harold, he was the only Saxon bishop not replaced by William the Conqueror—reportedly because of his "simple goodness." He joined with *Archbishop Lanfranc in successfully combating the slave trade.

WÜRTTEMBERG CONFESSION (1552). A statement of belief drafted by Johann *Brenz at the request of Duke Christopher, who became the leader of German *Protestantism. The document's thirty-five articles made some gestures to *Calvinism but are heavily weighted on the Lutheran side. They were said to have influenced the drafting of the *Thirty-Nine Articles.

WYCLIFFE, JOHN (c. 1329–1384). English Reformer. Priest and Oxford philosopher, he became widely known during his last ten years, when he was rector of Lutterworth in Leicestershire. Critical of the church's acquisitive attitude to property, he began to question other things publicly. Right thinking and right living were almost identical for Wycliffe. He instituted "simple" itinerant *priests to supplement church services by religious instruction in the vernacular. They were helped by an English translation of the *Bible and by Wycliffe's tracts and *sermons. His proclamation of a simple *gospel, though unwelcomed in England until the 16th century, greatly influenced Jan *Hus. Wycliffe has been called the "morning star of the *Reformation."

XYZ

XAVIER, FRANCIS (1506–1552). *Jesuit *missionary. Born in Spain, he was a student in Paris when he met *Ignatius of Loyola and, with six others, was associated with him in founding the Jesuits in 1534. Ordained in 1537, he went as a missionary to Goa in 1542 and baptized thousands of converts. He was just as successful during two years in Japan (1549–1551) but was driven out by Buddhist monks. He finally returned to Goa, where he died. His methods have been questioned, notably his use of the *Inquisition, but *Pius X gave him the title "*Patron of Foreign Missions."

XIMÉNIZ DE CISNEROS, FRANCISCO (c. 1436–1517). *Archbishop of Toledo. Born in Castile, he was educated at Salamanca. He was in Rome for some years, where he later became a *Franciscan of the most austere type. In 1492 he unwillingly became confessor and adviser to Queen Isabella, and three years later he was *primate of Spain as archbishop of Toledo. Created *cardinal in 1507, he never discarded his austere mode of life. His was also regent during the minority of *Charles V, a patron of learning, and an organizer of expeditions against the Moors.

YAHWEH The Hebrew name of *God formed from the four consonants YHWH. Another way of transliterating the Hebrew is JHVH, giving *Jehovah. In modern versions of the *OT, Lord is often used where this name occurs in the Hebrew text.

YAHWIST The supposed writer of the so-called *J source of the *Pentateuch. He is identified as such because of his use of the name *Yahweh of *God.

YOUNG, BRIGHAM (1801–1877). Second leader of the Mormons. Born in New York, he was converted from *Methodism after reading the Book of Mormon in 1832. An industrious worker who received quick promotion, he established a *mission in England in 1839. After the death of Joseph *Smith in 1844, he took command at a time of severe persecution and subsequently led his *Latter-Day Saints to Utah, where the main company arrived in 1848. He was the first governor of the territory of Utah (1850–1857) and a practical man who contributed much to the establishment of his church on a solid foundation.

YOUNG, EDWARD JOSEPH (1907–1968). American *OT scholar. After an extensive education, he taught *OT at Westminster Theological Seminary, Philadelphia, from 1936 until his death. A brilliant linguist and staunch upholder of the *inerrancy of *Scripture, he wrote many works that have been widely used, including *An Introduction to the Old Testament* (1949), *Thy Word is Truth* (1957), and volumes on Daniel (1949) and Isaiah (1965).

YOUNG MEN'S CHRISTIAN ASSOCIATION (YMCA) An interdenominational movement founded in London by George *Williams in 1844. The movement soon spread to other countries and by 1878 had established headquarters in Geneva. To its evangelistic and devotional activities were added recreation and relief work, and the YMCA's concerns were further expanded by the needs of the Armed Forces in World War I and by the increase in the number of young travelers or those who work or study away from home.

YOUNG WOMEN'S CHRISTIAN ASSOCIATION (YWCA) In America the first YWCA originated in New York City in 1858 from a prayer group led by Mrs. Marshall Roberts. A group in Boston first called itself a YWCA in 1866. The YWCA of the United States was founded in 1906. It is a worldwide organization, serving women in more than seventy countries. Generally its aims and facilities are those of the *Young Men's Christian Association, with headquarters also in Geneva.

ZACHARIAS (d. 752). Pope from 741. Born in Italy of Greek parents, he proved himself adept at foreign relations by effecting friendly links with Lombards, Franks, and the *Byzantine Empire. He encouraged the evangelistic outreach of *Boniface and had him anoint *Pepin III as Frankish ruler (who responded by recognizing him as ruler of the *Papal States), and he favored the use of *images in the *Iconoclastic Controversy.

ZEALOT Someone who is enthusiastically and with dedication bound to a particular cause. It is used particularly of a member of a Jewish nationalistic and revolutionary party or group in the period A.D. 66–70, when the fight with Rome was intense. In a more general way it is used of Jews who were zealous for the Law and for Jewish self-rule in the time of *Jesus. Certain zealots became *disciples of Jesus (Mark 3:18; Luke 6:15).

ZEISBERGER, DAVID (1721–1808). Moravian *missionary to American Indians. Born in Moravia and raised largely in *Herrnhut, he went to America in 1738 and began in Pennsylvania in 1745 the *mission work that was to continue until his death. He championed his Indians amid persecution and injustice, mastering their dialects and establishing a number of *Christian villages, most of which were destroyed by the colonists.

ZEPHYRINUS (d. 217). Pope from 198. Little is known about him. The Roman *priest *Hippolytus called him a weak man, "unskilled in the church's rule," and recorded that he compromised on *Sabellianism. Zephyrinus is said to have died a *martyr's death.

ZILLERTHAL EVANGELICALS A Protestant group that emigrated from the Austrian Tyrol to Prussia about 1837. Inhabitants of the Ziller valley, a few hundred in number, they had to endure harassment, which continued in the archdiocese of Salzburg even after a *toleration edict of 1781. A sympathetic Prussian ruler, Frederick William III, gave permission and material aid for their settlement at Erdmannsdorf in Silesia.

ZINZENDORF, NIKOLAUS LUDWIG, COUNT VON (1700–1760). Founder of the Moravian church. Born in Dresden and raised in Pietist circles, he studied law at Wittenberg and in 1721 entered Saxon government service. *Herrnhut, the famous *Christian community, emerged from his giving of refuge to a group of Bohemian refugees on his estate. He left government service in 1727 and was ordained as a Lutheran *pastor in 1734 and as *bishop of the *Unitas Fratrum in 1737. From Herrnhut, Zinzendorf sent his *missionaries to many countries; John *Wesley was only one from other *traditions who found his *heart "strangely warmed" through contact with the Moravians. Zinzendorf himself traveled extensively, notably in America, and spent five years ministering in England. It is hard to overestimate his contribution to the modern missionary movement.

ZION Used in the *OT in several ways with reference to all or part of Jerusalem and used in both the OT and *NT of the heavenly city of *God (Isa 60:14;

Heb 12:22; Rev 14:1). So it has been used in the church as an image of *heaven or of the people of God in heaven.

ZOSIMUS (d. 418). Pope from 417. The rule of this Greek-born *pontiff lasted only twenty-one months, but it saw turmoil in the church, much of it of his making. An unfortunate papal appointment in Gaul provoked a bitter crisis there. Zosimus was hoodwinked by *Celestius, a smooth-talking Pelagian, into sympathy for the *heresy after his predecessor and the African church had condemned it; Zosimus again interfered in Africa by giving support to an unworthy *priest. Even though he backtracked and condemned *Pelagianism, he had lost credibility through his unpredictable behavior.

ZWEMER, SAMUEL MARINUS (1867–1952). "*Apostle to Islam." Born into a Dutch Reformed family in Michigan, he early espoused the *mission movement, helped to form the Arabian Mission, and worked in the Gulf area, 1890–1905. Thereafter he traveled extensively through the Islamic world, making Cairo his base until his appointment as Princeton's professor of missions and comparative *religions (1929). He wrote many challenging books on Islam, founded *The Muslim World* in 1911, and edited it until just before his death.

ZWICKAU PROPHETS A name given by *Luther to three *Anabaptists: Nicholas *Storch, Marcus Stubner, and Thomas Drechsel. Expelled from Zwickau in Saxony, they visited Wittenberg in 1521. They sounded strong eschatological notes, claimed to have received special *revelations, and condemned more conventional beliefs. They were forced out of Wittenberg in 1522.

ZWINGLI, ULRICH (1484–1531). Swiss Reformer. An admirer of *Erasmus, he became chief preacher at Zurich's Great Münster (1518), where his *NT lectures marked the beginning of the Swiss Reformation. He attacked Roman Catholic *doctrine and practice; defeated its supporters in public debate; and supported by the civil authorities, suppressed the *Mass, celebrated the *Lord's Supper after a *Reformed manner, and established ecclesiastical independence. Zwingli's view of the *Eucharist as purely symbolic estranged him from *Luther and made a united *Protestantism impossible. The *Reformation divided Switzerland, and in the ensuing civil *war, Zwingli was killed while serving as chaplain and standard-bearer with the Protestant forces.

ZWINGLIANISM Either the total *theology of Ulrich Zwingli (1484–1531), the Zurich reformer, or, in particular, his supposed view of the *Eucharist as merely a memorial meal. The latter is the more common usage and is seen as the other end of the spectrum from such views as *transubstantiation. It is the view that bread is broken and wine poured merely and only to remember that *Christ died. There is no particular *grace given or presence of Christ promised or provided by *God.